BARRON'S

HOW TO PREPARE FOR THE

ASVAB

ARMED SERVICES VOCATIONAL APTITUDE BATTERY

For Reference

Not to be taken from this room

8TH EDITION

Compiled by the Editorial Department
of Barron's Educational Series, Inc.
Edited by Terry L. Duran

BARRON'S

The publisher acknowledges gratefully the following for permission to adapt material:

Barkus, Philip. HOW TO PREPARE FOR THE POSTAL CLERK-CARRIER EXAMINATION. Barron's Educational Series, Inc., Hauppauge, N.Y., 2000.

Delmar Publishers, Inc., for permission to reprint material from ENERGY: ELECTRICITY/ELECTRONICS by Rex Miller and Fred W. Culpepper, Jr., published by Delmar Publishers, Inc. Copyright 1982.

Edwards, Gabrielle I. BIOLOGY THE EASY WAY. Barron's Educational Series, Inc., Hauppauge, N.Y., 2000.

General Motors Corporation. WHAT MAKES AUTOS RUN. Detroit.

General Motors Corporation. MECHANICAL PRINCIPLES AND THE AUTOMOBILE. Detroit.

Lehrman, Robert L. PHYSICS THE EASY WAY. Barron's Educational Series, Inc., Hauppauge, N.Y., 1998.

Macmillan Publishing Company for permission to adapt material from GAS ENGINE MANUAL, Third Edition. Reprinted with permission of Macmillan Publishing Company from GAS ENGINE MANUAL, Third Edition by Edwin P. Anderson, revised by Charles G. Facklam. Copyright © 1962, 1965, 1977 by Howard W. Sams Co., Inc. Copyright © 1985 by G. K. Hall & Co.

Miller, Rex. ELECTRONICS THE EASY WAY. Barron's Educational Series, Inc., Hauppauge, N.Y., 2002.

U.S. Military Entrance Processing Command. ASVAB: YOUR FUTURE IS NOW. North Chicago, IL.

U.S. Military Entrance Processing Command. HOW TO USE YOUR ASVAB RESULTS. North Chicago, IL.

All inquiries should be addressed to:
Barron's Educational Series, Inc.
250 Wireless Boulevard
Hauppauge, New York 11788
www.barronseduc.com

Library of Congress Catalog Card No. 2005045316
ISBN-13: 978-0-7641-3281-0 (book only)
ISBN-10: 0-7641-3281-4 (book only)

ISBN-13: 978-0-7641-7880-1 (book with CD-ROM)
ISBN-10: 0-7641-7880-6 (book with CD-ROM)

Library of Congress Cataloging-in-Publication Data

Barron's how to prepare for the ASVAB Armed Services Vocational Aptitude Battery/
    compiled by the editorial department of Barron's Educational Series, Inc.—8th ed.
    p. cm.
    ISBN 0-7641-3281-4 (book)—ISBN 0-7641-7880-6 (Book with CD ROM)
    1. Armed Services Vocational Aptitude Battery—Study guides.   I. Title: How to prepare
for the ASVAB Armed Services Vocational Aptitude Battery.   II. Title: ASVAB.   III.
Barron's Educational Series, Inc. Editorial Dept.

U408.5.H69   2006   2005045316
355'.0076—dc22

PRINTED IN THE UNITED STATES OF AMERICA
9 8 7 6 5 4 3 2 1

CONTENTS

INTRODUCTION

CHAPTER

1 All About the ASVAB

What Is It?

The Armed Services Vocational Aptitude Battery, or ASVAB, is a series of ten subtests that measures your ability in separate career areas and provides an indication of your academic ability. It is used to determine if you qualify for military enlistment or for specific military specialties and programs, and to identify where your current aptitudes lie (in or out of the military). Everyone who enlists in the military must take the Armed Services Vocational Aptitude Battery.

ASVAB HISTORY

During World War I, the Army developed the Army Alpha Test to classify draftees. It consisted of 212 multiple-choice and true/false questions about vocabulary, sentence structure, arithmetic problems, number series, general knowledge, and "common sense."

When it became apparent that many draftees couldn't read or write—and therefore couldn't be properly classified using the Army Alpha Test—the Army developed the Army Beta Test, which minimized verbal knowledge and used only pictures and diagrams. The current ASVAB, originally developed by the Department of Defense in the 1960s, is an outgrowth of these classification initial tests.

ASVAB COMPOSITION AND VERSIONS

Currently, the ASVAB consists of ten individual subtests on the following subjects: General Science (GS), Arithmetic Reasoning (AR), Word Knowledge (WK), Paragraph Comprehension (PC), Auto Information (AI), Mathematics Knowledge (MK), Mechanical Comprehension (MC), Electronics Information (EI), Shop Information (SI), and Assembling Objects (AO).

There are currently three versions of the ASVAB. Results from any one of them can be used for military recruiting purposes.

Paper ASVAB for High School

The high school version is a paper-based test usually given to juniors and seniors in high school through a cooperative program between the Department of Defense and the Department of Education. The test is offered at more than 14,000 high schools and postsecondary schools in the United States. The primary purpose of this test is not for enlistment in the military—although the test scores can be used for military enlistment—but rather to help school counselors and students discover where a student's basic aptitudes lie. Almost a million students take the high school version of the ASVAB each year.

Paper ASVAB for Recruiting

This version is given by the Armed Forces for enlistment purposes only. While the questions on the high school version and the recruiting version are different, they are of equal difficulty. Fewer people take the paper recruiting version of the ASVAB because more people interested in joining the military take the computerized version at the Military Entrance Processing Station (MEPS), but both are equally valid.

Computer-Administered Test (CAT)-ASVAB

The third version of the test is the CAT-ASVAB. The CAT-ASVAB is adaptive, which means that it tailors questions to the ability level of each test taker (in the paper version, all test takers answer the same questions, regardless of their ability). For example, on the computer version, your first test question is given in the middle ability range, not too difficult and not too easy. If you answer it correctly, the next question is more difficult. If, however, you don't answer the first item correctly, the next item is less difficult. The test continues in this manner until your proficiency level is determined. You answer questions that are appropriate for your ability level, so you won't waste time answering questions that are too easy or too difficult—therefore, there are fewer questions and less time available in each section.

The CAT-ASVAB is advantageous in that you can finish it in less time, it can be scored immediately, and you don't need to wait for the next administered test. However, you can't skip around or go back to change an answer, and you can't go back and review your answers at the end of the test.

Unlike the paper ASVAB subtest raw scores, CAT-ASVAB subtest raw scores are not equal to the total number of correct answers. CAT-ASVAB subtest scores are computed using formulas that take into account the difficulty of the test item and the correctness of the answer. By equating CAT-ASVAB raw scores with paper-and-pencil ASVAB raw scores, both scores become equivalent.

ASVAB SCORING

Many people find that they score higher on the CAT-ASVAB than they do on the paper version. On overall ASVAB score calculation (not individual subtest scores, known as "line scores"), the mathematics knowledge (MK) and arithmetic reasoning (AR) questions on the ASVAB are "weighted," with harder questions worth more points than easier questions. However, the ASVAB is not an IQ or intelligence test. It was designed specifically to measure an individual's aptitude (i.e., probability of success) to be trained in a range of specific jobs.

Although there are minimum scores necessary for enlistment, there is no "failing grade" on the ASVAB. If you want to enlist in the military, you must achieve a minimum AFQT (Armed Forces Qualification Test) score—and then you may have to score at a certain level on particular subtests to qualify for certain specialties. The AFQT score is calculated from your scores on the WK, PC, AR, and MK subtests. Various combinations of all ten scores are used to determine qualification for particular specialties. For example, to qualify for a technical communications specialty, you might have to have sufficiently high scores on the math, electronics, and general science subtests.

THE TEST FORMAT

Subtest	Paper test minutes	CAT minutes	Paper questions	CAT questions	Emphasis
1. General Science	11	8	25	16	Knowledge of physical and biological sciences
2. Arithmetic Reasoning	36	39	30	16	Ability to solve arithmetic word problems
3. Word Knowledge	11	8	35	16	Ability to select correct meaning of words in context and to identify the best synonym for a given word

Subtest	Paper test minutes	CAT minutes	Paper questions	CAT questions	Emphasis
4. Paragraph Comprehension	13	22	15	11	Ability to interpret and obtain information from written passages
5. Automotive Information	8	6	15	11	Knowledge of automobiles
6. Mathematics Knowledge	24	18	25	16	Knowledge of high school mathematics principles
7. Mechanical Comprehension	19	20	25	16	Knowledge of mechanical and physical principles and ability to visualize how illustrated objects work
8. Electronic Information	9	8	20	8	Knowledge of electricity and electronics
9. Shop Information	8	5	15	11	Knowledge of tools and shop terminology and practices
10. Assembling Objects	20	9	20	16	How an object will look when its parts are mentally assembled

The overall minimum enlistment score, as well as the scores needed to qualify for particular jobs, vary from time to time based on the needs of the individual services.

If you've taken the ASVAB in high school, those scores (if they aren't over two years old) should be acceptable for enlistment. If you'd like a chance to increase your scores, you may want the recruiter to arrange for you to take the version of the ASVAB given to people who didn't take the high school version.

If you did well on the SAT or ACT, or if you get good grades in school, you should have no problem with the ASVAB math and verbal subtests; having a mechanical or electronics background will help you in the other ASVAB subtests.

The ASVAB is offered at many high schools across the country; if your high school isn't one of them, ask your guidance counselor for alternatives. If you are already out of high school, call a local military recruiter.

The information collected when someone takes the ASVAB is used by the Department of Defense for recruiting and research purposes. Scores and personal information obtained during the test are also released to the United States armed forces, the United States Coast Guard, and your local school.

WHY SHOULD I TAKE THE ASVAB?

An aptitude battery helps you measure your potential. It can give you a good indication of where your talents lie. By looking at your composite scores and your own personal interests, you can make more intelligent career decisions. The higher your score, the more choices you'll have when it comes to job specialties.

The ASVAB will also help predict your success in secondary and postsecondary courses and selected civilian career fields. If you're a high school senior trying to decide what to do after high school, your test scores can help you identify fields that you might explore. No matter what your age or inclination, the ASVAB can be valuable to you because it can tell you more about yourself.

If your score on a particular subtest is not as high as you would like, this book can help you raise your scores.

WHERE CAN I TAKE THE ASVAB?

The ASVAB is administered year-round at Military Entrance Processing Stations (MEPS) locations throughout the United States, as well as by mobile teams. Officials of the Military Entrance Processing Command proctor the tests.

HOW DO I APPLY?

Ask your guidance counselor to make arrangements for you, or contact the nearest recruiter of the service of your choice. There is no cost for this examination since the Department of Defense wants to tell you about military service opportunities and assist you in career exploration.

AM I OBLIGATED TO JOIN THE MILITARY?

No. Taking the ASVAB does not obligate you to the military in any way. You are free to use your test results in whatever manner you wish. Additionally, ASVAB results will *not* be used to enter your name in any draft registration system.

You will, however, be required to sign a statement authorizing the release of your test scores to representatives of all the military services, and (like the majority of high school students), if you are an upperclassman, you will probably be contacted by a recruiter sometime before you graduate. You should expect this whether or not you ever take the ASVAB.

Nevertheless, be sure to find out about the many job opportunities with the military services (Air Force, Army, Marine Corps, and Navy) and the U.S. Coast Guard.

Hundreds of thousands of students enter one of the military services each year. Your ASVAB test scores are good for enlistment purposes for two years after you take the test. Phone or visit a service recruiter to determine whether you would qualify to enter that service (assuming that you meet other qualifications such as age, physical requirements, etc.).

WHO SEES MY TEST SCORES?

The ASVAB is used by the Armed Services for recruiting purposes and by your counselor for guidance counseling. Therefore, your test scores will be provided to your counselor and to the recruiting services and the Coast Guard.

The personal information you will provide at the time of testing will be maintained in a computer file and on microfiche records. After two years, individual test scores, identified by student name and social security number, are retained by the Department of Defense only for research purposes to assist in evaluating and updating test materials.

Your personal identity information and related test information will not be released to any agency outside the Department of Defense and your school system. This information will not be used for any purpose other than recruiting by the Armed Services, counseling in your school, and research on test development and personnel measurement. Information on your test scores provided to your school will be handled and disposed of in accordance with the policies of the governing state or local school system.

WHAT EFFECT DO MY ASVAB SCORES HAVE?

If you plan to enter the military, your scores are very important. Your scores on the four subject tests that make up the AFQT determine whether or not you can enter the military at all. Once you have enlisted, your scores on the other subtests determine which military specialties you are eligible to be trained for.

HOW CAN I USE MY TEST SCORES?

Since the ASVAB is a vocational aptitude test, its primary value is in relating your test scores to jobs in the vocational-technical career fields. Whether or not you plan on going on to college, you should be aware of the range of jobs in the trades, what skills and training they require, and how much they can pay. (Some technical careers pay surprisingly well.) See Chapter 15 for a look at how your test scores can help you analyze your job opportunities and potential.

COMPUTERIZED ASVAB CAREER EXPLORATION SYSTEM (ACES)

For use on school computers, the software automatically matches a student's attributes to occupations. Each student is able to see which occupations have characteristics consistent with his or her own and which may not be such good matches. This system is currently available to schools for use with those students who participate in the ASVAB program. Call your local ASVAB representative for more information.

WHAT SHOULD I EXPECT ON THE DAY OF THE TEST?

When you go to the examining station to take the ASVAB, you will be given a booklet with ten short tests, each consisting of *practice questions* and *actual test questions*. You will also be given a separate answer sheet on which to mark your answers, a special pencil to use, and some scratch paper for doing any figuring you may want to do.

At the examining station, you will be given complete instructions as to what to do in taking the tests and how much time you have to work on each test. After you have been given the instructions, you will be allowed to practice by answering some sample questions. Finally, you will be given plenty of opportunity to ask questions before you start, so that you will understand exactly what you are supposed to do on the tests.

HOW TO TAKE THE TEST

In each of the ten ASVAB subtests, there are four possible answers, labeled A, B, C, and D, for each question. Only one answer in each question is correct or best. Your job is to read each question carefully and decide which of the answers given is the best. Then you record your choice on the separate answer sheet by blackening out the space which has the same number and letter as your choice.

In all cases, you should choose the best answer and mark your answer sheet in the space for it. Don't make any stray marks on the answer sheet because the scoring machine might record those marks as wrong answers. You also should not make any marks in the ASVAB test booklet.

On most of the tests, you will have enough time to try every question, and you *should* try every one. Be sure to work as quickly and accurately as you can. Do not go on to the next page until the examiner tells you to.

Some tests will be easier for you than others, but do the best you can on all of them. All are important. Your score on each test of the ASVAB will be based on the number of answers you mark correctly. *Wrong answers will not count against you.*

HOW TO USE THIS BOOK

To obtain maximum benefit from this book, we recommend the following approach:

- Read the sections "All About the ASVAB" and "Test-Taking Techniques," which appear on pages 1 and 12.
- Take Practice Examination One. This test, which is in the format used on the actual ASVAB, will give you a clear idea of what the examination is like. Take the test, following all the instructions given, including the time limits. After you complete the test, check your answers and record your scores on the Progress Chart on page 471. Your scores will enable you to see your strengths and weaknesses. You have thus diagnosed the problems you have and can now plan your study time.
- Use the guide on page 472 to plan your studies. Concentrate your study efforts in your weak areas but review other topics as well. Chapters 4 through 11 provide comprehensive review material.

- Take Practice Examination Two. Before you take it, reread the section "Test-Taking Techniques" on pages 9–12. After you finish this examination, check your answers, review the explained answers, and complete the Progress Chart on page 471. Then restudy the appropriate chapters in accordance with the advice given in the study guide.
- Take Practice Examination Three. After you have finished this examination, follow the same procedure that you followed after finishing Practice Examination Two. Continue to restudy material in your weak areas.
- Take Practice Examination Four. Again, follow the same procedure that you followed after finishing each of the other practice examinations. Your scores should improve with each test as you become familiar with the material and review your weak subjects.
- Analyze your job opportunities by studying *academic composites* and *occupational composites* charts on pages 472 and 473.

CHAPTER
2 Test-Taking Techniques

Many people incorrectly believe that the amount of time spent studying is the most important factor in test preparation. Efficient study habits are part of the key to successful test preparation. Of course, all else being equal, the amount of time you devote to your studies is a critical factor. But spending time reading is not necessarily studying. If you want to retain what you read, you must develop a system. For example, a person who devotes 60 minutes a day to uninterrupted study in a quiet, private area will generally retain more than someone who puts in twice that time by studying five or six times a day for 15 to 20 minutes at a time.

Rules for Studying More Effectively

We have listed a number of rules for you to follow to increase study time efficiency. If you use these rules, you will get the most out of this book.

- **MAKE SURE YOU UNDERSTAND THE MEANING OF EVERY WORD YOU READ.** Your ability to understand what you read is the most important skill needed to pass any test. Therefore, starting now, every time you see a word that you don't fully understand, write it down and make note of where you saw it. Then, when you have a chance, look up the meaning of the word in the dictionary. When you think you know what the word means, go back to the reading material that contained the word, and make certain that you fully understand the meaning of the word.

    Keep a list of all words you don't know and periodically review them. Also, try to use these words whenever you can in conversation. If you do this faithfully, you will quickly build an extensive vocabulary that will be helpful to you—not only when you take this examination, but for the rest of your life.

- **STUDY WITHOUT INTERRUPTION FOR AT LEAST 30 MINUTES.** Structure your schedule so that you can study for at least an uninterrupted period of 30 minutes. It is essential that you concentrate for extended periods of time. When you take the practice examinations, do a complete examination in one sitting, just as you must do at the actual examination.

- **SIMULATE EXAMINATION CONDITIONS WHEN STUDYING.** As much as possible, study under the same conditions as those of the examination. Eliminate as many outside interferences as you can. This means no TV, no radio, and staying out of the way of traffic.

- **FOLLOW THE RECOMMENDED TECHNIQUE FOR ANSWERING MULTIPLE-CHOICE QUESTIONS.** In this chapter we provide an invaluable technique for answering multiple-choice questions.

- **TIME YOURSELF WHEN DOING PRACTICE QUESTIONS.** Running out of time on a multiple-choice examination is a tragic error that can be easily avoided. Learn through practice to move to the next question after you've spent a reasonable period of time on any one question. When you are doing practice questions, time yourself so that you will stay within the recommended time limits.
- **CONCENTRATE YOUR STUDY TIME IN YOUR WEAKEST AREAS.** Practice Examination One will give you an idea of the most difficult question types for you. Though you should spend most of your time improving yourself in these areas, don't ignore the other types of questions.
- **EXERCISE REGULARLY AND STAY IN GOOD PHYSICAL CONDITION.** Students who are in good physical condition have an advantage over those who are not. Good physical health improves the ability of the mind to function smoothly and efficiently—you are more relaxed, your brain functions better with more oxygen, and your body secretes substances that make you feel better, which gives you more confidence.
- **ESTABLISH A SCHEDULE FOR STUDYING AND STICK TO IT.** Don't put off studying until those times when you have nothing else to do. Schedule your study time and try not to let anything else interfere with that schedule.

Test Day

1. Get a good night's rest before the test. Wake up in time to eat a sensible breakfast.
2. Wear comfortable clothes. Include a sweater or light jacket that can be added or removed according to room temperature.
3. Come early. If you are not certain about how to get to the test location or how long the trip will take, check these things out ahead of time. If you have to rush into the test worried and out of breath, you will not be in the best condition to do well.

Strategies for Handling Multiple-Choice Questions

The remainder of this chapter outlines a very specific test-taking strategy valuable for a multiple-choice examination. Study the technique, practice it, then study it again until you have mastered it.

1. **READ THE DIRECTIONS.** Do *not* assume that you know what the directions are without reading them. Make sure you read and understand them. This does not mean *spending* time so much as *investing* it in your success. Note particularly whether there are different directions from one section of the examination to another.
2. **TAKE A CLOSE LOOK AT THE ANSWER SHEET.** The answer sheets on your practice examinations are typical of the one you will see on your exam. However, do *not* take anything for granted. Review the directions on the answer sheet carefully, and familiarize yourself with its format.
3. **BE CAREFUL WHEN MARKING YOUR ANSWERS.** Be sure to mark your answers in accordance with the directions on the answer sheet.

   Be extremely careful that:
   ➤ you mark only one answer for each question,
   ➤ you do not make extra marks on your answer sheet,
   ➤ you completely darken the allotted space for the answer you choose,
   ➤ you erase completely any answer you want to change.

4. **MAKE ABSOLUTELY CERTAIN YOU ARE MARKING THE ANSWER TO THE RIGHT QUESTION.** Many multiple-choice tests have been failed because of carelessness in this area. All it takes is one mistake. If you put down one answer in the wrong space, you will probably continue the mistake for a number of questions until you realize your error. It's helpful to use the following procedure when marking your answer sheet:

➤ Select your answer and ask yourself what question number you are working on.
➤ If you select C as the answer for question 11, say to yourself, "C is the answer to question 11."
➤ Then find the space on your answer sheet for question 11, blacken choice C on the answer form, and again say "C is the answer to question 11" as you mark the answer.

While this might seem overly simple and repetitive, after a while it becomes automatic. If followed properly, it guarantees that you will not fail the examination because of a careless mistake.

5. **MAKE SURE THAT YOU UNDERSTAND WHAT THE QUESTION IS ASKING.** Read the stem of the question (the part before the choices) very carefully to make certain that you know what the examiner is asking. In fact, it's wise to read it twice—unless you are working on one of the "speeded" subtests.

6. **READ ALL THE CHOICES BEFORE YOU SELECT AN ANSWER.** Don't make the mistake of falling into the trap that the best distractor, or wrong answer, comes before the correct choice! Read all choices.

7. **BE AWARE OF KEY WORDS THAT OFTEN TIP OFF CORRECT AND INCORRECT ANSWERS.**

Absolute Words—*Usually a Wrong Choice*
(They are generally too broad and difficult to defend)

| never | nothing | always | everyone | only |
| none | nobody | all | everybody | any |

Limiting Words—*Often a Correct Choice*

| usually | few | some | many | often |
| generally | sometimes | possible | occasionally | |

8. **NEVER MAKE A CHOICE BASED ON FREQUENCY OF PREVIOUS ANSWERS.** Some students pay attention to the pattern of answers (A, B, C, and D) when taking the exam. Always answer the question without regard to what the previous choices have been.

9. **ELIMINATE CHOICES YOU KNOW ARE WRONG.** As you read through the choices, eliminate any choice you know is wrong. If you eliminate all but one of the choices, the remaining choice should be the answer. Read the choice one more time to satisfy yourself, and blacken its letter designation (if you still feel it is the best answer) on the answer sheet. If you were not able to narrow the choices to one, many times the second time you read the remaining choices, the answer is clear.

10. **SKIP OVER QUESTIONS THAT GIVE YOU TROUBLE.** The first time through the examination be certain not to dwell too long on any one question. Simply skip the question after blackening any answer on the answer sheet (to keep your answers from getting out of sequence), and go to the next question. Circle the question number in your test booklet so that you can go back to it if you have time.

11. **RETURN TO THE QUESTIONS YOU SKIPPED IN A SUBTEST AFTER YOU FINISH THAT PORTION OF THE EXAMINATION.** Once you have answered all of the questions you were sure of in a subtest of the examination, check the time remaining.

If time permits, return to each question you did not answer and reread the question and the choices. If the answer is still not clear and you are running out of time, make an "educated guess" among those choices. When making an educated guess, follow the guidelines in Strategy 13.

12. **NEVER LEAVE QUESTIONS UNANSWERED SINCE THERE IS NO PENALTY FOR WRONG ANSWERS.**

13. **RULES FOR MAKING AN EDUCATED GUESS.** Your chances of picking the correct answer to questions you are not sure of will be significantly increased if you use the following rules:

➤Never consider answer choices that you have already eliminated. (See Strategy 9.)

➤Be aware of key words that give you clues about which answer might be right or wrong. (See Strategy 7.)

➤If two choices have a conflicting meaning, one of them is probably the correct answer. And, if two choices are too close in meaning, probably neither is correct.

➤If all else fails and you have to make an outright guess at more than one question, guess the same lettered choice for each question. The odds are that you will pick up some valuable points.

14. **BE VERY RELUCTANT TO CHANGE ANSWERS.** Unless you have a very good reason, don't change an answer once you have chosen it. Studies have shown that all too often, people change their answer from the right one to the wrong one.

IDENTIFY AREAS
TO IMPROVE

ANSWER SHEETS—Practice Examination One

GENERAL SCIENCE—SUBTEST 1

1. Ⓐ Ⓑ Ⓒ Ⓓ	6. Ⓐ Ⓑ Ⓒ Ⓓ	11. Ⓐ Ⓑ Ⓒ Ⓓ	16. Ⓐ Ⓑ Ⓒ Ⓓ	21. Ⓐ Ⓑ Ⓒ Ⓓ
2. Ⓐ Ⓑ Ⓒ Ⓓ	7. Ⓐ Ⓑ Ⓒ Ⓓ	12. Ⓐ Ⓑ Ⓒ Ⓓ	17. Ⓐ Ⓑ Ⓒ Ⓓ	22. Ⓐ Ⓑ Ⓒ Ⓓ
3. Ⓐ Ⓑ Ⓒ Ⓓ	8. Ⓐ Ⓑ Ⓒ Ⓓ	13. Ⓐ Ⓑ Ⓒ Ⓓ	18. Ⓐ Ⓑ Ⓒ Ⓓ	23. Ⓐ Ⓑ Ⓒ Ⓓ
4. Ⓐ Ⓑ Ⓒ Ⓓ	9. Ⓐ Ⓑ Ⓒ Ⓓ	14. Ⓐ Ⓑ Ⓒ Ⓓ	19. Ⓐ Ⓑ Ⓒ Ⓓ	24. Ⓐ Ⓑ Ⓒ Ⓓ
5. Ⓐ Ⓑ Ⓒ Ⓓ	10. Ⓐ Ⓑ Ⓒ Ⓓ	15. Ⓐ Ⓑ Ⓒ Ⓓ	20. Ⓐ Ⓑ Ⓒ Ⓓ	25. Ⓐ Ⓑ Ⓒ Ⓓ

ARITHMETIC REASONING—SUBTEST 2

1. Ⓐ Ⓑ Ⓒ Ⓓ	7. Ⓐ Ⓑ Ⓒ Ⓓ	13. Ⓐ Ⓑ Ⓒ Ⓓ	19. Ⓐ Ⓑ Ⓒ Ⓓ	25. Ⓐ Ⓑ Ⓒ Ⓓ
2. Ⓐ Ⓑ Ⓒ Ⓓ	8. Ⓐ Ⓑ Ⓒ Ⓓ	14. Ⓐ Ⓑ Ⓒ Ⓓ	20. Ⓐ Ⓑ Ⓒ Ⓓ	26. Ⓐ Ⓑ Ⓒ Ⓓ
3. Ⓐ Ⓑ Ⓒ Ⓓ	9. Ⓐ Ⓑ Ⓒ Ⓓ	15. Ⓐ Ⓑ Ⓒ Ⓓ	21. Ⓐ Ⓑ Ⓒ Ⓓ	27. Ⓐ Ⓑ Ⓒ Ⓓ
4. Ⓐ Ⓑ Ⓒ Ⓓ	10. Ⓐ Ⓑ Ⓒ Ⓓ	16. Ⓐ Ⓑ Ⓒ Ⓓ	22. Ⓐ Ⓑ Ⓒ Ⓓ	28. Ⓐ Ⓑ Ⓒ Ⓓ
5. Ⓐ Ⓑ Ⓒ Ⓓ	11. Ⓐ Ⓑ Ⓒ Ⓓ	17. Ⓐ Ⓑ Ⓒ Ⓓ	23. Ⓐ Ⓑ Ⓒ Ⓓ	29. Ⓐ Ⓑ Ⓒ Ⓓ
6. Ⓐ Ⓑ Ⓒ Ⓓ	12. Ⓐ Ⓑ Ⓒ Ⓓ	18. Ⓐ Ⓑ Ⓒ Ⓓ	24. Ⓐ Ⓑ Ⓒ Ⓓ	30. Ⓐ Ⓑ Ⓒ Ⓓ

WORD KNOWLEDGE—SUBTEST 3

1. Ⓐ Ⓑ Ⓒ Ⓓ	8. Ⓐ Ⓑ Ⓒ Ⓓ	15. Ⓐ Ⓑ Ⓒ Ⓓ	22. Ⓐ Ⓑ Ⓒ Ⓓ	29. Ⓐ Ⓑ Ⓒ Ⓓ
2. Ⓐ Ⓑ Ⓒ Ⓓ	9. Ⓐ Ⓑ Ⓒ Ⓓ	16. Ⓐ Ⓑ Ⓒ Ⓓ	23. Ⓐ Ⓑ Ⓒ Ⓓ	30. Ⓐ Ⓑ Ⓒ Ⓓ
3. Ⓐ Ⓑ Ⓒ Ⓓ	10. Ⓐ Ⓑ Ⓒ Ⓓ	17. Ⓐ Ⓑ Ⓒ Ⓓ	24. Ⓐ Ⓑ Ⓒ Ⓓ	31. Ⓐ Ⓑ Ⓒ Ⓓ
4. Ⓐ Ⓑ Ⓒ Ⓓ	11. Ⓐ Ⓑ Ⓒ Ⓓ	18. Ⓐ Ⓑ Ⓒ Ⓓ	25. Ⓐ Ⓑ Ⓒ Ⓓ	32. Ⓐ Ⓑ Ⓒ Ⓓ
5. Ⓐ Ⓑ Ⓒ Ⓓ	12. Ⓐ Ⓑ Ⓒ Ⓓ	19. Ⓐ Ⓑ Ⓒ Ⓓ	26. Ⓐ Ⓑ Ⓒ Ⓓ	33. Ⓐ Ⓑ Ⓒ Ⓓ
6. Ⓐ Ⓑ Ⓒ Ⓓ	13. Ⓐ Ⓑ Ⓒ Ⓓ	20. Ⓐ Ⓑ Ⓒ Ⓓ	27. Ⓐ Ⓑ Ⓒ Ⓓ	34. Ⓐ Ⓑ Ⓒ Ⓓ
7. Ⓐ Ⓑ Ⓒ Ⓓ	14. Ⓐ Ⓑ Ⓒ Ⓓ	21. Ⓐ Ⓑ Ⓒ Ⓓ	28. Ⓐ Ⓑ Ⓒ Ⓓ	35. Ⓐ Ⓑ Ⓒ Ⓓ

PARAGRAPH COMPREHENSION—SUBTEST 4

1. Ⓐ Ⓑ Ⓒ Ⓓ	4. Ⓐ Ⓑ Ⓒ Ⓓ	7. Ⓐ Ⓑ Ⓒ Ⓓ	10. Ⓐ Ⓑ Ⓒ Ⓓ	13. Ⓐ Ⓑ Ⓒ Ⓓ
2. Ⓐ Ⓑ Ⓒ Ⓓ	5. Ⓐ Ⓑ Ⓒ Ⓓ	8. Ⓐ Ⓑ Ⓒ Ⓓ	11. Ⓐ Ⓑ Ⓒ Ⓓ	14. Ⓐ Ⓑ Ⓒ Ⓓ
3. Ⓐ Ⓑ Ⓒ Ⓓ	6. Ⓐ Ⓑ Ⓒ Ⓓ	9. Ⓐ Ⓑ Ⓒ Ⓓ	12. Ⓐ Ⓑ Ⓒ Ⓓ	15. Ⓐ Ⓑ Ⓒ Ⓓ

AUTOMOTIVE INFORMATION—SUBTEST 5

1. Ⓐ Ⓑ Ⓒ Ⓓ	4. Ⓐ Ⓑ Ⓒ Ⓓ	7. Ⓐ Ⓑ Ⓒ Ⓓ	10. Ⓐ Ⓑ Ⓒ Ⓓ	13. Ⓐ Ⓑ Ⓒ Ⓓ
2. Ⓐ Ⓑ Ⓒ Ⓓ	5. Ⓐ Ⓑ Ⓒ Ⓓ	8. Ⓐ Ⓑ Ⓒ Ⓓ	11. Ⓐ Ⓑ Ⓒ Ⓓ	14. Ⓐ Ⓑ Ⓒ Ⓓ
3. Ⓐ Ⓑ Ⓒ Ⓓ	6. Ⓐ Ⓑ Ⓒ Ⓓ	9. Ⓐ Ⓑ Ⓒ Ⓓ	12. Ⓐ Ⓑ Ⓒ Ⓓ	15. Ⓐ Ⓑ Ⓒ Ⓓ

MATHEMATICS KNOWLEDGE—SUBTEST 6

1. Ⓐ Ⓑ Ⓒ Ⓓ	6. Ⓐ Ⓑ Ⓒ Ⓓ	11. Ⓐ Ⓑ Ⓒ Ⓓ	16. Ⓐ Ⓑ Ⓒ Ⓓ	21. Ⓐ Ⓑ Ⓒ Ⓓ
2. Ⓐ Ⓑ Ⓒ Ⓓ	7. Ⓐ Ⓑ Ⓒ Ⓓ	12. Ⓐ Ⓑ Ⓒ Ⓓ	17. Ⓐ Ⓑ Ⓒ Ⓓ	22. Ⓐ Ⓑ Ⓒ Ⓓ
3. Ⓐ Ⓑ Ⓒ Ⓓ	8. Ⓐ Ⓑ Ⓒ Ⓓ	13. Ⓐ Ⓑ Ⓒ Ⓓ	18. Ⓐ Ⓑ Ⓒ Ⓓ	23. Ⓐ Ⓑ Ⓒ Ⓓ
4. Ⓐ Ⓑ Ⓒ Ⓓ	9. Ⓐ Ⓑ Ⓒ Ⓓ	14. Ⓐ Ⓑ Ⓒ Ⓓ	19. Ⓐ Ⓑ Ⓒ Ⓓ	24. Ⓐ Ⓑ Ⓒ Ⓓ
5. Ⓐ Ⓑ Ⓒ Ⓓ	10. Ⓐ Ⓑ Ⓒ Ⓓ	15. Ⓐ Ⓑ Ⓒ Ⓓ	20. Ⓐ Ⓑ Ⓒ Ⓓ	25. Ⓐ Ⓑ Ⓒ Ⓓ

MECHANICAL COMPREHENSION—SUBTEST 7

1. Ⓐ Ⓑ Ⓒ Ⓓ	6. Ⓐ Ⓑ Ⓒ Ⓓ	11. Ⓐ Ⓑ Ⓒ Ⓓ	16. Ⓐ Ⓑ Ⓒ Ⓓ	21. Ⓐ Ⓑ Ⓒ Ⓓ
2. Ⓐ Ⓑ Ⓒ Ⓓ	7. Ⓐ Ⓑ Ⓒ Ⓓ	12. Ⓐ Ⓑ Ⓒ Ⓓ	17. Ⓐ Ⓑ Ⓒ Ⓓ	22. Ⓐ Ⓑ Ⓒ Ⓓ
3. Ⓐ Ⓑ Ⓒ Ⓓ	8. Ⓐ Ⓑ Ⓒ Ⓓ	13. Ⓐ Ⓑ Ⓒ Ⓓ	18. Ⓐ Ⓑ Ⓒ Ⓓ	23. Ⓐ Ⓑ Ⓒ Ⓓ
4. Ⓐ Ⓑ Ⓒ Ⓓ	9. Ⓐ Ⓑ Ⓒ Ⓓ	14. Ⓐ Ⓑ Ⓒ Ⓓ	19. Ⓐ Ⓑ Ⓒ Ⓓ	24. Ⓐ Ⓑ Ⓒ Ⓓ
5. Ⓐ Ⓑ Ⓒ Ⓓ	10. Ⓐ Ⓑ Ⓒ Ⓓ	15. Ⓐ Ⓑ Ⓒ Ⓓ	20. Ⓐ Ⓑ Ⓒ Ⓓ	25. Ⓐ Ⓑ Ⓒ Ⓓ

ELECTRONICS INFORMATION—SUBTEST 8

1. Ⓐ Ⓑ Ⓒ Ⓓ	5. Ⓐ Ⓑ Ⓒ Ⓓ	9. Ⓐ Ⓑ Ⓒ Ⓓ	13. Ⓐ Ⓑ Ⓒ Ⓓ	17. Ⓐ Ⓑ Ⓒ Ⓓ
2. Ⓐ Ⓑ Ⓒ Ⓓ	6. Ⓐ Ⓑ Ⓒ Ⓓ	10. Ⓐ Ⓑ Ⓒ Ⓓ	14. Ⓐ Ⓑ Ⓒ Ⓓ	18. Ⓐ Ⓑ Ⓒ Ⓓ
3. Ⓐ Ⓑ Ⓒ Ⓓ	7. Ⓐ Ⓑ Ⓒ Ⓓ	11. Ⓐ Ⓑ Ⓒ Ⓓ	15. Ⓐ Ⓑ Ⓒ Ⓓ	19. Ⓐ Ⓑ Ⓒ Ⓓ
4. Ⓐ Ⓑ Ⓒ Ⓓ	8. Ⓐ Ⓑ Ⓒ Ⓓ	12. Ⓐ Ⓑ Ⓒ Ⓓ	16. Ⓐ Ⓑ Ⓒ Ⓓ	20. Ⓐ Ⓑ Ⓒ Ⓓ

SHOP INFORMATION—SUBTEST 9

1. Ⓐ Ⓑ Ⓒ Ⓓ	4. Ⓐ Ⓑ Ⓒ Ⓓ	7. Ⓐ Ⓑ Ⓒ Ⓓ	10. Ⓐ Ⓑ Ⓒ Ⓓ	13. Ⓐ Ⓑ Ⓒ Ⓓ
2. Ⓐ Ⓑ Ⓒ Ⓓ	5. Ⓐ Ⓑ Ⓒ Ⓓ	8. Ⓐ Ⓑ Ⓒ Ⓓ	11. Ⓐ Ⓑ Ⓒ Ⓓ	14. Ⓐ Ⓑ Ⓒ Ⓓ
3. Ⓐ Ⓑ Ⓒ Ⓓ	6. Ⓐ Ⓑ Ⓒ Ⓓ	9. Ⓐ Ⓑ Ⓒ Ⓓ	12. Ⓐ Ⓑ Ⓒ Ⓓ	15. Ⓐ Ⓑ Ⓒ Ⓓ

ASSEMBLING OBJECTS—SUBTEST 10

1. Ⓐ Ⓑ Ⓒ Ⓓ	5. Ⓐ Ⓑ Ⓒ Ⓓ	9. Ⓐ Ⓑ Ⓒ Ⓓ	13. Ⓐ Ⓑ Ⓒ Ⓓ	17. Ⓐ Ⓑ Ⓒ Ⓓ
2. Ⓐ Ⓑ Ⓒ Ⓓ	6. Ⓐ Ⓑ Ⓒ Ⓓ	10. Ⓐ Ⓑ Ⓒ Ⓓ	14. Ⓐ Ⓑ Ⓒ Ⓓ	18. Ⓐ Ⓑ Ⓒ Ⓓ
3. Ⓐ Ⓑ Ⓒ Ⓓ	7. Ⓐ Ⓑ Ⓒ Ⓓ	11. Ⓐ Ⓑ Ⓒ Ⓓ	15. Ⓐ Ⓑ Ⓒ Ⓓ	19. Ⓐ Ⓑ Ⓒ Ⓓ
4. Ⓐ Ⓑ Ⓒ Ⓓ	8. Ⓐ Ⓑ Ⓒ Ⓓ	12. Ⓐ Ⓑ Ⓒ Ⓓ	16. Ⓐ Ⓑ Ⓒ Ⓓ	20. Ⓐ Ⓑ Ⓒ Ⓓ

CHAPTER
3 Practice Examination One

GENERAL SCIENCE—SUBTEST 1

DIRECTIONS

This test has questions about science. Pick the best answer for each question, then blacken the space on your separate answer form that has the same number and letter as your choice.

Here is a sample question.

1. An example of a chemical change is

    A melting ice.
    B breaking glass.
    C rusting metal.
    D making sawdust from wood.

The correct answer is "rusting metal," so you would blacken the space for C on your answer form.

Your score on this subtest will be based on the number of questions you answer correctly. You should try to answer every question. Do not spend too much time on any one question.

When you begin, be sure to start with question number 1 in Part 1, and number 1 in Part 1 on your answer form.

THE ACTUAL TEST WILL SAY:

Do not turn this page until told to do so.

General Science

Time: 11 minutes; 25 questions

1. A ringing bell, placed in a vacuum under a glass bell jar, will

   A have the pitch of its sound raised.
   B crack the thick glass of the bell jar.
   C undergo no change.
   D be inaudible.

2. The light-year is used to measure

   A intensity of light.
   B distance.
   C time.
   D brightness.

3. If a piece of corundum weighs 4 ounces in the air but appears to weigh only 3 ounces when submerged in water, its specific gravity is

   A 1/4.
   B 1.
   C 3.
   D 4.

4. Which kind of time does a sundial keep?

   A legal
   B standard
   C solar
   D sonic

5. Of the following, the best conductor of heat is

   A asbestos.
   B copper.
   C brass.
   D glass.

6. Ecology can best be described as the study of

   A methods of fighting pollution.
   B erosion of land.
   C changes in plants.
   D the relationship between the environment and living things.

7. When a candle burns, the chief products are

   A carbon monoxide and nitrogen.
   B carbon dioxide and nitrogen.
   C carbon monoxide and water.
   D carbon dioxide and water.

8. Of the following, the one that yields the most energy per ounce as a result of normal metabolism is

   A protein.
   B sugar.
   C starch.
   D fat.

9. The half-life of radium is 1,620 years. What fraction of a radium sample will remain after 3,240 years?

   A 1/16
   B 1/8
   C 1/4
   D 1/2

10. Which is a chemical property of water?

    A It freezes.
    B It evaporates.
    C It condenses.
    D It decomposes into gases.

11. Which of the following statements correctly refers to the process of photosynthesis?

    A Light is necessary for the process to occur.
    B Oxygen is necessary for the process to occur.
    C Carbon dioxide is given off during this process.
    D The process is carried on by all protozoa.

12. The relative humidity of the air when dew forms is

    A 100%.
    B 75%.
    C 50%.
    D 25%.

13. To start a fire with the aid of the sun, one should use a

A concave lens.
B flat mirror.
C magnifying lens.
D concave mirror.

14. The change from daylight to darkness is caused by the

A inclination of the earth's axis.
B force of gravitation.
C rotation of the earth.
D revolution of the earth.

15. A substance that is readily absorbed through the walls of the stomach is

A a starch.
B alcohol.
C an amino acid.
D ascorbic acid.

16. The positively charged particle in the nucleus of an atom is a(n)

A proton.
B isotope.
C neutron.
D electron.

17. Which one is unrelated to the other three?

A Pluto
B Moon
C Neptune
D Uranus

18. Sulfur is mined chiefly for the production of

A sulfa drugs.
B sulfanilamide.
C sulfuric acid.
D superphosphates.

19. To which organism is the whale most closely related?

A tuna
B turtle
C dinosaur
D horse

20. A beam of parallel rays of light is reflected from a plane (flat) mirror. After reflection, the rays will be

A absorbed.
B converged.
C diffused.
D parallel.

21. How much voltage is needed to produce a current of 0.5 ampere in a circuit that has a resistance of 24 ohms?

A 6 volts
B 12 volts
C 24 volts
D 36 volts

22. Aeration of water will produce

A a loss of oxygen.
B a loss of methane.
C a gain of carbon dioxide.
D a gain of carbon dioxide and a loss of oxygen.

23. What is the correct formula for dry ice?

A HO_2
B H_2O_2
C CO
D CO_2

24. If a person lifts a 50-pound package to the top of a 25-foot ladder, how many foot-pounds of work are performed?

A 75 foot-pounds
B 500 foot-pounds
C 1,000 foot-pounds
D 1,250 foot-pounds

25. What chemical reaction is represented by the following equation?

$$2H_2S \rightarrow 2H_2 \uparrow + S_2 \uparrow$$

A composition
B decomposition
C replacement
D double replacement

ARITHMETIC REASONING—SUBTEST 2

DIRECTIONS

This test has questions about arithmetic. Each question is followed by four possible answers. Decide which answer is correct. Then, on your answer form, blacken the space that has the same number and letter as your choice. Use scratch paper for any figuring you wish to do.

Here is a sample question.

1. If 1 quart of milk costs $0.80, what is the cost of 2 quarts?

   A $2.00
   B $1.60
   C $1.20
   D $1.00

The cost of 2 quarts is $1.60; therefore, answer B is correct.

Your score on this test will be based on the number of questions you answer correctly. You should try to answer every question. Do not spend too much time on any one question.

Notice that Part 2 begins with question number 1. When you begin, be sure to mark your first answer next to number 1 on your answer form.

THE ACTUAL TEST WILL SAY:

Do not turn this page until told to do so.

Arithmetic Reasoning

Time: 36 minutes; 30 questions

1. The Parkers bought a table that was marked $400. On the installment plan, they made a down payment equal to 25% of the marked price, plus 12 monthly payments of $30 each. How much more than the marked price did they pay by buying it this way?

   A $25
   B $50
   C $60
   D $460

2. A scientist planted 120 seeds, of which 90 sprouted. What percentage of the seeds failed to sprout?

   A 25%
   B 24%
   C 30%
   D 75%

3. An airplane traveled 1,000 miles in 2 hours and 30 minutes. What was the average rate or speed, in miles per hour, for the trip?

   A 200 miles per hour
   B 300 miles per hour
   C 400 miles per hour
   D 500 miles per hour

4. What is the value of this expression?

$$\frac{0.05 \times 4}{0.1}$$

   A 20
   B 2
   C 0.2
   D 0.02

5. Joan Smith's bank balance was $2,674. Her bank balance changed as follows over the next 4-month period:

   −$348, +$765, +$802, −$518

What was her bank balance at the end of the 4-month period?

A $5,107
B $4,241
C $3,475
D $3,375

6. A snack bar sold 12½ gallons of milk at 35 cents a pint. How much did the snack bar receive for the milk?

A $33.60
B $34.00
C $35.00
D $32.20

7. A square measures 9 feet on a side. If each side of the square is increased by 3 feet, how many square feet are added to the area?

A 144
B 81
C 60
D 63

8. What is the average of 1/4 and 1/6?

A 5/24
B 7/24
C 5/12
D 1/5

9. Joe Gray's salary was increased from $260 per week to $290 per week. What was the increase in his salary to the nearest percent?

A 12%
B 11%
C 10%
D 9%

10. If 1 pound, 12 ounces of fish costs $2.24, what is the cost of the fish per pound?

A $1.20
B $1.28
C $1.24
D $1.40

11. A front lawn measures 25 feet in length and 15 feet in width. The back lawn of the same house measures 50 feet in length and 30 feet in width. What is the ratio of the area of the front lawn to the area of the back lawn?

A 1:2
B 2:3
C 3:4
D 1:4

12. The price of a used car was increased from $6,400 to $7,200. What was the percentage increase?

A 10%
B 11.25%
C 12.5%
D 15%

13. What is the next term in this series: 3½, 2¼, 13¼, 12, _____?

A 1¼
B 10¾
C 23
D 14½

14. A movie theater opens at 10:00 A.M. and closes at 11:30 P.M. If a complete showing of a movie takes 2 hours and 15 minutes, how many complete showings are given at the movie theater each day?

A 5
B 6
C 7
D 8

15. At a concert, orchestra seats sell for $20 each, and balcony seats sell for $10 each. If 324 orchestra seats were occupied, and the box office collected $10,000, how many balcony seats were sold?

A 375
B 352
C 330
D 310

16. In a certain city, taxicab fare is $0.80 for the first 1/4 mile, and $0.20 for each additional 1/4 mile. How far, in miles, can a passenger travel for $5.00?

A 5 miles
B 4¼ miles
C 5½ miles
D 5¾ miles

17. A scale drawing of a building plot has a scale of 1 inch to 40 feet. How many inches on the drawing represent a distance of 175 feet on the plot?

A 4⅛ inches
B 4⅜ inches
C 4½ inches
D 4¾ inches

18. The wholesale list price of a watch was $50. A dealer bought a shipment of watches at a discount of 20% and sold the watches at 10% above the wholesale list price. What was her profit on each watch?

A $8
B $10
C $12
D $15

19. The minute hand of a clock is missing, but the hour hand is on the 11-minute mark. What time was it when the clock broke?

A 5 minutes after 11
B 11 minutes after 12
C 12 minutes after 2
D 20 minutes after 1

20. During a season a professional basketball player tried 320 shots and made 272 of them. What percentage of the shots tried were successful?

A 85%
B 80%
C 75%
D 70%

21. A painter and a helper spent 3 days painting a house. The painter received twice as much as the helper. If the two men were paid $375 total for the job, how much did the painter receive?

A $175
B $200
C $225
D $250

22. What is the difference between a 50% discount and a discount of 33⅓%?

A 0.17
B 1/3
C 0.25
D 1/6

23. What is the value of $3a^2 - 2a + 5$ when $a = 4$?

A 43
B 45
C 61
D 21

24. This table gives the annual premiums for a life insurance policy based on the age of the holder when the policy is taken out.

Age in Years	Premium per $1,000
22	$18
30	$22
38	$28
46	$38

Over 20 years, how much is saved by taking out a $1,000 policy at age 30, rather than at age 46?

A $16
B $32
C $320
D $400

25. A chair was marked for sale at $240. This sale price was 25% less than the original price. What was the original price?

A $300
B $280
C $320
D $60

26. What is the quotient when 0.675 is divided by 0.9?

A 7.5
B 0.075
C 75
D 0.75

27. On May 15, an electric meter read 5,472 kilowatt-hours. The following month, on June 15, the meter read 5,687 kilowatt-hours. The utility charges the following rates for electric service.

First 10 kilowatt-hours—$2.48

Next 45 kilowatt-hours—$0.16 per kilowatt-hour

Next 55 kilowatt-hours—$0.12 per kilowatt-hour

More than 110 kilowatt-hours—$0.07 per kilowatt-hour

What was the total charge for the kilowatt hours consumed during the month from May 15 to June 15?

A $22.53
B $23.63
C $22.63
D $24.43

28. What is the difference between the square of 49 and the square of 31?

A 18
B 1.4322
C 1,440
D 2,056

29. An auditorium contains x rows, with y seats in each row. What is the number of seats in the auditorium?

A xy
B $x + y$
C $x - y$
D $y - x$

30. When a certain number is divided by 15, the quotient is 8 and the remainder is 7. What is the number?

A 127
B 8½
C 3⅗
D 77

WORD KNOWLEDGE—SUBTEST 3

DIRECTIONS

This test has questions about the meanings of words. Each question has an **underlined boldface word**. You are to decide which one of the four words in the choices most nearly means the same as the underlined boldface word; then mark the space on your answer form that has the same number and letter as your choice.

Now look at the sample question below.

1. It was a **small** table.

   A sturdy
   B round
   C cheap
   D little

The question asks which of the four words means the same as the boldface word, **small**. Little means the same as **small**. Answer D is the best one.

Your score on this test will be based on the number of questions you answer correctly. You should try to answer every question. Do not spend too much time on any one question.

When you begin, be sure to start with question number 1 in Part 3 of your test booklet and number 1 in Part 3 on your answer form.

THE ACTUAL TEST WILL SAY:

Do not turn this page until told to do so.

Word Knowledge

Time: 11 minutes; 35 questions

1. **Subsume** most nearly means

   A understate.
   B absorb.
   C include.
   D belong.

2. Our committee reached **consensus**.

   A accord
   B abridgment
   C presumption
   D quota

3. **Altercation** most nearly means

   A defeat.
   B concurrence.
   C quarrel.
   D vexation.

4. Don't accuse him of being **irresolute**.

   A wavering
   B insubordinate
   C impudent
   D unobservant

5. **Laconic** most nearly means

   A slothful.
   B concise.
   C punctual.
   D melancholy.

6. **Audition** most nearly means

   A reception.
   B contest.
   C hearing.
   D display.

7. The job was filled by a **novice**.

A volunteer
B expert
C beginner
D amateur

8. A **conciliatory** attitude sometimes helps.

A pacific
B contentious
C obligatory
D offensive

9. The drug will **counteract** any effect.

A undermine
B censure
C preserve
D neutralize

10. **Precedent** most nearly means

A example.
B theory.
C law.
D conformity.

11. **Diaphanous** most nearly means

A transparent.
B opaque.
C diaphragmatic.
D diffusive.

12. We **deferred** our judgment.

A reversed
B accelerated
C rejected
D delayed

13. To **accentuate** most nearly means to

A modify.
B hasten.
C sustain.
D intensify.

14. **Authentic** most nearly means

A detailed.
B genuine.
C valuable.
D practical.

15. **Unanimity** most nearly means

A emphasis.
B namelessness.
C disagreement.
D concurrence.

16. Their actions made them **notorious**.

A condemned
B unpleasant
C vexatious
D infamous

17. **Previous** most nearly means

A abandoned.
B former.
C timely.
D younger.

18. Use a **flexible** metal.

A breakable
B flammable
C pliable
D weak

19. **Option** most nearly means

A use.
B choice.
C value.
D preference.

20. You should **verify** the facts.

A examine
B explain
C confirm
D guarantee

21. Pert most nearly means

A ill.
B lazy.
C slow.
D saucy.

22. Aesthetic most nearly means

A sentient.
B sensitive.
C tasteful.
D inartistic.

23. Decimation most nearly means

A killing.
B annihilation.
C armistice.
D brawl.

24. She made an **indignant** response.

A angry
B poor
C indigent
D lazy

25. Cliché most nearly means

A commonplace.
B banality.
C hackney.
D platitude.

26. Harmony most nearly means

A rhythm.
B pleasure.
C discord.
D agreement.

27. Indolent most nearly means

A moderate.
B hopeless.
C lazy.
D idle.

28. His **respiration** was impaired.

A recovery
B breathing
C pulsation
D sweating

29. The job requires a **vigilant** attitude.

A sensible
B watchful
C suspicious
D restless

30. Incidental most nearly means

A independent.
B needless.
C infrequent.
D casual.

31. To **succumb** most nearly means to

A aid.
B oppose.
C yield.
D check.

32. That solution is not **feasible.**

A capable
B harmful
C beneficial
D practicable

33. Versatile most nearly means

A well-known.
B up-to-date.
C many-sided.
D ambidextrous.

34. His **imperturbability** helps in a crisis.

A obstinacy
B serenity
C sagacity
D confusion

35. Strident most nearly means

A swaggering.
B domineering.
C angry.
D harsh.

PARAGRAPH COMPREHENSION—SUBTEST 4

DIRECTIONS

This test is a test of your ability to understand what you read. In this section you will find one or more paragraphs of reading material followed by incomplete statements or questions.

You are to read the paragraph and select which of the four lettered choices best completes the statement or answers the question. When you have selected your answer, blacken the correct numbered letter on your answer sheet.

Now look at the sample question below.

In certain areas water is so scarce that every attempt is made to conserve it. For instance, on one oasis in the Sahara Desert the amount of water necessary for each date palm tree has been carefully determined.

1. How much water is each tree given?

    A no water at all
    B exactly the amount required
    C water only if it is healthy
    D water on alternate days

The amount of water each tree required has been carefully determined, so answer B is correct.

Your score on this subtest will be based on the number of questions you answer correctly. You should try to answer every question. Do not spend too much time on any one question.

When you begin, be sure to start with question number 1 in Part 4 of your test booklet and number 1 in Part 4 on your answer form.

THE ACTUAL TEST WILL SAY:

Do not turn this page until told to do so.

Paragraph Comprehension

Time: 13 minutes; 15 questions

1. Twenty-five percent of all household burglaries can be attributed to unlocked windows or doors. Crime is the result of opportunity plus desire.

To prevent crime, it is each individual's responsibility to

A provide the opportunity.
B provide the desire.
C prevent the opportunity.
D prevent the desire.

2. From a building designer's standpoint, three things that make a home livable are the client, the building site, and the amount of money the client has to spend.

According to the passage, to make a home livable

A the prospective piece of land makes little difference.
B it can be built on any piece of land.
C the design must fit the owner's income and the site.
D the design must fit the designer's income.

3. Family camping has been described as the "biggest single growth industry in the booming travel/leisure market." Camping ranges from backpacking to living in motor homes with complete creature comforts. It is both an end in itself and a magic carpet to a wide variety of other forms of outdoor recreation.

It can be inferred from the passage that the LEAST luxurious form of camping is

A backpacking.
B travel trailers.
C truck campers.
D motor homes.

4. Most drivers try to drive safely. A major part of safe driving is driving at the right speed. But what is the "right" speed? Is it 20 miles per hour, or 35, or 60? That question may be hard to answer. On some city streets and in heavy traffic, 20 miles per hour could be too fast, even if it's within the posted speed limit. On a superhighway, 35 miles per hour could be too slow. Of course, a good driver must follow the speed limit, but he must also use good judgment. The right speed will vary depending on the number of cars, the road surface and its condition, and the driver's visibility.

The general theme of this passage is that a good driver

A drives at 35 miles an hour.
B adjusts to different driving conditions.
C always drives at the same speed.
D always follows the speed limit.

5. Gardening can be an easygoing hobby, a scientific pursuit, an opportunity for exercise and fresh air, a significant source of food to help balance the family budget, a means of expression in art and beauty, an applied experiment in green plant growth, or all of these things together.

All of the following are made possible by gardening according to the passage EXCEPT

A relaxation.
B exercise.
C experimentation.
D hard work.

6. About three-fourths of the surface of the earth is water. Of the 336 million cubic miles of water, most (97.2%) is found in the oceans and is salty. Glaciers hold another 2% of the total. Less than 1% (0.8%) is available as freshwater for people to use—and much of that is not near people who need it.

The amount of freshwater available for people to use is

A 97.2%.
B 0.8%.
C 2%.
D 75%.

7. Early settlers in the United States made the most of the herring fishing season. When spring came, the fish arrived in great numbers in the rivers. No nets or hooks were needed. Men used what was called a *pinfold*, a large circular pen built in shallow water. It was made by driving stakes closely together in the floor of the river.

A pinfold was made with

A hooks and nets.
B only nets.
C stakes driven into the river bottom.
D fishing rods.

8. The powers of the United States government are divided. The legislative branch, composed of the two houses of Congress (the House of Representatives and the Senate), makes the laws. The executive branch, made up of the president and the heads of the different departments, put the laws into effect. The judicial branch, made up of the courts, tries cases when laws are broken. The idea behind this organization is to prevent one part or branch of government from having all the power.

As a result of the divided powers of government,

A Congress rules the United States.
B the president rules the United States.
C power is shared.
D no branch has power.

9. A narcotic is a drug that, in proper doses, relieves pain and induces profound sleep, but which, in poisonous doses, induces stupor, coma, or convulsions. Narcotics tend to be habit-forming and, in many instances, repeated doses lead to addiction.

A proper dose of narcotic induces

A coma.
B convulsions.
C deep sleep.
D stupor.

10. Because nitrogen, phosphorus, and potassium are used by plants in large amounts, these nutrients are likely to be deficient in the soil. When you buy a fertilizer, therefore, you generally buy it for its content of these materials.

Unfertilized soil naturally deficient in nitrogen, phosphoric oxide, and potash probably lacks these nutrients because

A they are not soluble.
B manufacturers do not recommend them to gardeners.
C they are rare elements never found in the earth.
D plants use them up in large quantities.

11. Where does pollution come from? It comes from a wide variety of sources, including furnaces, smokestacks, incinerators, power-generating stations, industrial plants, dirt and dust caused by tearing down old buildings and putting up new ones, ordinary street dirt, restaurants that emit smoke and odors, cars, buses, trucks, planes, and coal- or diesel-burning motor ships. Sixty percent of pollution is caused by motor vehicle exhausts, while another thirty percent is due to industry.

Most air pollution is caused by

A industry and incinerators.
B cars, trucks, and buses.
C airplanes.
D smokestacks of buildings.

12. The use of sunglasses as an aid to vision is important. For the most part, the eye is a daytime instrument: It requires light to work properly. However, too much bright light and glare can create discomfort; as a result the eyes blink, squint, get tears, or have trouble seeing well. Sunglasses help by keeping much of this bright light and glare from reaching the eyes.

The main purpose of sunglasses is to

A hide the eyes.
B screen out harmful rays of the sun.
C remove the need for regular glasses.
D protect the eyes from dirt.

13. Would you like to be good at a trade? Would you like to know a skill that pays well? One sure way to skill, good pay, and regular work is to train on the job. This is called *apprentice training*. While it is not the only way to learn, apprentice training has good points. You can earn while you learn. You will know the skill "from the ground up." You can advance on the job.

Apprentice training is described by discussing

A both sides.
B the good side.
C the bad side.
D a specific trade.

14. When you work at a job covered by social security, you and your employer contribute equal amounts. Your portion of the tax is taken from your wages or paycheck before you receive it. This is called a *deduction*.

Which of these statements is true according to the passage?

A Total tax rate is retirement rate plus insurance rate.
B Insurance rates are higher than retirement rates.
C Money taken from your pay is called a deduction.
D Only your employer contributes to social security.

15. Nucleic acids are found in all living organisms, from viruses to humans. Their name refers to their discovery in the nuclei of white blood cells and fish sperm by Swiss physiologist Johann Miescher in 1869. However, it is now well established that nucleic acids occur outside the cell nucleus as well.

Nucleic acids are found

A only in cells of humans.
B only in viruses.
C in all living cells.
D only in white blood cells.

AUTOMOTIVE INFORMATION—SUBTEST 5

DIRECTIONS

This test has questions about automobiles. Pick the best answer for each question, then blacken the space on your separate answer form that has the same number and letter as your choice.
Here is a sample question.

1. The most commonly used fuel for running automobile engines is

   A kerosene.
   B benzene.
   C crude oil.
   D gasoline.

Gasoline is the most commonly used fuel, so D is the correct answer.

Your score on this test will be based on the number of questions you answer correctly. You should try to answer every question. Do not spend too much time on any one question.

When you are told to begin, be sure to start with question number 1 in Part 5 of your test booklet and number 1 in Part 5 on your separate answer form.

THE ACTUAL TEST WILL SAY:

Do not turn this page until told to do so.

Automotive Information

Time: 8 minutes; 15 questions

1. Underinflating a tire will cause excessive wear on

   A the center of the tread.
   B both outside edges of the tread.
   C the bead.
   D the sidewalls.

2. A vehicle's "track" is measured from

   A bumper to bumper.
   B left front wheel to right rear wheel.
   C center of left wheel to center of right wheel.
   D fender to fender.

3. The resistor used to drop voltage to the ignition coil is called the

   A battery resistor.
   B ballast resistor.
   C ignition resistor.
   D dropping resistor.

4. Syncromesh units are used in standard transmissions because they

   A are stronger.
   B eliminate grinding of the gears.
   C cost less.
   D give an overdrive effect.

5. The vacuum modulator in an automatic transmission

   A allows the transmission only to downshift.
   B controls the shifts of the transmission while sensing the engine load.
   C creates a vacuum to shift the clutches.
   D modulates vacuum for ignition spark advance when overheating.

6. A clutch pedal must have free play so that

   A the clutch grabs early.
   B the clutch grabs late.
   C there is clearance between the disc and the flywheel.
   D there is clearance between the clutch fingers and the throwout bearing.

7. A limited slip differential is used to

   A allow a car to climb hills faster.
   B give better traction on ice.
   C keep the rear end cooler.
   D give a softer ride.

8. What are the two main functions of the ignition system?

   A to provide a primary arc and a secondary spark
   B to provide a spark and a means to decrease it
   C to provide a high-voltage spark and the means to time the engine
   D to provide a path for the wires and the spark plugs

9. In an ignition system using a resistor in the primary circuit, the resistor is located between the

   A battery and the ignition switch.
   B ignition switch and the coil.
   C coil and the distributor points.
   D distributor points and the condenser.

10. The magnetic field within an alternator is produced by the

    A rotor.
    B stator.
    C diodes.
    D heat sink.

11. If a horn sounds continuously but the horn relay is good, the most likely cause is

    A a short in the horn.
    B a grounded horn.
    C an open wire at the horn button.
    D a grounded wire at the horn button.

12. The purpose of the rubber cups in the brake wheel cylinders is to

    A push out the brake shoes.
    B prevent brake fluid from leaking out of the cylinder.
    C maintain the springs in position.
    D absorb the shock of the brake application.

13. The metering valve in a hydraulic brake system

    A holds off pressure to the front brakes.
    B holds off pressure to the rear brakes.
    C equalizes pressure to all four wheel brakes.
    D warns the driver of brake system failure.

14. The order in which the events occur in the four-stroke cycle engine are

    A intake, compression, exhaust, power.
    B intake, compression, power, exhaust.
    C intake, power, exhaust, compression.
    D intake, power, compression, exhaust.

15. If the piston and rod assembly is to be removed from an engine block, any ridge at the top of a cylinder

    A should be removed using a ridge reamer.
    B should be drilled out.
    C should be filed down with a single cut file.
    D does not interfere with the removal of the assembly.

MATHEMATICS KNOWLEDGE—SUBTEST 6

DIRECTIONS

This is a test of your ability to solve general mathematical problems. Each problem is followed by four answer choices. Select the correct response from the choices given, then mark the space on your answer form that has the same number and letter as your choice. Use scratch paper to do any figuring that you wish.

Now look at this sample problem.

1. If $x + 8 = 9$, then x is equal to

A 0.
B 1.
C –1.
D 9/8

The correct answer is 1, so B is the correct response.

Your score on this test will be based on the number of questions you answer correctly. You should try to answer every question. Do not spend too much time on any one question.

Start with question number 1 in Part 6. Mark your answer for this question next to number 1, Part 6, on your answer form.

THE ACTUAL TEST WILL SAY:

Do not turn this page until told to do so.

Mathematics Knowledge

Time: 24 minutes; 25 questions

1. Which of the following is the smallest prime number greater than 200?

   A 201
   B 205
   C 211
   D 214

2. If 40% is equal to the fraction $x/30$, what is the value of x?

   A 0.4
   B 15
   C 1,200
   D 12

3. The expression "5 factorial" equals

   A 125.
   B 120.
   C 25.
   D 10.

4. What is the result of subtracting $3x^2 - 5x - 1$ from $8x^2 + 2x - 9$?

   A $5x^2 - 3x - 10$
   B $-5x^2 - 3x - 10$
   C $5x^2 + 7x - 8$
   D $-5x^2 - 7x + 8$

5. What is the meaning of the statement $-30 < -5$?

   A 30 is greater than 5.
   B 30 is less than minus 5.
   C Negative 30 is less than negative 5.
   D Negative 30 is greater than negative 5.

6. Solve for x: $8x - 2 - 5x = 8$.

   A $x = 1.3$
   B $x = 2\frac{1}{2}$
   C $x = 3\frac{1}{3}$
   D $x = -7$

7. A woman has $500 in a bank account. Every week, she writes out a check for $50. If she doesn't make any new deposits, what will her bank account hold x weeks from now?

   A $500 + 50x$
   B $500 − 50x$
   C $550 − x
   D $500 + $50 + x

8. When the temperature is 20°C, what is it on the Fahrenheit (F) scale? (Use the following formula).

   $$F = \left(\frac{9}{5} \times C\right) + 32$$

   A 93⅗ degrees
   B 78 degrees
   C 62⅗ degrees
   D 68 degrees

9. The perimeter of a rectangle is 38 inches. If the length is 3 inches more than the width, find the width.

   A 17½ inches
   B 8 inches
   C 11 inches
   D 14½ inches

10. Find the square root of 85 correct to the nearest tenth.

    A 9.1
    B 9.2
    C 9.3
    D 9.4

11. If $5x = 30$, then x is equal to

    A 150
    B 25
    C 6
    D 0.6

12. What is the product of $(a − 5)$ and $(a + 3)$?

    A $a^2 − 15$
    B $a^2 + 2a − 15$
    C $a^2 − 2a − 15$
    D $a^2 − 2$

13. Solve for z: $3z − 5 + 2z = 25 − 5z$.

    A $z = 0$
    B $z = 3$
    C $z = −3$
    D no solution

14. A park commissioner designs a new playground in the shape of a pentagon. If he plans to have a fountain at every corner of the park, how many fountains will there be?

    A 4
    B 5
    C 6
    D 7

15. If one of the angles of a right triangle is 30 degrees, what are the other two angles?

    A 30 degrees, 120 degrees
    B 60 degrees, 45 degrees
    C 60 degrees, 90 degrees
    D 45 degrees, 90 degrees

16. What is the value of x in the equation $\frac{x}{2} = 7$?

    A $x = 14$
    B $x = 3½$
    C $x = 9$
    D $x = 5$

17. Divide $15a^3b^2c$ by $5abc$.

    A $10abc$
    B $3abc$
    C $5a^2b^2$
    D $3a^2b$

18. Two circles have the same center. If their radii are 7 inches and 10 inches, find the area that is part of the larger circle but not the smaller one.

A 3 square inches
B 17 square inches
C 51π square inches
D 70π square inches

19. My average grade on a set of five tests was 88%. I can remember only that the first four grades were 78%, 86%, 96%, and 94%. What was my fifth grade?

A 88
B 86
C 84
D 82

20. How many cubic yards of concrete are needed to make a cement floor that is 9 feet by 12 feet by 6 inches thick?

A 2
B 18
C 54
D 648

21. A wildlife preserve is laid out in the shape of a perfect circle whose radius is 14 miles. The lions' territory in this preserve is shaped like a wedge and has a fence around it. Two inner sides of a fence meet at a 90-degree angle in the center of the preserve. How much territory do the lions have?

A 140 square miles
B 3½ square miles
C 210 square miles
D 154 square miles

22. Find the value of $(-3)^4 + (-2)^4 + (-1)^4$.

A 98
B −98
C −21
D 21

23. A cylindrical can has a radius of 7 inches and a height of 15 inches. How many gallons of milk can it hold? (There are 231 cubic inches in a gallon.)

A 15 gallons
B 14 gallons
C 140 gallons
D 10 gallons

24. A 10-foot-high ladder is resting against an 8-foot-high wall surrounding a tennis court. If the top of the ladder is exactly even with the top of the wall, how far is the base of the ladder from the wall?

A 18 feet
B 6 feet
C 12 feet
D 9 feet

25. Ten ounces of liquid contain 20% fruit juice and 80% water. The mixture is diluted by adding 40 additional ounces of water. What is the percentage of fruit juice in the new solution?

A 4%
B 10%
C 20%
D 40%

MECHANICAL COMPREHENSION—SUBTEST 7

DIRECTIONS

This test has questions about general mechanical and physical principles. Pick the best answer for each question, then blacken the space on your separate answer form that has the same number and letter as your choice.

Here is a sample question.

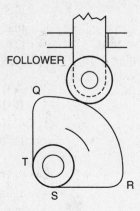

1. The follower is at its highest position between points

A Q and R.
B R and S.
C S and T.
D T and Q.

The correct answer is "between Q and R," so you would blacken the space for A on your answer form.

Your score on this test will be based on the number of questions you answer correctly. You should try to answer every question. Do not spend too much time on any one question.

When you are told to begin, be sure to start with question number 1 in Part 7 of your test booklet and number 1 in Part 7 of your answer form.

THE ACTUAL TEST WILL SAY:

Do not turn this page until told to do so.

Mechanical Comprehension

Time: 19 minutes; 25 questions

1. A ½-inch open end wrench will fit the head of one of the following N.F. cap screws.

   A 1/2 inch
   B 1/4 inch
   C 3/8 inch
   D 5/16 inch

2. Two parts are securely held together by a nut, bolt, and lock washer. The correct position for the lock washer is

   A between the two parts.
   B under the nut.
   C directly under the head of the bolt.
   D over a flat washer.

3. The following tools should be used to disconnect a gas line from a carburetor.

   A open-end and flare nut wrench
   B open-end wrench and plier
   C two open-end wrenches
   D pipe wrench and box wrench

4. Each line on the beveled edge of the thimble of a micrometer represents

   A 0.100 inch
   B 1 inch
   C 0.025 inch
   D 0.001 inch

5. A brake spoon is used to

   A adjust drum brakes.
   B adjust disc brakes.
   C remove cotter pins.
   D clean the backing plate.

6. The following instrument is used to test battery electrolyte specific gravity.

   A voltmeter
   B ammeter
   C ohmmeter
   D hydrometer

7. A starter armature is being tested on a growler. If the hacksaw blade vibrates when placed on the core of the armature, it indicates that the

   A field coils are grounded.
   B solenoid disc is burned.
   C armature is open.
   D armature is shorted.

8. The device used to check the runout of a disc brake rotor is a

   A torque wrench.
   B dial indicator.
   C micrometer.
   D feeler gage.

9. Which gage is used to check engine crankshaft endplay?

   A depth gage
   B plastigage
   C feeler gage
   D micrometer

10. An ohmmeter test of an electronic ignition pickup coil indicates an infinite reading. What does this reading indicate?

    A normal
    B shorted
    C open
    D grounded

11. A transmission

    A controls the speed of the engine.
    B trades speed for power.
    C transmits power at an angle.
    D trades power for speed.

12. If a rear axle ratio is 4 to 1,

    A the pinion gear has 4 times the number of teeth as the ring gear.
    B the ring gear has 4 times the number of teeth as the pinion gear.
    C the rear tire is 4 times larger than the brake drum.
    D the side gear has 4 times the number of teeth as the spider gear.

13. The motive power of the automotive cranking motor is created by the

    A field poles attracting the laminated iron core of the armature.
    B repelling force of like poles being formed in the armature opposite the field poles.
    C starter neutral safety switch.
    D starter drive.

14. Compressing air in a closed container

A increases the volume and lowers the temperature.

B lowers the temperature and decreases the volume.

C increases both temperature and volume.

D decreases the volume and increases the temperature.

15. The greatest amount of mechanical advantage of power is attained when an 11-tooth gear drives a

A 29-tooth gear.

B 11-tooth gear.

C 47-tooth gear.

D 15-tooth gear.

16. If the transmission ratio is 3.29 to 1, and the differential ratio is 3.85 to 1, then the final ratio is

A 7.14 to 1.

B 0.56 to 1.

C 12.67 to 1.

D none of these.

17. Pliers are an example of a

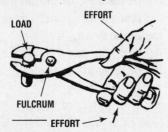

A first-class lever.

B second-class lever.

C third-class lever.

D first- and second-class lever.

18. The follower is at its highest position between points

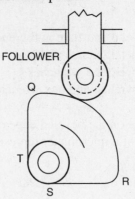

A Q and R.

B R and S.

C S and T.

D T and Q.

19. If pulley A is the driver and turns in direction 1, which pulley turns fastest?

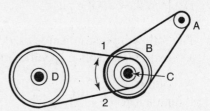

A A

B B

C C

D D

20. Which shaft or shafts are turning in the same direction as shaft X?

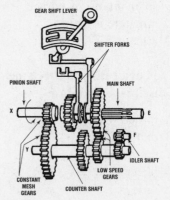

A Y

B Y and E

C F

D E and F

21. The human arm is an example of a

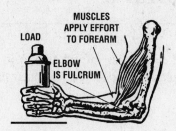

A first-class lever.
B second-class lever.
C third-class lever.
D second- and third-class lever.

22. If arm H is held fixed as gear B turns in direction 2, gear

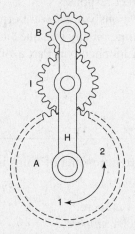

A A must turn in direction 1.
B A must turn in direction 2.
C I must turn in direction 2.
D A must be held fixed.

23. Gearset Y is

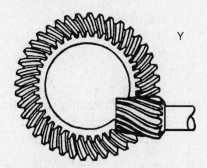

A rack and pinion.
B spur.
C hypoid bevel.
D spiral bevel.

24. If the force on piston X is 10 pounds, then the output force of piston Y will be

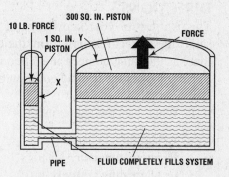

A 300 pounds
B 30 pounds
C 10 pounds
D 3,000 pounds

25. How much effort must be placed at point *A* to lift the weight at point *B*?

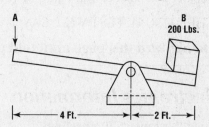

A 200 pounds
B 4,000 pounds
C 8,000 pounds
D 100 pounds

ELECTRONICS INFORMATION—SUBTEST 8

DIRECTIONS

This is a test of your knowledge of electrical, radio, and electronics information. You are to select the correct response from the choices given. Then mark the space on your answer form that has the same number and letter as your choice.

Now look at the sample question below.

1. What does the abbreviation AC stand for?

A additional charge
B alternating coil
C alternating current
D ampere current

The correct answer is "alternating current," so C is the correct response.

Your score on this test will be based on the number of questions you answer correctly. You should try to answer every question. Do not spend too much time on any one question.

When you are told to begin, be sure to start with question number 1 in Part 8 of your test booklet and number 1 in Part 8 of your answer form.

THE ACTUAL TEST WILL SAY:

Do not turn this page until told to do so.

Electronics Information

Time: 9 minutes; 20 questions

1. Flux is placed inside electrical solder in order to

A clean the connections during soldering and prevent oxidation.
B raise the melting point of silver.
C increase the conductivity of the connection.
D act as an insulator within the connection.

2. A cold solder connection is

A clean and shiny in appearance.
B dull and brittle in appearance.
C a connection that is properly soldered.
D a connection achieved with a low-wattage iron.

3. A current reading of 1 mA is equivalent to

A 0.1 ampere.
B 0.001 ampere.
C 1 ampere.
D 10 amperes.

4. An ohmmeter is used to check the condition of a fuse. If the fuse is good, the meter reading should be

A 100K ohms.
B 120 volts.
C zero.
D infinity.

5. Which of the following metals has the highest conductivity?

A silver
B copper
C aluminum
D zinc

6. Stranded wire is used in extension cords primarily because

A it costs less than solid wire.
B it is flexible.
C it is a better conductor than solid wire.
D it is the only type of wire available in that gauge.

7. A toaster is connected to 120 volts and draws 10 amperes when in use. How much power does this appliance consume?

A 12 watts
B 120 watts
C 110 watts
D 1,200 watts

8. How many cells does a 12-volt carbon-zinc car battery contain?

A 12
B 8
C 6
D 1

9. The property of a circuit that opposes any change in current is

A inductance.
B capacitance.
C resistance.
D reactance.

10. Of the choices listed below, which component is an example of a transducer?

A resistor
B switch
C diode
D speaker

11. The period of a sine wave is determined by

A its amplitude.
B the distance between the crests of the wave.
C the number of hertz in 1 second.
D the time it takes to complete 1 hertz.

12. What is the effective value of an AC signal of 141 volts peak value?

A 141 volts
B 100 volts
C 120 volts
D 56.5 volts

13. The frequency response of the human ear is in the range of

A 16 to 16,000 Hz.
B 20,000 to 30,000 Hz.
C 50 KHz to 1 MHz.
D 1 MHz to 1000 MHz.

14. One kilowatt is equivalent to

A 1 watt.
B 10 watts.
C 1,000 watts.
D 1,000 volts.

15. What is the total resistance in this circuit?

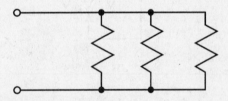

Each resistor = 900 ohms

A 100 ohms
B 300 ohms
C 900 ohms
D 1,000 ohms

16.

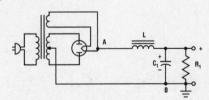

In the above schematic of a DC power supply, an oscilloscope connected at points A and B would display what type of waveform?

A square wave
B sine wave
C pulsating DC
D sawtooth wave

17. Referring to the schematic in question 16, what is the purpose of C_1?

   A to bleed R_1
   B to increase the output voltage
   C to change the incoming AC to DC
   D to filter the AC ripple voltage

18. Which is the correct schematic symbol for a tuning capacitor?

A

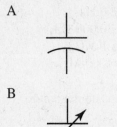

B

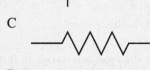

C

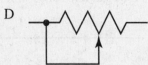

D

19.

What is the equivalent solid state component of the vacuum tube drawn above?

   A semiconductor rectifier
   B silicon-controlled rectifier
   C zener diode
   D transistor

20.

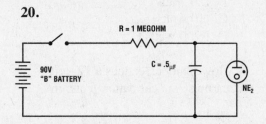

Which choice best describes the operation of the circuit drawn in the above schematic?

   A The lamp will light constantly when the switch is closed.
   B The lamp will light only when the switch is open.
   C The lamp will flash when the switch is closed.
   D The lamp will not light with the switch open or closed.

SHOP INFORMATION—SUBTEST 9

Shop Information

Time: 8 minutes; 15 questions

1. The mitre box is used for cutting

  A angles from 90 degrees to 45 degrees.
  B rafters.
  C joists.
  D logs.

2. The coping saw is for cutting

  A wood at any curve or angle desired.
  B steel at any curve or angle desired.
  C straight lines along a board.
  D cross-cutting along a straight line.

3. Another name for the wrecking bar is

  A lever.
  B crowbar.
  C slot maker.
  D plumb bob.

4. The screwdriver with a cross or X on the end is called a

  A Phillips head screwdriver.
  B standard screwdriver.
  C wrench.
  D plumb bob.

5. A chisel is used to cut wood by striking it with a

  A screwdriver.
  B hammer.
  C fist.
  D level.

6. A device with glass tubes that have air bubbles in them is used to indicate when a door or window is

  A nailed in place.
  B warped.
  C screwed in place.
  D level.

7. If you wanted to cut circular holes in wood or metal, which of the following tools would you use?

A coping saw
B cross-cut saw
C hole saw
D mitre box

8. The measuring edges of a steel rule are usually graduated in what increments?

A 1/8, 1/16, 1/32, and 1/64 inch
B 1/8, 1/4, 1/2, and 1 inch
C 1 mm, 10 mm, 100 mm, 1 cm
D 0.01 mm, 0.1 mm, 1 mm, 10 mm

9. The back saw has a(n) _____ tooth configuration and is used to cut _____, leaving a _____ piece of work.

A open, with the grain, smooth-finished
B fine, with the grain, unfinished
C fine, cross-grain, smooth-finished
D open, cross-grain, rough

10. If a cold chisel starts to "mushroom" at the head, you should remove the splintered ends with a

A band saw.
B file.
C grinder.
D pair of bolt cutters.

11. The speed bore, forstner, and brad point bits are used in

A a brace arrangement turned by hand.
B metal drilling.
C oil well drilling.
D electric hand drills or drill presses.

12. Curved claw hammers meant for carpentry use usually come in

A 20, 24, 28, and 32 ounce weights.
B 24, 28, 32 and 36 ounce weights.
C small and large sizes.
D three degrees of curvature.

13. The nail weight of *penny* is abbreviated as

A p
B d
C y
D n

14. Self-tapping screws are used to connect

A heavy wooden structural members.
B thin-gage sheet metal parts.
C parts made of softer metals more than 0.5 inch thick.
D PVC pipe when a seal is required.

15. Rubbing compounds have a(n) _____ base.

A cloth
B aluminum oxide.
C ceramic
D pumice

ASSEMBLING OBJECTS—SUBTEST 10

DIRECTIONS

This test measures your ability to picture how an object will look when its parts are put together mentally. Pick the best answer for each question, then blacken the space on the answer form that has the same number and letter as your choice.

Here is a sample question.

1. Which of the following shapes will complete this shape 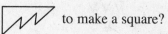 to make a square?

A

B

C

D

Choice D is the shape that, when added to the basic shape, will result in a square.

Your score on this test will be based on the number of questions you answer correctly. You should try to answer every question. Do not spend too much time on any one question.

When you are told to begin, be sure to start with question number 1 in Part 10 of your test booklet and number 1 in Part 10 on your separate answer form.

THE ACTUAL TEST WILL SAY:

Do not turn this page until told to do so.

Assembling Objects

Time: 20 minutes; 20 questions

1. Which of the following shapes will complete this shape to make a square?

   A

   B

   C

   D

2. Which of the following shapes will complete this shape to make a rectangle?

   A

   B

   C

   D

3. Which of the following shapes will complete this shape to make a circle?

A

B

C

D

4. Which of the following shapes will complete this shape to make a triangle?

A

B

C

D

5. Which of the following shapes will complete this shape to make a square?

A

B

C

D

6. Which of the following shapes will complete this shape to make a parallelogram?

A

B

C

D

7. Which of the following shapes will complete this shape to make a pentagon?

A

B

C

D

8. Which of the following shapes will complete this shape to make a circle?

A

B

C

D

9. Which of the following shapes will complete this shape to make a hexagon?

A

B

C

D

10. Which of the following shapes will fit together with this shape?

A

B

C

D

11. Which of the following shapes will fit together with this shape?

A

B

C

D

12. Which of the following shapes will fit together with this shape?

A

B

C

D

13. Which of the following shapes will fit together with this shape?

A

B

C

D

14. Which of the following shapes will fit together with this shape?

A

B

C

D

15. Which of the following shapes will fit together with this shape?

A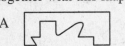

B

C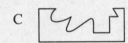

D

16. Which of the following shapes will fit together with this shape?

A

B

C

D

17. Which of the following shapes will fit together with this shape?

A

B

C

D

18. Which of the following shapes will fit together with this shape?

A

B

C

D

19. Which of the following shapes will fit together with this shape?

A

B

C

D

20. Which of the following shapes will fit together with these shapes?

A

B

C

D

ANSWERS AND ANSWERS EXPLAINED

GENERAL SCIENCE—SUBTEST 1

Answers

1. **D**   5. **B**   9. **C**   13. **C**   17. **B**   20. **D**   23. **D**
2. **B**   6. **D**   10. **D**   14. **C**   18. **C**   21. **B**   24. **D**
3. **D**   7. **D**   11. **A**   15. **B**   19. **D**   22. **B**   25. **B**
4. **C**   8. **D**   12. **A**   16. **A**

Answers Explained

1. **D** Sound cannot travel through a vacuum.

2. **B** A light-year is a convenient term to measure great distances. Since light travels at the rate of 186,282 miles per second, a light-year is equal to 186,282 miles, times 60, times 60, times 24, times 365—which equals 5,874,588,800,000, or almost 5.9 trillion miles!

3. **D** Specific gravity equals

$$\frac{\text{Weight of substance in air}}{\text{Loss of weight of substance in water}}$$

Since the weight of the corundum in air is 4 ounces and its weight in water is 3 ounces, the loss of weight in water is 1 ounce. Hence, the specific gravity of corundum is 4 ounces divided by 1 ounce, or 4.

4. **C** A sundial consists of a tilted rod that casts a shadow on a clockface. Solar noon is indicated when the rod casts the shortest shadow when the sun is at the highest point in the sky.

5. **B** Of the metals listed, copper is the best conductor of heat. Asbestos and glass are very poor conductors of heat, which is why they are used as insulation materials.

6. **D** Ecology is the study of the relations of living things with each other and with their environment. The incorrect choices are factors relating to ecology, but they do not describe ecology.

7. **D** The paraffin (wax) in the candle contains carbon, hydrogen, and oxygen. The products obtained when the candle burns are, therefore, the oxides of carbon (carbon dioxide) and hydrogen (water).

8. **D** Fat has the most carbon molecules in its composition of the substances listed and would therefore yield the most energy per ounce.

9. **C** The half-life of a radioactive element is the time it takes for one-half of a given mass of the element to change to something else. In 1,620 years, one-half of the sample radium "disintegrates." In another 1,620 years (making a total of 3,240 years), one-half of the remaining radium disintegrates. This leaves one-half of the remaining one-half in the form of radium.

$$1/2 \text{ of } 1/2 = 1/4$$

10. **D** When water disintegrates, it becomes molecules of hydrogen and oxygen. It no longer has the properties of water. This is an example of matter undergoing a chemical change. The other changes listed as choices are examples of physical change.

11. **A** Light is needed by plants in order to carry on the process of photosynthesis—the manufacture of carbohydrates. During this process green plants absorb carbon dioxide and give off oxygen. Protozoa are one-celled organisms.

12. **A** The dew point is the condition when air becomes saturated with moisture.

13. **C** To start a fire with the aid of the sun, it is necessary to concentrate, or converge, the rays of sunlight to a focal point. This is done with a convex lens, which is also known as a magnifying glass.

14. **C** The rotation of the earth on its axis exposes different parts of the earth to the sun's rays for different parts of each day.

15. **B** Alcohol does not have to be digested. The other substances are not broken down, nor are they ready for absorption, until they reach the small intestine.

16. **A** An atom contains several types of particles. Its central core, the nucleus, consists of positively charged particles, called protons, and uncharged particles, called neutrons. Surrounding the nucleus and orbiting it are negatively charged particles called electrons. Isotopes are atoms that contain the same number of protons as other atoms of the same element but have different numbers of neutrons.

17. **B** The moon is a satellite. The others are planets.

18. **C** Sulfuric acid is one of the most important acids used by industry.

19. **D** The whale and the horse are mammals. They have a four-chambered heart, mammary glands, and lungs. They bear live offspring, not eggs.

20. **D** In a beam of parallel rays, each ray strikes the mirror at a different point. Since the mirror has a plane surface, the rays are all parallel after reflection.

21. **B** According to Ohm's law, the voltage (V) needed to produce a current (C) is equal to the current times the resistance (R) that it meets: $V = CR$. In this case, the needed voltage would be

$$24 \text{ (ohms, a measure of resistance)}$$
$$\times\, 0.5 \text{ (ampere, a measure of current)}$$
$$12.0 \text{ (volts, a measure of electric potential)}$$

22. **B** During aeration of water, methane and carbon dioxide are liberated (eliminated) from the water, and oxygen is absorbed from the air.

23. **D** Dry ice is solid carbon dioxide (CO_2) made by cooling this gas to $-80°C$. In this case, CO_2 goes directly from a gaseous state to a solid.

24. **D** The scientific measure of work is the foot-pound, which is the force of 1 pound acting through a distance of 1 foot. To measure work (W) in a specific task, multiply the force (F) in pounds by the distance (D) in feet. Thus, in this example,

$$F \times D = W$$
$$50 \times 25 = 1{,}250 \text{ foot-pounds of work}$$

25. **B** Chemical reactions can be classified into four main types. In composition (direct combination), two or more elements or compounds combine to form a more complex substance. Decomposition (the reverse of composition) occurs when a complex compound breaks down into simpler compounds of basic elements. Replacement takes place when one substance in a compound is freed and another takes its place. Double (or ionic) replacement occurs when ions in a solution combine to form a new product, which then leaves the solution.

ARITHMETIC REASONING—SUBTEST 2

Answers

1. C	6. C	11. D	15. B	19. C	23. B	27. B
2. A	7. D	12. C	16. C	20. A	24. C	28. C
3. C	8. A	13. C	17. B	21. D	25. C	29. A
4. B	9. A	14. B	18. D	22. D	26. D	30. A
5. D	10. B					

Answers Explained

1. **C** The down payment was 25% (or 1/4) of the total payment.
$400 \times (1/4) = 100
$30 \times 12 = 360 (sum of monthly payments)
$360 + $100 = 460 (cost on installment plan)
$460 - $400 = 60 (extra cost on installment)

2. **A** The number of seeds that failed to sprout was
$$120 - 90 = 30$$
The percentage of seeds that failed to sprout was
$$\frac{30}{120} = \frac{1}{4} = 25\%$$

3. **C** To find the average rate of speed, divide the distance covered (1,000 miles) by the time spent traveling (2½ or 2.5 hours). Clear the decimal in the divisor.

$$\frac{1,000}{2.5} = \frac{10,000}{25} = 400 \text{ miles per hour}$$

4. **B** Solve by multiplying first and then dividing. Clear the decimal in the divisor.

$$\frac{0.05 \times 4}{0.1} = \frac{0.20}{0.1} = \frac{0.2}{0.1} = \frac{2}{1} = 2$$

5. **D** Find the sum of the deposits and the sum of the withdrawals.
$765 + $802 = $1,567 (deposits)
$348 + $518 = $866 (withdrawals)
Find the difference between deposits and withdrawals.
$1,567 − $866 = $701 (overall gain)
Add this gain to the original balance.
$701 + $2,674 = $3,375 (new balance)

6. **C** Change 12½ gallons into pints (8 pints = 1 gallon).
12½ × 8 =
²⁵⁄₂ × 8 = 100 (pints)
Multiply the cost of 1 pint by 100.
$0.35 × 100 = $35

7. **D** Multiply one side of a square by itself to find the area. Thus
9 feet × 9 feet = 81 square feet
By adding 3 feet to each side of the 9-foot square, you produce a 12-foot square. Thus
12 feet × 12 feet = 144 square feet
Find the difference between the areas of the two squares
144 − 81 = 63 square feet

8. **A** First, change both fractions to a common denominator (12) and add them.

$$\frac{1}{4} = \frac{3}{12} \qquad \frac{1}{6} = \frac{2}{12}$$

$$\frac{3}{12} + \frac{2}{12} = \frac{5}{12}$$

To get the average, divide the sum by 2.

$$\frac{5}{12} \div 2 = \frac{5}{12} \times \frac{1}{2} = \frac{5}{24}$$

9. **A** First find the salary increase.
$290 − $260 = $30 (amount of increase)
To find the percentage of increase, use the original salary as the base and carry the division out to three decimal places. Rounded to the nearest hundredth, 0.115 is 0.12.
0.12 = 12%

$$\frac{\text{(increase)}}{\text{(original salary)}} = \frac{\$30}{\$260} = \frac{3.000}{26} = 0.115$$

10. **B** Express the total weight of the fish in ounces.
1 pound = 16 ounces
16 ounces + 12 ounces = 28 ounces
Find the cost of 1 ounce and multiply it by 16 to find the cost of 1 pound.
$2.24 ÷ 28 = $0.08
$0.08 × 16 = $1.28

11. **D** Find the area of each lawn.
25 feet × 25 feet = 375 square feet (front lawn)
50 feet × 30 feet = 1,500 square feet (back lawn)
To find the ratio, divide one area by the other.

$$\frac{\text{(front lawn)}}{\text{(back lawn)}} = \frac{375}{1,500} = \frac{1}{4}$$

The ratio of the front lawn to the back lawn is 1:4.

12. **C** Find the amount of the price increase.
$7,200 − $6,400 = $800
To find the rate of increase, use the original price as your base.

$$\frac{\text{(increase)}}{\text{(original price)}} = \frac{\$800}{\$6,400} = \frac{1}{8}$$

$$\frac{1}{8} = 12\frac{1}{2}\% \quad \text{(rate of increase)}$$

13. **C** Find the relationship between each pair of numbers in the series. Thus
(3½; 2¼) 3½ − 1¼ = 2¼
(2¼; 13¼) 2¼ + 11 = 13¼
(13¼; 12) 13¼ − 1¼ = 12
The pattern so far is −1¼, +11, −1¼. To continue the series, add 11 to the fourth number in the series:
12 + 11 = 23

14. **B** Find the number of hours the movie house is open. From 10:00 A.M. to 10:00 P.M. is 12 hours. From 10:00 P.M. to 11:30 P.M. is 1½ hours.
12 + 1½ = 13½ hours
Divide this total by the length of time for a complete showing of the movie (2 hours and 15 minutes, or 2¼ hours).

$$13\frac{1}{2} \div 2\frac{1}{4} =$$
$$\frac{27}{2} \div \frac{9}{4} =$$
$$\frac{27}{2} \times \frac{4}{9} = 6 \text{ (showings)}$$

15. **B** Find the amount taken in for orchestra seats.
324 × $20 = $6,480
Out of $10,000, the remaining amount came from balcony seats.
$10,000 − $6,480 = $3,520
Divide this amount by $10 to find the number of balcony seat tickets that were sold.
$3,520 ÷ $10 = 352 balcony seats

16. **C** Since the first 1/4 mile costs $0.80, this leaves $4.20 for the balance of the trip. At $0.20 for each additional 1/4 mile, find the number of 1/4 miles that $4.20 will cover. (Clear the decimal in the divisor.)
$4.20 ÷ $0.20 =
4.2 ÷ 0.2 =
42 ÷ 2 = 21 additional 1/4 miles)

Add the first 1/4 mile (at $0.80) to this total.
21 + 1 = 22 (1/4 miles)
Change the 1/4 miles to miles.
22 ÷ 4 = 5½ (miles for $5)

17. **B** Divide the distance by the number of feet (40) to an inch.
175 feet ÷ 40 feet = $4\frac{15}{40}$ = 4⅜ (inches)

18. **D** Find the discounted price paid by the dealer.
$50 × 20% =
$50 × 0.2 = $10 (discount)
$50 − $10 = $40 (price paid by dealer)
Then find the dealer's selling price based on an increase over the original wholesale list price.
$50 × 10% =
$50 × 0.1 = $5 (increase over list price)
$50 + $5 = $55 (dealer's selling price)
Finally, find the dealer's profit.
$55 − $40 = $15 (dealer's profit)

19. **C** When the hour hand is on the 10-minute mark, it is actually on the number 2 (for 2 o'clock). The hour hand advances to a new minute mark every 12 minutes of actual time. Thus, when the hour hand stopped at the 11-minute mark, it was 12 minutes after 2.

20. **A** Divide the number of successful shots by the total number of shots the player tried. Change your answer to percent.

$$\frac{272}{320} = \frac{34}{40} = \frac{17}{20}$$
$$\frac{17}{20} = 0.85 = 85\%$$

21. **D** Let x equal the amount the helper receives. Let $2x$ equal the amount the painter receives. Write an equation to show that, together, they receive $375 for painting the house.
$$2x + x = \$375$$
Combine the similar terms, and then divide both sides of the equation by the number with x. (This is to undo the multiplication.)
$$3x = \$375$$
$$x = \$125 \text{ (the helper's wages)}$$
$$2x = \$250 \text{ (what the painter receives)}$$

22. **D** Find the difference between the two percentages. Divide the answer by 100% to change it to a simple fraction.

23. **B** To solve, substitute the number value for the letter and do the arithmetic operations.
$$3a^2 - 2a + 5 =$$
$$= (3 \times a^2) - (2 \times a) + 5$$
$$= (3 \times 4^2) - (2 \times 4) + 5$$
$$= (3 \times 16) - (2 \times 4) + 5$$
$$= 48 - 8 + 5$$
$$= 40 + 5 = 45$$

24. **C** Find the annual difference between the premium paid by someone who is 30 and the premium paid by someone who is 46.
$$\$38 - \$22 = \$16$$
Multiply the answer by 20 to find the total amount saved over 20 years by taking out a policy at an early age.
$$\$16 \times 20 = \$320 \text{ saved}$$

25. **C** On sale, the chair is 25% less than the original price. In other words, the sale price is a fraction of the original price.
$$100\% - 25\% = 75\% \text{ (or 3/4) of the original price}$$
If x equals the original price, then the sale price can be written as an equation.
$$(3/4)x = \$240$$

To solve for x, divide each side of the equation by 3/4. (This is to undo the multiplication.)
$$\frac{3}{4}x \div \frac{3}{4} = \$240 \div \frac{3}{4}$$
$$\frac{3}{4}x \times \frac{4}{3} = \$240 \times \frac{4}{3}$$
$$x = \$320 \text{ (original price)}$$

26. **D** The quotient is the answer in division. (Clear the decimal in the divisor before doing the arithmetic.)

27. **B** For the month between May 15 and June 15, the meter showed that the electric usage was
$$5,687 - 5,472 = 215 \text{ (kilowatt-hours)}$$
The first 10 kilowatt-hours cost $2.48
The next 45 kilowatt-hours cost $0.16 per kilowatt-hour $7.20
The next 55 kilowatt-hours cost $0.12 per kilowatt-hour $6.60
All usage over the first 110 kilowatt-hours was charged at a lower rate. Thus, 215 – 110, or 105 kilowatt-hours cost $0.07 per kilowatt-hour $ 7.35
TOTAL bill for the month $23.63

28. **C** To square a number, multiply it by itself.
$$49^2 = 49 \times 49 = 2,401$$
$$31^2 = 39 \times 39 = -961$$
$$\underline{1,440} \text{ (difference)}$$

29. **A** To find the number of seats in the auditorium, multiply the number of rows (x) by the number of seats in each row (y). This is expressed as xy.

30. **A** One way of checking a division example is to multiply the quotient (the answer) by the divisor. After multiplying, add the remainder (if there was one in the division answer). Thus

$$
\begin{array}{r}
15 \text{ (divisor)} \\
\times\,8 \text{ (quotient)} \\
\hline
120 \\
+\,7 \text{ (remainder, after division)} \\
\hline
127 \text{ (original number)}
\end{array}
$$

WORD KNOWLEDGE—SUBTEST 3

Answers

1. C	6. C	11. A	16. D	21. D	26. D	31. C	
2. A	7. C	12. D	17. B	22. C	27. C	32. D	
3. C	8. A	13. D	18. C	23. A	28. B	33. C	
4. A	9. D	14. B	19. B	24. A	29. B	34. B	
5. B	10. A	15. D	20. C	25. D	30. D	35. D	

Answers Explained

1. **C** To **subsume** means to include within a larger class or order.

2. **A** **Consensus**, like accord, means agreement.

3. **C** **Altercation**, like quarrel, means a disagreement.

4. **A** **Irresolute**, like wavering, means to hesitate between choices.

5. **B** **Laconic**, like concise, means to express much in a few words.

6. **C** **Audition**, like hearing, means an opportunity to be heard.

7. **C** **Novice** designates one who has no training or experience in a specific field or activity, and is hence a beginner.

8. **A** Pacific, like **conciliatory**, implies trying to preserve or obtain peace.

9. **D** To neutralize, like to **counteract**, means to render ineffective.

10. **A** **Precedent**, like example, refers to an individual instance (e.g., act, statement, case) taken as representative of a type.

11. **A** **Diaphanous** (*dia-* is a Greek prefix meaning "through, across"), like transparent, describes material that light rays can pass through.

12. **D** **Deferred**, like delayed, means postponed.

13. **D** **Accentuate**, like intensify, means to emphasize or increase in degree.

14. **B** **Authentic** (from the Greek for "warranted"), like reliable, means entitled to acceptance or belief.

15. **D** **Unanimity**, like concurrence, means complete accord.

16. **D** **Notorious** like infamous, means to be known widely and regarded unfavorably.

17. **B** Former means preceding in time and is synonymous with **previous**.

18. **C** Both pliable and **flexible** mean to be easily bent or yielding, usually without breaking.

19. **B** The opportunity to make a choice is equivalent to freedom to select or exercise an **option**.

20. **C** Confirm, like **verify**, means to make certain, to corroborate or authenticate.

21. **D** Saucy, like **pert**, means bold or impudent.

22. **C** Tasteful, similar to **aesthetic** (from the Greek for "perceptive"), means having the ability to appreciate what is beautiful.

23. **A** **Decimation** means to kill or otherwise remove a large part of a group.

24. **A** Angry, like **indignant** (from the Latin for "deeming unworthy"), implies deep and strong feelings aroused by injury, injustice, or wrong.

25. **D** Platitude, like **cliché** (originally, to pattern in clay), refers to a remark or an idea that has become trite through overuse and lost its original freshness and impressive force.

26. **D** Agreement means **harmony** among people, thoughts, or ideas.

27. **C** Lazy, like **indolent**, applies to one who is not active.

28. **B** Breathing, like **respiration**, means inhalation and exhalation of air.

29. **B** Watchful, like **vigilant**, means alert.

30. **D** Casual, similar to **<u>incidental</u>**, means happening by chance or without definite intention.

31. **C** To **<u>succumb</u>** is to cease to resist or contend before a superior force, hence to yield.

32. **D** **<u>Feasible</u>** describes that which is possible to bring about and is hence practicable.

33. **C** Many-sided, like **<u>versatile</u>** (from the Latin for "turning about"), means capable of turning with ease from one task to another.

34. **B** **<u>Imperturbability</u>** or calmness is almost synonymous with serenity.

35. **D** **<u>Strident</u>** (from the Latin for "creaking") means having an irritating or unpleasant—hence harsh—sound.

PARAGRAPH COMPREHENSION—SUBTEST 4

Answers

1. C	4. B	6. B	8. C	10. D	12. B	14. C
2. C	5. D	7. C	9. C	11. B	13. B	15. C
3. A						

Answers Explained

1. **C** Each individual should prevent the opportunity for crime to occur.

2. **C** The design must fit the owner's income and the building site.

3. **A** The selection describes a range of camping styles from backpacking to motor homes with complete creature comforts, so backpacking can be inferred to be the least luxurious.

4. **B** According to the selection, the right speed varies depending on the number of cars, the road surface, and the visibility, so a driver should adjust to different driving conditions.

5. **D** *Hard work* is the only term in the list not mentioned in the passage.

6. **B** The selection states that less than 1 percent (0.8%) is available as freshwater for people to use.

7. **C** A pinfold is described in the passage as a large circular pen made by driving stakes close together in the floor of the river.

8. **C** The division of powers prevents one part or branch of government from having all the power; therefore, power is shared.

9. **C** The passage states that a proper dose of narcotic relieves pain and induces profound sleep.

10. **D** The passage mentions that nitrogen, phosphorus, and potassium are used by plants in large amounts.

11. **B** The passage mentions that 60% of pollution is caused by motor vehicle exhausts, so the choice is B—cars, trucks, and buses.

12. **B** Since too much bright light can create discomfort for the eyes and create difficulty in seeing well, the main purpose of sunglasses is to screen out harmful rays.

13. **B** The selection mentions the good points of apprentice training but none of the negative points.

14. **C** The selection does not deal with insurance rates, tax rates, or retirement rates. It defines what a deduction from your paycheck is.

15. **C** The first sentence states that nucleic acids are found in all living organisms, from the simplest living things to the most complex.

AUTOMOTIVE INFORMATION—SUBTEST 5

Answers

1. B	5. B	9. B	13. A
2. C	6. D	10. A	14. B
3. B	7. B	11. D	15. A
4. B	8. C	12. B	

Answers Explained

1. **B** When a tire is underinflated, the center area of the tread moves upward as the sidewalls flex. This abnormal action places stress on the tire, causing wear to both outside edges.

2. **C** The vehicle "track" measurement is taken from the center of the left wheel to the center of the right wheel.

3. **B** The resistor inserted in series with the ignition coil is used to drop the 12-volt battery power supply to 6 volts, for which the coil was designed. This allows for the lower voltage from the battery during cranking operations. The coil can then produce the high voltage needed for the spark plugs.

4. **B** A syncromesh unit is designed to bring two gears to the same speed before engagement. A syncromesh unit does not change gear ratios.

5. **B** The modulator is a vacuum-operated device connected to a source of manifold vacuum. As vacuum changes in response to engine load, the modulator is actuated and sends a signal to the valve body, resulting in a different shift point. For example, when vacuum is low, as it normally is when the engine is accelerated, the modulator reacts and causes the transmission to shift at a higher vehicle speed. The higher shift point allows the engine to develop more torque, which increases engine power.

6. **D** Too much clearance will cause the clutch to grab early. Hard shifting and clashing gears are problems associated with too much free play. Insufficient clearance will cause the clutch to grab late. A slipping clutch usually results from no free play.

7. **B** The limited slip differential transmits power to the driving wheel that has traction. In a conventional differential, if one wheel begins to slip, the vehicle will not move. All power remains with the slipping drive wheel.

8. **C** The ignition circuit must transform 12 volts to more than 20,000 volts. It must also deliver this high-voltage spark to the spark plugs at the correct time.

9. **B** The purpose of the resistor is to lower and control voltage to the ignition coil. Since power for the coil comes through the ignition switch, the resistor is connected between the switch and coil.

10. **A** The magnetic field within an alternator is produced by the rotor. Electricity is produced in the stator. Diodes change voltage from AC to DC.

11. **D** Under normal operating conditions, whenever the horn button is depressed, a circuit in the relay is grounded and the horn sounds. If the wire to the button becomes permanently grounded due to an insulation breakdown, the horn will blow continuously.

12. **B** The rubber cups in the brake wheel cylinders are there to keep brake fluid from leaking out of the cylinder. Wheel cylinder pistons push the brake shoes outward toward the drum when the brakes are applied. Spring tension keeps the springs in place inside the cylinder.

13. **A** The metering valve is used on a disc/drum-type brake system. Its purpose is to hold off hydraulic pressure to the front disc brakes until the rear wheel cylinders overcome the tension of the brake shoe return springs. Disc brakes do not use return springs. The pads ride very close to the disc and make contact with the friction surface of the disc as soon as hydraulic pressure is applied.

14. **B** The air/fuel mixture is delivered to the cylinder on the intake stroke, compressed on the compression stroke, and ignited on the power stroke. Burned gases are pushed out of the cylinder on the exhaust stroke.

15. **A** In normal engine operation a ridge forms at the top of a cylinder bore. To properly remove a piston it is necessary to cut away this ridge. Failure to remove the ridge can result in damage to the piston. The

ridge reamer is designed to remove the ridge without damaging the cylinder bore. Filing can ruin a cylinder wall.

MATHEMATICS KNOWLEDGE— SUBTEST 6

Answers

1. C   5. C   9. B   13. B   17. D   20. A   23. D
2. D   6. C   10. B   14. B   18. C   21. D   24. B
3. B   7. B   11. C   15. C   19. B   22. A   25. A
4. C   8. D   12. C   16. A

Answers Explained

1. **C** A prime number is a number larger than 1 that has only itself and 1 as factors. (It can be evenly divided only by itself and by 1.) 201 is divisible by 3; 205 is divisible by 5; 211, however, is a prime number.

2. **D** Change 40% to a decimal and write an equation to solve for x.

$$0.4 = \frac{x}{30}$$

Multiply both sides by 30. You are "undoing" the division.

3. **B** The product of all integers from 1 to x is called the x *factorial*. The product of all numbers from 1 to 5 is 5 factorial. Thus

$$(5)(4)(3)(2)(1) = 20\,(3)(2)(1)$$
$$= 60\,(2)(1)$$
$$= 120\,(1) = 120$$

The expression "5 factorial" is equal to 120.

4. **C** To subtract one polynomial from another, you change the signs of the terms in the subtrahend. First write the example as a subtraction in arithmetic.
(From) $8x^2 + 2x - 9$
(Take) $3x^2 - 5x - 1$
Then change the signs of the terms in the bottom row (the subtrahend) and combine terms that are alike.

$$8x^2 + 2x - 9$$
$$\underline{-3x^2 + 5x + 1}$$
$$5x^2 + 7x - 8$$

5. **C** In deciding whether a number is greater or less than another, it helps to use a number line.

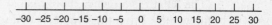

On the number line above, –5 is to the left of 0 and is, therefore, less than 0. But –30 is to the left of –5. This makes –30 less than –5. The < sign is a symbol of inequality, meaning "less than." The statement (–30 < –5) means "negative 30 is less than negative 5."

6. **C** To solve for x, combine all similar terms, and set the equation equal to zero.

$$(8x - 5x) + (-2 - 8) = 0$$

Do the operations inside the parentheses.

$$3x - 10 = 0$$

Next, add 10 to each side. You are undoing the subtraction.

$$3x - 10 + 10 = 0 + 10$$
$$3x = 10$$

Finally, divide each side by 3 to find the value of x. You are undoing the multiplication.

7. **B** In x weeks, she will make out checks for x times $50, or $50x$. To find out how much she still has after writing these checks, she would subtract $50x$ from $500. Thus her bank account will hold $500 - $50x$.

8. **D** Use the formula

$$F = \left(\frac{9}{5} \times C\right) + 32$$

Substitute 20 degrees for C.

$$F = \left(\frac{9}{5} \times 20\right) + 32$$

$$F = 36 + 32 = 68 \text{ degrees}$$

9. **B** The perimeter of a rectangle is the sum of its four sides. If x equals its width, then $x + 3$ equals the length. (The length is 3 inches more than the width.) From this, you can write an equation to find the perimeter. (Use the formula $2w + 2l = P$.)
$x + x + (x + 3) + (x + 3) = 38$
To solve for x, combine similar terms.
$$4x + 6 = 38$$
$$4x = 38 - 6$$
$$4x = 32$$
$$x = 8 \text{ (inches)}$$

10. **B** One way to solve this is to square each of the suggested answers to see which is close to 85. Thus

9.1	9.2	9.3	9.4
$\times 9.1$	$\times 9.2$	$\times 9.3$	$\times 9.4$
91	184	279	376
819	828	837	846
82.81	84.64	86.49	88.36

The squares of 9.2 and 9.3 are near 85. Find the difference between the square of each of these numbers and 85.

(9.2)	85.00	(9.3)	86.49
	-84.64		-85.00
	0.36		1.49

The square of 9.2 is closer to 85 than the square of 9.3. Therefore, the square root of 85, to the nearest tenth, is 9.2.

11. **C** The statement $5x = 30$ means "5 times a certain number is equal to 30." To find the number, divide each side by 5. This is to undo the multiplication.
$$\frac{5x}{5} = \frac{30}{5}$$
$$x = 6$$

12. **C** Set this up as a multiplication example in arithmetic. Remember that when you multiply terms with unlike signs, the product has a minus sign.
$$
\begin{array}{r}
a - 5 \\
\times\, a + 3 \\
\hline
3a - 15 \\
a^2 - 5a \\
\hline
a^2 - 2a - 15
\end{array}
$$

13. **B** Begin by combining like terms.
$$3z - 5 + 2z = 25 - 5z$$
$$5z - 5 = 25 - 5z$$
Next add $5z$ to each side to eliminate the $-5z$ from the right side.
$$5z - 5 + 5z = 25 - 5z + 5z$$
$$10z - 5 = 25$$
Now add 5 to each side to undo the remaining subtraction.
$$10z - 5 + 5 = 25 + 5$$
$$10z = 30$$
$$z = 3$$

14. **B** A pentagon is a five-sided figure. If the park commissioner places a fountain at every corner of the park, there will be 5 fountains.

15. **C** Every right triangle contains an angle of 90 degrees. This particular right triangle also has an angle of 30 degrees. To find the third angle, subtract the sum of these two angles from 180 degrees.
$180 - (30 + 90) = 180 - 120$
$= 60$ degrees in third angle
The other two angles are 60 and 90 degrees.

16. **A** To solve for x in this equation, multiply both sides by 2. This is to undo the division.
$$2 \times \frac{x}{2} = 2 \times 7$$
$$x = 14$$

17. **D** Divide only similar terms. First divide numbers, then letters. When dividing powers of a letter, just subtract the exponents.

$$\frac{15a^3b^2c}{5abc} = \frac{15}{5} \times \frac{a^3}{a} \times \frac{b^2}{b} \times \frac{c}{c} = 3a^2b$$

18. **C** The formula for the area of a circle is $\pi \times R^2$. Find the area of the larger circle first.

$\pi \times 10^2 = 100\pi$ square inches

Then find the area of the smaller circle.

$\pi \times 7^2 = 49\pi$ square inches

To find the part of the larger circle that the smaller one doesn't touch, subtract the two areas.

$100 - 49 = 51\pi$ square inches

19. **B** The easiest way to solve this is to form an equation using x as the unknown grade.

$$\frac{78 + 86 + 96 + 94 + x}{5} = 88$$

$$\frac{354 + x}{5} = 88$$

Multiply both sides by 5. This is to undo the division.

$$5 \times \frac{354 + x}{5} = 88 \times 5$$

Simplify both sides of the equation.

$354 + x = 440$

$x = 440 - 354$

$x = 86$ (grade)

20. **A** First change all measurements to yards

9 feet = 3 yards; 12 feet = 4 yards; 6 inches = 1/6 yard

To find the volume of the concrete, multiply the length by the width by the height.

$$3 \times 4 \times \frac{1}{6} =$$

$$12 \times \frac{1}{6} = 2 \text{ cubic yards}$$

21. **D** First find the area of the entire wildlife preserve. Since it is a circle, use the formula for the area of a circle. (Area equals π times the square of the radius.)

$A = \pi \times R^2$

$$= \frac{22}{7} \times (14)^2 = \frac{22}{7} \times 196$$

$$= 22 \times 28$$

$$= 616 \text{ square miles}$$

The lions' territory is a wedge formed by a 90-degree angle at the center of the circle. Since a circle has 360 degrees, we can find the part of the preserve inhabited by lions.

$$\frac{90}{360} = \frac{1}{4}$$

Next find what this equals in square miles.

$$\frac{1}{4} \times \frac{616}{1} = 154 \text{ square miles}$$

22. **A** Solve by doing each arithmetic operation and combining answers. Remember that the product of two negative or two positive numbers is a positive number. The product of a negative and a positive number is negative.

$(-3)^4 = (-3)(-3)(-3)(-3) = 81$

$(-2)^4 = (-2)(-2)(-2)(-2) = 16$

$(-1)^4 = (-1)(-1)(-1)(-1) = \dfrac{1}{98}$

23. **D** To find the volume (V) of a cylinder, multiply π times the square of the radius (r) times the height (h).

$$V = Pi \times r^2 \times h$$

$$V = \frac{22}{7} \times \frac{7}{1} \times \frac{7}{1} \times \frac{15}{1}$$

$$V = 154 \times 15$$

$$V = 2{,}310 \text{ cubic inches (volume)}$$

To find the number of gallons this cylinder will hold, divide its volume by 231.

$2{,}310 \div 231 = 10$ gallons

24. **B** The wall, the ladder, and the ground in the tennis court form a right triangle. The ladder is on a slant, and is opposite the right angle formed by the wall and the ground. In this position, the ladder is the "hypotenuse" of the right triangle. In geometry, the Pythagorean Theorem states that the square of the hypotenuse (c^2) equals the sum of the squares of the other two sides ($a^2 + b^2$).

Thus, $a^2 + b^2 = c^2$

$$8^2 + x^2 = 10^2$$

Solve by doing the arithmetic operations, and by clearing one side of the equation for x^2.

$$64 + x^2 = 100$$
$$x^2 = 100 - 64$$
$$x^2 = 36$$

Then find the square root of x^2 and of 36.

$$x = 6$$

The base of the ladder is 6 feet from the wall.

25. **A** First find how many ounces of the original mixture were fruit juice.

$10 \times 20\% = 10 \times .2 = 2$ ounces

Next find the total number of ounces in the new mixture.

$10 + 40 = 50$ ounces

Then find what part of the new mixture is fruit juice, and convert it to a percentage.

$$\frac{2}{50} = \frac{1}{25} = \frac{4}{100} = 4\%$$

MECHANICAL COMPREHENSION— SUBTEST 7

Answers

1. D   5. A   9. C   13. B   17. A   20. D   23. C
2. B   6. D   10. C   14. D   18. A   21. C   24. D
3. A   7. D   11. B   15. C   19. A   22. B   25. D
4. D   8. B   12. B   16. C

Answers Explained

1. **D** A 1/4-inch wrench fits the head of a 1/2-inch cap screw. A 7/16-inch wrench fits a ¼-inch screw. A 9/16-inch wrench fits a 1/8-inch screw. N.F. indicates a fine thread cap screw.

2. **B** The lock washer prevents the nut from loosening.

3. **A** The open-end wrench is used to hold the carburetor fitting while the flare nut wrench is turned to loosen the flare nut on the tubing. A flare nut wrench will not "round-off" the flare nut.

4. **D** Each line on the micrometer thimble equals 0.001 inch (one-thousandth of an inch).

5. **A** The brake spoon is used to turn the star wheel adjuster of a drum-type brake system. Turning the adjuster with the spoon decreases the clearance between the brake shoes and the drum. Disc type brakes are not adjustable.

6. **D** The hydrometer is used to test battery electrolyte specific gravity.

7. **D** "Opens" in an armature are found by using the meter on the growler.

8. **B** A micrometer is used to check rotor thickness and thickness variation.

9. **C** A feeler gauge is used to measure the clearance between the crankshaft and the main thrust bearing. This clearance determines the end play of the crankshaft. A plastigage is used to measure crankshaft bearing oil clearance. A micrometer is used to measure crankshaft journal diameter.

10. **C** An infinite reading indicates an open or incomplete circuit. A short would be indicated by a lower than normal reading.

11. **B** A transmission uses gear reduction to increase engine torque or turning force. During the time torque is increasing, speed decreases.

12. **B** The pinion, which connects to the

driveshaft, is the driving gear. The ring, which drives axles, is the driven gear. To calculate the gear ratio, divide the drive into the driven gear.

13. **B** When a starter is energized, the magnetic fields created in the armature and field coils produce the turning effect on the armature shaft. The starter drive engages the flywheel ring gear and cranks over the engine whenever the starter is energized.

14. **D** The diesel engine is an example of this principle. As a piston moves up on its compression stroke, air in the cylinder is compressed. Ignition takes place when the fuel is injected into the cylinder. The temperature of the compressed air provides the heat for combustion. A diesel engine does not use a spark plug.

15. **C** The greater the difference between the teeth of two meshed gears, the greater the torque increases.

16. **C** To calculate the final ratio of a transmission and differential, multiply the ratio of the transmission by the ratio of the differential.

$$3.29 \times 3.85 = 12.67$$

17. **A** The fulcrum is positioned between the effort and the load on a first-class lever.

18. **A** The pivot shaft is at T and S. The lobe (high spot) of the cam is between Q and R.

19. **A** The smallest pulley will turn the fastest. When a series of pulleys is connected by drive belts, the smallest diameter pulley rotates at the highest speed.

20. **D** A pair of meshed gears always turns in opposite directions. X and Y are turning in opposite directions. Since E and F are meshed with Y, both are turning in the direction of X.

21. **C** On a third-class lever, the fulcrum is placed at one end, the load is at the other end, and the effect is between the fulcrum and the load.

22. **B** Two meshed gears turn in opposite directions. When an idler gear (I is the idler) is placed between the two, both turn in the same direction. The idler gear turns in direction 1.

23. **C** The centerline of the small gear or pinion is below the center line of the larger ring gear.

24. **D** Pascal's law states that "pressure at any point in a body of fluid is the same in every direction." When a 10-pound force is placed on piston X, which measures 1 square inch, the same force is placed on every square inch of piston Y. Since Y is 300 square inches, then $10 \times 300 = 3000$-pound force.

25. **D** To calculate the effort needed to lift the load of 200 pounds, use this formula. The effort multiplied by the effort arm equals the load multiplied by the load arm or:
E = effort needed to lift the load
$E \times e = L \times w$
e = length of the effort arm
$E \times 4 = 200 \times 2$
w = load arm
$E \times 4 = 400; L = $ load
$E = \frac{400}{4}$
$E = 100$ pounds

ELECTRONICS INFORMATION— SUBTEST 8

Answers

1. A   4. C   7. D   10. D   13. A   16. C   19. D
2. A   5. A   8. B   11. D   14. C   17. D   20. C
3. B   6. B   9. A   12. B   15. B   18. B

Answers Explained

1. **A** Flux is the component in solder that, when liquid, removes the impurities present in the connection and helps prevent oxidation. After it has cooled, the remaining flux present around or between connections acts as an insulator. Tin increases the conductivity of the

connection, and it is the combination of tin and lead that results in the combined lower melting point for solder that is desired in electrical work.

2. **A** A connection that is clean and shiny in appearance is an example of a properly soldered connection. The wattage of the iron used has no effect on the resulting solder connection. The soldering procedure determines what the connection will look like.

3. **B** 1 ampere is equal to 1,000 mA. 0.1 ampere is equal to 100 mA. 0.01 ampere is equal to 10 mA. 0.001 ampere is equal to 1 mA.

4. **C** A good fuse will allow current to flow through it, or indicate continuity on a continuity check using an ohmmeter. If there is continuity, or if the fuse is good, the meter will read zero, or very low resistance. Choices A and D indicate a resistance reading that is very high. Choice B is not a reading found on an ohmmeter scale but rather during a voltage check.

5. **A** The material with the highest conductivity is silver, followed in order of conductivity by copper, aluminum, and zinc.

6. **B** Stranded wire and solid wire of the same gage do not differ in conductivity. Both are available in numerous gages, including the gage used in extension cords. However, solid wire of the gage needed for an extension cord is not nearly as flexible as stranded wire. Because an extension cord is often moved, stranded wire is preferable.

7. **D** The formula to calculate power consumption is power = current × voltage, or $P = I \times E$. Substituting the values given,
$P = I \times E$
$= 10 \text{ amperes} \times 120 \text{ volts}$
$= 1,200 \text{ watts}$

8. **B** A carbon-zinc cell has a voltage of approximately 1.5 volts. In a 12-volt carbon-zinc battery there are 8 cells or 1.5 volts × 8 = 12 volts.

9. **A** The circuit property that opposes any change in current is defined as inductance. Capacitance is the circuit property that opposes any change in voltage. Resistance is the opposition to the flow of electrons, and reactance is the opposition to the flow of an alternating current as a result of inductance or capacitance present in a circuit.

10. **D** A transducer is a component that converts one form of energy into another form of energy. A speaker converts the electrical energy at audio frequencies in the final stage of a radio receiver into sound energy. A resistor is used in a circuit to limit current flow and drop voltage or consume energy. A diode is used to block energy or rectify an AC signal, and a switch is a mechanical means of turning current on and off.

11. **D** The time it takes to complete one sine wave is known as the period of a wave. The distance between the crests of a wave is equal to 1 hertz, and the number of hertz completed in 1 second is known as the frequency. The amplitude of the wave is the distance between the ground line and the highest point of the wave in both the positive and the negative.

12. **B** The correct choice is B. To convert from AC peak value to AC effective value the formula is
$E_{eff} = 0.707 \times E_{peak}$
$= 0.707 \times 141 \text{ volts}$
$= 100 \text{ volts}$

13. **A** The term *frequency response* is used to denote the range of frequencies that a device, or in this case the human ear, is sensitive to. Sound or audio frequencies fall into the range of 16 to16,000 Hz.

14. **C** The term *kilo* represents a quantity of 1,000. Therefore 1 kilowatt is equal to 1,000 watts. Watts and voltage are not interchangeable terms. A watt is a unit of measurement for power, and a volt is a unit of measurement for voltage.

15. **B** The formula for parallel resistors is $R_T = R/n$, where R is equal to the value of one resistor and n is equal to the number of resistors that are of the same value in parallel. Substituting values into the equation:

$$R_T = \frac{900}{3}\ \text{ohms}$$

$$R_T = 300\ \text{ohms}$$

16. **C** The given schematic is of a full-wave DC power supply. At points A and B before the filter capacitor C_1, the waveform is that of a pulsating direct current. A sine wave could not be displayed because a sine wave indicates a voltage that alternates between positive and negative values. At points A and B the voltage present has been rectified to full-wave direct current by the duo-diode tube. This resultant waveform is known as pulsating direct current. A sawtooth or square wave, although both are examples of pulsating direct current, are waveforms resulting from the introduction of other components after the rectification stage.

17. **D** Capacitor C_1 is used to smooth out the AC ripple voltage from the output of the power supply. Choice A is incorrect, as a resistor is used to bleed a capacitor, not vice versa. R_1 is used as an output load resistor. Choice B is incorrect because a capacitor cannot amplify, and choice C is incorrect because a capacitor cannot rectify a signal; that is the purpose of the duo-diode tube.

18. **B** Choices C and D are schematics of resistors. C is a fixed resistor. D is a potentiometer or variable resistor. Choice A is a fixed-capacitor symbol. In choice B the arrow through the fixed capacitor symbol denotes variability. As a tuning capacitor is a variable capacitor, this is the correct choice.

19. **D** The schematic symbol drawn is of a triode tube. Its equivalent solid state component is the transistor. In the triode tube, the elements plate, cathode, and grid correspond to the elements collector, emitter, and base, respectively, in the transistor.

20. **C** When the switch is closed, the capacitor will charge through the resistor. When the voltage across the capacitor reaches the voltage necessary for the neon bulb to light, the lamp will glow. As the lamp glows, the capacitor discharges, resulting in a cycle of charge-discharge. This cycle will cause the neon bulb to flash.

SHOP INFORMATION—SUBTEST 9

Answers

1. B	4. B	7. B	10. A	13. A
2. C	5. D	8. A	11. B	14. A
3. B	6. B	9. D	12. A	15. B

Answers Explained

1. **A** The mitre box is used to cut angles from 45 degrees to 90 degrees in some cases where the angle is adjustable in a metal mitre. In the case of a wooden mitre box there are just two angles, 90 degrees and 45 degrees, cut in the sides of the box to hold the saw.

2. **A** The coping saw is used in carpentry to cut moldings to fit at corners. It can also be used to cut wood at any curve or angle desired.

3. **B** Other names for the crow bar are *pry bar* and *wrecking bar*. It has many uses and different names in different parts of the country.

4. **A** The screwdriver with a straight end is the standard type. The screwdriver with a cross or X on the end is referred to as a Phillips screwdriver. It comes in four different end sizes to fit different screw heads.

5. **B** In order to use a chisel to cut wood, it is usually necessary to strike it with some type of object to drive the cutting edge along the wood. This is usually done with a hammer.

6. **D** The level is made up of at least two glass tubes with air bubbles trapped in the tubes. As the level is moved, the air bubbles move. When the bubbles are aligned in between the two marks on each tube, the level is said to be level.

7. **C** The best way to cut circular holes in metal or wood is to use the hole saw. It has the blades shaped to cut the size you need. Just select the diameter you want, place the saw blade in the electric drill, and drill.

8. **A** The measuring edges of a steel rule are usually graduated in increments of 1/8, 1/16, 1/32, and 1/64 inch.

9. **C** The back saw has a <u>fine</u> tooth configuration and is used to cut <u>cross-grain</u>, leaving a <u>smooth-finished</u> piece of work.

10. **C** If a cold chisel starts to "mushroom" at the head, you should remove the splintered ends with a grinder.

11. **D** The speed bore, forstner, and brad point bits are used in electric hand drills or drill presses.

12. **A** Curved claw hammers meant for carpentry use usually come in 20-, 24-, 28-, and 32-ounce weights.

13. **B** The nail weight *penny* is abbreviated as d.

14. **B** Self-tapping screws are used to connect thin-gage sheet metal parts.

15. **D** Rubbing compounds have a <u>pumice</u> base. Aluminum oxide is used on sandpaper.

ASSEMBLING OBJECTS—SUBTEST 10

Answers

1. **B**	4. **B**	7. **D**	10. **B**	13. **D**	16. **C**	19. **A**
2. **A**	5. **A**	8. **A**	11. **A**	14. **D**	17. **B**	20. **D**
3. **D**	6. **C**	9. **C**	12. **B**	15. **D**	18. **B**	

IMPROVE YOUR RESULTS

CHAPTER
4 General Science Review

Before You Begin

The material in this section is a review of some of the basic concepts and terms taught in high school science courses. As you read these pages, concentrate on any topics you may not have studied in high school. Then try to find a textbook or one of Barron's review books on the particular field of science you think you need to study more intensely.

Spend about 90% of the time you can allot to general science reviewing life sciences and physical sciences and the remaining 10% of your time reviewing earth science. Pay special attention to terms in *italics* and to terms that are defined in clusters or groups. Often, exam questions ask you to distinguish between words that are related to the same concept, but have different meanings (for example, between *evaporation* and *condensation* or between the *proton* and *neutron* in the nucleus of an atom).

INTRODUCTION

Science can be divided into life, physical, and earth sciences. *Biology* is the general term for the study of life. It covers topics dealing with human health and medicine, and is closely related to the study of *botany* (the study of plants) and *zoology* (the study of animals). *Earth science* covers conditions affecting the earth (weather, climate, relation of people to their environment). *Chemistry* is a physical science that investigates the composition, structure, and properties of matter. It is also concerned with changes in matter and the energy released during those changes. *Physics*, like chemistry, is a physical science that deals with matter and energy. However, in physics, more attention is given to mechanical and electrical forces in areas such as light, sound, heat, motion, and magnetism.

THE SCIENTIFIC METHOD

Scientific problem solving depends upon accuracy of observation, precision of method and orderliness. Scientific problem solving follows a pattern of actions which are collectively known as the *scientific method*. Each of the sciences uses this way of solving problems. It involves several steps:

1. *Observation*. In a sense, the true scientist is always involved in this step. It requires the accurate sighting and recording of a particular occurrence. The accuracy of one observation is proved when a number of independent observers agree that they see the same set of circumstances occurring under the same conditions many times.

2. *Hypothesis*. A temporary set of conclusions drawn from a set of observations is known as a

hypothesis. It is usually a very general statement, and suggests the need for a particular experiment.

3. *Experiment*. To test a specific hypothesis, scientists perform experiments. The purpose of the experiments is to answer questions about data truthfully and carefully. Reliable experiments require controlled conditions.
4. *Theory*. When a hypothesis is supported by data obtained from experiments, the hypothesis becomes a theory.
5. *Law* or *principle*. When a theory stands up under the test of time and repeated experiments, it may be called a "law" or principle.

Life Science

BASIC CONCEPTS IN BIOLOGY

There are several basic principles, or concepts, that biologists must constantly deal with. *Homeostasis* refers to the balanced, internal environment of a human cell and of the human organism as a whole. To stay alive, cells must regulate their internal and external fluids according to temperature, acid-base balance, and the amount and content of salts and other vital substances.

Unity is shared by all living species insofar as they have certain biological, chemical, and other characteristics in common: there is the unity of the basic living substances (*protoplasm*). All living cells arise from preexisting living cells. All cells synthesize and use *enzymes*. (An enzyme is a substance which speeds up the reaction of chemicals without itself being changed.) The genetic (hereditary) information of all cells is carried by *DNA* molecules. DNA gives cells the ability to *replicate* (make exact copies of themselves).

Metabolism is a term related to all the biochemical activities carried on by cells, tissues, organs, and systems—activities that are necessary for life.

Adaptation refers to a trait that aids the survival of an individual or a species in a given environment.

The basic unit of classification among living things is the *species*. A species is a group of similar organisms that can mate and produce fertile offspring.

LIFE FUNCTIONS

To satisfy all the conditions necessary for life, all living systems must be able to perform certain biochemical and biophysical activities which together are known as *life functions*.

1. *Nutrition* includes all those activities through which a living organism obtains *nutrients* (food molecules) from the environment and prepares them for use as fuel and for growth. Included in nutrition are the processes of *ingestion, digestion,* and *assimilation.* Ingestion is the process of taking in or procuring food. Digestion refers to the chemical changes that take place in the body so that nutrients can be converted into forms that a cell can use. Assimilation involves changing nutrients into protoplasm.
2. *Circulation* is the movement of fluid and its dissolved materials throughout the body of an organism or within a single cell.
3. *Respiration* consists of *breathing* and *cellular respiration*. Breathing refers to the pumping of air into and out of the lungs of air-breathing animals or the movement of water over the gills of fish. During breathing, oxygen flows into air sacs in the lungs and diffuses into the blood. Carbon dioxide moves out of the blood into the lungs and out of the body through the nose and mouth. Cellular respiration is a combination of processes that release energy from glucose (sugar).
4. *Excretion* removes waste products of cellular respiration from the body. The lungs, the skin,

and the kidneys are excretory organs in humans. They remove carbon dioxide, water, and urea from the blood and other body tissues.

5. *Synthesis* involves those biochemical processes in cells by which small molecules are built into larger ones. As a result of synthesis, *amino acids*, the building blocks of proteins, are changed into enzymes, hormones, and protoplasm. (A *hormone* is a chemical "messenger" produced by the endocrine gland. It helps to control and coordinate the activities of the body.)

6. *Regulation* includes all processes that control and coordinate the many activities of a living thing. Chemical activities inside of cells are controlled by enzymes, vitamins, minerals, and hormones. The *nervous* and *endocrine* systems of higher animals coordinate body activities. The growth and development of plants is regulated by *auxins* and other growth-control substances.

7. *Growth* describes the increase of cell size and increase of cell numbers. The increase of cell numbers occurs when cells divide in response to a sequence of events known as *mitosis*.

8. *Reproduction* is the process by which new individuals are produced by parent organisms. There are two major kinds of reproduction: *asexual* and *sexual*. Asexual reproduction involves only one parent. The parent may divide and become two new cells, thus ending the parent generation. Or the new individual may arise from part of the parent cell; in such a case, the parent remains. In either case, replication of the *chromosomes* is involved. (Chromosomes are small rod-shaped bodies in cells. They contain the genes of heredity.) Sexual reproduction requires the participation of two parents, each producing special reproductive cells known as *sex cells*, or *gametes*. The continuation and survival of the species is dependent upon reproduction. Once a species has lost its reproductive potential, the species no longer survives and becomes extinct.

BASIC UNIT OF LIFE—THE CELL

The *cell* is the basic structural and functional unit of virtually all forms of life. It is the basic unit of structure, with its various shapes and sizes giving form to the body of an organism. It is the basic unit of function, acting as a biochemical factory to perform the basic metabolic functions of life. The cell is also a basic unit of growth, increasing in size and multiplying to form an organism of a specific size and shape. The cell is also a basic unit of heredity, producing cells identical to itself in hereditary makeup and carrying the code for all hereditary information.

Structure of a Cell

A cell is a membrane-enclosed unit containing *cytoplasm* and a *nucleus*. The parts of a cell are known as *organelles*, meaning "little organs." This term is appropriate because parts of the cell have special functions, somewhat like miniature body organs. Although there are some differences between plant and animal cells, all cells have the same basic structure. The major parts of a cell and the function of each follows.

➤ *Cell Membrane* – Also known as the *plasma membrane*, the cell membrane holds the cell together and controls the *selective passage* of certain materials into and out of the cell.

➤ *Cytoplasm* – The living material of the cell lying within the cell membrane but outside the nucleus, the cytoplasm contains many organelles, or little organs, each with its own specific function.

➤ *Nucleus* – The control center of the cell, the nucleus contains *chromosomes*, which carry the genetic, or hereditary, material of the cell.

➤ *Endoplasmic Reticulum* – A network of membranes extending from the nucleus to the cell membrane, the endoplasmic reticulum allows for the movement of materials within the cytoplasm and to the cell membrane.

➤ *Ribosome* – A small organelle, a ribosome is a site of protein synthesis within the cell. Ribosomes are very numerous in the cytoplasm.

➤ *Golgi Body* – A complex of membranes, the Golgi body, or Golgi apparatus, stores and transports materials formed in other parts of the cell.

➤ *Mitochondrion* – The largest organelle in the cell, the mitochondrion is the powerhouse of the cell, involved in cellular respiration. There are many mitochondria in each cell, and each one has a complex internal structure of folded membranes.

➤ *Lysosome* – A saclike structure, the lysosome functions in the release of enzymes within the cell.

Differences Between Plant and Animal Cells

Although the basic structure of plant and animal cells is very similar, there are a few differences. Plant cells have a *cell wall* outside the cell membrane. This wall is made up of *cellulose* and other compounds. It gives the plant cell a more rigid outer covering, helps to support it, and keeps it from drying out. Animal cells do not have a structure that can be compared to the cellulose cell wall. Plant cells also contain *chlorophyll*—containing *chloroplasts*, which function in the process of *photosynthesis*, by which green plants convert the energy of the sun into usable foodstuffs. Animal cells do not have chloroplasts and therefore cannot make their own food.

Animal cells sometimes have *flagella* or *cilia*, threadlike structures that function in the movement of simple organisms and the movement of particles in more complex organisms.

The Basic Chemistry of Cells

The cell is like a "chemical factory" that uses some of the elements present in the nonliving environment. Thus, in the living material of the cell, we find carbon, hydrogen, oxygen, and nitrogen in the greatest amounts, with smaller quantities of sulfur, phosphorus, magnesium, iodine, iron, calcium, sodium, chlorine, and potassium. In the cell, these elements are present in both *organic* and *inorganic compounds*. (A *compound* is a chemical union of two or more substances.)

An inorganic compound is one that does not have the elements carbon and hydrogen in its chemical combination. Inorganic compounds in living cells include water, mineral salts, and inorganic acids.

An organic compound has the elements carbon and hydrogen. Examples are *carbohydrates, lipids, proteins, and nucleic acids*.

1. Carbohydrates are composed of carbon, oxygen, and hydrogen. The hydrogen and oxygen atoms are usually present in the ratio of 2:1. For example *glucose* (a sugar) has 12 atoms of hydrogen and 6 atoms of oxygen (as well as 6 carbon atoms), $C_6H_{12}O_6$. Carbohydrates are used by cells primarily as sources of energy.

2. Lipids include fats and fat-like substances. Like carbohydrates, a lipid molecule contains carbon, hydrogen, and oxygen. But the ratio of hydrogen to oxygen is much greater than 2:1. Most lipid molecules provide twice as much energy per gram as do carbohydrate molecules.

3. Proteins are composed of carbon, hydrogen, oxygen, and nitrogen. Some proteins also contain sulfur. All proteins are built from amino acids, which are essential to life. Some proteins are involved in complex biochemical activities. Others contribute to the structure of cells.

4. Nucleic acids are essential to the continuance of life. They pass hereditary information from one generation to the next. This makes possible the continuance of life within each species of living things. *Deoxyribonucleic acid* (DNA) molecules are the particular type of nucleic acid out of which genes are made. *Genes* carry hereditary traits from parent to offspring.

Cells are always engaged in chemical activity. The major difference between living things and nonliving matter is that living systems carry out vital chemical activities on a controlled and continuous basis. The control of chemical processes in cells requires the work of enzymes. Enzymes are thus *organic catalysts*. (A catalyst, in this sense, is a molecule that controls the rate of a chemical reaction but is not, itself, used up in the process.)

Division of Cells

To ensure growth and reproduction, cells must divide. When a normal body cell reaches a certain size, it divides into two cells. These daughter cells are identical to each other and to the parent cell. In the basic cell division process—mitosis—the hereditary material in the nucleus replicates, or duplicates itself, and then pulls apart to form two separate nuclei, while the cytoplasmic material doubles and splits. The result is two cells identical to the original single cell.

To ensure that the characteristic species number of chromosomes is maintained generation after generation, sex cells, or *gametes* (egg cells and sperm cells), are produced through a special type of cell division known as *meiosis*. In this process, the number of chromosomes in each gamete is reduced to half, so that upon *fertilization* (the union of sperm and egg), the species chromosome number is maintained.

Cloning

By definition, a clone is an individual organism grown from a single body cell of its parent and genetically identical to that parent. Cloning involves stimulating the parent cell to reproduce by asexual (nonsexual) means. Over the past 50 years, tissue culture experiments have been carried out with plants in which single nonembryonic cells have been induced to develop in the same way as a fertilized egg. The results with species such as carrots, African violets, Boston ferns, and Cape sundews show that an entire plant can be reproduced from a single nonreproductive cell.

Among animals (including humans), twinning occurs naturally, producing two separate organisms with the same genetic makeup. Scientists in the 1950s, 1960s, and 1970s demonstrated that they could clone frog tadpoles from frog embryonic cells by transferring the nucleus of one cell into another. In the 1980s, scientists created clones of mammals by splitting embryos in a process called *artificial twinning*, or by nuclear transfer using embryonic cells.

A major breakthrough in animal cloning occurred in 1997 when Scottish researchers cloned a sheep using genetic material from a nonembryonic cell. Once it was proven possible to clone a new animal from a cell of an adult animal, other groups began to experiment with cloning different species. Cloning from adult cells means that it is possible to be more certain ahead of time what the cloned animal will be like. So far, successfully cloned animals include frogs, mice, rats, sheep, cattle, pigs, goats, cats, rabbits, mules, horses, and deer.

PLANT LIFE

The green *plant kingdom* includes species ranging from single-celled to *multicellular* (many-celled) plants. In multicellular plants, different cells are programmed to carry out special tasks. This is called cell *specialization*, and it goes hand-in-hand with a *division of labor*. According to this division, groups of cells work together to perform some special life function to benefit the entire organism.

Lower plant species such as the single-celled *algae* can live in fresh or salt water. But most species of plants (the higher forms) are "anchored" in one place. Higher plants are sometimes referred to as *terrestrial* (land-dwelling).

The bodies of these higher plants have parts known as *roots, stems,* and *leaves*. Roots anchor plants in the soil and absorb water and dissolved materials from the ground. Stems have three major functions: (1) they conduct water upward from the roots to the leaves and conduct dissolved food materials downward from the leaves to the roots; (2) they produce and support leaves and flowers; (3) they provide a means for storing food.

The most important function of green leaves is to carry out *photosynthesis*. This is the food-making process by which inorganic materials are changed into organic nutrients. Green leaves have a pigment called *chlorophyll*. In the presence of that pigment, leaves use the energy of sunlight to make carbohydrates from carbon dioxide (CO_2) and water. These carbohydrates are the food used by plants—and by the animals that eat the plants. During photosynthesis, the oxygen (O_2) needed by animals is released into the atmosphere.

ANIMAL LIFE

All animals are multicellular. One of the simplest forms of animal life is the sponge, which lives in water, attached to rocks. All animals are composed of cells without walls. They *ingest* (take in) food, digest it, and distribute it to cells that make up their body. Most animals can move. Some lower forms of animals reproduce by *budding*. (A new organism grows from cells of the parent, breaks off, and then continues its own existence.) Some forms reproduce through unfertilized eggs, while others reproduce sexually, using sperm and egg. About 90 percent are *invertebrates*—animals without backbones.

Vertebrates are animals with a true backbone made of cartilage or bone. They have a noticeable development of the head, where a brain is enclosed in a *cranium*. Blood is pumped through a closed *circulatory system* by means of a heart with two types of chambers: an *atrium* and a *ventricle*. Most vertebrates (except humans) have a tail. Another characteristic of vertebrates is a mouth that is closed by a movable lower jaw.

CLASSIFICATION

With well over a million different kinds of plants and animals living on earth, there is need for a system of classification. The system currently in use was developed by Carl Linne. It is based primarily on relationships and similarities in structure. The classification has 7 levels. The top, or broadest, containing the largest number of different kinds of organisms is called the kingdom. The bottom level, or the smallest number of different kinds of organisms, is called the species.

> Kingdom
> Phylum
> Class
> Order
> Family
> Genus
> Species

A SPECIAL TYPE OF ANIMAL—HUMANS

Humans belong to a special order of vertebrates called *primates*. What distinguishes primates from other vertebrates? Scientists believe that at one time all primates lived in trees. Over evolutionary time, species such as chimpanzees and humans left the trees and adapted successfully to life on land. Certain characteristics of their "tree life" remain, however. They have (a) hands able to grasp objects; (b) a well-developed sense of sight (primates can see in three dimensions, which enables them to see branches they are going to grasp); and (c) a larger brain with more surface for nerve cells. Primates also have teeth capable of chewing a variety of foods.

Humans are special primates, set apart from others in their species by special characteristics. They have *bipedalism* (the ability to walk on two legs, instead of four). They can adapt to living in almost any environment. And they have the power of speech, along with the ability to remember and to make associations between ideas. It is this that is the basis of culture and history.

The human organism has key systems:

- the *skeletal system* (carries the body and supports and protects the organs)
- the *muscular system* (about 40 percent of body weight, it enables the body to move)
- the *nervous system* (permits communication between the organism and its environment)
- the *endocrine system* (includes glands that regulate growth, blood pressure, etc.)
- the *respiratory system* (allows the body to inhale air and exhale carbon dioxide)
- the *circulatory system* (includes the heart and blood vessels)
- the *lymphatic system* (brings oxygen to cells and removes waste products from them)
- the *digestive system* (processes and distributes nutrients)
- the *excretory system* (removes wastes from the body)
- the *reproductive system* (allows humans to reproduce)

The human body has five major *senses*—sight, hearing, taste, smell, and touch—that transmit information about the environment to the nervous system, and eventually to the brain. Two of these senses show the "division of labor" in the body.

1. The human *eyeball* rests in a bony socket of the skull, and is attached to it by three pairs of small muscles. The colored portion of the front of the eye is the *iris*; in its center is a hole called the *pupil*. Behind the pupil is the *lens*, which flattens or thickens to focus on an object. Light enters the eye through the pupil. It passes through the *cornea* and *lens* (which turns the image upside down and reverses it from left to right), and sets up a barrage of signals in the *retina*. These signals pass through the *optic* nerve to the brain where the image is corrected and "recognized."

2. The *human ear* is made up of three divisions: the *outer ear*, the *middle ear*, and the *inner ear*. The outer ear catches sound waves and transports them to the *eardrum*, causing it to vibrate. Three bones in the middle ear—the *hammer*, *anvil*, and *stirrup*—transmit these vibrations to the *cochlea* in the inner ear. The fluid-filled cochlea is lined with hair cells which transmit the vibrations to the *auditory nerve* and, eventually, to the brain. (The air-filled middle ear is connected by the *Eustachian tube* to the throat. Thus, when you yawn or swallow, you help equalize the air pressure in the middle ear.)

Nutrition

Nutrition is the sum of all the methods by which an organism satisfies the needs of its body cells for energy, fuel, and regulation. Substances that contribute to the nutritional needs of cells are *nutrients* or (for animals) "food." Nutrients that are needed in large amounts are called *macronutrients*: carbohydrates, proteins, and fats. *Micronutrients*—vitamins and minerals—are needed in smaller amounts. Malnutrition results either from eating too little food or from eating an imbalanced diet. A *balanced diet* includes an appropriate number of daily choices from the five major food groups: (a) milk and other dairy products, (b) meat and other proteins, (c) vegetables and fruits, (d) breads, cereals, and other grain products, and (e) fats and oils, which occur most often in prepared foods.

Carbohydrates include starches and sugars. Their primary function is to serve as fuel for the body cells. When body cells receive more simple sugar than they can use, some of the excess sugar is stored in the liver and muscles as *glycogen* (animal starch). However, if the quantity of carbohydrates taken in is much too large, the body converts them to fat, which is stored under the skin and around the body's organs. Food sources of carbohydrates include potatoes, fruit, cereal grains, beans, baked goods, milk, etc.

Proteins are the most abundant of the organic compounds in body cells. Hair, nails, and other fibrous structures in the body are composed of proteins. They form part of certain hormones, are vital to the formation of DNA molecules, and help to build the body's resistance to disease. Food sources of proteins include meat, fish, eggs, milk, cheese, beans, nuts, etc.

Fats are also fuel foods. Certain fats are essential to the structure and function of body cells and to the building of cell membranes. Fats also aid in transporting fat-soluble vitamins. Foods rich in fats include butter, bacon, egg yolk, cream, and some cheeses. Fat-rich foods add to the caloric content of the human diet. A *calorie* is the unit of heat necessary to raise 1 liter of water 1 degree Celsius. One gram of fat provides 9 calories. One gram of protein or carbohydrates provides 4 calories.

Vitamins are organic compounds necessary for the proper functioning of the body. The following table summarizes the source and value of some major vitamins:

Vitamin	Necessary for	Some Food Sources
A	Healthy eyes and skin	Fish liver oil, butter, yellow fruits and vegetables
C (Ascorbic acid)	Healthy teeth, gums, and bones; resistance to infection	Citrus fruits, cabbage, green leafy vegetables
D	Strong bones and teeth; regulation of calcium and phosphorus metabolism	Fish liver oil, egg yolk, salmon
E	Prevention of oxidation by red blood cells; good muscle tone	Wheat germ, green leafy vegetables
K	Clotting of blood	Green vegetables, tomatoes
B (Thiamin, Niacin)	Growth; good digestion and appetite; normal nerve functions	Yeast, wheat germ, liver, bread, green vegetables
B (Riboflavin)	Health of skin and mouth; growth; healthy eyes	Same as for thiamin and niacin; meat

Minerals are inorganic compounds. *Calcium* regulates muscle activity and, together with *phosphorus*, is used in building bones and teeth. (Both calcium and phosphorus are found in dairy products. Calcium is also found in grains and green leafy vegetables.) *Sodium* functions in the regulation of body temperature: large amounts of the body's salts are excreted by the sweat glands. Nerve cells could not carry impulses, nor could muscles contract, without the assistance of sodium and *potassium*. (Potassium is found in beans, peas, and fruit.)

Other minerals include: *fluorine*, which helps resist tooth decay; *iodine* (found in fish and salts), which aids in metabolism; *magnesium* (found in green leafy vegetables), which is also good for metabolism and for healthy bones and teeth; and *iron* (found in liver, egg yolk, red meats, and grains), which is necessary for *hemoglobin*—a chemical that unites with oxygen in the blood.

Fiber in the human diet comes only from plant sources. Fiber is not a nutrient, but it is important for stimulating the normal action of the intestines in the elimination of wastes. Raw fruits and vegetables, whole cereals and bread, and fruits with seeds (figs, strawberries, and raspberries) are excellent sources of fiber.

Food Guide Pyramid

Since we are what we eat, it is obvious that our health depends to a large extent on our taking in the correct types of food. A vigorous, alert, disease-resistant condition can result from having the proper amounts of vitamins, water, minerals, proteins, fats, and carbohydrates in our diet.

The U.S. Department of Agriculture maintains and publishes a set of guidelines known as the Food Guide Pyramid for a person's daily diet. The large base of the pyramid advises that bread, cereals, rice, and pasta should make up most of the daily food choices; 6 to 11 servings should be eaten from this group every day. As one moves up the pyramid, specific servings of the different food groups are recommended, as can be seen in the accompanying illustration. At the top, the small peak of the pyramid suggests that fats, oils, and sweets be eaten only sparingly. Although the United States is the richest and best-fed nation on earth, the American way of eating fast food, large amounts of fat, protein, and carbohydrates) may be hazardous to health and may contribute to serious disorders such as heart disease, high blood pressure, cancer, obesity, stroke, and diabetes. The director of the Institute for Disease Prevention, Dr. Oliver Labaster, has provided evidence that more than 50 percent of heart disease and strokes and about 35 percent of cancers are caused by bad eating habits.

Calories

Your body needs to have the right amount of calories every day to get the nutrients it needs. How many calories that actually amounts to depends on a variety of factors, including your age, sex, height, weight, and activity level. Caloric needs are also different for people who have a long-term illness and women who are either pregnant or breastfeeding.

The National Academy of Sciences recommends the following calorie categories:

1,600 calories—Many sedentary (not very active) women, some older adults
2,200 calories—Children, teenage girls, active women, many sedentary men
2,800 calories—Teenage boys, active men, very active women

People in the lower-calorie category (1,600 calories a day) should aim for the lesser amount in the number of servings listed. For instance, someone in this category would want to normally have only about six servings of bread and grains a day; have three servings of vegetables; have two each of fruits, dairy products, and meats; and keep their fats and sweets to a minimum. A person in the middle group ought to have no more than about nine servings of breads and grains, four of vegetables, three of fruits, and so on—while someone in the upper category would aim for the upper end of the recommended ranges listed.

You may also be between calorie categories. If you are, you'll need to estimate your servings for each category. For example, some less active women may need only about 2,000 calories to get the nutrients they need and maintain a healthy weight. If you are at this calorie level, eight servings from the grain group would be about right.

Diseases

A *disease* is a disorder that prevents the body organs from working as they should. In general, diseases can be classified as *noninfectious* or *infectious*. Among the noninfectious causes of disease are malnutrition, poisoning, radiation, and the malfunctioning of the endocrine system. Infectious diseases can be caused by *germs* (bacteria), fungi, parasitic worms, and *viruses*. Viruses are inorganic, but they grow within living cells. Most infectious diseases are *contagious*—that is, they are spread by body contact or by droplet infection.

The human body has many powerful defenses against disease. The skin itself kills most germs that land on it. So does the saliva in our mouths, the acid in our stomachs, the mucus membrane in our nose and throat. If any germs do get past these defenses, our body releases chemicals to surround and destroy the germs. White blood cells, cells in the lymph vessels, and *antibodies* are also part of this defense. Antibodies are "tailor-made" by the body to fight specific germs.

Our communities can do a great deal to help prevent disease. One strategy is to require that all children be immunized against disease. *Immunization* is the injection of a *vaccine*—a weak agent of the disease—into a person's body. This stimulates the body to produce antibodies that will be ready to fight germs if they invade the body. Successful methods of immunization have been developed against smallpox, polio, measles, typhus, and other contagious diseases.

Another safeguard is to protect our water supply against contamination. There are several techniques. *Settling* is the process by which water is held in large tanks until suspended solids settle out. In *filtering*, water is allowed to trickle through sand beds several feet deep. This removes 90 to 95 percent of all bacteria as well as fine particles of solid matter. *Aeration* is the process by which water is sprayed into the air. This technique kills some bacteria and allows more air to dissolve into the water. In *chlorination,* some form of chlorine is added to the water to kill any remaining germs.

There are several ways to preserve food—some of them ancient, some very recent; drying, salting, smoking, fast-freezing, pickling, and sterilization by heat. Canning sterilizes food and seals it so that no germs can get in. To prevent the spread of disease through milk, dairies *pasteurize* it: They chill milk immediately after collecting it to kill some of the bacteria, and then heat it to a required temperature for a period of time. This kills all the disease-causing germs.

Genetics

Human genetics is the study of the mechanism by which characteristics are passed from parents to offspring. Every child develops from a fertilized egg which has 23 pairs of chromosomes for a total of 46. The basic principles of heredity were first established by Gregor Mendel in the late 18th century. Mendel formulated three basic laws of heredity: the *law of segregation,* which stated that individual heredity traits, or units, separate in the gametes; *the law of independent assortment,* which stated that each trait is inherited independently of other traits; and *the law of dominance,* which stated that when contrasting traits are crossed (e.g., trait for brown eyes and trait for blue eyes), one trait is *dominant* over the other, which is *recessive.* Subsequent research corrected and expanded these initial findings. The recognition that the hereditary units are discrete units, now known as genes, on the *chromosomes* opened the way for further studies. We now know that a gene is a unit of a *deoxyribonucleic acid (DNA)* molecule and that it carries a *code* for the production of a specific protein needed by the organism. A change in a gene (an error in DNA coding or duplication) is a *mutation.* As a rule, mutations occur randomly, and most are harmful to the organism.

In recent years, scientists have been able to identify the genetic basis of many diseases and attempts are being made to find ways of treating genetic disorders. Through a process known as *amniocentesis,* in which a small amount of amniotic fluid surrounding a fetus is removed from a pregnant woman and the fetal cells analyzed, some hereditary defects can now be diagnosed before birth.

ECOLOGY

Ecology is that branch of science that deals with the interaction of organisms and their environment. It is very dependent on knowledge of biology and chemistry. The interconnection of plant, animal, and human life is becoming more widely appreciated. Ecology, for example, focuses on the effects of chemical waste products on our air, sea, and land.

One of the most important concepts in ecology is that of an *ecosystem*, the system by which a particular living *community* of plant and animal *populations* interacts with its non-living environment. There is no size requirement for an ecosystem: It may be a forest, a pond, an unused city lot, or a crack in the sidewalk. The structure of an ecosystem is the same whether its location is on land or underwater. What really defines an ecosystem is a set of interacting forces:

1. The *air* is made up of 21 percent oxygen, 78 percent nitrogen, .03 percent carbon dioxide, and other inert gases.
2. The *soil* is the source of minerals that supply plants with compounds of nitrogen, zinc, calcium, phosphorus, and other minerals.
3. The *green plants* in an ecosystem are its *producers*, so-called because they make their own food.
4. *Primary consumers* in an ecosystem are its *herbivores* (plant-eaters). These include crickets, grasshoppers, and cattle, for example.
5. *Secondary consumers* (so-called because they feed on the herbivores) are flesh eaters, such as snakes, frogs, and coyotes. These are called *carnivores*.
6. *Tertiary consumers* are those that feed on the herbivores and carnivores.
7. *Scavengers*, such as earthworms and vultures, feed upon dead organic matter.
8. *Decomposers* are those bacteria and other organisms that break down dead organic matter, thus releasing minerals that are returned to the soil. Without the decomposers, valuable minerals would remain trapped in dead organic matter.

The source of all energy in an ecosystem is the sun. Green plants use the sun's light (its energy) to make their own food. This energy is then transferred from plants to the animals that consume them. Animals use energy to do work and, in the process, give off body heat, which radiates into the atmosphere. The cycles of *photosynthesis* (energy trapping) and *respiration* (energy release and use) must continue if the ecosystem is to continue. The flow of energy in the ecosystem can be studied by way of this *food chain* showing the transfer of energy from a producer, lettuce, to a tertiary consumer, the hawk. (Not all food chains are this simple.)

Lettuce → Rabbit → Snake → Hawk

Ecosystems that have become permanent in a broad geographical area are known as *biomes*. The earth is divided into several biomes:

1. The *arctic tundra* includes vast stretches of treeless plains around the Arctic Ocean. Here the temperature is the limiting factor in the ecosystem: It ranges from 60° F in the summer to −130° F in the winter. The ground is permanently frozen a few feet below the surface.
2. In the *taiga*, coniferous (evergreen) forests survive long, severe winters. Canada has a large taiga.
3. The *deciduous* (leaf-shedding) *forests* of the world are in regions with relatively temperate (mild) climates.
4. *Deserts* form in regions where the annual rainfall is less than 2.5 inches (6.5 centimeters)— or where rain is irregular, and the rate of evaporation is very high. The Sahara and Gobi Deserts are examples.
5. *Grasslands* occur where rainfall is low and irregular. In the United States, the Great Plains is a grasslands region; grasslands in the Soviet Union are called *steppes*.
6. *Tropical rain forests* are characterized by high temperatures and constant rainfall. This type of biome is found in Central and South America.
7. Oceans and seas form the *marine biome*, the thickest known layer of living things. Here, the depth of water determines where life flourishes.

Earth Science

The term *earth science* includes several related sciences such as *geology* (the study of the earth), *oceanography* (the study of the seas and oceans), *meteorology* (the study of weather and climate), and *astronomy* (the study of the earth as part of the universe).

GEOLOGY

Geology deals with the formation and composition of the earth. It relates to and borrows from other sciences such as chemistry, physics, and biology. Geologists determine the strength and behavior of rock formations and their reaction to stress. Such knowledge is essential for the design and construction of large-scale buildings, dams, bridges, and tunnels; for the prediction of earthquakes; and for the location and mining of petroleum, coal, and other minerals.

How were the hills and valleys of the earth's surface formed? Glacier National Park in Montana is an outdoor textbook on this question. For millions of years thick beds of ooze in this area solidified into limestone. Later, *sediments* (fragments of rocks and organic matter) covered the limestone and became mudstone. These, in turn, were overlaid with the other sediments that also became limestone.

About 70 million years ago, in what is now Montana, enormous stresses in the earth's crust acted on the deeply buried mudstones, sandstones, and limestones. As the tensions and strain became acute, the rock was warped and finally broken. The western part, more than 1/2 mile thick, slid over the eastern part. The pressures continued for millions of years until a gigantic 300-mile-long section of the earth's crust was moved more than 37 miles to the east. This section, with *strata* (layers) more than 1 billion years old, actually capped "younger" rock. The same process created other mountain systems throughout the world. However, few overthrusts have been as great as this, the Lewis Overthrust of Glacier National Park. The carving of the park's rugged landscape was principally the work of *glaciers* (slow-moving masses of ice) during the last 3 million years. The moving ice deepened the main valleys and cut back the base of the cliffs. As the ice melted, the strata of earth's oldest sediments appeared as streaks on the sides of the 900-foot-high precipices (overhanging cliffs) in the park.

On a geologic time scale, these different types of change in the earth's surface fall into four periods or eras:

1. The *Prepaleozoic* era, characterized chiefly by volcanic activity and the formation of great mountain ranges;
2. The *Paleozoic* era, with periodic submergence and emergence of continents and mountains;
3. The *Mesozoic* era, characterized by uplift (the elevation of land in a particular place), erosion, and more volcanic activity;
4. The *Cenozoic* era, with the rise and fall of coastal lands, general erosion, and the retreat of the glaciers.

The movement of the earth's seemingly solid crust is part of the theory of continental drift. Recent evidence seems to support the idea that at one time all the continents as we know them were joined in one large land mass, "Pangaea." Gradually—according to theory—this continent split into two land masses, with North America, Europe, and Asia in one mass, and the rest of today's continents in the other. Separations continued. The similarities in the Atlantic coastlines of Africa and South America suggest that they were once united. And recently, the fossil remains of a large reptile (Lystrosaurus) that was once common in Africa have been found in Antarctica. This suggests that these two continents were also once joined.

How old is the earth? Methods that have been used to determine the geologic age of earth include measuring *salinity, erosion, sedimentary layers*, and *radioactivity*. The salinity technique assumes that all oceans were originally fresh water. However, as rivers washed over the land, picking up minerals, they began to deposit accumulated salts in the oceans. The rate of this process can be calculated. Thus, the time for all oceans to reach their present degrees of salinity can be approximately figured.

The sedimentary layers method and the erosion method are opposites. The erosion method figures the rate at which a rock formation was worn away by wind or water. With sedimentary layers, the figuring is based on the present thickness of the layer and the assumed rate of its buildup through past deposits. These methods and the salinity technique have led geologists to place the age of the earth somewhere between 100 million and 1.5 billion years.

We now know that such figures are much too low. Dating by these methods is not reliable because they depend too heavily on rates that vary widely from place to place and through time. What was needed was a way to measure time by a process that does not vary, a process that runs continuously through time and leaves a record with no gaps in it. The discovery of radioactivity by A. H. Becquerel in 1896 provided the needed process.

The most recently developed technique uses the *radioactivity* or "half-life" of an element. By analyzing particular elements such as uranium, strontium, and thorium and by studying their decay products, geologists can figure the age of rock samples. Since each element has a specific *half-life* (the time needed for half the atoms in a mass to disintegrate), scientists using this method figure the age of the earth to be about 3.5 billion years.

The radioactive dating technique is helping paleontologists to establish the geologic age of *fossils*. Fossils are forms of plant and animal life preserved in rock. Since carbon is part of every organic compound, knowledge of the half-life of carbon-14 is effective in establishing when a particular fossil was actually a living plant or animal.

OCEANOGRAPHY

Using various related sciences, oceanography studies the oceans and seas. Although oceans cover more than three-fourths of earth's surface, only a small portion of this vast area is used by humans. Examination of the ocean floor, marine life, and mineral content of the water is important for the future development of essential materials, food, and medicines.

There are four major oceans on earth: the Pacific, Atlantic, Indian, and Arctic. Together, these bodies of water hold 97% of all water on earth. In the simplest terms, an ocean may be divided into the *shoreline,* the *water* itself, and the *seabed,* or bottom. However, these classifications need further division into zones (levels), shown in the following table.

MARINE ZONES

Zone	Average Depth	Average Temperature	Comment
Shore (between high, low tides)	Varies	Varies by season	Wave action, light for photosynthesis
Water (1) shore to continental shelf	600 feet (0–200 meters)	41°– 77° F (5°– 25°C)	Waves, currents, greatest amount of plant and animal life
(2) downward slope from continental shelf	600–18,250 feet (200–2,500 meters)	41°– 59° F (5°– 15°C)	Currents, almost dark, fewer marine animals, no plants
(3) deeper plain	8,000–21,250 feet (2,500–6,500 meters)	27°– 35° F (3°– 4°C)	Dark, limited animal life, no plants
(4) deepest trenches or canyons	21,250–37,350 feet (6,500–11,500 meters)	34°– 37° F (1°– 3°C)	Dark, very limited animal life, no plants

Oceans and Natural Resources

The oceans represent a vast source of information and natural resources that have not yet been fully tapped because the ocean environment is hostile and not readily accessible. The oceans contain information in the sedentary layers and fossils that line their floors. The core samples that have been retrieved by oceanographic research vessels reveal much information about the Earth's geologic history, and fossils found in these sediments record a history of life in the oceans. The information obtained from ocean sediments about past climates and the ways they have changed helps us to understand our present climate. Careful study of ocean bottoms also revealed the mechanism for continental drift, which led to the theory of plate tectonics.

The ocean is also an important source of valuable chemical and mineral resources such as bromine, iodine, magnesium, manganese, oil, natural gas, phosphorite, and metal-rich muds. Moreover, as desalination plants are made more efficient, the oceans are becoming a valuable source of fresh water in arid regions. The oceans are also a critical source of food, particularly animal protein. Although aquaculture, or farming the oceans, is still in its infancy, it is becoming an increasingly important source of animals such as clams, oysters, and shrimp, as well as such plants as kelp.

It is difficult to assess the mineral resources of the oceans because they are underwater, and the usual methods of mineral exploration and recovery cannot be used. However, the estimated value of the mineral resources of the oceans is staggering.

The most valuable resources that we know about are the oil and natural gas found in the sediments of the continental shelf. The value of oil and gas obtained from the oceans yearly is greater than the combined value of all biological resources taken from the ocean.

The rising of magma, or liquified rock material, in the ocean ridges and the movements of magma near the subduction zones create fluids enriched in minerals, which are then deposited on the ocean floor. The deposits found include such minerals as copper, iron, zinc, manganese, nickel, vanadium, lead, chromium, cobalt, silver, and gold.

Generally, animal life and plant life typical of one zone are not found in a different zone. However, there are exceptions; there are no exact boundaries between zones to prevent a sea creature from moving from one level to another. Knowledge of the deeper levels and the ocean bottom is still incomplete.

An important influence of the ocean on human life comes from tides. Tides are the alternate rising and falling of water levels in the oceans and other large bodies of water. They are the result of the gravitational pull of the sun and the moon on the freely moving waters of the earth. Since the moon is much closer to the earth than is the sun, the moon has a much greater effect on tides. Tides affect the movement of ships, especially when in port in shallow waters.

ASTRONOMY

Although astronomy is often considered part of physics, it is also related to earth science. The *rotation* of the earth on its *axis* (an imaginary line running through the earth from North to South Pole) causes day and night. The *revolution* of the earth around the sun affects the seasons of earth's year. The earth itself is part of a *solar system* with eight other planets, and is part of a *universe* of many stars and suns.

Planet	Average distance from the sun (million miles)	Rank by size	Time for revolution	Number of moons
Mercury	36.0	8	88 days	0
Venus	67.1	6	225 days	0
Earth	93.0	5	365¼ days	1
Mars	141.7	7	687 days	2
Jupiter	483.4	1	12 years	63 (12 major, 51 minor)
Saturn	886.1	2	29 years	33 (9 major, 24 minor)
Uranus	1,783.0	3	84 years	27 (5 major, 22 minor)
Neptune	2,793.0	4	164 years	13 (2 major, 11 minor)
Pluto	3,666.0	9	248 years	1

Occasionally, earth's moon goes into *eclipse*. An eclipse occurs when one astronomical body cuts off light from another. A *lunar eclipse* occurs when the earth comes directly between the sun and the moon, thus causing the earth's shadow (*umbra*) to fall directly on the moon. Since the moon shines only in light reflected from the sun, this position of the earth puts the moon into eclipse.

In a total *solar eclipse,* the moon is directly between the earth and the sun, so that the umbra of the moon's shadow that sweeps across the earth during a solar eclipse is very narrow. The shadow's maximum width is about 170 miles.

Two astronomical bodies that interest humans are the *comet* and *meteor.* Comets are mostly gaseous bodies that can be seen from earth for periods ranging from a few days to months at a time. The *comet head* contains a small bright nucleus that astronomers think contains ice, frozen gases, and other particles. When a comet approaches the sun, these gases and particles stream off in the form of a *tail,* sometimes as long as 100,000,000 miles (Halley's comet appeared in 1986).

A meteor is a small piece of extraterrestrial matter that becomes visible when it enters earth's atmosphere. In the friction that goes along with this entry, a meteor heats up intensely and usually disintegrates before it can reach the ground. Those meteors large enough to reach ground are called *meteorites.* The glow of a meteor's appearance has led it to be called (incorrectly) a *"shooting"* or *"falling star."*

METEOROLOGY

Meteorology is the study of *weather* and *climate.* Weather is the condition of the atmosphere at any given time and place. Climate is the average of weather conditions in a particular place over a period of time. The services of *meteorologists* in predicting the weather are critical to farmers, travelers, and people in many different kinds of business.

Weather is the description of several atmospheric conditions interacting with one another. These conditions—*temperature, air pressure, winds, humidity,* etc.—are themselves influenced by other factors.

1. The temperature of a place is affected by the angle of the sun's rays, the length of its daylight period, its altitude, and its closeness to bodies of water. Water heats and cools more slowly than land and affects the air above it in the same way. Therefore, breezes blowing off the water tend to moderate the temperature of air over faster-heating and faster-cooling land.
2. The pressure of the air depends on its temperature and humidity. Warm air is lighter than cold air, and moist air is lighter than dry air. Thus moist, warm air has very low pressure. Changes in atmospheric pressure are measured on a *barometer.* When meteorologists at the weather bureau see a "falling" barometer, they predict rain.
3. Wind is the movement of air from one place to another. Winds are caused by differences in air pressure. Winds always move from areas of higher pressure (cold, dry air) to areas of lower pressure (warm, moist air). Sometimes the difference in pressure between two areas is great enough to cause *hurricanes* or *tornadoes.* A hurricane is a wind of 74 miles or more per hour. A tornado is a wind with a funnel-shaped cloud that touches the ground.
4. Humidity refers to the amount of moisture in the air. When the air is warm and dry, moisture on the earth's surface tends to *evaporate* (turn into vapor). When the air is completely filled with moisture (when it is *saturated*), a drop in the temperature will cause the moisture in the air to *condense* (form droplets) and *precipitate* (fall) as rain, snow, sleet, hail, etc.

Chemistry

Chemistry is a physical science that investigates the composition, structure, and properties of *matter.* Chemistry is also concerned with changes in matter and the *energy* involved during those changes.

MATTER

Matter is defined as anything that occupies space and has mass. Mass is the quantity of matter that a substance possesses and, depending on the gravitational force acting on it, has a unit of weight assigned to it. Although the weight can vary, the mass of the body is a constant and can be measured by its resistance to a change of position or motion. For example, an astronaut who weighs 168 pounds on Earth weighs about 28 pounds on the moon, but still has the same mass. This property of mass to resist a change of position or motion is called *inertia*. Since matter does occupy space, we can compare the masses of various substances that occupy a particular volume unit. This relationship of mass to a volume unit is called the density of a substance.

Matter occurs in one of three *states*, or conditions: A substance may be a *solid*, a *liquid*, or a *gas*. A solid has both a definite size and shape (for example, an ice cube before it melts). A liquid has a definite volume, but it takes the shape of the container it's in. (For example, an ice cube is a solid with a definite shape. If it melts in a cup, the liquid water then takes the shape of the cup.) A gas has neither definite shape nor definite volume. Often, the state of matter that a particular substance is in can be changed by the addition or removal of *heat energy*. For example, water that is cooled sufficiently will freeze; heated sufficiently, it will turn into a gas.

Matter can be subdivided in another way: It may be either an *element*, a *compound*, or a *mixture*. An element is a substance that is made up of only one kind of atom. For example, gold, iron, sulfur, oxygen are all elements and each contains only one kind of atom. A compound is a substance composed of two or more kinds of atoms joined together in a definite pattern. For example, water (H_2O) always occurs in the relationship of two atoms of hydrogen to one atom of oxygen. A mixture is an indefinite blending of two or more substances. Sometimes the substances are very evenly distributed (food coloring in water). Other times, the mixture is uneven (raisins in cookie dough).

Matter undergoes two types of change: *physical change* and *chemical change*. In a physical change, the appearance of a substance may change, but its chemical composition remains the same (for example, broken glass, split wood, melted ice). A chemical change involves a change in the chemical makeup of a substance (for example, burning wood) and is always accompanied by either the release or absorption of energy.

In describing the state of matter and its changes we speak of the *physical* and *chemical properties* of matter. The physical properties of a substance are those we can observe with our senses: its color, taste, melting point, hardness, etc. The chemical properties of a substance are those that describe its reactions with other substances (for example, iron rusts in the presence of oxygen, gold does not, etc.). The smallest particle of a substance that has all the physical and chemical properties of the substance is called a *molecule*.

ENERGY

Energy is usually defined as the ability to do work. Energy may appear in a variety of forms—as *light, heat, sound, mechanical energy, electrical energy,* and *chemical energy*. Energy can be converted from one form to another. For example: (1) Heat from burning fuel is used to vaporize water (change it to steam); (2) this steam energy is used to turn turbine wheels to produce mechanical energy; (3) the turbine turns a generator to produce electricity; (4) this electricity is then available in homes for use as light, heat, or in the operation of appliances.

Two general classifications of energy are *potential energy* and *kinetic energy*. Potential energy is said to be due to the position of an object. Kinetic energy is energy of motion. The difference between the two can be illustrated by a boulder on the slope of a mountain. While it remains there, the boulder has high potential energy due to its position above the valley floor. If it falls, however, its potential energy is converted into kinetic energy.

What is the relationship between matter and energy? The *Law of Conservation of Mass and Energy* states that matter and energy are neither created nor lost during chemical reactions. The law also states that matter and energy are interchangeable under special conditions. Albert Einstein's formula for this interchange is $E = mc^2$

$$Energy = Mass \times (speed\ of\ light)^2$$

SYMBOLS AND EQUATIONS IN CHEMISTRY

Chemistry requires the understanding of *symbols* and *equations*. Symbols are short forms for expressing an idea or a term. Symbols in chemistry include the following examples:

→ means yields, or leads to (Arrows are also used in chemical equations, where they perform the same function as the equal sign in mathematics)

↑ means forms a gas

↓ means forms a *precipitate* (something that settles to the bottom of a liquid)

Element	Symbol	Element	Symbol
Magnesium	Mg	Gold	Au
Phosphorus	P	Barium	Ba
Sulfur	S	Arsenic	As
Mercury	Hg	Iron	Fe
Sodium	Na	Chlorine	Cl

An equation resembles a sentence. A sentence is made up of words. A chemical equation is made up of formulas of molecules. A formula may be of a compound—H_2O or NaCl, for example—or an element, Mg, O_2, etc. A *chemical equation* shows what happens when chemical elements or compounds interact. For example, you can read the following as a sentence:

$$2H_2 + O_2 \rightarrow 2H_2O$$

Translated, this chemical equation reads, "Four atoms (or two molecules) of the element hydrogen and one molecule or two atoms of the element oxygen combine to yield two molecules of a compound called H_2O, which is water." The basic features of a chemical equation are:

➤ A chemical equation shows a *chemical change*. Either a new chemical compound is formed, or a compound is separated into its elements.

➤ The equation must *balance:* The total quantities to the left of the arrow (→) must equal the total quantities to the right of the arrow. In the following equation, you have 2 hydrogen (H_2) and 2 chlorine (Cl_2) molecules yielding only one molecule of hydrogen chloride (HCl). This is, therefore, an *imbalanced equation:*

$$H_2 + Cl_2 \rightarrow HCl$$

If you place a 2 before the compound HCl, you make the 2 hydrogen and 2 chlorine atoms on the left equal to two hydrogen and two chlorine atoms contained in two hydrogen chloride molecules on the right. Thus, this equation is balanced:

$$H_2 + Cl_2 \rightarrow 2HCl$$

The periodic table of the elements was first used in 1869 by Dmitry I. Mendeleyev as a way of presenting all the elements in a way that shows their similarities and differences. The elements are arranged in increasing order of *atomic number* (Z) as you go from left to right across the table. The horizontal rows are called *periods*, and the vertical rows are known as *groups*.

A *noble gas* is found at the right side of each period. There is a progression from metals to nonmetals across each period. Elements found in groups (e.g., alkali, halogens) have a similar electronic configuration. The number of electrons in the outer shell is the same as the number of the group (e.g., lithium 2·1).

The block of elements between groups II and III are called *transition metals*. These are similar in many ways; they produce colored compounds, have variable valencies, and are often used as *catalysts*. Elements 58 to 71 are known as *lanthanides* or rare earth elements. These elements are found on earth in only very small amounts.

Elements 90 to 103 are known as the *actinide elements*. They include most of the well-known elements found in *nuclear reactions*. The elements with atomic numbers larger than 92 do not occur naturally. They have all been produced artificially by bombarding other elements with particles.

Periodic Table of the Elements

KEY

Atomic Mass → 12.0111
Selected Oxidation States → -4 / +2 / +4
Symbol → C
Atomic Number → 6
Electron Configuration → 2-4

Note: Mass numbers in parentheses are mass numbers of the most stable or common isotope.

Relative atomic masses are based on $^{12}C = 12.000$

*The systematic names and symbols for elements of atomic numbers above 109 will be used until the approval of trivial names by IUPAC.

**Denotes the presence of (2-8-) for elements 72 and above

Period	Group 1	Group 2											13	14	15	16	17	18
1	H 1																	He 2
2	Li 3	Be 4											B 5	C 6	N 7	O 8	F 9	Ne 10
3	Na 11	Mg 12	3	4	5	6	7	Group 8	9	10	11	12	Al 13	Si 14	P 15	S 16	Cl 17	Ar 18
4	K 19	Ca 20	Sc 21	Ti 22	V 23	Cr 24	Mn 25	Fe 26	Co 27	Ni 28	Cu 29	Zn 30	Ga 31	Ge 32	As 33	Se 34	Br 35	Kr 36
5	Rb 37	Sr 38	Y 39	Zr 40	Nb 41	Mo 42	Tc 43	Ru 44	Rh 45	Pd 46	Ag 47	Cd 48	In 49	Sn 50	Sb 51	Te 52	I 53	Xe 54
6	Cs 55	Ba 56	La 57	Hf 72	Ta 73	W 74	Re 75	Os 76	Ir 77	Pt 78	Au 79	Hg 80	Tl 81	Pb 82	Bi 83	Po 84	At 85	Rn 86
7	Fr 87	Ra 88	Ac 89	Rf 104	Db 105	Sg 106	Bh 107	Hs 108	Mt 109	Uun* 110	Uuu 111	Uub 112		Uuq 114				

Ce 58	Pr 59	Nd 60	Pm 61	Sm 62	Eu 63	Gd 64	Tb 65	Dy 66	Ho 67	Er 68	Tm 69	Yb 70	Lu 71
Th 90	Pa 91	U 92	Np 93	Pu 94	Am 95	Cm 96	Bk 97	Cf 98	Es 99	Fm 100	Md 101	No 102	Lr 103

Reference Tables for Physical Setting/Chemistry

MEASUREMENTS IN CHEMISTRY

The *metric system* of measurement is the one used by scientists all over the world. It is important for them to use the same units when communicating information. For this reason, scientists use the modernized metric system, designated in 1960 by the General Conference on Weights and Measures as the International System of Units. This is commonly known as the SI system, an abbreviation for the French *Systeme International d'Unites*. It is now the most common system of measurement in the world. The reason it is so widely accepted is twofold. First, SI uses the decimal system as its base. Second, in many cases units for various quantities are defined in terms of units for simpler quantities. There are seven basic units that can be used to express the fundamental properties of measurement. These are called the SI base units and are shown in the table below:

SI BASE UNITS

Property	Unit	Abbreviation
mass	kilogram	kg
length	meter	m
time	second	s
electric current	ampere	A
temperature	kelvin	K
amount of substance	mole	mol
luminous intensity	candela	cd

Some basic units and prefixes used with the units of the metric system are as follows:

LENGTH

10 millimeters (mm) = 1 centimeter (cm)
100 cm = 1 meter (m)
1,000 m = 1 kilometer (km)

A unit of length used especially in expressing the length of light waves is the *angstrom*, abbreviated Å and equal to 10^{-8} cm.

VOLUME

1,000 milliliters (mL) = 1 liter (L)
1,000 cubic centimeters (cm^3) = 1 liter
1 mL = 1 cm^3

MASS

1,000 milligrams (mg) = 1 gram (g)
1,000 g = 1 kilogram (kg)

CONVERSION TABLE

2.54 cm = 1 inch
1 meter = 39.37 inches (10% longer than 1 yard)
28.35 grams = 1 ounce
454 grams = 1 pound
1 kilogram = 2.2 pounds
.946 liter = 1 quart
1 liter (5% larger than a quart) = 1.06 quarts

TEMPERATURE

Temperature is measurable on three different scales—*Celsius* (or *centigrade*), *Fahrenheit*, and *Kelvin* (or *absolute*). Their respective freezing and boiling points are:

	Celsius	Fahrenheit	Kelvin
Boiling point of water	100°	212°	373°
Freezing point of water	0°	32°	273°

There are formulas for converting from one system to another:
Example: What is the Fahrenheit value of 30°C?

$$°F = \frac{9}{5} °C + 32°$$

$$°F = \frac{9}{\cancel{5}} (30°{}^{6}) + 32°$$

$$°F = 54° + 32° = 86° F$$

Thus,
$$30° C = 86° F$$

Similarly, the formula for converting from Celsius to Fahrenheit is:

$$°C = \frac{5}{9} (°F - 32°)$$

The formula for converting from Kelvin to Celsius is somewhat simpler:

$$°K = °C + 273°$$

Sometimes, when working with very "long" numbers, you may want to use *scientific notation system*. This system uses exponents to shorten the form of expressing numbers with many places in them. For example:

1. With very large numbers, such as 3,630,000, move the decimal point to the left. When only one digit remains to the left of the decimal point (3.630000), count the number of places you have moved (in this case, six places). Indicate this number of moves as the exponent of 10 (10^6). Then write the short form of your original number as 3.63×10^6.
2. With very small numbers, such as .000000123, move the decimal point to the right. When the first digit is to the left of the decimal (0000001.23), count the number of places you have moved (in this case, seven places). Indicate this number of moves as the negative exponent of 10 (10^{-7}). Then write the short form of your original number as 1.23×10^{-7}.

Prefix	Multiples	Scientific Notation	Abbreviation
mega-	1,000,000	10^6	m
kilo-	1,000	10^3	k
hecto-	100	10^2	h
. . . .	. . . .	. . . .	. . . .
deci-	. . . .	10^{-1}	d
centi-	.1	10^{-2}	c
milli-	.01	10^{-3}	m
nano-	.001	10^{-9}	n
	.000,000,001		

ATOMS AND MOLECULES

The idea of small, invisible particles being the building blocks of matter can be traced back more than 2,000 years to the Greek philosophers Democritus and Leucippus. These particles were supposed to be so small and indestructible that they could not be divided into smaller particles. They were called *atoms,* the Greek word for indivisible. The English word atom comes from this Greek word. An *atom,* then, is the smallest unit of an element that retains the general properties of that element. The core of the atom, the *nucleus,* is very dense and very small by comparison with the rest of the atom. It contains *protons* (positively charged particles) and *neutrons* (particles with no charge). Outside the nucleus are the atom's *electrons* (negatively charged particles). An atom has the same number of electrons as its protons. These electrons are arranged in "shell" layers around the nucleus. It's as though an atom were a marble inside a baseball inside a basketball, etc. Atoms tend to borrow, lend, or share electrons from these outer shells. These are called *valence electrons.*

On the basis of their atomic structure, atoms are considered *metals* if they lend electrons, *non-metals* if they borrow electrons, and *inert* if they neither borrow nor lend. The *atomic number* of an atom is the number of protons in its nucleus. All atoms of the same element have the same atomic number and each element's atomic number is different from all other elements. The *atomic mass* is the number of protons and neutrons in an atom's nucleus. An atom containing the same number of protons as other atoms of the same element, but having a different number of neutrons, is called an *isotope* of that element.

A *molecule* is the smallest particle of an element or compound that retains the characteristics of the original substance. A molecule of water is a *triatomic* ("three-atom") *molecule* since two hydrogen atoms and one oxygen atom must combine to form the substance water. When atoms do combine to form molecules there is a *chemical bonding.* When such a bonding takes place, there is an exchange of energy.

STATES OF MATTER
Matter exists in basically three states, or forms: gas, liquid, and solid. (A fourth state of matter, plasma, consists of very hot ionized gases.)

Gases
Of all the gases that occur in the atmosphere, the most important is *oxygen.* Although oxygen makes up only 21% of the atmosphere, it is equal in weight to all other elements on earth combined. About 50% of the earth's crust (including earth's waters and atmosphere) is oxygen. Most living things require it.

Properties of Oxygen
Physically, oxygen is colorless, tasteless, odorless, and slightly heavier than air. It supports the combustion of other substances but does not burn itself. When oxygen combines slowly with an element (so that no noticeable heat and light are given off), we call the process *slow oxidation.* A common example is rusting iron. (A substance loses electrons in oxidation, and gains them in *reduction.*) When the combination of oxygen with an element is so rapid that the released energy can be seen as light and felt as heat, the process is called *rapid oxidation* or *normal burning.* Oxygen occurs as molecules containing two oxygen atoms, O_2.

Ozone is a form of oxygen having three atoms in its molecular structure (O_3). Ozone is found in the upper atmosphere and can be formed in the lower atmosphere in the presence of high-voltage electricity.

Properties of Hydrogen
Physically, pure hydrogen is colorless, tasteless, and odorless. It is 1/14 as heavy as air and diffuses (moves from place to place) more rapidly than any other gas. Its chemical properties include burning in air or oxygen, giving off large amounts of heat. Hydrogen molecules also contain two atoms, H_2.

Hydrogen is the lightest of all known elements. The most abundant element in the universe, hydrogen is the major fuel in fusion reactions of the sun. Its ability to burn well makes it an important part of many fuels.

General characteristics of gases. Most gases behave according to these "laws":

1. The particles of a gas move in continuous, random, straight-line motion.
2. As the temperature of a gas increases, its kinetic energy increases, and this increases its random motion. As its temperature decreases, the kinetic energy of a gas decreases until it reaches the point where it liquifies.
3. If the pressure on a gas remains the same, its volume will increase with temperature, and vice versa.
4. If the temperature of a gas remains the same, its volume will decrease as pressure on it increases, and vice versa.
5. If the volume of a gas remains the same, its pressure will increase with temperature, and vice versa.

Liquids

A liquid *expands* (grows larger in volume) and *contracts* (grows smaller in volume) very slightly with a temperature change. Nevertheless, the molecules of a liquid are always in motion. If a particular molecule gains enough kinetic energy near the surface of a liquid, it can overcome the attraction of other molecules in the liquid and escape into a gaseous state. When this occurs, the average temperature of the remaining liquid molecules becomes lower than before the "escape."

In an enclosed area (when the temperature of a gas remains the same), opposing changes tend to take place at the same time: Liquid molecules escape into the gaseous stage (*evaporation*), and gas molecules return to the liquid stage (*condensation*). When these opposite changes take place at the same rate, we have what is called *equilibrium*.

When liquid is heated in an open container, equilibrium disappears and liquid molecules begin to pass rapidly into a gaseous stage. When this conversion begins to occur within the liquid as well as its surface, we have reached the liquid's *boiling point*. The temperature at which a gaseous substance cannot return to the liquid phase is called its *critical temperature*.

Water

Water is so often involved in chemistry that it is important to know how to obtain it chemically and how it is used in science. The method of obtaining pure water in the laboratory is by *distillation:* Water is heated (causing it to evaporate) and then cooled (causing it to condense).

Water has been used in the definition of various standards:

➤ For weight – 1 ml (cm^3) of water at 4° C is 1 gram
➤ For heat – (a) the heat needed to raise one gram of water one degree on the Celsius scale = 1 Calorie (cal); (b) the heat needed to raise one pound of water one degree on the Fahrenheit scale = 1 British thermal unit (BTU)
➤ Degree of heat – the freezing point of water = 0° C or 32° F
    – the boiling point of water = 100° C or 212° F

Water forms compounds that are classified as *bases* or *acids*. Metal oxides (compounds of oxygen and a metal) react with water to form bases, which have the following properties:

1. Bases can conduct electricity in a water solution. The degree of conduction depends on the *"ionization"* of a base—that is, its number of charged particles.
2. Bases react with acids to neutralize each other and form a *salt* and water.
3. They react with fats to form soaps.
4. They cause litmus paper to change from red to blue. (This is a test for the presence of a base.)

Examples of bases include:
$$2Na + 2H_2O \rightarrow 2NaOH + H_2 \text{ (sodium hydroxide)}$$
$$CaO + H_2O \rightarrow Ca(OH)_2 \text{ (calcium hydroxide)}$$
Nonmetal oxides react with water to form acids, which have the following properties:

1. Water solutions of acids conduct electricity. This conduction depends on an acid's ionization.
2. Some acids react with some metals and liberate hydrogen.
3. Acids react with bases to neutralize each other and form a salt and water.
4. Acids react with carbonates to release carbon dioxide.
5. They cause litmus paper to change to a pink-red color. (This is a test for the presence of an acid.)
6. Acids are corrosive.

Examples of acids include:
$$SO_3 + H_2O \rightarrow H_2SO_4 \text{ (sulfuric acid)}$$
$$P_2O_5 + 3H_2O \rightarrow 2H_3PO_4 \text{ (phosphoric acid)}$$
Water is often referred to as "the universal solvent" because of the number of common substances that dissolve in water. When substances are dissolve in water to the point that no more will dissolve at that temperature, the solution is said to be *saturated*. The substance dissolved is called the *solute*. The medium in which it is dissolved is called the *solvent*. When a small amount of solute is dispersed throughout the solvent, it is called a *dilute solution*. When a large amount of solute is dissolved in the solvent, it is called a *concentrated solution*.

Some substances form geometric ("building-block") patterns as they slowly come out of a solution (as they lose water). The process is called *crystallization*.

Solids

Particles at the *solid* stage have the most fixed position and maintain a collective shape. The temperature at which particles of a solid begin to break free from fixed positions and slide over each other is called its *melting point*. At certain pressures, some solids vaporize directly, without passing through the liquid stage. This is called *sublimation*. Solid carbon dioxide and solid iodine have this property.

CHEMICAL REACTIONS

One of the major interests in chemistry is the study of how different substances react with one another. Generally there are four basic types of *reaction*:

1. *Combination (synthesis)* is the formation of a compound from the union of its elements. For example:
$$C + O_2 \rightarrow CO_2 \text{ (carbon dioxide)}$$
2. *Decomposition (analysis)* is the breakdown of a compound to release its components as individual elements or simpler compounds. For example:
$$2H_2O \rightarrow 2H_2 \uparrow + O_2 \uparrow \text{ (electrolysis of water)}$$
3. *Single replacement (single displacement)* occurs when one substance replaces another in a compound. For example:
$$Fe + CuSO_4 \rightarrow FeSO_4 + Cu$$
(iron and copper sulfate) $\rightarrow$ (iron sulfate and copper)
4. In *double replacement (double displacement)* there is an actual exchange of "partners" to form new compounds. For example:
$$AgNO_3 + NaCl \rightarrow AgCl + NaNO_3$$
(silver nitrate and sodium chloride) $\rightarrow$ (silver chloride and sodium nitrate)

In general the *probability* that a specific chemical reaction will take place depends on the amount of heat needed to produce the reaction. The higher the amount of *heat of formation,* the greater the *stability* ("permanence") of a compound, and vice versa.

How long does it take for a chemical reaction to occur? The measurement of a *reaction rate* is based on the rate of formation of a product or the disappearance of a reactant (reacting substance). There are five important factors that control this rate:

1. The nature of the reactants. Some elements and compounds react very rapidly with each other.
2. The exposed surface areas of the reactants. Most reactions depend on the reactants coming into contact. Thus, the more exposure they have to each other at one time, the faster the reaction.
3. The concentrations. The reaction rate is usually proportional to the degree of concentration of the reactants.
4. The temperature. A temperature increase of 10° C above room temperature usually causes a reaction rate to double or triple.
5. The presence of a *catalyst.* A catalyst is a substance that speeds up or slows down a reaction, without being (permanently) changed itself.

Some reactions involve products that continuously interact with the original reactants. That is, reactants and their products interact in both directions. This is shown as follows:

$$A + B \leftrightarrows C + D$$

The double arrow indicates that substances C and D can react to form A and B, while A and B react to form C and D. Such a reaction is said to reach an *equilibrium* when the forward reaction rate is equal to the reverse reaction rate. The symbol *Ke,* the *"equilibrium constant,"* is a symbol for the point at which equilibrium occurs.

In many of the preceding predictions of reactions, we used the concept that reactions will occur when they result in the lowest possible energy state. There is, however, another driving force for reactions that relates to their state of disorder, or of randomness. This state of disorder is called *entropy.* A reaction is also driven, then, by a need for a greater degree of disorder.

KEY ELEMENTS AND THEIR FAMILIES

1. *Sulfur.* After oxygen, the most important element is sulfur. Sulfur is found in a free state in volcanic regions of Japan, Mexico, and Sicily. It can also be produced in the laboratory. Sulfur is used in making sprays to control plant disease and harmful insects. It is used in the manufacture of rubber, to *vulcanize* rubber (give it extra hardness). Sulfur is used in the preparation of medicines and gunpowder. It is also used in making *sulfuric acid, hydrogen sulfide,* and *sulfur dioxide.*

    Sulfuric acid (H_2SO_4) is called the "king of chemicals" because of its widespread industrial use. Some of these uses include:
    a. making other acids;
    b. freeing iron and steel metals of scale and rust;
    c. washing objectionable colors from gasoline made by the "cracking" process;
    d. acting as a dehydrating agent in the manufacture of explosives, dyes, and drugs.
    Hydrogen sulfide (H_2S) is used widely in laboratory tests (many sulfides precipitate with distinct colors) and in making paints. Sulfur dioxide (SO_2) is used as a bleach.
2. *Halogens. Fluorine* (F_2), the most active nonmetal, is a yellowish, poisonous, highly corrosive element. When it is added at 1 ppm (part per million) to water, it hardens tooth enamel and reduces tooth decay. *Chlorine* (Cl_2) is used to purify water supplies to act as a bleaching agent, and to prepare hydrochloric acid (which is used in the manufacture of

other chemicals). *Bromine* (Br_2) is used to keep anti-knock gasolines free of lead deposits. *Iodine* (I_2) is most widely known for its use as an antiseptic in tincture of iodine.

3. *Nitrogen*. The most common member of this family is *nitrogen* (N_2) itself. It is colorless, odorless, tasteless, rather inactive, and makes up about four-fifths of the air in our atmosphere. Nitrogen-fixing bacteria found in the roots of beans, peas, clover, and similar plants "fix" nitrogen. This means they use nitrogen from the air to form compounds that plants can use. Two important compounds of nitrogen are *nitric acid* and *ammonia*.

   Nitric acid (HNO_3) is useful in making dyes, celluloid film, and lacquers for cars. Nitric acid is also used in the manufacture of powerful explosives—for example, "TNT" and "nitroglycerine." Ammonia (NH_3) is one of the oldest known compounds of nitrogen. It is a colorless, pungent gas, extremely soluble in water. A water solution of ammonia is used as a cleanser. Another use of ammonia is as a fertilizer.

4. *Phosphorus* (P), a nonmetallic element, is yellow to white, waxy, and extremely poisonous. Because phosphorus ignites spontaneously when exposed to air, it is stored underwater. The principal use of phosphorus is in compounds which act as fertilizers, detergents, insecticides, soft drinks, and pharmaceuticals. Phosphorus compounds are essential to the diet. (They are important for our bones and teeth.) Phosphorus is a component of *adenosine triphosphate* (ATP), a fundamental energy source in living things.

METALS

Some physical properties of *metals* are: (1) they have a metallic luster or sheen; (2) they can conduct heat and electricity; (3) they can be pounded into sheets (metals are *malleable*) or drawn into wires (metals are *ductile*); (4) they are not soluble in any ordinary solvent without undergoing a chemical change. A general chemical property of metals is that they are *electropositive* (charged with positive electricity).

The outstanding properties of *aluminum* (Al) are: it is very light, has high strength, can resist oxidation, and can conduct an electric current. Aluminum is prepared from *bauxite ore*.

Magnesium (Mg), the eighth most abundant metal in the earth's crust, is found in plant chlorophyll. (Magnesium is necessary to the diet of humans and other animals.) It is light, rigid, and inexpensive, and is used in the manufacture of aircraft fuselages, cameras, and optical instruments.

Copper (Cu) has been known to humans since the Bronze Age. It is reddish, malleable, ductile, and is an excellent conductor of electricity. It is used in manufacturing wires, utensils, coins, etc. It also is important to the human diet.

Iron (Fe), a malleable, ductile, silver-gray metal, is abundant in the universe. (It is found in many stars, including the sun.) A good conductor of heat and electricity, iron is attracted by a magnet and is easily magnetized. It rusts very easily. Iron is extracted from ores in a blast furnace, after which it can be mixed with other substances to form ores in a blast furnace, after which it can be mixed with other substances to form steel. It is also important in the human diet.

Alloys are mixtures of two or more metals. *Bronze* (an alloy of copper and tin) and *brass* (an alloy of copper and zinc) are examples. Certain properties of metals are affected when they are mixed in an alloy. An alloy is usually harder than the metals which compose it, but its melting point is usually lower than that of its components.

CARBON AND ORGANIC CHEMISTRY

The element *carbon* (C) is present in all living things. It occurs in both crystalline and amorphous (noncrystal) forms.

1. Crystalline *diamonds*, found in South Africa and other regions, are the hardest form of carbon. They are brilliant, both reflecting and refracting light. Diamonds are used as gems and in the making of drills, saws, etc.

2. *Graphite* (a crystal) is prepared from hard coal in an electric furnace. It is soft, gray, and greasy, and forms a good electrical conductor. It is used as a lubricant, in making lead pencils, and in the construction of atomic reactors.
3. *Charcoal* is formed from the destructive distillation of soft coal. It burns with little smoke or flame and is used as a fuel.
4. *Coke* is formed from the destructive distillation of soft coal. It burns with little smoke or flame and is used as a fuel.
5. *Anthracite coal*, almost pure carbon, burns with little smoke and is used as a fuel.

Carbon dioxide (CO_2) is a widely distributed gas. The usual laboratory preparation of carbon dioxide consists of reacting calcium carbonate (marble chips) with hydrochloric acid. There are several important uses for carbon dioxide:

1. It is used to make carbonated beverages.
2. Solid carbon dioxide (at $-78°$ C), or "dry ice," is used as a refrigerant.
3. Fire extinguishers make use of carbon dioxide because of its weight and its property of not supporting ordinary combustion.
4. Plants use carbon dioxide in photosynthesis.

Organic chemistry may be defined as the chemistry of the compounds of carbon. Since Friedrich Wöhler synthesized urea in 1828, chemists have synthesized thousands of carbon compounds in the areas of dyes, plastics, textile fibers, medicines, and drugs. The number of organic compounds has been estimated to be in the neighborhood of a million and is constantly increasing.

Physics

Physics includes many topics that have been standard for years: *light, heat, mechanics, sound, electricity, magnetism*. Some of these topics have subdivisions. For example, mechanics includes the study of motion, forces, and statics (objects at rest). *Thermodynamics* deals with relations of heat and energy. Today, the study of the actions of particles within the nucleus of an atom has become especially important.

MEASURING FORCE

A *force* is a "push" or a "pull." If you hold a 5-pound bag of sugar in your hand, you are exerting a 5-pound force (a pull) on the bag to keep it from falling. In physics, it is possible to draw this effort symbolically—but not by showing a hand with a bag of sugar! Instead, you draw a diagram of two things: (1) the amount of pull; and (2) the direction of the pull.

To represent the amount of pull, make up a *scale* for one unit of the pull (in this case, one pound). Then draw five connected units (for the five pounds) in the direction of the pull (toward the bottom of the paper, representing the ground). When we deal with both the *magnitude* (size) of the pull and its *direction*, we are working with a *vector quantity*.

Sometimes, two or more forces work on an object. These are called *concurrent forces*. Scientists are interested in finding the combined effect (the *resultant*) of these forces. There are several ways to do this:

1. If both forces are exerted in exactly the same direction, add the forces. For example, if a 3-*newton* force and a 4-*newton* force act on an object in the same direction, the resultant force is 7 newtons. A newton (N) is a unit of measure in physics.
2. If the two forces act in opposite directions (at an angle of 180 degrees), subtract them. With a 3-newton force and a 4-newton force pulling in opposite directions, the resultant is a 1-newton force, exerted in the direction of the larger force (the 4-newton force).

3. If the two forces are pulling at an angle to one another, the solution requires a few steps. Suppose that a 3-newton force and a 4-newton force with a 60-degree angle between them are acting on an object: What is the resultant?

    (a) Select a scale for one unit of the force. (Let ¼ inch equal 1 newton.)
    (b) Draw the vector AB for the 3-newton force (¾ inch).
    (c) Using the same scale, draw the vector AC for the 4-newton force (1 inch). Start it from the same point as the first vector. Keep an angle of 60 degrees between both vectors.
    (d) Using AB and AC as the first two sides, draw the parallelogram ACDB.
    (e) Draw the diagonal AD and lay off ¼-inch units on it. In this example, the diagonal will be a little more than 6 of these units. Since each unit equals 1 newton, we can estimate that the resultant for a 3-newton force and a 4-newton force at a 60 degree angle to each other is about 6.1 newtons.

Sometimes the direction of a vector is given in terms of "north," "south," "east," or "west." In other examples, the direction of one vector is given by relating it to another vector (for example, "85 degrees apart"). If you find two vectors forming a right angle (90 degrees), you can treat the example as one involving a right triangle, and solve it by using the Pythagorean Theorem (*see Mathematics Review*). In such a case, the resultant you are looking for would be the hypotenuse of the right triangle.

If two equal and opposite parallel forces are applied to an object, their resultant force is zero. (Try pressing one hand against an open door while you press the other hand against the opposite side of the door. So long as you exert an equal force through both hands, the door won't move.)

If an object can rotate, we call the force that produces this rotation the *torque*, or the *moment of a force*. The magnitude of the moment of a force is equal to the product of the force and what is called the *length of the moment arm*. The length of the moment arm is the perpendicular distance from the *fulcrum* to the direction of the force. A fulcrum is a stationary point about which an object rotates. For example, the earth's axis is its fulcrum. A hinge is the fulcrum of the door.

SPEED AND VELOCITY

Speed is the distance covered per unit of time. Speed is *a scalar quantity*—it describes magnitude only, e.g., miles per hour. The *velocity* (v) of an object is its speed in a given direction. Thus velocity is a vector quantity—it has magnitude and direction. Velocity changes if either the speed, or the direction of motion, or both, change.

Sometimes we can think of the motion of an object as a *combination of velocities*. For example, if you walk 4 miles per hour from the last car of the train toward the front while the train is going 60 miles per hour, your velocity is 64 miles per hour in the direction of the train's motion.

Uniform motion is motion in which the velocity is constant. If the velocity changes, the motion is said to be accelerated. *Acceleration* (a) is the rate of change of velocity. Acceleration is a vector quantity. The formula for finding acceleration is

$$\text{acceleration} = \frac{\text{change in velocity}}{\text{time required for change}}$$

An example of how acceleration is expressed would be "four feet per second per second," which can be written as 4 ft/sec^2.

Uniformly accelerated motion is motion with constant acceleration. If an object is allowed to *fall freely* near the surface of the earth (to fall with its initial velocity at zero and with no forces other than gravity acting on it), the acceleration of the object remains constant and is independent of the mass of the object. The letter g is used universally for this acceleration. Usually, $g = 32$ ft/sec^2.

For all types of motion, the general formula is

$$\text{average speed} = \frac{\text{distance covered}}{\text{time required}}$$

NEWTON'S LAWS

Newton's first law of motion. This law states that if the net force acting on an object is zero, the velocity of the object does not change—that is, its speed and direction of motion remain constant. The term *net force* means the same as resultant force. This law can be stated in other ways: When a body is at rest, or moving with constant speed in a straight line, the resultant of all the forces acting on the body is zero.

An object at rest tends to remain at rest. An object in motion tends to remain in motion unless acted on by an unbalanced force. For example, passengers in a car lurch forward when the driver suddenly applies the brakes.

Newton's second law (F = ma). According to this law, if the net force acting on an object is not zero, the object will be accelerated in the direction of the force. Its acceleration will be proportional to the net force and inversely proportional to the mass of the object. For example, a push that is enough to give a 3,000-pound car an acceleration of 4ft/sec^2 will be able to give a 6,000-pound van an acceleration of 2 ft/sec^2.

Think of net force as being used to overcome the *inertia* of an object. The greater the *mass* of an object, the greater the force needed to produce a given acceleration. Mass is the measure of an object's inertia. Inertia is the property by which an object resists being accelerated.

Newton's third law. This law states that when one object exerts a force on a second object, the second object exerts an equal and opposite force on the first object. (This is sometimes stated: Action equals reaction.) This law is the principle underlying the operation of rockets and jet aircraft. As the hot gases are pushed out from the rear, they exert a forward push on the object from which they escape.

When an object moves with constant speed around a circle, the object's velocity is constantly changing, because its direction is constantly changing. Because the velocity is changing, the object is accelerated. This acceleration is produced by the *centripetal force*—the force which keeps an object moving around a circle in a circular path.

Newton's law of universal gravitation. According to this law, two objects attract each other with a force that is proportional to the product of their masses and inversely proportional to the square of the distance between them. The earth's attraction for objects is known as *gravity*. Gravity accounts for the *weight* of an object on earth—the earth's pull on an object. It is an attracting (force) that acts on every part of an object—a tree, for example. The attraction of the earth for a tree is actually a set of parallel forces. The resultant goes through a point in the tree known as its *center of gravity*. (We can increase the *stability* of objects by building them with a low center of gravity and with as big a base as possible.)

WORK

In physics we talk about *work* done on an object, or work done by an object or by a force. When a force moves an object, the force does work on the object. If a 20-pound force is used to pull an object 3 feet along a flat surface, we say 60 foot-pounds of work was done on the object. Thus, work is equal to the product of the force (in this case, a 20-pound force) and the distance the object moves in the direction of the force (in this case, 3 feet). The *units of work* obtained by multiplying a unit of force by a unit of distance may be expressed in terms of the *foot-pound* (ft-lb), the *joule (newton-meter),* or the *erg.*

ENERGY

In elementary physics, *energy* is defined as the ability to do work. *Potential energy* is defined as the energy possessed by an object because of its position or condition (for example, a ripe apple at the end of a tree branch). *Kinetic energy* is the energy possessed by an object in motion (for example, a bicycle in motion). When an object does work, it has less energy left after the work. In mechanics, work is done on an object for various reasons:

1. to give it potential energy;
2. to give it kinetic energy;
3. to overcome friction (friction is a force which always opposes motion or a tendency to motion);
4. to accomplish a combination of the three reasons just given.

Principle of *conservation of energy.* Energy cannot be created or destroyed but may be changed from one form into another. As a consequence of Einstein's theory of relativity, mass can be considered a form of energy. When mass is converted to forms of energy such as heat, the following formula applies (*m* is the mass converted, and *c* is the speed of light):

$$\text{energy produced} = mc^2$$

Units of energy are the same as units of work. When *m* is expressed in grams and *c* is expressed in meters per second (3×10^{10} cm/sec) the energy will be expressed in ergs. When *m* is expressed in kilograms and *c* is expressed in meters per second (3×10^8 m/sec), the energy is expressed in joules.

Power is the rate of doing work. Since work is calculated by multiplying the force by the distance that the force moves, we have the following formula:

$$\text{power} = \frac{\text{force} \times \text{distance}}{\text{time}}$$

Units of power are expressed as *foot-pounds per second, horsepower* (hp), or *watts:*

$$1 \text{ hp} = 550 \text{ ft-lb/sec}$$
$$1 \text{hp} = 746 \text{ watts}$$
$$1 \text{ watt} = 1 \text{ joule/sec}$$

SIMPLE MACHINES

Probably the most direct way of doing useful work on an object is to take hold of it and lift or move it. When this is difficult, we turn to *machines* to help us. A machine is a device that will transfer a force from one point of application to another for some practical advantage. There are six simple machines: lever, pulley, wheel and axle, inclined plane, screw, and wedge. The force that we apply to a machine in order to do the work is known as the *effort* (F_E). The force that we have to overcome is known as the *resistance* (F_R).

1. A *lever* is a rigid bar that is free to turn on or around a fixed point known as the *fulcrum* or *pivot.* Crowbars, bottle openers, and oars on a boat are examples of levers. So is a see-saw.

   What is the principle on which a lever operates? When a lever is perfectly balanced on its fulcrum, the force (effort) on one arm matches the force on the other. If a box (or other form of load) is placed on one end of such a lever, but not the other, the balance is upset. To restore the balance (actually, to lift the load) we exert a compensating force on the end without the box (the effort arm). To calculate this compensating force, we determine the length of each arm from the fulcrum to the end, and apply this equation:

$$\text{effort} \times \text{effort arm} = \text{load} \times \text{load arm}$$

Example: Assume that a lever 10 feet long has a carton (load) weighing 35 pounds on one end (the load arm). If the fulcrum is 3 feet from the end of the load arm, how much effort is needed on the effort arm to raise the carton?

$$E \times EA = L \times LA$$
$$E \times 7 = 35 \times 3$$
$$7E = 105$$
$$E = 15 \text{ pounds of effort}$$

2. A *pulley* is useful for lifting heavy objects a considerable distance. It consists of a wheel mounted in a frame in such a way that the wheel can turn readily on its axis. The wheel rim is usually grooved, to guide the rope (or wire, or string) used with it.

3. In a *wheel and axle,* the wheel is rigidly attached to an axle, which turns with it. Applications of the wheel-and-axle machine include the steering wheel of an automobile and a doorknob.

4. An *inclined plane* is a flat surface, one end of which is kept higher than the other. When heavy objects have to be raised to a platform or put into a truck, it is often convenient to slide these objects up along a board. The board in this case is an inclined plane. The effort to pull or push the object "up" along the plane is usually applied parallel to the plane.

5. A *screw* may be defined as a cylinder around which an inclined plane (a "thread") winds in spiral fashion. A screw can be used to connect one object to another.

6. A *wedge* may be thought of as a double inclined plane. It is used in devices like an axe to split wood. It is easy to use when its length is large compared to its thickness.

FLUID PRESSURE AND THE ATMOSPHERE

The term *fluid* refers to both gases and liquids. A liquid has definite volume, but takes the shape of its container, with its top surface tending to be horizontal. (A gas has neither definite shape nor volume, and expands to fill any container into which it is put.)

Fluids push against the container in which they are placed. *Pressure* (p) is the force per unit area. Liquid pressure is independent of the size or shape of the container. It depends only on the depth (or "height," h) and the *density* (d) of the liquid. (The density of a substance is the mass per unit volume.) Thus the formula for finding water pressure in a container is

$$p = hd.$$

There are several principles that derive from the nature of water pressure:

1. *Pascal's principle* states two ideas about pressure applied to a confined fluid (a fluid enclosed on all sides): (a) such pressure is transferred throughout the liquid without any loss; and (b) this pressure acts perpendicularly on all the surfaces of the liquid's container, regardless of their size.

   Imagine a water-filled, U-shaped container, one of whose arms is wider than the other. Each arm of the "U" is sealed by a *piston.* (A piston is a cylinder that slides inside another cylinder—something like a cork that moves easily in and out of the neck of a bottle.) If you exert a small force against the piston in the smaller arm of the "U," the resulting pressure travels through the water in both arms and acts on the underside of the larger piston. The resulting force in this second piston is then larger than the force applied to the first one.

2. *Archimedes' principle* states that the apparent loss in weight of an object immersed in a fluid equals the weight of the displaced fluid. For example, an object weighing 50 grams is placed in water, where it weighs 30 grams. Since the apparent loss of weight is 20 grams, we know that the weight of the displaced water is 20 grams.

3. *Bernoulli's principle* states that if the speed of a fluid is increased, its pressure is decreased. This principle is made use of in the design of airplane wings to give the plane "lift." The wing is designed so that the air will move faster over the top of the wing than across the

bottom. As a result, the pressure of the air on the top of the wing is less than on the bottom. This makes the upward push on the wing greater than the downward push, and keeps the plane aloft.

HEAT ENERGY

One way of defining *temperature* is to say it is the degree of hotness or coldness of an object. If we think of *kinetic energy*, however, we get a different definition.

The molecules of a substance are in constant random motion. If we heat a gas, its molecules move faster—that is, when the temperature of a gas goes up, the average speed of its molecules increases. When the speed of the motion of a molecule increases, its kinetic energy increases too. This leads to thinking of temperature as a measure of the average kinetic energy per molecule of a substance. Thus, a substance has *internal energy* as a result of its kinetic energy.

When a "hot" substance is brought into contact with a "cold" substance, the hot piece gets colder and the cold piece gets hotter. Thus we define *heat* as the form of energy which flows between two substances because they are at different temperatures.

Expansion and Contraction

When heated, most solids, liquids, and gases *expand* (increase in volume); when cooled, most solids, liquids, and gases *contract* (decrease in volume). Solids differ among themselves in their degree of expansion. For example, brass expands more than iron. And different liquids expand by different amounts when subjected to the same temperature change. Gases are more uniform in their expansion and contraction.

Water behaves strangely in this respect. As water is cooled from 100° C, it contracts until the temperature reaches 4° C. If it is cooled further the water will expand—until it freezes at 0° C. Thus, water is densest at 4° C.

Heat Engines

Heat engines are used to convert heat into *mechanical energy*. Examples of heat engines include the *gasoline engine, diesel engine, steam engine,* and the *steam turbine*. In these engines, hot gases are allowed to expand; as they expand they do work.

If the fuel is burned inside the cylinder of the engine itself, the engine is known as an *internal combustion engine*. The gasoline engine and the diesel engine are internal combustion engines. If the fuel is burned in a separate chamber outside the engine proper, the engine is known as an *external combustion engine*. Steam engines and steam turbines are examples of external combustion engines. In these, the fuel—which may be coal—is burned in a separate furnace and is used to heat water in a boiler. Steam from this process is then directed into the engine.

Methods of Heat Transfer

The three methods of heat transfer are *conduction, convention,* and *radiation*. Heat conduction is the process of transferring heat by the flow of "free" electrons through a medium. (Conduction also involves the bombardment of cool molecules by heated molecules.) For example, if we heat one end of a copper rod, the other end gets hot, too. Metals are good conductors of heat (and also good conductors of electricity). Silver is the best. Copper and aluminum are also very good. Liquids, gases, and nonmetallic solids are poor conductors of heat. Poor conductors are known as *insulators*.

Heat convection is the process of transferring heat in a fluid, which involves the motion of the heated portion toward the cooler portion of the fluid. The heated portion expands, rises, and is replaced by cooler fluid, thus giving rise to so-called *convection currents*. Radiators heat rooms chiefly by convection.

Heat radiation is a process of transferring heat by a *wave motion* similar to light. Radiation can occur through space and through a material medium. The higher the temperature of an object, the greater the amount of heat it radiates.

The *vacuum bottle (thermos bottle)* is designed with the three methods of heat transfer in mind. The bottle is made of glass—a good insulator. The stopper is made of cork or plastic—also good insulators. The space between the walls is evacuated, minimizing heat transfer by conduction or convection. And the inside surfaces (facing the vacuum) are shiny, reflecting radiation that might come from either side. This minimizes heat transfer by radiation.

ENERGY SOURCES

For heating buildings and operating machines, humans have depended almost solely on *fossil fuels* such as coal and oil. *Waterfalls* can be used in the regions where they are located. (Waterfalls and fossil fuels ultimately owe their energy to the sun.) In some parts, of the earth, huge *solar reflectors* trap the sun's radiant energy. The constant motion of the *tides* might also be a source of energy.

Some people think the hope of the future lies in *nuclear energy*—energy that is released when certain changes take place in the nucleus of an atom. We have already learned to obtain nuclear energy resulting from the splitting or *fission* of the nuclei of heavy elements, such as uranium. Only small quantities of such fissionable materials are available. Nuclear energy can also be obtained by the combining or *fusion* of the nuclei of light atoms, such as hydrogen. If this can be done in a controllable manner, a practically endless supply of energy will be available, because *hydrogen*, the necessary "fuel," is obtainable from the oceans in almost unlimited quantity.

WAVE MOTION AND SOUND

Wave motion in a medium is a method of transferring energy through a medium by means of a *distortion* (disturbance) of the medium; the distortion travels away from the place where it was produced. The medium itself moves only a little bit. For example, a pebble dropped into still water disturbs it. The water near the pebble does not move far, but the disturbance travels away from that spot. Energy lost by the pebble is carried by the wave, so that if there is a cork floating on the water in the path of the wave, the cork will be lifted by the wave. The cork gets some of the energy that the pebble lost. We can set up a succession of waves in the water by pushing a finger rhythmically through the surface of the water. Similarly, a vibrating tuning fork produces waves in air.

Two basic waves are the *longitudinal wave* and the *transverse wave*. A longitudinal wave is a wave in which the particles of the medium vibrate in the same direction as the path which the wave travels. The waves produced by a tuning fork are examples of a longitudinal wave; so are sound waves. A transverse wave is a wave in which the vibrations of the medium are at right angles to the direction in which the wave is traveling. A water wave is approximately transverse.

There are several important measurements related to wave motion. A *wavelength* can be measured as the distance between any two successive peaks of the wave. As we watch a wave moving past a given spot of the medium, we see peak after peak of the wave. The time required for two successive waves to pass a spot is known as the *period* of the wave. The *frequency* of the wave is the number of complete waves (periods) per second. Out of all these measurements comes a key equation:

$$\text{speed of wave} = \text{frequency of wave} \times \text{wavelength}$$

SOUND

In physics, when we speak about *sound,* we usually mean the *sound wave*. Sound waves are longitudinal waves in gases, liquids, or solids. Sound cannot be transmitted through a vacuum. If a sound wave begins in the air and then hits a solid, the frequency of the wave will be the same in the new medium (the solid) as in the air, but the new speed—and therefore the new wavelength—will be different. The *speed of sound* in air is approximately 1090 ft/sec or 331 meters/sec at 0°C. In general, sound travels faster in liquids and solids than in air.

Musical Sounds

Sounds produced by regular vibration of the air are said to be *musical*. (Irregular vibrations of the air are classified as unpleasant sounds, or "*noise*.") The *range of frequencies* in musical sounds is 20 to 20,000 cycles per second (Hertz). Longitudinal waves that are higher than those which people can hear are called *ultrasonic* frequencies. (Ultrasonic frequencies are used in *sonar* for such purposes as submarine detection.) The term *supersonic* refers to speed greater than the speed of sound. Mach 1 means a speed equal to that of sound. *Mach* 2 is twice the speed of sound. Some airplanes travel at supersonic speed.

Musical sounds have three basic characteristics: *pitch, loudness,* and *quality* (timbre). Pitch refers to frequency: the higher the frequency of a sound wave, the higher the pitch. Loudness depends on the amplitude of the wave reaching the ear. The quality of sound depends on the number of different overtones reaching the ear at the same moment.

When a sound wave reaches another medium, part of the wave is usually reflected. Where there is reflected sound, a distant *echo* is heard if the reflected sound reaches the ear at least $\frac{1}{10}$ second after the sound traveling directly from the vibrating source to the ear. The *Doppler effect* refers to the way we perceive pitch when the source of a sound is traveling toward or away from us. (This is something a jogger might notice as a car approaches on an otherwise empty road.) As the source of the sound approaches us, the pitch we hear grows higher than the actual frequency produced by the source of the sound. As the source of the sound moves away, the pitch appears to get lower than it actually is.

LIGHT AND ILLUMINATION

In many ways, *light* coming from the sun behaves like a wave. How can we explain a wave traveling through a vacuum? Electric fields and magnetic fields can exist in a vacuum. Light is considered to be one type of *electromagnetic wave,* along with X-rays and radio waves. The wavelength of light is rather short—about 5×10^{-5} cm. The exact wavelength depends on the color of the light. (The *quantum theory of light,* however, says that light is emitted and absorbed in little lumps or bundles of energy called *photons*.)

Illumination. A *luminous body* is one that emits light because it has been heated (for example, the filament in our electric light bulb). An *illuminated object* is one that is visible by the light that it reflects (for example, the moon).

Reflection

In discussing illumination, the term *ray* is used to represent the direction in which the light is traveling. (Light is considered to travel in a straight line.) When light hits a surface, some of it is reflected. We call the light that travels toward the surface the *incident light*, and the light that is reflected the *reflected light*. The angle of the incident light equals the angle of the reflected light. When parallel light rays strike a smooth surface, they are reflected as parallel rays.

In a *plane mirror* (a perfectly flat mirror), a ray of light striking the mirror is reflected without being changed. In a *convex mirror* (one in which the center bulges outward), the light rays are spread apart by reflection and the reflected image seems smaller than the object. In a *concave mirror* (one in which the center "caves in"), the light rays are focused by reflection and—at a close distance—the reflected image seems larger than the object.

Refraction

Refraction is the bending of a wave as it passes from one medium into another. Refraction occurs because of the different speeds at which the wave travels through the two denser media. The medium in which a light wave travels more slowly is known as the optically denser medium. The medium in which light travels faster is known as the optically rarer medium. Light travels faster in air than in liquids and solids. Light travels faster in water than in glass. A ray of light passing obliquely into a denser medium is bent toward the "*normal*" (that is, toward a perpendicular with the surface of the medium). A ray of light entering a rarer medium obliquely is bent away from the normal.

Lenses

A *lens* is a device shaped to *converge* (focus) or *diverge* (spread) a beam of light through it. Lenses are fashioned to be thin, spherical, transparent, and are usually glass. A *convex lens* is thicker at the middle than at the edge; it is a converging lens. A *concave* lens is thinner in the middle than at the edge; it is a diverging lens. Convex lenses form images similar to concave mirrors; concave lenses form images similar to convex mirrors. There is another important difference. Lenses let light through and refract it; mirrors reflect light.

Optical Instruments

The *camera* and the eye have many points of similarity. The camera has a *shutter* to admit the light, corresponding to the eyelid. Light goes through a camera's *convex lens* to the sensitive *film*. In the eye, light goes through the pupil and lens, falling on the retina where the image is formed. The image on both the film and the retina is real, reduced in size, and inverted.

The *astronomical telescope* is used by scientists who want to see very distant objects invisible to the naked eye. The *microscope* is used for examining small things close at hand. Both the microscope and the astronomical telescope employ a *magnifying eyepiece*. A *projector* is used to throw an enlarged picture on a screen.

Color and Light

If light goes through a (three-dimensional) glass *prism,* the emerging rays are bent away considerably from the original direction. If we use so-called *white light* (such as from an incandescent tungsten filament bulb), the light is dispersed (broken) into its component colors. The order of colors, from the one bent the least to the one bent the most is red, orange, yellow, green, blue, indigo, violet. We call this array of colors the *spectrum of visible light*. *Infrared light* has a greater wavelength than red; *ultraviolet light* has a shorter wavelength than violet. Both of these are invisible to the human eye.

The color of an opaque object is determined by the color of the light that it reflects. A red object, for example, reflects mostly red; it absorbs the rest. If an object reflects no light it is said to be black. If an object reflects all the light it is said to be white.

ELECTRICITY

Nearly all the *mass* of an *atom* is concentrated in the *nucleus*, which ordinarily contains *protons* and (except in the case of the hydrogen atom) *neutrons*. The atom's *electrons* form "shells" around the nucleus. A proton has a positive charge equal to the negative charge of an electron, but its mass is approximately 1,836 times as much as the mass of the electron. A neutron is electrically neutral; its mass is slightly greater than that of the proton. An *ion* is a charged atom or group of atoms.

Charging an object usually results in a gain or loss of electrons. In a solid, the positive charges do not move readily. A gain of electrons results in making an object more negative; a loss of electrons results in making it more positive. A neutral object usually acquires the same kind of *charge* as that of the charged object it touches.

An *electric field* is said to exist wherever an electric force acts on an electric charge. If a positive charge is released in an electric field, the positive charge will move in the direction of the electric field. A negative charge released in an electric field will move in the direction opposite to that of the field. The *potential difference* between two points in an electric field is the work-per-unit charge required to move a charge between the points. The unit of potential difference is the volt. The common flashlight cell supplies 1½ volts. A home outlet supplies 115 volts.

Electric Current

Current is the rate of flow of electric charge. Generally, we speak of *direct current* (DC) and *alternating current* (AC).

Direct current is a flow of current in one direction at a constant rate. To create a circuit for such flow, batteries, dynamos, and generators have two terminals—one, positive; the other, negative. The positive terminal has a deficiency of electrons; the negative terminal has an excess of electrons. Work has to be done to push electrons onto the negative terminal against the repulsion of electrons already there. (According to *Coulomb's law*, particles with the same charge repel one another; unlike particles are attracted to one another.) In this case, the potential difference is the work-per-unit charge that was done to get the terminals charged. This charge is now potentially available for doing work outside the battery (for example, operating a desk lamp).

Resistance of a device is its opposition to the flow of electric charges. Electric energy is converted to heat because of this opposition. *Conductance* is the reciprocal of resistance. The higher the conductance of a device (as with something made of copper or silver), the lower the resistance. According to *Ohm's law*, the current in a circuit is directly proportional to the potential difference that is applied to the circuit and inversely proportional to the resistance of the circuit.

As its name suggests, *alternating current* is a current that goes through a cycle: (a) it increases from zero to a certain maximum in one direction; (b) it decreases to zero; (c) it increases to a maximum in the opposite direction; (d) it decreases to zero. The number of repetitions of this cycle per second is the frequency of the current; in the United States this frequency is 60 cycles per second. AC current can do some things better than DC current. It can be transmitted more easily over long distances, and its voltage can be changed more easily. Only DC current can be used for charging batteries, for electroplating, and for operating some electronic circuits.

In today's computer age, *semiconductors* have become very important. A semiconductor is a material whose conductivity is very low by comparison with conductors like copper, but greater than that of insulators like glass. Common semiconductors are germanium and silicon. In practice a small, precise amount of an impurity is added to the pure semiconductor, to give it desired characteristics (for example, the ability to control precisely the flow of electrons).

MAGNETS

A *magnet* attracts iron and steel. A *magnetic substance* is one that can be attracted by a magnet. Magnetic materials include iron and alloys of iron. Examples of nonmagnetic substances are glass and wood. A *magnetized substance* is a magnetic substance which has been made into a magnet. A *magnetic pole* is the region of a magnet where its strength is concentrated. Every magnet has at least two poles, North and South. The *North pole* (N-pole) of a suspended magnet points toward the earth's magnetic pole in the northern hemisphere. (Magnetic poles do not coincide with the earth's geographic poles.) The *law of magnets* states that like poles repel; unlike poles attract. The *magnetic field* is the region around the magnet where its influence can be detected as a force on another substance. The direction of the field at any point is the direction in which the N-pole of a *compass* would point. A magnetic field can be used to produce an electric current.

CHEMICAL ENERGY

Another important source of electrical energy is *chemical energy*. A *voltaic cell* converts chemical energy into electrical energy. It consists of two dissimilar *electrodes* immersed in an *electrolyte* which acts on at least one of them. An electrolyte may be a liquid which conducts electricity by the motion of ions (such as would occur in a solution of salt in water). The electrodes are conductors. The electrode which is positively charged is called the *anode*. The electrode which is negatively charged is called the *cathode*.

A *primary cell* is a voltaic cell whose electrodes are consumed in an irreversible way when the cell is used. The *dry cell* used in a flashlight is a primary cell. A *secondary cell* is a voltaic cell whose electrodes can be used over and over again, with periodic recharging. The automobile battery is an example of a secondary cell.

CHAPTER
5 Mathematics Review

Tips for Studying

The material in this section is a review of basic terms and problem-solving methods taught in high school mathematics courses. You will find samples of math problems most often asked on the ASVAB exam, with an explanation of how to solve each. (You may find that you know one or several other ways for working out a problem.) Before you study the topics in this section, look over the following suggestions for how to do good work in mathematics.

A. Develop the habit of careful reading. As you read a problem, look for answers to these questions:
    1. What is given? (the facts in the problem)
    2. What is unknown? (the answer to be found)
    3. What do I use? (the best method or steps for solving the problem)
B. Pay careful attention to each word, number, and symbol. In mathematics, directions and problems are compressed into very few words. Sometimes, the principal direction is expressed as a symbol.
    Example: What is the value of 6 − 3? (The minus sign tells you to subtract.)
C. The reading of mathematics also requires close attention to relationships. How does one fact or idea lead to another? Which facts or ideas are connected? Take the following example:

    Mr. Brown and his partner worked for 5 hours on Monday. For his wages, Mr. Brown received $10 an hour. How much did he earn on Monday?

    To solve this problem, you can ignore the day of the week and the fact that there was a partner present. Just multiply the number of hours Mr. Brown worked (5) by the amount he received each hour ($10).

    $$5 \times \$10 = \$50 \text{ (Mr. Brown's earnings)}$$

Laws and Operations

The numbers 5 and 10 are *whole numbers*. So are 0, 1, 2, 3, 4, and so on. (By contrast, 3/4 is a fraction, and 6¾ is a mixed number—a whole number plus a fraction.) In mathematics, when we combine two or more whole numbers, we perform an *operation* on them. There are two such basic operations: *addition* and *multiplication*. In addition, we combine individual numbers (23 + 4) to find an answer called the *sum*. In multiplication, we combine groups of numbers for an answer called the *product*. For example, three times four (3 × 4) means three groups of four; their product is 12.

Subtraction and *division* are really *opposite*, or *inverse*, *operations* of addition and multiplication. Subtraction is performed to undo addition, and division is performed to undo multiplication. The answer in subtraction is called the *remainder*; in division, it is called the *quotient*. Consider these examples.

BASIC OPERATIONS	INVERSE OPERATIONS
Addition	Subtraction
23 + 4 = 27 (sum)	27 − 4 = 23 (remainder)
Multiplication	Division
4 × 3 = 12 (product)	12 ÷ 4 = 3 (quotient)

USE OF PARENTHESES: ORDER OF OPERATIONS

Sometimes, parentheses are used in a math problem to indicate which operation must be done first. For example, in the problem 3 + (5 × 2), you would first multiply 5 × 2, then add 3. Look at the different results you get when you work without the parentheses, and then with them.

$$3 + 5 \times 2 = \qquad 3 + (5 \times 2) =$$
$$8 \times 2 = 16 \qquad 3 + 10 \quad = 13$$

Even though we read a problem from left to right, there is an order in which we must perform arithmetic operations:

1. First, do all work within parentheses.
2. Next, do all multiplications and divisions. Do these in left-to-right order.
3. Finally, do additions and subtractions.

In the following example, notice the order in which arithmetic operations are carried out.

$(10 - 6) \times 5 - (15 \div 5) =$ (first do operations inside the parentheses)
    $4 \times 5 - \qquad 3 =$ (next do multiplication)
      $20 - \qquad 3 = 17$ (then do subtraction)

ROUNDING OFF NUMBERS

Occasionally, you are asked to *round off* answers to the nearest ten, hundred, or thousand, etc. We do this in everyday speech when we say that a pair of shoes priced at $37.50 cost "about $40." Rounding off, estimating, and approximating all mean the same thing. You make a guess as to the approximate value. There is a rule for rounding off numbers. First, look at these labels and the way that the number 195,426,874 is written below them.

millions   thousands   hundreds
1 9 5,   4 2 6,   8 7 4

If you are asked to round off 195,426,874 to the nearest hundred, you would first find the number in the highest hundred place (8), and then look at the number to its right (7). If the number to the right is 5, 6, 7, 8, or 9, you round off the hundreds to the next higher number—(9) and replace the 74 with 00. It's the same as saying that 874 is about 900. Your answer would be 195,426,900.

Suppose your original amount was 195,426,834. In that case, when you check the number to the right of 8, you would find 3. Since 3 is below 5, you would leave the 8 and replace the 34 with 00. Your answer would be 195,426,800.

PRIME AND COMPOSITE NUMBERS

Whole numbers are sometimes classified as either *prime* or *composite numbers*. A prime number is one that can be divided evenly by itself and 1—but not by any other whole number.
Examples: 2, 3, 5, 7, 11, 13
A composite number is one that can be divided evenly by itself, by 1, and by at least one other whole number.
Examples: 4, 6, 8, 10, 15, 27

FACTORS

When a whole number has other divisors besides 1 and itself, we call these other divisors *factors*. In other words, factors are numbers that we multiply to form a composite (whole) number.

Sometimes you will be asked to "factor" a number—for example, 6. The factors of 6 are the numbers that you multiply to produce 6. Since 3 times 2 equals 6, the factors of 6 are 3 and 2.

EXPONENTS

There is a short way of writing *repeated factors* in multiplication. For example we may write 5×5 as 5^2. The small 2 written to the right and slightly above the 5 is called an *exponent*. It tells us that 5 is used twice as a factor. You can read 5^2 as either "5 to the second power," or more briefly, "5 squared." Note that 5^2 does not represent "5×2." The expression 2^3 means "2 to the third power," or "2 cubed," and represents $2 \times 2 \times 2$.

n Factorial

Don't confuse these expressions of repeated factors with the term *factorial*. When you see "6 factorial," for example, it means "find the product of every number between 1 and 6." Thus, 6 factorial means $6 \times 5 \times 4 \times 3 \times 2 \times 1$. (The symbol for 6 factorial is 6!)

RECIPROCAL

You may also be asked to find the *reciprocal* of a number. To find the reciprocal of 5, look for the number that you multiply by 5 to get 1. The easiest way to work this out is to divide 1 by 5. You can express the answer either as 1/5 or as 0.2 (see the following sections on fractions and decimals). Remember that the product of a number and its reciprocal is always 1: the reciprocal of 1/4 is 4; the reciprocal of 2/4 is 2.

SERIES AND SEQUENCES

There is a popular type of question involving a *series* or *sequence* of numbers. You are given several numbers arranged in a pattern, and are asked to find the number that comes next. The way to solve this is to figure out the pattern. Try the following two examples:

> A. 2, 4, 6, 8, ?
> B. 3, 9, 4, 8, ?

Each number in sequence A is 2 higher than the number to its left. Thus, the missing term is 10. By testing the relationships between numbers in series B, you find the following pattern:

> 3 (+ 6) = 9   The first step is "add 6."
> 9 (− 5) = 4   The next step is "subtract 5."
> 4 (+ 4) = 8   The next step is "add 4."

To continue the pattern, the next step will have to be "subtract 3." Thus, the missing number is 5.

Fractions

Many problems in arithmetic have to do with fractions. (Decimals and percents are other ways of writing fractions.) There are at least four ways to think about fractions.

1. A fraction is a part of a whole. The fraction 2/3 means that something has been divided into 3 parts, and we are working with 2 of them. The number written above the fraction line (2) is the numerator, and the number below it (3) is called the denominator.
2. A fraction is the result of a multiplication. The fraction 3/4 means 3 times 1/4.
3. A fraction is an expression of division. Thus 2/5 is the quotient (result) when 2 is divided by 5. This can also be written as $2 \div 5$.

4. A fraction is an expression of a ratio. A ratio is a comparison between two quantities. For example, the ratio of 6 inches to 1 foot is 6/12, since there are 12 inches in a foot.

Using Arithmetic Operations with Fractions

There are special rules and some shortcuts, too, for multiplying, dividing, adding, and subtracting fractions and mixed numbers. (A *mixed number* is one that is made up of a whole number and a fraction—for example, $3\frac{2}{3}$.)

MULTIPLYING FRACTIONS

The general rule for multiplying two or more fractions is to multiply the numerators by one another, and then multiply the denominators by one another.

Example: $\frac{1}{2} \times \frac{3}{4} \times \frac{5}{8} = \frac{15}{64}$ (numerators)
(denominators)

Explanation: $1 \times 3 \times 5 = 15$; $2 \times 4 \times 8 = 64$

Sometimes, the product you get when you multiply two fractions can be expressed in simpler terms. When you express a fraction in its *lowest terms,* you put it in a form in which the numerator and denominator no longer have a common factor.

Example: Reduce 24/36 to lowest terms.

Step 1. Find a number which is a factor of both 24 and 36. Both numbers can be divided by 4.

Step 2. Divide 24 and then 36 by 4.

$$24 \div 4 = 6$$
$$36 \div 4 = 9$$
Thus, $\frac{24}{36} = \frac{6}{9}$

Step 3. Check again. Is there a number which is a factor of both 6 and 9? Yes, both numbers can be divided by 3. Divide 6 and then 9 by 3.

$$6 \div 3 = 2$$
$$9 \div 3 = 3$$
Thus, $\frac{6}{9} = \frac{2}{3}$

Answer: 24/36 can be reduced to its lowest terms, 2/3

CHANGING IMPROPER FRACTIONS TO MIXED NUMBERS

When the numerator of a fraction is larger than its denominator, it is called an *improper fraction.* An improper fraction can be changed to a mixed number.

Example: Change 37/5 to a mixed number.

Since a fraction is also an expression of division, 37/5 means $37 \div 5$. If 37 is divided by 5, the quotient is 7, and the remainder is 2. Thus, $\frac{37}{5} = 7\frac{2}{5}$

CHANGING MIXED NUMBERS TO IMPROPER FRACTIONS

In order to multiply or divide mixed numbers, it is necessary to change them into improper fractions.

Example: Change 8⅗ to an improper fraction.

Convert the whole number, 8, to fifths: 8 = 40/5. 40/5 and 3/5 is 43/5, an improper fraction. A shortcut for achieving the change from a mixed number to an improper fraction is to multiply the whole part of the mixed number by the fraction's denominator, and then add the result to the original numerator. Thus $8\dfrac{3}{5} = \dfrac{8 \times 5 + 3}{5} = \dfrac{43}{5}$.

MULTIPLYING MIXED NUMBERS

When multiplying or dividing with a mixed number, change the mixed number to an improper fraction before working out the problem.

Example: $2\dfrac{2}{3} \times \dfrac{5}{7} =$

$$\dfrac{8}{3} \times \dfrac{5}{7} = \dfrac{40}{21} = 1\dfrac{19}{21}$$

CANCELLATION

Cancellation is a shortcut you can use when multiplying (or dividing) fractions. Suppose you want to multiply 8/9 times 3/16. If you immediately multiply the numerators by each other, and the denominators by each other, you get an answer you have to reduce to lowest terms.

$$\dfrac{8}{9} \times \dfrac{3}{16} = \dfrac{24}{144} = \dfrac{1}{6}$$

An easier way to handle the problem is to see if there is any number you can divide evenly into both a numerator and a denominator of the original example. In this case, there is. You can divide 8 into both itself and 16.

Step 1. $\dfrac{\overset{1}{\cancel{8}}}{9} \times \dfrac{3}{\underset{2}{\cancel{16}}} =$

You can also divide 3 into the numerator 3 and the denominator 9. Solve the problem by multiplying the new numerators, and then the new denominators.

Step 1. $\dfrac{\overset{1}{\cancel{8}}}{\underset{3}{\cancel{9}}} \times \dfrac{\overset{1}{\cancel{3}}}{\underset{2}{\cancel{16}}} = \dfrac{1}{6}$

DIVIDING FRACTIONS

Division of fractions looks similar to their multiplication, but there is an important extra step. Dividing something by 3 is the same as multiplying it by 1/3. Therefore we can convert the division example 1/2 ÷ 3/1 into the multiplication example 1/2 × 1/3.

To divide with fractions, *invert* the second term, and change the division sign to a times sign. In other words, write the second term upside down and then treat the problem as a multiplication of fractions. This is also called multiplying the first fraction by the reciprocal of the second fraction. Note that in the example below, 3 can be written as 3/1.

$$\dfrac{1}{2} \div 3 = \dfrac{1}{2} \div \dfrac{3}{1} = \dfrac{1}{2} \times \dfrac{1}{3} = \dfrac{1}{6}$$

ADDING AND SUBTRACTING FRACTIONS

To add or subtract fractions, follow two basic rules:

(a) Add or subtract only those fractions which have the same denominator.

(b) Add or subtract only the numerators of the fractions. Keep the same denominator.

If two fractions you want to add or subtract do not have a *common denominator,* find a way to change them so that both denominators are the same. This is easy if one of the denominators divides evenly into the other. To add 5/6 and 1/12, you can work with the fact that 6 goes into 12 evenly. You can change the 5/6 to 10/12, a fraction with the same value.

Step 1. Write the fraction you have to change. Next to it, write the new denominator you want to use.

$$\frac{5}{6} = \frac{?}{12}$$

Step 2. To find the missing numerator: (a) divide the original denominator into the new denominator (6 into 12 = 2), then (b) multiply your answer by the original numerator ($2 \times 5 = 10$). Your new fraction is 10/12. By changing 5/6 to 10/12, you can now add it to 1/12.

$$\frac{10}{12} + \frac{1}{12} = \frac{11}{12}$$

If you cannot divide one of the denominators into the other, then you have to find a number that both will go into. If you are working with three fractions, you have to find a number that all three denominators can divide evenly.

Suppose you are asked to add 1/4, 1/5, and 1/6. One rule for finding a common denominator for several fractions is to take the largest denominator and start multiplying it by 2, 3, etc., until you find a number that the other denominators will also divide into evenly. In this case, 6 is the largest denominator. If you multiply 6 times 2, you get 12—a number that 5 does not divide into evenly. You have to keep trying until you reach 60—the first product that all three denominators divide evenly. Thus,

$$\frac{1}{4} = \frac{15}{60}$$
$$\frac{1}{5} = \frac{12}{60}$$
$$+\frac{1}{6} = \frac{10}{60}$$

By adding the converted fractions, you find that 1/4 + 1/5 + 1/6 = 37/60.

To add mixed numbers, follow these three steps:

Step 1. Add the whole numbers.

Step 2. Add the fractions. If the sum of these is an improper fraction, change the sum to a mixed number.

Step 3. Add the sum of the whole numbers to the sum of the fractions.

Example: $3\frac{2}{3} + 12\frac{2}{3}$

Step 1. $3 + 12 = 15$

Step 2. $\frac{2}{3} + \frac{2}{3} = \frac{4}{3} = 1\frac{1}{3}$

Step 3. $15 + 1\frac{1}{3} = 16\frac{1}{3}$

In subtracting mixed numbers, you may have to "borrow" as you do in subtracting whole numbers. For example, if you want to subtract 6¾ from 9¼, you realize you cannot take 3/4 from 1/4. (Try to get $.75 out of a quarter!) Thus, you borrow 1 from 9, and rewrite the example.

$$9\frac{1}{4}=8\frac{4}{4}+\frac{1}{4}= \quad 8\frac{5}{4}$$
$$-6\frac{3}{4}= \quad\quad -6\frac{3}{4}$$
$$\overline{\quad\quad\quad 2\frac{2}{4}=2\frac{1}{2}}$$

Decimals

DECIMAL FRACTIONS
Decimal fractions are special fractions whose denominators are always powers of ten. *Powers of ten* are easy to remember. The exponent tells you how many zeros there are in the power of ten. Thus,

$$10^1 = 10 \quad\quad = 10 \times 1$$
$$10^2 = 100 \quad\quad = 10 \times 10$$
$$10^3 = 1,000 \quad\quad = 10 \times 10 \times 10$$

You can tell the denominator of a decimal fraction by counting the places in the number to the right of its decimal point. When it is written as a fraction, the denominator has the same number of zeros as this number of places. That is, it has the same power of ten. Thus,

$$0.7 = \frac{7}{10^1} \text{ or } \frac{7}{10} \quad\quad \text{(seven tenths)}$$
$$0.07 = \frac{7}{10^2} \text{ or } \frac{7}{100} \quad\quad \text{(seven hundredths)}$$
$$0.007 = \frac{7}{10^3} \text{ or } \frac{7}{1,000} \quad\quad \text{(seven thousandths)}$$
$$0.0007 = \frac{7}{10^4} \text{ or } \frac{7}{10,000} \quad\quad \text{(seven ten-thousandths)}$$

CHANGING FRACTIONS TO DECIMALS
To change a fraction to a decimal, divide the numerator by the denominator. Place a decimal point to the right of the numerator, and add a zero for each decimal place you want in your answer.

Example: $\frac{2}{5}=5\overline{)2.0}$ with 0.4 above, 20 below. So $\frac{2}{5}=0.4$

Here's a short list of common fractions, converted to decimals.

$$\frac{1}{2}= .50 \quad\quad \frac{1}{3}= .33\frac{1}{3}$$
$$\frac{1}{4}= .25 \quad\quad \frac{3}{4}= .75$$
$$\frac{1}{5}= .20 \quad\quad \frac{3}{5}= .60$$
$$\frac{4}{5}= .80 \quad\quad \frac{1}{8}= .12\frac{1}{2} \text{ (or .125)}$$

CHANGING DECIMALS TO FRACTIONS

Every decimal is really a fraction whose denominator is a power of ten. For example,

$$0.0231 \text{ is } \frac{231}{10,000}; \quad 0.25 \text{ is } \frac{25}{100} \text{ or } \frac{1}{4}; \quad \text{and } 3.4 \text{ is } \frac{34}{10}$$

MULTIPLYING DECIMALS BY POWERS OF 10

Here is a shortcut for multiplying a decimal by a power of ten. Suppose you want to multiply .16 by 10^3.

Step 1. Count the number of zeros in the power of ten.
$$10^3 = 1,000 \quad (3 \text{ zeros})$$

Step 2. Move the decimal in .16 to the right. Move it as many places as this number of zeros.

Sometimes, you have to add one or more zeros so that you can move the correct number of places.
$$10^3 \times .16 = 10^3 \times .160 = 160$$
Other examples: $10^2 \times 2.1 = 10^2 \times 2.10 = 210$
$$10^4 \times .43 = 10^4 \times .4300 = 4300$$

DIVIDING DECIMALS BY POWERS OF 10

To divide a decimal by a power of ten, count the number of zeros in the power of ten, and move that many places to the left of the decimal.

Examples: $158.7 \div 10^1 = 158.7 \div 10 = 15.87$
$$.32 \div 10^2 = 00.32 \div 100 = .0032$$

ADDING AND SUBTRACTING DECIMALS

To add or subtract decimals, line up the numbers so that the decimal points are directly under one another. Then add or subtract as you would with whole numbers. Write zeros at the end of decimals if you find it easier to work with place holders.

Examples: Add $3.12 + 14.3 + 205.6 + 0.0324$, and subtract their sum from $1,000.55$. Remember to put the decimal point in the answers.

```
      3.1200          1,000.5500
     14.3000          − 223.0524
    205.6000           777.4976  (remainder)
  +   0.0324
    223.0524  (sum)
```

MULTIPLYING DECIMALS

Multiply two decimals as though they were whole numbers. Then use these steps to find out where to put the decimal point in your answer.

Step 1. Add the decimal places in both numbers, counting from the decimal point to the right.

Step 2. Count off this same number of places from right to left in the answer.

Step 3. Insert a decimal point where you finish counting off. Add extra zeros, if you need them, to fill out the correct number of places.

Examples: $.02 \times .12 = .0024$
$$30 \times 1.5 = 45.0$$

DIVIDING DECIMALS

To divide a decimal by a whole number, divide the numbers as though they were both whole numbers. Then place a decimal point in the answer directly above the decimal in the problem.

Example: 5.117 ÷ 17

$$17\overline{)5.117} \quad \begin{array}{r} 0.301 \\ \hline \end{array}$$

$$\begin{array}{r} 5\ 1 \\ \hline 17 \\ \underline{17} \end{array}$$

To divide one decimal by another, begin by making the divisor a whole number. Do this by moving the decimal in the divisor all the way to the right. Count the number of places you move it. Then move the decimal in the other number (the dividend) the same number of places.

Example: $\dfrac{1.8}{0.2} = \dfrac{18}{2} = 9$

ROUNDING OFF DECIMALS

Many math problems require a rounding-off process to reach an answer. Think about 3.7 yards. Is this closer to 3 yards or to 4 yards? $3.7 = 3\frac{7}{10}$, which is closer to 4 yards. How about 3.5 yards? This is exactly midway between 3 and 4 yards. We must make an agreement on rounding off a number of this type: We agree that 3.5 yards will be rounded off to 4 yards. Now round off 3.346 to the nearest tenth. This lies between 3.3 and 3.4, but is closer to 3.3. A common mistake in rounding off is to start from the right; in this case the 6 in the thousandths place will round the 3.346 off to 3.35. This causes our rounded off number to become 3.4 instead of 3.3. To round off a decimal to the nearest tenth, look at the number in the hundredths place (just to the right of the tenths). If it is 5 or more, round off upward. If it is less than 5, drop it and all numbers following it.

Percentages

A *percent* is a way to express a fraction. It simply means hundredths. To use a percent in solving a problem, change it to a fraction or a decimal.

To change a percent to a fraction, drop the percent sign and multiply by 1/100.

Examples: 5% means $5 \times \dfrac{1}{100}$ or $\dfrac{5}{100}$

20% means $20 \times \dfrac{1}{100}$ or $\dfrac{20}{100}$

100% means $100 \times \dfrac{1}{100}$ or $\dfrac{100}{100}$

CHANGING A PERCENT TO A DECIMAL

To change a percent to a decimal, drop the percent sign and move the decimal point two places to the left. Add extra zeros, if you need them, to fill out the correct number of places. If the percent is given as a fraction, first change the fraction to a decimal.

Examples: 3% = .03   1.2% = .012

75% = .75   1/4% = .25% = .0025

15% = .15   100% = 1.00 (or 1)

CHANGING A DECIMAL TO A PERCENT

To change a decimal to a percent, move the decimal point two places to the right and add the percent sign.

Examples: .23 = 23%   .05 = 5%

.5 = 50%   .66⅔ = 66⅔%

ARITHMETIC PROBLEMS USING PERCENT

An arithmetic problem using percent usually falls into one of three categories:

1. Find a number when you are told it is a certain percent of another number. This involves multiplication.

    Example: What is the amount of the discount on a hat marked $49.95 and discounted at 20%?

    Step 1.   Change the rate of discount to a fraction or decimal. 20% = .2

    Step 2.   Multiply the marked price by the rate of discount.

    $49.95 × .2 = $9.99 (discount)

2. Find what percent one number is of another. This involves division.

    Example: A baseball team played 20 games and won 17 of them. What percent of its games did it win?

    Step 1.   Express the games won by the team as a part of the total games they played. In other words, state the relationship between the two numbers by writing a fraction (a ratio).

    $$\frac{17}{20}$$

    Step 2.   Convert this fraction to a percent. Divide the numerator by the denominator. (Add a decimal point and zeros to carry the answer out two places.)

    $$\frac{17.00}{20} = 0.85$$

    Step 3.   Multiply the quotient by 100 to convert to percent.

    0.85 × 100 = 85% (games won)

3. Find a whole number when you know only a part of it and the percent that the part represents. This involves division.

Example: A family pays $5,000 a year in premiums for home insurance. If the rate of insurance is 12½%, how much is the insurance policy worth?

Step 1. Change the percent to a decimal.

12½% = 0.125 (rate of insurance)

Step 2. Divide the premium by the rate of insurance.

$$\$5{,}000 \div 0.125 = 125\overline{)\$5{,}000{,}000}^{\$40{,}000}$$

$$\underline{5\,00}$$

The home insurance policy is worth $40,000.

INTEREST

A percent problem you frequently see has to do with interest earned on a sum of money, the *principal*. A formula for finding interest is: principal (p) × rate of interest (r) × the period of time (t) = interest (i). *Time* is always time in years.

$$i = p \times r \times t$$

Example: How much interest will there be on $5,000 for 6 months at 5%?

Step 1. Change the rate of interest to a fraction: 5% = 5/100 (or 1/20)

Step 2. Express the time in terms of years. There are 12 months in a year, so 6 months is 6/12, or 1/2, of a year.

Step 3. Apply the formula for finding interest.

$$i = p \times r \times t$$

$$i = \frac{\$5,000}{1} \times \frac{1}{20} \times \frac{1}{2}$$

$$i = \frac{\overset{\$2,500}{\cancel{\$5,000}}}{1} \times \frac{1}{20} \times \frac{1}{\cancel{2}_1}$$

$$i = \frac{\overset{\overset{\$125}{\cancel{\$2,500}}}{\cancel{\$5,000}}}{1} \times \frac{1}{\cancel{20}_1} \times \frac{1}{\cancel{2}_1} = \$125$$

The interest on $5,000 for 6 months will be $125.

Square Roots

The square root of a number is one of the two equal factors (numbers) that, when multiplied together, give that number. For example, the square root of 9 is 3 since $3 \times 3 = 9$, and the square root of 49 is 7 since $7 \times 7 = 49$.

The square root of a number may be indicated by using a radical sign. For example, $\sqrt{81}$ means the square root of 81, that is, $\sqrt{81} = 9$. Similarly, $\sqrt{25} = 5$.

Only numbers that are perfect squares have exact square roots. Some perfect squares are 1, 4, 9, 16, 25, 36, 49, 64, 81, and 100.

FINDING THE SQUARE ROOT OF A NUMBER

You may be asked to find the square root of a number that is not a perfect square, giving your answer correct to the nearest tenth, for example. A trial-and-error procedure can be used to find a square root to the nearest decimal place. For example, suppose you are asked to find $\sqrt{29}$ to the nearest tenth: $\sqrt{29}$ is between $\sqrt{25}$, which we know is 5, and $\sqrt{36}$, which we know is 6. And $\sqrt{29}$ is nearer to $\sqrt{25}$ than it is to $\sqrt{36}$. Guess 5.3 as $\sqrt{29}$ to the nearest tenth. Divide 5.3 into 29:

$$
\begin{array}{r}
5.4 \\
53. \overline{)29\ 0.0} \\
\underline{26\ 5} \\
2\ 50 \\
\underline{2\ 12}
\end{array}
$$

This was a good guess. We now know that $\sqrt{29}$ is between 5.3 and 5.4. The results of multiplying 5.3×5.3 and 5.4×5.4 show that $\sqrt{29}$ is nearer to 5.4 than to 5.3:

$$
\begin{array}{r}
5.3 \\
\underline{5.3} \\
1\ 59 \\
\underline{26\ 5} \\
28.09
\end{array}
\qquad
\begin{array}{r}
5.4 \\
\underline{5.4} \\
2\ 16 \\
\underline{27\ 0} \\
29.16
\end{array}
$$

Algebra

Algebra is a way to reduce a problem to a small set of symbols. When we can state a problem with a few symbols, letters, and numbers, it seems easier to solve. The solution we are looking for is often an *"unknown"* quantity, and we speak of "finding the unknowns."

Take an example. We know that if a sweater is priced at $20, we have to pay $20 to buy one. If we want three sweaters, we pay three times that amount, or $60. How do we find the answer, $60? We multiply two numbers to find a third number. Using the style of algebra, we can express this operation briefly. Let p equal the price of one sweater, and let c (the "unknown") equal the cost of three sweaters. Here's an algebraic expression for how we find c.

$$c = 3 \times p \quad (\text{or}) \; c = 3p$$

In this expression, the letters c and p are called *literal numbers,* meaning they are letters that stand for numbers. Another word for such letters is *variables,* meaning that the numbers they stand for can change. (If the price of the sweater is discounted to $18, then p will equal $18, and c will equal $54.)

ARITHMETIC OPERATIONS IN ALGEBRA

All four arithmetic operations are possible in algebra: both basic operations (addition and multiplication), and inverse operations (subtraction and division). We can express these operations algebraically:

1. The sum of two numbers, x and y, is $x + y$
2. The difference between two numbers, x and y, is $x - y$
3. The product of two numbers, x and y, is $(x) \times (y)$ (or) $x \cdot y$ (or) xy
4. The quotient of two numbers, x and y, is $x \div y$ (or) $\dfrac{x}{y}$

EQUATIONS

An *equation* is a statement that two quantities are equal. This is clear when the quantities are expressed in numbers. Thus,

$$3 + 7 = 10 \qquad 7 \cdot 8 = 56$$
$$5 - 3 = 2 \qquad 18 \div 2 = 9$$

But in algebra, equations always include variables, or unknowns. Usually, you will be asked to "solve the equation" by finding the unknown number value. In this sense, the *solution* to an equation is the number which proves that the equation is true. (You show that it is true by substituting the number for the variable.) But how do you find the number?

Suppose you heard someone say, "I can't afford to buy a car for $8,000. That would leave me with only $5,000 in my bank account." How would we express his (or her) statement in algebra? (Remember, the "unknown" is the unstated amount, x, now in the bank account.) Here's one way of writing the expression:

$$x - \$8,000 = \$5,000$$

How do we solve for x?

Step 1. Think about what the expression now means: A certain number, minus $8,000, equals $5,000.

Step 2. Think of how you want to express the solution: x = (the amount in the bank)

Step 3. Think of how the statement of your solution will differ from the equation you begin with: $8,000 will no longer be on the same side of the equal sign as x.

Step 4. Now think about how to "get rid of" or "clear" the $8,000 from the side that shows x. Notice that the sign with $8,000 is a minus sign. If you add $8,000 to the left side of the equation, the two 8,000s will cancel each other. But remember that in a true equation, everything on the left side of the equal sign must have the same value as everything on the right side. If you add $8,000 to the left, you have to add it to the right. Thus,

$$x - \$8,000 = \$5,000$$
$$x - \$8,000 + \$8,000 = \$5,000 + \$8,000$$
$$x = \$13,000 \; (\text{amount in bank})$$

How is the equation solved? By performing an inverse operation on both sides of the equation. Thus, to solve for x, we go through three steps:

Step 1. We decide to "solve for x" by removing all other operations from the side of the equation where x is found.

Step 2. We remove an operation from one side of the equal sign by performing its inverse (opposite) operation on the same side.

Step 3. We then perform the same operation on the other side of the equal sign. (That is, if we subtract 3 from one side, we subtract 3 from the other side.)

EXAMPLES OF USING INVERSE OPERATIONS TO SOLVE EQUATIONS

1. The inverse of addition is subtraction.

    Solve: $x + 7 = 50$

    $x + 7 - 7 = 50 - 7$

    $x = 43$ (solution of equation)

2. The inverse of subtraction is addition.

    Solve: $x - 3 = 4$

    $x - 3 + 3 = 4 + 3$

    $x = 7$ (solution)

3. The inverse of multiplication is division.

    Solve: $0.05x = 4$

    $$\frac{0.05x}{0.05} = \frac{4}{0.05}$$

    $x = 80$ (solution)

    ($0.05 \div 0.05 = 1$. When you divide 4 by 0.05, you have to clear the decimal from the divisor first. Thus, 0.05 becomes 5, and 4 becomes 400.)

4. The inverse of division is multiplication.

    $$\text{Solve}: \frac{x}{2} = 7$$

    $$2\left(\frac{x}{2}\right) = 7 \times 2$$

    $x = 14$ (solution)

INVERSE OPERATIONS WITH MORE COMPLEX EQUATIONS

Sometimes, an equation shows x as part of more than one operation. There may also be negative terms (terms with a minus sign). The same basic steps are involved in finding the solution, but may have to be repeated. Remember, the goal is always to isolate x on one side of the equation.

Example: Solve: $3x + 7 = -11$

Step 1. Perform the inverse operation of + 7.

    $3x + 7 - 7 = -11 - 7$

    $3x = -18$

Step 2. Perform the inverse operation of $3x(3 \cdot x)$.

    $$\frac{3x}{3} = \frac{-18}{3}$$

    $x = -6$ (solution)

(Remember that in multiplication and division, if the signs of both terms are plus or minus, the answer is signed by a plus sign. If the two terms are different, the answer is signed by a minus sign.)

Sometimes, x appears on both sides of the original equation. In that case, the first step is to remove x from one side (or, "collect all xs on one side") of the equal sign.

Example: Solve: $-7x = 24 - x$

Step 1. Perform the inverse operation of $-x$.
$$-7x + x = 24 - x + x$$
$$-6x = 24$$

Step 2. Perform the inverse operation of $(-6)x$.
$$\frac{-6x}{-6} = \frac{24}{-6}$$
$$x = -4 \text{ (solution)}$$

ALGEBRAIC EXPRESSIONS

An *algebraic expression* in any collection of numbers and variables. This collection may have more than one variable. For example, $3x + 4y$ is an algebraic expression meaning "3 times one unknown number (x), plus 4 times another unknown number (y)."

ARITHMETIC OPERATIONS WITH ALGEBRAIC EXPRESSIONS

1. To add or subtract algebraic expressions, remember that only *similar*, or *"like"* terms can be combined. (Terms are similar if they have the same variable, raised to the same power.) Thus, we can subtract $3x$ from $5x$ to get $2x$, but we cannot get x^3 by adding x and x^2, or get $9zh$ out of $4z$ and $5h$.
   Example: Add: $3x + 2y - 4z + 2x - 5y$
   $$3x + 2x = 5x \text{ (partial sum)}$$
   $$2y - 5y = -3y \text{ (partial sum)}$$
   Therefore, $5x - 3y - 4z$ is the sum.
2. To multiply algebraic expressions, follow these steps.
   Step 1. Multiply the numbers of similar terms.
   Step 2. Multiply the letters of similar terms. When multiplying one power of x by another power of x, just add the exponents.
   Example: $(2x^2)(3x^5)$
   Step 1. $2 \times 3 = 6$ (partial product)
   Step 2. $x^2 \times x^5 = x^7$ (partial product)
   Thus, the product is $6x^7$

   Sometimes, you are asked to multiply more complex algebraic expressions. The rules are basically the same.
   Example: In $x^2y(3x - 5y)$, the parentheses tell you that x^2y is the multiplier for both $3x$ and $-5y$.
   Step 1. $x^2y \times 3x = 3x^3y$ (partial product)
   Step 2. $x^2y \times -5y = -5x^2y^2$ (partial product)
   The product is $3x^3y - 5x^2y^2$

   Example: In $(a + 2)(2a - 3)$, think of $(a + 2)$ as a two-place multiplier. An easy way to do this example is to set it up as an ordinary multiplication in arithmetic.

$$
\begin{array}{r}
2a - 3 \\
\times\, a + 2 \\
\hline
4a - 6 \quad \text{Multiply } (2a - 3) \text{ by } 2 \\
2a^2 - 3a \qquad \text{Multiply } (2a - 3) \text{ by } a \\
\hline
2a^2 + a - 6 \quad \text{Product}
\end{array}
$$

3. To divide algebraic expressions, follow these steps:
   Step 1. Divide the number of similar terms.
   Step 2. Divide the letters of similar terms. When dividing one power of x by another power of x, subtract the exponents.
   Example: $x^5 \div x^3 = x^2$

Example: $\dfrac{8x^3}{4x} = \dfrac{\overset{2}{\cancel{8}}}{\underset{1}{\cancel{4}}} \times \dfrac{\overset{x^2}{\cancel{x^3}}}{\underset{1}{\cancel{x}}} = 2 \times x^2 = 2x^2$

Sometimes, a divisor goes into several terms.

Example: $\dfrac{\overset{3x^2}{\cancel{24x^3}} - \overset{1}{\cancel{8x}}}{\underset{1}{\cancel{8x}}} = 3x^2 - 1$

EVALUATING ALGEBRAIC EXPRESSIONS

To evaluate an algebraic expression means to replace the letters with numbers, and then simplify (add, multiply, etc.).

Example: Evaluate the expression $(a + 2b)$ if $a = 3$ and $b = 2$.

$$a + 2b$$
$$= 3 + 2(2)$$
$$= 3 + 4$$
$$= 7$$

FACTORING IN ALGEBRA

Sometimes, you are given the answer to a multiplication example in algebra, and are asked to find the original multipliers. This is called *factoring*.

1. Factor the *highest common factor*. The highest common factor of an algebraic expression is the highest expression that will divide into every one of the terms of the expression.
    Example: $6x^2 + 3xy$
    Step 1. The highest number that will divide into the numerical coefficients, 6 and 3, is 3.
    Step 2. The highest literal factor that will divide into x^2 and xy is x. Note that y is not contained in the first term at all.
    Step 3. Divide the highest common factor, 3x, into $6x^2 + 3xy$ to find the remaining factor: The factors are $3x(2x + y)$.
    Example: $2a^2b^3 - 4ab^2 + 6a$.
    The highest common factor of the three terms is 2a, so the factors are $2a(ab^3 - 2b^2 + 3)$.

2. Factor the *difference of two squares*. In this case, your example contains the square of one number, minus the square of another number. (The square of another is the product you get when you multiply a number by itself. The *square root* of a number is the number that was multiplied by itself to produce the square.)
    Example: $x^2 - 9$
    Step 1. Find the square root of x^2 and place it to the left, within each of two "empty" parentheses. The square root of x^2 is x.

    $$(x \quad) (x \quad)$$

    Step 2. Find the square root of 9 and place it to the right, within each of these parentheses. The square root of 9 is 3.

    $$(x \quad 3) (x \quad 3)$$

    Step 3. Place a plus sign between one pair of terms, and a minus sign between the other pair of terms.

    $$(x + 3) (x - 3)$$

    The factors of $x^2 - 9$ are $(x + 3)$, $(x - 3)$.

3. Factor a *quadratic trinomial*. A quadratic trinomial is an algebraic expression of the form $ax^2 + bx + c$, where *a, b,* and *c* are numbers and *a* does not equal 0. Its factors are always two pairs of terms. The terms in each pair are separated by a plus or minus sign.

Example: Factor $x^2 - 11x + 30$.

Step 1. Find the factors of the first term in the trinomial. The factors of x^2 are x and x.

$$(x \quad)(x \quad)$$

Step 2. Look at the last term in the trinomial. It has a plus sign. This means that both factors of the trinomial are either plus or minus. Which one? Since the middle term ($-11x$) has a minus sign, both factors must have minus signs.

$$(x - \;)(x - \;)$$

Step 3. Find the factors of 30. There are several numbers you can multiply to get 30: 30×1, 10×3, etc. But the two multipliers you use must also combine somehow to give you 11, the middle term. When 5 and 6 are multiplied, they give you 30. When they are added, they give you 11. We know the factors have minus signs. So the factors of 30 are actually -6 and -5.

$$(x - 6)(x - 5)$$

The factors of $(x^2 - 11x + 30)$ are: $(x - 6)$, $(x - 5)$.

SOLVING QUADRATIC EQUATIONS

A *quadratic equation* is an equation that contains a term with the square of the unknown quantity and has no term with a higher power of the unknown. In a quadratic equation, the exponent is never higher than 2 (x^2, b^2, c^2, etc.). Examples of quadratic equations include:

$$x^2 + x - 6 = 0$$
$$3x^2 = 5x - 7$$
$$x^2 - 4 = 0$$
$$64 = x^2$$

How do we solve equations like this? Basically, we factor them, and then set each factor equal to zero. After that, it's easy to solve for x. Let's take it step by step.

Example: Solve: $x^2 = 3x + 10$

Step 1. Place all terms on one side of the equal sign, leaving the equation equal to 0. (Remember inverse operations.)

$$x^2 - 3x - 10 = 0$$

Step 2. Factor this equation.

$$(x - 5)(x + 2) = 0$$

Step 3. Set each factor equal to zero, and solve the equations.

$$x - 5 = 0 \qquad x + 2 = 0$$
$$x = +5 \qquad x = -2$$

Step 4. To check its accuracy, substitute each answer in the original equation.

$$x^2 = 3x + 10 \qquad\qquad x^2 = 3x + 10$$
$$(5)^2 = 3(5) + 10 \qquad (-2)^2 = 3(-2) + 10$$
$$25 = 15 + 10 \qquad\qquad 4 = -6 + 10$$
$$25 = 25 \text{ (proof)} \qquad\quad 4 = 4 \text{ (proof)}$$

The solution of the quadratic equation is $x = 5, -2$.

INEQUALITIES

Not everything in algebra is an equation! An *inequality* is a statement that two quantities are not equal to each other. With an inequality, one of these two things must be true:

1. The first quantity is greater than the second.

OR 2. The first quantity is less than the second.

A number line helps to show how this is true.

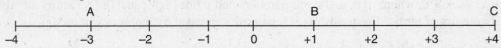

On the number line, A is to the left of B, and B is to the left of C. Whenever one variable is to the left of another on a number line, it is less than the other. Thus, –3 is less than +1, and +1 is less than +4. We can make a few general statements.

1. Any negative number is less than zero.
2. Zero is less than any positive number.
3. Any negative number is less than any positive number.

There are symbols for statements of inequality.

Symbols	Meanings
$6 \neq 7$	6 does not equal 7
$7 > 6$	7 is greater than 6
$6 < 7$	6 is less than 7
$x \geq 8$	x is greater than or equal to 8
$x \leq 8$	x is less than or equal to 8

SOLVING INEQUALITIES

The rules for solving inequalities are similar to those used for solving equations with one important difference, which is illustrated in the second of the two examples below. The difference is that when both sides of an inequality are multiplied or divided by a *negative* number, the direction of the inequality sign must be reversed. To illustrate, if $8 > 5$ has each side multiplied by –2, then $-16 < -10$.

Example: Solve: $x - 3 < 8$

"Clear" for x by transferring –3 to the other side of the inequality symbol. Do this by performing an inverse operation.

$$x - 3 + 3 < 8 + 3$$
$$x < 11 \text{ (solution)}$$

The solution means that any number less than 11 will make the original statement of inequality true. You can prove that by substituting numbers less than 11 for x. Try letting $x = 10$.

$$x - 3 < 8$$
$$10 - 3 < 8$$
$$7 < 8 \quad \text{This is certainly true!}$$

Example: Solve: $13 - 2x < 7$

"Clear" the x term by subtracting 13 from both sides of the inequality.

$$13 - 13 - 2x < 7 - 13$$
$$-2x < -6$$

To obtain x alone, divide both sides of the inequality by –2. Since division is by a *negative* number, the direction of the inequality sign must be reversed.

$$x > 3$$

The solution means that any number greater than 3 will make the original inequality true. To prove this, substitute any number greater than 3 for x. Try letting $x = 5$.

$$13 - 2x < 7$$
$$13 - 2(5) < 7$$
$$13 - 10 < 7$$
$$3 < 7$$

This is certainly true!

Geometry

Geometry has to do with the world around us. Some knowledge of geometry is necessary for everyone. Both arithmetic and algebra are used in solving geometry problems. Many geometry problems involve measurement, and use familiar words, such as line or point. An important term in geometry is *angle*.

ANGLES

An angle is formed by two lines meeting at a point. The point is called the *vertex* of the angle. You can name an angle in three ways.

1. By the point at the vertex (for example, angle B).

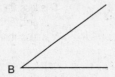

2. By the letter names of the lines that meet to form the angle, with the vertex in the middle (for example, angle ABC).

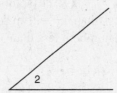

3. By a number inside the angle on a diagram (for example, angle #2).

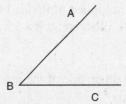

PROTRACTOR

To measure an angle, we use an instrument called a *protractor*. Angles are measured in *degrees* (°). Just as a foot is divided into 12 inches, a degree is divided into minutes (') and seconds ("). (Don't confuse these with time!)

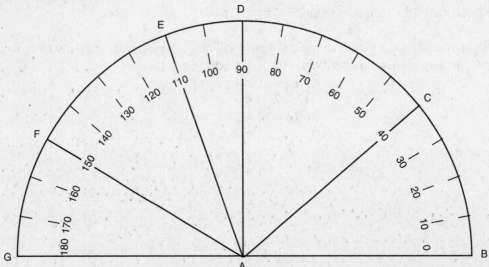

1. A *straight line* is an angle of 180 degrees.

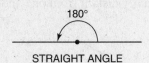

STRAIGHT ANGLE

2. A *right angle* is an angle of 90 degrees.

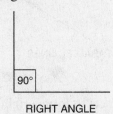

RIGHT ANGLE

3. An *obtuse angle* is an angle of more than 90 degrees, but less than 180 degrees.

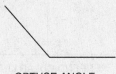

OBTUSE ANGLE

4. An *acute angle* is an angle of more than 0 degrees but less than 90 degrees.

ACUTE ANGLE

5. *Complementary angles* are two angles whose sum is 90 degrees.

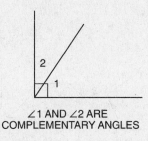

∠1 AND ∠2 ARE
COMPLEMENTARY ANGLES

6. *Supplementary angles* are two angles whose sum is 180 degrees.

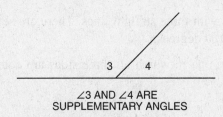

∠3 AND ∠4 ARE
SUPPLEMENTARY ANGLES

LINES

Parallel lines are two lines that are equally distant from one another at every point along the lines.

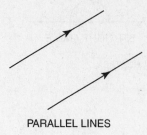

PARALLEL LINES

Perpendicular lines are two lines that meet to form a right angle.

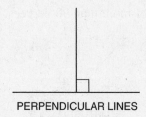

PERPENDICULAR LINES

POLYGONS

A *polygon* is composed of three or more lines, connected so that an area is closed in. There are several types of polygons.

1. A *triangle* has three sides.
2. A *quadrilateral* has four sides.
3. A *pentagon* has five sides.
4. A *hexagon* has six sides.
5. An *octagon* has eight sides.
6. A *decagon* has ten sides.

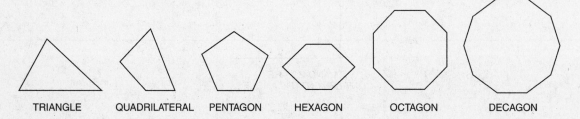

TRIANGLE   QUADRILATERAL PENTAGON   HEXAGON   OCTAGON   DECAGON

TRIANGLES

A triangle is a geometric figure with three straight lines. There are several ways to classify a triangle, but all triangles contain 180 degrees.

1. An *equilateral* triangle is one in which all three sides are equal, and all three angles are equal—60 degrees each.

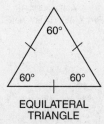

EQUILATERAL
TRIANGLE

2. An *isosceles* triangle is one in which two sides are equal. (The angles opposite these sides are also equal.)

ISOSCELES
TRIANGLE

3. A *scalene* triangle is one in which all the sides and all the angles are unequal.

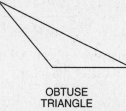

SCALENE
TRIANGLE

4. An *acute triangle* is one in which all three angles are acute (less than a right angle).

ACUTE
TRIANGLE

5. An *obtuse triangle* is one in which one angle is obtuse (greater than 90 degrees).

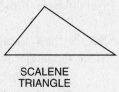

OBTUSE
TRIANGLE

6. A *right triangle* is one which includes a right angle (90 degrees). The longest side of a right triangle is called the *hypotenuse*. It is always the side opposite the right angle (side c). The other two sides are called *legs*.

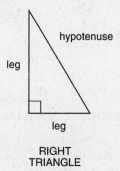

hypotenuse

leg

leg

RIGHT
TRIANGLE

There is a very important idea connected with right triangles. It is called the *Pythagorean Theorem*. It says that in a right triangle, the square of the hypotenuse is equal to the sum of the square of the legs. As an equation, the Pythagorean Theorem would be expressed as follows:

$$c^2 = a^2 + b^2$$

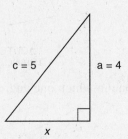

Example: A gardener placed a 5-foot ladder against a 4-foot wall. If the top of the ladder touched the top of the wall, how far away from the base of the wall was the bottom of the ladder?

Solution: The angle formed by the base of the wall and the ground is a right angle. Therefore, we can use the Pythagorean Theorem. Since the ladder was opposite the right angle, let c = 5.

$$c^2 = a^2 + b^2$$
$$5^2 = 4^2 + x^2 \text{ (Clear for x.)}$$
$$5^2 - 4^2 = 4^2 - 4^2 + x^2$$
$$25 - 16 = x^2$$
$$9 = x^2 \text{ (Find the square roots.)}$$
$$3 = x$$

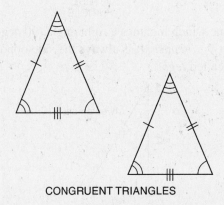

7. *Congruent triangles* are alike in every respect. All three sides and all three angles of one triangle are exactly the same as those of the other.

CONGRUENT TRIANGLES

8. *Similar triangles* are triangles with exactly the same shape, but not necessarily the same size. The angles of two similar triangles are the same.

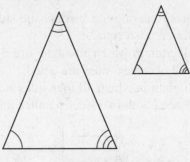

SIMILAR TRIANGLES

9. *Special lines in a triangle* include altitudes, medians, and angle bisectors.

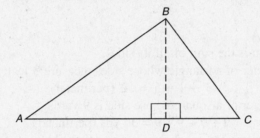

BD is an *altitude*

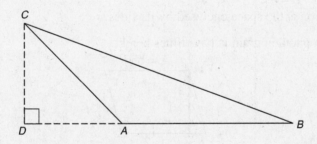

CD is an *altitude*. Notice that AB must be extended for the perpendicular to meet it at right angles.

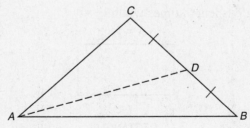

AD is a *median* if CD = BD.

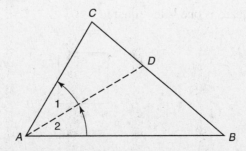

AD is an *angle bisector* of ∠A if ∠1 = ∠2.

QUADRILATERALS

There are several types of quadrilaterals, but all quadrilaterals contain 360 degrees.

1. A *parallelogram* is a quadrilateral with its opposite sides parallel. In a parallelogram the opposite sides and angles are also equal.
2. A *rectangle* is a parallelogram in which all angles are right angles.
3. A *square* is a rectangle all of whose sides are equal.
4. A *rhombus* is a parallelogram in which all four sides are equal.
5. A *trapezoid* is a quadrilateral with two sides parallel, and two sides not parallel.

   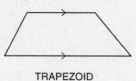

PARALLELOGRAM   RECTANGLE   SQUARE   RHOMBUS   TRAPEZOID

PERIMETER AND AREA

The *perimeter* of a polygon is the sum of all its sides.

Example: Find the perimeter of a triangle whose sides measure 3 feet, 4 feet, and 5 feet.

$$3' + 4' + 5' = 12' \text{ (perimeter)}$$

Example: Find the perimeter of a square whose side is 9 yards.

$$9 + 9 + 9 + 9 = 36 \text{ yds (perimeter)}$$

Since all four sides of a square are equal, you can use the rule "perimeter (P) of a square equals four times a side (s)": $P = 4s$.

The *area* of a polygon is the space enclosed by its sides.

1. The area of a parallelogram is base times height.

$$A = bh$$

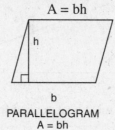

PARALLELOGRAM
$A = bh$

2. The area of a rectangle is length times width.

$$A = lw$$

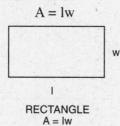

RECTANGLE
$A = lw$

3. The area of a square is one side "squared."

$$A = s^2$$

SQUARE
$A = s^2$

4. The area of a triangle is one-half the base times the height.

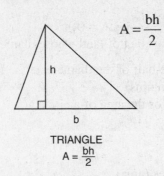

$$A = \frac{bh}{2}$$

TRIANGLE
$$A = \frac{bh}{2}$$

Example: Find the area of a room whose length is 20 feet and whose width is 18 feet.

A = lw
x = 20' × 18'
x = 360 square feet (area)

CIRCLES

A *circle* is a closed curved line, all of whose points are equally distant from the center. A circle contains 360 degrees. There are several special "parts" to a circle.

The *circumference* of a circle is its "length"—once around the rim.

The *radius* of a circle is a line drawn from the center to any point on the circumference.

The *diameter* is a line passing through the center of a circle, and is equal to twice the radius.

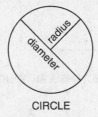

CIRCLE

Perimeter and Area of a Circle

To find the circumference (perimeter) of a circle, we use a new number, Pi (π). Pi is actually a Greek letter. In geometry it expresses an unchanging relationship between the circumference of a circle and its diameter. In other words, the circumference is always Pi times the diameter. Since the diameter is twice the radius, we can also say that the circumference of a circle is Pi times twice the radius. Thus,

$$C = (\pi)d \ OR \ C = (\pi)2r$$

When we do arithmetic operations with Pi, we use either 3.14 or 3½ for Pi.

Example: Find the circumference of an ice rink whose radius is 70 yards.

$$C = (\pi)2r$$
$$C = (\pi)(2 \times 70)$$
$$C = 3\frac{1}{7} \times 140$$
$$C = \frac{22}{7} \times \overset{20}{\cancel{140}}$$
$$C = 22 \times 20 = 440 \text{ yards}$$

The area of a circle also has a fixed relationship to Pi. The area equals Pi times the square of the radius. Thus,

$$A = (\pi)r^2$$

Example: Find the area of a circular tract of land whose diameter is 20 miles.

Step 1. Find the radius (one-half of the diameter).
$20 \div 2 = 10$ miles (radius)

Step 2. Apply the formula for the area of a circle.
$A = (\pi)r^2$
$A = 3.14 \times 10^2$
$A = 3.14 \times 100$
$A = 314$ square miles (area)

VOLUME

Volume is the space occupied by a solid figure. A *solid*, or three-dimensional object, has a flat base and height (sometimes called depth). Volume is measured in cubic units.

A *rectangular solid* has length, width, and height. The formula for finding its cubic measure is length times width times height. Thus,

$$V = lwh.$$

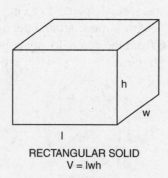

RECTANGULAR SOLID
$V = lwh$

A *cube* is a solid whose length, width, and height are the same. The volume of a cube is one side "cubed"—or one side raised to the third power. Thus,

$$V = s^3.$$

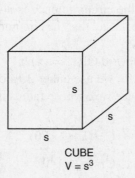

CUBE
$V = s^3$

A solid in which both bases are circles in parallel planes is called a *cylinder*. The volume of a cylinder is the area of its base (a circle) times its height. Thus,

$$V = (\pi)r^2h.$$

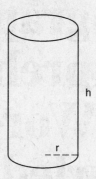

CIRCULAR CYLINDER
$V = \pi r^2 h$

Example: Find the difference between the capacity of a rectangular solid measuring 3' by 5' by 10' and a cylinder with a radius of 7' and a height of 3'.

Step 1. Find the volume of the rectangular solid.

$V = lwh$

$V = 3' \times 5' \times 10'$

$V = 150$ cubic feet

Step 2. Find the volume of the cylinder.

$V = (\pi)r^2h$

$V = 3\dfrac{1}{7} \times 7^2 \times 3$

$V = \dfrac{22}{7} \times 49 \times 3$

$V = 22 \times 7 \times 3$

$V = 462$ cubic feet

Step 3. Find the difference between both volumes.

$462 - 150 = 312$ cubic feet

6 Paragraph Comprehension and Word Knowledge Review

Paragraph Comprehension

The paragraph comprehension part of the ASVAB tests your ability to understand what you read. It does this by asking multiple-choice questions based on passages that vary in length from one to five paragraphs of about 30 to 120 words. Each passage is used for one to five questions.

Reading comprehension involves several abilities: the ability to recognize main ideas; the ability to recall details; the ability to make inferences about the material in a passage; the ability to apply the material in the passage to other material; the ability to recognize and understand sequential, cause/effect, and comparative relationships; and the ability to paraphrase or summarize a passage.

FINDING THE MAIN IDEA

The main idea is the most important point the author wants the reader to understand about the subject matter of a paragraph or passage. Sometimes the main idea is stated directly by the author and sometimes it is implied rather than stated.

Whenever you are asked to determine a passage's main idea, always check the opening and closing sentences of each paragraph. Authors typically provide readers with a "topic sentence" that expresses a paragraph's main idea succinctly. Although such topic sentences may appear anywhere in the paragraph, they often are the opening or closing sentence.

Example

The world faces a serious problem of overpopulation. Right now many people starve from lack of adequate food. Efforts are being made to increase the rate of food production, but the number of people to be fed increases at a faster rate.

In this paragraph, the main idea is stated directly in the opening sentence. You know that the passage will be about "a serious problem of overpopulation." Like a heading or caption, the topic sentence sets the stage, getting your mind ready for what follows in the paragraph.

Example

> During the later years of the American Revolution, the Articles of Confederation government was formed. This government suffered severely from a lack of power. Each state distrusted the others and gave little authority to the central, or federal, government. The Articles of Confederation produced a government that could not raise money from taxes, prevent Indian raids, or force the British out of the United States.

What is the topic sentence in the preceding paragraph? Certainly the paragraph is about the Articles of Confederation. However, is the key idea in the first sentence or in the second sentence? In this instance, the *second* sentence does a better job of giving you the key to this paragraph—the lack of centralized power that characterized the Articles of Confederation. The sentences that complete the paragraph relate more to the idea of "lack of power" than to the time when the government was formed. Don't assume that the topic sentence is always the first sentence of a paragraph.

Example

> They had fewer men available as soldiers. Less than one third of the railroads and only a small portion of the nation's industrial production was theirs. For most of the war their coastline was blockaded by Northern ships. It is a tribute to Southern leadership and the courage of the people that they were not defeated for four years.

In this case you will note that the passage builds up to its main point. The topic sentence is the last one.

As we mentioned previously, you may also find that the main idea is not expressed directly at all, but can only be inferred from the selection as a whole.

Example

> The plane landed at 4 P.M. As the door opened, the crowd burst into a long, noisy demonstration. The waiting mob surged against the police guard lines. Women were screaming. Teenagers were yelling for autographs or souvenirs. The visitor smiled and waved at his fans.

The main idea of the paragraph is not expressed, but it is clear that some popular hero or famous personality is being welcomed enthusiastically at the airport.

To help find the main idea in a reading passage on the test, ask yourself these questions:

1. Who or what is this paragraph about?
2. What aspect of this subject is the author talking about?
3. What is the author trying to get across about this aspect of the subject?

In addition, look for signal words in the passage—words like *again, also, as well as, furthermore, moreover,* and *significantly*. These signal words may call your attention to the main idea.

FINDING DETAILS

In developing the main idea of a passage, a writer will make statements to support his or her point. The writer may give examples to illustrate the idea, or facts and statistics to support it. She may give reasons why the statement that is the main idea is true, or arguments for or against a position stated as the main idea. The writer may also define a complex term, or give a number of qualities of a complicated belief (such as democracy). He may also classify a number of objects within a larger category, or use descriptive details to develop an idea and to help the reader envision the situation. Finally, the writer may compare two ideas or objects (show how they are similar) or contrast them (show how they are different).

Note how the author of the following paragraph uses supporting details.

Episodic memories relate to our individual lives, recalling what we have done and the kinds of experiences we have had. When you recall your first date, the time you fell off your bicycle, or what you felt like when you graduated from high school, you are recalling episodic memories. The information in episodic memory is connected with specific times and places....

To help you understand the term *episodic memory,* the author gives three examples in the second sentence. These examples are supporting details.

To answer questions about supporting details, you *must* find a word or group of words in the passage that supports your choice of answer. The following techniques should help:

1. Look for key words (nouns and verbs) in the question stem and the answer choices.
2. Run your eye down the passage, looking for those key words or their synonyms.
3. Reread the part of the paragraph or passage that contains the key word or its synonym.

MAKING INFERENCES

You make inferences by putting together ideas that are expressed by the author to arrive at other ideas that are not. In other words, you draw conclusions from the information the author presents. You do this by locating relevant details and determining their relationships—time sequence, place sequence, cause and effect, and so on.

In inference questions you must put two and two together and see what you get; the passage never tells you directly what the answer is. Inference questions require you to use your own judgment. You must not take anything directly stated by the author as an inference. Instead, you must look for clues in the passage that you can use in coming up with your own conclusion. You should choose as your answer a statement that is a logical development of the information the author has provided. Remember that in answering inference questions you must go beyond the obvious, beyond what the author explicitly states, to look for logical implications of what the author says.

Let's try to apply these skills to representative passages you will encounter in the paragraph comprehension part of the test.

Family camping has been described as the "biggest single growth industry in the booming travel/leisure market." Camping ranges from backpacking to living in motor homes with complete creature comforts. It is both an end in itself and a magic carpet to a wide variety of other forms of outdoor recreation.

It can be inferred from the passage that the LEAST luxurious form of camping is

A backpacking
B travel trailers
C camping trailers
D motor homes

The answer is A. This question requires you to make an inference from the information in the passage. The second sentence in the paragraph refers to the range of camping—from backpacking to the "creature comforts" of rolling homes. From this it can be inferred that backpacking is the least luxurious form of camping.

UNDERSTANDING THE ORGANIZATION OF THE MATERIAL

Questions on a reading passage may also test your understanding of the organization of the ideas presented and their relationship to one another. Authors generally organize material in predictable and logical ways to make it easier for the reader to understand. Recognizing common patterns of organization increases understanding, recall, and speed.

Ideas may be organized in a sequential or spatial pattern, or a cause-and-effect relationship can be expressed. Ideas may also be compared or contrasted with one another, perhaps in an arguable or opposing position. A reading passage may also present a solution to a problem or problems mentioned, or a conclusion may be drawn from ideas stated or implied.

Sequential Organization

A *sequence is a series of steps or events in which order is important.* If the sequence is chrono- logical, or time-based, the events are described or mentioned in the order in which they occurred. Clues to sequential organization of ideas include cardinal numbers (*1, 2, 3,* etc.), ordinal numbers (*first, second, third,* etc.), transition words (*next, later, then, finally*), and dates or other words referring to time (*next year, the following winter, in 1992, ten weeks later,* etc.).

Example

If you are stung by a bee, first remove the stinger. Next, apply a paste of baking soda and water. Then, apply ice or cold water to help reduce the pain. If the pain is severe or you are allergic to the insect, seek medical help immediately.

Spatial Organization

When the organization is spatial, the physical arrangement of a place or object is described. Clue words include *above, below, next to, in front of, in back of, to the right of, to the left of*.

Example

Taste buds are distributed across the tongue, but the distribution is uneven, and cer- tain areas of the tongue are more sensitive to certain fundamental tastes than other areas…. The tip of the tongue is most sensitive to sweetness, but the portion just behind the tip is most sensitive to salty tastes. Only the sides of the tongue are very sensitive to sour tastes, and the rear specializes in bitter tastes.

Cause and Effect

A reading passage may include reasons why something happened and the results that occurred. For example, a history passage may present the events leading up to a war, or a science passage may list causes of the greenhouse effect and its effect, in turn, on global climate. Often, the relationship is presented as a *chain of events,* with one or more events leading to or resulting in another. Clue words include *for this reason, resulted in, because, consequently, since, thus*.

Example

By the year 2020, there will be approximately one retired American for every two working Americans. In these large numbers, older Americans will become an increas- ingly powerful political force, and political issues of concern to the elderly—such as special housing, medical benefits, and reduced levels of employment—will become issues taken more seriously by elected officials.

Opposing or Similar Ideas

A reading passage may present the similarities or differences between ideas, people, places, or other things. The presentation may focus on similarities in a *comparison*; clue words include *like, similarly, likewise, in like manner, also.* Or, the presentation may focus on differences in presenting a *contrast*; clue words include *however, unlike, in contrast, on the other hand, versus, nevertheless*.

Example

> The American farm problem often centers on supply exceeding demand and farm policies that foster surplus production. This is not true in most other parts of the world, where countries cannot produce enough food to support their own population and must import food or face famine.

Solution to a Problem

In this organization pattern, the author presents a problem or describes a situation that is causing difficulty and presents or suggests solutions or remedies. Clue words include *problem, cause, effects, answers, remedies.*

Example

> In one study, students who lived in dormitories near an area in which earthquakes occurred frequently simply denied the seriousness of the situation and the possible danger they were in.

(In this case, the solution—an unrealistic one—was simply to ignore the problem.)

DRAWING A CONCLUSION

A conclusion is a logical inference based on information presented or implied. If you read a passage critically, you follow the author's train of thought and arrive at logical conclusions. An author may expect a reader to draw the conclusion, or he or she may state it, often using clue words such as *thus, therefore, in conclusion,* or *hence*.

The sample passage that follows is about disabled Americans. The reader can conclude that legislation has made progress in moving the disabled into society's mainstream, although the author does not say so directly. Incidentally, you should note the sequence pattern in this passage.

Example

> A major goal for the disabled is easier access to the mainstream of society. The 1973 Rehabilitation Act has moved them toward this goal. So has the Education for All Handicapped Children Act of 1975, which mandates that all children, however severe their disability, receive a free, appropriate education. Before the legislation, one million handicapped children were receiving no education and another three million were receiving an inappropriate one (as in the case of a blind child who is not taught Braille or is not provided with instructional materials in Braille). In 1987, Congress enacted the Employment Opportunities for Disabled Americans Act, which allows disabled individuals to earn a moderate income without losing their Medicaid health coverage.

How to Build Your Vocabulary

WHY VOCABULARY

In a classic study conducted by Johnson O'Connor of the Human Engineering Institute and reported in an article called "Vocabulary and Success," the main finding was that a good vocabulary was more frequently to be found among successful people (persons in important positions) than any other single factor. That doesn't mean that everyone with a good vocabulary is necessarily successful, but it is generally true that successful people have good vocabularies.

This discovery should really come as no surprise. A vocabulary is not merely a collection of words. It is all the ideas for which words stand. Take, for example, the following words taken from the study of government.

anarchy	fascism
autocracy	federal
autonomy	oligarchy
democracy	republic
dictatorship	totalitarian

These words all identify systems of government. Anyone who knows the meanings of these ten words has an understanding of the most widely known kinds of government and what each represents. Or, to choose a more technical (and more dramatic) area, that of space exploration, a knowledgeable person will have as part of his vocabulary such words as:

abort	injection
apogee	orbit
burnout	perigee
cislunar	phasing
docking	telemetry

among others. The point is that the person with a good vocabulary has more ideas (about government, for example) and more knowledge (about space exploration, for example) and such people are always in demand in business and in the professions.

HOW TO ADD A WORD TO YOUR VOCABULARY

The best way to find words to build your vocabulary is by reading, and not the most difficult books, either. Research has shown that, to build your vocabulary, it is better to read books just a little bit more difficult than the level you find to be easy. A few new words a page are better than many. Let's take a few examples of how reading can help you add words to your vocabulary.

A fine American short story starts with the sentence:

"It was late in the afternoon, and the light was *waning*."

The sentence itself provides a clue to the meaning of the word "waning." "Late in the afternoon" the light grows dim. Reference to the dictionary confirms this guess at the meaning from the clues provided in the sentence. One definition reads: "to grow dim, as a light." It will help you retain the meaning of the word if you jot it down in a small vocabulary notebook. The notation should include the following:

Word (correctly spelled)	Meaning	Example of use
wane	grow dim	The light began to *wane*.

The final clincher is your own proper use of the word in another sentence. One possibility might be: "His eyesight began to *wane*."

In the above example, you can find these five steps to take if you want to master a word.

1. Find the word as it is used in the company of other words on the printed page. Reading is the best way to do this.
2. Make a temporary judgment about the meaning of the word from the clues contained in the sentence where it is found—the context.
3. Check your opinion of its meaning by referring to a dictionary at your first opportunity.
4. If possible, add the word to a continuing list you develop in a small pocket-size notebook. Include the meaning and a typical context (the sentence in which it was found).
5. Use it yourself in the same or, preferably, in a new context (word setting).

Now try your hand at the next example.

This is taken from another fine American short story.

"It was a *desolate* country in those days; geographers still described it as The Great American Desert, and in looks it deserved the title."

How would you master the word "desolate"?

A temporary judgment about its meaning would be based on the clue in the sentence that it was similar to a desert. But what quality or characteristic of a desert does it stand for? You find out by checking with the dictionary. It is in its alphabetical place between Des Moines and desolation. Four meanings are given and you start with the first: "lonely; solitary." That is the original meaning and the most precise. It is best to choose the first definition in preference to the others if it fits the sentence. In this case, the others are all possible extensions of the main meaning, "lonely": uninhabited; laid waste; forlorn. Your notebook notation might read something like this:

Word	Meaning	Example of use
desolate	lonely	The station was in a desolate part of the city.

There is one more important dictionary clue in the entry for *desolate*. The origin of the word is given: [>L. *de-* intens. + *solus,* alone]. The word comes to us from Latin: *de* is an intensifier, meaning *very,* but the important clue is the Latin word *solus,* meaning *alone.* Other English words use forms of the Latin word *solus.* These are some that might occur to you: sole, solitaire, solitary, solitude, solo.

In fact, many English words include Latin, Greek, and other languages in their histories. One of our most frequently used words is an example of this. The word television came to English from the French: télévision. But télévision was not originally a French word. In fact, its journey through history includes both Latin and Greek.

> *tele* from the Greek *tele*, meaning at a distance, or far off
>
> *vision* from the Latin *visio*, meaning see

Put the two parts together and you have a good definition of television: pictures taken at a distance that you can see.

STUDY THE PARTS OF A WORD

This means of vocabulary building requires you to work with three elements of a word: root, prefixes, and suffixes.

The one essential part of any word is the root. It may be a word in itself (for example, *flex*) or a word element from which other words are formed (for example, *aud*). Knowing many word roots is one way of multiplying your vocabulary, for each root can lead you to the understanding of several words. We'll look at an example after we define the other two elements; prefixes and suffixes.

A prefix is a syllable or group of syllables added to the beginning of a word which changes its meaning. Let's return to the example *flex.* By itself, it means to bend or contract. The context is the human body. You can flex an arm; you can flex a muscle. If you add the prefix *re* to the beginning of the root, *flex*, you get a new word, *reflex*, with a new meaning. *Reflex* describes an action which you cannot control, such as a sneeze.

We can further change the meaning of the root *flex* by adding a suffix. A suffix is a word part (a syllable or group of syllables) added to the end of a word that changes its meaning. If you add the syllables *ible* to the end of the root, that is, if you add the suffix *ible*, you get another new word, *flexible*, with a new meaning. *Flexible* means *able to bend without breaking* or, in a broader meaning, *able to adjust to change*.

It is also possible to add both a prefix and a suffix to a root and get still another word. If you add both the prefix *in* (meaning *not*) and the suffix *ible* (meaning *able*), you get a new word, *inflexible. Inflexible* means *unbending* or, in a broader meaning, *stubborn* and *unable to adjust to change*.

To give you some idea of the *flex* family of words, here are a number of other words (*flect* is another form of *flex*).

flexibility	reflection
deflect	circumflex
inflection	genuflect

Here is a list of widely used prefixes in English. Make up at least one word using each prefix and check your accuracy in the dictionary.

Prefix	Meaning	Word
a	no, not	
ab	away, from	
ad	to	
amphi	both	
ante	before	
anti	against	
be	completely	
circum	around	
contra	against	
de	from, away	
dia	across	
eu	well	
ex	out of	
extra	beyond	
fore	before	
hyper	above	
hypo	below, under	
in	into	
in	not	
inter	between	
intra	within	
mis	wrong	
ob	against	
out	from, beyond	
over	above, too much	
para	beside	
peri	around	
poly	many	
post	after	
pre	before	
pro	forward	
re	back, again	
retro	back	
se	apart	
sub	under	
super	above, beyond	
syn	together, with	
trans	across	
ultra	beyond	
un	not	
under	below	

Here is a list of widely used word roots. Make up at least one word using each root and check your word in the dictionary. Try to combine the root with one of the prefixes we have listed for you.

Prefix	Meaning	Word
act	do	
anim	spirit, life	
anthro	man	
ann(u)	year	
aqua	water	
aud	hear	
bene	well	
cas	fall	
chrom	color	
chron	time	
ced(e)	go	
cid(e)	kill	
clud(e)	close	
cor	heart	
corp	body	
cred	believe	
curr	run	
dem	people	
dic(t)	say	
do(n)	give	
duc(t)	lead	
fac(t)	make	
fer	carry	
fin	end	
flect	bend	
flu(x)	flow	
fract	break	
frater	brother	
graph	write	
gress	walk	
hetero	different	
homo	same	
hydro(o)	water	
ject	throw	
jur(e)	swear	
litera	letter	
lith	stone	
magn	large, great	
mal	evil	
man(u)	hand	
mar	sea	
mater	mother	
ment	mind	
met(er)	measure	
micro	small	
mit	send	
mono	one	
mort	death	
mot	move	
multi	many	
nom(y)	science of	
norm	rule	
nov	new	
ortho	right	

Prefix	Meaning	Word
pan	all	
pater	father	
path	suffer, feel	
ped	foot	
pend	hang	
phil	love	
phon	sound	
psych	mind	
pugn	fight	
rupt	break	
sci	know	
scrib	write	
sect	cut	
sol	alone	
soph	wise	
spect	look	
struct	build	
tele	far	
temp	time	
tract	draw	
vad	go	
ven(t)	come	
vert	turn	
vis	see	
vict	conquer	
voc, voke	call	
volv	turn	

The following is a list of prefixes, both in Greek and Latin, that indicate a number. Find one word for each prefix and add it to your vocabulary.

Meaning	Latin		Greek	
half	semi	....	hemi	....
one	uni	....	mono	....
two	bi	....	di	....
three	tri	....	tri	....
four	quadr	....	tetra	....
five	quint	....	penta	....
six	sex	....	hexa	....
seven	sept	....	hepta	....
eight	oct	....	octa	....
nine	nona	....	(rarely used)	....
ten	dec	....	deca	....
hundred	cent	....	(rarely used)	....
thousand	mill	....	kilo	....

LEARN THE SYNONYMS AND ANTONYMS OF A WORD

A synonym is a word that has the same or nearly the same meaning as another word in the language. An antonym is a word that has the opposite or nearly the opposite meaning from another word. You may ask, "How do I find these synonyms and antonyms?" The answer is again: "In the dictionary." The paperback pocket-size dictionary, because of its size, will give you little help in this particular technique. You need to use a desk-size dictionary.

Let's take *Webster's New World Dictionary of the American Language*, College Edition's listing of synonyms for the word *happy*.

SYN.—happy generally suggests a feeling of great pleasure, contentment, etc. (a *happy* marriage); glad implies more strongly an exultant feeling of joy (your letter made her so *glad*), but both glad and happy are commonly used in merely polite formulas expressing gratification (I'm *glad*, or *happy*, that you could come); cheerful implies a steady display of bright spirits, optimism, etc. (He's always *cheerful* in the morning); joyful and joyous both imply great elation and rejoicing, the former generally because of a particular event, and the latter as a matter of usual temperament (the *joyful* throngs, a *joyous* family). See also *lucky.*—*ANT.* sad

In addition to giving you four synonyms for *happy*, the entry distinguishes among them. It also gives you a context (a group of words in which the synonym appears) for each synonym. And it refers you to *lucky*, under which you find two more synonyms—*fortunate* and *providential*. Finally, it gives you one antonym, *sad*, which itself becomes a clue to five other antonyms—*sorrowful, melancholy, dejected, depressed,* and *doleful*. From the one word, *happy*, the dictionary has led us to seven synonyms and five antonyms, an additional dozen words.

Similarly, the word *large* will lead you to synonyms *big* and *great* and to antonyms *small, little, diminutive, minute, tiny, miniature,* and *petite*.

It is easier to learn related words and remember them than to learn words in isolation. Surprisingly, it is often a fact that one sign you're learning the meaning of a word is when you make a mistake in using its antonym or opposite. You are associating the word incorrectly and incompletely, but the point is you *are* making an association.

LEARN HOMONYMS
English seems to have so many words that sound the same but are spelled differently and have different meanings. These are homonyms.

Examples:

1. A full moon *shone* brightly last night.
   The film was *shown* on TV last night.
2. Once we nail up this *board*, the tool shed will be finished.
   I was very *bored* during the speech.
3. The *pain* in my right shoulder gets worse in the cold.
   I have to replace the broken *pane* of glass.

LEARN TO ASSOCIATE WORDS BY TOPIC OR IDEA
One of the most helpful aids to vocabulary building is a book based on this principle. It is called *Roget's International Thesaurus* or the treasury of words of Peter Mark Roget, the man who first thought out the organization of words into 1,000 related groups. Roget's thesaurus can't be used by itself. It must be used together with a dictionary, since the thesaurus merely lists the words by idea. For example, under the idea of GREATNESS, the word *consummate* is listed as one of the adjectives. The word *consummate* fits into the general idea of greatness, but it refers to great mastery of a skill, both to be admired or to be disapproved of, as in "with consummate artistry" or "a consummate liar." That is why the thesaurus *must* be used together with a dictionary.

While we're on the subject of association as a way of learning new words, there is another kind of association that you can make: associate words that deal with a specific topic or subject. A good place to start is your own interests. Let's try foods and food preparation. Words such as the following might come to mind: *aspic, baste, sauté, truss, buffet, entrée, ragout, simmer, braise, compote, cuisine, curried, garnish, soufflé, meringue, hors d'oeuvres*.

Now for a subject that concerns all of us—health. The following words are the stock in trade of the medical doctor: *abscess, allergy, anemia, cataract, cyst, eczema, embolism, gangrene, hemorrhage, hepatitis, metabolism, neuralgia, pleurisy, sciatica, stroke, tumor*.

And anyone with an interest in motors and tools should be familiar with the terms *carburetor, condenser, compression, gear ratio, piston, socket wrench, dynamometer, emission, vacuum.*

Many books have glossaries, lists of difficult words with definitions. When you read a book on a particular subject, see if it has a glossary, and if it does, study the new words and their definitions.

LEARN TO USE CORRECT ABBREVIATIONS

Many people either misuse or don't correctly understand three common abbreviations: etc., e.g., and i.e.

Etc. is short for the Latin phrase *et cetera*, which means, "and so on," literally, "and other things." It should be used only after a series of at least three things, as in "people, animals, places, etc."

E.g. is short for the Latin phrase *exempli gratia*, which means "for example." It is used when you want to cite an example of a general statement, as in "Not all birds can fly, e.g., the ostrich, which can't fly but can run very fast."

I.e. is an abbreviation of the Latin *id est*, which means "in other words." This is the most misused abbreviation of the three, i.e., be careful how you use it.

LEARN ACTION AND DESCRIPTIVE WORDS

If you would like to build your vocabulary and work at improving your writing skills, try increasing the number of action and descriptive words you use. You can start by using the word *get* less frequently and using more precise verbs.

Less Interesting	Precise
We should **get** a new typewriter for the office.	We should (**buy, rent, lease**) a new typewriter for the office.
Milton tried to **get** me to take his side in the debate.	Milton tried to **persuade** me to take his side in the debate.
The first baseman **got** hit by the pitcher's fast ball.	The pitcher's fast ball **struck** the first baseman.

A Basic 1,100-Word Vocabulary

To help you build your vocabulary, we have selected 1,100 words which every high school graduate should know. They are grouped into lists of nouns, verbs, and adjectives. You should use these lists and definitions together with a good dictionary such as *Webster's New World Dictionary of the American Language*. For each word, we have provided a definition that is most widely used but is often far removed from the first or literal meaning. You may wish to study other meanings of each word. We have also provided many words, sentences, and phrases to show you how the particular word should be used.

300 USEFUL NOUNS

ACCESS (means of) approach or admittance (e.g., to records)

ACCORD agreement

ADAGE proverb (as "Better late than never")

AFFLUENCE abundance; wealth (e.g., age of ____)

AGENDA list of things to be done or discussed (e.g., at a meeting)

ALACRITY brisk willingness (e.g., agreed with ____)

ALIAS assumed name (e.g., Fred Henry, John Doe)

ANIMOSITY great hatred (e.g., toward strangers)

ANTHOLOGY collection of writings or other creative work such as songs

APATHY indifference (e.g., toward poverty)

APEX the highest point (e.g., ____ of a triangle)

ATLAS book of maps

AUDACITY boldness

AVARICE greed for wealth

AWE feeling of respect and wonder (e.g., in ____ of someone's power)

BEACON guiding light (e.g., of knowledge)

BENEDICTION blessing

BIGOTRY unwillingness to allow others to have different opinions and beliefs from one's own

BLEMISH defect (e.g., on one's record)

BONDAGE slavery

BOON benefit (e.g., a ____ to business)

BRAWL noisy fight

BREVITY shortness

BROCHURE pamphlet (e.g., a travel ____)

BULWARK strong protection (e.g., a ____ against corruption)

CALIBER quality (e.g., a person of high ____)

CAMOUFLAGE disguise, usually in war, changing the appearance of persons or equipment

CASTE social class or position

CATASTROPHE sudden disaster (e.g., an earthquake)

CHAGRIN feeling of deep disappointment

CHRONICLE historical record

CLAMOR uproar

CLEMENCY mercy (e.g., toward a prisoner)

CONDOLENCE expression of sympathy (e.g., extended ____ to a bereaved)

CONNOISSEUR expert judge (e.g., of paintings, food)

CONSENSUS general agreement

CONTEXT words or ideas just before or after a given word or idea (e.g., meaning of a word in a given ____)

CRITERION standard of judgment (e.g., good or poor by this ____)

CRUX the essential point (e.g., the ____ of the matter)

CYNIC one who doubts the good intentions of others

DATA known facts (e.g., ____ were found through research)

DEARTH scarcity (e.g., of talent)

DEBACLE general defeat (e.g., in a battle)

DEBUT first appearance before an audience (e.g., actor, pianist)

DELUGE great flood (e.g., rain or, in a special sense, mail)

DEPOT warehouse

DESTINY predetermined fate

DETRIMENT damage or loss (e.g., it was to his ____)

DIAGNOSIS determining the nature of a disease or a situation

DICTION manner in which words are used in speech (e.g., The radio announcer's ____ was excellent.)

DILEMMA situation requiring a choice between two unpleasant courses of action (e.g., He was in a ____.)

DIN loud continuing noise

DIRECTIVE a general order (e.g., from an executive or military commander)

DISCORD disagreement

DISCREPANCY inconsistency (e.g., in accounts, in testimony)

DISCRETION freedom of choice (e.g., He was given ____ to spend the money as he saw fit.)

DISSENT difference of opinion (e.g., from a decision by a higher authority)

DROUGHT long spell of dry weather

EGOTIST one who judges everything only as it affects his own interest; a self-centered person

ELITE choice part (e.g., of society)

ENTERPRISE an important project

ENVIRONMENT surrounding influences or conditions

EPITOME typical representation (e.g., She was the ____ of beauty.)

EPOCH period of time identified by an important person or event (e.g., the ____ of space flight)

ERA period of time marked by an important person or event (e.g., the Napoleonic ____)

ESSENCE basic nature (e.g., ____ of the matter)

ETIQUETTE rules of social behavior which are generally accepted

EXCERPT passage from a book or a document

EXODUS departure, usually of large numbers

FACET side or aspect (e.g., of a problem)

FACSIMILE exact copy

FALLACY mistaken idea; reasoning which contains an error

FANTASY imagination (e.g., He indulged in ____.)

FEUD continued deadly hatred (e.g., between two families)

FIASCO complete, humiliating failure

FIEND inhumanly cruel person

FINALE last part of a performance

FLAIR natural talent (e.g., for sports)

FLAW defect

FOCUS central point (e.g., of attention)

FOE enemy

FORMAT physical appearance or arrangement (e.g., of a book)

FORTE one's strong point (e.g., math, sports)

FORTITUDE steady courage (e.g., when in trouble)

FORUM a gathering for the discussion of public issues

FOYER entrance hall (e.g., to a building or dwelling)

FRAUD deliberate deception

FRICTION rubbing of the surface of one thing against the surface of another

FUNCTION purpose served by a person, object, or organization

FUROR outburst of excitement (e.g., over a discovery)

GAMUT the whole range (e.g., of experiences)

GAZETTEER geographical dictionary, usually accompanying an atlas

GENESIS origin (e.g., of a plan)

GHETTO section of a city where members of a particular group (formerly religious, now racial) live

GIST essential content (e.g., of a speech or an article)

GLUTTON one who overeats or who indulges in anything to excess

GRIEVANCE complaint made against someone responsible for a situation believed to be unjust

HAVOC great damage and destruction (e.g., wreak ____ on)

HAZARD danger

HERITAGE inheritance either of real wealth or of a tradition

HOAX deliberate attempt to trick someone, either seriously or as a joke

HORDE crowd, multitude

HORIZON limit (of knowledge, experience, vision, or ambition)

HUE shade of color

HYSTERIA wild emotional outburst

IDIOM expression peculiar to a language which has a different meaning from the literal meaning of the words which make it up (e.g., hit the road)

ILLUSION idea or impression different from reality

IMAGE likeness or reflected impression of a person or object

IMPETUS moving force

INCENTIVE spur or motive to do something (e.g., profit ____)

INCUMBENT present holder of an office

INFIRMITY physical defect

INFLUX flowing in (e.g., of money into banks, tourists into a country)

INFRACTION violation of a rule or a law

INITIATIVE desire or ability to take the first step in carrying out some action (often a new plan or idea)

INNOVATION introduction of a new idea or method

INTEGRITY moral and intellectual honesty and uprightness

INTERIM meantime (e.g., in the ____)

INTERLUDE period of time between two events (e.g., ____ between the acts of a play)

INTRIGUE secret plot

INTUITION knowledge through instinct rather than thought

IOTA very small amount

ITINERARY route followed on a trip, actual or planned

JEOPARDY risk of harm (e.g., put into ____)

KEYNOTE main theme (e.g., he sounded the ____ of the convention)

LARCENY theft (e.g., they couldn't decide whether it was grand or petty ____)

LAYMAN one who is not a member of a particular profession (e.g., from the point of view of a ____)

LEGACY material or spiritual inheritance (e.g., ____ from a parent)

LEGEND story or stories passed on from generation to generation and often considered to be true

LEGION large number

LIAISON contact between two or more groups (e.g., ____ between headquarters and field units)

LORE body of traditional knowledge (e.g., nature ____)

MALADY disease (e.g., incurable ____)

MANEUVER skillful move (e.g., a clever ____)

MANIA abnormal absorption (e.g., She had a ____ for clothes.)

MARATHON a foot race lasting 26 miles, 385 yards; any contest requiring endurance

MAVERICK one who acts independently rather than according to an organizational pattern

MAXIM a saying which provides a rule of conduct (e.g., Look before you leap.)

MEDIUM means of communication (e.g., the ____ of radio)

MEMENTO object which serves as a reminder (e.g., a ____ of the war)

METROPOLIS main city of a state or region; any very large city

MILIEU surroundings

MORALE state of mind as it affects possible future action (e.g., The troops had good ____.)

MORES well-established customs (e.g., the ____ of a society)

MULTITUDE a large number

MYRIAD a large number of varied people or things

MYTH a story which is a traditional explanation of some occurrence, usually in nature (e.g., the ____ of Atlas holding up the heavens on his shoulders)

NICHE a suitable and desirable place (e.g., He found his ____ in the business organization.)

NOMAD wanderer

NOSTALGIA desire to return to past experiences or associations

OASIS a place which provides relief from the usual conditions (e.g., an ____ of peace in a troubled world)

OBLIVION place or condition in which one is completely forgotten

ODYSSEY long journey

OMEN something which is believed to predict a future event (e.g., an evil ____)

OPTIMUM the best possible quantity or quality (e.g., He participated to the ____.)

OVATION enthusiastic reception usually accompanied by generous applause (e.g., He received a tumultuous ____.)

OVERSIGHT failure to include something through carelessness (e.g., His name was omitted because of an ____.)

OVERTURE first step, which is intended to lead to others in either action or discussion (e.g., He made a peace ____.); the introduction to an opera or other extended musical piece

PAGEANT public spectacle in the form of a stage performance or a parade (e.g., a historical ____)

PANACEA something considered a cure for all diseases or problems

PANORAMA a clear view of a very broad area

PARADOX statement of a truth which appears to contradict itself (e.g., a 20-year-old who had only five birthdays because he was born on February 29).

PASTIME way of spending leisure time (e.g., He took up golf as a ____.)

PAUCITY scarcity (e.g., a ____ of nuclear scientists)

PAUPER very poor person

PEER an equal in age, social standing, ability, or other feature

PHENOMENON a natural occurrence such as the tides

PHOBIA fear of something which is so great as to be unreasonable (e.g., ____ toward cats)

PHYSIQUE build (of the human body)

PILGRIMAGE long trip to some place worthy of respect or devotion

PINNACLE highest point (e.g., the ____ of power)

PITFALL trap

PITTANCE very small amount or sum of money (e.g., He survived on a ____.)

PLATEAU area of level land located at a height

PLIGHT condition, usually unfavorable (e.g., the sorry ____ of the refugees)

POISE calm and controlled manner of behavior (e.g., He showed ____ in difficult situations.)

POPULACE the common people

POSTERITY future generations (e.g., leave a peaceful world to our ____)

PRECEDENT event or regulation which serves as an example or provides the basis for approval of a later action (e.g., set a ____)

PREDICAMENT unpleasant situation from which it is difficult to free oneself (e.g., He found himself in a ____.)

PREFACE introductory statement to a book or speech

PRELUDE something which is preliminary to some act or work which is more important

PREMISE statement from which a conclusion is logically drawn (e.g., Granted the ____ that …, we may conclude ….)

PREMIUM amount added to the usual payment or charge (e.g., He paid a ____ for the seats.)

PRESTIGE respect achieved through rank, achievement, or reputation

PRETEXT reason given as a cover-up for the true purpose of an action (e.g., He gave as a ____ for stealing it his sentimental attachment to the ring.)

PRIORITY something which comes before others in importance (e.g., He gave ____ to his studies.)

PROCESS step-by-step system for accomplishing some purpose (e.g., the ____ of legislation)

PROSPECT possibility for the future (e.g., the ____ of peace)

PROVISO requirement that something be done, usually made in writing

PROWESS superior ability (e.g., ____ in athletics)

PROXIMITY nearness

PSEUDONYM assumed name, usually by an author (e.g., Mark Twain, ____ of Samuel Clemens)

PUN play on words depending on two different meanings or sounds of the same word (e.g., Whether life is worth living depends on the *liver.*)

QUALM uneasy doubt about some action (e.g., He had a ____ about running for office.)

QUANDARY uncertainty about a choice between two courses of action (e.g., He was in a ____ about whether to choose law or medicine.)

QUERY question

QUEST search (e.g., ____ for knowledge)

RAPPORT harmonious relationship (e.g., ____ between teacher and pupil)

RARITY something not commonly found (e.g., A talent like his is a ____.)

REFUGE place to which one can go for protection (e.g., He found ____ in the church.)

REMNANT remaining part (e.g., ____ of the troops)

REMORSE deep feeling of guilt for some bad act (e.g., He felt ____ at having insulted his friend.)

RENDEZVOUS a meeting or a place for meeting

RENOWN fame (e.g., an actor of great ____)

REPAST meal

REPLICA an exact copy (e.g., ____ of a painting)

REPRIMAND severe criticism in the form of a scolding (e.g., He received a ____ from his superior.)

REPRISAL return of something in kind (e.g., ____ for an injury—"An eye for an eye")

RESIDUE remainder, what is left over

RESOURCES assets, either material or spiritual, which are available for use

RESPITE temporary break which brings relief (e.g., ____ from work)

RESUMÉ summary of work experience and education

REVERENCE feeling of great respect (e.g., ____ for life)

ROBOT one who acts mechanically or like a mechanical person; a self-directed mechanical person

ROSTER list of names (e.g., ____ of guests)

SABOTAGE deliberate damage to vital services of production and supply, usually to those of an enemy in wartime

SAGA long tale, usually of heroic deeds

SALUTATION greeting, written or spoken (e.g., The ____ of a letter may be "Dear Sir.")

SANCTION approval, usually by proper authority

SARCASM cutting remarks

SATIRE attack on someone's behavior by making it appear to be ridiculous

SCAPEGOAT someone who is blamed for the bad deeds of others

SCENT distinctive smell

SCOPE entire area of action or thought (e.g., the ____ of the plan)

SCROLL roll of paper or parchment containing writing

SECT group of people having the same beliefs, usually religious

SEGMENT part or section of a whole (e.g., ____ of a population)

SEMBLANCE outward appearance (e.g., He gave the ____ of a scholar.)

SEQUEL something that follows from what happened or was written before (e.g., ____ to a novel)

SHAM false imitation (e.g., His devotion was a ____ of true love.)

SHEAF bundle either of grain or of papers

SHEEN luster (e.g., of polished furniture)

SILHOUETTE outline drawing in black

SITE location of an object or an action (e.g., original ____ of a building)

SLANDER untruth spoken or spread about someone which damages his reputation

SLOGAN motto which is associated with an action or a cause (e.g., Pike's Peak or Bust!)

SLOPE slant (e.g., ____ of a line); measured from 0 degrees to 90 degrees

SNARE trap

SOLACE comfort (e.g., She found ____ in work.)

SPONSOR one who endorses and supports a person or an activity

SPUR something which moves one to act (e.g., a ____ to sacrifice)

STAMINA ability to fight off physical difficulties such as fatigue

STATURE height reached physically or morally (e.g., a man of great ____)

STATUS standing, social or professional

STIGMA mark of disgrace

STIMULUS any encouragement to act

STRATEGY skillful planning and execution (e.g., the ____ in a battle)

STRIFE conflict (e.g., ____ between labor and management)

SUMMIT the highest point (e.g., the ____ of his career)

SUPPLEMENT amount added to complete something (e.g., ____ to a budget)

SURVEY broad study of a topic (e.g., a ____ of employment)

SUSPENSE tenseness brought about by uncertainty about what will happen

SYMBOL something which is used to stand for something else (e.g., Uncle Sam is a ____ of the United States.)

SYMPTOM indication of something (e.g., ____ of disease)

SYNOPSIS brief summary

TACT ability to say and do the right thing without causing undue offense

TACTICS skillful actions to achieve some purpose (e.g., The ____ he used to win were unfair.)

TALLY record of a score or an account (e.g., the ____ of the receipts)

TANG strong taste or flavor

TECHNIQUE method or skill in doing work (e.g., the ____ of an artist)

TEMPERAMENT natural disposition to act in a certain manner (e.g., He displayed a changeable ____.)

TEMPO pace of activity (e.g., The ____ of life is increasing.)

TENSION mental or emotional strain (e.g., He was under great ____.)

THEME topic of a written work or a talk

THRESHOLD the starting point (e.g., the ____ of a career)

THRIFT ability to save money or spend wisely (e.g., He became wealthy because of ____.)

TINT a shade of a color

TOKEN sign which stands for some object or feeling (e.g., a ____ of esteem)

TONIC something which is a source of energy or vigor

TRADITION customs and beliefs that are transmitted from one generation to another

TRAIT distinguishing feature (e.g., ____ of character)

TRANSITION movement from one situation to another (e.g., ____ from dictatorship to democracy)

TRIBUNAL place of judgment, such as a court

TRIBUTE showing of respect or gratitude (e.g., He paid a ____ to his parents.)

TURMOIL disturbance (e.g., great ____ at the meeting)

TUTOR a private teacher

TYCOON wealthy and powerful businessman

ULTIMATUM a final condition or demand ("Take it or leave it!")

UNREST restless dissatisfaction

UPHEAVAL sudden overthrow, often violent

USAGE established practice or custom

UTENSIL implement which is of use (e.g., a spatula is a common kitchen ____)

UTOPIA ideal place or society

VALOR courage

VENTURE something involving risk

VICINITY neighborhood

VICTOR winner

VIGOR vitality

VIM energy

VOW solemn pledge

WAGER bet

WHIM sudden notion or desire

WOE great sorrow (e.g., He brought ____ to his friends.)

WRATH intense anger (e.g., He poured his ____ on his enemies.)

ZEAL eager desire

ZENITH the highest point

ZEST keen enthusiasm (e.g., ____ for competition)

300 USEFUL VERBS

ABHOR hate

ABSOLVE free from guilt (e.g., for a crime)

ACCEDE agree to (e.g., a request)

ACCELERATE speed up

ACCOST go up and speak to

ADHERE give support to (e.g., a cause)

ADJOURN put off to a later time (e.g., a meeting)

ADVOCATE act in support of (e.g., revolution)

ALLAY calm (e.g., fears)

ALLEGE claim

ALLOT assign (e.g., a share)

ALLUDE refer to (e.g., a book)

ALTER change

ASSENT agree

ATONE make up for (e.g., a sin)

AUGMENT add to

AVERT prevent

BAFFLE puzzle

BAN forbid

BAR exclude

BEFALL happen to

BERATE scold

BESEECH plead

BESTOW grant (used with on or upon)

CEDE give up (e.g., territory)

CENSURE blame

CHAR scorch

CHASTISE punish

CHIDE scold

CITE mention in order to prove something

COERCE force

COLLABORATE work with someone

COMMEND praise

COMPLY act in answer to (e.g., a request)

CONCEDE admit that something is true (e.g., an argument)

CONCUR agree

CONSTRICT squeeze

CULL pick out

CURTAIL cut short or reduce

DEDUCE come to a conclusion from given facts

DEEM consider

DEFER postpone

DEFRAY pay at least part of

DELETE remove or erase (e.g., a word)

DELVE investigate

DEPLETE use up

DEPLORE be sorry about

DEPRIVE keep someone from having or getting something

DESPISE scorn

DETAIN delay temporarily

DETECT uncover something that is not obvious

DETER keep someone from doing something

DETEST hate

DETRACT take away from

DEVOUR eat up greedily

DIGRESS depart from the subject under consideration

DILUTE weaken by adding something less strong to the original (e.g., a mixture)

DISBURSE pay out

DISCERN make out clearly (e.g., a pattern)

DISDAIN look down on with scorn

DISINTEGRATE fall apart

DISMAY dishearten

DISPEL drive away

DISPERSE scatter

DISRUPT break up

DISTORT present incorrectly (e.g., facts)

DIVERGE go in different directions

DIVERT turn from a course (e.g., a stream)

DIVULGE reveal

DON put on (e.g., clothing)

EFFACE blot out

EFFECT bring about (verb); result (noun)

EJECT throw out

ELATE make happy

EMIT give forth (e.g., sounds)

ENCOUNTER meet

ENCROACH intrude on (e.g., property)

ENDEAVOR try

ENDOW provide with (e.g., a desirable quality)

ENHANCE increase the value of

ENSUE follow as a result

ENTREAT plead

ERR make a mistake

ERUPT break out

ESTEEM value

EVADE avoid or escape from someone or something

EVICT expel

EXALT raise to greater heights

EXCEED surpass

EXPEDITE speed up the handling of

EXPLOIT take advantage of a situation or a person

EXTOL praise highly

FALTER stumble

FAMISH starve

FEIGN pretend

FLAUNT show off

FLOURISH thrive

FLOUT defy mockingly

FOIL prevent

FORGO do without

FORSAKE abandon

FRUSTRATE prevent someone from achieving something

GAUGE estimate; measure

HARASS disturb constantly

HEAVE lift and throw

HEED pay attention to (e.g., advice)

HINDER keep back

HOVER hang in the air above a certain spot

HURL throw with force

IGNITE set fire to

IMMERSE plunge completely into a liquid

IMPAIR damage

IMPEDE stand in the way of

IMPLY suggest

INCITE arouse

INCUR bring upon oneself (e.g., criticism)

INDUCE persuade

INDULGE satisfy (e.g., a desire)

INFER come to a conclusion based on something known

INHIBIT restrain

INSTIGATE spur to action

INSTILL put a feeling into someone (e.g., fear)

INTERCEPT interrupt something (or someone) which is on its (his/her) way

INTERROGATE question

INTIMIDATE frighten by making threats

INVOKE call upon

IRK annoy

JAR shake up (e.g., as in a collision)

JEER poke fun at (e.g., as by sarcastic remarks)

LAMENT feel sorrow for

LAUNCH set in motion

LOOM appear in a threatening manner

LOP cut off

LURE tempt

LURK remain hidden

MAGNIFY make larger

MAIM cripple

MIMIC imitate

MOCK ridicule

MOLEST bother

NARRATE tell (e.g., a story)

NAVIGATE steer (e.g., a ship)

NEGATE deny

ORIENT adjust oneself or someone to a situation

OUST expel

PARCH make dry

PEER look closely

PEND remain undecided; hang

PERFECT complete; flawless

PERPLEX puzzle

PERSEVERE continue on a course of action despite difficulties

PERTAIN have reference to

PERTURB upset to a great extent

PERUSE read carefully

PINE long for

PLACATE make calm

PONDER think through thoroughly

PRECLUDE prevent something from happening

PRESCRIBE order (e.g., for use or as a course of action)

PRESUME take for granted

PREVAIL win out over

PROBE investigate thoroughly

PROCURE obtain

PROFESS claim

PROSPER be successful

PROTRUDE project

PROVOKE arouse to action out of irritation

PRY look closely into

QUELL subdue

RAVAGE ruin

REBATE give back, usually part of an amount paid

REBUFF repulse

REBUKE disapprove sharply

RECEDE move backward

RECOMPENSE repay

RECONCILE bring together by settling differences

RECOUP make up for (e.g., something lost)

RECTIFY correct

RECUR happen again

REDEEM buy back; make good a promise; regain honor or reputation

REFRAIN keep from

REFUTE prove false

REIMBURSE pay back

REITERATE repeat

REJECT refuse to take or accept

RELINQUISH give up

REMINISCE recall past happenings

REMIT send (e.g., money)

REMUNERATE pay for work done

RENOUNCE give up (e.g., a claim)

RENOVATE restore (e.g., a house)

REPENT feel regret for (e.g., a sin)

REPLENISH make full again

REPOSE rest

REPRESS hold back (e.g., a feeling)

REPROACH blame

REPUDIATE reject the validity of

REPULSE drive back

RESCIND cancel (e.g., a rule or regulation)

RESPIRE breathe

RESTRAIN hold back

RETAIN keep

RETALIATE return in kind (e.g., a blow for a blow)

RETARD delay

RETORT answer sharply

RETRACT take back (e.g., something said)

RETRIEVE get back

REVERE have deep respect for

REVERT go back to a former condition

REVOKE withdraw or cancel a law or rule

RUPTURE break

SALVAGE save something out of a disaster such as fire

SCALD burn painfully with steam or hot liquid

SCAN look at closely

SCOFF mock

SCORN treat with contempt

SCOUR clean thoroughly; move about widely in a search

SCOWL make an angry look

SECLUDE keep away from other people

SEEP ooze

SEETHE boil

SEVER divide

SHEAR cut with a sharp instrument

SHED throw off (e.g., clothing)

SHIRK seek to avoid (e.g., duty or work)

SHRIVEL contract and wrinkle

SHUN avoid

SHUNT turn aside

SIFT sort out through careful examination (e.g., evidence)

SIGNIFY mean

SINGE burn slightly or around the edges

SKIM read over quickly

SMITE hit hard

SMOLDER give off smoke after the fire is out

SNARL tangle

SOAR fly high in the air

SOJOURN live temporarily in a place

SOLICIT ask for (e.g., help)

SPURN reject scornfully

STARTLE surprise

STIFLE suppress (e.g., feelings)

STREW scatter

STRIVE try hard

STUN daze

SUBSIDE lessen in activity

SUBSIST continue to live with difficulty

SUCCUMB yield to

SUFFICE be enough

SUPPRESS put down (e.g., a revolt)

SURGE increase suddenly

SURMOUNT overcome (e.g., an obstacle)

SUSTAIN support

SWARM move in great numbers

SWAY move back and forth

TAMPER meddle with

TARNISH discolor

TAUNT reproach mockingly

THAW melt

THRASH defeat thoroughly

THRIVE prosper

THROB beat or pulse insistently

THROTTLE choke

THRUST push forcefully and suddenly

THWART prevent someone from achieving something

TINGE color slightly

TORMENT afflict with pain

TRANSFORM change the appearance of

TRANSMIT send along

TRANSPIRE come to light; occur

TRAVERSE cross over

TRUDGE walk with difficulty

UNDERGO experience

UNDO return to condition before something was done

USURP seize power illegally

UTILIZE make use of

UTTER speak

VACATE make empty

VANQUISH conquer

VARY change

VEND sell

VERGE be on the point of

VERIFY prove the truth of

VEX annoy

VIBRATE move back and forth rapidly

VIOLATE break (e.g., a law)

VOUCH guarantee

WAIVE give up (e.g., a right or privilege)

WANE decrease in strength

WARP twist out of shape

WAVER sway back and forth

WHET sharpen

WIELD put to use (e.g., power or a tool such as a club)

WILT become limp

WITHER dry up (e.g., a flower)

WITHSTAND hold out against (e.g., pressure)

WREST pull violently

WRING force out by squeezing

WRITHE twist and turn about

YEARN long for

YIELD give up

500 USEFUL ADJECTIVES

ACRID sharp to taste or smell (e.g., odor)

ADAMANT unyielding

ADEPT skilled

ADROIT skillful

AESTHETIC having to do with beauty

AGILE nimble

AMBIDEXTROUS equally skilled at using both hands

AMENABLE disposed to follow (e.g., advice)

AMIABLE friendly

APT suitable

AQUATIC living in or practiced on water

ARDENT passionate

ARROGANT overly proud

ARTICULATE able to express oneself clearly

ASTUTE shrewd

AUSPICIOUS favorable (e.g., circumstances)

AUSTERE harsh

AUTHENTIC genuine

AUXILIARY helping

BARREN unfruitful

BIZARRE strange

BLAND gentle

BLATANT overly loud

BOISTEROUS rambunctious

BRUSQUE rudely brief

CALLOUS unfeeling

CANDID honest

CASUAL offhand

CHIC stylish

CHRONIC continuing over a long period of time

CIVIC municipal

CIVIL courteous

COGENT convincing (e.g., argument)

COHERENT clearly holding together

COLLOQUIAL conversational, informal

COLOSSAL huge

COMPATIBLE capable of getting along together

COMPLACENT satisfied with oneself

CONCISE brief but complete

COPIOUS plentiful

CRAFTY sly

CREDIBLE believable

CREDULOUS given to believing anything too easily

CUMBERSOME bulky

CURSORY done quickly but only on the surface (e.g., an examination)

CURT rudely brief

DEFT skillful

DEFUNCT dead; broken, no longer working

DEMURE overly modest

DEROGATORY belittling

DESOLATE lonely

DESPONDENT depressed

DESTITUTE poverty-stricken

DETERGENT cleansing

DEVIOUS indirect

DEVOID completely free of (e.g., feeling)

DEVOUT very religious

DIFFIDENT shy

DIMINUTIVE tiny

DIRE dreadful

DISCREET careful

DISCRETE distinctly separate

DISINTERESTED impartial

DISMAL gloomy

DISTRAUGHT driven to distraction

DIVERSE varied

DOCILE easily led

DOGMATIC stubbornly positive (e.g., opinion)

DOMESTIC having to do with the home

DOMINANT ruling

DORMANT sleeping

DRASTIC extreme (e.g., changes)

DREARY gloomy

DUBIOUS doubtful

DURABLE lasting

DYNAMIC energetic

EARNEST intensely serious; sincere

EBONY black

ECCENTRIC peculiar (e.g., behavior)

EDIBLE fit to be eaten

EERIE weird

ELEGANT tastefully fine

ELOQUENT powerfully fluent in writing or speech

ELUSIVE hard to get hold of

EMINENT distinguished (e.g., author)

EPIC heroic in size

ERRATIC not regular

ETERNAL everlasting

ETHNIC having to do with race

EXORBITANT unreasonable (e.g., price)

EXOTIC foreign

EXPEDIENT suitable in a given situation but not necessarily correct

EXPLICIT clearly indicated

EXQUISITE extremely beautiful

EXTEMPORANEOUS spoken or accomplished with little preparation

EXTENSIVE broad

EXTINCT no longer existing

EXTRANEOUS having nothing to do with the subject at hand

FANATIC extremely emotionally enthusiastic

FEASIBLE possible to carry out (e.g., a plan)

FEEBLE weak

FERTILE productive

FERVENT warmly felt

FESTIVE in the spirit of a holiday (e.g., celebration)

FICKLE changeable

FLAGRANT noticeably bad (e.g., violation)

FLEET swift

FLIMSY not strong (e.g., platform)

FLUENT smooth (e.g., speech)

FORLORN hopeless

FORMIDABLE fear-inspiring because of size or strength (e.g., enemy)

FRAGILE easily broken

FRAIL delicate

FRANK outspoken

FRATERNAL brotherly

FRIGID extremely cold

FRUGAL thrifty

FUTILE useless

GALA festive

GALLANT courteously brave (e.g., conduct)

GAUDY tastelessly showy

GAUNT overly thin and weary-looking

GENIAL kindly

GERMANE pertinent

GHASTLY frightful (e.g., appearance)

GIGANTIC huge

GLIB fluent but insincere

GLUM gloomy

GORY bloody

GRAPHIC vividly realistic

GRATIS free

GRIEVOUS causing sorrow

GRIM sternly forbidding

GROSS glaringly bad (e.g., injustice)

GROTESQUE distorted in appearance

GRUESOME horrifying

GULLIBLE easily fooled

GUTTURAL throaty (e.g., sound)

HAGGARD worn-looking

HALE healthy

HAPHAZARD chance; disorganized

HARDY having endurance

HARSH disagreeably rough

HAUGHTY overly proud

HEARTY friendly (e.g., welcome)

HECTIC feverish

HEINOUS outrageous (e.g., crime)

HIDEOUS extremely ugly

HILARIOUS very funny

HOMOGENOUS of like kind (e.g., group)

HORRENDOUS horrible

HOSTILE unfriendly

HUMANE merciful

HUMBLE modest

HUMID damp

ILLICIT illegal

IMMACULATE spotlessly clean

IMMENSE very large

IMMINENT about to happen (e.g., storm)

IMPARTIAL unbiased, fair

IMPERATIVE necessary

IMPERTINENT rude

IMPETUOUS acting on impulse

IMPLICIT implied

IMPROMPTU without any preparation (e.g., remarks)

IMPUDENT rudely bold

INANE silly

INCENDIARY causing fire (e.g., bomb)

INCESSANT uninterrupted

INCLEMENT rough (e.g., weather)

INCOGNITO with real identity hidden

INCOHERENT not clearly connected or understandable

INDELIBLE unable to be erased

INDIFFERENT showing no interest

INDIGENT poor

INDIGNANT very angry

INDISPENSABLE absolutely necessary

INDUSTRIOUS hard-working

INEPT ineffective

INFALLIBLE unable to make a mistake

INFAMOUS having a bad reputation

INFINITE endless

INFINITESIMAL very, very small

INFLEXIBLE unbending

INGENIOUS clever

INGENUOUS naturally simple

INHERENT existing in someone or something

INNATE inborn

INNOCUOUS harmless

INSIPID uninteresting (e.g., conversation)

INSOLENT boldly rude

INTEGRAL essential to the whole

INTENSIVE concentrated

INTERMITTENT starting and stopping (e.g., rain)

INTOLERANT unwilling or unable to respect others or their beliefs

INTRICATE complicated

INVINCIBLE unable to be conquered

IRATE angry

IRRATIONAL unreasonable

JOVIAL good-humored

JUBILANT joyous

JUDICIOUS showing good judgment

LABORIOUS demanding a lot of work

LANK tall and thin

LATENT hidden (e.g., talent)

LAUDABLE worthy of praise

LAVISH extremely generous (e.g., praise)

LAX loose (e.g., discipline)

LEGIBLE easily read (e.g., print)

LEGITIMATE lawful (e.g., claim)

LETHAL fatal

LISTLESS lacking in spirit

LITERAL following the exact words or intended meaning of the original (e.g., translation)

LITERATE being able to read and write (e.g., person)

LIVID discolored by a bruise (e.g., flesh)

LOATH reluctant

LOFTY very high

LOQUACIOUS talkative

LUCID clear

LUCRATIVE profitable (e.g., business)

LUDICROUS ridiculous

LURID shockingly sensational (e.g., story)

LUSTY vigorous

MAJESTIC grand (e.g., building)

MALICIOUS spiteful

MALIGNANT harmful

MAMMOTH gigantic

MANDATORY required

MANIFEST evident

MANUAL done by the hands (e.g., labor)

MARINE of the sea (e.g., life)

MARTIAL warlike

MASSIVE bulky and heavy

MEAGER scanty

MENIAL lowly (e.g., task)

MERCENARY working only for financial gain (e.g., soldier)

METICULOUS extremely careful

MILITANT aggressive

MOBILE movable (e.g., home)

MOOT unresolved; of only academic importance (e.g., a _____ point)

MORBID unhealthily gloomy

MUTUAL reciprocal (e.g., admiration)

NAIVE innocently simple

NAUSEOUS disgusting

NAUTICAL having to do with ships and sailing

NEGLIGENT neglectful

NEUROTIC describing the behavior of a person suffering from an emotional disorder

NIMBLE moving quickly and easily

NOCTURNAL of the night (e.g., animal)

NOMINAL small in comparison with service or value received (e.g., fee)

NONCHALANT casual and unexcited

NOTABLE important (e.g., person)

NOTORIOUS well-known in an unfavorable way (e.g., criminal)

NULL having no effect

OBESE overly fat

OBJECTIVE free from prejudice (e.g., analysis)

OBLIQUE indirectly indicated (e.g., suggestion)

OBNOXIOUS extremely unpleasant (e.g., behavior)

OBSOLETE out-of-date (e.g., machine)

OBSTINATE stubborn

OMINOUS threatening (e.g., clouds)

ONEROUS burdensome (e.g., task)

OPPORTUNE timely

OPULENT wealthy

ORNATE elaborately decorated

ORTHODOX usually approved; conventional (e.g., religious beliefs)

OSTENSIBLE apparent

OUTRIGHT complete

OVERT open

PALTRY insignificant (e.g., sum of money)

PARAMOUNT chief (e.g., importance)

PASSIVE not active (e.g., participation)

PATENT obvious

PATHETIC pitiful, weak

PEDESTRIAN unimaginative (e.g., ideas)

PEEVISH irritable

PENITENT repentant

PENSIVE thoughtful

PERENNIAL lasting for a long time (e.g., problem)

PERILOUS dangerous

PERTINENT relevant

PETTY relatively unimportant

PICAYUNE petty

PIOUS devoutly religious

PLACID calm (e.g., waters)

PLAUSIBLE apparently true (e.g., argument)

PLIABLE flexible

POIGNANT keenly painful to the emotions; intense

POMPOUS self-important (e.g., person)

PORTABLE capable of being carried (e.g., radio)

POSTHUMOUS taking place after a person's death (e.g., award)

POTENT powerful (e.g., drug)

POTENTIAL possible (e.g., greatness)

PRACTICABLE capable of being done

PRAGMATIC practical

PRECARIOUS risky

PRECISE exact

PRECOCIOUS advanced to a level earlier than is to be expected (e.g., child)

PREDOMINANT prevailing

PREPOSTEROUS ridiculous

PREVALENT widespread

PRIMARY fundamental (e.g., reason)

PRIME first in importance or quality

PRIMITIVE crude (e.g., tools)

PRIOR previous (e.g., appointment)

PRODIGIOUS extraordinary in size or amount (e.g., effort)

PROFICIENT skilled

PROFUSE abundantly given (e.g., praise)

PROLIFIC producing large amounts (e.g., author)

PRONE disposed to (e.g., accidents)

PROSAIC ordinary

PROSTRATE laid low (e.g., by grief)

PROVINCIAL narrow (e.g., view of a matter)

PRUDENT discreet (e.g., advice)

PUGNACIOUS quarrelsome (e.g., person)

PUNGENT sharp to taste or smell (e.g., odor)

PUNITIVE inflicting punishment (e.g., action)

PUNY small in size or strength (e.g., effort)

PUTRID rotten

QUAINT pleasantly odd (e.g., custom)

RADIANT brightly shining

RAMPANT spreading unchecked (e.g., violence)

RANCID having the bad taste or smell of stale food (e.g., butter)

RANDOM decided by chance (e.g., choice)

RANK complete (e.g., incompetency)

RASH reckless

RAUCOUS harsh (e.g., sound)

RAVENOUS extremely hungry

REFLEX involuntary response (e.g., action)

REGAL royal

RELENTLESS persistent (e.g., chase)

RELEVANT pertinent

REMISS careless (e.g., in one's duty)

REMOTE far distant (e.g., time or place)

REPLETE filled (e.g., with thrills)

REPUGNANT extremely distasteful

REPULSIVE disgusting

REPUTABLE respectable (e.g., doctor)

RESIGNED submitting passively to (e.g., to one's fate)

RESOLUTE firmly determined

RESONANT resounding (e.g., sound)

RESTIVE restless (e.g., pupils)

RETICENT speaking little (e.g., child)

RIGID stiff

ROBUST strong and healthy

ROWDY rough and disorderly (e.g., mob)

RUGGED rough

RUSTIC of the country (e.g., life)

RUTHLESS pitiless (e.g., dictator)

SAGE wise (e.g., advice)

SALIENT prominent (e.g., points)

SALUTARY healthful (e.g., climate)

SANE mentally sound

SANGUINARY bloody

SANGUINE cheerfully hopeful

SCANTY meager

SCHOLASTIC having to do with school and education (e.g., record)

SCRAWNY thin

SCRUPULOUS careful and honest (e.g., accounting)

SECRETIVE given to secrecy; purposely not made public

SECULAR not religious (e.g., education)

SEDATE dignified

SERENE calm

SHEER very thin (e.g., stockings); utter (e.g., nonsense)

SHIFTLESS lazy

SHIFTY tricky

SHODDY inferior in quality (e.g., material)

SHREWD clever in one's dealings (e.g., businessman)

SIMULTANEOUS happening at the same time (e.g., events)

SINGULAR remarkable; strange (e.g., behavior)

SINISTER threatening evil

SKEPTICAL showing doubt (e.g., attitude)

SLACK not busy (e.g., business season); loose (e.g., rope)

SLEEK smooth and glossy (e.g., appearance)

SLENDER small in size or amount (e.g., contribution)

SLOVENLY untidy

SLUGGISH slow-moving

SMUG self-satisfied

SNUG comfortable

SOBER serious

SOLEMN grave; serious (e.g., occasion)

SOLITARY lone

SOMBER dark and gloomy (e.g., outlook)

SOPHISTICATED wise in the ways of the world

SORDID wretched (e.g., condition)

SPARSE thinly scattered

SPIRITED lively

SPIRITUAL of the spirit or soul

SPONTANEOUS happening as a result of natural impulse (e.g., reaction)

SPORADIC happening at irregular times (e.g., shooting)

SPRY nimble

STACCATO with breaks between successive sharp sounds

STAGNANT not moving or circulating (e.g., water)

STALWART robust

STAUNCH firm (e.g., friend)

STARK bleak (e.g., outlook)

STATELY dignified

STATIC stationary

STATIONARY not moving

STEADFAST firm

STERN severe (e.g., look)

STOCKY short and heavily built

STODGY uninteresting

STOICAL unmoved emotionally

STOUT fat; firm (e.g., resistance)

STRAIGHTFORWARD honest (e.g., answer)

STRENUOUS demanding great energy (e.g., exercise)

STUPENDOUS amazing (e.g., effort)

STURDY strongly built

SUAVE smoothly polite

SUBLIME inspiring admiration because of noble quality (e.g., music)

SUBSIDIARY of less importance (e.g., rank)

SUBSTANTIAL of considerable numbers or size

SUBTLE suggested delicately (e.g., hint)

SULLEN resentful

SULTRY extremely hot and humid (e.g., weather)

SUMPTUOUS costly (e.g., meal)

SUNDRY various

SUPERB of a high degree of excellence

SUPERFICIAL not going beyond the obvious; only on the suface (e.g., examination)

SUPERFLUOUS beyond what is needed

SUPERLATIVE superior to all others (e.g., performance)

SUPPLE limber, flexible

SURLY offensively rude

SUSCEPTIBLE easily affected by (e.g., to colds)

SWARTHY dark-skinned

TACIT not openly said but implied (e.g., approval)

TANGIBLE capable of being touched; actual (e.g., results)

TARDY late (e.g., student)

TART having a sharp taste

TAUT tightly stretched (e.g., rope)

TEDIOUS long and tiresome (e.g., study)

TEMPERATE moderate (e.g., climate)

TENACIOUS holding fast

TENTATIVE for a temporary period of trial (e.g., agreement)

TEPID lukewarm (e.g., water)

TERMINAL concluding

TERSE brief but expressing a good deal (e.g., comment)

THANKLESS unappreciated (e.g., task)

TIDY neat (e.g., appearance)

TIMELESS eternal (e.g., beauty)

TIMELY happening at a desirable or appropriate time (e.g., arrival)

TIMID shy

TIRESOME making one weary; boring

TITANIC of enormous size or strength

TORRID intensely hot

TRANQUIL calm (e.g., waters)

TRANSIENT passing away after a brief time

TRIFLING of little importance

TRITE ordinary (e.g., remark)

TRIVIAL insignificant

TURBULENT agitated

ULTIMATE final (e.g., conclusion)

UNANIMOUS in complete agreement (e.g., decision)

UNASSUMING modest

UNCANNY unnatural (e.g., accuracy)

UNCONDITIONAL absolute (e.g., surrender)

UNCOUTH crude and clumsy

UNDAUNTED not discouraged

UNDERHANDED sly

UNDULY overly (e.g., concerned)

UNEASY disturbed

UNGAINLY awkward

UNIQUE only one of its kind (e.g., specimen)

UNKEMPT messy; not well taken care of

UNRULY disorderly (e.g., crowd)

UNSCATHED uninjured

UNWIELDY clumsy to use, usually because of size (e.g., implement)

UPRIGHT honest (e.g., citizen)

UTMOST most extreme (e.g., in distance, height, or size)

UTTER complete (e.g., failure)

VAIN futile (e.g., attempt); conceited (e.g., person)

VALIANT brave

VALID (legally) sound (e.g., argument)

VAST very large in extent or size (e.g., distances)

VEHEMENT violent in feeling (e.g., protest)

VERBATIM word for word (e.g., report)

VERSATILE able to perform many tasks well (e.g., athlete)

VIGILANT watchful (e.g., sentry)

VILE highly disgusting (e.g., conduct)

VISIBLE able to be seen (e.g., object)

VITAL essential (e.g., contribution)

VIVACIOUS lively

VIVID bright (e.g., color)

VOID not binding legally (e.g., contract); empty

VOLUMINOUS very great in size (e.g., writings)

VORACIOUS greedy for food (e.g., appetite)

VULNERABLE open to attack (e.g., position)

WARY cautious

WEARY tired

WEE very small

WEIGHTY important (e.g., decision)

WHOLESOME causing a feeling of well-being (e.g., entertainment); not crude or dirty

WILY cunning (e.g., magician)

WISHFUL showing desire that something be so (e.g., thinking)

WITTY amusingly clever (e.g., remark)

WORDY using too many words (e.g., reply)

WORLDLY knowledgeable of and enjoying pleasures and experiences of this world (e.g., person)

WORTHY deserving (e.g., choice)

WRETCHED miserable

7 Electronics Information Review

The Greeks are believed to have discovered electricity in the process of conducting some of their experiments. While working with a piece of amber (the fossilized resin from an ancient species of tree), which is translucent and golden in color, they found that if the amber was rubbed briskly, it would exhibit an attraction for tiny bits of lightweight material. You have probably seen this happen when you run a comb through your hair on a dry day and then pick up bits of paper with the comb. The Greeks believed that the "forces of amber" were at work in this phenomenon. Similarly, the Romans found that rubbing lignite (a form of coal) could produce, by friction, the same reaction. However, it is the Greeks who have been given credit for the first experiments that led, in 1600, to the work of the Englishman William Gilbert with friction and static electricity. Gilbert wrote a book on the substances with which he had experimented. He showed that amber was not the *only* material that produced an attraction for bits of paper. Gilbert has been called the father of electricity, since he was the first to classify objects that would produce an electrostatic field when rubbed. He called these substances *electrics*.

Over the years, scientists learned more and more about this phenomenon called electricity. They learned that how it acts can be described in certain principles. They also learned how to generate, distribute, and use electricity. *Electronics* is the application of the principles of electricity.

Basic Atomic Structure

Electricity is defined as the flow of electrons along a conductor. A *conductor* is an object that allows electrons to pass easily. That means electrons must be organized and pushed toward a goal. This is done in a number of ways, but we must first know what electrons are before we can start working with them.

Elements are the most basic materials in the universe. There are more than 120 elements, including some that have been made in the laboratory. Elements such as iron, copper, gold, lead, and silver have been found in nature. Others have been made in the laboratory. Every known substance—solid, liquid, or gas—is composed of elements.

An *atom* is the smallest particle of an element that retains all the properties of that element. Each element has its own kind of atom. That is, hydrogen atoms are alike, and they are different from the atoms of all other elements. However, all atoms have certain things in common. They all have an inner part, the *nucleus*. The nucleus is composed of very small particles called *protons* and *neutrons*. An atom also has an outer part, consisting of other small particles. These very small particles are called *electrons*. The electrons orbit around the nucleus. (See Fig. 7.1.)

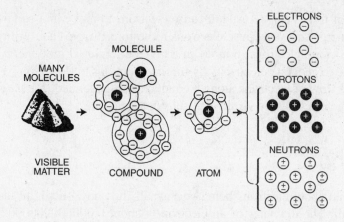

Fig. 7.1. Molecular structure. The negative (–) particles are electrons.

Protons have a positive charge, electrons a negative charge. Neutrons have no charge. Because of their charges, protons and electrons are particles of energy. That is, these charges form an electric field of force within the atom. These charges are always pulling and pushing one another; this action produces energy in the form of movement.

The atoms of each element have a definite number of electrons, and they have the same number of protons. (See the Periodic Table on page 84.) A hydrogen atom has one electron and one proton (Fig. 7.2). The aluminum atom has 13 of each (Fig. 7.3). Opposite charges—negative electrons and positive protons—attract each other and tend to hold electrons in orbit. As long as this arrangement is not changed, an atom is electrically balanced.

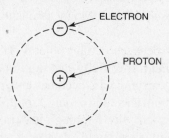

Fig. 7.2. The hydrogen atom has one electron and one proton.

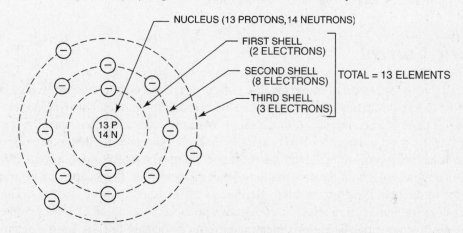

Fig. 7.3. The aluminum atom has 13 electrons and 13 protons.

When electrons leave their orbits, they move from atom to atom at random, drifting in no particular direction. Electrons that move in such a way are referred to as *free electrons*. Electrons in copper drift along in a random fashion when at room temperature.

Different kinds of forces can be used to cause electrons to move in a certain direction. Heat is only one type of energy that can cause electrons to be forced from their orbits. A magnetic field can also be used to cause electrons to move in a given direction. Light energy and pressure on a crystal are also used to generate electricity by forcing electrons to flow along a given path. That is how electricity (the flow of electrons along a conductor) is generated. A *conductor* is any material that has many free electrons by virtue of its physical makeup.

Electric Energy

So far you have read about electrons being very small. Just how small are they? Well, electrons are incredibly small. The diameter of an electron is about 0.00000000000022 inch or 200 trillionths of an inch. You may wonder how anything so small can be a source of energy. Much of the answer lies in the fact that electrons move at nearly the speed of light, or 186,282 miles per second (mi/sec). In metric terms that is 300 million meters per second (m/sec). As you can see from their size, billions of them can move at once through a wire. The combination of speed and concentration together produces great energy.

When a flow of electrons along a conductor occurs, this is commonly referred to as *current flow*. Thus, you can see that the movement of electrons is related to current electricity.

Magnetism and Electricity

Magnetism and electricity are closely related. Magnetism is used to generate electricity, and electricity produces a magnetic field.

Magnetism is a force that acts between certain objects. The area around a magnet where the force is felt is called a *magnetic field*. Electricity flowing through a wire sets up a magnetic field around the wire. A coil of current-carrying wire becomes an *electromagnet* with the magnetic field strongest at the two ends of the coil, the "north" and "south" *poles*. The electromagnet remains magnetic only as long as the electricity flows through it. A magnetic field can also produce electricity. If you pass a wire across a magnetic field, electricity will be generated in the wire. Electric generators are based on this principle. The relationship between electricity and magnetism is also used in transformers, relays, solenoids, and motors.

Electric Current

In the early years of electrical study, electric current was erroneously thought to be a movement of positive charges from positive to negative. This assumption, termed *conventional current flow,* is a concept that became entrenched in the minds of many scientists. Consequently, conventional current flow is found in many textbooks and the theory's existence should be taken into account.

Since it has been proven that electrons (negative charges) move through a wire, *electron current* will be used throughout the explanation of electric current in this chapter and throughout the remainder of the text. Electron current is defined as the directed flow of electrons. The direction of electron movement is from a region of negative potential to a region of less negative potential or more positive potential. Therefore, electric current can be said to flow from a negative potential to a positive potential. The direction is determined by the polarity of the voltage source.

Electric current is generally classified into two general types—direct current and alternating current. A *direct current* flows continuously in the same direction, whereas an *alternating current* periodically reverses direction.

A *circuit* is a pathway for the movement of electrons. An external force exerted on electrons to make them flow through a conductor is known as *electromotive force,* or *emf.* It is measured in volts. Electric pressure, potential difference, and emf mean the same thing. The words *voltage drop* and *potential drop* can be interchanged.

For electrons to move in a particular direction, it is necessary for a potential difference to exist between two points of the emf source. If 6,250,000,000,000,000,000 electrons pass a given point in one second, there is said to be one *ampere* (A) of current flowing. The same number of electrons stored on an object (a static charge) and not moving is called a *coulomb* (C).

MEASUREMENT OF CURRENT

The magnitude of current is measured in *amperes*. A current of one ampere is said to flow when one coulomb of charge passes a point in one second. Expressed as an equation:

$$I = \frac{Q}{T}$$

Where: I = current in amperes
                                                      Q = charge in coulombs
                                               T = time in seconds

Frequently, the ampere is much too large a unit. Therefore the *milliampere* (mA), one thousandth of an ampere, or the *microampere* (μA), one millionth (0.000001) of an ampere, is used.

Current flow is assumed to be from negative (–) to positive (+) in our explanations here. Electron flow is negative (–) to positive (+), and we assume that current flow and electron flow are one and the same. It makes explanations simpler as we progress into electronics. The *conventional* current flow is the opposite, or positive (+) to negative (–).

An *ammeter* is used to measure current flow in a circuit. A *milliammeter* is used to measure smaller amounts, while the *microammeter* is used to measure very small amounts of current.

A *voltmeter* is used to measure voltage. In some instances it is possible to obtain a meter which will measure both voltage and current plus resistance. This is called a *multimeter,* or *volt-ohm-milliameter* (VM).

Conductors

A material through which electricity passes easily is called a *conductor* because it has free electrons. In other words, a conductor offers very little resistance or opposition to the flow of electrons.

All metals are conductors of electricity to some extent, but some are much better than others. Silver, copper, and aluminum let electricity pass easily. Silver is a better conductor than copper. However, copper is used more frequently because it is cheaper. Aluminum is used as a conductor where light weight is important.

Why are some materials good conductors? One of the most important reasons is the presence of free electrons. If a material has many electrons which are free to move away from their atoms, that material will be a good conductor of electricity.

Although free electrons usually move in a haphazard way, their movement can be controlled. The electrons can be made to move in the same direction, and this flow is called *electric current*.

Conductors may be in the form of bars, tubes, or sheets. The most familiar conductors are wire. Many sizes of wire are available. Some are only the thickness of a hair. Other wire may be as thick as your arm. To prevent conductors from touching at the wrong place they are usually coated with plastic, rubber, or cloth material. This covering on the conductor is called an *insulator*.

WIRE GAGE

Various electrical applications require different *conductor* sizes. Some wires are extremely large, and others are almost as fine as human hair. All wire is designed by definite gage sizes. Each number designates a wire of a specific diameter. As the diameter of the wire decreases, the gage number increases. The following table, which refers to standard annealed solid copper wire, illustrates some various wire sizes, their comparative areas, and resistance per 1,000 ft. These resistance values apply only to copper conductors.

Gage Number	Diameter (mils)	Cross Section Circular (mils)	Ohms per 1000 ft 25°C (= 77°F)
0000	460.0	212,000.0	.0500
2	258.0	66,400.0	.159
6	162.0	26,300.0	.403
10	102.0	10,400.0	1.02
14	64.0	4,110.0	2.58
18	40.0	1,620.0	6.51
22	25.3	642.0	16.51
26	15.9	254.0	41.6
30	10.0	101.0	105.0
36	5.0	25.0	423.0
38	4.0	15.7	673.0
40	3.1	9.9	1,070.0

Much wire in common use today, however, is not solid; it is stranded.

STRANDED WIRE

Copper wire is stranded for one reason: Stranded wire is easily bent. In order to bend or flex wire constantly it is necessary to make many smaller strands into a cable or bundle. This allows for flexing of the cable or wire. The lamp cord in your home is made of many fine strands of copper wire. This allows it to be flexible and bend where you want it on the way from the plug to the lamp.

Larger wires used for wiring commercial or industrial buildings are also stranded. Any number of smaller wires are grouped in a cable to carry the same amount of current as a solid conductor wire in a solid mass. The larger cables have to be stranded or it would be next to impossible to bend them or work with them.

The physical size of flexible wire is greater than the same size, electrically, of solid wire. A solid No. 18 wire is easily bent, but is not as flexible as a multiple-strand cable made up of smaller gage wire to equal the No. 18 wire used in a lamp cord.

Insulators

An insulator is a material with very few, if any, free electrons. No known material is a perfect insulator. However, there are materials that are such poor conductors that they are classified as insulators. Glass, dry wood, rubber, mica, and certain plastics are insulating materials.

Semiconductors (I)

So far you have looked at insulators and conductors. In between the two extremes are semiconductors. Semiconductors in the form of transistors, diodes, and integrated circuits or chips are used every day in electronic devices. Now is the time to place them in their proper category.

Materials used in the manufacture of transistors and diodes have a conductivity halfway between that of a good conductor and a good insulator. Therefore, the name *semi*conductor has been given to them. Germanium and silicon are the two most commonly known semiconductor materials. Through the introduction of small amounts of other elements (called impurities), these nearly pure (99.999999%) elements become *limited* conductors. The opposite of conductors are *resistors*. Resistors are devices used to give a measured amount of opposition or resistance to the flow of electrons. This opposition to current flow is measured in ohms (Ω) and indicates the amount of resistance a piece of material offers to the flow of electrons. Take a look at Fig. 7.4 to see how these semiconductor materials are placed between good conductors and poor conductors.

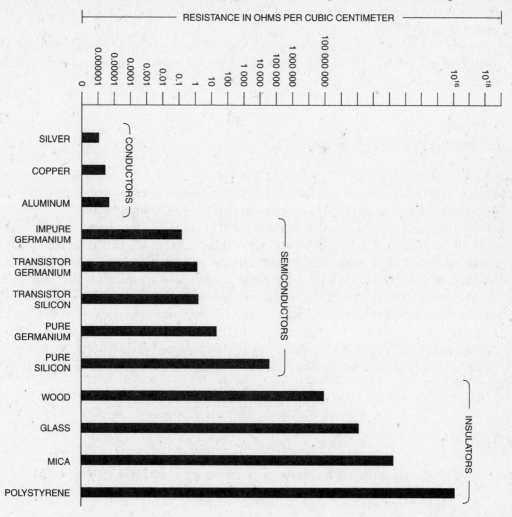

Fig. 7.4. Location of insulators, semiconductors, and conductors in relation to one another in terms of inherent resistance.

Power

Power is defined as the *rate* at which work is done. It is expressed in metric measurement terms of watts (W) for power and joules (J) for energy work. A *watt* is the power which gives rise to the production of energy at the rate of one joule per second (W = J/s). A *joule* is the work done when the point of application of force of one newton is displaced a distance of one meter in the direction of the force (J = N • m).

It has long been the practice in this country to measure work in terms of horsepower (hp). Electric motors are still rated in horsepower and probably will be for some time, since the United States did not adopt metric standards for everything.

Power can be electric or mechanical. When a mechanical force is used to lift a weight, *work* is done. The rate at which the weight is moved is called *power*. *Horsepower* is defined in terms of moving a certain weight over a certain distance in one minute (e.g., 33,000 lb lifted 1 ft in 1 min equals 1 hp). Energy is consumed in moving a weight or when work is done. The findings in this field have been equated with the same amount of work done by electric energy. It takes 746 W of electric power to equal 1 hp.

The horsepower rating of electric motors is calculated by taking the voltage and multiplying it by the current drawn under full load. This power is measured in watts. In other words, one volt times one ampere equals one watt. When put into a formula it reads:

$$\text{Power} = \text{volts} \times \text{amperes or } P = E \times I$$

where E = voltage, or emf
I = current, or intensity of electron flow

Kilowatt

The kilowatt is commonly used to express the amount of electric energy used or available. The term *kilo* (k) means one thousand (1,000). A kilowatt (kW) is one thousand watts.

When the kilowatt is used in terms of power dissipated or consumed by a home for a month it is expressed in kilowatt-hours. The unit kilowatt-hour is abbreviated as kWh. It is the equivalent of one thousand watts used for a period of one hour. Electric bills are calculated or computed on an hourly basis and then read in the kWh unit. The entire month's time is equated to one hour's time.

Milliwatt is a term you will encounter when working with electronics. The *milliwatt* (mW) means one-thousandth (0.001) of a watt. The milliwatt is used in terms of some very small amplifiers and other electronic devices. For instance, a speaker used on a portable transistor radio will be rated as 100 milliwatts, or 0.1 W. Transistor circuits are designed in milliwatts, but power line electric power is measured in kilowatts. Keep in mind that *kilo* means 1,000 and *milli* means 0.001 (one-thousandth).

Resistance

Any time there is movement there is resistance. This resistance is useful in electric and electronic circuits. Resistance makes it possible to generate heat, control electron flow, and supply the correct voltage to a device.

Resistance in a conductor depends on four factors: material, length, cross-sectional area, and temperature.

Material
Some materials offer more resistance than others, depending on the number of free electrons present in the material.

Length

The longer the wire or conductor, the more resistance it has. Resistance is said to vary *directly* with the length of the wire.

Cross-Sectional Area

Resistance varies *inversely* with the size of the conductor in cross section. In other words, the larger the wire, the smaller the resistance per foot of length.

Temperature

For most materials, the higher the temperature, the higher the resistance. However, there are some exceptions to this in devices known as *thermistors*. Thermistors change resistance with temperature. They *decrease* in resistance with an increase in temperature. Thermistors are used in certain types of meters to measure temperature.

Resistance is measured by a unit called the *ohm*. The Greek letter omega Ω is used as the symbol for electrical resistance.

RESISTORS

Resistors are devices which provide measured amounts of resistance. They are valuable when it comes to making sure the proper amount of voltage is present in a circuit. They are useful when generating heat.

Resistors are classified as either *wirewound* or *carbon-composition*. The symbol for a resistor of either type is ⎓⋀⋀⋀⎓ .

Wirewound resistors are used to provide sufficient opposition to current flow to dissipate power of 5 W or more. Remember, a watt is a unit of electric power equal to one volt times one ampere.

Wirewound resistors are made of wire that has controlled resistance per unit length.

Resistance causes a voltage drop across a resistor when current flows through it. The voltage is dropped or dissipated as heat and must be eliminated into the air.

Some variable resistors can be varied but can also be adjusted for a particular setting. Resistors are available in various sizes, shapes, and wattage ratings.

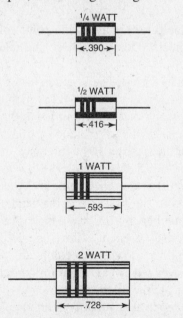

Fig. 7.5. Wattage ratings of carbon-composition resistors. All measurements shown here are in inches.

Carbon-composition resistors are usually found in electronic devices. They are of low wattage. They are made in 1/8-W, 1/4-W, 1/2-W, 1-W, and 2-W sizes. The physical size determines the wattage rating or their ability to dissipate heat.

Carbon-composition resistors are usually marked according to their ohmic value with a *color code*. The colors are placed on the resistors in rings (Fig. 7.6).

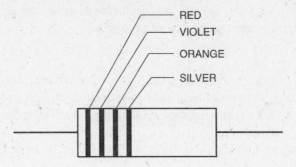

RED
VIOLET
ORANGE
SILVER

Fig. 7.6. A 27,000-ohm (Ω) resistor.

The table below shows the values for reading the color code of carbon-composition resistors.

Resistor Color Code

0 Black	5 Green
1 Brown	6 Blue
2 Red	7 Violet
3 Orange	8 Gray
4 Yellow	9 White

Take a close look at a carbon-composition resistor. The bands should be to your left. Read from left to right. The band closest to one end is placed to the left so you can read it from left to right. The first band gives the first number according to the color code. In this case it is red, or 2. The second band gives the next number, which is violet, or 7. The third band represents the multiplier or divisor.

If the third band is a color in the 0 to 9 range in the color code, it states the number of zeros to be added to the first two numbers. Orange is 3; so the resistor in Fig. 7.5 has a value of 27,000 Ω of resistance.

The 27,000 Ω is usually written as 27 kΩ. The k stands for thousand; it takes the place of three zeros. In some cases, resistors are referred to as 27 MΩ (which means 27,000,000, or 27 million Ω), because the M stands for *mega*, and that is the unit for million.

If there is no fourth band, the resistor has a tolerance rating of ± 20 percent (± means plus or minus). If the fourth band is silver, the resistor has a tolerance of ± 10 percent. If the fourth band is gold, the resistor has a tolerance of ± 5 percent.

Silver and gold may also be used for the *third* band. In this case, according to the color code, the first two numbers (obtained from the first two color bands) must be divided by 10 or 100. Silver means divide the first two numbers by 100. Gold means divide the first two numbers by 10. For example, if the bands of the resistor are red, yellow, and gold, then the value is 24 divided by 10, or 2.4 Ω. If the third band is silver and the two colors are yellow and orange, then the 43 is divided by 100 to produce the answer of 0.43 Ω. Keep in mind, though, that the fourth band will still be either gold or silver to indicate the tolerance.

Resistors marked with the color code are available in hundreds of size and wattage rating combinations. Wattage rating refers to the wattage or power consumed by the resistor.

Conductance

Electronics is frequently explained in terms of opposites. The opposite of resistance is conductance. Conductance is the ability of a material to pass electrons. The factors that affect the magnitude of resistance are exactly the same for conductance, but they affect conductance in the opposite manner. Therefore, conductance is directly proportional to area, and inversely proportional to the length and specific resistance of the material. The temperature of a material is definitely a factor, but assuming a constant temperature, the conductance of a material can be calculated if its specific resistance is known.

The formula for conductance is:

$$G = \frac{A}{pL}$$

where:

G = conductance measured in siemens (S)
A = cross-sectional area in cir mils
L = length measured in feet
P = specific resistance

The unit of conductance is the *siemen* (formerly the mho, which is ohm spelled backwards). Whereas the symbol used to represent the magnitude of resistance is the Greek letter omega (Ω), the symbol used to represent conductance is S. The relationship that exists between resistance and conductance is a reciprocal one. A reciprocal of a number is one divided by that number. In terms of resistance and conductance:

$$R = \frac{1}{G}$$
$$G = \frac{1}{R}$$

If the resistance of a material is known, dividing its value into one will give its conductance. Also, if the conductance is known, dividing its value into one will give its resistance.

Ohm's Law

A German physicist by the name of Georg Ohm discovered the relationship between voltage, current, and resistance in 1827. He found that in any circuit where the only opposition to the flow of electrons is resistance, there is a relationship between the values of voltage, current, and resistance. The strength or intensity of the current is directly proportional to the voltage and inversely proportional to the resistance.

It is easier to work with Ohm's law when it is expressed in a formula. In the formula, E represents emf, or voltage; I is the current, or the intensity of electron flow; R stands for resistance. The formula is $E = I \times R$. It is used to find the emf (voltage) when the current and the resistance are known.

To find the current, when the voltage and resistance are known, use

$$I = \frac{E}{R}$$

To find the resistance, when the voltage and current are known, use

$$R = \frac{E}{I}$$

Ohm's law is very useful in electrical and electronics work. You will need it often to determine the missing value. In order to make it easy to remember the formula, take a look at Fig. 7.7. Here the formulas are arrived at by placing your finger on the unknown and the other two will have their relationship displayed.

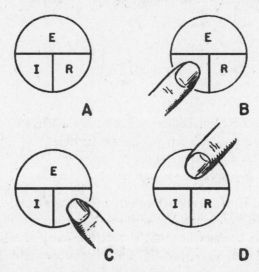

Fig. 7.7. Ohm's law. Place your finger on the unknown value and the remaining two letters will give the formula to use for finding the unknown value.

The best way to become accustomed to solving problems is to start with something simple, such as:

1. If the voltage is given as 100 V and the resistance is 25 Ω, it is a simple problem and a practical application of Ohm's law to find the current in the circuit. Use

$$I = \frac{E}{R}$$

Substituting the values in the formula,

$$I = \frac{100}{25}$$

means 100 is divided by 25 to produce 4 A for the current.

2. If the current is given as 2 A (you may read it on an ammeter in the circuit), and the voltage (read from the voltmeter) is 100 V, it is easy to find the resistance. Use

$$R = \frac{E}{I}$$

Substituting the values in the formula,

$$I = \frac{100}{2}$$

means 100 divided by 2 equals 50 Ω for the circuit.

3. If the current is known to be 10 A, and the resistance is found to be 50 Ω (measured before the circuit is energized), it is then possible to determine how much voltage is needed to cause the circuit to function properly. Use

$$E = I \times R$$

Substituting the values in the formula,

$$E = 10 \times 50$$

means 10 times 50 produces 500, or that it would take 500 V to push 10 A through 50 Ω of resistance.

Circuits

There are a number of different types of circuits. Circuits are the pathways along which electrons move to produce various effects.

The *complete* circuit is necessary for the controlled flow or movement of electrons along a conductor (Fig. 7.8). A complete circuit is made up of a source of electricity, a conductor, and a consuming device. This is the simplest of circuits. The flow of electrons through the consuming device produces heat, light, or work.

In order to form a complete circuit, these rules must be followed:

1. Connect one side of the power source to one side of the consuming device: *A* to *B* (see Fig. 7.8).
2. Connect the other side of the power source to one side of the control device, usually a switch: *C* to *D* (see Fig. 7.8).
3. Connect the other side of the switch to the consuming device it is supposed to control: *E* to *F* (see Fig. 7.8). When the switch is closed, the circuit is complete.

However, when the switch is open, or not closed, there is no path for electrons to flow, and there is an *open circuit* condition where no current flows.

This method is used to make a complete path for electrons to flow from that side of the battery with an excess of electrons to the other side which has a deficiency of electrons. The battery has a negative (–) charge where there is an excess of electrons and a positive (+) charge where there is a deficiency of electrons. Yes, you read it right; the – means excess and + means deficiency. This is due to the fact that we are using the current flow and electron flow as both the same and from – to + in the circuit.

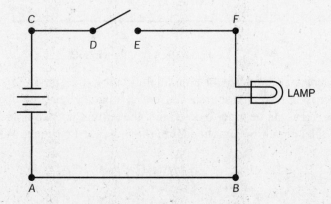

Fig. 7.8. A simple circuit with a switch.

A single path for electrons to flow is called a *closed,* or *complete,* circuit. However, in some instances the circuit may have more than one consuming device. In this situation we have what is called a *series circuit* if the two or more resistors or consuming devices are placed one after the other as shown in Fig. 7.9.

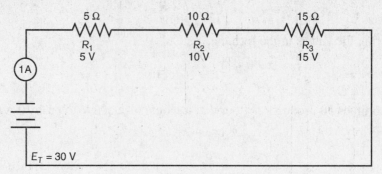

Fig. 7.9. A series circuit with three resistors.

SERIES CIRCUIT

Fig. 7.9 shows a series circuit. The three resistors are connected in series, or one after the other, to complete the path from one terminal of the battery to the other. The current flows through each of them before returning to the positive terminal of the battery.

There is a law concerning the voltages in a series circuit. *Kirchhoff's voltage law* states that the sum of all voltages across resistors or loads is equal to the applied voltage. Voltage drop is considered across the resistor. Fig. 7.9 shows the current flow through three resistors. The voltage drop across R_1 is 5 V. Across R_2 the voltage drop is 10 V. And across R_3 the voltage drop is 15 V. The sum of the individual voltage drops is equal to the total or applied voltage of 30 V. E_T means total voltage. It may also be written as E_A for applied voltage or E_S for source voltage.

To find the total resistance in a series circuit, just add the individual resistances, or $R_T = R_1 + R_2 + R_3$. In this instance (Fig. 7.9), the total resistance is 5 + 10 + 15, or 30 Ω.

PARALLEL CIRCUITS

In a parallel circuit each resistance is connected directly across the voltage source or line. There are as many separate paths for current flow as there are branches (Fig. 7.10).

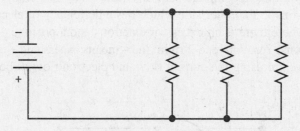

Fig. 7.10. A parallel circuit.

The voltage across all branches of a parallel circuit is the same. This is because all branches are connected across the voltage source. Current in a parallel circuit depends on the resistance of the branch. Ohm's law can be used to determine the current in each branch. You can find the total current for a parallel circuit by simply adding the individual currents. When written as a formula it reads

$$I_T = I_1 + I_2 + I_3 + ...$$

The total resistance of a parallel circuit cannot be found by adding the resistor values. Two formulas are used for finding the total resistance (R_T). If there are *only* two resistors in parallel, a simple formula can be used:

$$R_T = \frac{R_1 \times R_2}{R_1 + R_2}$$

If there are more than two resistors in a parallel, you can use the following formula. This formula may also be used with two resistors in parallel. In fact it can be used for *any* number of resistors.

$$\frac{1}{R_T} = \frac{1}{R_1} + \frac{1}{R_2} + \frac{1}{R_3} + \frac{1}{R_4} + \ldots$$

One thing should be kept in mind in parallel resistances: The total resistance is *always* less than the smallest resistance. However, this is not true if one of the resistances is negative. The condition occurs only in active circuits, so for most applications the statement is true enough to be used for quick checks of your math.

SERIES-PARALLEL CIRCUITS

The series-parallel circuit is a combination of the series and the parallel arrangement. Fig. 7.11 shows an example of the series-parallel circuit. It takes a minimum of three resistances to make a series-parallel circuit. This type has to be reduced to a series equivalent before it can be solved in terms of resistance. The parallel portions are reduced to the total for the part of the circuit, and then the equivalent resistance is added to the series part to obtain the total resistance.

Total current flows through the first series resistor but divides according to the branch resistances after that. There are definite relationships which must be explored here before that type of circuit can be fully understood. This will be done in a later part of this book.

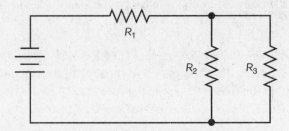

Fig. 7.11. A series-parallel circuit.

OPEN CIRCUITS

An open circuit is an incomplete circuit. Fig. 7.12 shows an open circuit that will become a closed circuit once the switch is closed. A circuit can also become open when one of the leads is cut or when one of the terminals has the wire removed. A loose connection can cause an open circuit.

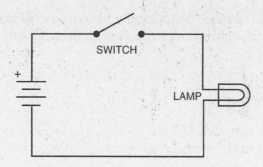

Fig. 7.12. An open circuit produced by an open switch.

SHORT CIRCUITS

The short circuit is something to be avoided because it can cause a fire or overheating. A short circuit has a path of low resistance to electron flow. This is usually created when a low-resistance wire is placed across the consuming device (see Fig. 7.13). The greater number of electrons will flow through the path of least resistance rather than through the consuming device. A short usually generates an excess current flow, which can result in damage to a number of parts of the circuit. If you wish to prevent the damage caused by short circuits, use a fuse.

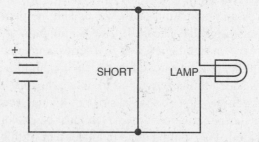

Fig. 7.13. A short circuit. The wire has less resistance than the lamp.

FUSES

Fuses are available in a number of sizes and shapes. They are used to prevent the damage done by excess current flowing in a circuit. They are placed in series with the consuming devices. Once too much current flows, it causes the fuse wire inside the fuse case to melt. This opens the circuit and stops the flow of current and prevents the overheating that occurs when too much current is present in a circuit.

The symbol for a fuse is ⌐⌐⌐ . It fits into a circuit as shown in Fig. 7.14.

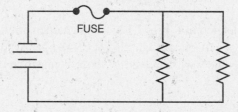

Fig. 7.14. The location of the fuse in a circuit.

Resistors and resistance are very important in the study of electricity and electronics. However, when two other devices are introduced into the circuits, there is the possibility of various combinations that can produce rather interesting final results. One of these devices is the inductor, which produces inductance.

Inductance

Inductance is the ability of a coil, or choke, or inductor (all three mean the same thing and are interchangeable) to oppose any change in circuit current. This is not so important in a direct current (DC) circuit because the current flows in only one direction, from negative to positive, when it is first turned on, and then it stops when it is turned off. The collapsing magnetic field that was produced by the coil of wire with a current through it produces an emf in the coil when it decays or collapses. This emf is in the opposite polarity to that which caused it to be produced. The emf is called a *counter emf,* abbreviated as *cemf.*

Michael Faraday was an Englishman who performed early experiments with coils of wire and electric current. Faraday started to experiment with electricity about 1805. It was not until 1831 that he performed experiments on magnetically coupled coils. A voltage was induced in one of the coils by means of a magnetic field created by current flow in the other coil. From this experiment came the induction coil. Faraday's experiment and discovery made possible many of our modern conveniences. The automobile, doorbell, automobile radio, and television are all possible because of inductance.

Faraday also invented the first *transformer*. A transformer changes electricity into a higher or lower voltage. At that time it had very few practical uses. At the time Faraday was working in England, Joseph Henry was making almost the same discoveries in the United States. Henry worked in New York and discovered the property of self-inductance before Faraday. The unit of measurement for inductance is the henry (H). The symbol for inductance is L.

An inductor has an inductance of one *henry* if an emf of one volt is induced in the inductor when the current through the coil is changing at the rate of one ampere per second. Keep in mind that the one-volt, one-ampere, and one-henry relationship deals with the basic units of measurement of voltage, current, and inductance.

Inductors come in many sizes and shapes. Air-core inductors are coils that are wound without a core. They are used in circuits where the frequencies cannot be heard, such as radio frequencies. Radio frequencies are above the human hearing range. The symbol for a radio frequency coil is ⌐000⌐. Note how the radio frequency air-core inductor is very small and resembles a resistor. The size of the color band to the left is larger than the others. This indicates that it is an inductor of a resistor. The color code tells the size in microhenrys (μH).

• Moisture Resistant

Iron core RF chokes are designed to meet demand for high-reliability ultraminiature components. Suited to network and filter design, delay lines, and computer applications. Coils are impregnated with moisture-resistant laquer.

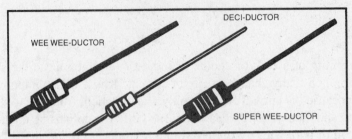

WEE WEE-DUCTOR

DECI-DUCTOR

SUPER WEE-DUCTOR

THE SMALLEST SHIELDED INDUCTOR FOR HIGH DENSITY CIRCUITS 0.10 TO 1000μH, THIS GRADE 2 CLASS B INDUCTOR IS DESIGNED TO SOLVE DENSITY CIRCUIT APPLICATION PROBLEMS.

Fig. 7.15. Radio frequency chokes.

Inductors are also called *chokes* because of the way they hold back current or choke it. They are also called *coils* for the simple construction technique used to make them. They are nothing more than a coil of wire.

Inductors with iron cores are used in circuits where the frequencies can be heard. These are called *audio frequencies* and they are referred to as audio chokes or audio inductors. The iron core is usually laminated sheets of iron. The iron is specially made silicon steel. Silicon steel is used because it can change its magnetic orientation rapidly without causing too much opposition to the changing field or polarity reversals. The symbol for an iron core choke is ⎓⎓⎓ .

When two coils are placed near one another, *mutual induction* occurs. A change in the flux or magnetic field in one coil will cause an emf to be induced in the other coil. The two coils have mutual inductance. The amount of mutual inductance depends on the distance between the two coils. If the coils are separated a considerable distance, the amount of flux common to both coils is small and the mutual inductance is low. If the coils are close together nearly all the flux on one coil will link the turns of the other. The mutual inductance can be increased greatly by mounting both coils on the same iron core.

Mutual inductance of two adjacent coils depends upon the physical size of the two coils, the number of turns in each coil, the distance between the two coils, the distance between the axes of the two coils, and the permeability of the cores. *Permeability* is the ease with which magnetic lines of force distribute themselves throughout a material.

Alternating Current

Most of us have grown up with alternating current (AC). We are used to the 60-hertz (Hz) line current that is furnished to every house in the United States. It is much better than direct current (DC) when it comes to transporting power over long distances without huge losses. It is also important since electronics devices rely so heavily on alternating current. The radio frequencies which bring us radio and television are also AC. In order to get a better understanding of AC, we should look at how it is generated and distributed.

Alternating current has a distinct advantage over direct current. Alternating current can be stepped up to obtain higher voltages and lower currents and still produce the same amount of power at the other end of the line. It can be transported over long distances through small wires because of the higher voltages and lower currents. Current determines the size of the wire. Then it is stepped down for local distribution. Since transformers are very efficient machines, very low losses are experienced with AC.

Usually, alternating current is generated at 13,800 volts (V). This is then stepped up to at least 138,000 V for distribution. The most commonly used high voltages for long-distance transmission are 138,000, 250,000, and 750,000 V. Once the power reaches its destination, it is reduced to as low as 240 V for home use. This is further split for home circuits of 120 V.

AC GENERATOR

Alternating current is produced in an AC generator, or *alternator*, through the interaction of magnetic fields and electric conductors. Basically, the voltage and current that result from this *electromagnetic induction* is called AC electricity. (When necessary, it can be converted to DC.)

Alternating current can be produced by simply rotating one or more turns of wire in a magnetic field. The arrangement shown in Fig. 7.16A demonstrates the principle involved in the generation of alternating current. The flux density is a constant that depends on the strength of the permanent magnet or electromagnet. The length of the conductor in the magnetic field is also constant. The loop is revolved at a constant speed by some external mechanical force, such as an internal combustion engine, steam engine, water turbine, or electric motor. It is important to keep in mind that one factor that does change as the coil is rotated is the angle at which the conductor moves in relation to the magnetic lines of force. The angle changes 360 degrees as the coil is rotated.

Figure 7.16A shows the single turn of wire rotated in the magnetic field. This will generate only a small amount of electrical energy. Nonetheless, such a loop or turn becomes part of a complete electrical circuit whenever a load is connected across the terminals of the loop. In Fig. 7.16A, the ends of the loop are connected to a pair of slip rings. Power from the loop is then conducted to the load through a pair of brushes. The current in the load is the same as the current induced in the rotating loop.

Fig. 7.16B shows the loop in the vertical position at 0 degrees and the rotating conductors are shown moving parallel to the lines of magnetic force. For a brief period the conductors are not cutting any lines of force, so no current is induced.

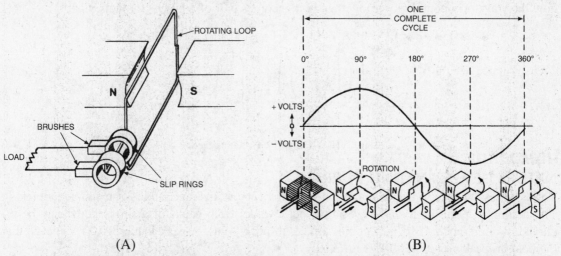

(A) (B)

Fig. 7.16. A simple AC generator. (A) Power from the loop is conducted to the load through a pair of brushes. The current in the load is the same as the current induced in the rotating loop. (B) The position of the conductor while rotating in a magnetic field determines the magnitude and direction of the induced current.

As long as the loop is rotated in the magnetic field, electricity is produced. The amplitude and direction of the current produced changes with time, forming a characteristic *waveform,* or pattern, known as a *sine wave*. The sine wave is the basic waveform of alternating current or voltage. See Fig. 7.17 for sine wave generation. As the generator loop continues to turn in a 360° circle, the output of the generator resembles the sine wave shown. Note how the various points on the circuit are shown in relationship to the sine wave.

One complete cycle of the generator is one *hertz*. A hertz (Hz) is a measurement of *frequency,* or the number of times the alternating current changes direction in 1 second. (The time base of 1 second is standard in the electrical field.) 60 Hz means the generator makes 60 complete cycles in 1 second. The word hertz means "frequency (cycles) per second" so the words "1 second" are not used with it.

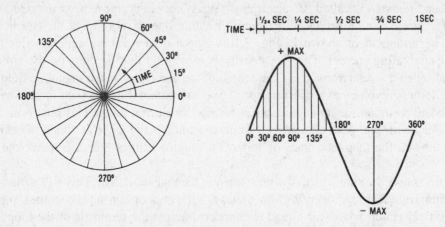

Fig. 7.17. A 360° rotation of the loop will produce a sine wave output.

Frequency can also be expressed in megahertz, or MHz; this is 1 million hertz. It can also be expressed in kilohertz, which means 1000 times or hertz. Kilohertz is abbreviated kHz. (Note that k is a lowercase letter.)

Fig. 7.18 shows the difference between 4 Hz and 1 Hz. Note that both of them occur in 1 s. Note how the waveform comes closer together as it becomes part of a higher frequency.

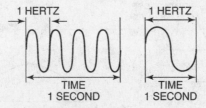

Fig. 7.18. 4 Hz and 1 Hz compared.

NATURE OF ALTERNATING CURRENT

Three values are used to describe alternating current; peak, average, and root-mean-square (rms). The maximum point on a sine wave is the peak value. Both peaks of a single hertz may be included in a reference. If so, it becomes a peak-to-peak value. A peak value of 100 V means that the peak-to-peak value is 200 V (Fig. 7.19).

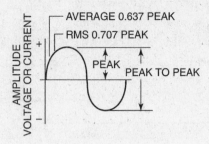

Fig. 7.19. AC sine wave values

The average of all instantaneous values of a generator is measured at regular intervals. The values are taken at selected points in the generating process. The average of these is the average value of AC current. The average value is 0.637 times the peak. This means that a peak of 100 V is equal to 63.7 V average. However, average is not often used in reference to AC. Instead, root-mean-square (rms) is used more often.

Root-mean-square is a method used for equating alternating current to direct current. Since AC is constantly changing, it forms a sine wave. The values used for rms figuring are taken from selected points in the sine wave generating process. The AC is constantly changing and does not have the heating value of DC. That is because DC comes up to its peak and stays there until turned off. Therefore, if you take the AC sine wave and break it into four parts, each containing 90° of the complete cycle needed to generate 1 Hz, you will find that the instantaneous voltage and current when taken 90 times (once of each degree) and squared, then averaged (*mean* means average) and the square root taken of the average, you will have 0.7071 times the peak value of the sine wave. This shows that rms, effective heat, and heating effect all mean the same thing. You could also get the rms, or 0.7071 value, by taking the *sine* of 45°. Since 45° is one-half of the 90° to the peak of the waveform, it makes more sense mathematically. It also makes sense because the shape of the waveform is not a semicircle, but is shaped more like the mathematical equivalent of a sine value.

Transformers

A transformer is used to step up or step down alternating current voltages. It is not used with direct current.

A transformer is a device consisting of two coils that can change voltages. The voltage put into a transformer is either stepped up or stepped down. (In some instances, however, isolation transformers are used so that they have the same output as input voltage. They are used to eliminate the ground convention line current. That way you must come across both terminals to receive a shock instead of any ground and the hot side of the line.)

Fig. 7.20 shows how transformers are used to distribute electric power from the generator to the consumer. Note that the symbols used for the transformer are two coils of wire with straight lines in between to designate the iron core.

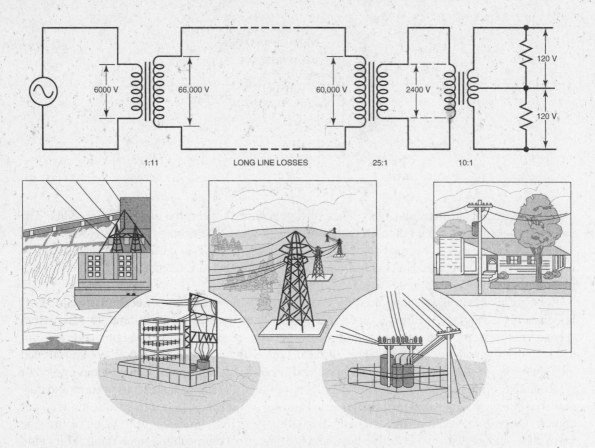

Fig. 7.20. Using transformers to distribute alternating current over long distances.

A transformer has a primary winding and a secondary winding. A transformer is simply a coil when it has no load on the secondary. When a load is placed on the output side (the secondary winding), the device actually becomes a transformer.

Transformers come in many sizes and shapes. They may be used on alternating currents at power line frequencies of 25, 50, or 60 and also on frequencies of more than 1 million Hz. The transformers used on radio frequencies do not have cores. They have air for a core, and their physical size is much smaller than power frequency transformers.

Since there are no moving parts in a transformer, it can be up to 99 percent efficient. The only moving part is the current. Losses are eliminated by using silicon steel for the core laminations. The silicon steel reduces the losses due to hysteresis caused by changing the polarity many times per second. Eddy currents are small currents induced in the metal by the changing magnetic field. Laminations eliminate the losses caused by eddy currents. Copper losses are reduced to a minimum by using the proper size wire for the amount of current being handled.

POWER TRANSFORMERS

A power transformer can be both a step-up and a step-down unit (Fig. 7.19). The secondary windings can furnish a number of different voltages. These voltages may be either higher or lower than the primary voltage. This type of transformer is used in electronics equipment where a number of different voltages are needed.

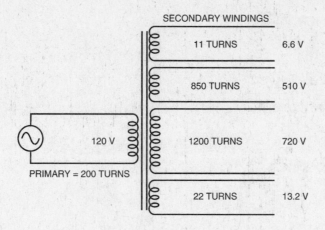

Fig. 7.21. Power transformer schematic.

Inductive Reactance

Inductive reactance is the opposition put up to alternating current by a coil. The coil has a definite time or delay built in due to the ratio of inductance to resistance. This built-in delay of current comes in conflict with the AC since the current is constantly changing and not necessarily at the same rate as the natural tendency of the coil. Therefore, the reaction or reactance is in the form of an opposition. Since it is an opposition, it is measured in ohms. Reactance is represented by the symbol X. Inductance is represented by its symbol L. When the inductive reactance is represented, it is written as X_L. It is measured in ohms.

A number of factors determine X_L. One is the frequency of AC, which affects reactance. Another is the size of the inductor. The formula used to calculate X_L is

$$X_L = 2\pi f L$$

In this equation, f is the frequency, measured in Hz. L is inductance, measured in henrys (H). Pi (π) is a standard mathematical terms with a value of 3.141592654. Thus, 2π equals 6.28 when rounded off for quick answers.

By increasing the f, the X_L increases. If the f is decreased, the X_L decreases. The same is true for L, or inductance. Since the 2π is a constant, it does not change. Therefore, the only two variables for X_L are frequency and inductance. Keep in mind that the voltage and current are 90 degrees out of phase whenever there is an inductor in the circuit. The voltage leads the current by 90 degrees in a purely inductive circuit.

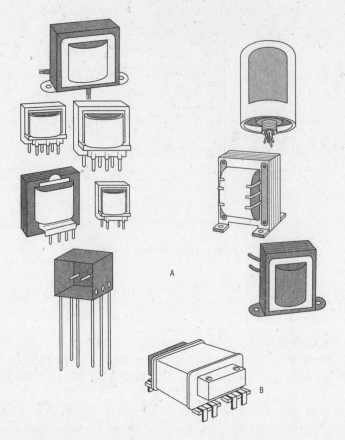

Fig. 7.22. A. Various sizes and types of transformers. (B) Power transformer.

Resistors and inductive reactances both produce opposition, and both are measured in ohms. This means that inductive reactances which are in series are simply added to obtain the total inductive reactance in a circuit:

$$X_{LT} = X_{L1} + X_{L2} + X_{L3} + \dots$$

Inductive reactances which are in parallel are treated the same as resistors in parallel. You can use the product divided by the sum formula or the reciprocal formula:

$$X_{LT} = \frac{X_{L1} \times X_{L2}}{X_{L1} + X_{L2}}$$

$$\frac{1}{X_{LT}} = \frac{1}{X_{L1}} + \frac{1}{X_{L2}} + \frac{1}{X_{L3}} + \dots$$

The major use of inductance is to provide a minimum reactance for low frequencies. Inductors produce high opposition to higher frequencies.

One specific use of inductance is in filters. Filters are used when certain frequencies are desired and others are to be avoided. An inductor is used that has an X_L that passes certain frequencies and opposes others.

The main use for inductive reactance is in electronic circuits. Such circuits, along with capacitors, tune in certain frequencies and reject others. An example is the tuner of your radio or television.

Capacitors

Capacitors play an important role in the building of circuits. A capacitor is a device that opposes any change in circuit voltage. That property of a capacitor which opposes voltage change is called *capacitance*.

Capacitors make it possible to store electric energy. Electrons are held within a capacitor. This, in effect, is stored electricity. It is also known as an *electrical potential,* or an *electrostatic field*. Electrostatic fields hold electrons. When the buildup of electrons becomes great enough, the electric potential is discharged. This process takes place in nature: clouds build up electrostatic fields. Their discharge is seen as lightning.

Fig. 7.23 shows a simple capacitor. Two plates of a conductor material are isolated from one another. Between the two plates is a dielectric material. The dielectric conducts electrons easily. Electrons are stored on the plate surfaces. The larger the surface, the more area is available for stored electrons. Increasing the size of the plates therefore increases the capacitance.

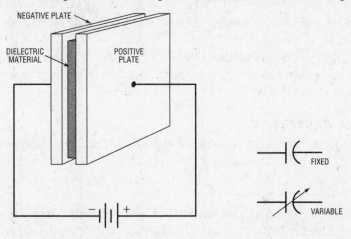

Fig. 7.23. Design of a capacitor.   **Symbols for a capacitor.**

OPERATION OF THE CAPACITOR

If a capacitor has no charge of electrons, it is uncharged. This happens when there is no voltage applied to the plates. An uncharged capacitor is shown in Fig. 7.24A. Note the symbol for a capacitor in this drawing. This is the preferred way to show a capacitor: a straight line and a curved line facing each other. Note that the circuit has a DC source and a three-position switch that is in the open position.

In Fig. 7.24B, the switch has been closed to position 1. This causes current to flow. A difference in potential is created by the voltage source. This causes electrons to be transferred from the positive to the negative plate. This transfer continues as long as the voltage source is connected to the two plates and until the accumulated charge becomes equal to the potential difference of the applied voltage. That is, charging takes place until the capacitor is charged.

In Fig. 7.24C, the voltage has been removed. The switch is open. At this point, the potential difference, or charge, across the capacitor remains. That is, there is still a surplus of electrons on the negative plate of the capacitor. This charge remains in place until a path is provided for discharging the excess electrons.

In Fig. 7.24D, the switch is moved to position 3. This opens the path for discharging the surplus electrons. Notice that the discharge path is in the opposite direction from the charge path. This shows how a change in circuit voltage results in a change in the capacitor charge.

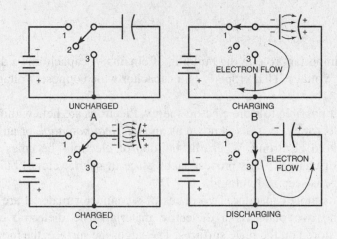

Fig. 7.24. Charge and discharge of a capacitor.

Some electrons leave the excess (negative) plate. They do this in an attempt to keep the voltage in the circuit constant.

As you can see from the foregoing, the ability of a capacitor to charge and discharge can be useful in many types of circuits. Its ability to oppose any change in the circuit voltage can also be helpful. All this will be put to work later in electronic circuits.

CAPACITY OF A CAPACITOR

The two plates of the capacitor may be made of almost any material. The only criterion is that the material will allow electrons to collect on it. The dielectric may be air, vacuum, plastics, wood, or mica.

Three factors determine the capacity of a capacitor: the area of the plates, the distance between the plates, and the material used as a dielectric. The larger the plate area, the greater the capacity, or capacitance. The distance between the plates of a capacitor determines the effect that electrons have upon one another. That is because electrons possess a charge, or field, around them that can react with those close by. Capacitance increases when the plates are brought close together. One of the effects of the dielectric materials is determined by its thickness. The thinner the dielectric, the closer the plates will be. A thin dielectric can thus increase capacitance. Some dielectrics have better insulating qualities than others and will allow greater voltages to be applied between the plates before breaking down. Take a look at the dielectric materials listed in the table below to see how various materials affect the capacitance of a capacitor.

Material	Dielectric Constant (*K*)
Air or vacuum	1
Rubber	2–4
Oil	2–5
Paper	2–6
Mica	3–8
Glass	8
Ceramics	80–1,200

WORKING VOLTAGE DC

The maximum safe working voltage of a capacitor in a direct current circuit is identified as the working voltage DC, or WVDC. Above this voltage, a capacitor is expected to puncture or develop a short circuit. If the temperature in which a circuit operates reaches 140°F (60°C) or higher, the voltage rating is lowered.

Voltage ratings for mica, paper, and ceramic capacitors are usually 200, 400, and 600 V DC. Oil-filled capacitors have voltage ratings ranging up to 7500 V. As the voltage ratings become higher, the physical size of the capacitors becomes greater. Never operate a capacitor above its rated WVDC. It is customary to use a capacitor in a circuit with about 50 to 75 percent of its rated voltage.

Capacitors in Series

Capacitors can be connected in series, but the series reduces the capacitance. The formula used for finding capacitance for two capacitors in series is

$$C_r = \frac{C_1 \times C_2}{C_1 + C_2}$$

$$\frac{1}{C_r} = \frac{1}{C_1} + \frac{1}{C_2} + \frac{1}{C_3} + ...$$

As you increase the distance between the plates, effectively, when placing them in series, you also increase the WVDC rating. Just add the WVDC ratings of the capacitors to obtain the higher value created with the placement in series.

Capacitors in Parallel

Capacitors can be connected in parallel if their polarity is observed in the case of electrolytics. For standard, nonpolarized types, it is not necessary to observe any particular connection procedure except to place the leads together in order to produce a parallel connection. Placing capacitors in parallel *increases* the capacitance. Just add the individual capacitances to obtain the total capacitance. However, keep in mind that the WVDC will be the rating of the *smallest* value of voltage in the WVDC ratings.

MEASURING CAPACITANCE

Capacitance is measured in farads (F). The *farad* is defined as having the ability to store enough electrons to produce a voltage difference of one volt across the terminals while producing one ampere of current for one second.

The farad is a very large unit of capacitance. The capacitors we use in electricity and in electronics are much, much smaller. They are measured in *microfarads* (0.000001 F) and in micro-microfarads, now called *picofarads* (0.000000000001 F).

It is often necessary to interpret or change values. This occurs as you read circuit drawings or markings on capacitors. You may, for example, find yourself working with capacitors marked in terms of pF and drawings indicated μF. Keep in mind the following to make sure you get the conversion correct and that you are tuned in to the correct formulas.

- pF to μF, move the decimal six places to the left.
- μF to F, move the decimal six places to the left.
- F to μF, move the decimal six places to the right.
- μF to pF, move the decimal six places to the right.
- pF to F, move the decimal 12 places to the left.
- F to pF, move the decimal 12 places to the right.

SPECIAL PURPOSE CAPACITOR

People in electronics have long dreamed of having a source of power other than a battery to power devices that may require small currents for long periods of storage time, such as the case with the memory of computers or calculators. This is now possible with the production of a capacitor of sufficient strength (one Farad). The 1-Farad capacitor has long been thought of as a desirable thing for many uses. It is now possible to package a capacitor in the 1-Farad size in a 1.1 inch diameter unit only 0.55 inch high (see Figure 7.25).

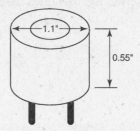

Fig. 7.25. Electrolytic capacitor of 1 Farad fits a package 1.1" diameter and 0.55" high.

This energy source makes it possible to support digital system backup application without batteries. It has fast recharge time, easy interface and virtually unlimited life. It is especially well suited for applications where the energy of a battery is not required, and reliability, long life, low cost, and simple design and implementation are of primary importance.

DIP capacitors can now be purchased in dual in-line packages. They resemble the standard IC chip packaging. However, they contain capacitors connected between the pins as shown in the following figure:

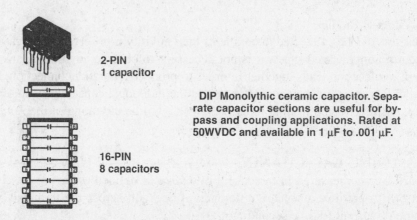

2-PIN
1 capacitor

DIP Monolythic ceramic capacitor. Separate capacitor sections are useful for bypass and coupling applications. Rated at 50WVDC and available in 1 µF to .001 µF.

16-PIN
8 capacitors

Fig. 7.26. DIP monolythic ceramic capacitor. Separate capacitor sections are useful for bypass and coupling applications.

Capacitive Reactance

Capacitive reactance is that opposition that a capacitor presents to alternating current (AC). A capacitor has a definite time period for charging: $T = R \times C$. The time T in seconds (s) is equal to the resistance (Ω) times the capacitance (F). This produces a time constant which is 63.2 percent of the maximum voltage presented to the capacitor. It takes five time constants for a capacitor to charge to its full, or 99.3 percent, level. It also takes the same amount of time to discharge when presented with a resistance across its terminals.

When AC is present across the terminals of a capacitor, it changes faster than the capacitor can charge and discharge. This reaction or reactance is determined by the frequency of the AC and the capacity of the capacitor. A formula used to express capacitive reactance is

$$X_c = \frac{1}{2\pi fC}$$

where f = frequency, expressed in hertz

C = capacitance, expressed in farads

X_c = capacitive reactance, expressed in ohms since it is opposition to current flow

The following are conditions which occur when a capacitor is introduced into an AC circuit.

1. If the capacitance decreases, the capacitive reactance will increase for the same frequency.
2. If the capacitance increases, the capacitive reactance will decrease as long as the same frequency is presented to the capacitor.
3. If the frequency is decreased and the capacitor is the same, then the capacitive reactance will increase.
4. If the frequency is increased, then the capacitive reactance will decrease provided the capacitance stays the same.

As you can see from these statements and observations, the increase or decrease of the frequency or capacitance will cause the reverse reaction with the X_c.

Resonance

Resonance is a very important part of electronics. It is necessary for the operation of the many types of television receivers and FM and AM radios. Resonance is created through the proper arrangement of a coil and capacitor.

Circuits with resistance, capacitance, and inductance behave differently from those with only one or two of these factors. For instance, a circuit with resistance reacts to alternating current (AC) and direct current (DC) the same way. However, when both a resistor and inductor are in a circuit, another factor is introduced because AC is applied to the combination. It behaves completely different from the DC circuit consisting of only a resistor and coil. The same is true with a resistor and capacitor combination. The AC introduces the capacitive reactance, but DC causes only the charging of the capacitor at a time determined by the values of the resistor and the capacitor.

It becomes important, then, for us to look closely at the combination of devices connected to a circuit. It is very evident that AC and DC cause different things to happen in an electric circuit.

The use of vectors will aid in the understanding of phase angle introduced by various combinations of these three devices (inductors, capacitors, and resistors).

RESISTANCE, CAPACITANCE, AND INDUCTANCE

Resistance produces an opposition to current flow in a circuit. The resistor is the device that produces the opposition. It behaves the same with either AC or DC.

Capacitive reactance produces an opposition to current flow in a circuit. The capacitor is the device that produces the opposition. The capacitor behaves differently with AC than with DC. Remember (just as in resistance), the opposition, or capacitive reactance, is measured in ohms.

Inductive reactance produces an opposition to current flow in a circuit. The inductor is the device that produces the opposition. The inductor behaves differently with AC than with DC. Inductive reactance is also measured in ohms.

Bear in mind, also, that the capacitor opposes any *change* in circuit *voltage*. The inductor opposes any *change* in circuit *current*. These two simple statements make a great deal of difference between understanding resonance and not being able to visualize it. So reread them to make sure you have them clearly in mind.

The relationship between current and voltage is vital to an understanding of electronics and electric circuits.

IMPEDANCE

The *total* opposition to current flow within a circuit is impedance. The symbol for impedance is Z. Impedance impedes or opposes current flow. It is a term used when either resistance, capacitive reactance, inductive reactance, or any combination of the three is used. In DC circuits, opposition to voltage and current is resistance only, since capacitors and inductors do not have reactance with DC—only AC. Z is measured in ohms.

Impedance can be R and X_L. It can be R and X_C, or it can be R and X_C and X_L. Impedance (Z) can also be used when there is X_L and X_C. Any combination of these oppositions can be referred to as an impedance.

Voltage lags the current in a capacitive circuit. Current lags the voltage in an inductive circuit. Voltage lagged the current in a capacitor by 90° in a purely capacitive circuit. Voltage led the current in a purely inductive circuit. That is another way of saying that the current lagged the voltage by 90°. This leading and lagging is very important in any understanding of impedance for it takes into account the *phase angle*.

The phase angle is the difference between the voltage and the current in a circuit caused by either capacitance or inductance in an AC circuit. If we want to combine these phase angles, such as when a capacitor and inductor are in a circuit, we have to do it vectorially (see Fig. 7.27). Fig. 7.27 is a diagram of how impedance is represented by Z, resistance by R, and reactance by X_L. Note the angle formed by lines *BA* and *AD*. Z is shown halfway between the two lines and as a result shows a phase angle of 45°. This happens when the resistance (R) and inductive reactance (X_L) are equal. As you can see, impedance is the *vector sum* of resistance and reactance. A *vector* is a line segment used to represent a quantity that has both direction and magnitude. Vectors are used to represent a quantity that has both direction and magnitude. Vectors are used to represent current, voltage, or any combination of the electrical quantities encountered.

A vector can show direction of current flow. It can also show the magnitude, or amount, of current flowing. A vector sum is a line representing the total of two or more vectors. Impedance is stated in terms of a vector sum.

Inductive reactance causes the current in an inductor to lag 90° behind the voltage. Therefore, a graphic way of presenting the impedance of current can be drawn as shown in Fig. 7.27. In this illustration, resistance is plotted on the horizontal line *AD*. The length of the line *AD* is proportional to the amount of resistance in the circuit. Proportional means that the quantity of resistance within the circuit is represented by line *AD*. Zero resistance is indicated by point *A*. The value of resistance in the circuit is indicated at point *D*. Using the same scale, the amount of inductive reactance is plotted on a line 90° from the resistance line. This is because the voltage and current in the resistor are in phase with one another. This means that the resistance line *AD* can be used as the horizontal reference and everything else will be plotted up or down in reference to this horizontal reference.

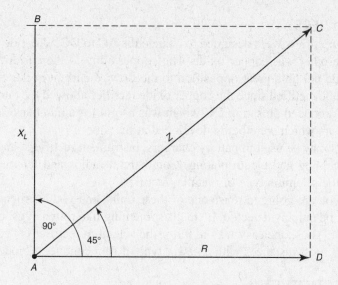

Fig. 7.27. Impedance shown in vector form.

The vertical line *AB* represents the inductive reactance. This is also proportional. Zero inductive reactance is shown at point *A*. The value of inductive reactance is indicated at point *B*.

The impedance *Z* is the vector sum of the two lines. It is represented by line *AC*. To find the value of *C*, begin by constructing a parallelogram. This is shown in Fig. 7.27 by the dotted lines finishing up the Figure. A *parallelogram* is a four-sided figure whose opposite sides are parallel and equal. In Fig. 7.27, the dotted line *CD* is parallel to *AB*, and *BC* is parallel to *AD*.

C is the point where the parallelogram is completed. The value of *Z* is found by drawing a straight line between *C* and *A*. This line can be measured and the value of *Z* found by equating it to the units used in X_L and *R*.

The value of this graphic method is that it helps you to visualize the procedure. In practice there are faster methods for calculating impedance. This is a simple operation on most calculators. Using a calculator becomes even easier once you can visualize and understand the values involved.

Changing Alternating Current to Direct Current

Since alternating current (AC) is inexpensive, it is used in thousands of devices. It can be stepped up or stepped down by using a transformer. It is a versatile type of power that can easily be changed to fit the voltage or current needs of particular circuits. However, direct current (DC) is also useful for many devices. Electronics depend upon DC for many of its circuit components. This dependence upon DC requires a source of inexpensive direct current for a variety of voltages and currents.

Historically the changing of AC to DC began around the turn of the century when AC became available at Niagara Falls, New York, but was not easily transported to Buffalo (26 miles away) where it was needed by the milling industry. The demand for soap products became rather important in our country around 1900 when the newly "arrived" middle class was demanding the cleanliness of everything, and it became apparent that DC current could be used to produce any number of soap products from various cheap chemicals. Niagara Falls, with its inexpensive source of falling water-generated AC, would easily become one of the chemical centers of the country if only the AC could be converted to DC. The change was vital because DC was much more easily used in the chemical processes of the time.

METALLIC RECTIFIERS

Large copper oxide rectifiers were designed to change the AC to DC. One side of the rectifier disk was copper, and the other was copper oxide. The copper allowed the current to flow easily, but the copper oxide side put up a great opposition to the flow of current in the other direction. This meant the AC could be rectified since the copper oxide rectifier allowed the current to flow in only one direction. This produced pulsating DC which was useful for a number of chemical processes and for driving motors which were being developed at the time.

Metallic rectifiers may be used in battery chargers, instrument rectifiers, and many other applications including welding and electroplating. Commercial radios and television sets have been designed to utilize the selenium type of metallic rectifier.

One caution: If you are going to reuse one of these units, and you overheat the selenium type, a pungent odor will be quickly detected. It smells something like rotten eggs, or hydrogen sulfate, or like molten sulfur. Thus, one easy way to tell if the selenium rectifier is "gone" is by the odor. It can be replaced in most instances with a newer type of semiconductor diode.

SOLID STATE RECTIFIERS

Semiconductor materials are used to make a diode. A *diode* is a device which allows current to flow in one direction and not the other. Germanium and silicon are used as the materials for semiconductor diodes.

Crystals of germanium or silicon are grown from a *melt* which includes small quantities of impure substances such as phosphorus, indium, boron, and other *impurity* atoms. The crystal structure of the resulting metallic chips or wafers permits current flow in one direction only.

Historically, the crystal diode dates to the crystal set used by the first amateurs who worked on making their own receivers of radio signals. Fig. 7.28 shows how a crystal set may have looked in early days of radio. Note particularly the crystal and cat whisker. This was the forerunner of today's crystal diodes.

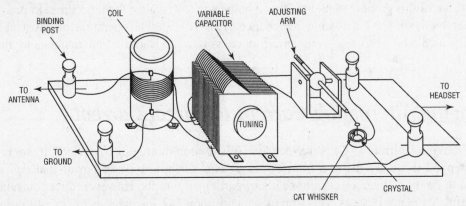

Fig. 7.28. Early receiver consisting of a crystal, cat whisker, coil, and capacitor, known as the *crystal set* to early radio buffs.

The first use of the crystal semiconductor as a rectifier (detector) was in the early days of radio. A crystal was clamped in a small cup or receptacle and a flexible wire (cat whisker) made light contact with the crystal. Tuning the receiver was accomplished by operating the adjusting arm until the cat whisker was positioned on a spot of the crystal that resulted in a sound in the headset. Tuning the variable capacitor provided maximum signal in the headset. Trying to find the correct or loudest point on the crystal was quite time-consuming. Today's point contact diode is identical to the crystal diode of yesteryear (see Fig. 7.29).

The development of the point contact transistor was announced in 1948. The physical construction of the point contact transistor is similar to that of the point contact diode except that a third lead with a metallic point contact is placed near the other metallic point contact on the semiconductor.

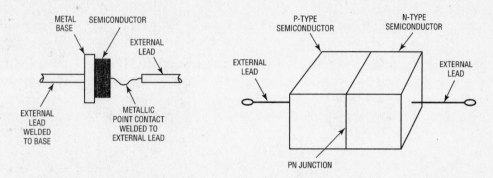

Fig. 7.29. Physical construction of the point contact diode.

Physical construction of the junction diode.

The junction diode was first announced in 1949. The junction diode consists of a junction between two dissimilar sections of semiconductor material. One section, because of its characteristics, is called a P semiconductor. The connections to the junction diode consist of a lead to the P semiconductor material and a lead to the N semiconductor. The P material has a deficiency of one electron for every covalent bond of the material. The N material has an extra electron [therefore the (–) or N designation] for every covalent bond of the material. *Covalent* means that the atoms share electron orbits with adjacent atoms.

The junction diode handles larger power than the point contact diode, but the junction diode has a larger shunt capacitance.

Many types of semiconductor diodes are available. They vary in size from those so small that they are hard to see to those as large as 2 in. in diameter. They can withstand high voltages and carry large currents. The improvement of the semiconductor material creates better-quality diodes.

VACUUM TUBE DIODE

The electron tube is considered by many as the primary starting point for electronics. It is responsible for the rapid advancement of electronics up to the invention of the transistor.

The electron tube is made up of a highly evacuated glass or metal shell, which encloses several elements. The elements consist of the cathode that emits electrons when hot, the plate, and sometimes one or more grids. The diode does not have a grid. The *di* part of the name means *two*; *ode* is short for *electrode*. Put them together and you have two electrodes in an envelope. Fig. 7.30 shows a typical example of a two-element tube.

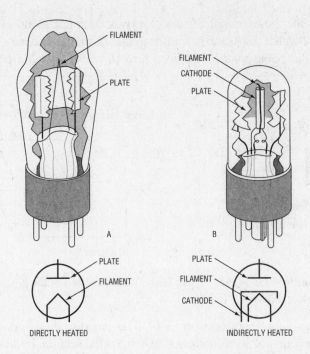

Fig. 7.30. Cutaway view of a diode or vacuum tube rectifier.

Construction Details

The original diode was constructed by Thomas Edison, inventor of the incandescent lamp, shortly after his invention of the lamp itself. He added a metal plate inside his evacuated lamp and provided an external terminal from it for use as an electrode. Then he used his heated filament as another electrode and arranged that diode as shown in Fig. 7.31.

Operation of the Vacuum Tube Diode

The operation of the tube can be observed when it is connected in a circuit. Fig. 7.31 is composed of a diode vacuum tube, a battery, a milliammeter, and a resistor. Note what happens to the meter in A as compared with B in Fig. 7.31. As the battery polarity is changed, the action of the vacuum tube changes. When the cathode is negative, the electrons flow through the vacuum from the cathode (K) to the plate (P). The plate has a positive potential applied.

When the plate is connected to the negative potential and the cathode to the positive terminal of the battery, the electrons—being of a negative charge—are repelled by the like potential on the plate. Therefore, there is no current flow (or electron flow) through the tube when it is *reverse-biased*.

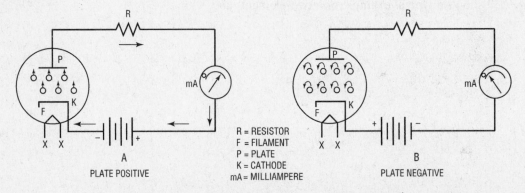

Fig. 7.31. Operation of the vacuum tube diode circuit.

Now try to visualize how an alternating current (AC) is applied between the cathode and plate. As the polarity reverses itself in AC, the tube will conduct and not conduct according to the polarity of the two elements. Thus, the current will flow during one-half of the hertz applied to the tube and not conduct when the other half is applied. That action produces a half-wave rectified output from the circuit (see Fig. 7.32).

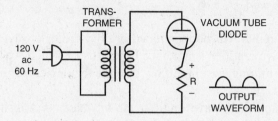

Fig. 7.32. Output of the rectifier when connected to an AC source.

How does the vacuum tube operate? Well, now that we have seen some of its action, let's take a closer look at the inside workings of the device. First, we'll need a source of electrons. The electrons are obtained by heating a cathode made up of a nickel sleeve or cylinder coated with thoriated tungsten. The thoriated tungsten gives off electrons when heated to about 2,000°C (3,657.6°F). The cathode (emitter) is brought up to temperature by applying the rated voltage across the heater terminals marked with an X in Fig. 7.31.

If the battery is connected so that the plate is positive and the cathode is negative, the meter will indicate a current flow in the external circuit. This phenomenon, the emission of electrons from a hot body, was first observed by Edison in 1883 and is called the *Edison effect*. However, if the battery is reversed in its connection to the electrodes of the tube, there is no current flow.

The total number of electrons emitted by the hot electrode at a given operating temperature is always the same, regardless of the plate voltage. This same condition exists regardless of the plate polarity because the electrons fly into the space surrounding the emitter to produce a cluster or cloud, which is in turbulence or great agitation. This could constitute a negative space charge that constantly tends to repel the electrons toward, and into, the emitter as fast as they are being emitted. The negative charge on the plate only repels the nearby electrons within the cloud, but the action is so effective that none of the electrons reach the plate regardless of the plate voltage, as long as the plate remains negative.

Examine Fig. 7.31A again. With low values of positive plate voltage, only those electrons of the space-charged cloud that are nearest to the plate are attracted to it, and the plate current is low. As the plate voltage is increased (the cathode temperature remaining constant), greater numbers of electrons are attracted to the plate and, correspondingly, fewer of those being emitted are repelled back into the cathode.

If the plate voltage is gradually increased, eventually a plate voltage value (saturation voltage) is reached at which all the electrons being emitted are in transit to the plate and none is repelled back into the cathode.

When as many electrons as possible are attracted by the plate and it absorbs them, the saturation current is reached. Any further increase in plate voltage can cause no further increase in plate current flowing through the tube.

Power Supply Rectifiers

Older electronics equipment needed a power supply that would furnish more than one voltage. Most of the vacuum tubes needed filament voltages of 5.0, 6.3, or 12.6 volts (V). A winding on the power transformer had to provide these voltages and the current necessary to heat the filaments to boil off the electrons to cause the tubes to operate. Also on the power transformer was a high-voltage winding that would take the 120 V AC put into the primary of the transformer and step it up to over 300 V. This 300 V AC coming out of the transformer had to be changed to DC before the tubes could utilize it on their plates and screen grids. This changing of AC to DC was the job of the diode or rectifier tube.

RECTIFIER CIRCUITS

Three types of rectifier circuits will be mentioned briefly: the half-wave, the full-wave, and the bridge rectifier. A half-wave rectifier is a device by means of which AC is changed to pulsating direct current (pdc) by permitting current to flow through the device during one-half of the power supply hertz.

Fig. 7.33 shows a simple half-wave rectifier circuit. Note that inside the diode there is a vacuum or a gas, according to which type is needed. The electrons are attracted to the plate of the diode when it is more positive than the cathode. When the plate becomes negative with respect to the cathode, electrons are repelled by it, and no electron stream can flow in the tube. Therefore, a single diode may be used as a half-wave rectifier because the electrons can flow in the tube during only the half of the hertz when the plate is positive relative to the cathode.

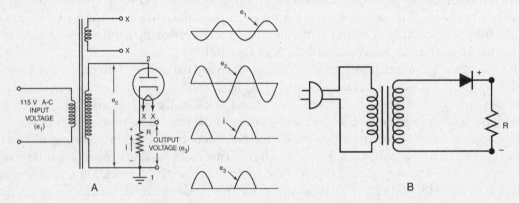

Fig. 7.33. (A) Half-wave vacuum tube rectifier circuit with waveforms. (B) Semiconductor half-wave rectifier circuit (waveforms are same as vacuum tube rectifier in A).

A full-wave rectifier is a device that has two or more elements so arranged that the current output flows in the same direction during each half-hertz of the AC power supply. Full-wave rectification may be accomplished by using two diodes in the same envelope (a duo-diode) with a common cathode connected to one end of the load resistor, such as shown in Fig. 7.34. The other end of the load resistor is connected to the center tap of the transformer.

Take a look at Fig. 7.35 for a four-vacuum-tube-diode arrangement referred to as a *bridge rectifier circuit*. This is a full-wave rectifier; the output is full-wave as shown in the previous two-diode circuit. There are a couple of advantages to the bridge rectifier over the regular two-tube, or semiconductor, diode, full-wave rectifier. First, the bridge arrangement allows for twice the voltage output from the same power transformer. Secondly, a bridge rectifier circuit is so designed that it has only half the peak inverse voltage impressed on a tube as the full-wave rectifier with only two diodes. *Peak inverse voltage* (piv) is a negative voltage applied across the tube when there is no current flowing through the tube, or diode in the case of semiconductor diodes.

The bridge rectifier that uses vacuum tubes has a disadvantage since it needs three filament transformer windings. This disadvantage, of course, does not apply to the bridge circuit composed of dry-disk or semiconductor diodes, since they do not have filaments to contend with.

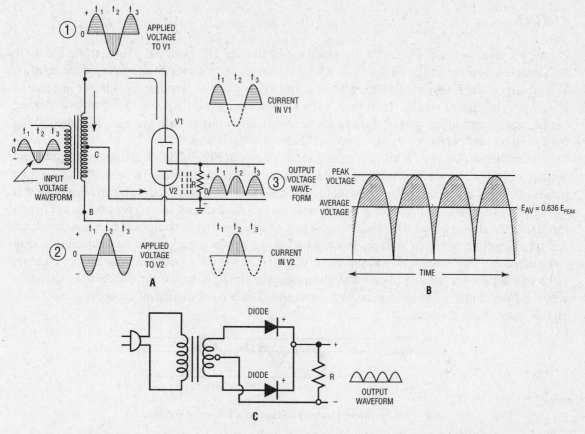

Fig. 7.34. (A and B) Full-wave vacuum tube rectifier with waveforms. (C) Semiconductor diodes used in full-wave rectifier circuit.

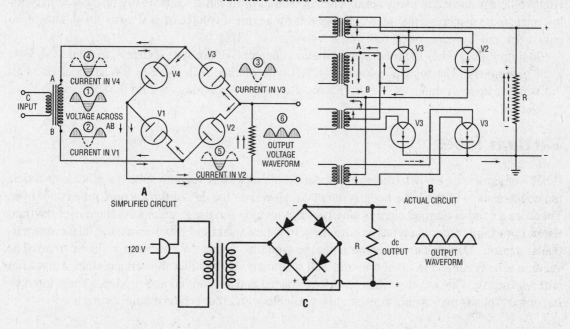

Fig. 7.35. Bridge-rectifier circuit using vacuum tubes (A and B) and semiconductor diodes (C).

Filters

Up to this point we have discussed the making of pulsating DC from AC. This is fine for some uses, but for most electronic circuits it is not pure enough DC for proper operation of the circuits. Too much pulsating will make a high level of hum, and in some—computer circuits, for instance—it will give unreliable results. That, then, calls for something a little purer in the way of making the DC usable and of the proper form to do the work. Filter circuits are the answer to smoothing out the ripple and pulsations of full-wave and half-wave rectifiers.

The unfiltered output of a full-wave rectifier is shown in Fig. 7.36. The polarity of the output voltage does not reverse, but its magnitude fluctuates about an average value as the successive pulses of energy are delivered to the load. In Fig. 7.36 the average voltage is shown as the line that divides the waveform so that area *A* equals area *B*. The fluctuations of voltage above and below this average value is called the *ripple*. The output of any rectifier is composed of a direct voltage and an alternating or ripple voltage. For most uses, the ripple voltage must be reduced to a very low amplitude. The amount of a ripple that can be tolerated varies with different uses of electron tubes and semiconductors. A circuit that eliminates the ripple voltage from the rectifier output is called a *filter*. Filter systems in general are composed of a combination of capacitors, inductors, and in some cases, resistors.

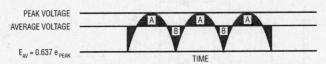

Fig. 7.36. Unfiltered output voltage of a full-wave rectifier.

VOLTAGE MULTIPLIERS

High voltage is needed in many circuits and devices. For instance, cathode ray tubes used in oscilloscopes, radar displays, and video displays call for a typical voltage of skV up to 20kV. They need only a few milliamperes of current and a regulation of ±1%.

Photomultiplier tubes are used in scintillation counters, flying spot scanners, as well as in low-level photometry. The typical voltages for this type of tube is 1 kV to 3 kV at about one-half milliampere up to as much as 5 milliamperes. Required regulation is within the 0.1% range.

Vacuum Tubes

When someone who knows something about electronics sees vacuum tubes in a book or article today, he or she will think the book is outdated. However, the day of the vacuum tube is not over. There are a number of good circuits which a vacuum tube can use to great advantage over the transistor. For example, certain types of amplifiers in the musical field contain vacuum tubes for a particular reason: Design engineers want the best-quality sound by the most reliable route. The vacuum tube is rugged in operation and will take many abuses that the semiconductor amplifier will not forgive. The vacuum tube can be overloaded and overdriven and produces some interesting output sounds that are not consistently available with other types of amplification.

Another important application of vacuum tubes is in the field of television. The vacuum tube is used for the *picture tube* in every television set made of any size. The cathode ray tube (CRT) is very much in evidence in computers and terminals located in all types of equipment. The basic knowledge that comes with understanding the vacuum tube should not be ignored if you wish to become a well-rounded, capable electronics technician or engineer.

Vacuum tubes and gas-filled tubes are not a thing of the past. They are used in many sophisticated pieces of equipment even today. The picture tube of the television set and the CRT monitor of the computer are tubes.

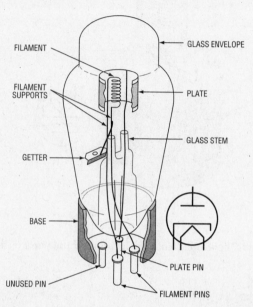

**Fig. 7.37. Early model of the diode with a single plate and cathode.
The filament was also the cathode in this directly heated tube.**

The *diode* (Fig. 7.37) is a tube with two elements. It is used primarily as a rectifier. It comes in both signal types for low voltages and currents and also in a larger variety that can handle power-line frequencies and rectify them to provide high voltages and higher currents than signal diodes. Electrons are boiled off the cathode, and the emitted electrons are attracted to the plate of the tube by the high positive voltage.

The *triode* (Fig. 7.38) is made up of three electrodes. It contains a control grid that can cause the tube to amplify signals presented between the grid and the cathode. The output of the triode has a load resistance that usually has a high voltage drop, which varies with the signal applied between the grid and the cathode. This increase in voltage from the input to the output results in amplification. The primary purpose of the triode is amplification, but it does have some frequency limitations that have to be corrected. This is where the tetrode and pentode enter the picture. They were designed to eliminate the interelectrode capacitance between the grid and the plate that could cause feedback and unwanted oscillations, producing squeals and howls.

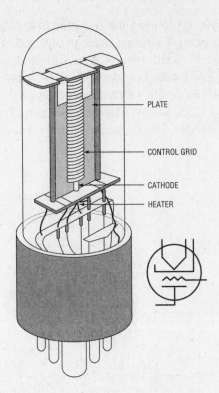

Fig. 7.38. The triode. Note the location of the parts of the tube.

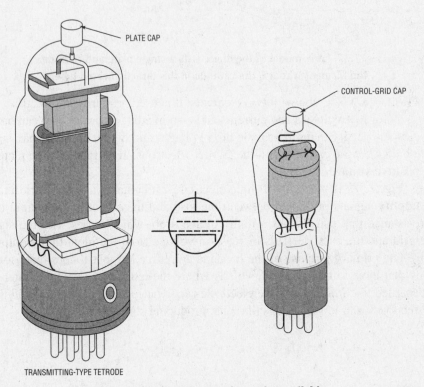

TRANSMITTING-TYPE TETRODE

Fig. 7.39. Various shapes of tetrodes available.

The *tetrode* (Fig. 7.39) has four elements. It has a screen grid added with a positive potential to get rid of some of the interelectrode capacitance of the triode. This additional grid did produce some rather unwanted results, such as a dip in the plate current at the beginning of the characteristic curve. It was overcome by the addition of another grid called the suppressor grid. With the addition of another grid it became the *pentode*, or five-element, tube. The pentode (Fig. 7.40) has a suppressor placed near the plate that has a negative potential on it so that the electrons emitted from the plate are kept near the plate and will not get in the way of the stream of electrons from the cathode. The unit of measure for transconductance, or the ability of a tube to conduct current, is the siemen (S) (formerly the mho, or the reverse of ohm).

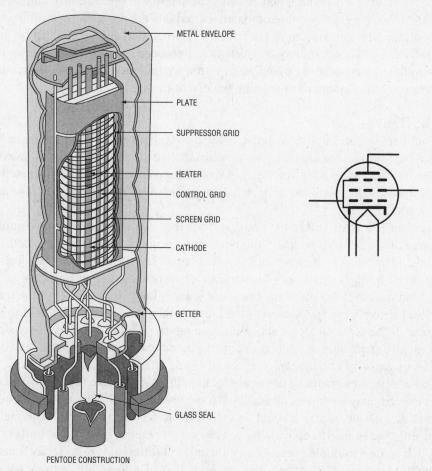

METAL ENVELOPE

PLATE

SUPPRESSOR GRID

HEATER

CONTROL GRID

SCREEN GRID

CATHODE

GETTER

GLASS SEAL

PENTODE CONSTRUCTION

Fig. 7.40. Construction details of a metal-enveloped pentode.

The beam power tube is a pentode with beam-forming plates instead of a suppressor grid. The tube is capable of handling relatively high levels of electric power for use in output stages of receivers and amplifiers. It is used in parts of transmitters and for power-handling requirements in amplifiers. The ability of the beam power tube to handle power or larger currents makes it ideal as a power amplifier tube.

A number of tubes have more than one tube in an envelope. They have several purposes and can be found in many pieces of electronic equipment. A multiunit, or dual-purpose, tube is one in which two or more individual tubes are combined within a single envelope, resulting in economy, compactness, and more satisfactory operation for certain purposes.

The filament voltage of a vacuum tube is given in the numbers preceding the first letter in its designation; that is, a 5U4 has a 5.0-volt filament.

Semiconductors (II)

The term *semiconductor* is applied to both diodes and transistors, as well as to certain special types of electronic devices. The word is based on the fact that germanium and silicon perform somewhere between the level of a conductor and an insulator in terms of opposition to current flow. The amount of opposition is programmed into or manufactured into the device by controlling the impurities introduced into pure germanium or pure silicon. Germanium and silicon can be purified to better than 99.999999%. Therefore, any other element introduced is called an *impurity* or *doping agent*. By controlling the amount of doping agent introduced into each crystalline structure, manufacturers can control the amount of opposition to current flow.

A BIT OF HISTORY

In 1833 Michael Faraday, an English scientist, made a contribution to the crystalline amplifier in his work with silver sulfide. He learned that the resistance of silver sulfide varies inversely with the temperature. As the temperature increases, the resistance decreases. This was noted as being different, since most conductors show an increase in resistance along with an increase in temperature.

It took more than 100 years before the Faraday discovery was utilized in any meaningful way. The development of the *crystal amplifier* (the transistor's original name) by three Bell Laboratory scientists utilized the work of Faraday and expanded on it. In June 1948 John Bardeen, William Shockley, and W. H. Brattain shared an office and rode to work together at Bell Labs in New Jersey. Their work on the development of the transistor led to a joint Nobel Prize for the team. From the day the Nobel Prizes were announced to the present, there has been no letup in the research and development of the semiconductor and solid state physics. Transistors have become increasingly sophisticated and reliable as their refinement has increased and their size has decreased. Modern transistors are very durable, are very small (some smaller than a human hair), are inexpensive, and have a high resistance to physical shock and impact. At one time, only discrete (separate) devices existed; they were usually sealed in a ceramic material with a wire extending from each segment to the outside, where it could be connected to an electric circuit. Although discrete transistors are still used in many applications, most transistors today are built as parts of integrated circuits, which contain multiple transistors (sometimes of different types). Today transistors are found in virtually every type of electronic device, as well as in automobile engines, smoke detectors, and lasers.

SEMICONDUCTOR DIODES

A semiconductor diode is made by joining a piece of P material with a piece of N material. The place where the two materials are joined is referred to as the *junction*. This junction is very thin, and each end has a piece of wire attached for connecting the diode, thus making a circuit. Fig. 7.41 shows how the two pieces of material form a diode junction.

Both holes and electrons are involved in conduction in the PN junction diode. There are minority carriers in both regions: holes in the N material and electrons in the P material. The holes produced in the N material near the junction are attracted by the negative ions on the P side of the junction and pass across the junction. These holes tend to neutralize the negative ions on the P side of the junction. Similarly, free electrons produced on the P side of the junction pass across the junction and neutralize positive ions on the N side. This action is an example of intrinsic conduction, which is undesirable.

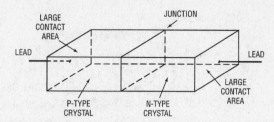

Fig. 7.41. Pictorial representation of a PN junction diode.

This flow of minority carriers weakens the potential barrier around the atoms that they neutralize. When this happens, majority carriers are able to cross the junction at the location of the neutral atom. This means that holes from the P material can cross over to the N material, and electrons from the N material can cross over to the P material.

This action results in both holes and electrons crossing the junction in both directions. These motions cancel each other, and the net movement contributes nothing toward the net charge or current flow through the junction. Because of intrinsic conduction, the junction is no longer a rectifier when an external voltage is applied across it. It is analogous to an electron tube diode in which not only the cathode emits electrons, but the plate is heated to the point where it also emits enough electrons to break down the rectifying properties of the diode.

OPERATION OF THE JUNCTION DIODE

When an electron leaves the donor atom in the N region and moves over to the P region (Fig. 7.42), the atom has fewer electrons than it needs to neutralize the positive charge on the nucleus, and it becomes charged (ionized). It has one extra positive charge equal to the negative charge of the electron that it lost.

Similarly, when a hole leaves an acceptor atom in the P region, the atom takes on a negative charge because the hole has been filled by an electron, and the atom has one more electron than it needs to neutralize the charge on its nucleus.

These charged atoms, or *ions* as they are called, are fixed in place in the crystal lattice structure and cannot move. Thus, they make up a layer of fixed charges on both sides of the junction. On the N side of the junction there is a layer of positively charged ions; on the P side there is a layer of negatively charged atoms or ions.

In Fig. 7.42 there is a barrier of negative ions on the P side of the junction. This negative barrier repels electrons from the immediate vicinity of the junction and prevents the diffusion of any more electrons from the N side over into the P side of the crystal. Similarly, on the N side of the junction there is a barrier of positive ions that repels holes away from the immediate vicinity of the P side of the junction and prevents the diffusion of any additional holes across the junction from the P material into the N material.

The two layers of ionized atoms form a barrier to any further diffusion across the junction. Because the charges at the junction force the majority carriers away from the junction, the barrier is known as the *depletion layer*. It is also known as the barrier layer or barrier potential.

The charge on the impurity atoms is distributed across the PN junction as shown in Fig. 7.42. In the P region the ionized acceptors have a negative charge, and in the N region the ionized donor atoms have a positive charge. At the junction, the charge is zero.

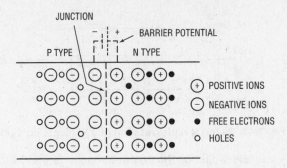

Fig. 7.42. Location of the ions and carriers in the junction diode.

However, in the P region there are holes that have a positive charge, and in the N region there are free electrons that have a negative charge. The distribution of holes and free electrons is shown in the illustration.

The potentials at the junction have driven the holes away from the junction in the P region, and the electrons away from the junction in the N region, so that the charges in the P region and the N region are moved farther apart. The charge at the junction is zero. The net charges on the crystal in the P region are equal to the difference between the charges on the ionized acceptor atoms and the electrons. These charges cancel except in the immediate region of the junction.

In the area near the junction there is a negative charge in the P region and a positive charge in the N region. As stated previously, they act as a barrier to prevent further diffusion of holes from the P region into the N region and diffusion of electrons from the N region into the P region. This potential barrier is a potential difference, or voltage, across the junction and is on the order of a few tenths of a volt. It can be represented as a dotted battery with the negative terminal connected to the P material and the positive terminal connected to the N material.

This barrier potential is like the plate-cathode voltage of a diode. If the plate is made positive and the cathode is made negative, the diode can be made to conduct a current. If the plate is negative with respect to the cathode, the diode will block the flow of current. Thus, the diode tube is a rectifier. The semiconductor diode also is a rectifier.

The Point Contact Diode

There are a number of diodes (Fig. 7.43). They are designed for special applications in some cases. The point contact diode is a very small (physically speaking) unit that is used for rectifying signals. The junction diode is used for rectifying power-line frequencies and higher currents.

Fig. 7.43. Symbol for a diode. The + end is the cathode.

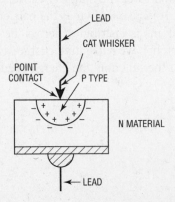

Fig. 7.44. A point contact diode.

Unlike the junction diode, the point contact type (Fig. 7.44) depends on the pressure or contact between a point and a semiconductor crystal for its operation. One section consists of a small, rectangular crystal of N material (either germanium or silicon) and a fine beryllium-copper, phosphor-bronze, or tungsten wire called the *cat whisker*. The cat whisker presses against the semiconductor material and forms the other part of the diode. The reason for using a fine-pointed wire instead of a flat metal plate is to produce a high-density electric field at the point of contact without using too large an external voltage source. The opposite end of the cat whisker is used as the diode terminal for connection purposes.

Both contacts with the external circuit are low-resistance connections. During the manufacture of the point contact diode, a relatively large current is passed through the cat whisker to the silicon crystal. The result of this large current is the formation of a small region of P material around the crystal in the vicinity of the point contact. Thus, there is a PN junction formed that behaves in the same way as the PN junction described for the junction diode operation.

This very small contact area has a reduced capacitance effect (over the junction type with two pieces of material actually touching along a wide surface) that can be used for rectifying higher frequencies than the junction diode. However, since the size of the cat whisker is limited, the amount of current the diode can handle is also limited.

Tunnel Diodes

Tunnel diodes can be used in extremely small spaces, such as part of an integrated circuit (IC) or chip. They can switch at very high rates [2 to 10 gigahertz (GHz)]. A gigahertz is 1,000 megahertz (MHz). A *megahertz* is 1 million times per second, and a *gigahertz* is 1,000 times faster than that, or 1 billion times per second.

Tunnel diodes are doped by using gallium arsenide, gallium antimonide, and indium antimonide.

The Silicon-Controlled Rectifier

Another type of specialized rectifier or diode is the silicon controlled rectifier (SCR). It was originally called the *thyrister*, but the SCR term was coined by General Electric (GE) and has persisted. Inasmuch as GE dominated the marketplace, it soon became known by GE's abbreviated name.

The SCR is a four-layer device. That is, it has either an NPNP or a PNPN arrangement for the semiconductor materials. It is a specialized type of device used for the control of current on its cathode-to-anode path. A gate is used to control the resistance between the cathode and the anode. By applying a small voltage between the gate and the cathode, it is possible to control this resistance and, as a result, the amount of current flow through the device. An SCR conducts current in the *forward* direction only. The symbol for the device is shown in Fig. 7.45.

Fig. 7.46 shows a circuit with an SCR. The function of an SCR is current control. Examples of this are a light dimmer and the speed control for an electrically powered small hand drill or other hand tool. The resistor is a rheostat. This adjustable resistor is used to control the amount of voltage delivered to the gate of the SCR. The greater the voltage, the less the anode-to-cathode resistance and the greater the amount of current allowed to flow through the cathode-anode connection. By adjusting the rheostat, it is possible to control the amount of current flow through the device. As the current increases, the load—the device that is being powered—gets brighter if it is a lamp or increases speed if it is a drill or electric motor. Thus, the SCR can be used to control either type of circuit. Other control circuits also use the SCR as their main operating device. Fig. 7.47 shows two of the design packages for SCRs.

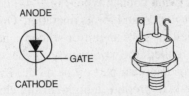

Fig. 7.45. Symbol for an SCR, or thyrister.

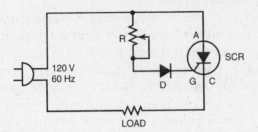

Fig. 7.46. A circuit with the SCR as a control device.

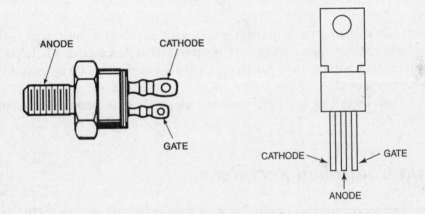

Fig. 7.47. Two packages used for SCRs.

Transistors

The word *transistor* comes from two other words: *transfer* and *resistor*. Thus, it is a transfer resistor or a device that has more impedance (resistance) in the input than in the output, or the other way around depending on its use. By having a difference in impedance between the input and the output, it is able to amplify.

There are two ways in which transistors are used. One is in switching, and the other is in amplifying a signal. The switching ability of a semiconductor has previously been discussed in the section on diodes in this chapter. However, we will mention it briefly here in the study of transistors. The main emphasis will be on the ability of the transistor to amplify and thereby to serve as a replacement for the vacuum tube.

Transistors are made from N and P materials, such as the semiconductor diode. Once they are joined, they resemble two diodes back to back (Fig. 7.48).

Transistors have an emitter, a base, and a collector. These are the connections to the N and P materials that make up the device. We will look at two types of transistors here: the point contact and the junction transistor.

The point contact was developed first, and the junction transistor followed later. Transistors are classified as PNP or NPN according to the arrangement of the impurities in the crystal. Symbols used for transistors are shown in Fig. 7.49.

The *point contact transistor* is similar to the point contact diode except that it has two cat whiskers instead of one. The two cat whiskers are placed with their point contacts very close together (about 0.002 inch). The diameter of the contacts is about 0.005 inch. The contacts are arranged to provide a springlike pressure on the flat surface of the crystal (Fig. 7.50). The crystal may be either N or P germanium.

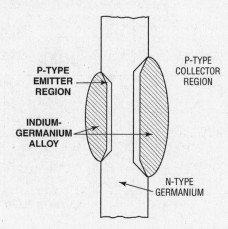

Fig. 7.48. PNP transistor junction formation.

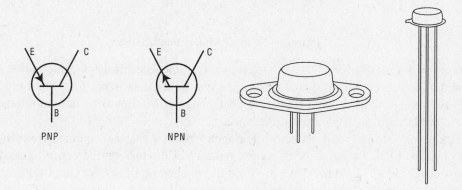

Fig. 7.49. Transistor symbols.

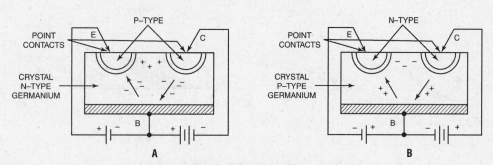

Fig. 7.50. Point contact transistors.

A wide variety of types of transistors have been developed since they were invented in the late 1940s. In addition to the point contact transistor, you should be aware of a few other main types in your study of electronics.

JUNCTION TRANSISTORS

Fig. 7.51 shows the current flow in the external circuit of a PNP junction transistor. The junction transistor uses the same semiconductor materials as the point contact transistor but is arranged in the form of a sandwich. There are also transistors with NPN or the opposite configuration. This means that the polarity of the power source is opposite that of the PNP transistor. The silicon transistor is usually NPN. A few are made with PNP, but in most instances the PNP is the germanium.

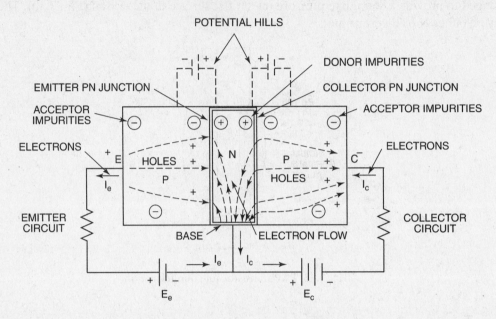

Fig. 7.51. Current flow in a PNP junction transistor.

Other types of transistors are alloy transistors, grown-junction transistors, microalloy transistors, germanium mesa and silicon planar transistors, and field-effect transistors. Field-effect transistors, or FETs, are small in size and are mechanically rugged. Similar to vacuum tubes, they have low power consumption and high input impedance.

MOS means *metal-oxide semiconductor*. The metal control gate is separated from the semiconductor channel. FETs are not affected by the polarity of the bias on the control gate. But are affected by changes in temperature. They are used in voltage amplifiers, RF amplifiers, and voltage-controlled attenuators. To attenuate means to reduce.

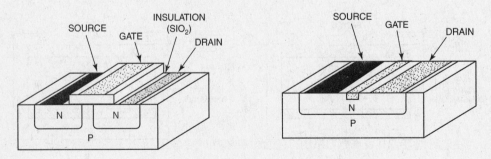

Fig. 7.52. The PN junctions of FET transistors.

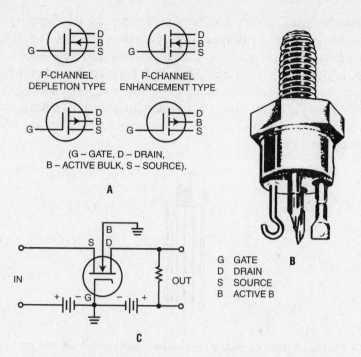

Fig. 7.53. (A) Symbols for FET transistors. (B) MOS (metal-oxide semiconductor) transistor. (C) An FET transistor in a circuit configuration.

There are four distinct types of MOS transistors. These classifications are based on the sources of conduction. The units make use of either electrons (N channel) or holes (P channel) for conduction. Symbols for the four types of MOS field-effect transistors (MOSFETs) are shown in Fig. 7.53A. The direction of the arrowhead in the symbol indicates the difference between N- and P-channel types. A solid channel line in the symbol indicates normally on. A dotted line indicates normally off.

MOSFETs are used in broadcast band receivers in low-power circuits. They can be found in RF amplifiers and converters. They are also used in IF stages and in the first audio. In other words, they are used in almost all the circuits in a broadcast receiver except the output stage that drives the speaker.

Fig. 7.53C shows a circuit with a MOSFET transistor. Note the parts and how they are connected in the circuit. They can be used in FM receivers as well as in AM receivers. FM receivers use FETs in the RF amplifier, conversion stages, IF stages, and limiter stages. They are as versatile as vacuum tubes and can be substituted almost directly in the circuits designed for tubes. However, the voltages are different, and there is no need for a filament in an FET.

Integrated Circuits

The integrated circuit (IC) is a single, monolithic (one-piece) chip made of semiconductor material. Transistors, diodes, resistors, and capacitors can all be deposited on a chip instead of having to be wired separately, as was the case when these transistors were relatively new. Diodes can be produced in many groups to do different things. Photolithography, a combination of photographic and printing techniques, has been used to make the complete circuit. This type of printing has made it possible to produce some very sophisticated ICs with very high reliability.

There are three standard packages for ICs. The multipin circular IC resembles a transistor package (Fig. 7.54); however, it has more leads than the transistor. The flat pack (Fig. 7.55) is a hermetically sealed package; that means it is vacuum-packed and heat-sealed. The dual inline package (DIP) (Fig. 7.56) has legs like a caterpillar; each leg is connected to some spot inside that is critical to the functioning of the chip. In many cases, the cost of the packaging can significantly exceed the actual cost of the chips, inside, but modern manufacturing has greatly improved the quality and reliability of the chips, and greater improvements in quality, capability, and reduced size are being made all the time.

Fig. 7.54. The multipin circular IC enclosure resembles a transistor package.

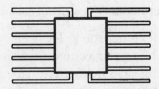

Fig. 7.55. The flat pack IC is hermetically sealed.

Fig. 7.56. This DIP package has become the standard for chips.

Today, ICs are used in almost every type of electronic device from simple toys to control circuits, television sets, FM receivers, hearing aids, car engines, and sophisticated missile guidance systems. They are used in great numbers in computers. ICs have a million uses—with probably many more yet to be discovered.

Batteries

A *battery* is a device in which chemical energy is converted to electrical energy. Batteries can also be defined as one or more galvanic cells connected in series or in parallel; a galvanic cell is simply one in which chemical energy is converted to electrical energy. Batteries are used in many products, from cars and boats to radios, clocks, computers, toys, and many household items.

A battery usually consists of two or more galvanic cells. Each cell provides from 1.2 to 2.2 volts of electricity. The number and type of cells determine the voltage of the battery.

A simple cell consists of two *electrodes* in a solution called an *electrolyte* or *electrolytic solution* (Fig. 7.57). The two electrodes are made of unlike metallic materials, and the electrolyte is nonmetallic, usually an acid or a salt dissolved in water. In the solution, the acid or salt *dissociates*, or separates, into positive and negative ions. The chemical reaction between the electrodes and the solution causes a movement of ions, and the *terminals* (electrodes) of the cell are positive or negative because of this chemical activity. There is an excess of electrons at the negative terminal and a lack of electrons at the positive terminal.

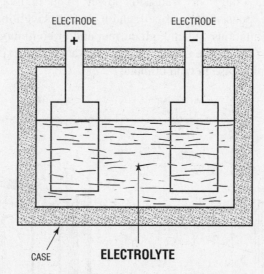

Fig. 7.57. Two electrodes and an electrolyte make up a cell, or battery.

When an external circuit is connected between the two terminals, the excess electrons at the negative electrode flow through the external circuit to the positive electrode. This flow of electrons is an *electric current*.

Continuing chemical activity in the cell provides a supply of electrons, and the cell is said to be *discharging*. Because of the chemical activity, however, one or both of the electrodes is eventually consumed or chemically changed. When the available chemical energy is gone, no more electrical power can be drawn from the cell, and the cell is said to be *discharged* (dead).

There are two general types of electrical cells: primary and secondary. In a *primary cell*, chemical energy is converted to electrical energy and the process cannot be reversed. Once the cell is discharged, it is no longer usable and cannot be regenerated as a source of electrical power.

A *secondary cell*, also known as a storage battery, is rechargeable; it is usually designed to have a lifetime of between 100 and 1,000 recharge cycles, depending on the composite materials used. The chemical action in the cell is reversible, and the electrodes and electrolyte can be restored to the same makeup that existed before the discharge; this is done by using an outside source of electricity. Although primary batteries are often made from the same basic materials as secondary (rechargeable) batteries, the design and manufacturing processes are different. Secondary cells are often more cost-effective over a long period of time than primary batteries since the battery can be recharged and reused. A single discharge cycle of a primary battery, however, provides more current for a longer period of time than a single discharge cycle of an equivalent secondary battery— a regular household alkaline battery provides about 50% more energy density than the best equivalent secondary or rechargeable version.

A PRIMARY CELL—THE DRY CELL

There are several types of primary cells, including wet cells, reserve cells, and fuel cells. However, the most common type of primary cell, which has now largely replaced all others, is the *dry cell*. A dry cell is unspillable and nonrefillable. The electrolyte is rather dry or pasty. There are many types of dry cells, differing mainly in the types of electrodes and electrolyte.

The Carbon-Zinc Primary Cell

Carbon-zinc (also called zinc-carbon or Leclanche) cells were the first widely used household batteries (Fig. 7.58). There are still lots of these around—the package in the grocery or electronics store may be labeled "heavy duty" or "transistor power." This is the type of cell found in most flashlights. It is the least expensive type of cell, and it performs well in many applications. However, it does have some limitations. When high current and/or continuous operation is required, it often costs less in the long run to use a higher-capacity—and more expensive—dry cell; the carbon-zinc cell is also of limited use in cold climates.

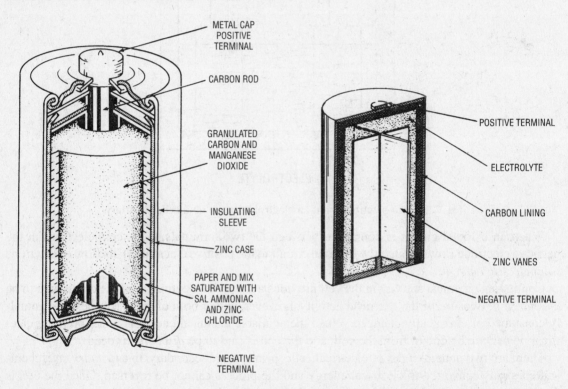

Fig. 7.58. Two views of the construction of a carbon-zinc cell.

In the standard round carbon-zinc cell, the positive electrode is a carbon rod mounted in the center of the cell. The negative electrode is a zinc can that also serves as the container for the cell. The electrolyte is a moist, black paste of salt ammoniac (ammonium chloride), chlorine, zinc chloride, and manganese dioxide. To prevent short circuits, all but the positive electrode and the bottom of the zinc can are covered by an insulation jacket.

The chemical activity that takes place at the carbon electrode releases hydrogen gas. If the hydrogen gas collects around the carbon electrode, a condition known as *polarization* can develop, in which the output voltage is reduced because the hydrogen partially insulates the carbon rod from the electrolyte. However, the presence of a *depolarizer*—manganese dioxide—contributes oxygen, which combines with the hydrogen gas to form water. The water not only prevents polarization but also serves to keep the electrolyte moist.

The chemical action during discharge decomposes the zinc electrode. Therefore, the cell has a definite life, which depends on the discharge current and the rate at which the zinc electrode is decomposed. As the zinc container is being consumed, the electrolyte often leaks into the surrounding area, causing corrosion damage. Thus, it is important to remove this type of cell from the circuit or device as soon as possible after its useful life has ended.

Carbon-zinc cells produce 1.5 volts. The materials in the cell and the chemicals, not the size of the cell, determine the voltage. A small cell has the same voltage as a large one made of the same materials. However, the larger cell has more materials and therefore produces more electrical energy. A large cell can supply more current than a smaller cell during the same period of time.

Popular sizes of dry cells are shown in Fig. 7.59. The n-type cell has about 0.02 ampere, and the D cell has about 0.15 ampere. Other batteries are available in various shapes and sizes.

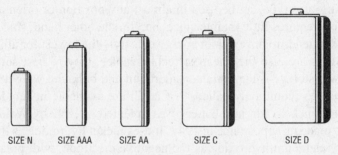

SIZE N   SIZE AAA   SIZE AA   SIZE C   SIZE D

Fig. 7.59. Standard dry cell sizes.

Other Types of Primary Cells

Probably the most common type of dry cell now is the alkaline cell, which has a lower internal resistance and can deliver a much higher current on a continuous basis than a carbon-zinc cell. Alkaline cells deliver about four times the energy of carbon-zinc cells. In "high-drain" applications such as toys, cameras, and CD players, the difference is even greater—carbon-zinc batteries in these cases can deliver only about one-tenth (10%) of that available from an alkaline cell.

Another type of dry cell used in electronic equipment is the mercury or mercuric oxide cell. The mercury cell can be made very small, which is an advantage for use in hearing aids and other miniature electronic devices. These cells are also available in the standard cylindrical shapes, providing high current capacity and long life. The unit cost for the mercury cell is the highest of the three types of dry cells discussed here, but the mercury cell has a higher efficiency than the other two types. The output voltage remains almost constant until the end of the useful life of the cell. Also, mercuric oxide batteries have a long shelf life, sometimes up to 10 years.

Silver oxide cells are commonly found as "button" cells that power small electronic devices such as watches, calculators, hearing aids, and other small specialty devices. Rated at 1.55 volts per cell, their advantages are small size, high energy density, and a long shelf life.

Lithium primary batteries are also available in a variety of chemistries combining lithium with sulfur dioxide, thionyl chloride, manganese dioxide, copper oxide, and iodine. Some of these styles are also rechargeable.

SECONDARY CELLS

There are several types of secondary cells, also known as "storage" or "rechargeable" batteries.

The *lead-acid battery* is the type of battery used in cars, small boats, and other vehicles. They are also known as "flooded" batteries because the electrolyte is liquid and, because of this, the battery usually needs to be maintained in a more-or-less upright position. This is the oldest type of secondary battery, developed in the mid-1800s. It has a positive electrode of lead oxide, a negative electrode of porous metallic lead, and sulfuric acid as the electrolyte. Although a separate storage battery is sometimes used to power the electronic equipment in a car, most often the battery that is part of the car's electrical system is also used to supply power for the radio, tape deck, and other electronic equipment. To charge the battery, a direct current of the opposite direction is passed through the cell, and this reverses the chemical activity.

A lead-acid battery must be protected from overheating and overcharging. Be sure to discharge the battery slowly rather than quickly. Charging too rapidly is also harmful and reduces the life of the battery. When storing a battery, make sure it is fully charged; a battery lasts longer in storage if it is fully charged.

Sealed lead-acid (SLA) batteries (sometimes called "gel cells") were developed from the familiar flooded lead-acid battery used for many years in cars and trucks. The SLA form uses a gel-type electrolyte instead of a liquid and electrodes made from lead alloys designed to never reach the stage during charging where gas is generated. This allows it to be sealed (i.e., no safety valve is needed), and therefore this type can be used in almost any position or orientation. Since water is not lost, the SLA also requires little maintenance, but, on the other hand, since it's never (theoretically) fully charged, it tends to have a poor energy density—the lowest for all the sealed rechargeables. But, since SLAs are also the cheapest rechargeables, they're best suited for applications where low-cost power storage is the main consideration and bulk and weight are not issues.

Nickel–cadmium cells (commonly called "NiCads") are available in standard household sizes and shapes. The basic nickel-cadmium battery was invented in 1899 by Waldmar Junger, but the modern sealed type made its appearance in 1947. It uses nickel hydroxide as the positive electrode and cadmium metal-cadmium hydroxide as the negative electrode, with potassium hydroxide as the electrolyte. The voltage of a nickel-cadmium cell is 1.25 volts, and its output is constant. It can be recharged often, and it can have a long, active life. Like SLAs, sealed NiCads can be used in just about any position, and they have up to double the energy density. However, they have a higher self-discharge rate than SLAs—about 10% in the first 24 hours after charging and about 10% per month thereafter—and the rate gets even higher in warmer conditions. However, this type of cell can also be discharged completely without being damaged.

Rechargeable alkaline–manganese (RAM) batteries have been relatively recently developed from the alkaline manganese-zinc primary battery; in alkaline secondary batteries, the voltage decreases slowly as power is consumed. It should never be discharged below 0.9 volt per cell because the battery life will be shortened. If an alkaline rechargeable cell is completely discharged, it will be impossible to recharge. Typical output voltage in the D-cell size is 1.5 volts. Like its primary cell cousin, it uses a manganese dioxide positive electrode and a potassium hydroxide electrolyte, but the negative electrode is a special porous zinc gel designed to absorb hydrogen during the charging process. RAM batteries are generally cheaper than NiCads and have a much lower self-discharge rate (i.e., a decreased charge over time when not used) than either NiCad or NiMH batteries—but they have a somewhat shorter life cycle than NiCads.

Nickel-metal hydride (NiMH) batteries are in many ways an evolution from NiCads, although they're also related to the hydrogen-nickel oxide batteries used in communication satellites. Like NiCads, NiMH batteries use a nickel-nickel hydroxide positive electrode and potassium hydroxide as the electrolyte. However, instead of a cadmium-cadmium hydroxide negative electrode, NiMH batteries have an electode made from a hydrogen storage alloy such as zirconium-nickel or lanthanum-nickel. NiMH batteries have up to a 30% higher energy density than NiCads, but they can be charged at only about half the speed. Charging NiMH batteries is also more complicated and ideally involves temperature sensing. The NiMH self-discharge rate is also about 50% higher than that of NiCads, and they cost significantly more.

Lithium-ion (Li-ion) rechargeable batteries are a relatively recent development from the lithium primary cell, which was invented in 1912 but not marketed commercially until the early 1970s. Lithium is the lightest of all metals and has the highest electrochemical potential, which gives it the potential for extremely high energy density. However, the metal itself is highly reactive, and while this isn't a problem with primary cells, it poses an explosion risk with rechargeable types. In order to be safe, lithium ions from chemicals such as lithium-cobalt dioxide are used instead of the metal itself. Typical Li-ion batteries have a negative electrode of aluminum coated with a lithium compound such as lithium-cobalt dioxide, lithium-nickel dioxide, or lithium-manganese dioxide. The positive electrode is generally copper coated with carbon (usually either graphite or coke), while the electrolyte is a lithium salt. Li-ion batteries have about twice the energy density of NiCads and have a relatively low self-discharge rate. However, they can't be charged as quickly as NiCads, and they cost more than either NiCads or NiMH batteries, making them the most expensive rechargeables of all. Part of the reason for this is that they must be provided with built-in protection against both excessive discharging and overcharging—both of which pose a safety risk. Most Li-ion batteries thus come in self-contained battery packs complete with "smart" protective circuitry.

Electric Motors

An electric motor changes electrical energy into mechanical energy to do work. It allows electric power to be used to run machinery. Basically, a motor connected to a source of electric power develops a twisting effort, or *torque*, that usually rotates the shaft of the motor. When this shaft is connected, belted, or geared to a machine, it drives the machine to do work.

An electric motor illustrates basic principles of electricity and magnetism. When an electric current is passed through a conductor (coil of wire), the conductor becomes an electromagnet, inducing a magnetic field around it. The direction of the current determines the poles of the magnet. When the current-carrying coil is placed between magnets, it rotates based on the principle that opposite poles attract and like poles repel each other.

There are two basic types of electric motors: direct current motors and alternating current motors.

DC MOTORS

A direct current (DC) motor is powered by direct current. It includes a stationary magnet, known as a *field magnet*; a current-carrying coil, known as an *armature*, that rotates between the poles of the stationary magnet; a device called a *commutator* that changes the direction of current in the armature; and *brushes* that form a sliding contact between the commutator and the direct current power supply. The armature is usually mounted on a drive shaft that can be used to transmit power to other machines.

Current passes through the armature, making it an electromagnet. The armature rotates so that its poles are next to opposite poles on the stationary magnet. Then the commutator reverses the direction of the current, and the armature rotates so that its poles are again next to the opposite poles of the magnet. When the armature turns, it turns a shaft that runs a machine. There are three basic types of direct current motors: shunt, series, and compound.

Shunt DC Motors

The *shunt DC motor* is one of the most versatile of DC motors. It is a relatively constant-speed motor with solid state circuitry used to control its speed over a wide range. The shunt motor is reversible at rest or during operation. It can be used for many purposes, such as windshield wipers on cars, fans in a car heater or air conditioning unit, and in special types of printing equipment. The brushes and commutator must be maintained.

Series DC Motors

The *series DC motor* is the most widely used motor; it is the most popular motor in smaller than 1-horsepower sizes. It can deliver high speed and a wide variety of speeds when used with speed controllers. However, the series motor does not have good speed regulation; it varies with the load applied. Many home appliances have series motors. They usually provide from 200 to 1,200 hours of operation before the brushes need to be replaced. Brush replacement is the most common maintenance concern with this type of motor.

Compound DC Motors

The *compound DC motor* has characteristics of both shunt and series motors. It has a constant speed and a high starting torque. Usually made in larger than 1-horsepower sizes, it can be used for such things as elevators, grain mill operations, and other uses where good starting torque and fairly constant speed are important.

CHARACTERISTICS OF DC MOTORS

	Shunt Wound	Series Wound	Compound Wound
Duty	Continuous	Intermittent	Continuous
Power supply	DC	DC	DC
Reversibility	At rest or during rotation	Usually unidirectional	At rest or during rotation
Speed	Relatively constant and adjustable	Varying with load	Relatively constant and adjustable
Starting torque	125 to 200% of rated torque	175% and up of rated torque	125% and up of rated torque
Starting current	Normal	High	Normal

AC MOTORS

Alternating current (AC) *motors* are more commonly used than direct current motors because almost all electric supply systems are alternating current systems. In the United States and Canada, electrical power—alternating current—is produced as three-phase (3 Ø). It is used in commercial and industrial applications as it is generated. Three-phase power has many advantages, but it is expensive to distribute to every home and business. Therefore, it is distributed from the generating source to substations where it is converted to single-phase (1 Ø) for local use in homes and small power consumption locations (Fig. 7.60).

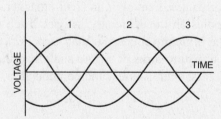

Fig. 7.60. Three-phase waveform. Electric power in the United States is generated as three-phase.

AC motors are three-phase and single-phase. *Three-phase motors* have good overall characteristics. They are ideal for driving machines in industrial applications. They can be reversed while running. Reversing any two of the three connections to the power line causes the motor to be reversed. See Fig. 7.61, where *a*, *b*, and *c* provide the three-phase power and *a* to *o* and *b* to *o* and *c* to *o* provide the single-phase connections.

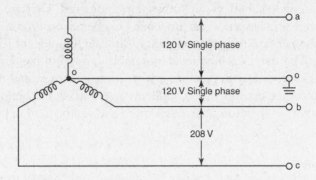

Fig. 7.61. Three-phase power to single-phase power.

The three-phase motor has a high starting torque and is very efficient to operate. It is also rather simple in construction since it has no starting mechanism. Neither does it have a commutator or brushes or a centrifugal switch to cause problems. Thus, it is comparatively easy to maintain. Three-phase motors are available in 208–230/460-volt sizes, with horsepower ratings varying from 1/4 to hundreds and can be obtained for operation on 50 or 60 hertz. The three-phase motor is the workhorse of industry (Fig. 7.62).

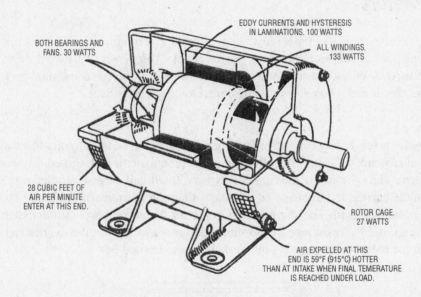

Fig. 7.62. Cutaway view of a three-phase motor.

Single-phase motors are more expensive to purchase and maintain than are three-phase motors. They are also less efficient, and their starting currents are relatively high. Single-phase motors are often selected because three-phase power is not available. Most small plants are equipped with single-phase motors, and the motors in all household appliances are single-phase.

Two of the commonly used AC motors are induction motors and synchronous motors.

Induction AC Motors

Induction motors are the most commonly used AC motors and are relatively simple to build. They are rugged, and they operate at a constant speed if they are not overloaded.

There are several types of induction motors. *Shaded pole motors* have a low starting torque and are used in small fans, clocks, pencil sharpeners, and can openers. Many types of *split-phase motors* have been manufactured. Split-phase motors are used where there is no need to start under load. They are used on grinders, buffers, and other similar devices. They are available in fractional horsepower sizes with various speeds and are wound to operate on 120 or 240 volts AC. *Capacitor-start motors* are another type of induction motor. Almost all motors of less than 1 horsepower used in refrigerators, oil burners, washing machines, table saws, drill presses, and similar devices are capacitor-start. A capacitor-start motor has a high starting current and the ability to develop about four times its rated horsepower if it is suddenly overloaded. Capacitor-start motors have a starting torque comparable to their torque at rated speed and can be used in places where the starting load is heavy.

Synchronous AC Motors

Synchronous AC motors have special uses because of their constant speed. These motors are used in factories and plants where large-horsepower motors with very stable rotating speeds are required for various processes. Speed can be controlled by varying the frequency of the power supplied to the motor. However, expensive equipment is needed to provide the variation in power frequencies. Synchronous motors are not self-starting and must have some kind of starting device such as another motor or a modification of the rotor.

Electric Meters

The performance of electrical circuits must be monitored. The monitoring of circuit operation may require a voltage check, current check, or power check. *Voltmeters* are used to check voltage; *ammeters* are used to check current; and *watt-hour meters* are used to monitor performance in terms of power consumed. *Ohmmeters* are designed to check resistance.

AMMETERS

The term *ammeter* refers to any current-indicating meter that can be used to measure amperes, milliamperes, or microamperes (Fig. 7.63). In most ammeters, the coil is designed for about 100 milliamperes or less. The wire in the moving coil is very small and cannot handle large amounts of current. When the current to be measured is greater than the capacity of the meter coil, a special circuit called a *shunt* is used. The shunt bypasses part of the current around the meter. The resistance of the meter and the resistance of the shunt path are selected to give the desired division of current so that the meter movement is not overloaded and burned out.

Fig. 7.63. 0–1 milliampere panel meter.

VOLTMETERS

A *voltmeter* is a high resistance current meter that is calibrated in volts (Fig. 7.64). Remember Ohm's law: If the current and the resistance of a circuit are known, the voltage can be determined. The voltmeter thus solves the Ohm's law problem. The resistance of the voltmeter is a known value, and the current in this resistance is indicated by the needle deflection. To find the voltage, simply mark the meter scale in volts and read it directly. The voltmeter is connected directly across the voltage source or across the circuit component and should draw as little current as possible. For this reason it should contain a sensitive meter movement and a high resistance.

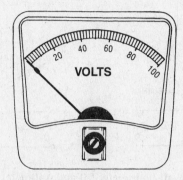

Fig. 7.64. Milliammeter with a voltage calibration.

OHMMETERS

It is possible to use resistors with a battery and a meter movement to make a circuit for measuring resistance, or ohms. The meter for measuring ohms is called an *ohmmeter*.

The principle of the ohmmeter is another application of Ohm's law: If the voltage and the current are known, the resistance can be found. In the ohmmeter, the voltage of the battery and the current needed to produce full-scale deflection are known. The meter scale can be calibrated in ohms, and the value can be read directly (Fig. 7.65).

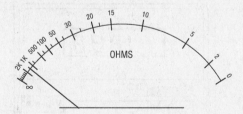

Fig. 7.65. Ohmmeter scale.

WATT-HOUR METERS

Watt-hour or *kilowatt-hour meters* are used primarily by power companies to record the total amount of energy used by a customer during a 1-month period. *Kilo* means "thousand," so a kilowatt-hour meter measures total energy consumed in thousands of units. A *wattmeter* is used to measure power as energy is being used on a per second basis. Fig. 7.66A shows the schematics of a kilowatt-hour meter and a wattmeter. Fig. 7.66B shows how the wattmeter works. It has a fixed coil and a moving coil arrangement. The fixed coils are connected directly across the power source and are usually made of many turns of fine wire. The current coil is usually made of a few turns of heavy wire connected in series.

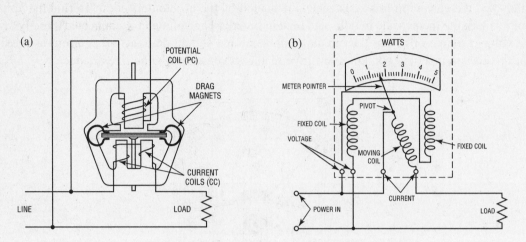

Fig. 7.66. Kilowatt-hour meter (A) and wattmeter (B) hookups.

DIGITAL MULTIMETERS

Digital multimeters have replaced many of the older types of mechanical meter movements. A digital meter makes it possible to measure the circuit workings more accurately since it utilizes electronic circuits that require very small amounts of current to indicate the presence of voltage or current. Fig. 7.67 shows one of the many types of digital meters available. The digital readouts are easy to read, not like trying to guess what the value is when reading "between the lines" on an analog-type meter.

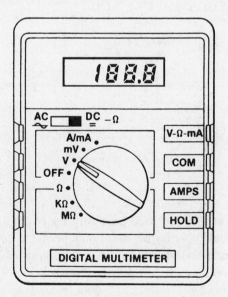

Fig. 7.67. Digital multimeter.

CLAMP-ON METERS

Clamp-on-type ammeters are used to check the current flowing through a wire without having to cut the wire and insert an ammeter. They use the transformer principle to detect the presence of the current, and their sensitive meter movement is calibrated to indicate the correct amount (Fig. 7.68). This type of meter is also available in digital readout.

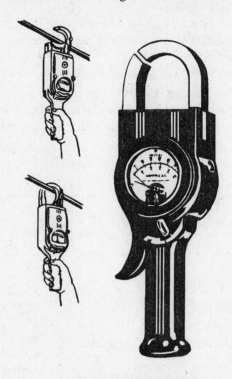

Fig. 7.68. Clamp-on meter.

Amplitude-Modulated Receivers

In this discussion, we will limit our study to the six-transistor AM receiver most often purchased at a discount store for less than $30. Communications receivers have some special circuits that are not important to the basics of AM reception at this time.

The block diagram of an AM receiver (Fig. 7.69) will give us some idea of how the entire unit operates; then we will look at it stage by stage to obtain the circuit functions.

Note how the signal is injected from the antenna into the RF amplifier. This is the case in most communications receivers and more expensive sets. If you have a standard six-transistor type, there will be no RF amplifier. The mixer will be the first stage to view. However, in the interest of getting a better look at the receiver, we will take a closer look at the RF amplifier when we analyze the circuit functions later in the chapter.

The RF amplifier takes the antenna signal and selects it. The broadcast AM band covers a wide-band of frequencies (535 to 1,605 kHz). This wideband of frequencies has to be beaten down to one in order for selectivity to be improved. This is where the principle of heterodyning comes in.

Heterodyning takes place in the mixer stage. This is where two frequencies (in this case the incoming frequency from the antenna, which is selected by the first tuning circuit) are mixed or beaten against a local oscillator frequency. The local oscillator puts out a nonmodulated frequency. However, the incoming frequency is modulated. The beating of the two frequencies produces the sum and difference frequencies, and the original two are also present. All four frequencies are now modulated in the collector tank circuit, which is the output of the mixer stage. Once the proper frequency [455 kHz is the usual *intermediate frequency* (IF) selected for AM] is chosen, it is passed on to the IF amplifier because of signal loss during the previous processing. There can be a minimum of two IF amplifiers to amplify the signal; each time there is a tuned circuit tuned to only 455 kHz with ±5 kHz for sidebands.

After the IF with the sidebands or modulation is amplified to the desired level, it is put through the detector stage where the modulation is taken from the RF carrier and passed on to the audio amplifiers. This audio amplification causes the signal to be of the proper level to drive a speaker.

The automatic volume control (AVC) or automatic gain control (AGC) is part of the detector stage and feeds back a strong bias voltage when the signal is too strong and cuts down on amplification of the signal before it can be heard by the human ear as being too loud. The power supply is needed to furnish the proper voltages for operation of the various stages.

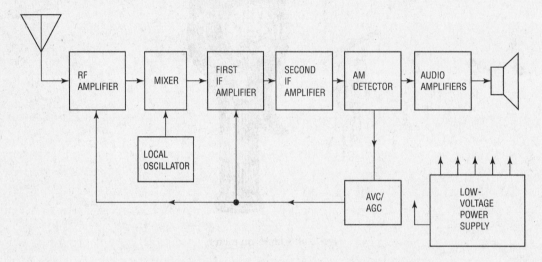

Fig. 7.69. Block diagram of an AM receiver with an RF stage.

The first stage in an AM receiver is the RF amplifier. The major assignment of the RF amplifier is to amplify the incoming signals from the antenna after a particular one has been selected. Four characteristics of the RF stage are very important in any receiver. It should have the ability to amplify or produce the required gain; it should have a low noise output since the signal itself has a certain amount of noise depending on the signal-to-noise ratio of the received signal; it needs to be selective since it has the entire band to select from; it also needs to have a linear characteristic throughout the entire band of AM frequencies.

Keep in mind that the RF amplifier stage is not a common stage for less expensive portable radios used for local reception. It is used in military equipment, ham radios, and advanced communications receivers and in more demanding situations where special equipment is needed for receiving weak signals.

The oscillator stage is required whenever heterodyning is used to improve the selectivity of a receiver. It produces the beat frequency used to beat against the incoming frequency to produce the IF.

The purpose of combining an RF with an oscillator frequency to produce an IF is called *mixing* or *frequency conversion*.

There is usually a minimum of two IF amplifiers. The major function of the IF amplifier is to give the signal good linear amplification through the range of frequencies it will be handling. The main objective of the amplifier after its use as an amplifier is to provide selectivity. By using a couple of additional tuned circuits tuned to the same frequency, it is possible to become very selective. This is one of the reasons for using superheterodynes rather than some earlier type of receiver. The 455-kHz signal has been chosen as the input to the first IF, and the output of this stage is also tuned. The 455-kHz signal is fed to the second IF and amplified further so that it is sufficient to be rectified by the detector to provide an audio signal that is not too noisy.

In most AM receivers the bandwidth is about 3 kHz. This severely limits the quality of music heard from the speakers. It means the IF cans have to be tuned to 455 kHz ± 3 kHz.

Now, let us back up for a minute and look at the automatic gain control, or as it is sometimes called, the automatic volume control. This stage is used to adjust the amplification of the RF and IF stages. The strength of the input signal determines the loudness of the speaker. Therefore, controls must be placed on the RF and IF stages if we want to control the volume. If the signals that reach the antenna are weak, the signal amplitude reaching the detector will also be weak, producing a low output volume. If strong signals are received, they will create overload signal conditions in the amplifiers and cause distortion. To correct this, a feedback signal is used to adjust bias on the first IF amplifier.

Finally, it is now possible to place the entire AM radio on one integrated-circuit chip. This can be done with one 14-pin DIP. This particular chip does not contain the audio output stages, which means that another chip of the desired audio power can be connected to allow it to operate as a radio.

Frequency-Modulated Receivers

The FM receiver is not as simple as the AM receiver. The method used to produce FM and then to produce stereo is somewhat more complicated than the operation of the AM receiver. There are some interesting integrated circuits used to decode the stereo signal and produce output sufficient to drive two (or more) speakers. In fact, the whole realm of FM electronics is constantly changing and improving, yielding improved sensitivity and selectivity as well as noise reduction.

Keep in mind that the FM band is used not only for wideband transmission of music for home receivers. Narrowband FM, where only the voice is used, can be made to serve a number of purposes. For instance, the commercial broadcast band covers 88 to 108 MHz with 200-kHz channel sidebands. Television audio signals use 50-kHz channel sidebands at 54 to 88 MHz, 174 to 216 MHz, and 470 to 890 MHz. The narrowband amateur radio channels are at 29.6 MHz, 52 to 53 MHz, 146 to 147.5 MHz, 440 to 450 MHz, and in excess of 890 MHz for experimental purposes.

There is a reason for not using FM on frequencies lower than 30 MHz. The earth's ionosphere introduces phase distortion in FM signals at frequencies below 30 MHz. The line-of-sight method of transmission is used for signals above 30 MHz because of nature's way of not reflecting these signals and allowing them to continue through the ionosphere. Since the earth curves, it limits the communications range of FM to about 80 miles. This is especially true of the narrowband public service channels that operate at 108 to 175 MHz, in between channels 6 and 7 on TV (broadcast, not cable). The narrowband is also assigned to frequencies in excess of 890 MHz. Output power from a TV FM transmitter is about 50 kW, while amateurs use some walkie-talkies with only 100 mW of power.

Of course, one of the main advantages of FM over AM is its ability to transmit music with very little noise, or static, being heard in the receiver.

Fig. 7.70 shows a block diagram of the FM receiver with the stages needed for reception of the standard monaural signal.

The antenna is usually a piece of wire where the signal is very strong, but a folded dipole is needed if any type of signal strength is desired at the front end of the receiver. The first two stages are called the front end of the receiver, which usually includes the RF amplifier and the mixer.

The RF amplifier, or preselector, performs the same function in the FM receiver as it does in the AM receiver, that is, it increases the sensitivity of the receiver. Such an increase in sensitivity is often a practical necessity in fringe areas. However, the gain of the IF stages is relatively much greater, perhaps 100 times that of the preselector, since the chief advantage of the superheterodyne lies in the uniformity of response and gain of the IF stages within the receiver band. The principal functions of the RF stage are to discriminate against undesired signals and to increase the amplitude of weak signals so that the signal-to-noise ratio will be improved.

Mixing the incoming FM signal with the set's oscillator frequency is basically the same in principle, but the frequencies are changed. FM for home use employs the 10.7-MHz IF. The beating together of the incoming frequency and the oscillator frequency produces the 10.7-MHz IF. This signal is passed on the IF strip where it is amplified. IFs are important here since they take the signal from the mixer and amplify it sufficiently for detection. They also increase the selectivity of the set since the heterodyning principle produces the IF for the purpose of allowing it to be amplified by stages which are tuned slightly off their normal 10.7 MHz. This detuning produces a wide enough bandwidth to allow the modulation (up to 200 kHz) to pass through the IF cans.

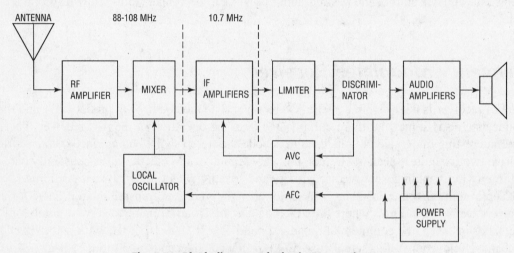

Fig. 7.70. Block diagram of a basic FM receiver.

The IF cans in the IF stages are stagger-tuned to produce a wide enough bandpass for the music to pass through. This means that there are usually three IF stages in an FM receiver.

A limiter puts out a signal with a constant amplitude. This eliminates any noise that may be riding on the incoming signal. A good limiter is essential to the proper operation of an FM receiver. The limiter stage also provides automatic gain control since its signals are from minimum value up to a maximum value constant in amplitude. This provides a constant input level to the discriminator. Limiters require an input signal voltage of at least 1 volt. This is why the IFs are used to boost the signal from the antenna (which may be about 1.5 mV) to this level. The sensitivity of an FM set refers to how much input signal is required to produce a specific level of quieting. This is normally 30 decibels (dB). A good-quality receiver has a sensitivity of 1.5 mV with a background noise 30 dB down from the input signal level of 1.5 mV. Most IF stages in today's receivers are made in integrated circuits that have built-in limiting action.

Translation of the FM variations into audio is the function of the discriminator, ratio detector, or slope detector. The detection takes place at the 10.7-MHz level of the IF. The IF has the modulation (±75 kHz) on it and must be separated to obtain good audio for the audio stages.

In order for the receiver to operate properly, the local oscillator that beats against the incoming frequency must be stable in its output frequency to produce the 10.7 MHz needed for the IFs. One way of keeping an oscillator frequency stable is to keep the voltages applied to the transistor (or vacuum tube) constant. This source of voltage correction can be obtained from the output of the audio stage. This direct current produced by the audio signal is taken and fed back to the local oscillator to keep it on frequency.

The AFC may cause the receiver to miss some weak stations when tuning. This is why a *defeat switch* is used. FM and AFC are the switch labels used to designate this condition. The FM or defeat position means that weaker stations can be tuned in and then the AFC turned on to capture or hold the stations.

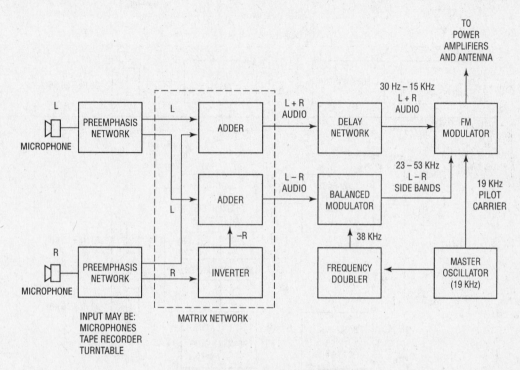

Fig. 7.71. FM stereo transmitter.

Current receivers don't use the AFC system of control since the problem of keeping an oscillator above 100 MHz from drifting is no longer the problem it once was. Current chips and phase-locked loops have automatic correction for frequency drift.

Once the signals have been detected, the audio is coupled to the audio amplifiers. In AM-FM sets the same audio section takes care of both the AM and FM outputs. However, they are switched with an external source usually mounted so that the AM, FM, and stereo are marked on the switch. FM stereo calls for two speakers and two amplifiers for the audio.

FM Stereo

Today's FM receivers are virtually all made with stereo, although this was not always the case. For the receiver to receive and decode this stereo signal, several stages have to be added to the basic monaural FM receiver.

Fig. 7.71 shows a typical block diagram. The FCC authorized FM stereo in 1961. This made it possible for home receivers to obtain the complete information on records and tapes that were already available. Stereo uses two separate signals to produce a spatial dimension in music or speech. This also called for another channel to be added to FM single-channel transmissions. Stereo high fidelity requires two channels of 30-Hz to 15-kHz signals to modulate the carrier frequency in such a way that the receiver can separate them and reproduce the outputs in a left and a right speaker.

More efficient use of the 200-kHz bandwidth was the answer to the stereo problem. This was achieved by the process of multiplexing. *Multiplexing* is the simultaneous transmission of two different signals on one carrier. It is also possible to broadcast more than two under the right conditions. The FCC has approved a compatible system for stereo broadcasts, which means that stereo and FM monaural signals can be received on receivers that normally receive monaural signals. Or, the stereo receiver can receive the monaural signal and reproduce it properly.

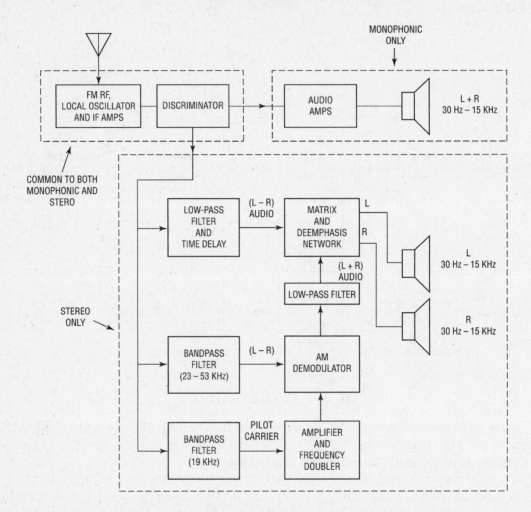

Fig. 7.72. Comparison of the stages needed for mono and stereo reception.

The FM receiver and the FM stereo receiver are the same up to the discriminator stage. At this point the stereo signal must be detected and processed properly to add the missing channel.

Take a look at Fig. 7.72 to see the common stages and those needed to obtain the extra channel. The output of the discriminator is 30 Hz to 15 kHz, or the audio frequencies normally transmitted by the monaural transmitter, but there is also the 19-kHz subcarrier and the 23- to 53-kHz $(L - R)$ signal. The 30-Hz to 15-kHz signal is called the $(L + R)$ signal. Keep in mind that 19 kHz is above the human hearing range and that in most instances audio amplifiers are not capable of amplifying it.

The basic monaural receiver reproduces the 30-Hz to 15-kHz $(L + R)$ signal and is not aware of the other frequencies. That makes it compatible with stereo signals; since it does not have the stages to reproduce it, the other channel is ignored, and the $(L + R)$ signal is sufficient to broadcast what is normally heard through one channel or speaker.

It is now possible to place the entire FM radio on one or two integrated-circuit chips. This can be done with two 14-pin DIPs. These chips do not contain the audio output stage but do have the preamplifier for the audio. That means another chip of the desired audio power can be connected to allow this to operate as a radio.

Other FM Users

There are other users of FM. The FCC allows some stations to multiplex music on a channel with no commercials, and the station owner can charge customers for the music they use as background for workers in plants, on elevators, and in offices. This kind of service is also now available from satellite broadcasting units.

This multiplexing system is referred to as the *subsidiary communication authorization* (SCA). It usually employs a 67-kHz carrier and a ±7.5-kHz (narrowband) deviation. Decoders, usually using the NE 565 IC chip, which is a phase-locked loop, perform the demodulation and filtering. However, this is beyond the realm of this discussion.

Keep in mind that television uses FM for the audio portion of its programs. TV FM is not as broadband as regular FM at 88 to 108 MHz. The FM standard deviation is limited to ±25 kHz to conserve the bandwidth. FM uses a ±75-kHz deviation. The television receiver is able to produce better-quality sound if it has a better audio amplifier and speaker system.

We have already mentioned the use of FM transmission by people who wish to communicate for distances of less than 80 miles. Amateurs use these frequencies for short distances; walkie-talkies are limited to a 100-mW output, and this further reduces their range. They come in handy for people enjoying the outdoors and for those who must work at two different locations at the same time (such as putting up a TV antenna on the roof and checking its performance inside the house). This type of communication provides comparatively low noise levels and is satisfactory for many purposes.

Stereo Equipment

For a "stereo" effect, we needed at least two amplifiers and two speakers to reproduce sound that has good fidelity to the original, giving you a feeling of "being there" when the music was recorded. Recording and reproducing high-quality sound dates back to the 1930s when Edwin Armstrong transmitted high-fidelity ("hi-fi") musical programs over his FM station. Some record companies produced long-playing 33⅓ records during this period for those who wanted to pay the higher prices and had the equipment to play them. World War II put the development of high-fidelity equipment on hold until 1946, when the FM band was shifted and people could buy the equipment to hear the better-fidelity FM sound. In 1947 the variable reluctance pickup for the phonograph (record player) gave the high-fidelity movement a boost. The development of the Williamson amplifier and the use of two-speaker systems launched the movement toward today's high-quality sound, which has continued with the development of compact discs (CDs) and digital recordings such as MP3s.

The word *stereo* is derived from a Greek word meaning "solid" or "three-dimensional" space. When properly reproduced, stereophonic sound creates an aural perspective and produces a feeling of presence and an illusion of depth. It causes the ear to reject distortion and helps it to hear a wider range of frequencies.

There are a number of types of microphones—carbon, dynamic, velocity, ribbon, and crystal. Preamplifiers are usually needed to amplify the inputs to stereo power amplifiers. The vacuum tube push-pull amplifier was one of the standbys of olden days for power amplification. Transistors and integrated circuits have long since replaced the vacuum tube in most applications.

The *permanent magnet* (*PM*) *speaker* is the most common today and comes in a wide variety of diameters and shapes. The size of voice coil wire limits the amount of current a speaker can handle. Crossover networks control which speaker reproduces the various frequencies. There are a number of different speaker enclosures. One of them is the bass-reflex type which has a ducted port or hole in the front. Other types include the infinite baffle and the plane baffle.

Transducers

Transducers are devices that convert pressure, light, heat, and sound to electrical energy. A microphone is a good example. It uses the pressure waves of sound to produce a varying electrical current. This varying current is then amplified and fed to a speaker so it can be heard, or it is recorded on tape, disc, or wire. The oil pressure gauge in an automobile has a transducer that allows it to operate. The transducer responds to the pressure of the oil on a diaphram that causes a change in resistance in the circuit, thereby allowing the meter or gauge to read the pressure of the oil. The same is true with the temperature gauge in a car. Heat causes the resistance of the transducer to change, which in turn causes a change in current in the circuit as indicated by the movement of the meter needle. The meter is calibrated in degrees Fahrenheit instead of milliamperes.

Transducers take many forms and are used in any number of electronic devices. Without transducers, the electrical control and operation of devices would be extremely limited.

Television

A number of basic elements must be considered in setting up any television system:

1. Camera and scanning
2. Sync signals
3. Video amplifiers
4. Audio amplifiers
5. An FM transmitter for audio
6. An AM transmitter for video.

CAMERA TUBES

Several different camera tubes were tried before the ones available today, which can work in low levels of light, were produced. The oldest was the *iconoscope*, developed in 1933 by Zworykin. The iconoscope tube had an electron gun with a magnetic beam deflection yoke located in the handle (Fig. 7.73). The photosensitive mosaic consisted of silver globules sensitized with cesium and deposited on one side of a mica sheet; the other side had a metallic backing. The mica was the dielectric of the capacitor formed by the silver deposit and the metal plate. When light struck the silver surface, it produced photoemission at each of the silver globules. An electron beam scanned the surface and struck each globule that was charged by the light striking it. The electrons from the scan replaced the electrons lost by photoemission. This caused a proportionate current pulse to flow in the signal plate. The amplitudes of the pulses from the signal plate current then represented the relative brightnesses of the mosaic elements as the beam scanned across them.

The iconoscope had some very strict light requirements and was replaced by the *image orthicon* (Fig. 7.74). This tube worked basically the same way, with some improvement in light levels. It was bulky, temperamental, and costly. It was the standard tube used in television studios for a number of years. However, another type of camera tube was the *vidicon*. It was smaller, simpler, and more rugged than the image orthicon. Its operation was somewhat different also, since its target depends on photoconductivity rather than photoemission.

The vidicon works by having an image focused through a transparent conductive film, which acts as the signal electrode. The image is impressed on the photoconductive target, which is biased slightly positive. When the layer is not exposed to light, such as in darkness, it acts as an insulator. The electron gun provides a beam. The beam is slowed by the wall coating and screen to a moderate velocity and deflected magnetically. Once the scanning beam strikes the back of the target, it neutralizes the charge on the target. This causes the target to give up just enough electrons to make up for those that have leaked through the partially conductive coatings since the last scan. As the brightness of the target area increases, so does the conductivity of the target. This produces a larger leakage current and a greater number of electrons taken from the beam. This action produces a burst of current at the signal electrode in proportion to the brightness of the spot being scanned.

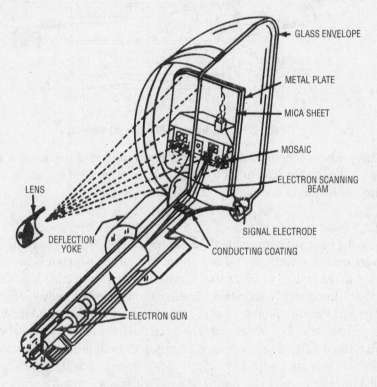

Fig. 7.73. The iconoscope.

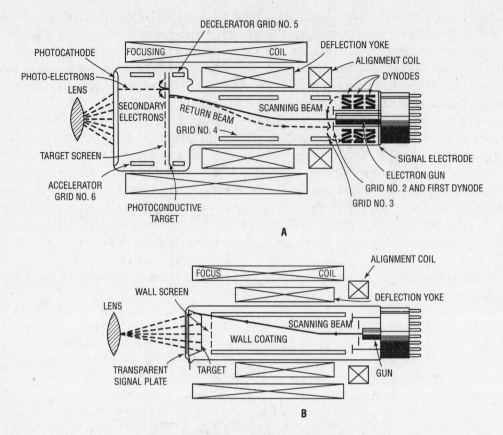

Fig. 7.74. (A) Image orthicon. (B) Vidicon.

More sensitive tubes are being developed. It is now possible to make color television programs at night using available light. The tubes have become more rugged for use in portable home cameras. They also use less light to obtain an acceptable picture.

SCANNING

In order to have the camera tube operate, it has to be scanned. The beam of light that scans the target area is swept back and forth and up and down. The rate at which it is moved from left to right and from the top to the bottom of the area determines the type of picture reproduced at the receiver.

The Electronics Industries Association standard for the United States is 525 lines horizontally (Fig. 7.75). The 525 lines are produced as the beam scans from the top to the bottom of the image area. This scanning is done in 1/30 second. This scan from top to bottom is called *one frame*. However, in the interlaced method, the sweep is from top to bottom in 1/60 second. This means that the odd-numbered lines are swept from top to bottom, and then the beam returns to sweep the even-numbered lines from top to bottom. The two fields make up a frame.

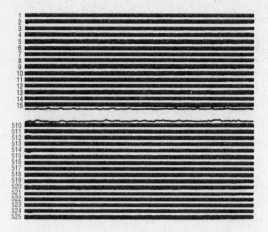

Fig. 7.75. The 525 scan lines for a TV picture.

This type of scanning, interlaced, has a tendency to reduce the flickering effect produced by the succession of pictures. The receiver uses the same scanning technique. That is why sync signals are produced: to keep the transmitter scanning rate in step with the scanning rate of the receiver's picture tube. If they are not in step, the picture will become scrambled. If the receiver's vertical scan is out of step with the transmitter's vertical scan, the picture on the tube at the receiver will roll slowly. If the horizontal scans are out of sync, the picture will become diagonally slanted and will not be recognizable. As you can see, the synchronization of the camera tube scan and the receiver tube scan is very important.

There are 60 fields each second. The vertical sweep frequency is 60 Hz, and the horizontal sweep frequency is 15,750 Hz. The latter is based on the fact that 30 frames times 525 lines equals 15,750. The sweep voltages are in a sawtooth waveform.

The odd-numbered lines are scanned first, and then the even-numbered. During the odd-numbered scanning the even-numbered lines are not illuminated, and so they appear black on the screen. Thus, you actually see only half of the lines at one time; that is, 262.5 lines make up a field.

TV TRANSMITTER

A television transmitter is really two transmitters in one (Fig. 7.76). The picture information (called video) is transmitted with its synchronization signals, both horizontal and vertical, by way of an amplitude-modulated transmitter. The audio information is transmitted by a frequency-modulated transmitter. They both use the same antenna. The band of frequencies that contain both picture and audio is 6 MHz wide.

The critical part of the video transmitter is the sync generator. It provides all the critical timing functions to both the local camera's sweep circuits and to the mixer for transmission to the receiver's sync circuits. The output of the camera is amplified and mixed, with the sync signals forming the composite video signal. The rest of the video transmitter is like any other AM transmitter, except that it operates in the TV frequency band and has a sideband filter to suppress the lower video sidebands.

As you can see, there is a lot of information in the video signal. On each side of the video is a guard band to prevent interference with the audio and to guard against interfering with adjacent channels.

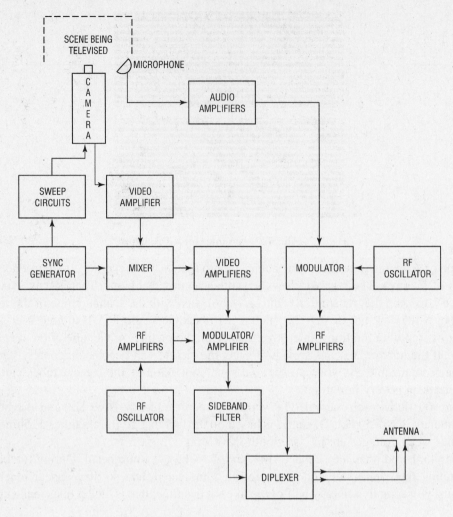

Fig. 7.76. Black-and-white TV transmitter block diagram.

Color Television

The monocolor, or black-and-white, television was first on the scene. Once it was developed, people began to look for better-quality pictures, and also pictures in color. Thus, the millions of TV sets that were purchased for black-and-white reception also had to be able to receive the color-transmitted programs in black and white. This produced a problem or two since the bandwidth had already been assigned and filled with information for black and white pictures and for the sound. There simply was not any space to add color signals. However, a few people had ideas that would make color and black and white compatible.

Color television relies on the principle that any visible color can be reproduced by using the proper combinations of the three primary or chromatic colors: red, blue, and green. All systems of transmitting color television signals use some method of analyzing the colors of the scene being scanned in terms of these three colors and of converting the information to electric signals. Fig. 7.77 shows how color separators work to produce the color TV picture. Three monochrome cameras view each scene through the same lens. The color of the scene is then divided into red, green, and blue light by the dichroic mirrors. A mirror of this type is a plate of glass coated with a thin, metallic layer. It then reflects one of the primary colors while allowing the others to pass through. The camera has three outputs corresponding to the three primary colors. The picture is transmitted by converting these signals into other signals that correspond to the brightness, hue, and saturation of the scene.

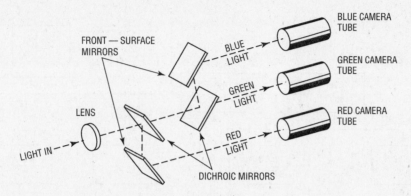

Fig. 7.77. Color separator system for a color camera.

In color television the brightness signal, called the *luminance signal,* is represented by the letter Y. Signals that correspond to the hue and saturation are called the *chrominance signals*. The process of combining the outputs of the cameras to form chrominance signals is called *encoding* and is accomplished in a circuit called a *matrix*.

There is no difference between the luminance, or Y, signal and the monochrome camera signal. It is all that's needed to produce a black-and-white picture. The luminance signal is made up of 30% of the output of the red camera, 59% of the output of the green camera, and 11% of the output of the blue camera. These are roughly the rates or percentages that the human eye responds to for the various colors.

THE TELEVISION RECEIVER

There is no difference between the television receiver and the AM and FM receivers. For now, we will take a look at the color receiver to see how it works in principle. These basics are the same whether the TV receives the signal from a broadcast station by means of an aerial or an antenna, through a cable interface (analog or digital), or from a satellite dish receiver.

Fig. 7.78 shows the black-and-white television set in block diagram form. The audio is separated at the video detector and sent to an FM section, which demodulates the signal and produces the sound. The picture information is sent to the cathode ray tube, where it is displayed as the signal dictates. In order to keep the picture synchronized properly, sync signals are picked from the incoming signal and fed to the deflection coils around the neck of the tube. These signals cause the beam of electrons in the picture tube to be moved back and forth and up and down by the sawtooth waveform fed into them. The scanning of the phosphorus coating on the picture tube causes it to glow or not glow according to the intensity of the beam. If the beam is not too bright, it will show as a gray. This produces a white-and-gray rather than a black-and-white picture.

Now that you have taken a quick look at the monochrome television receiver, let's modify the receiver slightly to enable it to receive the color signal and produce a picture and sound. First, though, let's review some information on color and how the eye perceives it. In order for color television to be developed, three things had to be understood and incorporated into the signal to be broadcast: (1) color has hue, or chroma, (2) color has saturation, or purity, and (3) color has brightness. *Hue* is the basic characteristic that gives color its name, such as orange or purple. *Saturation* indicates how much the color is diluted with white.

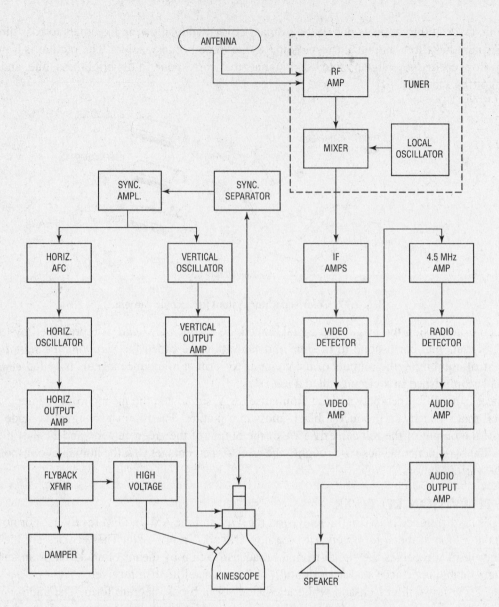

Fig. 7.78. Block diagram of a black-and-white TV receiver.

For instance, red can be seen in tomatoes and blood, while the less-saturated color would appear as pink in bubble gum, a pink hair ribbon, or anything with a lower intensity of red. *Brightness* refers to the brilliance of the color. Brilliance is a whole range of colors from white to dark grays to black. These three characteristics of color have to be taken into consideration for the purposes of reproducing a color television picture.

Now take a look at the other colors that will have to be understood before a device can be designed to reproduce all the colors known today. White, of course, is not a color—it is the *presence of all the colors*. Therefore, it can be reproduced if all the colors are mixed together. Black is not a color either; it is the *absence of light*. Gray is a weak white. Browns are reds, oranges, and yellows of low brightness. When a beam of light is broken up by a prism, six colors emerge: red, orange, yellow, green, blue, and violet. They are called the *spectral colors*. By mixing the red and the violet, purple and magentas can be formed from the various proportions of red and violet. These are called the *nonspectral colors*.

When you take three colors—red, green, and blue—and project them until they overlap, some interesting combinations result. The overlap of the red and green produces a yellow area.

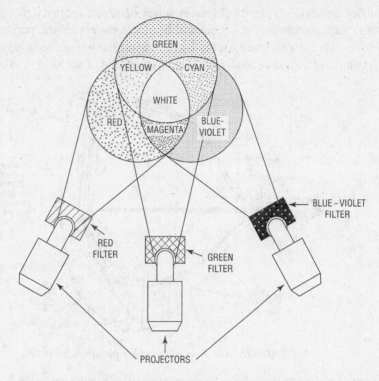

Fig. 7.79. Mixing the primary colors in an additive mode.

The red and blue-violet mix to form a magenta. The blue-violet with green combinations produces an aqua color which is called cyan in the printing business. By adjusting the brightness of the various lamps, you can obtain any color. This is the additive process of producing color. Keep in mind that the chrominance signals produced by the camera and transmitted by the color TV station are called orange-cyan and blue-green-magenta. (See Fig. 7.79.)

PHASE MODULATION

The subcarrier generated at the studio and modulated with the various outputs from three sources of color is filtered out before the TV signal is broadcast. It must be regenerated at the receiver by an oscillator. The oscillator has a tendency to drift if not kept at a perfectly stable temperature. This is why the 3.58-MHz burst is transmitted from the transmitter to keep the oscillator operating properly in the receiver. The two chrominance signals are blended with the subcarrier, but they are 90 degrees out of phase with one another. Once the subcarrier is removed at the transmitter, it leaves only these two sidebands with the chrominance signals 90 degrees apart. These become part of the sidebands of the regular carrier frequency assigned to the channel. They are placed on the regular carrier frequency by the process of phase modulation. Thus, the black-and-white receiver ignores them completely since it has no way of recognizing their existence.

The amplitude of the combined chrominance signal carries the saturation information, and the phase angle carries the hue. The sync signals and the luminance signal, along with the picture information, are broadcast over the assigned frequency for the channel (or sent through a cable distribution system, or routed to the appropriate satellite, and so on). The receiver picks them up and starts the process of demodulation and of putting the information where it will be used to produce a color picture.

THE COLOR PICTURE TUBE

The color picture tube has three guns that emit electrons in the end of the tube. There are three cathodes and three filament windings. The filaments heat up the tube (this is the red glow at the base of the tube) and boil off the electrons. A series of plates properly placed inside the neck of the picture tube, called a *kinescope*, accelerate the electrons toward the phosphorus coating on the front of the tube. Two coils are used for the horizontal deflection of the beam of electrons, and two vertical deflecting coils are used to deflect the beam up and down (Fig. 7.80).

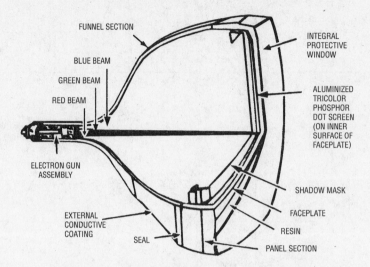

Fig. 7.80. Cutaway view of the color picture tube (RCA).

Another name for the picture tube is the kinescope. The kinescope made for the reproduction of color pictures needs some explanation so that you can understand how it reproduces all the colors needed for any picture. Fig. 7.80 shows the way the phosphors are placed on the inside of the tube. The inside face of the screen is coated with three different kinds of phosphors, which glow when struck with an electron beam. The phosphors are put on the screen in a three-dot pattern. The shadow mask is placed near the phosphor-coated screen and is located between the screen and the guns. The mask has about 250,000 holes in it. Each hole is there for a purpose. There is a red, a blue, and a green dot on the screen for each hole in the shadow mask. Thus, there are 750,000 dots on the screen.

A convergence electrode is operated at about 11,000 volts to cause the red, blue, and green beams to pass through the same shadow mask hole. Once the beams are through the shadow mask, the blue hits the blue dot, the red hits the red dot, and the green hits the green dot in any given pattern. The dots, however, are too small to be seen by the human eye. If the same beam intensity hits all three dots, it produces a white dot. However, if the red and green are the only ones hitting their dots within the pattern of that hole, a yellow dot is produced. This goes on for all the various combinations of colors. The color signal is then displayed on the phosphors of the tube in accordance with what they were in the studio or where the camera saw them. (See Fig. 7.81.)

The most common type of computer monitor, known as a cathode ray tube or a CRT, works in basically the same way as conventional TV screens. CRTs have the advantage of responding quickly when you turn on the switch, and high resolution is possible. They can produce the full range of both saturated and natural colors, and they are capable of both high contrast and brightness. They are—perhaps most importantly—a mature, relatively inexpensive, low-maintenance, widely accepted technology. On the other hand, they are relatively heavy, require lots of power (usually about 140 volts), and produce potentially harmful DC and AC electromagnetic fields. They can also have geometrical image errors at the edge of the screen.

Liquid crystal display screens, or LCDs, were for years able to be used practically only for such things as calculator displays and signs. LCDs use organic molecules that, in the absence of external forces, tend to align themselves in crystalline structures. When an external force is applied, however, they rearrange themselves as if they were a liquid. Some liquid crystals respond to heat (for example, mood rings), while others respond to electromagnetic forces. When used as optical or light modulators, LCDs change polarization instead of transparency (at least, this is true of the most popular type of LCD known as supertwisted nematic liquid crystals). In their unexcited or crystalline state, LCDs rotate the polarization of light by 90 degrees. In the presence of an electric field, the small electrostatic charges of the molecules align with the impinging electric-field. LCDs are typically slower to come "on" than CRTs, but they also take up only about one-sixth the space and weigh about one-fifth as much, while consuming only about one-fourth of the power a CRT requires. Their completely flat screens preclude geometrical errors at the edges, they don't emit electromagnetic waves, and they can be used with a fully digital signal. Pictures are also seen to be crisper. However, they usually cost two to three times what a CRT costs and have a narrower viewing angle, as well as lower available contrast and luminance.

Plasma screens or *plasma display panels* (PDPs) are essentially matrices of very small fluorescent tubes with red, green, and blue phosphors. As in ordinary tubes, a discharge is initiated by a high voltage that excites a mixture of inert gases such as helium and xenon. Upon relaxation, ultraviolet (UV) radiation is generated, which excites the phosphors. PDPs have a wider viewing angle but consume twice the voltage and have lower luminance than CRTs. And, they are not only more expensive, but also are not yet practicable for smaller screens such as workstation monitors; they are also not yet fully compatible with the sharper digital images of high-definition television (HDTV).

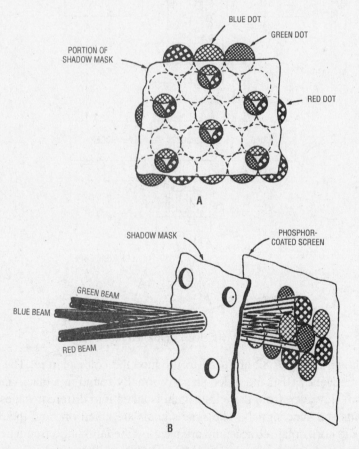

Fig. 7.81. (A) Shadow mask aligned with the color dot pattern.
(B) The three beams passing through the shadow mask.

RECEIVER STAGES

Fig. 7.82 shows the block diagram of the color TV receiver. In it you will notice some differences from that of the black-and-white receiver.

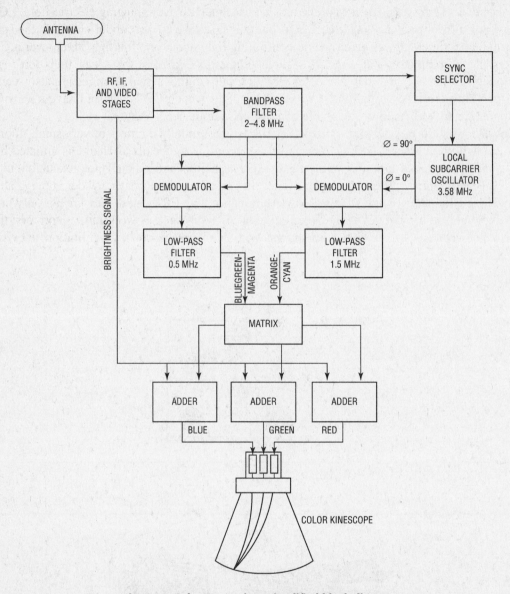

Fig. 7.82. Color TV receiver, simplified block diagram.

All the stages shown in Fig. 7.82 are used to produce the color picture. The radio frequency (RF), intermediate frequency (IF), and video stages normally found in a black-and-white receiver are located here also. However, from there the signal is taken into different stages to be processed for color components and sync signals. The sync signals are taken off, and the 3.58-MHz bursts that appear during the horizontal retrace time are used by the automatic frequency control circuit to check and compare with the receiver's 3.58-MHz crystal oscillator and to keep it in phase with that which is broadcast with the color information. The subcarrier (3.58 MHz) is again added to the sidebands that contain the color information. This allows the color information to be extracted. The subcarrier oscillator stage puts out two signals for the two modulators, and the signals are 90 degrees out of phase with one another. A low-pass filter of 0.5 MHz then puts out the blue-green-magenta signal, while the other low-pass filter of 1.5 MHz produces the orange-cyan signal.

These two signals are fed into the matrix. After demodulation, the R − Y (red minus luminance) and B − Y (blue minus luminance) signals are matrixed to produce a G − Y (green minus luminance) signal. All three signals are then applied to the picture tube where the positive Y signal from the video amplifier cancels all the −Y components. Keep in mind that the third signal, or brightness, is added after the matrix. From the matrix the signals are fed to the individual adders. The adders add the brightness signal (a positive Y signal), and this removes the −Y signals. This in turn produces a blue, a green, and a red to drive the individual color guns in the base of the kinescope.

When the tint or hue control is adjusted, it changes the phase angle slightly so that the exact color match can be obtained.

Solder and Soldering

The most common technique for joining wires, lugs, and terminals in electrical and electronics circuits is soldering.

Solder is an alloy metal made from tin and lead. There are three standard alloy mixtures for solder, which are given as percentages; the tin percentage is always stated first. Thus, a 40/60 solder contains 40% tin and 60% lead. There are also 50/50 and 60/40 solders. In general, the more tin contained in solder, the higher the quality. In industry, 60/40 solder is used by quality manufacturers.

Soldering is the technique of joining electrical or electronic connections where solder is melted to form a coating over the connection point, forming a joint. Standard solders melt at between 450°F and 600°F (232.2°C and 315.5°C).

Most solder contains a chemical, which is called *flux*. The purpose of the flux is to clean the area of the connection. This allows the melted solder to flow easily and also prevents oxidation. Two types of flux are available. One is an acid core flux used primarily in sheet metal soldering. Never use acid core flux when soldering copper. For electrical and electronics work, only rosin flux is used. Rosin flux can be purchased as a paste. However, the most common form is as part of the solder. Flux is built into soldering wire, which is then known as rosin-core solder.

There are three methods of applying solder: contact, dip, and wave.

CONTACT SOLDERING

Contact soldering uses a soldering iron or soldering pencil. A complete soldering station (Fig. 7.83) includes a soldering iron, a power supply that controls the current used to heat the iron, and a wet sponge used to clean the tip of the iron.

Fig. 7.83.

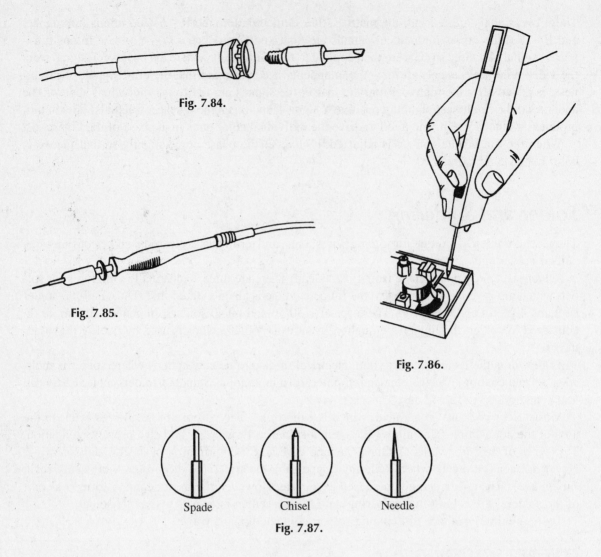

Fig. 7.84.

Fig. 7.85.

Fig. 7.86.

Spade Chisel Needle

Fig. 7.87.

Other types of equipment are also available for contact soldering. A soldering iron (Fig. 7.84) is a self-contained unit that simply plugs into an outlet for use. Soldering irons come in a variety of power ratings. For work on electronics, a low-wattage iron with a rating between 20 and 30 watts is recommended. The wattage may be higher for heavy-duty electrical devices—up to 500 watts. A soldering pencil (Fig. 7.85) is similar to a soldering iron but is smaller and is used for finer work. A portable soldering pencil (Fig. 7.86) is convenient and easy to use; it has no electric cord but is powered by a rechargeable cell in the handle.

Three types of tips are commonly used for soldering irons and pencils: spade, chisel, and needle (Fig. 7.87). Any of these can be used for any soldering job.

Soldering guns are popular with many hobbyists. The trigger of the gun activates a transformer within the unit, and heat is generated through induction.

To form a solder connection, follow a series of steps:

1. Clean the soldering iron or pencil.
2. Make sure the connection to be soldered is *clean*.
3. *Tin* the iron. To do this, touch the tip of the iron with solder wire, assuming you are using rosin-core solder. If not, dip the tip of the wire into the flux first. A small spot of solder

will form on the tip of the iron or pencil. Wipe the tip with a rag to cause the solder to coat or "tin" the tip. With the iron tinned, you are ready to solder.

4. Touch the connection with the tip of the iron or pencil. Simply allow the solder to flow into the connection. The flowing solder makes the connection.

5. Check the quality of your work. A good solder connection should be clean and shiny. There should be no cracks. If the solder is cracked or dull, this indicates a cold solder connection. A cold solder connection is unsatisfactory and should be reheated. Also, be careful that the solder does not bridge. *Bridging* occurs when solder runs across copper strips along a printed circuit board. This can cause a short circuit.

DIP SOLDERING

For mass production, it is possible to solder a number of connections in one operation—*dip soldering*. This is done to secure components onto printed circuit boards. All the components are put in position first. Then the bottom of the board is lowered into liquid solder contained in a pot. The leads of the connecting wires pick up solder. When the board is removed from the pot, the solder cools and the components are held in place.

WAVE SOLDERING

Wave soldering is a faster, more advanced, mass-production technique. Boards are prepared in the same way as described above for dip soldering. However, there is a pressure mechanism in the pot that causes the hot solder to flow upward in waves. Circuit boards with components in position are placed just above the level of the hot solder. The waves cause the solder to touch the connection. Soldering is clean and fast. The wave soldering process is illustrated in Fig. 7.88.

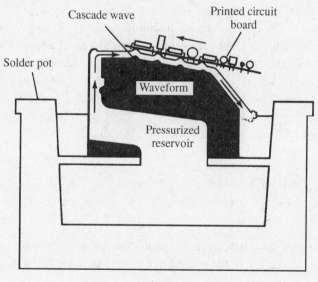

Fig. 7.88.

CHAPTER

8 Basic Mechanics Review

The ASVAB subtest on Mechanical Comprehension tests knowledge of basic mechanical and physical principles and the ability to visualize how illustrated objects and simple machines work. This chapter reviews some basic principles of physics and how some simple machines make work easier.

Force

One of the basic concepts of physics is the concept of force. *Force* is something that can change the velocity of an object by making it start, stop, speed up, slow down, or change direction. Let's think for a minute of a car. When you take your foot off the gas pedal, your car does not suddenly come to a stop. It coasts on, only gradually losing its velocity. If you want the car to stop, you have to do something to it. That is what your brakes are for: to exert a force that decreases the car's velocity. A spacecraft also illustrates the point. Voyager has been coasting through the solar system for years; nothing is pushing it. However, when we want it to speed up, slow down, or change direction, we send it signals that fire control rockets—in other words, we exert a force on it to change its velocity.

There are many types of force, some of which we will discuss.

Kinds of Force

FRICTION

Your car has two controls whose functions are to change the car's velocity: the gas pedal and the brake pedal. The brakes make use of the same force that stops your car if you just let it coast: friction.

Sliding friction is a force that is generated whenever two objects are in contact and there is relative motion between them. When something is moving, friction *always* acts in such a direction as to retard (slow down or decrease) the relative motion. Therefore, the direction of the force of friction on a moving object is always directly opposite the direction of the velocity. The brake shoes slow down the rotation of the wheels, and the tires slow the car until it comes to rest.

In the simplest case, the force of friction can be easily measured by using a *spring scale* (Fig. 8.1). (A spring scale can be used to measure all kinds of forces. Basically, it measures the force pulling on its shackle.) A spring scale is calibrated in force units—*pounds* or (in the SI) *newtons*. A newton (abbreviated N) is a fairly small unit of force; it takes 4.45 newtons to equal 1 pound.

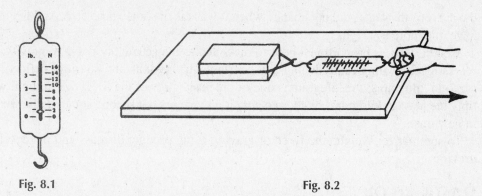

Fig. 8.1   Fig. 8.2

Figure 8.2 shows a spring scale being used to measure the force of sliding friction between a brick and the horizontal surface on which it is resting. The scale is pulling the brick along at constant speed. In this condition, the brick is said to be in *equilibrium*. Since its velocity is not changing, we can conclude that the net force acting on it is zero.

However, the spring scale *is* exerting a force, which is shown on its face; this force is pulling the brick to the right. The brick can remain in equilibrium only if there is an equal force pulling it to the left, so that the net force (the sum of forces acting on it in all directions) acting on it is zero. In the situation shown, the only force pulling the brick to the left is the frictional force between the brick and the surface. Therefore, the reading on the spring scale is equal to the force of friction.

Anyone who has ever moved furniture around, or slid a box across the floor, knows that the frictional force is greater when the furniture or the box is heavier. The force of friction does not change much as the object speeds up, but it depends very strongly on how hard the two surfaces are pressed together.

When a solid moves through a liquid, such as a boat moving through the water, there is a frictionlike force retarding the motion of the solid. It is called *viscous drag*. Like friction, it always acts opposite velocity. Unlike friction, however, it increases greatly with speed, and it depends more on the shape of the object and on the nature of the liquid than on the object's weight. Gases also produce viscous drag; the example of this you are probably most familiar with is the air resistance that acts on a car at high speed.

To summarize, friction and viscous drag are forces that act to retard motion.

GRAVITY

Probably the first law of physics that everyone learns is this: If you drop something, it falls. Since its velocity keeps on changing as it falls, there must be a force acting on it all the while. That is the force we call *gravity*.

You can measure gravity by balancing it off with a spring scale. When you hang something on a spring scale and read the scale in pounds or newtons, you usually call the force of gravity acting on the object by a special name—you call it the *weight* of the object.

Weight is not a fixed property of an object; it varies with location. A person who weighs 160 pounds at the North Pole will check in at 159.2 pounds at the equator. If he should step on a scale on the moon, it would read only 27 pounds. Everything weighs less where the acceleration due to gravity is smaller. Weight, in fact, is directly proportional to the acceleration of an object due to gravity.

Obviously, weight also depends on something else, since things have different weights even if they are all at the same place. Weight depends on how much "stuff" there is in the object. When you buy 10 pounds of sugar, you expect to get twice as much as if you buy 5 pounds. And if you take both sacks to the moon, one will still weigh twice as much as the other. The amount of sugar, the *mass* of the sugar, did not change when it was taken somewhere else. And the more sugar you have, the more it weighs.

Weight, then, is proportional both to mass and to the acceleration due to gravity. This equation works nicely, without introducing any constants, if the units are carefully defined. Mass is measured in kilograms; the kilogram is one of the basic units of the SI. By definition, when you multiply the mass in kilograms by the acceleration in meters per second squared, the weight comes out in newtons.

To summarize: Weight, the force of gravity, is the product of mass and the acceleration due to gravity.

ELASTIC RECOIL

The basic feature of a solid, as opposed to a liquid or a gas, is that it has a definite shape. It resists changes in its shape and, in so doing, exerts a force against whatever force is applied to it.

For example, look at the meter bar supported at its ends shown in Fig. 8.3. If you push down on it, you bend it, and you can feel it pushing back on you. The harder you push, the more the bar bends and the harder it pushes back. It bends just enough to push on you with the same force that you exert on it. The force it exerts is called *elastic recoil*.

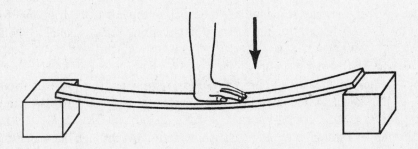

Fig. 8.3

The same thing happens when you stand on the floor or on the ground. You can't see the floor bend, but it bends just the same, although not very much. Even a feather resting on the floor bends it a little. The elastic recoil force needed to support the feather is very small, so the amount of bending is too small to detect.

A rope does not resist bending, but it certainly does resist stretching. When a rope is stretched, it is said to be in a state of *tension*. The tension can be measured by cutting the rope and inserting a spring scale into it, as shown in Fig. 8.4. The spring scale reads the tension in the rope in pounds or newtons. If you pull with a force of 30 N, for example, the tension in the rope is 30 N, and that is what the scale will indicate. Something, such as the elastic recoil of the wall to which the scale is attached, must be pulling on the other end with a force of 30 N. The tension in the rope is the same throughout and is equal to the elastic recoil force that the rope exerts at its ends.

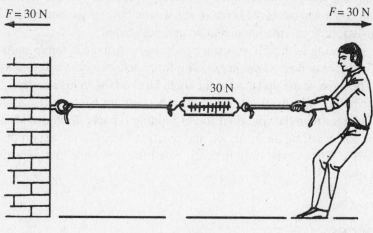

$F = 30$ N $F = 30$ N

30 N

Fig. 8.4

To summarize: A force applied to a solid distorts the shape of the solid, causing it to exert a force back on the force that distorted it.

BUOYANCY

If you take a deep breath and dive into a pool, you will have a lot of trouble keeping yourself submerged. Something keeps pushing you up. That force is called *buoyancy*.

The force of buoyancy acts in an upward direction on anything submerged in a liquid or a gas. Buoyancy is the force that makes ships float and helium-filled balloons rise. A rock sinks because its weight is greater than the buoyancy of the water. A submerged cork rises because the buoyancy is greater than its weight. When it reaches the surface, some of it emerges, but the rest is still under water. The amount under water is just enough to produce a buoyant force equal to its weight, so it stays put.

OTHER FORCES

There are some other familiar forces, and some not so familiar. You know about magnetism, which attracts iron nails to a red horseshoe. You have met electric force, which makes a nylon shirt cling to you when you try to take it off, or which refuses to release the dust particles from your favorite CD or DVD. Airplanes stay up because of the lift force generated by the flow of air across their wings. A rocket takes off because of the force generated by the gases expanding in it and coming from its exhaust. This chapter will illustrate other examples of force, but we have enough to get along with for now.

Action and Reaction

A batter steps up to the plate and takes a healthy swing, sending the ball into left field. The bat has exerted a large force on the ball, changing both the magnitude and the direction of its velocity. But the ball has also exerted a force on the bat, slowing it down. The batter feels this when the bat hits the ball.

Next time up, he strikes out. He has taken exactly the same swing but exerts no force on anything. (Air in this example is small enough not to count.) The batter has discovered that it is impossible to exert a force unless there is something there to push back. Forces exist *only* in pairs. When object A exerts a force on object B, then B must exert a force on A. The two forces are sometimes called *action* and *reaction*, although which is which is often somewhat arbitrary. The two parts of the interaction are equal in magnitude, are opposite in direction, and act on different objects.

The law of action and reaction leads to an apparent paradox if you are not careful how it is applied. A horse pulls on a wagon. If the force of the wagon pulling the horse the other way is the same, as the law insists, how can the horse and wagon get started?

The error in the reasoning is this: If you want to know whether the horse starts to move, you have to consider the forces acting *on the horse*. The force acting on the wagon has nothing to do with the question. The horse starts up because the force he exerts with his hooves is larger than the force of the wagon pulling him back. And the wagon starts up because the force of the horse pulling it forward is larger than the frictional forces holding it back. To know whether something moves, consider the forces acting *on it*. Action and reaction forces *never* act on the same object.

Again, to summarize, forces exist only in pairs, equal in magnitude and opposite in direction, acting on different objects.

Balanced Forces

If a single force acts on an object, the velocity of the object must change. If two or more forces act, however, their effects may eliminate each other. This is the condition of equilibrium in which there is no net force and the velocity does not change. We saw such a condition in the case in which gravity is pulling an object down and a spring scale, used for weighing it, is pulling it upward.

An object in equilibrium may or may not be at rest. A parachutist descending at a constant speed is in equilibrium. Her weight is just balanced by the viscous drag on the parachute, which is why she put it on in the first place. A heavier parachutist falls a little faster; his speed increases until the viscous drag just balances his weight.

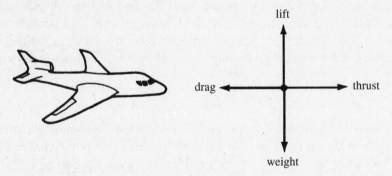

Fig. 8.5

Balancing the vertical forces is not enough to produce equilibrium. An airplane traveling at a constant speed is in equilibrium under the influence of four forces, two vertical and two horizontal. Vertical: Gravity (down) is just balanced by the lift produced by the flow of air across the wing. Horizontal: Viscous drag is just balanced by the thrust of the engines. Both the vertical and the horizontal velocities are constant.

The brick in Fig. 8.2, resting on a tabletop and being pulled along at a constant speed, is another example. Vertical: The downward force of gravity is balanced by the upward force of the elastic recoil of the tabletop. Horizontal: The tension in the spring scale, pulling to the right, is balanced by the friction pulling it to the left, opposite the direction of motion.

If an object is in equilibrium—at rest or moving at a constant speed in a straight line—the total force acting on it in any direction is exactly equal in magnitude to the force in the opposite direction.

Components of a Force

The crate in Fig. 8.6 is being dragged along the floor by means of a rope that is not horizontal. The rope makes an angle q with the floor.

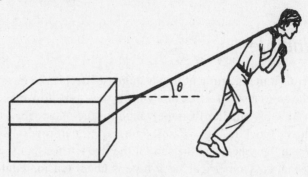

Fig. 8.6

The tension in the rope, acting on the crate, does two things to it. First, it drags the crate across the floor. Second, it tends to lift the crate off the floor. The smaller the angle q, the larger the effective force dragging the crate, and the smaller the effective force lifting it. When $q = 0$, the entire force is dragging and there is no lifting at all. Conversely, when $q = 90°$, the entire force is lifting the crate.

The Inclined Plane

A wagon rolls downhill, propelled only by its own weight. But gravity pulls straight down, not at an angle downhill. What makes the wagon go is a *component* of its weight, a part of its weight acting downhill, parallel to the surface the wagon rests on.

A component of a force can act in any direction, not just vertically or horizontally. On an inclined plane, the weight of the wagon has two different effects: it acts *parallel* to the surface of the hill, pushing the wagon downhill; and it acts perpendicular (or *normal*) to the surface, pushing the wagon into the surface. As the hill gets steeper, the parallel component becomes larger and the perpendicular component decreases.

When the wagon is resting on the surface, the elastic recoil of the surface is just enough to cancel the normal component of the wagon's weight. If the wagon is to stay in equilibrium, you have to pull on it, uphill, to prevent it from running away. If there is no friction, the uphill force needed is the same whether the wagon is standing still or going either uphill or downhill at constant speed.

The situation is different if the wagon is moving and there is friction. If the wagon is going uphill, you have to pull harder because the friction is working against you, holding it back. The total force you need to keep the wagon going is then equal to the parallel component of the weight plus the friction. On the other hand, if you are lowering the wagon down the hill, holding the rope to keep it from running away from you, friction is acting uphill, helping you to hold the wagon back. Then the force you must exert is the parallel component of the weight *minus* the friction.

Simple Machines

There are devices that make work easier. These devices are known as *simple machines*. Without thinking about it, everybody uses a hundred simple machines every day—a light switch, a doorknob, a pencil sharpener, to name just a few.

A pulley illustrates how machines make work easier. After discussing the pulley principle and learning some basic work terms, we will go on to discuss briefly some other simple machines—levers, hydraulic jacks, loading ramps, vises, and machines that spin (for example, winches and gears).

The Pulley Principle

A piano mover, unable to fit the instrument into a staircase, decides to raise it outside the building to a window. He attaches it to a set of ropes and wheels that somehow make it possible for him to lift it with a force considerably smaller than the weight of the piano. How does it work?

Consider first the heavy block in Fig. 8.7 suspended from two ropes. The upward force on the block is the tension (T) in the ropes, and the sum of the two tensions must equal the weight of the block. If the whole system is symmetrical, each rope is under tension equal to half the weight of the block.

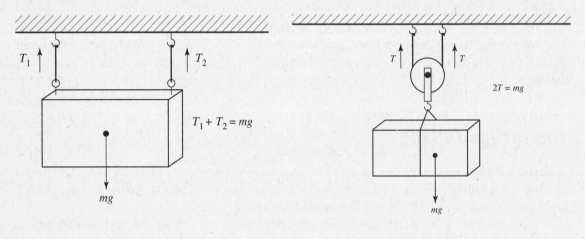

Fig. 8.7   Fig. 8.8

Now look at Fig. 8.8 where the block has been attached to a wheel. There is now only one rope, which passes over the wheel. The tension in the rope is the same throughout; if it were different on one side than on the other, the wheel would turn until the tension on the two sides equalized. The tension in the rope is still only half the weight of the block since it exerts *two* upward forces on the block. Now you have a system that helps in lifting things. Just fasten one end of the rope to a fixed support and pull on the other end (Fig. 8.9). Now you can raise the block with a force equal to only half its weight.

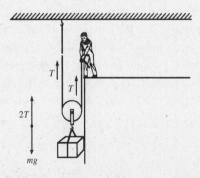

Fig. 8.9

Are you getting something for nothing? Well, yes and no. True, you can now lift the weight with less force, but you have to pull the rope farther than you would if you lifted the block directly.

Every time you pull 10 feet of rope through your hands, the block rises 5 feet. You might look at it this way: If the block rises 5 feet, *both* sides of the supporting rope have to shorten 5 feet, and the only way to accomplish this is to pull 10 feet of rope through. You raise the block with only half the force, but you have to exert the force through twice the distance.

You might prefer to pull in a downward direction rather than upward, and you can manage this by attaching a fixed wheel to the support and passing the rope around it as in Fig. 8.10. The tension in the rope is still only half the weight of the block; the fixed pulley does nothing but change the direction of the force you exert.

Let's adopt some vocabulary. The weight of the object being lifted we will call the *load*, and the distance it rises is the *load distance*. The force you exert on the rope is the *effort*, and the distance through which you exert that effort is the *effort distance*. With a single movable pulley in use, the effort is half the load and the effort distance is twice the load distance.

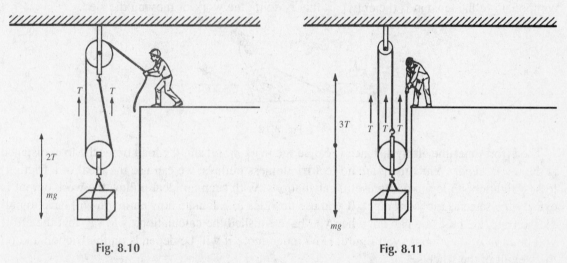

Fig. 8.10   Fig. 8.11

There are ways to string up a system of pulleys that will reduce the effort still further. Figure 8.11 shows how the same two pulleys can be connected to a rope in such a way as to divide the load among three strands instead of two. This is done by fastening one end of the rope to the load instead of to the fixed support. Unfortunately, when you do this, you have to shorten all three strands when you raise the object, and the effort distance becomes three times the load distance. By using more pulleys you can reduce the effort still further. Unfortunately, there is a limit to how much you can reduce the effort. The analysis we have done so far neglects a few things, such as friction and the weight of the movable pulleys themselves. Every time you add a pulley, you increase the friction in the system; if it is a movable pulley—the only kind that produces a reduction in force—you have to lift it along with the load. The effort in any real system is always larger than the ideal effort we calculated by dividing up the load. If there are a lot of pulleys, it may be considerably larger. And friction, while it increases the force you must exert, has no effect on the distance you have to pull the rope.

Effort distance is load distance times the number of supporting strands; effort is larger than load divided by the number of strands.

The Work Principle

While pulleys are useful, they don't really give you something for nothing. Ignoring the problem of friction, the input and output forces are in inverse ratio to the respective distances:

$$\frac{\text{effort}}{\text{load}} = \frac{\text{load distance}}{\text{effort distance}}$$

Or, to put it another way,

$$(\text{effort})(\text{effort distance}) = (\text{load})(\text{load distance})$$

A frictionless pulley, then, does not alter the product of force and distance; it is the same for the mover who pulls on the rope as it is for the piano. This product occurs repeatedly in physical situations, so it is given a special name. Force times distance is called *work*.

Work is done whenever a force moves something through a distance. If you stand still holding a boulder over your head, you might get tired, but—in the physical sense—you are doing no work.

There is another limitation on the definition of work. Only the force in the direction of motion counts. For example, look at Fig. 8.12—a child on a sled. The tension in the rope is pulling the sled, but it is also lifting the sled. Only the component of the force that is acting in the direction the sled is going is doing work on the sled. Since the sled is moving horizontally, the horizontal component of the tension is the only part that is doing the work of moving the sled.

Fig. 8.12

The effort times the effort distance is called the *work input*, and the load times the load distance is the *work output*. While there are no real frictionless pulleys, we can use the ideal of a frictionless, weightless pulley in doing useful calculations. With such an ideal pulley, the work output is exactly the same as the work input. If you use this idea to calculate how hard you will have to pull on the rope, the best you can do, when you have finished the calculation, is to say that the effort will be *at least* the amount you figure. How much more it will be depends on the friction and on the weight of the wheels.

With a real pulley, you always have to pull a little harder than the calculated value. The work input is therefore always more than the work output. The ratio between the work output and the work input is called the efficiency of the machine:

$$\text{efficiency} = \frac{W_{\text{out}}}{W_{\text{in}}}$$

Efficiency is usually expressed as a percent. It tells you what fraction of the work that you put into a machine comes out as useful work at the other end. Or, in other words, *efficiency* is the fraction of the work input that emerges as useful work output.

Levers

Another type of simple machine is a *lever*. A lever consists of a rigid bar pivoted at some point. An effort force applied to the bar at some point produces a different force on a load at some other position on the bar. The crowbar in Fig. 8.13 is typical. The load is the weight of the rock being lifted. The effort is the force exerted by the person who is trying to move the rock.

Fig. 8.13

Usually, the purpose of a machine is to make it possible to exert a large load force with a smaller effort. The machine magnifies force. The amount of this magnification, the ratio of load to effort, is called the *mechanical advantage* of the machine. It can be defined algebraically as the ratio of the two forces:

$$MA = \frac{F_L}{F_E}$$

In a pulley, the mechanical advantage is equal to the number of strands of rope supporting the load. For a lever, it can be found by considering the torques acting on the bar. The torque around the pivot that is exerted by the worker is $F_E r_E$, where r_E (the *effort arm*) is the distance from the point where the effort is applied to the pivot. Similarly, the torque produced by the weight of the rock is $F_L r_L$, where r_L is the load arm. If the system is rotating in equilibrium, these two torques must have the same magnitude, so

$$F_E r_E = F_L r_L$$

from which we find that the mechanical advantage, F_L/F_E, is given by

$$MA_{lever} = \frac{r_E}{r_L}$$

Or, in other words, in a lever the mechanical advantage is equal to the ratio of the effort arm to the load arm.

For many kinds of levers, friction at the pivot is very small, so efficiencies approach 100% and the arm ratio is very near the force ratio. Usually, no correction is needed.

Levers are classified according to the relative positions of the pivot, load, and effort. The three classes are represented by the tools shown in Fig. 8.14. In the pliers (first class) the pivot is between the effort and the load. In the nutcracker (second class) it is the load that is between the other two. And in the sugar tongs (third class), the effort is in the middle.

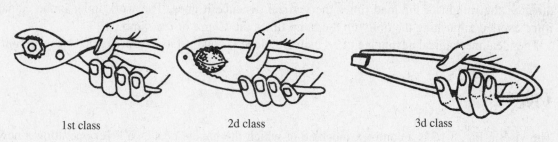

1st class   2d class   3d class

Fig. 8.14

Note that in the third-class lever (the sugar tongs), the load arm is longer than the effort arm, so the mechanical advantage is less than 1. This lever magnifies distance at the expense of force.

Mechanical advantage is the ratio of load to effort; in a lever, it is equal to the ratio of the effort arm to the load arm.

Hydraulic Jack

Liquids are nearly incompressible. This property makes them suitable as a means of transforming work.

A *hydraulic jack* is a device in which force is applied to the oil in a small cylinder. As shown in Fig. 8.15, this force causes some of the oil to be transferred to a larger cylinder. This forces the piston in the larger cylinder to rise, lifting a load.

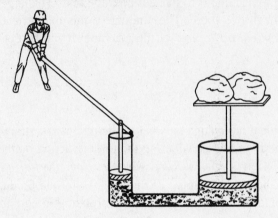

Fig. 8.15

This device takes advantage of the fact that oil, being nearly incompressible, transmits whatever pressure is applied to it. The pressure applied in the small cylinder appears unchanged in the big one, pushing up its piston.

Ideal mechanical advantage is the ratio between effort distance and load distance; for a hydraulic jack, it is equal to the ratio of the area of the load piston to that of the effort piston.

Loading Ramp

A *ramp* is a device commonly used to aid in lifting. To raise a heavy load a few feet onto a platform, it is common practice to place it on a dolly and wheel it up an inclined plane.

The work output of an inclined plane is the work that would have to be done to lift the load directly: the weight of the load times the vertical distance it goes. The work input is the actual force exerted in pushing the dolly up the ramp times the length of the ramp.

The ideal mechanical advantage of an inclined plane is equal to its length divided by its height.

Vise

The vise in Fig. 8.16 is a complex machine in which the handle acts as a lever operating a new kind of machine: a screw. How can we calculate the constants of this gadget?

It would be very difficult to calculate the ratio of the force the jaws apply to the force on the handle. The best we can do is work with the distances.

A *screw* consists of a single continuous spiral wrapped around a cylinder. The distance between ridges is known as the *pitch* of the thread, as shown in Fig. 8.17. Every time the screw makes one complete turn, it advances a distance equal to the pitch. In a vise, one complete turn is made when the end of the handle travels in a circle whose radius is the length of the handle (l). Therefore, when the effort moves a distance $2\pi\, l$, the load moves a distance equal to the pitch of the thread. Therefore, for a screw,

$$\text{ideal MA} = \frac{2\pi\,(\text{length of handle})}{\text{pitch of thread}}$$

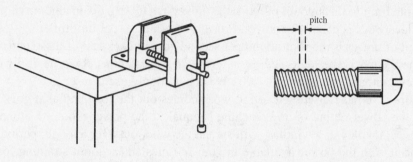

Fig. 8.16

Fig. 8.17

However, if you use this expression to calculate the forces, you will get it all wrong. A vise is a high-friction device. It has to be because it is the friction that keeps it from opening when you tighten it. A vise is a self-locking machine because its efficiency is considerably less than 50%.

Machines That Spin

What is the mechanical advantage of a winch, such as that shown in Fig. 8.18? The principle is not much different from that of a lever. Since the crank and the shaft turn together, the torque exerted by the effort (the force on the handle) must be equal to the torque exerted by the load (the tension in the rope). The mechanical advantage is then the ratio of the radius of the crank to the radius of the shaft.

Fig. 8.18

Fig. 8.19

In mechanical devices, gears are commonly used to change torque. Consider the gears in Fig. 8.19, for example. We assume that both gears are mounted on shafts of equal diameter and that the small gear is driving the large one. What is the mechanical advantage of this combination?

First of all, the teeth must have the same size and spacing on both gears in order for them to mesh properly. With 12 teeth in the large gear and only 4 in the small one, the small gear has to make three complete revolutions to make the big one turn once. The large, load gear moves only one-third as far as the smaller, effort gear. And the ratio of the two distances is the same as the ratio of the number of teeth in the two gears. Then we can say that the ideal mechanical advantage of a gear is the ratio of the number of teeth in the load gear to the number of teeth in the effort gear.

Power

When a piano mover rigs his tackle, he has to consider many factors. For one, the more pulleys he puts in, the longer it will take him to get the job done. If he has to pull more rope—using less force, though—he will have to keep pulling for a longer time.

There is a definite limit to the amount of work the mover can do in a given amount of time. The rate at which he does work is called the power. *Power* is work done per unit time.

The English unit of power is the foot-pound per second, and it takes 550 of these units to make 1 horsepower. The SI unit is the joule per second, or *watt* (W). A horsepower is 746 watts. The watt is a very small unit, and the kilowatt (1,000 W) is commonly used.

In all the machines we have discussed so far, work comes out the load end as it goes in at the effort end. Thus, the power output of any machine is equal to the power input. Machines do not increase your power. A pulley or a windlass will spread the work out over a longer period of time, so that you can do it with the power available in your muscles and without straining for a force larger than convenient.

CHAPTER

9 Shop Information Review

A person interested in making or repairing things is lost without tools. Tools make the difference between a person who works efficiently and one who struggles laboriously. There are some tools that are basic to any home shop and are generally used for simple carpentry work. Others are used for more specialized purposes. General shop knowledge also involves knowing basic facts about commonly used materials and about how design and layout are transferred from an idea to a finished product.

Tools

Common hand tools may be grouped under several headings: measuring and layout tools, cutting and shaping tools, drilling or boring tools, fasteners and fastening tools, clamping tools, pliers and wrenches, digging tools, grinding and sanding tools, and specialized tools like plumbers' or electricians' tools.

MEASURING AND LAYOUT TOOLS

Some of the most important tools, regardless of trade area, are measuring devices. They may take the form of *folding rules* and *tape measures* (Fig. 9.1) or steel rules and precision measuring instruments.

Fig. 9.1. Tape measure and folding rule

When using a folding, or zigzag, rule, place it flat on the work. The "0" end of the rule should be exactly even with the end of the space or board to be measured. The correct distance is indicated by the reading on the rule.

A very accurate reading may be obtained by turning the edge of the rule toward the work. In this position, the marked graduations of the face of the rule touch the surface of the board. With a sharp pencil, mark the exact distance desired. Start the mark with the point of the pencil in contact with the mark on the rule. Move the pencil directly away from the rule while making the mark.

You may notice a problem with a folding rule: if it gets twisted, it breaks. This happens commonly when folding or unfolding the rule and may not be noticed at the time. You should keep the joints oiled lightly so that the rule operates more easily.

Beginners may find a pocket tape the most useful measuring tool for all types of work. It extends smoothly to full length. It returns quickly to its compact case when the return button is pressed. Steel tapes are available in a variety of lengths. For most work, a tape 6, 8, 10, 12, or 25 feet long is suggested.

A *steel rule* (Fig. 9.2) is a very accurate version of the common notebook ruler. The measuring edges are usually graduated in 1/8, 1/16, 1/32, and 1/64 of an inch. In addition to being an accurate measuring device, a steel rule can also be used as a *straight edge* to draw or scribe a straight line. This tool is available in lengths ranging from 6 to 48 inches.

Fig. 9.2. Steel rule

Squares are used to set or check 90° angles. The two most common types are the *steel square*, also referred to as a *framing square*, and the *combination square* (Fig. 9.3). Because of its size, the steel square is used to check the squareness of large frames. It is also used by carpenters to lay out rafters and staircases. The combination square is used to lay out 90° and 45° angles and is equipped with a sliding steel rule, usually 12 inches in length.

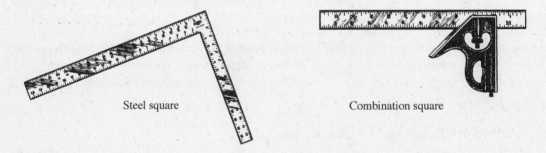

Steel square   Combination square

Fig. 9.3. Squares

Micrometers and *calipers* (Fig. 9.4) are precision instruments used to make very close tolerance measurements. In layout situations, calipers are used to transfer measurements from one location to another. These tools can be used to make measurements to one-thousandth of an inch. They are commonly used in precision metal machining and auto engine rebuilding.

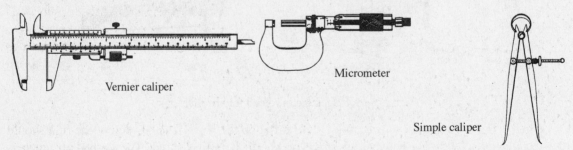

Vernier caliper   Micrometer   Simple caliper

Fig. 9.4. Micrometers and calipers

Levels are used for a number of purposes. The most important one is to make sure that things are properly oriented so that mechanisms will work correctly. A refrigerator, for example, usually has to be level for it to operate correctly; doors and windows have to be level to move up and down or open and shut smoothly, and, of course, things look better when they are level. A level has a vertical indicator and a horizontal indicator (Fig. 9.5). The bubbles in the glass tubes in the level tell you if the level is obtained. The carpenter's level is used to make sure windows and doors are properly installed. If the vertical and horizontal bubbles are lined up between the lines, then the window or door is plumb. Being plumb means that the window is vertical.

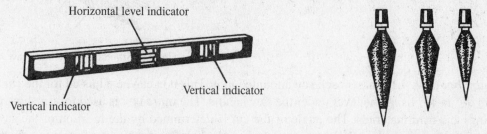

Fig. 9.5. Level

Fig. 9.6. Plumb bobs

A *plumb bob* is a small, pointed weight (Fig. 9.6). It is attached to a string and dropped from a height. If the bob is just above the ground, it will indicate the vertical direction by its string. Keeping windows and doors and frames square and level makes a difference in fitting. It is much easier to fit prehung doors into a frame that is square.

A *scratch awl* is a handy tool for a carpenter. It can be used to mark wood with a scratch mark. It can also be used to produce pilot holes for screws. Once it is in your tool box, you can think of a hundred uses for it. Since it has a very sharp point, it is best treated with respect. Fig. 9.7 shows the point.

Fig. 9.7. Scratch awl

CUTTING AND SHAPING TOOLS

Wood, metal, and other materials must often be cut and shaped. Saws, chisels, files, and planes are some of the tools used to cut, shape, and shave material. (Tools specifically designed to be used in cutting and shaping metal are also discussed in the section Working with Metal later in this chapter.)

Saws

Many home mechanics and carpenters use saws to cut wood or metal. There are different types made for wood or metal and different types designed for specific types of work. The blade determines the use of the saw.

The *back saw* (Fig. 9.8) gets its name from the piece of heavy metal that makes up the top edge of the cutting part of the saw. It has a fine tooth configuration. This means it can be used to cut cross-grain—cut wood across the grain—and it leaves a smooth finished piece of work. This type of saw is used by finishing carpenters who want to cut trim or molding.

The standard *skew-back saw* (Fig. 9.9) has a wooden handle. It has a 22-inch length. A 10-point saw (with 10 teeth per inch) is suggested for *crosscutting*. The 26-inch length, 5½ point saw is suggested for *ripping*—cutting with the wood grain. This saw is used in places where an electric saw cannot be used. The sharpness of the blade makes a difference in the quality of the cut and the ease with which the saw can be used.

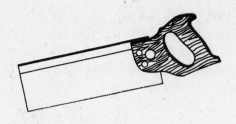

Fig. 9.8. Back saw

Fig. 9.9. Standard skew-back saw

The *mitre box* (Fig. 9.10) has a back saw mounted in it. This box can be adjusted for the cut you wish from 90° to 45° using the lever under the saw handle. The mitre box is used for finishing cuts on moldings and trim materials. The angle of the cut is determined by the location of the saw in reference to the bed of the box. Release the clamp on the bottom of the saw support to adjust the saw to any degree desired. The wood is held with one hand against the fence of the box and the bed. Then the saw is used by the other hand. As you can see from the setup, the cutting should take place when the saw is pushed forward. The backward movement of the saw should be made with the pressure on the saw released slightly. If you try to cut on the backward movement, you will just pull the wood away from the fence and decrease the quality of the cut.

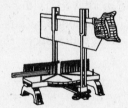

Fig. 9.10. Mitre box

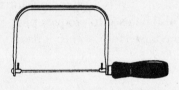

Fig. 9.11. Coping saw

The *coping saw* (Fig. 9.11) comes in handy to make cuts that are not straight. The coping saw can cut small thicknesses of wood at any curve or angle desired. It can be used to make a piece of paneling fit properly or a piece of molding fit another piece in the corner. The blade is placed in the frame with the teeth pointing toward the handle. This means it cuts only on the downward stroke. Make sure you properly support the piece of wood being cut. A number of blades can be obtained for this type of saw. The number of teeth in the blade determines the smoothness of the cut.

A *compass saw* (Fig. 9.12) is used to cut holes, such as those needed for electrical outlets.

Fig. 9.12. Compass saw

Hacksaws (Fig. 9.13) are primarily used for cutting metal. The teeth on a hacksaw blade are much smaller than those on a wood-cutting saw. The blade is made of hardened steel and is either 10 or 12 inches in length. The hacksaw frame can be adjusted to accommodate both sizes. Blades are classified by the number of teeth per inch and are always positioned in the frame so that they are pointed away from the handle.

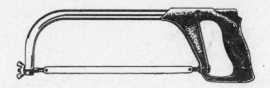

Fig. 9.13. Hacksaw

Files

Files are used to produce finished or semifinished surfaces. A number of different types of files are available (Fig. 9.14), each designed for a specific purpose. Machinist's files and curved tooth files are widely used in machine shops and industrial facilities for a variety of repair work. Some files are used for sharpening saws and touching up cutting edges. One type of wood file, known as a *rasp*, is coarse and designed for rough work, while other wood files are used to produce smooth and fine surfaces.

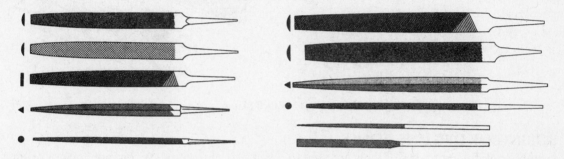

Fig. 9.14. Files

Chisels

Chisels are used to cut wood. They are sharpened on one end. When the other end is struck with a hammer, the cutting end will do its job—that is, of course, if you have kept it sharpened. Fig. 9.15 shows a wood chisel.

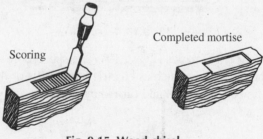

Scoring

Completed mortise

Fig. 9.15. Wood chisel

Fig. 9.16. Cold chisel

The *cold chisel* (Fig. 9.16) is made with a very sharp edge that can cut metal. This means it can be used to remove a nail. The nail head may have been broken off and the nail must be removed. The chisel can cut the nail and permit separation of the wood pieces. Cold chisels are used for many operations involving the removal of small amounts of metal.

If a chisel of this type starts to "mushroom" at the head, you should remove the splintered ends with a grinder. Hammering on the end can produce a mushrooming effect. These pieces should be taken off since they can easily fly off when hit with a hammer. This is just one reason for wearing eye protection when using tools.

Planes

Planes are used in carpentry work to shave off material of different thicknesses. They are used to smooth and straighten wood, to bevel it, and to make moldings and special shapes. A *jack plane* is an all-purpose plane, about 12 to 15 inches in length, that smooths boards and other wood pieces. A *block plane* (Fig. 9.17) is similar to a jack plane but smaller, about 6 inches long. Block planes are used for small smoothing and fitting jobs because of their small size and because they can be operated with one hand.

Fig. 9.17. Block plane

BORING OR DRILLING TOOLS

A number of different types of tools are used to bore holes in material. A common type of drilling tool is a *bit brace*, basically a type of hand drill, equipped with different types of tips, or *bits*.

Drill bits are made to cut or bore accurate round holes. Bits made to drill holes in metal are different in design from those used to bore holes in wood. Metals are much tougher to drill; therefore, metal cutting drill bits are made of hardened steel. These bits are commonly referred to as *twist drills* (Fig. 9.18) and are sized by diameter.

Fig. 9.18. Twist drill

Wood bits come in a variety of shapes (Fig. 9.19). The speed bore, forstner, and brad point bits are used in power drilling equipment, such as electric hand drills or drill presses. The *auger bit* is made to be used with a brace (Fig. 9.20) and turned by hand.

Forstner bit   Brad point bit   Speed bore

Fig. 9.19. Wood bits

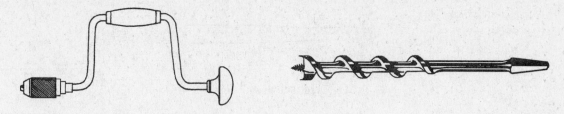

Fig. 9.20. Brace and auger bit

Hole cutters, or *hole saws* (Fig. 9.21), are used in the metal-cutting, electrical, plumbing, and automotive trades. The high-speed steel-cutting edge, welded to a tough alloy back, will cut clean, round holes in any machinable material up to 1 inch in depth and from 9/16 to 6 inches in diameter. Similar designs can be used for cutting holes in wood.

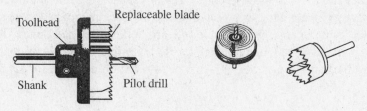

Fig. 9.21. Hole saw

FASTENERS AND FASTENING TOOLS

Many different types of tools and devices are used to fasten objects together or to drive or push one object into another.

Hammers

Hammers are used to drive nails into objects, to strike other tools such as chisels, and to form or shape metal and other materials. Hammers come in many sizes and shapes, each made for specific jobs. The basic parts of a hammer are shown in Fig. 9.22.

A *curved claw hammer* (Fig. 9.22) is commonly used by carpenters. It can be used to pull and extract nails that have been put in the wrong way or are bent. These hammers come in 20-ounce, 24-ounce, 28-ounce, and 32-ounce weights for carpentry use; the usual carpenter's choice is the 20-ounce.

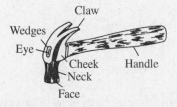
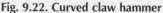
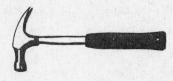

Fig. 9.22. Curved claw hammer   **Fig. 9.23. Straight claw hammer**

The *straight claw hammer*, also known as the *ripping hammer* (Fig. 9.23), is used for rough work. Because of its straight claw, it can easily be driven between boards and used to separate them and can also be used to split wood.

The *ball peen hammer* (Fig. 9.24), also known as a *machinist's hammer*, is used in metalworking and in mechanical work. It is used to drive punches and chisels and to shape metal parts. It can also be used to set and peen rivets.

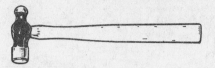

Fig. 9.24. Ball peen hammer

Other types of hammers include the *mallet*, often made with a wood, plastic, or rubber head, used to drive chisels and shape metal without marring the work surface, and the *sledgehammer*, used to break concrete and do other heavy, rough work.

Nails

Nails (Fig. 9.25) are driven by hammers. Note the relationship between gage, penny (*d*), and inches. The *d* after the number means penny. This is a measuring unit inherited from the English in the colonial days. There is little or no relationship between penny and inches. If you want to be able to talk about it intelligently, you'll have to learn both inches and penny. The gage is nothing more than the American Wire Gage number for the wire that the nails are made from originally. Finish nails have the same measuring unit (the penny) but do not have the large flat heads.

Nail Sets

Nail sets are used to drive finish nails below the surface of the wood. The nail set is placed on the head of the nail. The large end of the nail set is struck by the hammer. This causes the nail to go below the surface of the wood. Then the hole left by the countersunk nail is filled with wood filler and finished off with a smooth coat of varnish or paint.

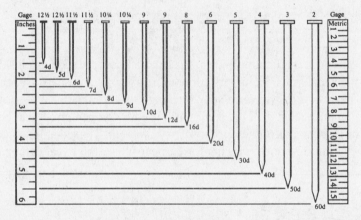

Fig. 9.25. Nails

Screwdrivers

This is one tool that shouldn't be left out of a tool box for a mechanic, carpenter, or anyone doing work around the house. It can be used for many things other than turning screws. There are two types of screwdrivers. The standard, most common type has a straight, slot-fitting blade at its end. The Phillips-head screwdriver has a cross or X on the end; this fits a screw head of the same design. Fig. 9.26 shows the two types of screwdrivers.

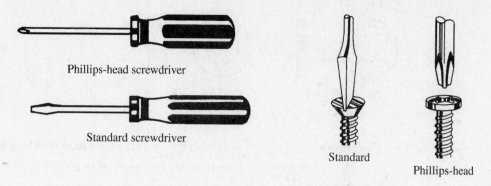

Fig. 9.26. Screwdrivers, standard and Phillips-head

Other Fasteners

The most common forms of threaded fasteners used are bolts, nuts, and machine screws.

Bolts and *machine screws* are available in a variety of shapes and sizes (Fig. 9.27) and are classified by head shape, diameter, and length. Most bolts have a hexagonal head. Coarse threads are cut deeper and are fewer in number per inch than are fine threads. Coarse thread nuts and bolts are used when the connection must be extremely tight. A fine thread is used for parts that must withstand a great deal of vibration, such as aircraft parts.

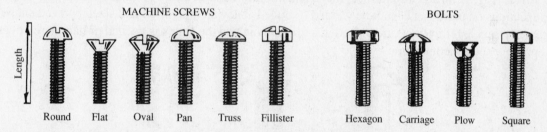

Fig. 9.27. Bolts and machine screws

Nuts are made with a hexagonal, square, or self-locking head (Fig. 9.28). *Self-locking nuts* are designed to jam against the bolt thread and will not vibrate loose. The *wing nut* is the only nut designed to be tightened by hand. It is used on connections that must be frequently disassembled and do not require excessive tightening.

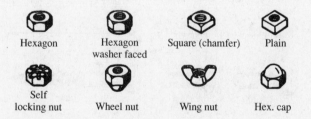

Fig. 9.28. Nuts

Washers are available as either flat or locking (Fig. 9.29). *Flat washers* are used to evenly distribute the compressive load of a bolted connection over a wider area or to compensate for an oversized hole. *Lock washers* are designed to exert force between the bolted connection and the workpiece, preventing the bolt and nut from loosening.

Plain steel washers   Lock washers

Fig. 9.29. Washers

Self-tapping screws, also called *sheet metal screws*, are used to connect thin gauge sheet metal parts (Fig. 9.30). The hardened steel screw actually cuts its own thread as it is inserted. These screws have either a hexagonal or slotted head.

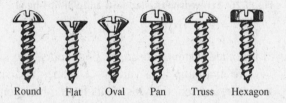

Round   Flat   Oval   Pan   Truss   Hexagon

Fig. 9.30. Self-tapping screws

Rivets (Fig. 9.31) are used in sheet metal and aircraft manufacturing to make solid, high strength connections on parts that cannot be welded or bolted. They are classified and sized by head shape, diameter, and length. Rivets are placed in a drilled hole and the shank is peened or hammered over to produce a tight connection.

Button head structural   Countersunk head   Cone head boiler

Fig. 9.31. Rivets

Wood screws (Fig. 9.32) are used in place of nails when a much tighter and stronger connection is needed. Screws are much more time-consuming to install and are mainly used in furniture construction or on connections that must be taken apart and reassembled. Wood screws are classified by the shape of the screw head, shank diameter, and length.

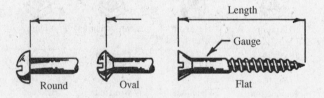

Round   Oval   Flat

Fig. 9.32. Wood screws

Clamps are used to hold parts together. They are most frequently used to hold glued pieces together while they are drying. There are several types of clamps (Fig. 9.33). A *C-clamp* is versatile, with many different sized jaw openings available. This type of clamp can also be used as a vise to hold an object to a work surface. A *spring clamp* has a pincer action. Small, this type of clamp is best suited for fast-setting glue jobs that require quick action.

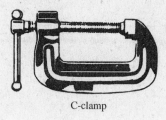

C-clamp

Spring clamp

Fig. 9.33. Clamps

PLIERS AND WRENCHES

Pliers extend a worker's grip and hand length. They are designed to do one of two things—grip or cut. The *slip joint, channel lock,* and *vise grip pliers* (Fig. 9.34) have serrated teeth and can grip parts securely. *Diagonal cutting* and *end cutting pliers* (Fig. 9.35) have sharpened jaws and are made for cutting. *Electrician's pliers* and *wire stripping pliers* (Fig. 9.36) are special tools used by electricians to cut wire and strip wire insulation; both are equipped with insulated handles.

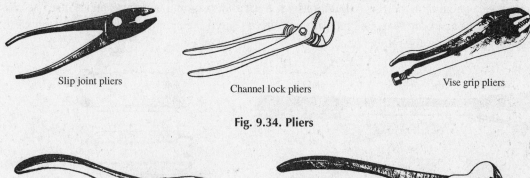

Slip joint pliers   Channel lock pliers   Vise grip pliers

Fig. 9.34. Pliers

Diagonal cutting pliers   End cutting pliers

Fig. 9.35. Cutting pliers

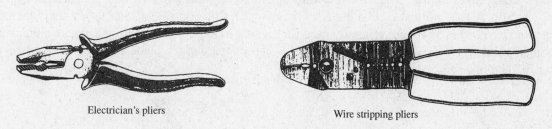

Electrician's pliers   Wire stripping pliers

Fig. 9.36. Electrician's pliers and wire stripping pliers

Wrenches are used to tighten or loosen nuts and bolts. They are classified as open end, box end, combination, or adjustable (Fig. 9.37). The *open end wrench* holds the bolt head or nut on two sides only; therefore, it is generally used only for snugging up bolted connections. If secure tightening is attempted, the open end wrench may slip and round off the bolt head or nut. The *box wrench* grips the nut on all six sides, allowing the user to tighten the connection securely without having the wrench slip. The *combination wrench* has an open end on one side and a box end on the other. *Adjustable wrenches* can be adjusted to fit a variety of nut and bolt sizes.

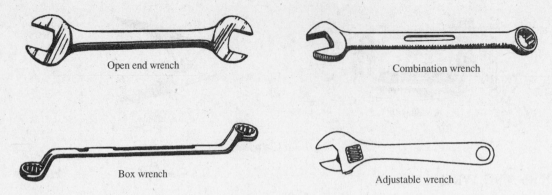

Fig. 9.37. Wrenches

Ratchet and *socket wrenches* (Fig. 9.38) are designed to do the same job as the box end wrench, but they can turn the bolt and nut continuously without repeated removal. Because of this feature, the tightening sequence is much faster. Socket wrenches are generally classified as six or twelve point and are available in metric or standard sizes to fit all hexagonal head nuts and bolts. The most common ratchet sizes are 1/4, 3/8, and 1/2 inch drive. The drive size refers to the diameter of the square drive shank on the ratchet head.

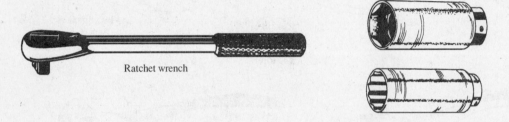

Fig. 9.38. Ratchet and socket wrenches

DIGGING TOOLS

Common digging tools are classified as either picks or shovels. The pickax and mattock (Fig. 9.39) have sharp edges and are used for breaking up tightly compacted soil. The pickax also has a pointed tip at one end that can be used for breaking up thin concrete slabs. Square and tapered mouth *shovels* (Fig. 9.40) are generally used for digging in loose soil or mixing and shoveling wet cement. The *digging spade* has a flat shoulder along the back of the blade so that it can be easily pushed into the soil by foot.

Fig. 9.39. Pickax and mattock

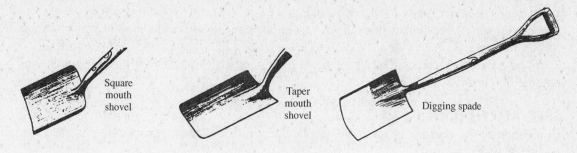

Fig. 9.40. Shovels

GRINDING AND SANDING TOOLS

Grinders and *sanding machines* are used to remove excess material or smooth rough edges. The machines are abrasive disks or pads similar in texture to sandpaper. *Angle grinders* and *sanders* (Fig. 9.41) are primarily used on hard materials such as metals. The *orbital vibrating sander* (Fig. 9.42) is most often used for smoothing wood surfaces.

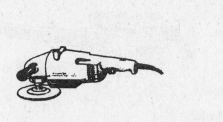

Fig. 9.41. Angle grinder/sander

Fig. 9.42. Orbital vibrating sander

The *bench grinder* (Fig. 9.43) is a more precise machine. It is equipped with two grinding wheels and is mainly used for sharpening cutting tools and drill bits.

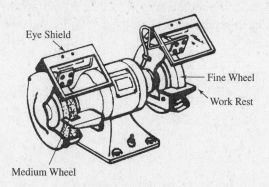

Fig. 9.43. Bench grinder

Abrasives are used to wear down or smooth the surface of another part. The most common of these are sandpaper, emery cloth, and rubbing compound. Abrasives are also used to machine very hard materials such as glass, ceramics, and hardened steel.

Aluminum oxide is the abrasive material used on most *sandpaper*. It is made by fusing bauxite, coke, and iron filings. Aluminum oxide paper can be used for sanding wood or metal. This type of sandpaper is very durable and ideal for use on electric sanders.

Emery cloth is similar to sandpaper except it has a cloth backing and is only used for smoothing or polishing metal parts. Emery is a very hard natural material. The advantage of the cloth backing is that it will not tear when used on curved or irregular surfaces. Emery cloth is often lubricated with water or oil for polishing operations.

Rubbing compounds have a pumice base. Pumice is made from granulated volcanic rock or ash. These compounds are primarily used for smoothing the finish on automobile paint and hand-rubbed furniture.

All abrasives are classified by texture or grit. A number 10 grit is the most coarse and a number 600 is the finest.

SPECIALIZED TOOLS

In addition to the commonly used shop tools, each trade has tools specifically designed for its particular type of work.

Plumbing Tools

Many common hand tools have been adapted to fit the requirements of fitting, measuring, cutting, and working with pipes and plumbing fixtures.

Pipe wrenches (Fig. 9.44) are made to firmly grip pipe and pipe fittings so that they may be tightened or loosened. The pipe wrench, also commonly known as a *stilson wrench*, has serrated teeth and a pivoting jaw that grips the pipe more securely as pressure is applied to the handle. The *chain wrench* is used primarily for gripping and turning very large diameter pipes.

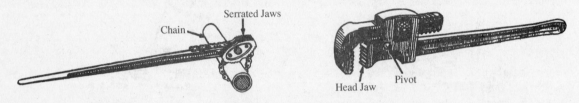

Fig. 9.44. Pipe wrenches

Pipe cutting tools are used for fast, clean pipe cutting by hand or power. Two rollers are adjusted to come in contact with the pipe (Fig. 9.45). They are then pushed against the pipe until the cutting tool (a small wheel on the outside of the tool) comes in contact with the pipe. As the cutter is turned around the pipe the handle is tightened until the cutting edge has penetrated the pipe lining and caused it to have a complete ring around it. When enough pressure is applied and the cutting edge has penetrated through the metal body of the pipe, the pieces separate with a smooth edge.

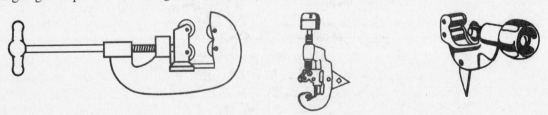

Fig. 9.45. Pipe cutter

Fig. 9.46. Tubing cutter

Tubing cutters are smaller versions of the pipe cutters. They are about 5 inches long with a lightweight frame of aluminum alloy. They are used to cut brass, copper, aluminum tubing, and thinwall conduit. Rollers smooth the tubing and make it ready for soldering. A reamer folds in when the cutter is in use. They are also designed to cut stainless steel tubing. Capacity is usually limited to tubing up to 2½ inches in diameter (Fig. 9.46).

Electrical Tools

Many of the tools used by electricians are designed to draw and position cable and wire and to attach electrical boxes. Others are measuring devices, designed to measure the output of an electrical circuit. Commonly used electrical measuring devices, or meters, such as the voltmeter, ammeter, and ohmmeter, are discussed in Chapter 7, "Electronics Information Review."

Materials

Various materials are used in general shop and construction work. Among the materials most often used are concrete, wood, metal, glass, plastics, and adhesives.

CONCRETE

Concrete is a mixture of cement, sand, and water. The cement and water form a paste that binds the other materials together as the concrete hardens. Hardened concrete is very strong, and it is both waterproof and fireproof. It also lasts a long time and is easy to maintain. There are special types of concrete, including *precast concrete*, which is cast and hardened into beams, girders, or other units before being used as a building material, and *reinforced concrete*, which is made by casting concrete around steel bars or rods to add strength to it.

You can order concrete ready-mixed and delivered by a truck that keeps it properly mixed until needed; or you can prepare it from a concrete mix by adding water; or you may mix cement, gravel, sand, and water. The ingredients must be added in the proper proportions and mixed to form the correct consistency.

In most instances you will want to place the concrete in a *form* that has previously been prepared for it. You first have to excavate the site. This calls for outlining with stakes the area to be covered with concrete. The area should extend at least 1 foot beyond the edge of a planned site—a patio, for instance. This helps prevent undercutting, which can occur when a base has eroded or fallen away, leaving the slab without sufficient base. Tie a string tautly between all stakes. To make the pattern for digging, simply sprinkle sand or lime over the string onto the ground, thus outlining the pattern for digging.

Then you must prepare the base. This means you should remove all grass, roots, and other organic matter from the surface. Dig to a depth of 6 to 8 inches, sloping gently away from the nearest building. Use sand, gravel, or other fill with a minimum of four inches to bring the site to a uniform grade. Compact the fill with a tamper or similar device, such as a concrete block or 4" × 4" piece of wood. Dampen the fill to aid in packing. The base should be uniform, hard, and free from foreign matter.

Make the form to fit the pattern needed. Dampen the forms and base thoroughly, but leave no puddles. Shovel or place the mix into the form. Fill to the full depth of the forms. Start at a corner and do not drag or flow the concrete unnecessarily. After the concrete has been spread, completely filling the forms, strike off and float immediately (Fig. 9.47).

To "strike off" means to use a 2" × 4" × 6' board, moving the edge back and forth with a saw-like motion, smoothing the surface. Then use a "darby" (made from a smooth, flat board approximately 3½ inches wide and 3½ feet long with a handle on top) to float the surface. This helps level any ridges and fills voids left by the straight edge. These two procedures help embed all particles of coarse stone or gravel slightly below the surface. Do not "overwork" the concrete. This can cause separation and create a less durable surface.

Fig. 9.47. Striking off concrete

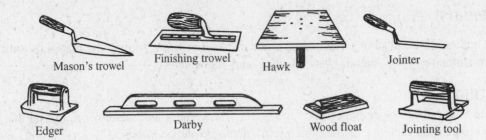

Fig. 9.48. Concrete finishing tools

Before finishing the concrete, allow it to stiffen slightly. This allows all water to evaporate from the surface before troweling. When the surface has turned dull, smooth and compact the concrete with a trowel. For best results keep the trowel pressed firmly and flat. Sweep it back and forth, each pass overlapping half of the previous pass. Good results can be attained by using a trowel measuring 4" × 14" (Fig. 9.48). Use an edging tool to round the edges along all forms. An edger with a half-inch radius is recommended. To produce a textured, non-skid surface, use a wood float for final troweling. Then use a wet broom to place the marks in the surface that are needed for your purposes.

Fig. 9.49. Buttering a concrete block

Other tools used by persons working with concrete and masonry are the *mason's trowel* which is used to "butter" a block or brick (Fig. 9.49). The *jointer* is used to finish up the joints between the blocks (Fig. 9.50). When a wall needs to be covered with mortar, the *hawk* can be used to keep enough near at hand so it can be spread on the surface of the blocks (Fig. 9.51).

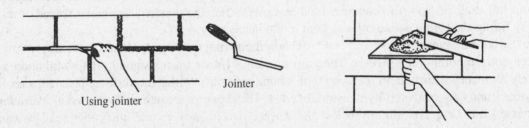

Fig. 9.50. Using a jointer   **Fig. 9.51. Hawk being used to hold mortar**

In order to cure concrete properly you should keep it damp for a period of five to seven days after it has been poured. This helps the hardening (hydrating) process, thus producing a more durable surface. Proper curing of all cement mixes is necessary for maximum strength. Concrete that has been moisture cured will be approximately 50% stronger than that exposed to dry air. Concrete reaches 98% of its strength in 28 days.

WOOD

Wood is the basic substance of trees, and there are many types of wood used for different purposes—furniture making, home building, and many other uses. Wood is easy to work with. It is made up of long cells that grow closely together, forming a compact, yet porous, material. It is elastic, plastic, and honeycomb. The relatively light weight of wood is explained by the fact that approximately half of its volume is made up of hollow cells. If wood is dried and crushed into solid material, it weighs approximately 1.5 times as much as an equal volume of water and consequently sinks in water. It is because of its hollow cell structure that most woods are buoyant, can take finishing materials, and can hold nails, screws, glue, and other fasteners.

Wood is named and classified as hard or soft according to the species of tree from which it is cut. Hardwood comes from the deciduous or broad-leaved trees and softwood comes from the coniferous or needle-bearing trees. This classification does not, however, indicate the degree of hardness of the wood. Some woods classified as hardwoods are actually soft. The pines, firs, and other evergreens are softwoods, and the maples, oaks, elms, poplars, and other shade and fruit trees are the hardwoods.

Trees are cut into logs, usually eight or more feet long. The individual logs are squared by slabbing, or the log is first split through the center and squared into a *cant*. In most cases, the cant is then sawed into timbers, planks, and boards. Sometimes logs are selected for special purposes and cut accordingly.

New lumber contains an excess of moisture. This may run as high as 200% when a freshly cut log is sawed. The evaporation of this moisture must be controlled if good lumber is to be obtained for building or furniture making. Rapid drying causes checking and cracks (Fig. 9.52). To help prevent rapid drying, freshly cut logs are often submerged in water until they are to be cut into lumber.

Warp due to shrinkage   Shrinkage in circumference   Shrinkage in quartered logs

Fig. 9.52. Warpage and shrinkage of wood

Controlled drying conditions reduce the intensity of the forces acting on the logs. Drying must be done by air seasoning or by the modern, faster method of kiln drying. Air-dried lumber is better for use outside and kiln-dried lumber is better for use inside. Kiln drying is done by using forced air or fans. It reduces the moisture content to 5 to 8 percent within two to three weeks for one-inch lumber.

Recent developments have produced lumber that will not rot quickly when left outside. Dipping the wood in polyethylene glycol or other chemicals has been found to stabilize the wood over a wide range of relative humidity conditions. The solution replaces most of the water in the wood and causes a reduction of shrinkage.

Wood has often been called nature's most versatile building material. Throughout history, it has been used to construct everything from buildings, ships, and machinery to furniture and airplanes. Because so many types of wood are available, construction applications are almost limitless. Wood can be pressure treated with a preservative to withstand rotting in damp soil for up to thirty years. By-products such as plywood and particle board are commonly used in house construction. Wood, however, does not have the load-carrying capacity or fire resistance of reinforced concrete and structural steel, nor the strength-to-weight ratio of modern plastics. Therefore, applications for wood in modern office buildings are restricted to interior trim and it is not used at all in automobile or airplane construction.

METAL

Metal is the most common material used in manufacturing. There are many different types of metals, ranging from heavy-weight iron to lightweight aluminum and titanium. Since some metals are too soft, rust too easily, or have other characteristics that make them hard to work with, they are combined into *alloys* with specific characteristics. Steel, for example, is an alloy of iron (made with carbon and magnesium) that does not rust and that has added strength.

Cast iron, steel, steel alloys, magnesium, and aluminum are some of the metals commonly used in industry. Cast aluminum and cast iron are used by automobile manufacturers to make engine blocks. Steel beams are used to construct the framework of buildings and bridges. Steel plate is used in shipbuilding, and lightweight metals like aluminum and magnesium are used in many aircraft and aerospace components.

Sheet metal is the most widely used form of metal. It is used to make the bodies of automobiles and aircraft, as well as in duct work for heating and ventilation systems. Special tools have been developed for use on sheet metal. Many of these tools are now also used in other trades to work with metals of different thicknesses and forms.

Special Tools

Special hammers—wooden *mallets* and soft-faced hammers—are used in forming sheet metal because they do not stretch, expand, or scratch the metal as much as do metal hammers. Other hammers—*peen* (or machinist's) *hammers*—are used for riveting or to indent or compress metal. A *bumping hammer* is used by auto body repair workers to smooth out dents.

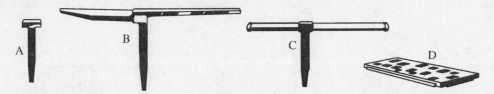

Fig. 9.53. Stakes (A) Square stake (B) Beakhorn stake (C) Double-seaming stake (D) Stake holder

Stakes are used so that sheet metal can be formed by hammering it over T-shaped anvils of steel (Fig. 9.53). *Punches* are used to make holes in sheet metal. It is safer to punch a hole in sheet metal than to drill it. A *groover* is used to lock seams together. You use one that fits the seam and tap it with a mallet as you slide it along the seam. Lay the seam over an anvil while tapping (Fig. 9.54).

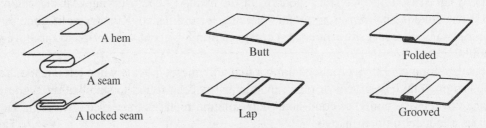

Fig. 9.54. Sheet metal seams

Tin snips, another sheet metal tool, are similar to scissors. They shear sheet metal just as scissors cut paper or cloth. To cut sheet metal, lay the sheet on a bench and slide snip jaws over the sheet at the side of the cutting mark. Press down on the top handle and let the bench push against the bottom (Fig. 9.55).

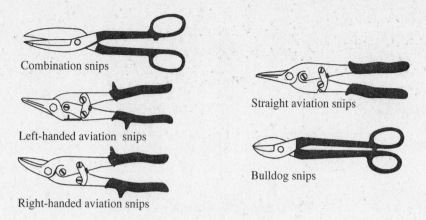

Combination snips

Straight aviation snips

Left-handed aviation snips

Right-handed aviation snips

Bulldog snips

Fig. 9.55. Tin snips

Sheet metal is also processed by hand-driven and automatic machines. A *squaring shear* cuts off sheet metal in a straight line. Edges are turned and hems formed on *bar folders* and *brakes*. Sheet metal can also be formed into round cylinders on a *slip roll*. Turned and wired edges are made on a *rotary machine*, and sheet is pressed into form on *presses* and cut to shape on *punch presses*.

Processes

Metals and alloys can be formed into a variety of shapes and joined or separated by a number of processes, including bolting, riveting, welding, soldering, and flame cutting.

Bolting and *riveting* provide a temporary or semipermanent connection. In these processes, fasteners—bolts, nuts, and rivets—are used, much like screws and nails, to hold two pieces of metal together. The connection is strong, but it can be broken if necessary by removing the bolt or by breaking the head of the rivet and pushing the rivet through the metal. Riveting is less commonly used today, now that welding has been improved.

Welding produces a permanent connection between two metals. The metal parts are melted and fused to form one piece that is very difficult to take apart. In *arc welding*, the intense heat of an electric arc melts the surface of the metalwork pieces and fuses them. This process is commonly used in heavy sheet fabrication and building and bridge construction. In *gas welding*, an oxygen and acetylene mixture in a welding torch produces a flame hot enough to melt and fuse metals. Thinner metals, such as sheet metal, are usually gas-welded.

Soldering is another way of joining metals; it is commonly used to bond sheet metal, wires, and metal pipes. Solder is an alloy made from tin and lead. It is available in different mixtures, each with its own characteristics. In soldering, first the metals to be joined must be cleaned thoroughly, usually with *flux*. Then, using a *soldering gun, soldering iron,* or *soldering pencil*, allow heated solder to flow between the joints of the metals to join them. Hems and seams are the joints in such products as tin cans, pails, boxes, and air conditioning and heating ducts.

Sheet metal work means working with patterns in much the same way as dressmaking or box folding work involves patterns. A seam is folded, whether it is in cloth or in metal. You may not have thought of the medieval armorer as a tailor, but he was, and a metalworker, too. A hem in cloth is sewn in place. In metal, the ends are folded, or hemmed, and then hooked together and locked, making a seam. To stiffen the joint even more and to make sure it holds water, solder is made to flow into the folds.

Galvanized and tin-plated steel can be soldered with a soldering iron (in this case the *soldering copper*). These metals do not conduct heat away as rapidly as do copper and brass. Brass usually requires a flame to solder rather than a copper-tipped iron (Fig. 9.56).

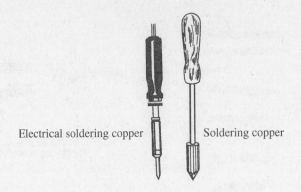

Electrical soldering copper   Soldering copper

Fig. 9.56. Soldering copper

When using the soldering copper to solder sheet metal, first heat the copper until it will melt solder. This is at about 450°F. Then wipe the tip clean with a damp cloth, and dip the hot tip into flux and rub on a small amount of solder. If the tip does not take the solder all over, rub it on a block of wood until it does. This is called *tinning*. A well-tinned copper holds solder better and transfers more heat to the metal than does a dirty one. You are now ready to solder with the tinned end of the soldering copper.

Clean the surfaces of the metal to be soldered. Do not use steel wool on galvanized metal or tin plate. Apply flux to the joint. Hold the tip of the copper against the joint until the metal is hot enough to melt the solder. Then add as much solder as needed to cover the area to be joined.

Flame cutting is a process used to cut heavy steel pieces apart. A high-pressure stream of oxygen in a cutting torch is designed to melt and blow away the molten metal. This process can be used to cut the bolts on a rusty car muffler or steel plate several inches thick.

GLASS

Glass is one of the least expensive and most abundant of all materials. It is made from the fusion of silica, which is found in sand. Glass has almost limitless uses. Glass products make up the windows in our homes, drinking glasses, optical lenses, automobile windshields, mirrors, television screens, and electrical insulators. Glass blocks, similar in shape to concrete blocks, are used in building construction to make a wall transparent to light.

The major disadvantage of glass is its brittleness. Glass can chip, crack, or break very easily if dropped or subjected to sudden impact. Glass, however, can be treated to improve its toughness. The process is called *tempering*, and it is used to make safety eyeglass lenses and tempered glass door panels.

Glassworking tools are specialty items. The *glass cutter* (Fig. 9.57) has a hardened steel wheel mounted on a handle. When this tool is drawn across a piece of glass, a line is scored on the surface of the glass, which can be snapped to produce a clean cut. *Glazier's pliers* (Fig. 9.58) have broad flat jaws designed to grasp a piece of glass on the cut line for the purpose of snapping a cut on very small or narrow pieces. Holes can be drilled through glass by using a *carbide tip spear point drill bit* (Fig. 9.59). During the drilling operation, the bit must be lubricated with water or kerosene.

Fig. 9.57. Glass cutter

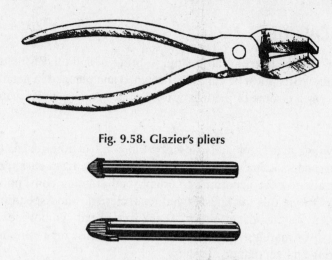

Fig. 9.58. Glazier's pliers

Fig. 9.59. Carbide tip spear point drill bits

PLASTICS

Plastics in one form or another are used in just about every type of manufacturing. They are light in weight and fairly impact resistant, and they can be easily and inexpensively formed into almost any shape. Hand tools, auto parts, machinery covers, and electronic components are just a few examples of the uses of plastics in modern industry.

Plastics have a very high corrosion resistance and excellent electrical insulating qualities. The corrosion resistance of plastic has made this material a popular choice in the manufacture of pipe. It is now used extensively in plumbing applications, particularly in underground systems. Plastic pipe can be quickly and easily glued together with special adhesives. Plastics do not, however, have the strength characteristic of many metals and cannot be used for structures that must withstand heavy loads.

GLUES AND ADHESIVES

Glues and adhesives are now used to join virtually any material or combination of materials. Most are very easy to apply and have the advantage of joining very thin materials or materials so different that they could not be joined any other way (e.g., steel to glass, wood to rubber, plastic to metal). A disadvantage of most adhesives is the inability to maintain strength at high temperatures.

There are several general types of adhesives, each with its own characteristics and uses. *Contact cement* is used when a strong bond is needed, as in bonding laminates to countertops or metal to wood. It is extremely flammable and must be used in a well-ventilated area.

Epoxy adhesives create a strong, moisture-resistant bond between almost any kind of material. They do not set instantly, which is an advantage when parts must be movable until a final fit is made. Too expensive for general use, epoxy adhesives are used when strong holding power is necessary.

Silicone sealants are used to keep moisture away from a structure, such as where a sink meets a wall or around a bathtub. These sealants usually come in tubes and are easy to apply.

Mastic adhesives are pasty adhesives applied with a *caulking gun* or trowel to glue such things as ceiling tiles, wallboards, and panels.

Polyvinyl resin glues, the typical white glue in a squeeze bottle, can be used to glue everything from paper to wood joints. They dry clear and form a strong bond.

Design and Layout

The construction and maintenance of all buildings, bridges, and other structures, as well as of all machines and machine parts, must be carefully designed and planned in detail. Blueprints, layouts, templates, and patterns are some of the means used in design and layout work.

BLUEPRINTS

Blueprints are drawings that graphically describe the construction, installation, maintenance, or repair of structures and machines. Blueprints may be done from different views and angles. However, virtually all are done according to established drawing conventions and use standardized symbols. Lines of various thicknesses and characteristics and specific symbols specify the size, shape, and other features of an object. There are special symbols for various architectural materials (e.g., wood or marble), for electrical configurations, for plumbing fixtures, for appliances, and for heating and ventilation systems.

There are different types of blueprints. Architectural drawings may be site, foundation, or construction plans. Other blueprints may be floor plans or plans that detail the electrical or plumbing systems. HVAC plans describe the heating, ventilation, and air conditioning system.

A basic blueprint is shown in Fig. 9.60. Blueprint reading is a skill that requires intensive training.

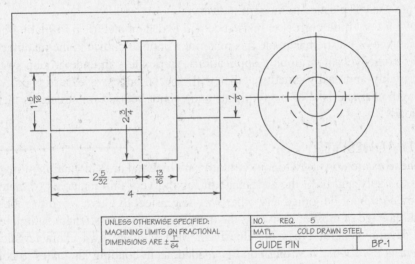

Fig. 9.60. Blueprint

LAYOUT

A *layout* is the transfer of dimensions and lines specified on a blueprint to the material being worked on. For example, if the blueprint specifies that a piece of wood be cut to a length of four feet, you must measure the desired length and draw a line on the spot where the cut must be made and also perhaps on the spot where the piece of wood is to be placed.

PATTERNS AND TEMPLATES

Patterns and templates are models by which parts are made. Fig. 9.61 is an example of a *flat pattern*. Commonly used in the fabrication of sheet metal parts, flat patterns represent the shape of the part before it is rolled or bent into final form. *Templates* are a gauge or guide used to check the size and shape of parts so that each will be exactly the same. For example, when a carpenter is building a house, the roof rafters require careful layout and cutting. Each must be cut at the same angle and length to ensure that the roof line will be straight. After the first rafter is cut and checked for accuracy, it is used as the template or pattern for every other rafter.

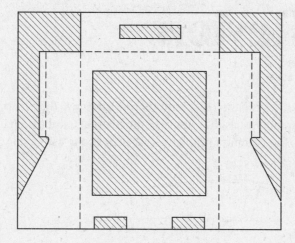

Fig. 9.61. Flat pattern

10 Automotive Information Review

This section explains the basic parts of an automobile and how they operate, discusses in some detail basic mechanical principles as they apply to the internal combustion engine, and finally provides a guide to recognizing common problems that may occur with a car or truck.

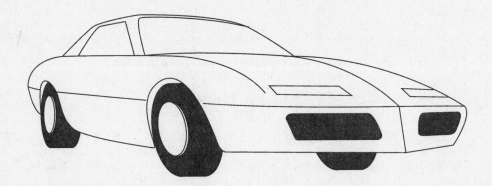

Parts of an Automobile

Fundamentally, an automobile is a compartment mounted on wheels with some self-contained means for propelling it over the ground. "Left" and "right" are determined by your perspective as you are sitting in the driver's seat.

The very least we need to make an automobile go is an engine and some means of connecting the engine—and the power it provides—to the wheels. Generally speaking, the engine turns a shaft that connects to the front or rear pair of wheels, or both. The shaft has a gear on the end that meshes with a gear on the axle connecting the drive wheels together. As the first shaft turns, it rotates the axle and the wheels propel the car. If there were no hills around, and we didn't want to go very fast or turn any corners, this arrangement might work. But in an actual automobile, we have some more parts between the engine and the wheels.

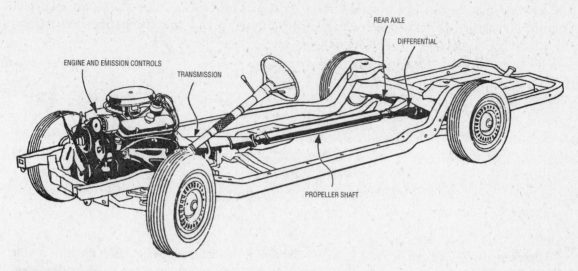

The Engine

The power of an automobile engine comes from the burning of a mixture of gasoline and air in a small, confined space. When this mixture burns, it expands greatly and pushes out in all directions very rapidly—so rapidly that when it happens in an uncontrolled or open environment, this rapid burning is more usually known as an explosion. This push or pressure can be used to move a part of the engine, and the movement of this part is eventually transmitted to the wheels to move the car.

When we first look at the engine under the hood of a truck or car, it seems to be a complicated piece of machinery with hundreds of pieces and attachments, and each auto's engine seems different from the others. However, almost all engines operate on the same basic principles and with the same kinds of basic parts; this is where we will concentrate our attention. Further, the primary difference between the different types of automobiles today is whether the vehicle's power is sent to the rear wheels (rear-wheel drive), the front wheels (front-wheel drive), or both (all-wheel or four-wheel drive). Most of the parts—especially when it comes to the engine itself—are otherwise the same.

First, let's get some terminology straight. To start with, an *engine* is any machine that uses energy to develop mechanical power, while a *motor* is a machine that converts electrical energy into mechanical energy. This means that a car or truck uses an engine, rather than a motor, to move the wheels and make the car go. However, most people use the terms interchangeably.

Going from the inside out—first, we have a cylinder where the controlled explosion, known as *combustion*, takes place; that's why the cylinder is also known as the combustion chamber. The cylinder is something like a tall metal can, or a pipe closed at one end. In fact some early automobiles used cast-iron pipe for cylinders.

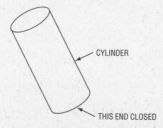

Inside the cylinder we have a piston. This is a plug that is close-fitting but that can slide up and down easily in the cylinder—think of the top of the piston as the movable floor in the combustion chamber. Fuel sprays into the chamber through a valve that functions as an automatic door in the top of the cylinder. When the piston has moved up as far as it can go—making the space in the chamber as small as it can get—an electric spark ignites the fuel and causes a controlled explosion. This explosion causes outward pressure in all directions inside the chamber, but only the bottom "wall" of the cylinder—the piston—can move, so it is pushed down.

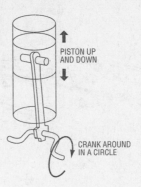

There are also intake and exhaust valves in the top of the cylinder. Metal disks are arranged to fit tightly over the holes to close them, but when pushed down, they open the holes to allow passage of the gases through them. This lets out the burned gases and lets fresh air in to begin the combustion cycle all over again.

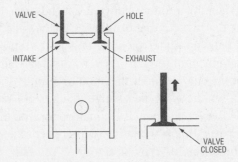

Now, in order to change this up-and-down motion to rotary motion to propel the car, we have a connecting rod and a crankshaft. The *crankshaft*, below the pistons, looks like a straight rod with a series of bends—called throws—in it, one for each cylinder. A *connecting rod* connects the bottom of the piston to one of the throws in the crankshaft. The top end of the connecting rod is fastened to the piston, so it goes up and down in a straight line. The bottom end is fastened to the crank, so that end has to go around in a circle as the piston moves up and down.

Downward pressure from the piston rotates the throw in the crankshaft and thus rotates the crankshaft itself. This is the most common way of changing straight-line motion to rotary motion. Familiar examples of it are found in a kitchen meat grinder and in a bicycle. In the latter, the foot pedal is the crank, and the rider's leg is the connecting rod. The rider's knee moves up and down in a straight line while his or her foot goes around in a circle.

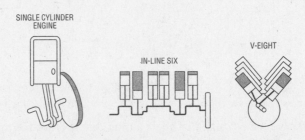

On one end of the crankshaft is a heavy wheel called the *flywheel*. If we turn a grindstone or emery wheel rapidly by hand and then let go, the wheel will keep on rotating. This is the same action as that of the flywheel. It keeps the engine turning between power impulses from the combustion in each cylinder.

These are the basic parts of an engine. However, these parts would make only a single-cylinder engine. All automobile engines today have at least three, and usually four or more, cylinders; motorcycles and other smaller engines often have just two. They can be arranged in one straight row, which we call an *in-line engine*, or in two rows set at an angle, described as a *V-type engine* (so a V-8 engine is one with eight cylinders, four each set in two rows at an angle to each other). In either case there is only one crankshaft, but it has a number of cranks instead of only one. With a number of cylinders the flywheel does not have such a big job to do because the power impulses occur more often and thus keep the crankshaft turning. By simply timing the controlled explosions (combustion) in each cylinder and placing the crankshaft throws at the appropriate angles, the crankshaft's rotation can be controlled so that it isn't fighting itself and all the cylinders are firing in the proper sequence—making a smooth, continuous cycle.

The valves in the top of each cylinder mentioned earlier are controlled by rocker arms and rods, which are moved by a camshaft. This is a shaft with "cams" or bumps on it—one bump for each valve—that push up on the rods to open the valves. The camshaft is driven by the crankshaft at one-half speed. The cams are accurately shaped and located, and the shaft rotates at just the proper speed so that the valves open and close at exactly the right time.

CARBURETORS AND FUEL PUMPS

In order to produce power, the engine needs a supply of gasoline and air mixed in the proper proportions. Up until the early 1980s, a mechanism known as a *carburetor* did the mixing job. Gasoline was pumped from the tank to the carburetor by the fuel pump, working in much the same way as an old-fashioned water pump—each stroke pushing a little fuel on to the carburetor where it went first to the float chamber. Air entered the carburetor through the air cleaner, being pulled in by the pumping action of the pistons working in the cylinders. The air flowed through a venturi (a reduced-width passage in the carburetor that made the flow speed up) at high speed, then past the end of a tube leading from the float chamber. This sucked the fuel out into the airstream, breaking the liquid up into a fine mist and mixing it thoroughly with the air (an atomizer or garden sprayer works in a similar way). Then the fuel/air mixture went on into the engine. The amount of the mixture going into the engine was controlled by a throttle valve at the base of the carburetor, which was opened or closed by the movement of the accelerator pedal.

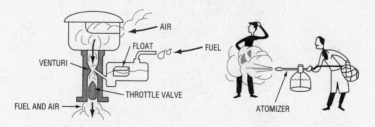

In the 1980s, automakers developed electronically controlled carburetors. This type of carburetor integrates the sophisticated electronics used in electronic fuel injection with the basic carburetor. The primary difference between a basic carburetor and an electronic carburetor is the addition of an electrically operated device called a *fuel solenoid*. The fuel solenoid is an electronically controlled valve used to regulate the amount of fuel delivered to the engine through the main metering circuit.

FUEL INJECTION SYSTEMS

There are three basic types of fuel injection in use today: (1) multi-injector electronic, (2) mono-injector electronic, and (3) manual continuous flow. The two electronic types are very similar and use most of the same components. They differ mainly in the number of injectors used. The multi-injector, the first electronic fuel injection system used and still popular, uses one injector for each cylinder, all connected to a common fuel rail. Each individual injector has a separate internal solenoid and fuel valve, yet all are connected to one control system.

A typical fuel injection system control usually contains most of the following units, which are interconnected by an electrical harness:

1. A manifold absolute pressure sensor, or vacuum transducer, that controls the basic quantity of fuel at each engine speed.
2. An engine speed, or timing, sensor that determines exactly when each injector valve is to be opened (or, as is generally the case, two or four valves can be opened simultaneously).
3. A throttle-position switch that controls the amount of fuel needed for the engine speed called for by the throttle position.
4. Temperature sensors for engine coolant and intake air that vary the basic fuel quantity in accordance with immediate engine operating temperatures.
5. An airflow sensor for determining the volume of air entering the cylinders and controlling the basic quantity of fuel delivered.
6. A fast-idle valve that increases the normal (warm engine) idle speed during periods of cold starting and warm-up. In some systems, an air solenoid valve is also used to supplement the fast-idle valve.
7. An oil-pressure sensor that closes down the system if the oil pressure becomes dangerously low.
8. Finally, a control unit (ECU) that converts all the aforementioned signals into the pulses that operate the injector valves.

In manual fuel injection systems the function of a manifold absolute pressure can be accomplished by a pressure sensor and a pressure switch. There can also be more than two temperature sensors. And a fuel injection pump, to which the various system signals are transmitted, can replace the control unit and injector valves and meter fuel directly to the injection nozzles.

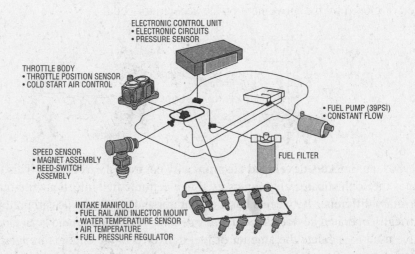

Fuel injector valves are used with electronic fuel injection systems. They are solenoid-operated pintle valves with integral fine-mist nozzles that project into the intake manifold above the respective intake ports. Each valve is operated by a pulsed signal from the control unit, which opens the valve for the proper time interval (pulse width) to deliver the amount of fuel determined by the control unit.

Fuel for the valves of an engine (one valve for each cylinder) is delivered by fuel rails, which are attached to the tops of the valve bodies and in which fuel is kept at a constant, predetermined pressure. Generally with V-type engines, the fuel rail is divided into two parts, each of which serves half the total number of valves. The two parts are usually assembled so that one pressure regulator, installed in the complete assembly, serves both halves.

FUEL PUMPS

Two electric *fuel pumps* are usually used. The first, located in the fuel tank, is generally a diaphragm-type booster pump that is integral with the fuel gage and a simple, replaceable-element filter. The second, located in the fuel line ahead of the pressure regulator, is usually a roller-vane pump driven by a motor and designed to produce a constant displacement. This second pump has a check valve (one-way pressure-opened) at the output side that prevents backflow to maintain pressure in the line when the pump is not operating. In general, a pump has built-in design factors that cannot be altered by service procedures. It is generally contained within a compact housing designed for mounting as desired and for connection, by a designed electrical harness, to the other components of a system. It is a nonserviceable unit that must be replaced if it becomes faulty.

FUEL PRESSURE REGULATOR

Because the second fuel pump operates continuously at maximum output, regardless of engine speed or load, the engine seldom requires all the fuel the pump makes available. It is the function of the pressure regulator to return excess fuel through a bypass line back to the tank and thus to maintain a constant pressure in the fuel rail.

ELECTRONIC CONTROL UNIT

The *electronic control unit* can be an analog or digital computer (with electronic circuits) that is preprogrammed by the manufacturer to accept certain signals from the various sensors of the system and to translate them into a pulsed signal for operation of the fuel injection valves. It is generally contained within a compact housing designed for mounting as desired and for connection, by a designed electrical harness, to the other components of the system. It is a nonserviceable unit that must be replaced if faulty.

ENGINE IGNITION

Now we have everything we need to make an engine run except something to start the mixture burning in the cylinder. In a cigarette lighter we make a spark by creating friction against a special metal; in an engine we do it electrically. The two main functions of the *ignition system* are to provide a high-voltage spark for combustion and to furnish the means to time the engine. A *spark plug* is inserted in the top of each cylinder, and a spark is created by electricity jumping across the gap between the two electrodes of the plug. The *battery*, using a 60% to 40% water-sulfuric acid mixture, furnishes the electricity, but several additional pieces of equipment are necessary for a complete ignition system.

The *coil* and the *breaker* cooperate to develop a very high voltage, and the *distributor* is responsible for getting the high-voltage electricity to the right spark plug at the right time. On a conventional ignition coil, the two small studs at the top of the coil are the primary or low-voltage terminals; the center tower is the secondary or high-voltage terminal. The ignition circuit has to transform 12 volts from the battery into more than 20,000 volts. It also has to deliver this high-voltage spark to the spark plugs at just the right time. The spark plug leads must be installed in the correct tower of the distributor cap to ensure the proper firing order. The firing order is the order in which the spark plugs ignite the fuel/air mixture in the cylinder or combustion chamber. A typical firing order for a six-cylinder engine is 1-5-3-6-2-4.

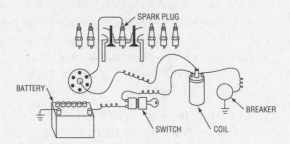

However, to lower and control voltage to the ignition coil, the ignition system has a resistor located between the ignition switch and the coil. This prevents the coil from burning out.

All of this must take place very rapidly. In an eight-cylinder engine driving a car 55 miles per hour, the ignition system has to furnish about 7,350 sparks per minute, or 123 sparks each second. And it must do this at exactly the right time and without a miss.

The reason the valve mechanism and ignition system must perform their duties at just the right time is that an engine operates with a certain definite cycle of events—over and over again, at a high rate of speed.

HOW AN ENGINE WORKS

Most automobile engines are four-cycle engines. This means they operate on a four-stroke cycle, requiring four strokes of the piston—down, up, down, up—for one complete cycle of events.

On the first stroke the intake valve is open and the piston moves down, pulling in the fuel/air mixture until the cylinder is full. This is the *intake stroke*.

Then the intake valve closes and the piston starts up on the *compression stroke*. It squeezes the mixture into a small space at the top of the cylinder, which increases the pressure in the cylinder to almost 200 pounds per square inch (psi). Between the second and third strokes, ignition takes place. Jumping the gap of the spark plug, the spark ignites the mixture of fuel and air squeezed at the top of the cylinder. In burning, the mixture of course gets very hot and tries to expand in all directions. The pressure rises to about 600 or 700 psi. The piston is the only thing that can move, so the expanding gases push it down to the bottom of the cylinder. This is the power stroke.

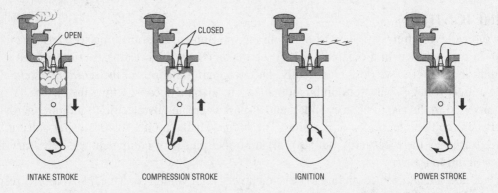

The fuel is burned, and the energy in the gases has been used up in pushing the piston downward. Now it is necessary to clear these burned gases out of the cylinder to make room for a new charge. On the *exhaust stroke*, the exhaust valve opens and the piston pushes the gases out through the opening.

So the cycle is completed, and we are ready to start over again with the intake stroke of the next cycle: intake–compression–power–exhaust, over and over again through the same series of actions. The crankshaft is going around continuously while the piston is going up and down, but we should note that it is only on the power stroke that the piston is driving it around. On the other three strokes, the crankshaft is driving the piston. There is one power stroke for every two revolutions of the crankshaft. This is for each cylinder, of course; with an eight-cylinder engine there are four power strokes for each revolution.

We have described what happens on the compression stroke, but we did not go into detail as to its importance. We hear talk of "compression ratio" and "high compression ratio," all of which have to do with how much we squeeze the mixture in the cylinder before igniting it. It is a fundamental fact of internal combustion engines that the more we compress the mixture—the harder we squeeze it—the more power we get from it.

The compression ratio is a measure of how much we squeeze the mixture. If the cylinder holds 100 cubic inches when the piston is all the way down in its lowest position, and 10 cubic inches when the piston is up as far as it can go, we say the compression ratio is 10 to 1. The mixture has been compressed into a space 110 times as large as it originally occupied. Fifty years ago 4 to 1 was a common figure for the compression ratio of automobile engines. This has increased over the years, and today compression ratios range upward of 8 to 1.

COOLING THE ENGINE

So far we've put together the main parts of an automobile engine. Such an engine would run—but it wouldn't run for very long. When the mixture of fuel and air burns in the cylinder, it creates a temperature of 4000° to 4500°F. This is almost twice the temperature at which iron melts. So it is easy to see that if we did not have a cooling system, our engine would not last very long.

The usual way of cooling an engine is to put water jackets around the hottest parts. Water is constantly circulated through these jackets by a small pump. The heat of the cylinder makes the water hot, and it then goes to the radiator where it is cooled by the outside air passing through. Then it starts back to the engine again to do more cooling. This process actually works very much like a steam or hot water heating system in a home. The engine is our boiler, which heats up the water, that then goes to a radiator where it gives up its heat to the air.

LUBRICATING THE ENGINE

The engine also needs a lubrication system. If all the rotating and reciprocating parts were running metal against metal with no film of oil between them to reduce friction, they would soon heat up and stick, or "seize." The friction would also make it harder for the parts to turn. So we have a reservoir of oil in the crankcase; a pump forces it from the crankcase to the bearings and other critical points in the engine. Some of it flows through tubes, and some through passages drilled in the crankshaft and connecting rods. The lubrication system might be compared to the water system in a house. The liquid is forced from one central place through pipes to many different locations where it is needed.

STARTING THE ENGINE

We must have some way of starting the engine. It has to be turning over before it can run under its own power, and we have to give it this initial start by means of an electric motor called the starter. The starter is an electric motor that engages, spins, and disengages the engine's flywheel in order to start the engine. This is somewhat similar to the motor in a vacuum cleaner or washing machine. It runs on electricity from the battery, and the starter switch is similar to the electric wall switch that turns on the lights in our homes.

There is one more important piece of electrical equipment: the alternator. It looks something like the starter motor, but its job is just the opposite. Instead of taking electricity from the battery to start the engine, the alternator is driven by the engine and generates electric current which feeds back into the battery to keep it charged for starting. The alternator also supplies power from the ignition system, lights, radio, and other electrical units. There are two slip rings mounted on the alternator's rotor shaft. Two brushes ride on the slip rings and deliver electrical energy to the rotor windings. Therefore, the magnetic field within an alternator is produced by the rotor.

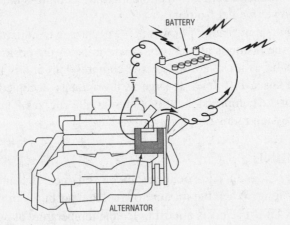

There is a resistor known as a *ballast resistor* that is inserted in series with the ignition coil; its purpose is to drop the 12-volt battery power supply to 6 volts, which is the voltage for which the coil was designed. This allows for the lower voltage from the battery when you crank up the vehicle; the coil can then produce the high voltage it needs for the spark plugs.

Controlling Engine Emissions

We have put together a complete automobile engine—at least enough parts of one so that it will start and keep on running. But before we talk about how power from the engine is sent back to the wheels to drive the car, let's look briefly at the systems used to control the emission of pollutants into the atmosphere.

Three major pollutants are emitted from automobiles into the atmosphere—hydrocarbons, carbon monoxide, and oxides of nitrogen. Hydrocarbons, which we can think of as essentially unburned gasoline, come from the exhaust pipe and the engine's crankcase as a result of the combustion process. They also enter the atmosphere from the fuel system through an evaporation process. Carbon monoxide (CO) results from partially burned fuel when rich fuel/air mixtures do not allow complete combustion all the way to carbon dioxide (CO_2). Oxides of nitrogen, on the other hand, are gases formed during combustion due to the high temperatures.

Modern autos have built-in systems designed to reduce the three major types of pollutants. The systems may vary somewhat among different makes of cars, but they all work to perform the same job—reducing emissions of hydrocarbons, carbon monoxide, and oxides of nitrogen.

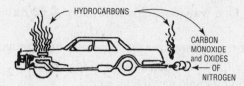

The first emission control applied to automobile engines was called the *positive crankcase ventilation* (PCV) system. This system, introduced in the early 1960s, is still in use today. During the compression strokes of the pistons, small amounts of gasoline vapor are forced past the piston rings out of the combustion chamber and into the engine crankcase. These infinitesimal amounts of vapor expelled during each engine cycle would add up to significant quantities of hydrocarbon (HC) emissions if they were allowed to enter the atmosphere. They aren't, however, because the PCV system directs these vapors back into the intake system so that they are burned in the combustion chambers. The system also increases gas mileage since the fuel vapors are not lost but are burned in the engine.

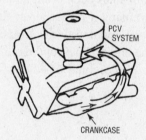

Another system—*air injection*—helps control hydrocarbon and carbon monoxide (CO) emissions in the exhaust. Air is injected by a pump into the engine's exhaust ports to cause further burning of the hot gasoline vapors before they pass out the exhaust pipe.

As government emission standards have become more strict, engineers and scientists have had to find new ways to achieve the required control. At the same time, they have had to come up with systems that would provide good fuel economy and not affect a vehicle's smooth operation.

The result was the development of a device called a *catalytic converter*, which was first introduced on most 1975-model cars made in the United States. This emission control system oxidizes hydrocarbons and carbon monoxide into harmless water vapor and carbon dioxide as the exhaust gases pass through a canister containing pellets coated with a catalyst material. A *catalyst* promotes chemical reactions, allowing them to take place at much lower than normal temperatures and more rapidly than a chemical reaction ordinarily would proceed. In the case of the catalytic converter emission control system, this means that catalysts allow more nearly complete oxidation of hydrocarbons and carbon monoxide at a much lower temperature than ordinary burning.

The catalytic converter has played a major role in reducing the emission of hydrocarbons and carbon monoxide from vehicle exhausts into the atmosphere. It has also promoted improved fuel economy and has helped engineers tune the engine for a more pleasant, better-performing car to drive. However, it reaches high temperatures while it's doing its job and has to be shielded from the car body by a heat deflector. An air pump on most cars adds to the combustion that takes place inside the converter and helps to reduce the amount of nitrogen oxides coming from the exhaust pipe.

Although the present catalytic converter, an oxidizing converter, does an excellent job in controlling hydrocarbon and carbon monoxide emissions, it isn't effective in controlling oxides of nitrogen (NO_x), the third type of pollutant in exhaust gases. Oxides of nitrogen are different from hydrocarbons and carbon monoxide because they will not burn to harmless combustion products.

Instead, controlling oxides of nitrogen in the engine exhaust usually requires doing something to prevent their formation. One way to do this is to dilute the air/fuel mixture as it enters the combustion chamber.

Oxides of nitrogen are formed anytime there are very high temperatures in the oxidation process (usually above 3000°F or 1090°C) when air is used to provide the oxygen. Air contains 79% nitrogen and 21% oxygen, so you could say the air burns.

The formation of oxides of nitrogen in an engine is minimized by diluting the fuel/air mixture entering the combustion chamber. This helps reduce the peak combustion temperature. One system being used is called *exhaust gas recirculation* (EGR). With this system, small quantities of exhaust gases are recirculated back into the intake system of the engine to dilute the fuel/air mixture. Some other systems use a single catalytic converter to remove the majority of all three types of pollutants.

To reduce hydrocarbons that evaporate from the fuel system when the engine is not running, there's a system that vents gasoline vapors into a canister filled with carbon granules. These granules act like a sponge and soak up the fumes and store them while the car is parked. When the engine starts up, the fumes are fed back to the engine and burned.

Further control of exhaust emissions has been brought about within the engine by changing the shape of the combustion chambers, using a leaner air-to-fuel ratio (more air in the mixture that goes to the cylinders for combustion), regulating the temperature of the air entering the carburetor, increasing the speed at which the engine idles, and modifying spark timing for stop-and-go driving. These changes to the engine all combine to help achieve more complete combustion and decrease exhaust emissions.

Shafts and Universal Joints

For rear-wheel-drive autos, the *propeller shaft*, or drive shaft, goes from the transmission back to the rear axle. It is a hollow or solid steel shaft, sometimes enclosed in an outer tube, sometimes left open. At the front end is a universal joint, and in many cars there is another universal joint at the rear end of the shaft. The *universal joint* allows the rear axle to move up or down in relation to the transmission without bending or breaking the shaft. It is something like the gimbals of a compass on a boat, which allow the compass to remain level at all times no matter how much the boat rolls or pitches. These universal joints are usually made up of two U-shaped pieces at right angles to each other and fastened together by a cross having arms of equal lengths. The U-shaped yokes pivot on the arms of the cross. Since there are two of these pivots, the two shafts can be at an angle to one another and still turn around and transmit power. They don't have to be in a straight line. This is very important because even if we could design the car to have them in a straight line to begin with, every time we went over a bump they would get out of line. The rear axle moves with the wheels, up and down with every bump, while the transmission does not move as much, being fastened to the frame. So the universal joint lets the propeller shaft keep on turning even though its two ends are moving around relative to each other.

Fastened at the rear end of the propeller shaft is a short shaft carrying a gear on the end. This is a bevel gear and is called the *pinion*. It meshes with the *ring gear* which is mounted on the rear axle. The job of the pinion and ring gear combination, or *final drive* as it often is called, is to take the torque provided by the propeller shaft, increase it, and turn it at right angles so that it can twist the wheels and drive the car.

For many years these rear axle gears were of the spiral bevel type. But now most cars use what are called *hypoid gears*. These are about the same as spiral bevel gears, except that the pinion does not meet the ring gear at its centerline. It meets it at a lower point, which means that the shape of the teeth must be different. This allows the propeller shaft to be lowered and, in turn, the overall car height.

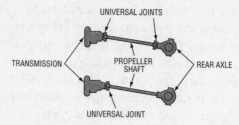

Since the pinion is much smaller than the ring gear, we know immediately that there is a speed reduction here, and an increase in torque. In today's passenger cars the rear axle ratios generally average about 3 to 1. The axles and wheels turn only about one-third as fast as the propeller shaft. It should be noted that this speed reduction and torque increase are always there and always stay the same. Even when we say that we are in direct drive, we are referring only to the transmission, and its rear axle ratio is still effective. And if the transmission is in low gear, say a ratio of 3 to 1 (it is actually less than this in most of today's cars), the overall ratio between the engine and rear wheels will be 3×3 (or 9), to 1.

Axles and Wheels

The *axles* are relatively slender steel shafts. They have a flange at the outer end to which the wheel and brake drum are bolted. Around the axle is the axle housing. This holds the parts of the brake that do not turn with the wheel and supports the bearing in which the outer end of the axle shaft runs.

The wheel itself is essentially a metal disk with a rim around the outside into which the tire fits. It is the outside surface of the tire that pushes on the ground and really makes a car move. But the engine furnishes the force, and all the other things just mentioned have a certain part of the job to do in getting that force from one place to the other.

Tracking, in terms of wheel alignment, means that the rear wheels follow the front wheels correctly. Tracking is correct when both rear wheels are parallel to, and the same distance from, the vehicle centerline (an imaginary line drawn down the center of the vehicle). A bent frame or twisted body structure can cause improper tracking.

However—and this can be just a little confusing—a vehicle's *track* is measured from the center of the left wheel to the center of the right wheel.

Tires are rated in several areas, and it's important to have the right kind of tires for your car and the conditions you drive in. The rating is listed on the tire's sidewall. For instance, if your sidewall reads, "P 185/70 R 14," this is what it all means:

P means this is a passenger car tire, as opposed to a tire made for a truck or other vehicle. P-metric is the U.S. version of a metric tire-sizing system.

185 is the section width. This is the width of the tire in millimeters from sidewall to sidewall. This measurement varies depending on the width of the rim to which a tire is fitted—larger on a wide rim, smaller on a narrow rim. The number on the tire shows the width measured when the tire is fitted to the recommended rim width.

70 is the aspect ratio, the ratio of height to width. This tire's height is 70% of its width.

R refers to construction, how the plies are constructed in the body of the tire. R indicates a radial; B means the tire has belted bias construction; D means diagonal bias construction.

14 is the rim diameter, the diameter of the wheel in inches.

It's important to keep your tires inflated to the proper pounds per square inch (psi). When a tire is underinflated, the center area of the tread moves upward as the sidewalls flex. This abnormal action places undue and unnecessary stress on the tire, causing excess wear to both outside edges. It also decreases the traction and worsens the gas mileage.

Shock absorbers are cylinders connected to each wheel that use hydraulic fluid to lessen the up-and-down movement of the wheel (and therefore the vehicle) caused by traveling over uneven road surfaces. A car with worn-out shock absorbers will bounce a lot on a rough road.

The Braking System

We've shown how to get the car to move, but another very important point is to be able to stop it. This is done by the *brakes*—one in each of the four wheels—which are simply a method of applying friction to the rotating wheels to stop them. It's like rubbing a stick against the rim of the wheels on a kid's wagon.

There are two types of brake systems—drum brake and disc brake. In the *drum brake system*, two stationary brake shoes covered with a special friction material (called the brake lining) are forced outward by hydraulic pressure against the inside of a metal drum that rotates with the wheel. A system of steel tubes filled with a particular type of hydraulic fluid (brake fluid) runs from a master cylinder to each brake. When the driver steps on the brake pedal, pressure is built up in the master cylinder and this pressure is transmitted through the tubes, called brake lines, to pistons located inside a hydraulic cylinder in each wheel. The pistons move outward and push the shoes against the brake drum. As a safety feature, most cars have a dual master cylinder that provides two independent hydraulic systems, one for the front wheels and one for the rear wheels.

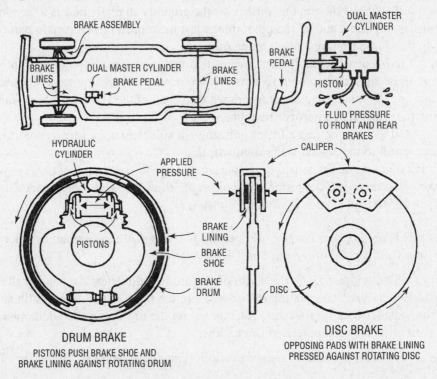

DRUM BRAKE
PISTONS PUSH BRAKE SHOE AND
BRAKE LINING AGAINST ROTATING DRUM

DISC BRAKE
OPPOSING PADS WITH BRAKE LINING
PRESSED AGAINST ROTATING DISC

In the *disc brake system*, the brake lining is bonded to brake shoes positioned on each side of a rotating disc located in the wheel. When the brake pedal is applied, hydraulic pressure transmitted from the dual master cylinder causes a caliper to clamp the opposing shoes against the disc—it's like taking your thumb and forefinger and squeezing them together against a rotating plate. However, if air gets into the hydraulic brake system, the brake pedal action will be spongy or soft because air is much more compressible than hydraulic fluid.

Brakes are friction devices that convert work into heat, and the amount of heat created by the brakes during a fast stop from a high speed is very significant. Because of this, proper cooling of the brakes is an important consideration during their design.

The Drive System

The first thing needed in the *drive system* is a device that will completely disconnect the engine from the drive wheels and the rest of the power transmission system. This allows the engine to run when the car is standing still, instead of having to turn the engine completely off whenever we stop. And it would be a problem to start the engine while it is connected to the drive system. Also, with manual shift transmissions, we have to disconnect it from the engine to shift gears easily.

There are various ways in which we could take care of these problems, but we need something else. We need something that will take hold gradually, that will not jump abruptly from no connection at all to a direct, solid connection. When we want to start a car, we have to speed the engine up to get enough power to move it. At the same time the wheels are standing still. We cannot, in one moment, bring the speed of the wheels up to the speed of the engine; there would be a terrible jerk. And when we shift gears after the car is moving, we have almost the same situation—the wheels and propeller shaft are not turning at the same speed as the engine. So we want something that will slip a little, that will take hold gently at first and gradually grab harder and harder. Thus the rear wheels can start to move slowly and gradually pick up speed until finally everything is turning at the same rate and the clutch is solidly engaged. From then on, of course, we do not want any slipping because that just wastes power and heats things up.

The kind of clutch we are talking about depends on friction for transmitting power. In fact, its full name is *friction clutch*, as there are other types of devices commonly called clutches.

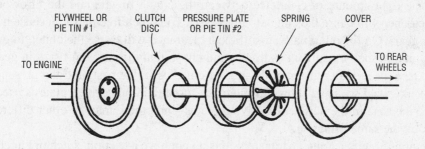

Suppose we mount two ordinary pie plates or tins, each on a shaft, as shown. As long as they are not touching each other, we can spin one as fast as we want to without affecting the other at all. But if we move them together when one of them is spinning, the other will begin to turn and almost immediately both shafts will start turning together as one unit. This is the general operating principle of the disc, or friction, clutch used in automobiles with manual transmissions. The discs are forced together by strong springs and are separated by pushing down on the clutch pedal in the driver's compartment. It is sometimes said that a good clutch must slip while being engaged and must not slip when it is engaged.

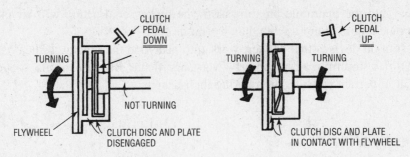

In most automobiles the clutch consists of one plate squeezed tightly between two other plates. The one in the middle is the driven member; it is connected to a shaft leading back into the transmission. The other two are the driving members; they are connected directly to the engine. A strong spring, or springs, forces the two driving members together. This tightens their grip on the middle plate until they are all turning together as one unit.

The *engine flywheel* is used for the first driving member. Its surface is made very smooth where the driven plate pushes up against it. The other driving member is called the *pressure plate*. It is a fairly heavy ring of cast iron that is smooth on one side. It is fastened to the cover, which is bolted to the flywheel, so they all turn together. It is fastened in such a way that it can slide back and forth. The driven plate is a flat disc of steel with friction facing fastened on each side. The plate is fastened by splines to a shaft going to the transmission. This means it fits into grooves on the shaft so that they must turn together, but the plate can slide forward and backward on the shaft. A series of coil springs, or sometimes one large, flat spring, are present between the clutch cover and the pressure plate. They push the pressure plate toward the flywheel, squeezing the driven plate between the two. The springs are always trying to engage the clutch, and they are strong enough to keep it from slipping under ordinary conditions. To disengage the clutch, the driver pushes on the pedal. This works through levers to pull back the pressure plate against the force of the springs. This loosens the driven plate and disconnects the transmission shaft from the engine crankshaft.

It's important to remember that a clutch pedal must have the proper amount of free play so that there is the right amount of clearance between the clutch fingers and the throwout bearing. Too much clearance will cause the clutch to grab early. Too much free play can cause hard shifting and clashing gears. On the other hand, insufficient clearance will cause the clutch to grab late, and no free play at all usually results in a slipping clutch, so that the car won't stay in gear.

There have been many different designs of clutches in the past, and the present ones don't all look just like what we have shown. Sometimes more than one driven plate is used, with a corresponding increase in the number of driving plates—and there may be other differences. But they all work on the same principle.

Cars equipped with automatic transmissions do not have a friction clutch or clutch pedal. We will discuss those shortly, but first we will cover the manual shift type transmission and drive system.

Manual Transmissions

A *transmission* is used in automobiles to enable us to change the speed of the engine in relation to the speed of the rear wheels. When a car is starting up or in heavy going at low speed, we need more twisting force on the rear wheels to make it go than we need if we're cruising along a good highway at constant speed. The transmission gives us this increased twisting force (torque) and also allows the engine to run faster. The latter is important because an internal combustion engine does not develop very much power at low speed. When the car picks up speed, the transmission is shifted to change the speed ratio between the engine and the wheels, and eventually is shifted into its highest gear.

The transmission is a system of gears. Suppose we have a small gear with 12 teeth driving a larger gear with 24 teeth. When the first gear has made one complete revolution, we might say that it has gone around a distance equivalent to 12 teeth. The second one has gone around the same distance—12 teeth—but this means only one-half a revolution for the larger gear. So this second gear, and the shaft it is fastened to, always turn at one-half the speed of the first gear and its shaft.

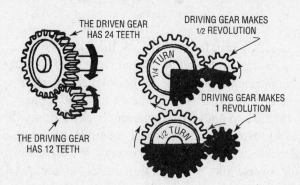

A familiar household example of gears is a hand-operated eggbeater. We can turn the large gear fairly slowly and the small gears meshing with it turn rapidly to drive the beaters at high speed.

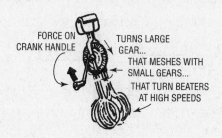

The transmission is a case full of gears located behind the clutch. The case is usually fastened to the clutch housing, so the whole unit looks like an extension of the engine. The purpose of the transmission, as mentioned, is to vary the speed and torque of the rear axle in relation to the speed and torque of the engine.

In a manual shift automobile transmission we have several combinations of gears arranged so that we can select the one we want to use at any moment. For *low or first gear*, a small gear on the engine shaft drives a large gear on another shaft. This reduces the speed and increases the twisting force; this is used for starting and for steep hills or heavy going in sand or mud. It lets the engine run fast while the car moves slowly. Then a small gear on the second shaft drives a large gear on the drive shaft, which goes to the drive axle. This reduces the speed and increases the torque still more, giving a ratio of about 3 to 1 for starting up or heavy pulling.

Second or intermediate gear works about the same way. The first two gears are the same as in low gear. The next pair are different, however. They are almost the same size, and sometimes the countershaft gear may be the larger. Thus the countershaft runs at the same speed as before, but there is little if any additional reduction from that to the third shaft. So the wheels run faster for the same engine speed than they did in low gear. The usual ratio in second gear is about 1⅔ to 1. This means that the propeller shaft will run at 1,000 rpm when the engine is running at 1,670 rpm.

Third or high speed is direct drive. The transmission does not do anything. We simply connect the first and third shafts together, and they turn as one. The propeller shaft turns at the same speed as the engine and delivers engine torque. Sticking to figures, we can say the ratio is 1 to 1.

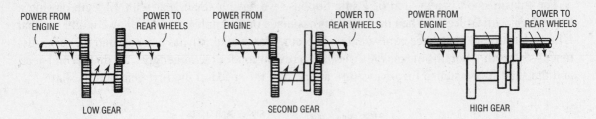

LOW GEAR   SECOND GEAR   HIGH GEAR

Besides the three (and usually more) forward speeds, there are two other possible combinations in a transmission. There is *neutral*, in which the transmission shaft is entirely disconnected from the clutch shaft and the engine cannot drive the propeller shaft or anything beyond the transmission. It has about the same effect as disengaging the clutch. And there is *reverse*. It is a complicated matter to make an internal combustion engine run backward, so we run it in one direction all the time and use gears to reverse the direction of rotation. We put an extra gear between the countershaft and the final drive shaft called the *reverse idler*. We drive the countershaft in the same way as before; it drives the reverse idler, which in turn drives the low speed gear on the final drive shaft. The system is just like low gear except for this extra gear. This changes the direction of rotation, and we can see that the final shaft is turning opposite what it was in all the previous cases. The ratio of reverse is about the same as for low gear, or even lower. This is logical because we may want to pull hard in reverse but we never want to back up very fast.

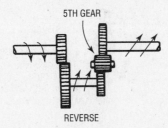

REVERSE

We have described a complete manual shift transmission of the conventional type, with three speeds forward and one reverse. The gears are mounted in a metal case filled with oil to lubricate the gears and bearings. The various speeds are selected by moving a gearshift in the driver's compartment—don't forget to put in the clutch first, though.

Most manual transmissions today have four or five speeds (some even have six); the higher gears—if they are differentiated from the first three—are sometimes called *overdrive* because at these higher gear ratios the engine is actually turning slower than the drive shaft and rear axle. With higher gear ratios and lower engine speeds, fuel economy can be significantly improved—this is why you get the best mileage cruising at a reasonable speed down a highway, not in stop-and-go city driving.

All manual shift transmissions are not exactly like those we have discussed. Some, particularly those in trucks, have a larger number of forward speeds, and the gears may be arranged in a different order on the shafts. Most manual transmissions, however, operate on the principles discussed. There are a number of gears that can be connected together in different ways to give us the different ratios we want. Except in direct drive, a certain amount of torque comes in at the front end from the clutch shaft, and a different amount goes out the back end to the propeller shaft.

Most standard (manual) transmissions have what is known as a *synchromesh* unit that helps eliminate grinding the gears when shifting. It's designed to bring two gears to the same speed before engagement, but it does *not* change gear ratios.

We have described to some extent the main parts of the power path in a car with a manual shift transmission—the clutch and transmission gearing. We covered the propeller shaft, universal joints, axles, differential, and wheels and tires earlier. We will soon discuss automatic transmissions and how they make the power path different from those in cars with manual shift transmissions. Before we do that, however, it would be best to spend a little time talking about planetary gears since they play such an important role in the operation of an automatic transmission.

Planetary Gears

Planetary gears are used in a variety of arrangements in the automobile. Probably the main reason for this is that we can make them do a number of different things, depending on how we connect them into the power system. This is what makes a planetary gear set so interesting. But first, let's look at one and see what it is.

In its simplest form, a planetary gear set is comprised of three gears. There is a sun gear, or pinion, in the center. Then there is a small planet gear meshing with it. (We show two examples on page 298 but usually there are three or four.) On the outside is the ring gear, an internal gear meshing with the planet gears. The planet gears are fastened together by the planet carrier, which holds them in place but lets them rotate. Just how these gears and carriers are fastened to the shafts depends on what we want the mechanism to do.

Suppose we connect the sun gear to the input, or driving shaft, and the planet carrier to the output, or driven shaft. We put a brake band around the outside of the ring gear and hold it tight so it cannot move.

If the engine drives the sun gear, the planet gears must turn around. But they cannot stand still and rotate on their shafts because that would mean the ring gear must move, and we are holding that with the brake. So they have to move around the ring gear, and the planet carrier moves with them. It is something like the differential we described. There are two motions in the planet gears. Each one is rotating about its own shaft, and at the same time they are all moving around in a circle on the teeth of the ring gear. This is where this type of gearing gets its name. The motion is much the same as that of Earth and the other planets about the sun. Each one rotates on its own axis, but they also continually circle around the sun.

The planet carrier, and thus the driven shaft, turns much more slowly than the sun gear and drive shaft and in the same direction. Just what the ratio is depends on the size of the gears, and we will not go into the details of how it is figured. As an example, however, with the smallest practical planets, the ratio cannot be less than 2½ to 1. When the planet and the sun gears are the same size, the ratio is 4 to 1. This of course means that speed is reduced to ¼ and the torque is increased 4 times.

To shift into direct drive, we release the brake on the ring gear and engage a clutch connecting the drive shaft directly to the driven shaft. This can be done by clutching the planet carrier to either the sun gear or the ring gear. In either case, none of the gears can turn on each other, so the whole mechanism is locked and rotates all together without affecting the drive. We mentioned that we can get various results with a planetary transmission by connecting it up in different ways. If we drive the ring gear and hold the sun gear still, we will still increase the torque as we did in the case just described, but it will not be increased as much. With other arrangements we can increase the speed and reduce the torque, and by still other means we can get reverse. We have three units, any one of which we can hold stationary and either of the other two can be the driving member. So there are six possible combinations. Practically all of them are used in transmissions in one way or another.

There are various modifications of this simple planetary gear. There are some with double planets of different sizes, and there are compound planetary gears, which consist of two planetary gear sets with certain gears of one connected to certain gears of the other. These act in fundamentally the same way as the simple planetary gear, but following the power flow through them is rather complicated and figuring the gear ratio is not worth the trouble unless we are in the business of designing transmissions.

PLANETARY GEAR COMBINATIONS

There are three units in a planetary gear set—a sun gear, planet gears and carrier, and a ring gear. To get various results we can hold any of these units stationary and either of the other two can be the driving or driven member. So there are six possible combinations. We show two examples on page 298, with labels telling what kind of gear results from each arrangement. They are all planetary gears, but a number of different results are obtained by hooking them up differently.

Automatic Transmissions

Most cars built today have some form of automatic transmission that eliminates the clutch and the need to shift gears manually to obtain the right gear ratios. There are various types, but most of them are similar in the way they affect the driving of the car. They usually have a hydraulic drive of some sort. The type that is in wide use today is the three-element *torque converter*. Imagine taking a doughnut, slicing it in two, and putting blades on the inside of each half. Both halves represent two elements of the torque converter—the *pump*, or driving element, and the *turbine*, or driven element.

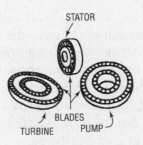

Now, between these two halves place a plate that also has blades. This is the third element of the converter and is called the *stator*. All three elements are in a casing filled with oil, which is circulated by means of the blades.

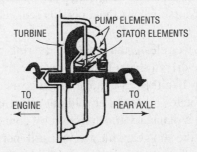

The park (or P) position on an automatic transmission gear selector represents the position that locks up the transmission (without damaging it) and stops the wheels from rolling. The car can be started only when it is in park or neutral (N).

Let's see what happens when we place the automatic transmission selector in the drive position. The pump is mechanically connected to the engine's crankshaft, so it always rotates when the engine runs. When the engine is started, the pump begins rotating and sends oil, spinning in a clockwise direction, against the blades of the turbine to start it turning. The spinning oil has energy that the turbine absorbs and converts into torque, or twisting force, which is then sent to the drive wheels. When the oil leaves the turbine, it spins in a counterclockwise direction, and if it went back to the pump spinning in this direction it would slow it down—we would lose any torque that had been gained. To make sure this doesn't happen, we use the blades of the stator, which does not rotate (not just yet, anyway), to change the direction of the oil flow so that it again spins in a clockwise direction. When the oil enters the pump, it adds to the torque the pump receives from the engine, the pump starts to turn faster, and we start to obtain torque multiplication. The cycle of oil going from the pump to the turbine, through the stator, and then back to the pump is repeated over and over until the car reaches a speed where torque multiplication is no longer needed. When this happens, the stator starts to turn freely (it's fixed to rotate only clockwise). The pump and the turbine then rotate at nearly the same speed and act like a fluid coupling, or clutch. We now have a situation similar to high gear in a manual shift transmission where the crankshaft is connected directly to the drive shaft and both revolve at nearly the same speed. The stator rotates when torque multiplication is needed again.

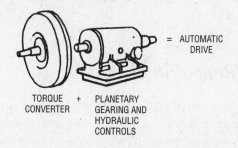

TORQUE CONVERTER + PLANETARY GEARING AND HYDRAULIC CONTROLS = AUTOMATIC DRIVE

The turbine is connected by a shaft to a gear transmission location behind the converter. The transmission usually used contains planetary gear sets and provides the desired number of forward speed gear ratios automatically. These gear ratios can also be selected manually for greater engine braking or exceptionally hard pulling. A reverse gear and neutral gear are also provided. The planetary type of gear transmission has its gears in mesh at all times. Gear ratios for different driving conditions are obtained using hydraulic controls that cause friction bands and clutches to grab and hold certain gears of the set stationary while the others rotate.

An interesting item in automatic transmissions is the *vacuum modulator*, which helps to control the shifting point of the transmission by sensing the engine load at any given moment. The modulator is a vacuum-operated device connected to a source manifold vacuum. As the vacuum changes in response to the engine load, this actuates the modulator, which sends a signal to the valve body, resulting in a different shift point. For instance, when vacuum is low—as it usually is when the engine is accelerated—the modulator reacts and causes the transmission to shift at a higher vehicle speed. The higher shift point allows the engine to develop more torque, which increases engine power.

Hydraulic torque converters can have variations in the design of their basic components. Some elements may have their blades set at a fixed angle to the flow of oil. Others may have blades that are hydraulically operated to provide varying blade angles automatically. For example, a stator could have a low angle for maximum efficiency during the average operating range of the transmission and a high angle for increased acceleration and performance (when more torque is needed at the drive wheels). There are also variations in the way the components are arranged in hydraulic torque converters. Some have two stators, while others have multiple sets of pump and turbine blades. Differences can exist, too, in the way the planetary gears are combined with the pump, turbine, and stator elements.

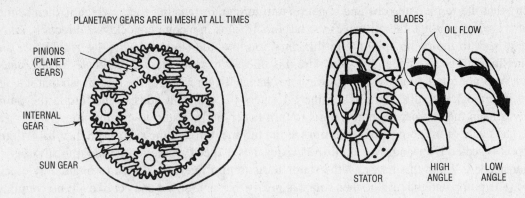

Under ordinary circumstances, however, these variations do not make a great deal of difference to the driver of the car. He still will find no clutch pedal and will have no shifting to do except when he wants to back up. And for forward driving, all he has to do is step on the accelerator to go and on the brake pedal to stop.

The Rear Axle (Rear-Wheel Drive)

In the rear axle we have two sets of gears. The first—a ring gear and a pinion—is simply to transmit the power around a corner. It enables the propeller shaft to drive the axle shafts that are at right angles to it. An old-fashioned ice cream freezer has a set of gears that do the same thing.

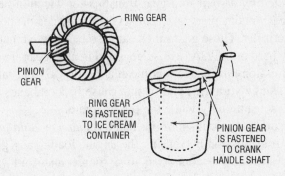

If we didn't ever have to turn a corner, that is all the gearing we would need in the rear axle. But when we turn a corner, the outside wheel has to travel farther than the inside wheel, and so it has to go faster during that time. It's like a squad of soldiers making a turn: The outside person has to march much faster than the one on the inside just to stay lined up and even. We have a set of gears called the differential to take care of this.

The *differential* consists of two small bevel gears on the ends of the axle shafts meshed with two bevel gears (for simplicity we show only one) mounted in the differential frame. This frame is fastened solidly to the ring gear.

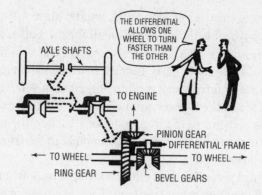

When a car is going straight ahead, the frame and the gears all rotate as a unit, with no motion between one another. But when the car is turning, one wheel must go faster than the other, so the gears on the axle shafts rotate relative to the other small gear. If the ring gear were stationary, one axle would turn frontward and the other one backward. But since the ring gear is turning the whole unit, it means that one axle is turning faster than the ring gear and the other is turning slower by the same amount. This can be carried to the point where one wheel is stationary and the other one is turning at twice ring gear speed, which is the situation we sometimes get when one wheel is on a slippery spot and the other isn't. Some cars, however, can be equipped with a limited slip differential, a type of differential that allows the major driving force to go to the wheel having greater traction.

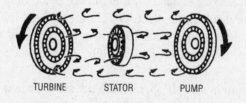

The axle shafts, of course, drive the wheels and make the car move, which is the point we have been getting to all this time. We have now described a complete rear-wheel-drive system, just as outlined at the beginning. Power starts at the engine and eventually gets to the rear wheels after passing through various mechanisms so that it will arrive there in proper form.

Front-Wheel Drive

As mentioned before, most cars today use front-wheel drive. The same basic components are used as for the rear wheel drive system, but all the components are arranged up in front of the driver and the constant velocity (CV) joint transmits power to the drive (front) wheels while allowing the wheels to be steered and the suspension to respond to bumps in the road—taking the place of a universal joint, of which it is a more complex version. The power flow from the engine is to the front-wheel axle shafts. Instead of the rear wheels pushing the car forward, the front wheels pull the car along. The CV joint is housed in a rubber boot (an all-around rubber covering with bellows that allows flexibility while still protecting the joint).

Four-Wheel and Six-Wheel Drive

Trucks and other utility vehicles often are driven in places where the going is rough. Sometimes better traction than usual is needed. For example, two wheels might get stuck in a mud hole and not be able to pull out of it. So instead of having the engine drive just two wheels, it drives four wheels or six wheels. A four-wheel vehicle driving on all four wheels is known as a 4 × 4, and one with six wheels, all driving, is a 6 × 6. A 4 × 6 is a six-wheel truck with four driving wheels.

To get such a drive we use a transfer case. In back of a regular transmission is another set of gears. Essentially this consists of three gears meshing together in series, extending out to one side of the transmission. The first and third gears are the same size. From each side of the third gear a propeller shaft extends, one forward to the front axle, one back to the rear axle. Each axle is driven just as we have shown in the two-wheel drive, except that in the front axle we must have some universal joints in order to steer.

For a six-wheel drive a third propeller shaft extends straight back from the first gear in the transfer case, that is, in line with the regular transmission. Thus, we have one input shaft into the transfer case and three output shafts.

With the first and third gears the same size we have no change of speed or torque in the transfer case. Usually, however, there is another pair of gears in it that can be shifted to give us a different ratio. A two-speed transfer case doubles the number of gear ratios available in the regular transmission.

Lights

Stoplights are usually controlled by spring-loaded electrical switches. Most cars have mechanically operated switches operated by contact with the brake pedal or with a bracket attached to the pedal. When the brakes are released, the electrical circuit through the stoplight is open—broken. When the brake is applied, the circuit through the switch closes and the stoplight lights. A loose or corroded headlight connection can cause a dim light. If the switch itself is faulty, all the lights will be affected.

The hydraulic type of stoplight switch operates on the same principle; its operation depends on hydraulic pressure in the master cylinder of the brake.

CHAPTER

11 Assembling Objects

Overview

The Assembling Objects (AO) subtest of the ASVAB is a relatively recent addition that tests *spatial apperception*—your ability to visualize how an object will look when its parts are put together. Think of a section of a jigsaw puzzle in separate pieces and then put together. Initially, this subtest was included only in the computer version, but it is now in the paper version, too, so expect it no matter which version you take. Currently, only the Navy uses the AO score to specifically qualify service members for a particular specialty (operational and some mechanical jobs), but that could and probably will change.

Much of what needs to be done mentally when taking this subtest will seem to be intuitive—either you'll get it right away, or you won't. It's a proven fact that some people are just naturally better at seeing patterns, grasping spatial relationships, and so forth. But it's also a proven fact that most of the rest of us can learn to get better at these skills, too—so don't give up hope.

The test will show you three to five shapes and then give you four choices, all of which are trying to persuade you that they are the final result of assembling the shapes.

This test measures your ability to picture how an object will look when its parts are mentally put together. Each question will show you several separate shapes; you will then pick the choice that best represents how the pieces would look if they were all fitted together correctly. There is only one best answer for each shape. Pick the best answer for each question, then blacken the space on the answer form that has the same number and letter as your choice.

Here is a sample question.

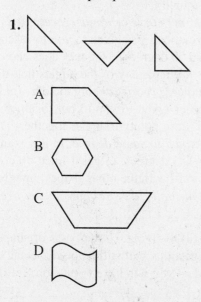

Choice A is the shape that will result when the three initial shapes are assembled correctly.

Tips and Techniques

For those who aren't naturally good at jigsaw puzzles—who don't or can't immediately and consistently come up with the right answers to these kinds of questions (and maybe for some of those who can)—here are some suggestions:

1. ***Don't try to assemble the pieces in your head—let the test do it for you.*** There is more than one way to assemble the pieces the test shows you, but only one of the choices is one of those ways—only one choice is correct. Therefore, what you have to do is disqualify three out of the four choices and then confirm that the remaining choice is, in fact, one way to assemble the parts you started out with.

   Referring to the example from page 301, here are *some* of the ways that the three initial shapes *could* be assembled:

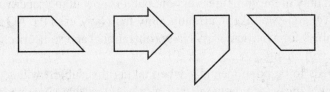

2. ***See which of the choices has the right amount of area or mass.*** Potential choices that are much bigger or smaller than the pieces given to you to assemble are usually pretty easy to identify. For instance, in the example above, choice B is much too small to be the result of putting the three initial shapes together, while choice C is much too large. Therefore, they are easy to disqualify.
3. ***Disqualify the choices that have a shape or external curve or angle that is not in the pieces given to you to assemble.*** For instance, choice D in the example above has two wavy lines, whereas the disassembled pieces given to you have no curves, only straight lines and sharp angles. Therefore, you know choice D is *not* the answer. Likewise, besides being too small, choice B has too many angles and is therefore easy to disqualify.
4. ***Disqualify the choices that*** **don't** ***have an unusual or distinct curve or angle represented in the pieces given to you to assemble.*** In the example above, the pieces given to you to assemble all have one right angle and two acute angles (less than 90 degrees). Not only does choice D have curves that the pieces don't have, choice D does *not* have any of the angles that the assembled object would have to have. In the same way, choice C (besides being too big—having too much area to result from the assembly of the pieces given to you to put together—doesn't have enough angles to be the result of putting all those pointy triangles together.
5. ***Expect that some or all of the pieces to assemble are rotated to some degree.*** In the example above, the middle shape has been rotated clockwise 135 degrees; to get it lined up correctly, you have to be able to imagine rotating the shape to fit with the other shapes. Imagine those jigsaw pieces again, lying flat on a table—but *don't mentally flip any of the shapes over*. Leave them flat on the imaginary table.

The exact format of the Assembling Objects subtest is still evolving, so the types of shapes and illustrations you see here may change, but these suggestions will still help you. None of the ASVAB subtests, however, exist to give you a free ride—you will have to put some effort into deducing the correct answer to each question. This means that more than one of the choices may be plausible at first glance. However, if you follow these steps—and especially if you use them to practice this skill of assembling objects in each of the four practice tests in this book—you should do well on the actual ASVAB.

TEST YOURSELF

ANSWER SHEETS—Practice Examination Two

GENERAL SCIENCE—SUBTEST 1

1. Ⓐ Ⓑ Ⓒ Ⓓ   6. Ⓐ Ⓑ Ⓒ Ⓓ   11. Ⓐ Ⓑ Ⓒ Ⓓ   16. Ⓐ Ⓑ Ⓒ Ⓓ   21. Ⓐ Ⓑ Ⓒ Ⓓ
2. Ⓐ Ⓑ Ⓒ Ⓓ   7. Ⓐ Ⓑ Ⓒ Ⓓ   12. Ⓐ Ⓑ Ⓒ Ⓓ   17. Ⓐ Ⓑ Ⓒ Ⓓ   22. Ⓐ Ⓑ Ⓒ Ⓓ
3. Ⓐ Ⓑ Ⓒ Ⓓ   8. Ⓐ Ⓑ Ⓒ Ⓓ   13. Ⓐ Ⓑ Ⓒ Ⓓ   18. Ⓐ Ⓑ Ⓒ Ⓓ   23. Ⓐ Ⓑ Ⓒ Ⓓ
4. Ⓐ Ⓑ Ⓒ Ⓓ   9. Ⓐ Ⓑ Ⓒ Ⓓ   14. Ⓐ Ⓑ Ⓒ Ⓓ   19. Ⓐ Ⓑ Ⓒ Ⓓ   24. Ⓐ Ⓑ Ⓒ Ⓓ
5. Ⓐ Ⓑ Ⓒ Ⓓ   10. Ⓐ Ⓑ Ⓒ Ⓓ   15. Ⓐ Ⓑ Ⓒ Ⓓ   20. Ⓐ Ⓑ Ⓒ Ⓓ   25. Ⓐ Ⓑ Ⓒ Ⓓ

ARITHMETIC REASONING—SUBTEST 2

1. Ⓐ Ⓑ Ⓒ Ⓓ   7. Ⓐ Ⓑ Ⓒ Ⓓ   13. Ⓐ Ⓑ Ⓒ Ⓓ   19. Ⓐ Ⓑ Ⓒ Ⓓ   25. Ⓐ Ⓑ Ⓒ Ⓓ
2. Ⓐ Ⓑ Ⓒ Ⓓ   8. Ⓐ Ⓑ Ⓒ Ⓓ   14. Ⓐ Ⓑ Ⓒ Ⓓ   20. Ⓐ Ⓑ Ⓒ Ⓓ   26. Ⓐ Ⓑ Ⓒ Ⓓ
3. Ⓐ Ⓑ Ⓒ Ⓓ   9. Ⓐ Ⓑ Ⓒ Ⓓ   15. Ⓐ Ⓑ Ⓒ Ⓓ   21. Ⓐ Ⓑ Ⓒ Ⓓ   27. Ⓐ Ⓑ Ⓒ Ⓓ
4. Ⓐ Ⓑ Ⓒ Ⓓ   10. Ⓐ Ⓑ Ⓒ Ⓓ   16. Ⓐ Ⓑ Ⓒ Ⓓ   22. Ⓐ Ⓑ Ⓒ Ⓓ   28. Ⓐ Ⓑ Ⓒ Ⓓ
5. Ⓐ Ⓑ Ⓒ Ⓓ   11. Ⓐ Ⓑ Ⓒ Ⓓ   17. Ⓐ Ⓑ Ⓒ Ⓓ   23. Ⓐ Ⓑ Ⓒ Ⓓ   29. Ⓐ Ⓑ Ⓒ Ⓓ
6. Ⓐ Ⓑ Ⓒ Ⓓ   12. Ⓐ Ⓑ Ⓒ Ⓓ   18. Ⓐ Ⓑ Ⓒ Ⓓ   24. Ⓐ Ⓑ Ⓒ Ⓓ   30. Ⓐ Ⓑ Ⓒ Ⓓ

WORD KNOWLEDGE—SUBTEST 3

1. Ⓐ Ⓑ Ⓒ Ⓓ   8. Ⓐ Ⓑ Ⓒ Ⓓ   15. Ⓐ Ⓑ Ⓒ Ⓓ   22. Ⓐ Ⓑ Ⓒ Ⓓ   29. Ⓐ Ⓑ Ⓒ Ⓓ
2. Ⓐ Ⓑ Ⓒ Ⓓ   9. Ⓐ Ⓑ Ⓒ Ⓓ   16. Ⓐ Ⓑ Ⓒ Ⓓ   23. Ⓐ Ⓑ Ⓒ Ⓓ   30. Ⓐ Ⓑ Ⓒ Ⓓ
3. Ⓐ Ⓑ Ⓒ Ⓓ   10. Ⓐ Ⓑ Ⓒ Ⓓ   17. Ⓐ Ⓑ Ⓒ Ⓓ   24. Ⓐ Ⓑ Ⓒ Ⓓ   31. Ⓐ Ⓑ Ⓒ Ⓓ
4. Ⓐ Ⓑ Ⓒ Ⓓ   11. Ⓐ Ⓑ Ⓒ Ⓓ   18. Ⓐ Ⓑ Ⓒ Ⓓ   25. Ⓐ Ⓑ Ⓒ Ⓓ   32. Ⓐ Ⓑ Ⓒ Ⓓ
5. Ⓐ Ⓑ Ⓒ Ⓓ   12. Ⓐ Ⓑ Ⓒ Ⓓ   19. Ⓐ Ⓑ Ⓒ Ⓓ   26. Ⓐ Ⓑ Ⓒ Ⓓ   33. Ⓐ Ⓑ Ⓒ Ⓓ
6. Ⓐ Ⓑ Ⓒ Ⓓ   13. Ⓐ Ⓑ Ⓒ Ⓓ   20. Ⓐ Ⓑ Ⓒ Ⓓ   27. Ⓐ Ⓑ Ⓒ Ⓓ   34. Ⓐ Ⓑ Ⓒ Ⓓ
7. Ⓐ Ⓑ Ⓒ Ⓓ   14. Ⓐ Ⓑ Ⓒ Ⓓ   21. Ⓐ Ⓑ Ⓒ Ⓓ   28. Ⓐ Ⓑ Ⓒ Ⓓ   35. Ⓐ Ⓑ Ⓒ Ⓓ

PARAGRAPH COMPREHENSION—SUBTEST 4

1. Ⓐ Ⓑ Ⓒ Ⓓ   4. Ⓐ Ⓑ Ⓒ Ⓓ   7. Ⓐ Ⓑ Ⓒ Ⓓ   10. Ⓐ Ⓑ Ⓒ Ⓓ   13. Ⓐ Ⓑ Ⓒ Ⓓ
2. Ⓐ Ⓑ Ⓒ Ⓓ   5. Ⓐ Ⓑ Ⓒ Ⓓ   8. Ⓐ Ⓑ Ⓒ Ⓓ   11. Ⓐ Ⓑ Ⓒ Ⓓ   14. Ⓐ Ⓑ Ⓒ Ⓓ
3. Ⓐ Ⓑ Ⓒ Ⓓ   6. Ⓐ Ⓑ Ⓒ Ⓓ   9. Ⓐ Ⓑ Ⓒ Ⓓ   12. Ⓐ Ⓑ Ⓒ Ⓓ   15. Ⓐ Ⓑ Ⓒ Ⓓ

AUTOMOTIVE INFORMATION—SUBTEST 5

1. Ⓐ Ⓑ Ⓒ Ⓓ   4. Ⓐ Ⓑ Ⓒ Ⓓ   7. Ⓐ Ⓑ Ⓒ Ⓓ   10. Ⓐ Ⓑ Ⓒ Ⓓ   13. Ⓐ Ⓑ Ⓒ Ⓓ
2. Ⓐ Ⓑ Ⓒ Ⓓ   5. Ⓐ Ⓑ Ⓒ Ⓓ   8. Ⓐ Ⓑ Ⓒ Ⓓ   11. Ⓐ Ⓑ Ⓒ Ⓓ   14. Ⓐ Ⓑ Ⓒ Ⓓ
3. Ⓐ Ⓑ Ⓒ Ⓓ   6. Ⓐ Ⓑ Ⓒ Ⓓ   9. Ⓐ Ⓑ Ⓒ Ⓓ   12. Ⓐ Ⓑ Ⓒ Ⓓ   15. Ⓐ Ⓑ Ⓒ Ⓓ

MATHEMATICS KNOWLEDGE—SUBTEST 6

1. Ⓐ Ⓑ Ⓒ Ⓓ	6. Ⓐ Ⓑ Ⓒ Ⓓ	11. Ⓐ Ⓑ Ⓒ Ⓓ	16. Ⓐ Ⓑ Ⓒ Ⓓ	21. Ⓐ Ⓑ Ⓒ Ⓓ
2. Ⓐ Ⓑ Ⓒ Ⓓ	7. Ⓐ Ⓑ Ⓒ Ⓓ	12. Ⓐ Ⓑ Ⓒ Ⓓ	17. Ⓐ Ⓑ Ⓒ Ⓓ	22. Ⓐ Ⓑ Ⓒ Ⓓ
3. Ⓐ Ⓑ Ⓒ Ⓓ	8. Ⓐ Ⓑ Ⓒ Ⓓ	13. Ⓐ Ⓑ Ⓒ Ⓓ	18. Ⓐ Ⓑ Ⓒ Ⓓ	23. Ⓐ Ⓑ Ⓒ Ⓓ
4. Ⓐ Ⓑ Ⓒ Ⓓ	9. Ⓐ Ⓑ Ⓒ Ⓓ	14. Ⓐ Ⓑ Ⓒ Ⓓ	19. Ⓐ Ⓑ Ⓒ Ⓓ	24. Ⓐ Ⓑ Ⓒ Ⓓ
5. Ⓐ Ⓑ Ⓒ Ⓓ	10. Ⓐ Ⓑ Ⓒ Ⓓ	15. Ⓐ Ⓑ Ⓒ Ⓓ	20. Ⓐ Ⓑ Ⓒ Ⓓ	25. Ⓐ Ⓑ Ⓒ Ⓓ

MECHANICAL COMPREHENSION—SUBTEST 7

1. Ⓐ Ⓑ Ⓒ Ⓓ	6. Ⓐ Ⓑ Ⓒ Ⓓ	11. Ⓐ Ⓑ Ⓒ Ⓓ	16. Ⓐ Ⓑ Ⓒ Ⓓ	21. Ⓐ Ⓑ Ⓒ Ⓓ
2. Ⓐ Ⓑ Ⓒ Ⓓ	7. Ⓐ Ⓑ Ⓒ Ⓓ	12. Ⓐ Ⓑ Ⓒ Ⓓ	17. Ⓐ Ⓑ Ⓒ Ⓓ	22. Ⓐ Ⓑ Ⓒ Ⓓ
3. Ⓐ Ⓑ Ⓒ Ⓓ	8. Ⓐ Ⓑ Ⓒ Ⓓ	13. Ⓐ Ⓑ Ⓒ Ⓓ	18. Ⓐ Ⓑ Ⓒ Ⓓ	23. Ⓐ Ⓑ Ⓒ Ⓓ
4. Ⓐ Ⓑ Ⓒ Ⓓ	9. Ⓐ Ⓑ Ⓒ Ⓓ	14. Ⓐ Ⓑ Ⓒ Ⓓ	19. Ⓐ Ⓑ Ⓒ Ⓓ	24. Ⓐ Ⓑ Ⓒ Ⓓ
5. Ⓐ Ⓑ Ⓒ Ⓓ	10. Ⓐ Ⓑ Ⓒ Ⓓ	15. Ⓐ Ⓑ Ⓒ Ⓓ	20. Ⓐ Ⓑ Ⓒ Ⓓ	25. Ⓐ Ⓑ Ⓒ Ⓓ

ELECTRONICS INFORMATION—SUBTEST 8

1. Ⓐ Ⓑ Ⓒ Ⓓ	5. Ⓐ Ⓑ Ⓒ Ⓓ	9. Ⓐ Ⓑ Ⓒ Ⓓ	13. Ⓐ Ⓑ Ⓒ Ⓓ	17. Ⓐ Ⓑ Ⓒ Ⓓ
2. Ⓐ Ⓑ Ⓒ Ⓓ	6. Ⓐ Ⓑ Ⓒ Ⓓ	10. Ⓐ Ⓑ Ⓒ Ⓓ	14. Ⓐ Ⓑ Ⓒ Ⓓ	18. Ⓐ Ⓑ Ⓒ Ⓓ
3. Ⓐ Ⓑ Ⓒ Ⓓ	7. Ⓐ Ⓑ Ⓒ Ⓓ	11. Ⓐ Ⓑ Ⓒ Ⓓ	15. Ⓐ Ⓑ Ⓒ Ⓓ	19. Ⓐ Ⓑ Ⓒ Ⓓ
4. Ⓐ Ⓑ Ⓒ Ⓓ	8. Ⓐ Ⓑ Ⓒ Ⓓ	12. Ⓐ Ⓑ Ⓒ Ⓓ	16. Ⓐ Ⓑ Ⓒ Ⓓ	20. Ⓐ Ⓑ Ⓒ Ⓓ

SHOP INFORMATION—SUBTEST 9

1. Ⓐ Ⓑ Ⓒ Ⓓ	4. Ⓐ Ⓑ Ⓒ Ⓓ	7. Ⓐ Ⓑ Ⓒ Ⓓ	10. Ⓐ Ⓑ Ⓒ Ⓓ	13. Ⓐ Ⓑ Ⓒ Ⓓ
2. Ⓐ Ⓑ Ⓒ Ⓓ	5. Ⓐ Ⓑ Ⓒ Ⓓ	8. Ⓐ Ⓑ Ⓒ Ⓓ	11. Ⓐ Ⓑ Ⓒ Ⓓ	14. Ⓐ Ⓑ Ⓒ Ⓓ
3. Ⓐ Ⓑ Ⓒ Ⓓ	6. Ⓐ Ⓑ Ⓒ Ⓓ	9. Ⓐ Ⓑ Ⓒ Ⓓ	12. Ⓐ Ⓑ Ⓒ Ⓓ	15. Ⓐ Ⓑ Ⓒ Ⓓ

ASSEMBLING OBJECTS—SUBTEST 10

1. Ⓐ Ⓑ Ⓒ Ⓓ	5. Ⓐ Ⓑ Ⓒ Ⓓ	9. Ⓐ Ⓑ Ⓒ Ⓓ	13. Ⓐ Ⓑ Ⓒ Ⓓ	17. Ⓐ Ⓑ Ⓒ Ⓓ
2. Ⓐ Ⓑ Ⓒ Ⓓ	6. Ⓐ Ⓑ Ⓒ Ⓓ	10. Ⓐ Ⓑ Ⓒ Ⓓ	14. Ⓐ Ⓑ Ⓒ Ⓓ	18. Ⓐ Ⓑ Ⓒ Ⓓ
3. Ⓐ Ⓑ Ⓒ Ⓓ	7. Ⓐ Ⓑ Ⓒ Ⓓ	11. Ⓐ Ⓑ Ⓒ Ⓓ	15. Ⓐ Ⓑ Ⓒ Ⓓ	19. Ⓐ Ⓑ Ⓒ Ⓓ
4. Ⓐ Ⓑ Ⓒ Ⓓ	8. Ⓐ Ⓑ Ⓒ Ⓓ	12. Ⓐ Ⓑ Ⓒ Ⓓ	16. Ⓐ Ⓑ Ⓒ Ⓓ	20. Ⓐ Ⓑ Ⓒ Ⓓ

CHAPTER
12 Practice Examination Two

GENERAL SCIENCE—SUBTEST 1

DIRECTIONS

This test has questions about science. Pick the best answer for each question, then blacken the space on your separate answer form that has the same number and letter as your choice.

Here is a sample question.

1. The planet nearest to the sun is

A Venus.
B Mars.
C Earth.
D Mercury.

Mercury is the correct answer, so you would blacken the space for D on your answer form.

Your score on this test will be based on the number of questions you answer correctly. You should try to answer every question. Do not spend too much time on any one question.

When you begin, be sure to start with question number 1 in Part 1, and number 1 in Part 1 on your answer form.

THE ACTUAL TEST WILL SAY:

Do not turn this page until told to do so.

General Science

Time: 11 minutes; 25 questions

1. Sound travels fastest through

   A air.
   B steel.
   C water.
   D a vacuum.

2. In order to use seawater onboard ship for boilers, the water must first be

   A distilled.
   B aerated.
   C chlorinated.
   D refined.

3. The most abundant metal in a free state in the earth's crust is

   A nitrogen.
   B aluminum.
   C copper.
   D iron.

4. An object will most effectively absorb the sun's rays if it is

   A polished, and dark in color.
   B polished, and light in color.
   C rough, and light in color.
   D rough, and dark in color.

5. The most effective farming method for returning minerals to the soil is

   A crop rotation.
   B strip farming.
   C contour plowing.
   D furrowing.

6. An example of a lever is

   A a wedge.
   B a crowbar.
   C a saw.
   D an escalator.

7. A lunar eclipse occurs when the

   A earth casts its shadow on the sun.
   B sun casts its shadow on the moon.
   C earth casts its shadow on the moon.
   D moon casts its shadow on the earth.

8. The part of the body that would suffer most from a diet deficient in calcium is the

   A pancreas.
   B stomach.
   C skeleton.
   D skin.

9. Which of the following is found in greatest quantities in automobile exhaust gases?

   A sulfur dioxide
   B sulfur trioxide
   C carbon monoxide
   D water

10. Which common electrical device contains an electric magnet?

    A flatiron
    B lamp
    C telephone
    D toaster

11. In a vacuum, radio waves and visible light waves must have the same

    A intensity.
    B frequency.
    C wavelength.
    D speed.

12. The most accurate description of the earth's atmosphere is that it consists

    A mostly of oxygen, argon, carbon dioxide, and water vapor.
    B entirely of ozone, nitrogen, and water vapor.
    C of a mixture of gases, liquid droplets, and minute solid particles.
    D of gases that cannot be compressed.

13. Object A with a mass of 2 kilograms and object B with a mass of 4 kilograms are dropped simultaneously from rest near the surface of the earth. Neglecting air resistance, at the end of 3 seconds, what is the ratio of the speed of object A to the speed of object B?

    A 1:4
    B 1:2
    C 1:1
    D 2:1

14. In June, a weather station in a New England city reports a falling barometer and southeast winds. The best weather forecast is probably

    A fair and warmer.
    B fair and colder.
    C rain and warmer.
    D rain and colder.

15. Which substance can be removed from water by filtration?

    A sand
    B ink
    C alcohol
    D sugar

16. As a balloon rises, the gas within it

    A solidifies.
    B freezes.
    C condenses.
    D expands.

17. The best estimate of the age of the earth comes from the study of

    A the salt content of the oceans.
    B the thickness of sedimentary rock.
    C radioactive material.
    D the rate of erosion of the land.

18. The presence of coal deposits in Alaska shows that, at one time, Alaska

    A was covered with ice.
    B was connected to Asia.
    C was connected to Europe.
    D had a tropical climate.

19. When an airplane is in flight, the air pressure on the top surface of the wing is

    A less than on the bottom surface.
    B the same as on the bottom surface.
    C slightly more than on the bottom surface.
    D more or less than on the bottom surface, depending on the shape of the wing.

20. In the human eye, which structure is like the film in a camera?

    A pupil
    B retina
    C lens
    D cornea

21. When water is taken apart by electricity, what two substances are formed?

    A carbon and oxygen
    B hydrogen and oxygen
    C oxygen and nitrogen
    D hydrogen and nitrogen

22. Which of the following statements is true for the right side of this equation?

    $$Fe + H_2SO_4 \rightarrow FeSO_4 + H_2$$

    A There are two elements on the right side.
    B There are two compounds on the right side.
    C There are an element and a gas on the right side.
    D There are a compound and an element on the right side.

23. The three elements found most commonly in commercial fertilizers are

    A calcium, phosphorus, iron.
    B phosphorus, nitrogen, sulfur.
    C nitrogen, phosphorus, potassium.
    D magnesium, iron, calcium.

24. Two nonporous rocks seem to lose the same weight when a string is attached to each and they are submerged in water. These two rocks must have the same

A weight in air.
B weight in water.
C volume.
D chemical and physical properties.

25. The thermos bottle is most similar in principle to

A storm windows.
B the freezing unit in an electric refrigerator.
C solar heating systems.
D radiant heaters.

ARITHMETIC REASONING—SUBTEST 2

DIRECTIONS

This test has questions about arithmetic. Each question is followed by four possible answers. Decide which answer is correct. Then, on your answer form, blacken the space that has the same number and letter as your choice. Use scratch paper for any figuring you wish to do.

Here is a sample question.

1. If 10 pounds of sugar cost $2.00, what is the cost of 1 pound?

   A 90 cents
   B 80 cents
   C 50 cents
   D 20 cents

The cost of 1 pound is 20 cents; therefore, the answer D is correct.

Your score on this test will be based on the number of questions you answer correctly. You should try to answer every question. Do not spend too much time on any one question.

Notice that Part 2 begins with question number 1. When you begin, be sure to mark your first answer next to number 1 on your answer form.

THE ACTUAL TEST WILL SAY:

Do not turn this page until told to do so.

Arithmetic Reasoning

Time: 36 minutes; 30 questions

1. You need 8 barrels of water to sprinkle ½ mile of roadway. How many barrels of water do you need to sprinkle 3½ miles of roadway?

   A 7
   B 15
   C 50
   D 56

2. A snapshot 8 inches long and 6 inches wide is to be enlarged so that its length will be 12 inches. How many inches wide will the enlarged snapshot be?

   A 8
   B 6
   C 9
   D 10

3. Lee Robinson has an ordinary life insurance policy with a face value of $10,000. At her age, the annual premium is $24.00 per $1,000. What is the total premium paid for this policy every 6 months?

   A $100
   B $120
   C $240
   D $400

4. If 2 pounds of cottage cheese cost $3.20, what is the cost of a 3-ounce portion of cottage cheese?

   A $0.30
   B $0.20
   C $0.25
   D $0.15

5. Mr. Green drove for 12 hours at a speed of 55 miles per hour. If his car covered 22 miles for each gallon of gas used, how many gallons of gas did he use?

A 32 gallons
B 34 gallons
C 36 gallons
D 30 gallons

6. Matty Smith earns $7.50 per hour. If he works from 8:45 A.M. until 5:15 P.M., with one hour off for lunch, how much does he earn in one day?

A $58.50
B $56.25
C $55.00
D $53.75

7. If 5 shirts and 3 ties cost $52 and each tie costs $4, what is the cost of a shirt?

A $6
B $8
C $10
D $7.50

8. What is the fifth term in the series: 5; 2; 9; 6; _____?

A 16
B 15
C 14
D 13

9. In a theater audience of 500 people, 80% were adults. How many children were in the audience?

A 20
B 50
C 100
D 125

10. A table usually sells for $240, but because it is slightly shopworn, the store manager lets it go for $210. What is the percentage of reduction?

A 12½%
B 14⅞%
C 16⅔ %
D 18¾%

11. Mr. and Mrs. Turner bought a home for $55,000. It was assessed at 80% of the purchase price. If the real estate tax was $4.74 per $100, how much realty tax did the Turners pay?

A $2,085.60
B $1,985.60
C $2,607.00
D $285.60

12. A scale on a map is 1 inch to 50 miles. On the map, two cities are 2½ inches apart. What is the actual distance between the two cities?

A 75 miles
B 100 miles
C 225 miles
D 125 miles

13. A shipment of 2,200 pounds of fertilizer is packed in 40-ounce bags. How many bags are needed for the shipment?

A 800
B 880
C 780
D 640

14. A television set priced at $400 was reduced 25% during a weekend sale. In addition, there was a 10% discount for paying cash. What was the cash price of the set during the sale?

A $130
B $260
C $270
D $320

15. In a store four clerks each receive $255.00 per week, while two part-timers each earn $120.00. What is the average weekly salary paid these six workers?

   A $200.00
   B $210.00
   C $187.50
   D $190.00

16. The perimeter of a rectangle is 40 feet. If the length is 15 feet, 6 inches, what is the width of the rectangle?

   A 4 feet, 6 inches
   B 9 feet, 6 inches
   C 5 feet, 6 inches
   D 5 feet

17. What is the result of dividing 0.675 by 0.9?

   A 7.5
   B 0.075
   C 75
   D 0.75

18. Two planes leave the same airport traveling in opposite directions. One is flying at the rate of 340 miles per hour, the other at 260 miles per hour. In how many hours will the two planes be 3,000 miles apart?

   A 5
   B 4
   C 6
   D 10

19. What is the cost of 5 feet, 3 inches of plastic slipcover material that sells for $8.00 per foot?

   A $14.00
   B $42.00
   C $23.00
   D $21.12

20. If 1 gallon of milk costs $3.84, what is the cost of 3 pints?

   A $1.44
   B $2.82
   C $2.04
   D $1.96

21. A man left $72,000 to his wife and son. The ratio of the wife's share to the son's share was 5:3. How much did his wife receive?

   A $27,000
   B $14,000
   C $45,000
   D $54,000

22. A recipe calls for 2½ ounces of chocolate and ½ cup of corn syrup. If only 2 ounces of chocolate are available, how much corn syrup should be used?

   A ½ cup
   B ⅓ cup
   C ⅖ cup
   D ³⁄₁₀ cup

23. A ship sails x miles the first day, y miles the second day, and z miles the third day. What was the average distance covered per day?

   A $\dfrac{xyz}{3}$

   B $\dfrac{x+y+z}{3}$

   C $3xyz$
   D none of these

24. A man invests $6,000 at 5% annual interest. How much more must he invest at 6% annual interest so that his annual income from both investments is $900?

   A $3,000
   B $5,000
   C $8,000
   D $10,000

25. Which of these is an example of similar figures?

   A a plane and a scale model of that plane
   B a pen and a pencil
   C a motorcycle and a car
   D an equilateral triangle and a right triangle

26. Find the numerical value of $5a^2b - 3ab^2$ if $a = 7$ and $b = 4$.

   A 846
   B 644
   C 488
   D 224

27. If the circumference of a circle is divided by the length of its diameter, what is the result?

   A 2
   B 27
   C π
   D 7

28. A businesswoman spends ⅕ of her income for rent, and ⅜ of the remainder of her income for salaries. What part of her income does she spend for salaries?

   A 23/40
   B 3/10
   C 1/2
   D 3/4

29. Using the following formula, find the value of C when $F = 50$.

$$C = \frac{5}{9}(F - 32)$$

   A 10
   B 18
   C 90
   D 40

30. What is the average of these temperature readings, taken on a cold day last winter?

6:00 A.M.	−12 degrees
7:00 A.M.	−7 degrees
8:00 A.M.	−2 degrees
9:00 A.M.	0 degrees
10:00 A.M.	+6 degrees

   A 0 degrees
   B 2 degrees
   C −1 degree
   D −3 degrees

WORD KNOWLEDGE—SUBTEST 3

DIRECTIONS

This test has questions about the meanings of words. Each question has an **underlined bold-face word**. You are to decide which one of the four words in the choices most nearly means the same as the underlined boldface word and then mark the space on your answer form that has the same number and letter as your choice.

Now look at the sample question below.

1. It was a **small** table.

    A sturdy
    B round
    C cheap
    D little

The question asks which of the four words means the same as the boldface word, **small**. Little means the same as **small**. Answer D is the best one.

Your score on this test will be based on the number of questions you answer correctly. You should try to answer every question. Do not spend too much time on any one question.

When you begin, be sure to start with question number 1 in Part 3 of your test booklet and number 1 in Part 3 on your answer form.

THE ACTUAL TEST WILL SAY:

Do not turn this page until told to do so.

Word Knowledge

Time: 11 minutes; 35 questions

1. Opulence most nearly means

    A affluence.
    B generosity.
    C poverty.
    D luxury.

2. Mimesis most nearly means

    A impersonation.
    B pretense.
    C cartoon.
    D imitation.

3. Her **languid** appearance was revealing.

    A sad
    B energetic
    C healthy
    D listless

4. Inherent most nearly means

    A essential.
    B intrinsic.
    C accidental.
    D necessity.

5. Anomie most nearly means

    A essential.
    B vacuum.
    C control.
    D anonym.

6. Tenuous most nearly means

    A tensile.
    B tentative.
    C ethereal.
    D substantial.

7. Most letters require a **salutation**.

   A offering
   B greeting
   C discussion
   D appeasement

8. **Mesmerize** most nearly means

   A hypnotize.
   B hypostatize.
   C metabolize.
   D change.

9. A **panoply** of flowers covered the shelf.

   A pansophy
   B display
   C resistance
   D parry

10. **Syntactic** most nearly means

    A morphological.
    B grammatical.
    C standard.
    D inflexional.

11. **Umbrage** most nearly means

    A resentment.
    B umbo.
    C impertinence.
    D pleasure.

12. **Raucous** most nearly means

    A ravenous.
    B harsh.
    C pleasing.
    D rankling.

13. **Prosecution** most nearly means

    A protection.
    B imprisonment.
    C trial.
    D punishment.

14. The **miasma** of modern cities causes discomfort.

    A pollution
    B fumes
    C exhalations
    D stench

15. **Paragon** most nearly means

    A paradox.
    B model.
    C prototype.
    D ideal.

16. She has **innate** talent.

    A eternal
    B well-developed
    C temporary
    D native

17. **Urbanity** most nearly means

    A loyalty.
    B refinement.
    C weakness.
    D barbarism.

18. We all **encounter** difficulties.

    A recall
    B overcome
    C retreat from
    D meet

19. **Banal** most nearly means

    A commonplace.
    B forceful.
    C tranquil.
    D indifferent.

20. **Small** most nearly means

    A sturdy.
    B round.
    C cheap.
    D little.

21. The accountant **discovered** an error.

A searched
B found
C enlarged
D entered

22. You must **inform** us.

A ask
B turn
C tell
D ignore

23. The wind is **variable** today.

A shifting
B chilling
C steady
D mild

24. **Cease** most nearly means

A start.
B change.
C continue.
D stop.

25. Drinking can **impair** your judgment.

A direct
B improve
C weaken
D stimulate

26. We knew the **rudiments** of the program.

A basic methods and procedures
B politics
C promotion opportunities
D minute details

27. **Imprudent** most nearly means

A reckless.
B unexcitable.
C poor.
D domineering.

28. **Dissension** stimulated the discussion.

A friction
B analysis
C injury
D slyness

29. **Disconnect** most nearly means

A separate.
B cripple.
C lesson.
D dismiss.

30. **Rudimentary** most nearly means

A discourteous.
B brutal.
C displeasing.
D elementary.

31. The commission made **autonomous** decisions.

A self-improvement
B self-educated
C self-explanatory
D self-governing

32. **Meander** most nearly means

A grumble.
B wander aimlessly.
C come between.
D weigh carefully.

33. **Destitution** most nearly means

A fate.
B lack of practice.
C extreme poverty.
D recovery.

34. Do not **malign** his name.

A slander
B prophesy
C entreat
D praise

35. **Impotent** most nearly means

A unwise.
B lacking strength.
C free of sin.
D commanding.

PARAGRAPH COMPREHENSION—SUBTEST 4

DIRECTIONS

This test is a test of your ability to understand what you read. In this section you will find one or more paragraphs of reading material followed by incomplete statements or questions. You are to read the paragraph and select one of four lettered choices that best completes the statement or answers the question. When you have selected your answer, blacken in the correct numbered letter on your answer sheet.

Now look at the sample question below.

In certain areas water is so scarce that every attempt is made to conserve it. For instance, for one oasis in the Sahara Desert the amount of water necessary for each date palm tree has been carefully determined.

1. How much water is each tree given?

    A no water at all
    B exactly the amount required
    C water only if it is healthy
    D water on alternate days

The amount of water each tree requires has been carefully determined, so the answer B is correct.

Your score on this sheet will be based on the number of questions you answer correctly. You should try to answer every question. Do not spend too much time on any one question.

When you begin, be sure to start with question number 1 in Part 4 of your test booklet and number 1 in Part 4 on your answer form.

THE ACTUAL TEST WILL SAY:

Do not turn this page until told to do so.

Paragraph Comprehension

Time: 13 minutes; 15 questions

1. The duty of a lighthouse keeper is to keep the light burning no matter what happens, so that ships will be warned of the presence of dangerous rocks. If a shipwreck should occur near the lighthouse, even though he would like to aid in the rescue of its crew and passengers, the lighthouse keeper must

    A stay at his light.
    B rush to their aid.
    C turn out the light.
    D quickly sound the siren.

2. In certain areas water is so scarce that every attempt is made to conserve it. For instance, for one oasis in the Sahara Desert the amount of water necessary for each date palm tree has been carefully determined.

How much water is each tree given?

    A no water at all
    B exactly the amount required
    C water only if it is healthy
    D water on alternate days

3. Plants should be gradually "hardened," or toughened for 2 weeks before being moved outdoors. This is done by withholding water and lowering the temperature. Hardening slows down the plants' rate of growth to prepare them to withstand such conditions as chilling, drying winds, or high temperatures.

You toughen a seedling

A by putting it in a cooler environment.
B by putting it in a 6-inch pot.
C by watering it thoroughly.
D by using ready-made peat pellets.

4. At depths of several miles inside the earth, the weight of rocks causes great pressure. This rock pressure, as well as other forces, sometimes causes rocks to break and slip. Faults (great cracks) form. When slippage occurs, shock waves are felt and can be detected with seismographs thousands of miles away.

The most frequent cause of major earthquakes is

A faulting.
B folding.
C landslides.
D submarine currents.

5. A leaf can catch sunlight and turn this energy into food which is stored in a tree or plant. To run this factory the leaf must have air, water, and sunlight. By a chemical process called *photosynthesis,* the leaf combines the air and water with the energy of the sun.

The process of *photosynthesis*

A combines air, water, and sun to make food.
B makes leaves grow in fancy shapes.
C causes water to form in clouds.
D is a physical process.

6. Most telephone sales are made by reputable persons who try to sell in an honest manner. These persons use the telephone as an aid to business, and they know success depends on being fair and reasonable. The opposite of reputable salesmen are overaggressive talkers who try to force you to make up your mind quickly.

The word *reputable* is closest in meaning to

A reasonable.
B trusted.
C friendly.
D aggressive.

7. When someone in your family suffers a minor burn, reach for an ice cube fast. Place it directly over the burn until the sting is gone when the cube is removed. Ice is great first aid for burns and kills the pain. Afterward you'll be amazed to discover there is very little swelling, blisters probably won't appear, and healing will be much faster.

The topic sentence or key idea in this paragraph is that

A ice prevents burn blisters.
B ice cubes remove the pain.
C ice is great first aid for burns.
D ice reduces swelling.

8. A stranger meets you and shows you some cash he has just "found." He wants to divide it with you. He says that you must show your "good faith" and put up some of your own money. When you agree to give him your money, the stranger finds some reason to leave for a while. Do you see him again? Not likely; you have just been cheated or swindled.

The main theme of this passage is

A do not speak to strangers.
B be careful of "get-rich-quick" plans.
C how to make money.
D do not believe strangers.

9. Statistically, by far the most common types of home accidents are falls. Each year over 15,000 Americans meet death in this way, within the four walls of their homes or in yards around their houses. Nine out of 10 of the victims are over 65, but people of all ages experience serious injuries as a result of home falls.

Falls most frequently result in death for

A children.
B adults under 35.
C all age groups.
D adults older than 65.

10. "Gray water" is slightly used water—the water you have collected at the bottom of the tub after you have showered or the rinse water from the washing machine. It is still useful, and we cannot afford to let it go down the drain.

Which of the following is an example of gray water?

A carbonated water
B rainwater
C soapy water
D tap water

11. Glaciers are frozen masses of snow and ice. As the weight of the snow increases each year, the lower layers become hard-packed like ice. The weight also causes the glacier to move slowly downhill. Speeds of glaciers are usually figured in inches per day rather than miles per hour.

A glacier moves as a result of its

A speed.
B weight.
C temperature.
D layers.

12. It is time to get this country moving again. No American wants to stand by and see this country go the other way. The men who have been elected are no longer in touch. A fresh point of view, new ideas, and more action are needed. The voters should finally wake up and give power to those who will make changes.

This passage tries to make you believe that

A changes are needed.
B no changes are needed.
C changes will never happen.
D no action is needed.

13. Up until a few years ago most parents, teachers, baby doctors, and coaches felt that right was right. There was even an old wives' tale that left-handed people did not learn as well. But, I'm happy to report, this right-thinking is gone. Today parents and teachers understand left-handedness, and our number is rising.

The main idea of this passage is that the feelings about left-handedness

A have not changed at all.
B have completely changed.
C have partly changed.
D will not change.

14. According to Newton's Third Law, to each action there is an equal and opposite reaction. You can illustrate the principle by blowing up a rubber balloon and then allowing the air to escape. Notice that the balloon moves forward as the air escapes in the opposite direction.

Which of the following describes Newton's Third Law?

A an object at rest
B gravitational force
C falling bodies
D action equals reaction

15. Water is a good conductor of sound waves. If you were swimming underwater while someone struck two rocks together underwater 10 feet away, you would be surprised at how loud the sound was. The U.S. Navy makes use of this knowledge in detecting enemy submarines.

Of the following, which is the best restatement of the main idea?

A Fish cannot hear ordinary sounds.
B Sound waves become compressed in very deep water.
C Water is a good conductor of sound waves.
D Submarines cannot detect sound waves.

AUTOMOTIVE INFORMATION—SUBTEST 5

DIRECTIONS

This test has questions about automobiles. Pick the best answer for each question, then blacken the space on your separate answer form that has the same number and letter as your choice.
Here is a sample question.

1. The most commonly used fuel for running automobile engines is

    A kerosene.
    B benzene.
    C crude oil.
    D gasoline.

Gasoline is the most commonly used fuel, so D is the correct answer.
Your score on this test will be based on the number of questions you answer correctly. You should try to answer every question. Do not spend too much time on any one question.

When you are told to begin, be sure to start with question number 1 in Part 5 of your test booklet and number 1 in Part 5 on your separate answer form.

THE ACTUAL TEST WILL SAY:

Do not turn this page until told to do so.

Automotive Information

Time: 8 minutes; 15 questions

1. Which is the right side of an engine?

    A the right side when you stand in front and look at the engine
    B the side that the distributor is on
    C depends on the manufacturer
    D the right side when you stand in the back and look at the engine

2. The letter and numbers G 78-14, printed on a tire, refer to

    A load, width, diameter.
    B diameter and air pressure.
    C cubic inch displacement.
    D price code.

3. "Tracking," in terms of front-end alignment, means that

    A each wheel travels independently of the other.
    B the wheels follow well on ice or in snow.
    C the front tires leave stronger tracks than the rear tires.
    D the rear wheels follow the front wheels correctly.

4. A car with worn-out shock absorbers

    A cannot carry a heavy load.
    B will bounce a lot on a rough road.
    C sags very low to the ground.
    D will have no traction on a wet road.

5. In a three-speed transmission, the cluster gear is supported by the

    A pinion shaft.
    B countershaft.
    C main shaft.
    D output shaft.

6. A clutch release bearing

A rotates whenever the engine is turning.
B rotates when only the clutch is engaged.
C rotates whenever the clutch pedal is depressed.
D holds the clutch shaft in alignment.

7. The general procedure to follow when adjusting a band on an automatic transmission is to

A loosen, tighten to a specified torque, loosen a specified number of turns, and lock.
B tighten to a specified torque with a torque wrench and lock.
C tighten to a specified torque, loosen 5 turns, and lock.
D loosen, tighten to a specified torque, and lock.

8. The purpose of the drive shaft is to connect the

A piston to the transmission.
B differential to the transmission.
C flywheel to the crankshaft.
D camshaft to the crankshaft.

9. The order in which the spark plugs in the engine fire is established by the order in which the

A plugs are mounted in the engine.
B plug leads are connected to the distributor cap.
C condenser is connected.
D contact points are opened.

10. The terminals exposed on the ignition induction coil are

A two secondary and one primary.
B one secondary and one primary.
C one secondary and two primary.
D two secondary and two primary.

11. Battery electrolyte is a mixture of distilled water and

A baking soda.
B sulfuric acid.
C lead peroxide.
D carbon particles.

12. The brushes in an alternator ride on

A the commutator.
B the stator.
C slip rings.
D the heat sink.

13. When all other lights show normal illumination but one headlight is dim, it is a good indication that the

A battery is weak.
B headlight switch is defective.
C headlight unit needs adjustment.
D headlight has a poor ground connection.

14. Should air get into the hydraulic brake system,

A brake application will be hard.
B it will have no effect.
C brake pedal action will be spongy.
D the brake pedal will stick.

15. The proportioning valve in a hydraulic brake system

A reduces pressure to the front brakes.
B controls the brake warning switch.
C is used only on a drum-type brake system.
D reduces pressure to the rear brakes.

MATHEMATICS KNOWLEDGE—SUBTEST 6

DIRECTIONS

This is a test of your ability to solve general mathematical problems. Each problem is followed by four answer choices. Select the correct response from the choices given. Then mark the space on your answer form that has the same number and letter as your choice. Use scratch paper to do any figuring that you wish.

Now look at this sample problem.

1. If $x + 8 = 9$, then x is equal to

A 0.
B 1.
C –1.
D 9/8.

The correct answer is 1, so B is the correct response.

Your score on this test will be based on the number of questions you answer correctly. You should try to answer every question. Do not spend too much time on any one question.

Start with question number 1 in Part 6. Mark your answer for this question next to number 1, Part 6, on your answer form.

THE ACTUAL TEST WILL SAY:

Do not turn this page until told to do so.

Mathematics Knowledge

Time: 24 minutes; 25 questions

1. If $b - 3 = 7$, then b is equal to

A 10.
B 4.
C 21.
D 8.

2. What is the product of $(z + 2)(2z - 3)$?

A $3z - 6$
B $z + 4z - 3$
C $z^2 + 4z - 6$
D $2z^2 + z - 6$

3. Smith Township has a public pool in the shape of a quadrilateral. If the town wants to put a lifeguard on each side of the pool, how many lifeguards are needed?

A eight
B six
C four
D three

4. If the largest possible circular tabletop is cut from a square whose side is 2 feet, how much wood is wasted? (Use 3.14 for π.)

A 1 square foot
B 1.86 square feet
C 5.86 square feet
D 0.86 square feet

5. Solve for x: $3x + 2 = -13$.

   A $x = 13$
   B $x = -4\frac{1}{3}$
   C $x = 8$
   D $x = -5$

6. An artist sold 4 of his paintings. These represented 0.05 of all the artwork he had done. How many paintings had he made?

   A 100
   B 80
   C 50
   D 20

7. One of the equal angles of an isosceles triangle is 40 degrees. What is the angle opposite the unequal side?

   A 40 degrees
   B 90 degrees
   C 100 degrees
   D 140 degrees

8. If you divide $24x^3 + 16x^2 - 8x$ by $8x$, how many x's will be there in the quotient?

   A 0
   B 5
   C 2
   D −1

9. A room is 19 feet long, 10 feet wide, and 8 feet high. If you want to paint the walls and ceiling, how many square feet of surface will you have to cover with paint?

   A 232 square feet
   B 422 square feet
   C 464 square feet
   D 654 square feet

10. If a car traveled 200 miles at an average rate of speed of r miles per hour, the time it took for the trip could be written as

    A 200/r
    B r/200
    C 200r
    D r/60

11. An equilateral triangle has the same perimeter as a square whose side is 12 inches. What is the length of a side of the triangle?

    A 9 inches
    B 12 inches
    C 18 inches
    D 16 inches

12. What is the value of $(0.1)^3$?

    A 0.3
    B 0.003
    C 0.1
    D 0.001

13. How many inches are contained in f feet and i inches?

    A $f \times i$
    B $f + i$
    C $f + 12i$
    D $12f + i$

14. A good rule of thumb is that a house should cost no more than 2½ times its owner's income. How much should you be earning to afford a $64,000 home?

    A $20,500
    B $25,000
    C $32,000
    D $160,000

15. What is the value of $(+2)(-5)(+3)(-3)$?

    A +90
    B +60
    C −13
    D −3

16. Solve for x: $x^2 = 3x + 10$.

   A $x = 3; x = 10$
   B $x = -3; x = -10$
   C $x = -2; x = 5$
   D $x = 2; x = -5$

17. Which of these is a cylinder?

   A a stick of butter
   B an orange
   C compact disc
   D a frozen-juice can

18. Solve the following formula for R.

$$N = \frac{CR}{C+R}$$

   A $R = \dfrac{C}{C+N}$

   B $R = \dfrac{NC}{C-N}$

   C $R = \dfrac{N}{C-R}$

   D $R = \dfrac{C-N}{R}$

19. What is the reciprocal of 5/3?

   A 0.6
   B 1⅔
   C 2
   D 1

20. What is the value of $(\sqrt{13})^2$?

   A 26
   B 13
   C 87
   D 169

21. Mr. Larson drove his car steadily at 40 miles per hour for 120 miles. He then increased his speed and drove the next 120 miles at 60 miles per hour. What was his average speed?

   A 48 miles per hour
   B 52 miles per hour
   C 50 miles per hour
   D 46 miles per hour

22. An architect designs two walls of a museum to meet at an angle of 120 degrees. What is an angle of this size called?

   A acute
   B obtuse
   C right
   D straight

23. Solve the following equations for x.

$$5x + 4y = 27$$
$$x - 2y = 11$$

   A $x = 3$
   B $x = 9$
   C $x = 4.5$
   D $x = 7$

24. If a is a negative number, and ab is a positive number, then which of the following must be true?

   A b is positive.
   B a is greater than b.
   C b is negative.
   D b is greater than a.

25. Solve the following inequality.

$$x + 5 > 7$$

   A $x = 2$
   B $x > 2$
   C $x - 7 > 5$
   D $x - 5 > 7$

MECHANICAL COMPREHENSION—SUBTEST 7

DIRECTIONS

This test has questions about general mechanical and physical principles. Pick the best answer for each question, then blacken the space on your separate answer form that has the same number and letter as your choice.

Here is a sample question.

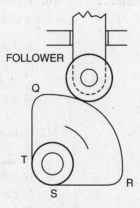

1. The follower is at its highest position between points

A Q and R.
B R and S.
C S and T.
D T and Q.

The correct answer is between *Q* and *R*, so you would blacken the space for A on your answer form.

Your score on this test will be based on the number of questions you answer correctly. You should try to answer every question. Do not spend too much time on any one question.

When you are told to begin, be sure to start with question number 1 in Part 7 of your test booklet and number 1 in Part 7 of your answer form.

THE ACTUAL TEST WILL SAY:

Do not turn this page until told to do so.

Mechanical Comprehension

Time: 19 minutes; 25 questions

1. Cap screws are ordered by

A wrench size.
B diameter and wrench size.
C diameter and number of threads.
D wrench size and kind of threads.

2. A round piece of stock having a different type of thread at each end is called a

A head bolt.
B stud.
C screw.
D cap screw.

3. The measurement across the flats of a cap screw head determines the

A wrench size.
B bolt size.
C thread size.
D diameter.

4. Ring and pinion backlash is checked with

A a micrometer.
B a round feeler gauge.
C Prussian blue.
D a dial indicator.

5. The clutch aligning arbor is used to align the clutch disc to the

A transmission.
B pilot bearing.
C pressure plate.
D main drive gear.

6. An oscilloscope is used to diagnose problems in which automotive system?

A charging
B starting
C fuel
D ignition

7. Which tool is used to adjust the preload on a front wheel bearing?

A pliers
B torque wrench
C dial indicator
D bearing cup driver

8. Which device measures electrical resistance?

A an ammeter
B a voltmeter
C an ohmmeter
D a hydrometer

9. The tool used to tighten a cylinder head bolt is a

A box wrench.
B breaker bar.
C ratchet.
D torque wrench.

10. The strength of the antifreeze solution is tested with a

A thermometer.
B thermostat.
C voltmeter.
D hydrometer.

11. Helical gears have

A slanted teeth.
B straight teeth.
C curved teeth.
D beveled teeth.

12. A gear train that uses a sun gear, internal gear, and three pinion gears is known as

A bevel spiral pinion.
B worm and sector.
C planetary gears.
D differential gears.

13. Reciprocating motion is changed into rotary motion by which one of the following engine parts?

A camshaft
B connecting rod bearings
C pistons
D crankshaft

14. Moisture forming on the inner surface of a windshield on a cold day is an example of

A vaporization.
B evaporation.
C distillation.
D condensation.

15. Which of the following statements concerning the poles of a magnet is correct?

A South repels north.
B Like poles attract.
C North attracts north.
D Unlike poles attract.

16. Torque means

A number of cylinders.
B turning effort.
C ratio of drive shaft to rear axle.
D drive shaft.

17. Water in an automobile engine may cause damage in cold weather because

A ice is a poor conductor of heat.
B water expands as it freezes.
C cold water is compressible.
D ice is denser than water.

18. What is the rear axle ratio in a standard differential with 11 teeth on the pinion gear and 43 teeth on the ring gear?

A 4.10 to 1
B 3.90 to 1
C 3.73 to 1
D 3.54 to 1

19. Gear B is intended to mesh with

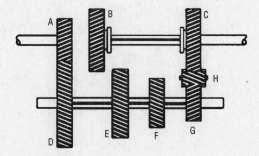

A gear A only.
B gear D only.
C gear E only.
D all of the above gears.

20. As cam A makes one complete turn, the setscrew hits the contact point

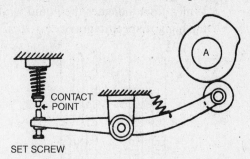

A once.
B twice.
C three times.
D not at all.

21. If gear A makes 14 revolutions, gear B will make

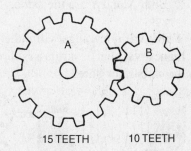

15 TEETH   10 TEETH

A 21.
B 17.
C 14.
D 9.

22. Which of the other gears is moving in the same direction as gear 2?

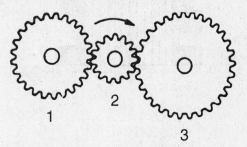

A gear 1
B gear 3
C neither of the other gears
D both of the other gears

23. Floats X and Y are measuring the specific gravity of two different liquids. Which float indicates the liquid with the highest specific gravity?

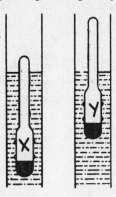

A Y
B X
C neither X nor Y
D Both X and Y are the same.

24. Which vacuum gauge will indicate the highest vacuum as air passes through the carburetor bore?

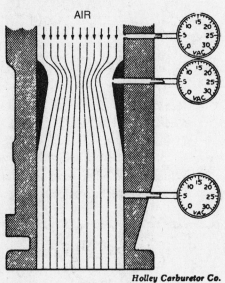

Holley Carburetor Co.

A X
B Y
C Z
D X and Z

25. The wheel barrel is an example of a

A first-class lever.
B second-class lever.
C third-class lever.
D first- and third-class lever.

ELECTRONICS INFORMATION—SUBTEST 8

DIRECTIONS

This is a test of your knowledge of electrical, radio, and electronics information. You are to select the correct response from the choices given. Then mark the space on your answer form that has the same number and letter as your choice.

Now look at the sample question below.

1. What does the abbreviation AC stand for?

A additional charge
B alternating coil
C alternating current
D ampere current

The correct answer is alternating current, so C is the correct response.

Your score on this test will be based on the number of questions you answer correctly. You should try to answer every question. Do not spend too much time on any one question.

When you are told to begin, be sure to start with question number 1 in Part 8 of your test booklet and number 1 in Part 8 of your answer form.

THE ACTUAL TEST WILL SAY:

Do not turn this page until told to do so.

Electronics Information

Time: 8 minutes; 20 questions

1. A 9-volt transistor contains how many cells?

   A one
   B four
   C six
   D nine

2. Compared to a number 12 wire, a number 22 wire is

   A longer.
   B shorter.
   C larger in diameter.
   D smaller in diameter.

3. A resistor marked "1.5K Ω" has a value of

   A 1.5 ohms
   B 105 ohms.
   C 1,500 ohms.
   D 1,500 watts.

4. An equivalent term for electromotive force is

   A voltage.
   B current.
   C resistance.
   D reactance.

5. The property of a circuit that opposes any change in voltage is

   A conductance.
   B capacitance.
   C resistance.
   D inductance.

6. The composition of 60/40 rosin core solder is

   A 60% lead, 40% tin.
   B 60% tin, 40% lead.
   C 60% silver, 40% rosin.
   D 60% lead, 40% silver.

7. A hair dryer is rated at 1,200 watts. Assuming it is operated at 120 volts, how much current will this appliance draw?

A 10 amps
B 100 amps
C 1,000 amps
D 144,000 amps

8. Another term for cycles per second is

A hertz.
B henry.
C kilo.
D mega.

9. A crystal microphone is an example of what electrical phenomenon?

A thermoionic emission
B piezoelectric effect
C inductance
D hysteresis

10. The process of transmitting voice by varying the height of a carrier wave is known as

A frequency modulation.
B amplitude modulation.
C demodulation.
D detection.

11. The primary of a transformer is connected to 120 volts. The voltage across the secondary is 40 volts. This transformer has a turns ratio of

A 1:1.
B 1:4.
C 1:3.
D 3:1.

12. A carbon resistor marked with the color bands of red, red, red, gold is of what value and tolerance?

A 2,000 ohms ± 5%
B 222 ohms ± 5%
C 2,200 ohms ± 5%
D 6 ohms ± 5%

13. Which is the correct schematic symbol of a tetrode tube?

A

B

C

D

14. What is the total resistance in this circuit if all resistors are 500 ohms?

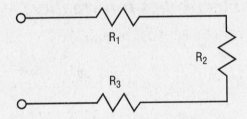

A 1,500 watts
B 1,500 ohms
C 1.5 ohms
D 500 ohms

15.

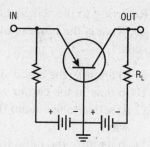

The above schematic represents which transistor configuration?

A common gate
B common collector
C common base
D common emitter

16. Which choice correctly identifies the waveform pictured?

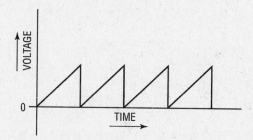

A sine wave
B square wave
C sawtooth wave
D pure DC

17. Of the choices illustrated, which is the correct schematic symbol for a potentiometer?

A

B

C

D

18. A component on a parts list has the following specifications, "1µF, 50 wvdc." The component specified is a

A potentiometer.
B coil.
C transistor.
D capacitor.

19.

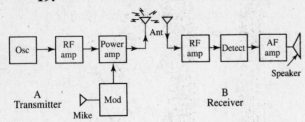

A
Transmitter

Mike

B
Receiver

The illustration is a block diagram of a transmitter and receiver. What is the purpose of the oscillator?

A to generate a radio frequency
B to produce a carrier wave for the intelligence
C to produce a high-frequency current
D all of the above choices

20. Referring to the schematic in question 19, what is the purpose of the detector stage?

A to amplify the audio signal
B to tune in the carrier wave
C to separate the audio from the radio wave
D to amplify the radio frequency

SHOP INFORMATION—SUBTEST 9

DIRECTIONS

This test has questions about your knowledge of tools, as well as common shop terminology and practices. Pick the best answer for each question, then blacken the space on the answer form that has the same number and letter as your choice.

Here is a sample question.

1. A hammer is most commonly used for driving

   A nails.
   B Miss Daisy.
   C nine irons.
   D to Las Vegas.

A hammer is most commonly to drive nails, so A is the correct answer.

Your score on this test will be based on the number of questions you answer correctly. You should try to answer every question. Do not spend too much time on any one question.

When you are told to begin, be sure to start with question number 1 in Part 9 of your test booklet and number 1 in Part 9 on your separate answer form.

THE ACTUAL TEST WILL SAY:

Do not turn this page until told to do so.

Shop Information

Time: 8 minutes; 15 questions

1. A coping saw blade is placed in the saw

   A with the teeth pointing upward.
   B with the teeth pointing toward the handle.
   C so it cuts with the wood grain.
   D so it cuts across the wood grain.

2. Carpenters use

   A ball peen hammers.
   B chisel point hammers.
   C claw hammers.
   D planishing hammers.

3. The term *penny* is used

   A to designate the cost of a nail.
   B to designate the size of a nail.
   C to indicate a rosin-coated nail.
   D to indicate a galvanized nail.

4. A tool used to cut sheet metal is a

   A bar folder.
   B box and pan brake.
   C slip roll.
   D squaring shear.

5. One of the most common ways to fasten sheet metal today is to

   A solder it.
   B braze it.
   C spot-weld it.
   D glue it.

6. A welding torch can also be used as a

   A light source.
   B burning tool.
   C cutting torch.
   D pipe wrench.

7. Tubing cutters are smaller versions of

A pipe cutters.
B ring cutters.
C hole cutters.
D glass cutters.

8. If you "overwork" concrete, it will cause

A loss of a smooth surface.
B separation and create a less durable surface.
C loss of strength throughout the slab.
D puddles in the middle of the slab.

9. Concrete reaches 98% of its strength in

A 3 days.
B 50 days.
C 28 days.
D 10 days.

10. Deciduous trees produce

A softwood.
B deadwood.
C hardwood.
D conifers.

11. The combination square is used to lay out angles of what measurement?

A 90 and 180 degreees
B 45 and 90 degrees
C 45, 90, and 135 degrees
D π and 2π

12. Most bolts have what shape head?

A round
B hexagonal
C square
D octagonal

13. Self-locking nuts are designed to

A be tightened by hand.
B be frequently disassembled.
C require periodic tightening.
D jam against the bolt thread and not vibrate loose.

14. Wood floats in water because

A of its hollow cell structure.
B it weighs 1.5 times as much as an equal volume of water.
C its cells are nonporous.
D it has short, compact cells with air in between them.

15. Flat washers may be used to

A prevent the bolt and nut from loosening.
B exert force between the bolted connection and the workpiece.
C compensate for an oversized hole.
D connect thin-gauge metal parts.

ASSEMBLING OBJECTS—SUBTEST 10

DIRECTIONS

This test measures your ability to picture how an object will look when its parts are mentally put together. Each question will show you several separate shapes; you will then pick the choice that best represents how the pieces would look if they were all fitted together correctly. There is only one best answer for each shape. Pick the best answer for each question, then blacken the space on the answer form that has the same number and letter as your choice.

Here is a sample question.

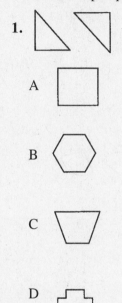

1.

A

B

C

D

Choice A is the shape that will result when the two initial shapes are assembled correctly.

Your score on this test will be based on the number of questions you answer correctly. You should try to answer every question. Do not spend too much time on any one question.

When you are told to begin, be sure to start with question number 1 in Part 10 of your test booklet and number 1 in Part 10 on your separate answer form.

THE ACTUAL TEST WILL SAY:

Do not turn this page until told to do so.

Assembling Objects

Time: 20 minutes; 20 questions

1.

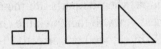

A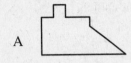

B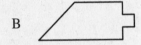

C

D

2.

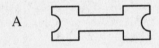

A

B

C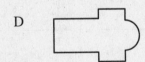

D

3.

A

B

C

D

4.

A

B

C

D

5.

A

B

C

D

6.

A

B

C

D

7.

A

B

C

D

8.

A

B

C

D

9.

A

B

C

D

10.

11.

12.

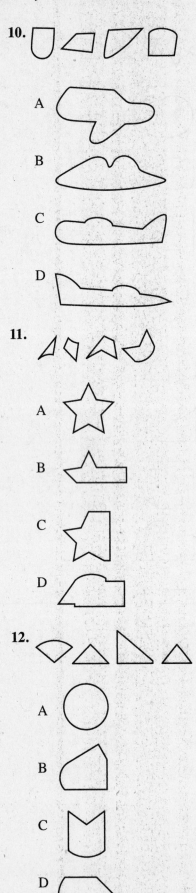

13.

14.

15.

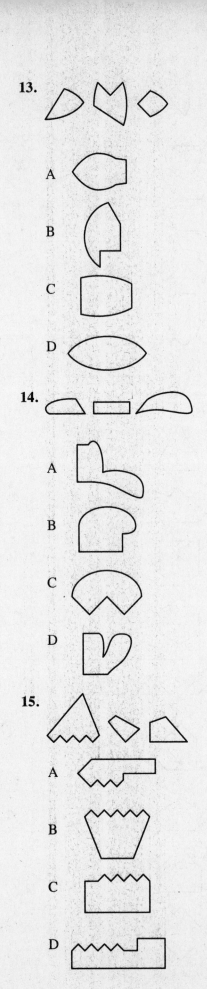

16.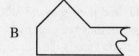

A

B

C

D

17.

A

B

C

D

18.

A

B

C

D

19.

A

B

C

D

20.

A

B

C

D

ANSWERS AND ANSWERS EXPLAINED

GENERAL SCIENCE—SUBTEST 1
Answers

1. B 5. A   9. D 13. C 17. C 20. B 23. C
2. A 6. B 10. C 14. C 18. D 21. B 24. C
3. C 7. C 11. D 15. A 19. A 22. D 25. A
4. D 8. C 12. C 16. D

Answers Explained

1. **B** Sound travels fastest in the densest, or heaviest, materials. The molecules in heavy materials are closer together and transmit sound vibrations more rapidly than the molecules in light materials. Sound does not travel through a vacuum.

2. **A** In the process of distillation, a liquid is evaporated by heat and then condensed by cooling. When seawater is distilled, the salt remains behind as a residue, and the distilled water is very pure. Seawater is distilled before it is used in a ship's boilers in order to get rid of the salt, which would form a scale and ruin the boilers.

3. **C** Nitrogen is a gas. Iron is seldom found in a free state, aluminum occurs in combination with other elements in the earth's crust. Copper is found in combination with other elements and also in a free state.

4. **D** When the sun's rays strike a surface that is smooth, shiny, or light in color, the rays are reflected. When the sun's rays strike a surface that is rough and dark, the rays are absorbed.

5. **A** In crop rotation, plants such as legumes are planted periodically to add nitrogen to the soil after other crops have exhausted it. None of the other methods returns minerals to the soil.

6. **B** A crowbar is a form of lever. By placing a crowbar over a support, you can exert pressure on one end and overcome resistance at the other. A crowbar can be balanced on the surface of one rock, for example, and then pressed hard to dislodge another rock on top.

7. **C** The lunar surface is darkened when the earth comes between the sun and the moon. This is caused by the fact that the shadow of the earth falls on the moon's surface.

8. **C** Calcium is a very important constituent of bone. Without it, the bones in our skeleton become brittle.

9. **D** The oxidation of the gasoline, which contains hydrogen, produces moisture. There is also an oxidation of the carbon in gasoline, which produces carbon dioxide (not mentioned in the question) and traces of carbon monoxide. These traces can be dangerous when the engine of a car is running in a confined, poorly ventilated place.

10. **C** The telephone receiver has an electromagnet with a metal diaphragm mounted close to it. The metal diaphragm vibrates (moves back and forth) and reproduces the sounds spoken into the transmitter. The sound waves produced by the speaker's voice cause the transmitter to make the current in the wires weaker and stronger. These changes occur thousands of times per second. These changes in current affect the electromagnet in the receiver at the other end of the phone call. The receiving electromagnet affects its diaphragm strongly or weakly as the current changes. This in turn reproduces the sound waves made originally by the speaker's voice.

11. **D** Radio and light waves are two forms of electromagnetic radiation. In a vacuum, all electromagnetic

waves have the same speed—that is, the speed of light.

12. **C** The earth's atmosphere consists of a mixture of nitrogen (about 78% by volume); oxygen (about 21%); carbon dioxide (about 0.03%); small amounts of rare gases such as neon, xenon, krypton, and helium; and some water vapor and dust particles.

13. **C** All freely falling objects, regardless of their masses near the earth, fall toward the earth with equal acceleration. Any two objects at rest that begin to fall at the same instant will have equal velocities at the end of 3 seconds, or at any other time interval. Thus the ratio of their speeds will be 1:1.

14. **C** A falling barometer indicates the approach of low pressure and rising air. The rising of warm, moist air usually results in precipitation. We have reason to assume that the air is warm since we know that southeast winds come from lower latitudes where the air was warmed, picking up moisture when it passed over the Atlantic Ocean.

15. **A** Sand particles are visible and comparatively large. They can be caught in the small holes of a filter. Sugar, alcohol, and most inks form true solutions in which the particles are of molecular size. These pass through filters.

16. **D** Barometric pressure decreases 1 inch for every 900 feet of altitude. The gas in the balloon expands because it enters regions of lower and lower pressure. Balloons being prepared for ascent are only partially filled with helium. The balloonist knows that the gas will expand and fill the balloon completely at higher altitudes.

17. **C** The analysis of radioactive material has given scientists an accurate estimate of the age of the earth.

18. **D** Coal deposits were formed when layers of giant ferns as well as other vegetation were compressed into layers of coal by the earth's movement. Its coal deposits tell us that Alaska must have had a tropical climate.

19. **A** The curve in the top of an airplane wing forces the air to flow faster over the top of the wing than below it. This faster flowing air results in less pressure above the wing. The principle behind this was first described by Bernoulli. In any flowing liquid, the pressure becomes less as the speed of the flowing liquid becomes greater.

20. **B** The lens focuses the light on the retina, which "records the image," sending impulses along the optic nerve to the brain. The cornea is the transparent tissue covering the eyeball. The pupil is the opening through which light enters the eye.

21. **B** When water is decomposed by electrolysis, the water breaks up into hydrogen and oxygen; the ratio is two volumes of hydrogen to one of oxygen.

$$2H_2O \rightarrow 2H_2 \uparrow + O_2 \uparrow$$

22. **D** $FeSO_4$ is a compound of three different elements—iron (Fe), sulfur (S), and oxygen (O). Hydrogen (H) is a separate element.

23. **C** Nitrogen is needed most by plants. They also have some need for phosphorus and potassium. Only traces of the other elements are needed by plants; they are not a major concern for companies that produce fertilizers.

24. **C** When an object is placed in water, it loses the exact same weight as the weight of the water it displaces. If two objects that are placed in water appear to lose the same weight, then they must have both displaced the same amount of water. That means that they are equal in size, or volume.

25. **A** A thermos is made with a vacuum between its double walls. In this vacuum, there are no molecules to receive the transfer of heat energy from the wall near the contents of the thermos. Thus, the vacuum prevents the loss of heat. Even though a storm window allows some air between it and the "year-round" window, it is the closest match to a thermos, among the choices given.

ARITHMETIC REASONING—SUBTEST 2
Answers

1. **D** 6. **B** 11. **A** 15. **B** 19. **B** 23. **B** 27. **C**
2. **C** 7. **B** 12. **D** 16. **A** 20. **A** 24. **D** 28. **B**
3. **B** 8. **D** 13. **B** 17. **D** 21. **C** 25. **A** 29. **A**
4. **A** 9. **C** 14. **C** 18. **A** 22. **C** 26. **B** 30. **D**
5. **D** 10. **A**

Answers Explained

1. **D** You need 8 barrels of water to sprinkle 1/2 mile.
You need 16 barrels of water to sprinkle 1 mile.
You need 3×16 (or 48) barrels to sprinkle 3 miles.
You need $48 + 8$ (or 56) barrels to sprinkle 3½ miles.

2. **C** Since the picture and its enlargement are similar, the lengths have the same ratio as the widths.

$$\frac{\text{length of picture}}{\text{length of enlargement}} = \frac{\text{width of picture}}{\text{width of enlargement}}$$

$$\frac{8}{12} = \frac{6}{\text{width of enlargement } (x)}$$

To solve this, cross-multiply the measurements, using x for the one you don't know.
$8 \times x = 12 \times 6 = 72$
$x = 72/8 \quad = 9$ (width)

3. **B** There are 10 units of $1,000 in $10,000. Thus, Lee Robinson pays $10 \times 24 (or $240) each year in premiums. That means that every 6 months, Lee Robinson pays 1/2 of $240, or $120.

4. **A** There are 16 ounces in 1 pound. Therefore, if 2 pounds of cottage cheese costs $3.20, then 1 pound of cottage cheese costs $1.60.
1 ounce costs $1.60 ÷ 16 (or $0.10).
3 ounces cost $3 \times 0.10 (or $0.30).

5. **D** To find the distance Mr. Green drove, multiply the hours by the miles per hour. Thus,
$12 \times 55 = 660$ (distance covered)
To find the number of gallons he used, divide the distance by the miles for each gallon. Thus,
$660 ÷ 22 = 30$ (gallons used)

6. **B** From 8:45 A.M. to 4:45 P.M. is 8 hours.
From 4:45 P.M. to 5:15 P.M. is 1/2 hour.
Subtract Matty's lunch hour.
$8½ – 1 = 7½$ (or 7.5 hours)
Multiply his work hours by his hourly rate.
$7.5 \times $7.50 = 56.25 (day's salary)

7. **B** Find the cost of 3 ties: $3 \times $4 = 12
Find the cost of the shirts alone:
$$52 – $12 = $40$$
Find the cost of 1 shirt:
$$40 ÷ 5 = $8$$

8. **D** Find the relationship between each pair of numbers in the series. Thus,
(5; 2) $5 – 3 = 2$
(2; 9) $2 + 7 = 9$
(9; 6) $9 – 3 = 6$
The pattern so far is $– 3, + 7, – 3$.
To continue the series, add 7 to the fourth number in the series:
$6 + 7 = 13$

9. **C** If 80% of the audience were adults, then the percentage of children was
$100\% – 80\% = 20\%$ (0.2)
To find the number of children, multiply
$500 \times 0.2 = 100.0 = 100$ children

10. **A** Find the amount of reduction by subtracting.
$$240 – $210 = 430$$
To find the percentage of reduction, divide it by the original price.
$$\frac{\text{(reduction) } \$30}{\text{(original price) } \$240} = \frac{1}{8} = 12\,½\%$$

11. **A** Multiply the cost of the home by the assessment rate.

$55,000 × 80% =

$55,000 × 0.8 = $44,000

The realty tax is $4.74 for each $100 in $44,000.

$44,000 ÷ 100 = 440 (hundreds)

$4.74 × 440 = $2,085.60 (tax)

12. **D** If 1 inch equals 50 miles, then 2½ inches equal 2½ times 50.

$$\frac{50}{1} \times \frac{5}{2} = 125 \text{ (miles)}$$

13. **B** One pound equals 16 ounces. Find the number of ounces in 2,200 pounds by multiplying.

2,200 × 16 = 35,200 (ounces)

Find the number of 40-ounce bags needed to pack 35,200 ounces by dividing.

35,200 ÷ 40 = 880 (bags)

14. **C** Find the first reduction and the weekend sale price. (25% = 1/4)

$400 × 1/4 = $100 (first reduction)

$400 − $100 = $300 (weekend sale price)

Use this weekend sale price to find the reduction for paying cash and the final price. (10% = 0.1)

$300 × 0.1 = $30 (second reduction)

$300 − $30 = $270 (cash price)

15. **B** Find the combined salaries of the 4 clerks.

$255 × 4 = $1,020

Find the combined salaries of the part-timers.

$120 × 2 = $240

Add both totals and divide by 6 for the average.

$1,020 + $240 = $1,260

$1,260 ÷ 6 = $210 (average salary)

16. **A** The perimeter of a rectangle is equal to the sum of two lengths and two widths. If 15 feet, 6 inches (15½ feet) equal 1 length, then

2 × 15½ = 31 feet (2 lengths)

40 − 31 = 9 feet (both widths)

9 ÷ 2 = 4½ feet (1 width)

17. **D** Before dividing by a decimal, clear the decimal point in both the divisor and the dividend.

$$\frac{0.675}{0.9} = \frac{6.75}{9} = 0.75$$

18. **A** In the first hour, the two planes will be a combined distance of 340 miles plus 260 miles apart. Thus,

340 + 260 = 600 miles apart in 1 hour

Find how many hours it will take them to be 3,000 miles apart by dividing.

3,000 ÷ 600 = 5 (hours)

19. **B** Multiply the cost per foot by the length of the material.

12 inches equal 1 foot.

3 inches equal 1/4 foot.

5 feet, 3 inches equal 5¼ feet (or 5.25 feet)

$8 × 5.25 = $42

20. **A** Find the cost of 1 pint. (There are 8 pints in 1 gallon.)

$3.84 ÷ 8 = $0.48

Find the cost of 3 pints.

$0.48 × 3 = $1.44

21. **C** Begin by letting x equal 1 share of the inheritance. According to the ratio, the widow received 5 shares ($5x$), and the son received 3 shares ($3x$). Together, they inherited $72,000. This can be written as an equation:

$5x + 3x = $72,000

Solve for x by combining similar terms.

$8x = $72,000

$x = $9,000 (one share)

Multiply the value of 1 share by the number of shares the mother received.

$5x = $45,000 (mother's share)

22. **C** Begin by setting up a statement of proportion.

$$\frac{\text{chocolate}}{\text{chocolate}} = \frac{\text{corn syrup (recipe)}}{\text{corn syrup (amount available)}}$$

$$\frac{2\frac{1}{2}}{2} = \frac{\frac{1}{2}}{x} \text{ (or) } \frac{\frac{5}{2}}{2} = \frac{\frac{1}{2}}{x}$$

Simplify each side of the proportion.

(a) $\dfrac{5}{2} \div \dfrac{2}{1} = \dfrac{5}{2} \times \dfrac{1}{2} = \dfrac{5}{4}$

(b) $\dfrac{1}{2} \div \dfrac{x}{1} = \dfrac{1}{2} \times \dfrac{1}{x} = \dfrac{1}{2x}$

Then solve the proportion by cross-multiplying

$$\frac{5}{4} = \frac{1}{2x} \text{ (or) } 10x = 4$$

Divide each side of the equation by 10 to find the value of x.

$$10x = 4$$
$$x = 4/10$$
$$= 2/5 \text{ cup of corn syrup}$$

23. **B** To find the average of three numbers, divide their sum by 3.

$x + y + z$ (sum of three numbers)

$\dfrac{x + y + z}{3}$ (sum of numbers, divided by 3)

24. **D** First find the income he gets on the $6,000 at 5% annual interest.

$6,000 × 0.05 = $300.00 (income)

Next find how much more interest he wants to earn in a year.

$900 − $300 = $600 (additional interest)

This $600 will equal 6% of the amount (x) he has to invest. Write this as an equation.

$$\$600 = 0.06 \text{ times } x$$
$$\$600 = 0.06\, x$$

To solve for x, divide each side of the equation by 0.06. (Clear the decimal in the divisor.)

$$\frac{\$600.00}{0.06} = \left(\frac{0.06}{0.06}\right)x$$

$$\$10,000 = x$$

(new amount needed) $x = \$10,000$

25. **A** Two figures are similar if they have the same shape. They may or may not have the same size. A plane and a scale model of that plane have the same shape and are therefore similar.

26. **B** Solve by substituting number values for letters and then doing the arithmetic operations.

$$5a^2b - 3ab^2$$
$$= (5 \times a^2 \times b) - (3 \times a \times b^2)$$
$$= (5 \times 7^2 \times 4) - (3 \times 7 \times 4^2)$$
$$= (5 \times 49 \times 4) - (3 \times 7 \times 16)$$
$$= 980 - 336 = 644$$

27. **C** The formula for the circumference (C) of a circle can be written in terms of its radius (R) or its diameter (D).

$$C = 2 \times R \times \pi \text{ (or) } C = D \times \pi$$

Thus, if you divide the circumference of a circle by its diameter, you are left with π.

$$\frac{C}{D} = \frac{D \times Pi}{D}$$
$$\frac{C}{D} = Pi$$

28. **B** If the businesswoman spends 1/5 of her income for rent, she has 4/5 of her income left.

$$\frac{5}{5} - \frac{1}{5} = \frac{4}{5} \text{ (remainder)}$$

She then spends 3/8 of the remainder on salaries.

$$\frac{4}{5} \times \frac{3}{8} = \frac{12}{40} = \frac{3}{10} \text{ (salaries)}$$

29. **A** Solve by substituting the number value for F and then doing the arithmetic operations.

$$C = \frac{5}{9}(F - 32)$$
$$C = \frac{5}{9}(50 - 32)$$
$$C = \frac{5}{9} \times (18)$$
$$C = 10$$

30. **D** To obtain the average, add the five temperatures and divide the total by 5.

Add: $-12 + (-7) + (-2) + 0 + 6$
$= -21 + 6$
$= -15$

Divide:

WORD KNOWLEDGE—SUBTEST 3
Answers

1. **A**	6. **C**	11. **A**	16. **D**	21. **B**	26. **A**	31. **D**
2. **D**	7. **B**	12. **B**	17. **B**	22. **C**	27. **A**	32. **B**
3. **D**	8. **A**	13. **C**	18. **D**	23. **A**	28. **A**	33. **C**
4. **B**	9. **B**	14. **A**	19. **A**	24. **D**	29. **A**	34. **A**
5. **B**	10. **B**	15. **B**	20. **D**	25. **C**	30. **D**	35. **B**

Answers Explained

1. **A** Luxury, like **opulence** (from the Latin for "rich, wealthy"), is conducive to sumptuous living.
2. **D** **Mimesis** (from the Greek for "imitation") means reproduction of the supposed words of another, usually in order to represent his or her character.
3. **D** **Languid** means weak, indifferent, weary, or exhausted, implying a languid person.
4. **B** **Inherence** (from the Latin for "sticking in or to") means the state of existing in something as a permanent and inseparable element, quality, or attribute, and thus, like *intrinsic*, implies belonging to the nature of a thing itself.
5. **B** **Anomie** (from the Greek for "lawlessness") describes a social condition marked by the absence of social norms or values, and therefore, like vacuum, implies the absence of components from an area.
6. **C** Ethereal describes something that is light and airy and thus may be unsubstantial, as implied by **tenuous** (from the Latin for "thin").
7. **B** Like **salutation**, greeting means to address with some expression of pleasure.
8. **A** Hypnotize, like **mesmerize**, means to put in a condition or state allied to sleep.
9. **B** Display, similar to **panoply**, means an impressive array of assembled persons or things.
10. **B** Like **syntactic** (from the Greek for "arrangement"), which pertains to patterns of formation of sentences and phrases in a particular language, grammatical pertains to the sound, formation, and arrangement of words.
11. **A** Resentment, like **umbrage**, describes a feeling of indignation at something regarded as an injury or insult.
12. **B** Harsh means rough to any of the senses, while **raucous** denotes hoarseness, or harshness, of voice or sound.
13. **C** Trial, like **prosecution**, means determining a person's guilt or innocence by due process of law.
14. **A** Pollution, which means defiling, rendering impure, making foul, unclean, dirty, is closely related to **miasma** (from the Greek for "pollution").
15. **B** Model, like **paragon**, is a pattern of excellence for exact imitation.
16. **D** **Innate**, like native, means belonging by birth.
17. **B** **Urbanity** indicates elegant courtesy or politeness, hence refinement.
18. **D** To **encounter** means to come upon, hence to meet.
19. **A** **Banal**, like commonplace, characterizes as lifeless and uninteresting.
20. **D** **Little**, like small, means not much in comparison to other things.
21. **B** **Found**, like discover, means to unearth something hidden or lost.
22. **C** **Tell**, like inform, means to communicate knowledge or give information.
23. **A** **Shifting**, like variable, means subject to change.
24. **D** **Stop**, like cease, means to end.

25. **C** <u>Weaken</u>, like impair, means to worsen or to damage.
26. **A** <u>Rudiments</u> are fundamental skills or basic principles, like *basic methods and procedures*.
27. **A** <u>Reckless</u>, like imprudent, means lacking discretion.
28. **A** <u>Friction</u>, like dissension, both refer to quarreling.
29. **A** <u>Separate</u>, like disconnect, means to become detached.
30. **D** <u>Elementary</u>, like rudimentary, refers to something fundamental or imperfectly developed.
31. **D** <u>Self-governing</u>, like autonomous, means governing without control.
32. **B** <u>Wander aimlessly</u>, like meander, means to follow a winding course without a definite destination.
33. **C** <u>Extreme poverty</u>, like destitution, characterizes the state of lacking resources and possessions.
34. **A** <u>Slander</u>, like malign, means to speak misleading or false reports about someone.
35. **B** <u>Lacking strength</u>, like impotent, means lacking power or vigor.

PARAGRAPH COMPREHENSION— SUBTEST 4
Answers

1. **A**	4. **A**	6. **B**	8. **B**	10. **C**	12. **A**	14. **D**
2. **B**	5. **A**	7. **C**	9. **D**	11. **B**	13. **C**	15. **C**
3. **A**						

Answers Explained

1. **A** The first sentence states that the duty of the lighthouse keeper is to keep the light burning no matter what happens.
2. **B** The second sentence mentions that the exact amount of water needed has been carefully determined.
3. **A** "Hardening" or toughening seedlings is done by reducing the water the seedlings obtain and lowering the temperature.
4. **A** Earthquakes occur when rock layers break and slip, forming cracks or faults.

5. **A** Photosynthesis combines air, water, and energy from the sun to make food.
6. **B** In this selection reputable means honest or trusted.
7. **C** The main idea of the selection is that ice can relieve many of the effects of a burn and is therefore great first aid.
8. **B** The main idea of the selection is to warn you to be careful of "get-rich-quick" plans.
9. **D** The third sentence mentions that 9 out of 10 victims of fatal falls are older than 65.
10. **C** "Gray water" is defined as slightly used water. The only choice that represents used water is soapy water.
11. **B** The third sentence specifies that a glacier moves because of its weight.
12. **A** Every sentence of the selection expresses disapproval of the present state of things and implies that changes are needed.
13. **C** The selection states that some categories of people have changed, but the fact that the "number is rising" implies that not everyone has changed.
14. **D** According to the first sentence, Newton's Third Law is that to each action there is an equal and opposite reaction, or action equals reaction.
15. **C** The first sentence, and main idea of the paragraph, states that water is a good conductor of sound waves.

AUTOMOTIVE INFORMATION— SUBTEST 5
Answers

1. **D**	5. **B**	9. **B**	13. **D**
2. **A**	6. **C**	10. **C**	14. **C**
3. **D**	7. **A**	11. **B**	15. **D**
4. **B**	8. **B**	12. **C**	

Answers Explained

1. **D** When viewed from the rear, the side to your right is the right side of an engine. This method is used by all manufacturers.

2. **A** G indicates the load-carrying capacity of a tire. 78 is the aspect ratio. The aspect ratio is the relationship between the tire height and width. When a tire is marked 78, the height is 78% of the width. 14 indicates that the tire will fit a 14-inch rim.

3. **D** Tracking is correct when both rear wheels are parallel to, and the same distance from, the vehicle centerline (an imaginary line drawn through the center of the vehicle). A bent frame or twisted body structure will cause improper tracking.

4. **B** Shock absorbers control spring oscillation. Original equipment shocks that do not use air or spring assist are not designed to control vehicle height.

5. **B** The countershaft is pressed into the transmission case and supports the cluster gear. The main shaft or output shaft is splined with the driveshaft.

6. **C** When a clutch pedal is depressed, the release bearing comes in contact with the fingers of the clutch pressure plate and rotates.

7. **A** To properly adjust an automatic transmission band, loosen the adjusting screw locknut. Then tighten the adjusting screw to the specified torque with a torque wrench. Next, loosen the adjusting screw the specified number of turns. Complete the job by holding the adjusting screw and tightening the locknut.

8. **B** On a rear-wheel-drive vehicle, the driveshaft transmits power from the transmission to the differential. The flywheel is bolted directly to the crankshaft.

9. **B** Spark plug leads must be installed in the correct tower of the cap to ensure the proper firing order. The firing order is the order that the spark plugs ignite the air/fuel mixture in the combustion chamber. A typical firing order for a six-cylinder engine is 1-5-3-6-2-4.

10. **C** On a conventional ignition coil the center tower is the secondary or high-voltage terminal. The two small studs at the top of the coil are primary or low-voltage terminals.

11. **B** Battery electrolyte is a mixture of approximately 60% distilled water and 40% sulfuric acid.

12. **C** Two slip rings are mounted on the rotor shaft. Two brushes ride on the slip rings and deliver electrical energy to the rotor windings.

13. **D** A loose or corroded headlight ground connection will cause a dim light. If the headlight switch is faulty, all lights will be affected, not just the headlight.

14. **C** Air is compressible and will cause a spongy or soft brake pedal action.

15. **D** A proportioning valve is commonly used on a vehicle equipped with front disc and rear drum-type brakes. The valve reduces hydraulic pressure to the rear drum brakes to prevent rear wheel lockup and skidding during heavy brake pedal application.

MATHEMATICS KNOWLEDGE— SUBTEST 6
Answers

1. **A**	5. **D**	9. **D**	13. **D**	17. **D**	20. **B**	23. **D**
2. **D**	6. **B**	10. **A**	14. **B**	18. **B**	21. **A**	24. **C**
3. **C**	7. **C**	11. **D**	15. **A**	19. **A**	22. **B**	25. **B**
4. **D**	8. **C**	12. **D**	16. **C**			

Answers Explained

1. **A** This equation means "a number, decreased by 3, is equal to 7."
$$b - 3 = 7$$
To arrive at a true statement for b, we want to eliminate -3 on the left side of the equation. We do this by adding 3. (This is undoing the subtraction.) We then add 3 to the other side so that the statement remains an equation.
$$(b - 3) + 3 = 7 + 3$$

By simplifying both sides, we isolate b and thus find the solution.
$$b = 10$$

2. **D** An easy way to perform the multiplication is to do four separate multiplications. Then the procedure looks like ordinary multiplication in arithmetic.

$$2z - 3$$
$$\underline{z + 2}$$
$4z - 6$ Multiply $(2z - 3)$ by 2
$\underline{2z^2 - 3z}$ Multiply $(2z - 3)$ by z
$2z^2 + z - 6$ Add the partial products as you do in arithmetic.

3. **C** Since a quadrilateral is a four-sided figure, the township will need four lifeguards. (If the sides of a quadrilateral are parallel, it is also called a parallelogram. If all four sides are equal and all four angles are right angles, it is called a square.)

4. **D** Step 1: Find the area of the square.
2 feet × 2 feet = 4 square feet
Step 2: Find the area of the circle, using the formula $A = \pi \times R^2$. (The radius equals half the diameter; the diameter of this circle is 2 feet— the same length as one side of the square.)
$3.14 \times 1^2 = 3.14$ square feet
Step 3. Subtract 3.14 square feet from 4 square feet to find the wood that is wasted, 0.86 square feet.

5. **D** Step 1: Subtract 2 from each side of the equation in order to eliminate + 2 from the left side. (You are undoing the addition.)
$$3x + 2 - 2 = -13 - 2$$
$$3x = -15$$
Step 2: Now divide each side by 3 to find x. (You are undoing the multiplication.)
$$\frac{3x}{3} = \frac{-15}{3}$$
$$x = -5$$

6. **B** Let p stand for the number of paintings the artist made. The 4 paintings he sold are equal to 0.05 of all his paintings. This can be expressed as an equation.
$$0.05p = 4$$
To solve for p, divide both sides by 0.05. You are undoing the multiplication of 0.05 and p.
$$\frac{0.05p}{0.05} = \frac{4}{0.05}$$ (Clear the decimal in the divisor.)
$$\frac{1p}{1} = \frac{400}{5}$$
$$p = 80$$ (paintings made)

7. **C** In an isosceles triangle, two of the sides are equal. This means that the angles opposite them are equal, too. If one is 40 degrees, then so is the other. To find the angle opposite the unequal side, begin by adding the equal angles.
$$40 + 40 = 80 \text{ degrees}$$
To find the third angle, subtract this amount from 180 (the number of degrees in any triangle).
$$180 - 80 = 100 \text{ degrees (third angle)}$$

8. **C** An easy way to do this example is to break it into three examples, dividing each term by $8x$. Divide the numbers first, and then the letters. However, to divide the exponents of x, just find the difference between them. (Thus, $x^3 \div x = x^{(3-1)} = x^2$.)
$$\frac{24x^3}{8x} + \frac{16x^2}{8x} - \frac{8x}{8x} =$$
$$3x^2 + 2x - 1$$
Since the question asks only how many x's there are in the quotient (not how many x^2's), the answer is 2.

9. **D** First, find the area (surface) of the ceiling. Since it is opposite the floor, it has the same length and width ($A = I \times w$).
19 feet × 10 feet = 190 square feet (ceiling)
Next find the combined area of two matching (opposite) walls. Start with the walls formed by the length and height of the room.

19 feet × 8 feet = 152 square feet
(first wall)
152 feet × 2 = 304 square feet
(matching walls)
Then find the area of the walls formed by the width and height of the room.
10 feet × 8 feet = 80 square feet
(second wall)
80 feet × 2 = 160 square feet
(matching walls)
Finally, combine all surfaces to be painted.
190 + 304 + 160 = 654 square feet

10. **A** The basic formula for travel is "distance equals rate multiplied by time," or $D = rt$. The car traveled 200 miles (D); therefore $200 = rt$. To solve for t (time), divide both sides of the equation by r. (You are undoing the multiplication.)

$$\frac{200}{r} = \frac{rt}{r}$$

$$\frac{200}{r} = t \quad \text{(time it took for trip)}$$

11. **D** The perimeter of a square is 4 times a side. Therefore, the perimeter of this square is 4 × 12 feet or 48 feet. The equilateral triangle has the same perimeter as the square. Since the 3 sides of an equilateral triangle are equal, divide by 3 to find the length of one side.
(48 feet) ÷ 3 = 16 feet (length of one side)

12. **D** The exponent in $(0.1)^3$ means you use 0.1 as a multiplier 3 times.
$(0.1)^3 = (0.1)(0.1)(0.1) = 0.001$
When multiplying decimals, count off one decimal place in the answer for each decimal place in the numbers you multiply.

13. **D** In 1 foot, there are 12 inches (12 × 1). In 2 feet, there are 24 inches (12 × 2). Therefore, in f feet, there are $12 \times f$ or $12f$ inches. Add $12f$ inches to i inches to obtain the total of $12f + i$.

14. **B** Use m as the owner's income. According to the rule of thumb, a house costing \$64,000 should be no more than 2½ times an owner's income, or 2½m (2.5m). This can be stated as an equation.
$$2.5m = \$64,000$$
To solve for m, divide both sides by 2.5. You are undoing the multiplication.
$$\frac{2.5m}{2.5} = \frac{\$64,000}{2.5m} \text{(Clear the decimal in the divisor.)}$$
$$m = \frac{\$640,000}{25} = \$25,600 \text{ (owner's income)}$$

15. **A** To find the product of more than two numbers, work on only two numbers at a time. If both of these numbers have plus signs (+), their product has a plus sign. If both have minus signs (–), their product has a plus (not a minus) sign. But if their signs are different, the product has a minus sign.
$$(+2)(-5)(+3)(-3)$$
$$= (-10)(+3)(-3)$$
$$= (-30)(-3)$$
$$= +90$$

16. **C** To solve the equation $x^2 = 3x + 10$, turn it into an equation equal to 0, find the two factors of the new equation, and then set each factor equal to 0, to solve for x.
Step 1: Move all expressions to one side of the equal sign. Change the signs of terms that are moved.
$$x^2 - 3x - 10 = 0$$
Step 2: Find the two factors that you would multiply to produce this polynomial. Do this one expression at a time. What gives you x^2? The answer is x times x. Therefore place an x at the beginning of each factor.
$$(x \quad)(x \quad)$$
Next find the two numbers you would multiply to get 10. They could be 10 and 1, or 5 and 2, but remember that the two numbers also have to produce 3, the middle term in the polynomial. The differ-

ence between 5 and 2 is 3. Therefore 5 and 2 are the numbers that complete the factors.

$$(x \quad 5)\,(x \quad 2)$$

Now decide the signs that belong in each factor. The appearance of −10 in the polynomial means that 5 and 2 have different signs. The −3x in the polynomial indicates that 5 (the larger number) has the minus sign, and that 2 has a plus sign. Thus

$$(x-5)\,(x+2)$$

Step 3: Set each factor equal to zero and solve the equations.

$$x - 5 = 0 \qquad x + 2 = 0$$
$$x = 5 \qquad\qquad x = -2$$

Check. Substitute each answer in the original equation.

$$x^2 = 3x + 10 \qquad x^2 = 3x + 10$$
$$(-2)^2 = 3(-2) + 1 \quad (5)^2 = 3(5) + 10$$
$$4 = -6 + 10 \qquad 25 = 15 + 10$$
$$4 = 4 \qquad\qquad 25 = 25$$

This proves that x is equal to −2 and 5.

17. **D** A cylinder is a solid figure whose upper and lower bases are circles. A small can of frozen-juice concentrate is an example of a cylinder. (An orange is a sphere. A stick of butter is a rectangular solid. A compact disc is a combination of different objects.)

18. **B** Your goal is to find the value of R in terms of the other letters in the equation.

$$N = \frac{CR}{C+R}$$

Begin by multiplying both sides of the equation by (C + R). You are undoing the division.

$$N(C+R) = \frac{CR}{(C+R)} \times (C+R)$$

$$N(C + R) = CR$$
$$NC + NR = CR \text{ (isolate terms}$$
$$\text{with } R)$$

Next, gather all terms with R on one side of the equation. To do this, subtract NR from both sides. You are undoing the addition.

$$NC + NR - NR = CR - NR$$
$$NC = CR - NR$$
$$NC = R(C - N)$$
$$\text{(simplify for } R)$$

Finally, divide both sides of the equation by (C − N). You are undoing the multiplication.

$$\frac{NC}{(C-N)} = \frac{R(C-N)}{(C-N)}$$

$$\frac{NC}{(C-N)} = R \text{ (transpose the statement)}$$

$$R = \frac{NC}{(C-N)}$$

19. **A** When the product of two numbers is 1, each number is the reciprocal of the other. In the following equation, r is the reciprocal you want to find.

$$r \times \frac{5}{3} = 1$$

To isolate r, divide each side by 5/3. This is undoing the multiplication.

$$r \times \frac{5}{3} \div \frac{5}{3} = 1 \div \frac{5}{3}$$

$$r \times \frac{5}{3} \times \frac{3}{5} = 1 \times \frac{3}{5}$$

$$r = \frac{3}{5} \text{ (reciprocal of 5/3)}$$

Written as a decimal, 3/5 equals 0.6.

20. **B** This problem does not have to be computed, because the two symbols cancel each other. The radical sign $\left(\sqrt{}\right)$ in $\left(\sqrt{13}\right)^2$ tells you to find the square root of 13. But the exponent (^{2}) tells you to square the answer—that is, to multiply the square root of 13 by itself. This would get you back to 13.

21. **A** To find the average rate of speed (mph), divide the distance he covered by the time he spent traveling (R = D/T). In this example, begin by finding the distance traveled.

120 + 120 = 240 miles (distance)

Next find the length of time he traveled. At the beginning of his trip, he drove 120 miles at 40 mph.

$\dfrac{120}{40} = 3$ hours (first part of trip)

Later, he increased his speed.

$\dfrac{120}{60} = 2$ hours (second part of trip)

Altogether, he traveled for 5 hours. Now apply the formula for finding his average rate of speed.

$\dfrac{D}{T} = \dfrac{240}{5} = 48$ mph (rate of speed)

22. **B** An angle of 180 degrees is a straight angle.

An angle of 90 degrees is a right angle.

An angle greater than 90 degrees but less than 180 degrees is an obtuse angle.

An angle less than 90 degrees is an acute angle.

23. **D** To solve these equations for x, begin by finding a way to eliminate y. Multiply both sides of the second equation by 2.

$$2(x - 2y) = 2 \times 11$$
$$2x - 4y = 22$$

Add the new form of the second equation to the first equation, and solve for x.

$$5x + 4y = 27$$
$$\underline{2x - 4y = 22} \text{ (+4 cancels –4)}$$
$$7x \quad\quad = 49$$
$$x = 7$$

24. **C** The product of a negative number and a positive number is always negative. The product of two negative numbers is always a positive number. Since ab is positive and a is negative, b must be negative, too.

25. **B** The expression $(x + 5 > 7)$ is a statement of inequality. It means that x plus 5 is greater than 7—not equal to it. To solve this inequality, subtract 5 from both sides of the statement.

$$x + 5 > 7$$
$$x + 5 - 5 > 7 - 5$$
$$x > 2$$

Thus the statement of inequality is true for any value of x that is greater than 2. Try it with 3, for example.

$$3 + 5 > 7$$
$$8 > 7, \text{ a true statement}$$

MECHANICAL COMPREHENSION—SUBTEST 7
Answers

1. C	5. B	9. D	13. D	17. B	20. A 23. A
2. B	6. D	10. D	14. D	18. B	21. A 24. B
3. A	7. B	11. A	15. D	19. C	22. C 25. B
4. D	8. C	12. C	16. B		

Answers Explained

1. **C** Cap screws are identified by diameter, pitch (threads per inch), material, hardness, and length. Two common types of threads are national coarse (NC) and national fine (NF).

2. **B** A stud is a headless bolt that has threads on both ends. Usually one side has NF threads, and the other side, NC threads.

3. **A** To find the wrench size of a cap screw, and so on, measure across the flats of its hexagon head.

4. **D** The dial indicator uses a gage to register movement. It is used to measure variations in dimensions and backlash (clearance) between two meshed gears.

5. **B** A pilot bearing is pressed into a hole at the end of the engine crankshaft. The purpose of the bearing is to support the tip of the transmission input (clutch) shaft. During the installation of a new clutch assembly, it is necessary to line up the clutch disc with the pilot bearing. If these parts are not aligned, the transmission will not slide into place on the engine.

6. **D** The oscilloscope, or scope, is a special type of voltmeter that displays traces and oscillations on a TV-type picture tube. The scope has the

capability of showing the rapid changes in voltage that occur in the ignition system. This is helpful in diagnosing problems in the circuit.

7. **B** A torque wrench is a special type of turning tool that is equipped with a gage. It is used to tighten nuts and bolts to a specified torque or tightness.

8. **C** An ohmmeter is a test instrument that measures the resistance in an electrical circuit. Resistance is the opposition to the flow of current through a circuit.

9. **D** A cylinder head must be tightened in a specific sequence using a torque wrench. Failure to tighten the head properly can result in a blown head gasket. *Note*: See the answer to question 7 for additional information.

10. **D** The specific gravity of an antifreeze solution is tested with a special hydrometer. It compares the weight of the antifreeze solution to that of water.

11. **A** Spur gears have straight teeth. Hypoid and spiral gears have curved or beveled teeth.

12. **C** Planetary gears are used in an automatic transmission. The three members are in constant mesh and provide gear reduction and reverse without shifting. To obtain a gear reduction or reverse, one member must be held stationary by a band or clutch assembly. Worm and sector gears are used in some types of steering gear assemblies. Differential or spider gears are used in a rear end assembly.

13. **D** The crankshaft changes the reciprocating (up and down) motion of the piston to rotary motion.

14. **D** Condensation takes place when a gas or vapor changes to a liquid. Moisture on the windshield is the result of water vapor in the air changing back to liquid.

15. **D** Unlike poles attract; like poles repel.

16. **B** The differential, which connects the driveshaft to the rear axle, increases engine torque through gear reduction. Engine torque is increased because the driveshaft turns faster than the rear axles.

17. **B** Water expands as it freezes. Water is not compressible.

18. **B** To calculate the gear ratio of a rear axle assembly, divide the number of teeth on the pinion gear into the number of teeth on the ring gear: 43 divided by 11 = 3.90.

19. **C** A and D are in constant mesh and F is too small.

20. **A** When the lobe (high spot) on cam A makes contact with the follower (roller) on the contact arm, the contacts will close. Since cam A has only one lobe, the contacts will close one time per revolution.

21. **A** To calculate the revolutions of gear B, use this formula: $r = (D \times R)$ divided by d.
D = number of teeth on gear A;
R = revolutions of gear A;
d = number of teeth on gear B;
r = revolutions of gear B;
$r = (D \times R)$ divided by d.

$$r = \frac{15 \times 14}{10}$$
$$r = \frac{210}{10}$$
$$r = 21$$

22. **C** Gears that are meshed turn in opposite directions. Gear 2 is turning clockwise; gears 1 and 3 are turning counterclockwise.

23. **A** Hydrometers use floats to measure specific gravity. Specific gravity is the weight of a liquid compared to the weight of water. The liquid with the highest specific gravity will cause the float to rise higher in the glass tube.

24. **B** Vacuum is greatest at the narrow or restricted area of an air passage.

The narrow area is called a venturi. Gage Z will also indicate a vacuum, but it will read lower than Y.

25. **B** On a second-class lever, the fulcrum is at one end, the effort is at the other end, and the load is between.

ELECTRONICS INFORMATION— SUBTEST 8
Answers

1. C 4. A 7. A 10. B 13. C 16. C 19. D
2. D 5. B 8. A 11. D 14. B 17. B 20. C
3. C 6. B 9. B 12. C 15. C 18. D

Answers Explained

1. **C** A cell has a voltage of approximately 1.5 volts. A 9-volt battery therefore contains 6 cells, or 1.5 volts $\times$ 6 = 9 volts.

2. **D** The higher the gage number of a wire, the smaller its diameter.

3. **C** The symbol K represents "kilo" or 1,000. A 1.5K-ohm resistor therefore has a value of $1.5 \times 1,000$ or 1,500 ohms. Choice D is incorrect because the unit of measurement for resistance is ohm. Watts is a unit of measurement for power.

4. **A** The interchangeable terms for voltage are electrical pressure, electromotive force, potential difference, difference of potential, and electrical force. The other choices are incorrect because they represent other circuit properties that cannot be substituted for the property of voltage.

5. **B** Capacitance can be defined as the circuit property that opposes any change in voltage. Inductance is the circuit property that opposes any change in current. Resistance is the circuit property that opposes the flow of electrons, and reactance is the opposition to the flow of an alternating current as a result of inductance or capacitance present in a circuit.

6. **B** Choice A has the quantities reversed, and choices C and D are incorrect because the amount of silver present in solder is minute, and rosin is a substance in the center of solder added to aid in the soldering process.

7. **A** To calculate the current requirement of an appliance, the power law can be applied.
power = current $\times$ voltage
$P = I \times E$

8. **A** Henry is the unit of measurement for inductance. Kilo represents a quantity of 1,000 and mega represents a quantity of 1 million.

9. **B** The piezoelectric effect is the property of certain crystalline substances to change shape when a voltage is impressed upon them, as in the crystal microphone. Thermoionic emission is the escape of electrons from a surface because of the presence of heat. Inductance is the circuit property that opposes any change in current, and hysteresis is the property of a magnetic substance that causes magnetization to lag behind the force that produces it.

10. **B** The height of a wave is known as the wave's amplitude. Varying the height of a carrier wave is known as AM or amplitude modulation. Frequency modulation transmits intelligence by varying the frequency of the carrier wave. Demodulation is the process of separating the intelligence from the carrier wave. Another term for this process is detection.

11. **D** The primary of this transformer has three times the voltage of its secondary. Therefore, the primary must have three times as many turns of wire as the secondary, or a turns ratio of 3:1. If its turns ratio was 1:1, the primary and secondary would have the same voltage. In choice B, a turns ratio of 1:4 would

result in an output voltage of 480 volts. In choice C a turns ratio of 1:3 would result in a secondary voltage of 360 volts.

12. **C** Reading the resistor color code, the first two bands indicate numbers; the third band is the multiplier or the number of zeros to write after the first two numbers. The fourth band indicates the tolerance of the resistor. Following the color code, the value of this resistor is 2,200 ohms ± 5%. Red, representing a number value of 2 and a multiplier value of 100 (or two zeros to write after the first two numbers) would indicate a resistor coded as follows:

2	2
Band 1 - red	Band 2 - red
00	±5%
band 3 - red	band 4 - gold

The tolerance of a fixed carbon resistor is a ± value. Gold represents 5% tolerance.

13. **C** Choice A = diode; choice B = triode; choice D = pentode.

14. **B** In a series circuit, the total resistance is equal to the sum of the individual resistors, or $R_T = R_1 + R_2 + R_3 + \ldots + R_n$. As all resistors have a value of 500 ohms, the total resistance in this circuit is equal to
$R_T = R_1 + R_2 + R_3$
$= 500 + 500 + 500$
$= 1,500$ ohms
Choice A is incorrect because watts is a unit of power, not a unit of resistance.

15. **C** The base element is common or shared by both circuits. Choice A is not a transistor circuit configuration as there is no gate element in a transistor.

16. **C** The waveforms corresponding to the other choices are given in the review section on waveforms.

17. **B** A potentiometer is a variable resistor. Choice A is the symbol for a fixed resistor, and choice B is the symbol for a variable resistor; note the arrow connected to the fixed symbol. Choice C is a fixed capacitor, and choice D is the symbol for a variable capacitor.

18. **D** The unit of measurement for capacitance is the farad, abbreviated F. A potentiometer would be specified in ohms, a coil in henrys, and a transistor by its type or generic number.

19. **D** The purpose of the local oscillator is to generate a high frequency, also known as a radio or carrier wave.

20. **C** A detector demodulates a signal. This is the process of separating the audio or intelligence from the radio wave. An AF amp is used to amplify the audio signal, and the RF amp is used to amplify the radio frequency. A tuner is used to tune in a frequency, making choices A, B, and D incorrect.

SHOP INFORMATION—SUBTEST 9
Answers

1. B	6. C	11. B
2. C	7. A	12. B
3. B	8. B	13. D
4. D	9. C	14. A
5. C	10. C	15. C

Answers Explained

1. **B** A coping saw blade is placed in the saw with the teeth of the blade facing the handle. That means that you cut with a coping saw on the downward stroke. It also calls for a special type of vise to hold whatever it is you are cutting.

2. **C** Carpenters use claw hammers so they can remove nails if they don't go where they belong or are bent on the way into the wood. Machinists use ball peen hammers. Planishing hammers are used by people trying to flatten or shape sheet metal. There is no such thing as a chisel point hammer.

3. **B** The term *penny* is an old English way to designate the size of a nail. It has no definite relation to today's measuring units. You can, however, keep in mind that the larger the number, the larger the nail.

4. **D** A squaring shear is used to shear or cut sheet metal.

5. **C** One of the most common ways to fasten sheet metal is by spot-welding it. This is done with the bodies of automobiles to make them sturdier.

6. **C** A welding torch can be used as a cutting torch when the proper amount of oxygen is used.

7. **A** A tubing cutter is nothing more than a smaller version of a pipe cutter.

8. **B** If you overwork concrete, it brings up all the water to the surface and the cement comes to the surface also. The heavier particles settle farther down into the slab, and you wind up with separation and create a less durable surface when it is dry.

9. **C** Concrete reaches 98% of its strength in 28 days.

10. **C** Deciduous trees are those that produce leaves that drop off in the fall. The wood produced by this type of tree is usually hard when properly dried.

11. **B** A combination square is used to lay out 45- and 90-degree angles of measurement.

12. **B** Most bolts have a hexagonal head.

13. **D** Self-locking nuts are designed to jam against the bolt thread and will not vibrate loose. The wing nut is the only nut designed to be tightened by hand. It is used on connections that must be frequently disassembled and do not require excessive tightening.

14. **A** Wood floats in water because of its hollow cell structure.

15. **C** Flat washers are used to evenly distribute the compressive load of a bolted connection over a wider area or to compensate for an oversized hole. Lock washers are designed to exert force between the bolted connection and the workpiece, preventing the bolt and nut from loosening.

ASSEMBLING OBJECTS—SUBTEST 10
Answers

1. A	6. A	11. A	16. C
2. C	7. A	12. C	17. D
3. D	8. D	13. D	18. A
4. B	9. B	14. A	19. B
5. C	10. C	15. B	20. B

ANSWER SHEETS—*Practice Examination Three*

GENERAL SCIENCE—SUBTEST 1

1. Ⓐ Ⓑ Ⓒ Ⓓ	6. Ⓐ Ⓑ Ⓒ Ⓓ	11. Ⓐ Ⓑ Ⓒ Ⓓ	16. Ⓐ Ⓑ Ⓒ Ⓓ	21. Ⓐ Ⓑ Ⓒ Ⓓ
2. Ⓐ Ⓑ Ⓒ Ⓓ	7. Ⓐ Ⓑ Ⓒ Ⓓ	12. Ⓐ Ⓑ Ⓒ Ⓓ	17. Ⓐ Ⓑ Ⓒ Ⓓ	22. Ⓐ Ⓑ Ⓒ Ⓓ
3. Ⓐ Ⓑ Ⓒ Ⓓ	8. Ⓐ Ⓑ Ⓒ Ⓓ	13. Ⓐ Ⓑ Ⓒ Ⓓ	18. Ⓐ Ⓑ Ⓒ Ⓓ	23. Ⓐ Ⓑ Ⓒ Ⓓ
4. Ⓐ Ⓑ Ⓒ Ⓓ	9. Ⓐ Ⓑ Ⓒ Ⓓ	14. Ⓐ Ⓑ Ⓒ Ⓓ	19. Ⓐ Ⓑ Ⓒ Ⓓ	24. Ⓐ Ⓑ Ⓒ Ⓓ
5. Ⓐ Ⓑ Ⓒ Ⓓ	10. Ⓐ Ⓑ Ⓒ Ⓓ	15. Ⓐ Ⓑ Ⓒ Ⓓ	20. Ⓐ Ⓑ Ⓒ Ⓓ	25. Ⓐ Ⓑ Ⓒ Ⓓ

ARITHMETIC REASONING—SUBTEST 2

1. Ⓐ Ⓑ Ⓒ Ⓓ	7. Ⓐ Ⓑ Ⓒ Ⓓ	13. Ⓐ Ⓑ Ⓒ Ⓓ	19. Ⓐ Ⓑ Ⓒ Ⓓ	25. Ⓐ Ⓑ Ⓒ Ⓓ
2. Ⓐ Ⓑ Ⓒ Ⓓ	8. Ⓐ Ⓑ Ⓒ Ⓓ	14. Ⓐ Ⓑ Ⓒ Ⓓ	20. Ⓐ Ⓑ Ⓒ Ⓓ	26. Ⓐ Ⓑ Ⓒ Ⓓ
3. Ⓐ Ⓑ Ⓒ Ⓓ	9. Ⓐ Ⓑ Ⓒ Ⓓ	15. Ⓐ Ⓑ Ⓒ Ⓓ	21. Ⓐ Ⓑ Ⓒ Ⓓ	27. Ⓐ Ⓑ Ⓒ Ⓓ
4. Ⓐ Ⓑ Ⓒ Ⓓ	10. Ⓐ Ⓑ Ⓒ Ⓓ	16. Ⓐ Ⓑ Ⓒ Ⓓ	22. Ⓐ Ⓑ Ⓒ Ⓓ	28. Ⓐ Ⓑ Ⓒ Ⓓ
5. Ⓐ Ⓑ Ⓒ Ⓓ	11. Ⓐ Ⓑ Ⓒ Ⓓ	17. Ⓐ Ⓑ Ⓒ Ⓓ	23. Ⓐ Ⓑ Ⓒ Ⓓ	29. Ⓐ Ⓑ Ⓒ Ⓓ
6. Ⓐ Ⓑ Ⓒ Ⓓ	12. Ⓐ Ⓑ Ⓒ Ⓓ	18. Ⓐ Ⓑ Ⓒ Ⓓ	24. Ⓐ Ⓑ Ⓒ Ⓓ	30. Ⓐ Ⓑ Ⓒ Ⓓ

WORD KNOWLEDGE—SUBTEST 3

1. Ⓐ Ⓑ Ⓒ Ⓓ	8. Ⓐ Ⓑ Ⓒ Ⓓ	15. Ⓐ Ⓑ Ⓒ Ⓓ	22. Ⓐ Ⓑ Ⓒ Ⓓ	29. Ⓐ Ⓑ Ⓒ Ⓓ
2. Ⓐ Ⓑ Ⓒ Ⓓ	9. Ⓐ Ⓑ Ⓒ Ⓓ	16. Ⓐ Ⓑ Ⓒ Ⓓ	23. Ⓐ Ⓑ Ⓒ Ⓓ	30. Ⓐ Ⓑ Ⓒ Ⓓ
3. Ⓐ Ⓑ Ⓒ Ⓓ	10. Ⓐ Ⓑ Ⓒ Ⓓ	17. Ⓐ Ⓑ Ⓒ Ⓓ	24. Ⓐ Ⓑ Ⓒ Ⓓ	31. Ⓐ Ⓑ Ⓒ Ⓓ
4. Ⓐ Ⓑ Ⓒ Ⓓ	11. Ⓐ Ⓑ Ⓒ Ⓓ	18. Ⓐ Ⓑ Ⓒ Ⓓ	25. Ⓐ Ⓑ Ⓒ Ⓓ	32. Ⓐ Ⓑ Ⓒ Ⓓ
5. Ⓐ Ⓑ Ⓒ Ⓓ	12. Ⓐ Ⓑ Ⓒ Ⓓ	19. Ⓐ Ⓑ Ⓒ Ⓓ	26. Ⓐ Ⓑ Ⓒ Ⓓ	33. Ⓐ Ⓑ Ⓒ Ⓓ
6. Ⓐ Ⓑ Ⓒ Ⓓ	13. Ⓐ Ⓑ Ⓒ Ⓓ	20. Ⓐ Ⓑ Ⓒ Ⓓ	27. Ⓐ Ⓑ Ⓒ Ⓓ	34. Ⓐ Ⓑ Ⓒ Ⓓ
7. Ⓐ Ⓑ Ⓒ Ⓓ	14. Ⓐ Ⓑ Ⓒ Ⓓ	21. Ⓐ Ⓑ Ⓒ Ⓓ	28. Ⓐ Ⓑ Ⓒ Ⓓ	35. Ⓐ Ⓑ Ⓒ Ⓓ

PARAGRAPH COMPREHENSION—SUBTEST 4

1. Ⓐ Ⓑ Ⓒ Ⓓ	4. Ⓐ Ⓑ Ⓒ Ⓓ	7. Ⓐ Ⓑ Ⓒ Ⓓ	10. Ⓐ Ⓑ Ⓒ Ⓓ	13. Ⓐ Ⓑ Ⓒ Ⓓ
2. Ⓐ Ⓑ Ⓒ Ⓓ	5. Ⓐ Ⓑ Ⓒ Ⓓ	8. Ⓐ Ⓑ Ⓒ Ⓓ	11. Ⓐ Ⓑ Ⓒ Ⓓ	14. Ⓐ Ⓑ Ⓒ Ⓓ
3. Ⓐ Ⓑ Ⓒ Ⓓ	6. Ⓐ Ⓑ Ⓒ Ⓓ	9. Ⓐ Ⓑ Ⓒ Ⓓ	12. Ⓐ Ⓑ Ⓒ Ⓓ	15. Ⓐ Ⓑ Ⓒ Ⓓ

AUTOMOTIVE INFORMATION—SUBTEST 5

1. Ⓐ Ⓑ Ⓒ Ⓓ	4. Ⓐ Ⓑ Ⓒ Ⓓ	7. Ⓐ Ⓑ Ⓒ Ⓓ	10. Ⓐ Ⓑ Ⓒ Ⓓ	13. Ⓐ Ⓑ Ⓒ Ⓓ
2. Ⓐ Ⓑ Ⓒ Ⓓ	5. Ⓐ Ⓑ Ⓒ Ⓓ	8. Ⓐ Ⓑ Ⓒ Ⓓ	11. Ⓐ Ⓑ Ⓒ Ⓓ	14. Ⓐ Ⓑ Ⓒ Ⓓ
3. Ⓐ Ⓑ Ⓒ Ⓓ	6. Ⓐ Ⓑ Ⓒ Ⓓ	9. Ⓐ Ⓑ Ⓒ Ⓓ	12. Ⓐ Ⓑ Ⓒ Ⓓ	15. Ⓐ Ⓑ Ⓒ Ⓓ

MATHEMATICS KNOWLEDGE—SUBTEST 6

1. Ⓐ Ⓑ Ⓒ Ⓓ	6. Ⓐ Ⓑ Ⓒ Ⓓ	11. Ⓐ Ⓑ Ⓒ Ⓓ	16. Ⓐ Ⓑ Ⓒ Ⓓ	21. Ⓐ Ⓑ Ⓒ Ⓓ
2. Ⓐ Ⓑ Ⓒ Ⓓ	7. Ⓐ Ⓑ Ⓒ Ⓓ	12. Ⓐ Ⓑ Ⓒ Ⓓ	17. Ⓐ Ⓑ Ⓒ Ⓓ	22. Ⓐ Ⓑ Ⓒ Ⓓ
3. Ⓐ Ⓑ Ⓒ Ⓓ	8. Ⓐ Ⓑ Ⓒ Ⓓ	13. Ⓐ Ⓑ Ⓒ Ⓓ	18. Ⓐ Ⓑ Ⓒ Ⓓ	23. Ⓐ Ⓑ Ⓒ Ⓓ
4. Ⓐ Ⓑ Ⓒ Ⓓ	9. Ⓐ Ⓑ Ⓒ Ⓓ	14. Ⓐ Ⓑ Ⓒ Ⓓ	19. Ⓐ Ⓑ Ⓒ Ⓓ	24. Ⓐ Ⓑ Ⓒ Ⓓ
5. Ⓐ Ⓑ Ⓒ Ⓓ	10. Ⓐ Ⓑ Ⓒ Ⓓ	15. Ⓐ Ⓑ Ⓒ Ⓓ	20. Ⓐ Ⓑ Ⓒ Ⓓ	25. Ⓐ Ⓑ Ⓒ Ⓓ

MECHANICAL COMPREHENSION—SUBTEST 7

1. Ⓐ Ⓑ Ⓒ Ⓓ	6. Ⓐ Ⓑ Ⓒ Ⓓ	11. Ⓐ Ⓑ Ⓒ Ⓓ	16. Ⓐ Ⓑ Ⓒ Ⓓ	21. Ⓐ Ⓑ Ⓒ Ⓓ
2. Ⓐ Ⓑ Ⓒ Ⓓ	7. Ⓐ Ⓑ Ⓒ Ⓓ	12. Ⓐ Ⓑ Ⓒ Ⓓ	17. Ⓐ Ⓑ Ⓒ Ⓓ	22. Ⓐ Ⓑ Ⓒ Ⓓ
3. Ⓐ Ⓑ Ⓒ Ⓓ	8. Ⓐ Ⓑ Ⓒ Ⓓ	13. Ⓐ Ⓑ Ⓒ Ⓓ	18. Ⓐ Ⓑ Ⓒ Ⓓ	23. Ⓐ Ⓑ Ⓒ Ⓓ
4. Ⓐ Ⓑ Ⓒ Ⓓ	9. Ⓐ Ⓑ Ⓒ Ⓓ	14. Ⓐ Ⓑ Ⓒ Ⓓ	19. Ⓐ Ⓑ Ⓒ Ⓓ	24. Ⓐ Ⓑ Ⓒ Ⓓ
5. Ⓐ Ⓑ Ⓒ Ⓓ	10. Ⓐ Ⓑ Ⓒ Ⓓ	15. Ⓐ Ⓑ Ⓒ Ⓓ	20. Ⓐ Ⓑ Ⓒ Ⓓ	25. Ⓐ Ⓑ Ⓒ Ⓓ

ELECTRONICS INFORMATION—SUBTEST 8

1. Ⓐ Ⓑ Ⓒ Ⓓ	5. Ⓐ Ⓑ Ⓒ Ⓓ	9. Ⓐ Ⓑ Ⓒ Ⓓ	13. Ⓐ Ⓑ Ⓒ Ⓓ	17. Ⓐ Ⓑ Ⓒ Ⓓ
2. Ⓐ Ⓑ Ⓒ Ⓓ	6. Ⓐ Ⓑ Ⓒ Ⓓ	10. Ⓐ Ⓑ Ⓒ Ⓓ	14. Ⓐ Ⓑ Ⓒ Ⓓ	18. Ⓐ Ⓑ Ⓒ Ⓓ
3. Ⓐ Ⓑ Ⓒ Ⓓ	7. Ⓐ Ⓑ Ⓒ Ⓓ	11. Ⓐ Ⓑ Ⓒ Ⓓ	15. Ⓐ Ⓑ Ⓒ Ⓓ	19. Ⓐ Ⓑ Ⓒ Ⓓ
4. Ⓐ Ⓑ Ⓒ Ⓓ	8. Ⓐ Ⓑ Ⓒ Ⓓ	12. Ⓐ Ⓑ Ⓒ Ⓓ	16. Ⓐ Ⓑ Ⓒ Ⓓ	20. Ⓐ Ⓑ Ⓒ Ⓓ

SHOP INFORMATION—SUBTEST 9

1. Ⓐ Ⓑ Ⓒ Ⓓ	4. Ⓐ Ⓑ Ⓒ Ⓓ	7. Ⓐ Ⓑ Ⓒ Ⓓ	10. Ⓐ Ⓑ Ⓒ Ⓓ	13. Ⓐ Ⓑ Ⓒ Ⓓ
2. Ⓐ Ⓑ Ⓒ Ⓓ	5. Ⓐ Ⓑ Ⓒ Ⓓ	8. Ⓐ Ⓑ Ⓒ Ⓓ	11. Ⓐ Ⓑ Ⓒ Ⓓ	14. Ⓐ Ⓑ Ⓒ Ⓓ
3. Ⓐ Ⓑ Ⓒ Ⓓ	6. Ⓐ Ⓑ Ⓒ Ⓓ	9. Ⓐ Ⓑ Ⓒ Ⓓ	12. Ⓐ Ⓑ Ⓒ Ⓓ	15. Ⓐ Ⓑ Ⓒ Ⓓ

ASSEMBLING OBJECTS—SUBTEST 10

1. Ⓐ Ⓑ Ⓒ Ⓓ	5. Ⓐ Ⓑ Ⓒ Ⓓ	9. Ⓐ Ⓑ Ⓒ Ⓓ	13. Ⓐ Ⓑ Ⓒ Ⓓ	17. Ⓐ Ⓑ Ⓒ Ⓓ
2. Ⓐ Ⓑ Ⓒ Ⓓ	6. Ⓐ Ⓑ Ⓒ Ⓓ	10. Ⓐ Ⓑ Ⓒ Ⓓ	14. Ⓐ Ⓑ Ⓒ Ⓓ	18. Ⓐ Ⓑ Ⓒ Ⓓ
3. Ⓐ Ⓑ Ⓒ Ⓓ	7. Ⓐ Ⓑ Ⓒ Ⓓ	11. Ⓐ Ⓑ Ⓒ Ⓓ	15. Ⓐ Ⓑ Ⓒ Ⓓ	19. Ⓐ Ⓑ Ⓒ Ⓓ
4. Ⓐ Ⓑ Ⓒ Ⓓ	8. Ⓐ Ⓑ Ⓒ Ⓓ	12. Ⓐ Ⓑ Ⓒ Ⓓ	16. Ⓐ Ⓑ Ⓒ Ⓓ	20. Ⓐ Ⓑ Ⓒ Ⓓ

13 Practice Examination Three

GENERAL SCIENCE—SUBTEST 1

DIRECTIONS

This test has questions about science. Pick the best answer for each question, then blacken the space on your separate answer form that has the same number and letter as your choice.

Here is a sample question.

1. An example of a chemical change is

   A melting ice.
   B breaking glass.
   C rusting metal.
   D making sawdust from wood.

The correct answer is rusting metal, so you would blacken the space for C on your answer form.

Your score on this test will be based on the number of questions you answer correctly. You should try to answer every question. Do not spend too much time on any one question.

When you begin, be sure to start with question number 1 in Part 1, and number 1 in Part 1 on your answer form.

THE ACTUAL TEST WILL SAY:

Do not turn this page until told to do so.

General Science

Time: 11 minutes; 25 questions

1. Which of the following determines the sex of a human offspring?

   A egg cell
   B polar body
   C egg nucleus
   D sperm

2. Rocks are frequently split apart by

   A running water.
   B wind.
   C sudden changes in temperature.
   D meteorites.

3. Sand is made up of colorless crystals of

   A iron.
   B mica.
   C shale.
   D quartz.

4. Which material is an acid?

   A ammonia water
   B baking soda
   C vinegar
   D rainwater

5. Isotopes of the same element have the same number of

   A protons only.
   B electrons and protons only.
   C neutrons only.
   D neutrons and protons only.

6. As heat is applied to boiling water, the temperature remains the same. The best explanation for this is that

   A convection increases at the boiling point of water.
   B radiation increases at the boiling point of water.
   C escaping vapor is taking away energy.
   D the applied heat is absorbed quickly by the surroundings.

7. Which of the following is outside the solar system?

   A Mars
   B nebulae
   C satellites
   D asteroids

8. Solar energy is transmitted through space by

   A convection.
   B radiation.
   C reflection.
   D absorption.

9. Which is an example of a sex-linked trait?

   A eye color
   B anemia
   C height
   D hemophilia

10. A fact that supports the position that viruses are living is that viruses

    A are made of common chemicals.
    B cause disease.
    C duplicate themselves.
    D are protein molecules.

11. A thermometer that indicates the freezing point of water at 0 degrees and the boiling point of water at 100 degrees is called a

    A Centigrade thermometer.
    B Fahrenheit thermometer.
    C Kelvin thermometer.
    D Reaumur thermometer.

12. Vegetation should be kept on slopes because

    A plants aid weathering.
    B runoff increases.
    C plant roots hold the soil.
    D plants enrich the soil.

13. A 25-pound force has two components at right angles to each other. If one component is 15 pounds, the other component is

A 10 pounds.
B 20 pounds.
C 40 pounds.
D 25 pounds.

14. What device is used to test the solution in a storage battery?

A voltmeter
B hydrometer
C ammeter
D anemometer

15. Fluorides are added to drinking water in order to

A improve taste.
B increase metabolism.
C prevent caries.
D prevent typhoid fever.

16. Blinking in response to bright light is an example of a(n)

A phototropism.
B habit.
C reflex.
D instinct.

17. The Rh factor is important in the study of

A fingerprinting.
B the blood.
C the acidity of a solution.
D the determination of sex.

18. What mineral element is part of hemoglobin?

A calcium
B fluorine
C carbon
D iron

19. In the winter the coldest areas are usually

A island coasts.
B continental interiors.
C oceans.
D hilltops.

20. If the mass of an object were doubled, its acceleration due to gravity would be

A halved.
B doubled.
C unchanged.
D quadrupled.

21. Respiration in plants takes place

A only during the day.
B only in the presence of carbon dioxide.
C both day and night.
D only at night.

22. Wind is mainly the result of

A clouds.
B storms.
C high humidity.
D unequal heating of air.

23. Which appeared most recently on the earth?

A reptiles
B mammals
C amphibians
D insects

24. When all the colors of the spectrum are mixed, the light is

A yellow.
B black.
C white.
D blue.

25. A solution that has a high ratio of solute to solvent is said to be

A unsaturated.
B saturated.
C dilute.
D concentrated.

ARITHMETIC REASONING—SUBTEST 2

DIRECTIONS

This test has questions about arithmetic. Each question is followed by four possible answers. Decide which answer is correct. Then, on your answer form, blacken the space that has the same number and letter as your choice. Use scratch paper for any figuring you wish to do.

Here is a sample question.

1. If 1 quart of milk costs $0.80, what is the cost of 2 quarts?

   A $2.00
   B $1.60
   C $1.20
   D $1.00

The cost of 2 quarts is $1.60; therefore, answer B is correct.

Your score on this test will be based on the number of questions you answer correctly. You should try to answer every question. Do not spend too much time on any one question.

Notice that Part 2 begins with question number 1. When you begin, be sure to mark your first answer next to number 1 on your answer form.

THE ACTUAL TEST WILL SAY:

Do not turn this page until told to do so.

Arithmetic Reasoning

Time: 36 minutes; 30 questions

1. Mr. Winter bought a $500 TV set that was marked at a 15% discount. He made a down payment of $65 and agreed to pay the balance in 12 equal monthly installments. How much was each installment?

   A $25.00
   B $30.00
   C $42.50
   D $360.00

2. A farmer uses 2 gallons of insecticide concentrate to spray each 1/4 acre of his land. How many gallons of the concentrate will he need to spray 10½ acres?

   A 80
   B 80¼
   C 82
   D 84

3. An engineering drawing on a sheet of paper that measures 12 inches by 18 inches is to be enlarged so that the length is 45 inches. How many inches wide will the enlarged drawing be?

   A 30
   B 39
   C 66
   D 33

4. In a quality control test at a factory, of 280 products inspected at random, 266 were found to be acceptable. What percentage of the items inspected were found acceptable?

   A 66%
   B 95%
   C 5%
   D 86%

5. A candy store sells 3 pounds of a candy mix for $4.80. What is the price of a 5-ounce bag of this mix?

A $1.00
B $2.40
C $0.25
D $0.50

6. The perimeter of a square is 13 feet, 8 inches. What is the length of one side of the square?

A 3 feet, 2 inches
B 3 feet, 5 inches
C 3 feet, 3 inches
D 3 feet, 6 inches

7. A military unit has 360 members, and 20% are officers. How many members of the unit are enlisted personnel?

A 90
B 270
C 72
D 288

8. Marcella Jones earns $8.50 per hour with time and a half paid for overtime in excess of 8 hours on any one day. One day she worked 10 hours. How much did she earn on that day?

A $85.00
B $117.50
C $97.75
D $93.50

9. What is the next term in the series:

2¼, 3¾, 3¼, 4¾, _____?

A 4¼
B 6¼
C 5¼
D 3¼

10. Tickets for movie admission for adults are $4.00 each, but half-price is charged for children. If 265 adult tickets were sold and the box office collected $1,200, how many children's tickets were sold?

A 70
B 35
C 280
D 140

11. A woman budgets her income so that she spends 1/4 of it for rent and 2/5 of the remainder for food. What part of the total income does she budget for food?

A 1/10
B 1/5
C 3/20
D 3/10

12. A survey of a small group of people found that 3 of them each watched 2 hours of TV per day. Two of them watched 1 hour per day, and 1 watched 4 hours per day. What is the average number of hours of TV watched by members of this group?

A 1⅓
B 2⅔
C 2
D 3

13. What is the cost of 3 yards, 2 feet of an upholstery edging material that costs $9 per yard?

A $30
B $36
C $29
D $33

14. A partnership agreement calls for the two partners to share the profits of their business in the ratio 4:5. If the profit for the year is $63,000, what is the share paid to the partner who gets the smaller portion?

A $28,000
B $7,000
C $35,000
D $15,750

15. A courier leaves an office driving at an average rate of 30 miles per hour but forgets part of the material he was supposed to take with him. An hour later, a second courier is dispatched with the missing material and is instructed to overtake the first courier in 2 hours more. How fast must the second courier travel?

A 90 miles per hour
B 60 miles per hour
C 45 miles per hour
D 40 miles per hour

16. A merchant buys radios listed wholesale for $60 a piece at a 25% discount. He sells these radios at a 20% markup above the original wholesale price. What is his profit on each radio?

A $9.00
B $27.00
C $12.00
D $18.00

17. An airplane travels a distance of x miles in y hours. What is its average rate of speed in miles per hour?

A $\dfrac{xy}{y}$

B $\dfrac{yx}{x}$

C $\dfrac{y}{x}$

D $\dfrac{x+y}{2}$

18. The cost of sending a telegram is $1.50 for the first 10 words and $0.05 for each additional word. How many words can be sent by telegram for $4.00?

A 51
B 60
C 81
D 90

19. A mapmaker is told to prepare a map with a scale of 1 inch to 40 miles. If the actual distance between two points is 110 miles, how far apart should the mapmaker show them on the map?

A 7 inches
B 3½ inches
C 2½ inches
D 2¾ inches

20. In the town of Hampshire, houses are assessed at 75% of the purchase price. If Mr. Johnson buys a house in Hampshire for $80,000 and real estate taxes are $4.83 per $100 of assessed valuation, how much realty tax must he pay?

A $2,898
B $3,864
C $600
D $604.83

21. The ingredients in a cake recipe include 4½ cups of flour and 3/4 cup of sugar. It is desired to make a cake that will require only 1/4 cup of sugar. How much flour should be used?

A 1¼ cups
B 1½ cups
C 4 cups
D 1¾ cups

22. When the tolls on a bridge were increased, the traffic declined from 1,200 cars crossing per day to 1,044. What was the percentage of the decline in traffic?

A 87%
B 156%
C 13%
D 15%

23. If a 2-gallon bucket of liquid floor polish costs $19.20, how much should a 1-quart can cost?

A $4.80
B $2.40
C $1.20
D $0.60

24. A man takes a trip in which he first drives for 3 hours at 50 miles per hour. He then drives for 2 hours more at 55 miles per hour. If his car gets 20 miles per gallon, how manly gallons of gas did he use for the trip?

A 10
B 9.5
C 26
D 13

25. A woman has $5,000 invested at 8% annual interest. At what rate must she invest an additional $10,000 so that her annual income from both investments is equivalent to 9% of her total investment?

A 10%
B 10½%
C 9%
D 9½%

26. The fuel tank of a gasoline generator contains sufficient capacity to operate the generator for 1 hour and 20 minutes. How many times must the fuel tank be filled to run the generator from 9:15 A.M. to 3:55 P.M.?

A 5
B 6
C 4½
D 4

27. A nursery employee mixes 10 pounds of hardy grass seed worth $1.20 per pound with 8 pounds of premium grass seed worth $3.00 per pound. At what price per pound should she sell the mixture?

A $2.10
B $2.00
C $1.90
D $2.50

28. What is the value of $\dfrac{0.02 \times 3}{0.001}$

A 60
B 6
C 0.6
D 0.06

29. Find the numerical value of $1 + 5xy^2 - 3x^2y$ if $x = 3$ and $y = 2$.

A 25
B 18
C 739
D 7

30. Using the formula $I = \sqrt{\dfrac{P}{R}}$, find the value of I when $P = 48$ and $R = 3$.

A 12
B 8
C 4
D 4/3

WORD KNOWLEDGE—SUBTEST 3

DIRECTIONS

This test has questions about the meanings of words. Each question has an **underlined bold-face word**. You are to decide which one of the four words in the choices most nearly means the same as the underlined boldface word; then mark the space on your answer form that has the same number and letter as your choice.

Now look at the sample question below.

1. It was a **small** table.

    A sturdy
    B round
    C cheap
    D little

The question asks which of the four words means the same as the boldface word, **small**. *Little* means the same as **small**. Answer D is the best one.

Your score on this test will be based on the number of questions you answer correctly. You should try to answer every question. Do not spend too much time on any one question.

When you begin, be sure to start with question number 1 in Part 3 of your test booklet and number 1 in Part 3 on your answer form.

THE ACTUAL TEST WILL SAY:

Do not turn this page until told to do so.

Word Knowledge

Time: 11 minutes; 35 questions

1. Inform most nearly means

    A ask.
    B heed.
    C tell.
    D ignore.

2. The dress was **crimson**.

    A crisp
    B neatly pressed
    C reddish
    D colorful

3. Caution most nearly means

    A signals.
    B care.
    C traffic.
    D haste.

4. Rain fell **intermittently**.

    A constantly
    B annually
    C using intermediaries (to stay)
    D at irregular intervals

5. Occurrence most nearly means

    A event.
    B place.
    C occupation.
    D opinion.

6. The disguise was a clever **deception**.

    A secret
    B fraud
    C mistrust
    D hatred

7. **Cease** most nearly means

   A start.
   B change.
   C continue.
   D stop.

8. **Acclaim** most nearly means

   A amazement.
   B laughter.
   C booing.
   D applause.

9. The city plans to **erect** a civic center.

   A paint
   B design
   C destroy
   D construct

10. **Relish** most nearly means

    A care.
    B speed.
    C amusement.
    D enjoy.

11. **Sufficient** most nearly means

    A durable.
    B substitution.
    C expendable.
    D appropriate.

12. **Fortnight** most nearly means

    A 2 weeks.
    B 1 week.
    C 2 months.
    D 1 month.

13. That action was a **blemish** on his record.

    A defect
    B mixture
    C accusation
    D decoration

14. Rules **impose** order on the group.

    A disguise
    B escape
    C require
    D purchase

15. **Jeer** most nearly means

    A peek.
    B scoff.
    C turn.
    D judge.

16. **Alias** most nearly means

    A enemy.
    B sidekick.
    C hero.
    D other name.

17. **Impair** most nearly means

    A direct.
    B improve.
    C weaken.
    D stimulate.

18. **Itinerant** most nearly means

    A traveling.
    B shrewd.
    C insurance.
    D aggressive.

19. I don't often **abandon** a good idea.

    A relinquish
    B encompass
    C infiltrate
    D quarantine

20. The association met to **resolve** the issue.

    A end
    B understand
    C recall
    D forget

21. Ample most nearly means

A plentiful.
B enthusiastic.
C well-shaped.
D fat.

22. The chemical spill left a **stench**.

A puddle of slimy water
B pile of debris
C foul odor
D dead animal

23. Sullen most nearly means

A grayish-yellow.
B soaking wet.
C very dirty.
D angrily silent.

24. Rudiments most nearly means

A basic methods and procedures.
B politics.
C promotion opportunities.
D minute details.

25. Clash most nearly means

A applaud.
B fasten.
C conflict.
D punish.

26. Camaraderie most nearly means

A interest in photography.
B close friendship.
C petty jealousies.
D arts and crafts projects.

27. The report was **superficial**.

A excellent
B official
C profound
D cursory

28. Tapestry most nearly means

A fabric of woven designs.
B tent.
C piece of elaborate jewelry.
D exquisite painting.

29. The response was **terse**.

A pointed
B trivial
C oral
D lengthy

30. We had never seen such a **concoction**.

A combination of ingredients
B appetizer
C drink made of wine and spices
D relish tray

31. Brevity most nearly means

A boldness.
B shortness.
C nearness.
D length.

32. Clemency most nearly means

A justice.
B punishment.
C mercy.
D dismissal.

33. That was an act of **insubordination**.

A humiliation
B rejection
C disobedience
D carelessness

34. She advised against **preferential** treatment.

A weekly
B constant
C unlimited
D special

35. Doldrums most nearly means

A fearful.
B diseased.
C low spirits.
D embarrassment.

PARAGRAPH COMPREHENSION—SUBTEST 4

DIRECTIONS

This is a test of your ability to understand what you read. In this section you will find one or more paragraphs of reading material followed by incomplete statements or questions. You are to read the paragraph and select one of four lettered choices that best completes the statement or answers the question. When you have selected your answer, blacken in the correct numbered letter on your answer sheet.

Now look at the sample question below.

In certain areas water is so scarce that every attempt is made to conserve it. For instance, on one oasis in the Sahara Desert the amount of water necessary for each date palm tree has been carefully determined.

1. How much water is each tree given?

A no water at all
B exactly the amount required
C water only if it is healthy
D water on alternate days

The amount of water each tree requires has been carefully determined, so answer B is correct.

Your score on this test will be based on the number of questions you answer correctly. You should try to answer every question. Do not spend too much time on any one question.

When you begin, be sure to start with question number 1 in Part 4 of your test booklet and number 1 in Part 4 on your answer form.

THE ACTUAL TEST WILL SAY:

Do not turn this page until told to do so.

Paragraph Comprehension

Time: 13 minutes; 15 questions

1. Professional drivers, people who drive trucks and buses for a living, have a low opinion of the average motorist. They complain that the average driver does not maintain proper speed, changes lanes without signaling, and stops without warning.

The topic sentence or key idea in this paragraph is that

A professional drivers do not think much of the average driver.
B people who drive trucks are professional drivers.
C the average driver is not a good driver.
D the average driver does not like professional drivers.

2. The trees stood quietly under the dark gray clouds. Their bare branches shuddered as the cold wind slipped around them. Sailing along on the wind a few birds flew to shelter. No other animals were to be seen.

In this paragraph the word *shuddered* means:

A fell.
B shook.
C cracked.
D remained still.

3. Many think of the log cabin as a New England invention. Others feel it was first made by the pioneers who crossed the Appalachian Mountains. According to one authority, the log cabin was introduced to America by the Swedes. The area around the Delaware River was settled by Swedes and Finns. These two European peoples were first to use the log cabin.

According to this passage, the log cabin was introduced to this country by

A New England colonists.
B Swedes and Finns.
C Appalachian Mountain pioneers.
D the English.

4. Down the gently drifting stream, the boat glided softly. Soft breezes and warm sun bathed him. The fishing pole lay unused. The floppy hat shaded his half-closed eyes and much of his face. Only his lower features, framed in a pleasant smile, could be seen.

This passage describes a man who is

A sad.
B active.
C contented.
D exhilarated.

5. Would you like to be good at a trade? Would you like to know a skill that pays well? One sure way to skill, good pay, and regular work is to train on the job. This is called apprentice training. While it is not the only way to learn, apprentice training has good points. You can earn while you learn, can learn the skill "from the ground up," and can advance on the job.

Apprentice training is described in this paragraph by

A discussing both sides.
B discussing only the good side.
C discussing only the bad side.
D comparing it to other types of training.

6. Move into a house with 6 closets and all of them will be jammed in a short time. Move into a house with 15 closets and the same thing will happen. In short, we never have enough closets no matter how many closets we have. But there's one thing we can do. We can make better use of the space within a closet.

The author of this paragraph suggests that we

A should build more closets in houses.
B never have enough things to fill the closets.
C usually fill every closet in the house.
D make the best use of space within a closet.

7. There is a big difference between a liberal and a reactionary. The person who favors new ideas, tries to change, and looks for new ways is more free or liberated. On the other hand, a person may look back or want to return to the way things used to be. This person does not like progress and resents change.

The word *reactionary* can be used to describe a person who

A looks ahead to the future.
B looks back to the past.
C favors new ideas.
D likes change.

8. This forest must be preserved. These trees have stood against natural forces for over a hundred years. Within the area wildlife flourishes and the streams are clear and sparkling. Thousands of people can find pleasure through camping or walking in a spot of unspoiled nature. The beauty and peace of this forest can renew the spirit of many a person.

This passage was probably written by a

A lumber company spokesperson.
B religious society.
C house-building company.
D conservation group.

9. There has been enough talk. The problem has been studied from every viewpoint. The figures add up to the need for the bridge. When the bonds are approved their cost will be met by future tolls. All groups favor this and no property owners will be hurt by it. The time for action has come.

According to this paragraph, the next logical step would be to

A build the bridge
B pass a law to raise the money
C decide how to collect the tolls
D have a meeting of property owners

10. Lightning is a gigantic spark, a tremendous release of energy between earth and cloud. The shorter the gap between earth and cloud, the greater the chances of discharge. Thus, lightning tends to favor objects that thrust above the surrounding terrain. This might mean you sitting in a boat or the lone tree on the golf course.

Lightning is described as

A man-made energy.
B a bolt from heaven.
C a release of electrical energy.
D a poorly understood phenomenon.

11. Every large city has problems of traffic and people trying to use transportation. The problem is at its worst in the 2 hours before 9 A.M. and the 2 hours after 4 P.M. So many businesses, stores, and companies start work and end work at the same time. This becomes a very great problem in the downtown business centers with their many-storied skyscrapers and their thousands of workers.

The morning transportation rush starts at

A 9 A.M.
B 7 A.M.
C 8 A.M.
D 6 A.M.

12. A vision care technician assists the patient in frame selection and fitting and provides instruction in the use of contact lenses. Such a technician works with children in visual training programs and assists with testing for corneal curvature, visual acuity, and eye pressure.

The word *acuity* means

A cuteness.
B strength.
C sharpness.
D pressure.

13. An agricultural research scientist wishes to test the germination power of a particular strain of wheat. That is, he wants to know what proportion of the seeds will grow to maturity. He picks one seed at random from a bunch of wheat and that particular grain of wheat produces a strong and healthy stalk of wheat.

We can conclude from this experiment that

A the rest of the seeds are the same.
B this seed is the only healthy one.
C more seeds must be tested.
D it was an accident that this seed was good.

14. Most breads and cereals are well-liked, fit easily into meal plan, and cost little per serving. These foods, with whole-grain or enriched bread as examples, provide good food value. Mostly they give food energy, but they also supply vitamins and minerals. According to a recent survey, bread and cereal products provided 40% of the thiamine (a B vitamin) and 30% of the iron needed daily by a person.

What percent of the daily needs of a B vitamin come from bread and cereals?

A 30%
B more than half
C 40%
D 70%

15. In the many years before 1800 there was a great fear of plague and other illnesses. Most of the problem came from poor medical knowledge and no scientific way to fight the diseases. People knew the results of plague would be suffering and death. Naturally they tried to stay away from infection or they tried to keep the danger away from them.

The main reason for the fear of plague before 1800 was

A crowded cities and seaports.
B little medical or scientific knowledge.
C long time needed for quarantine.
D difficulty in avoiding infection.

AUTOMOTIVE INFORMATION—SUBTEST 5

DIRECTIONS

This test has questions about automobiles. Pick the best answer for each question, then blacken the space on your separate answer form that has the same number and letter as your choice.

1. The most commonly used fuel for running automobile engines is

  A kerosene.
  B benzene.
  C crude oil.
  D gasoline.

Gasoline is the most commonly used fuel, so D is the correct answer.

Your score on this test will be based on the number of questions you answer correctly. You should try to answer every question. Do not spend too much time on any one question.

When you are told to begin, be sure to start with question number 1 in Part 5 of your test booklet and number 1 in Part 5 on your separate answer form.

THE ACTUAL TEST WILL SAY:

Do not turn this page until told to do so.

Automotive Information

Time: 8 minutes; 15 questions

1. The universal joint is needed to

  A allow the drive shaft to flex.
  B hold the drive shaft rigid.
  C make the transmission shift.
  D make the differential turn corners.

2. Three major pollutants emitted by a gasoline engine are

  A carbon dioxide, carbon monoxide, and oxygen.
  B hydrocarbons, nitric acid, and nitrogen.
  C hydrocarbons, carbon monoxide, and oxides of nitrogen.
  D nitrogen, oxygen, and carbon monixide.

3. The catalytic converter

  A converts gasoline to the air/fuel ratio needed.
  B reduces the input pressure of exhaust gases to the muffler.
  C converts intake manifold pressure to a lower value.
  D converts exhaust gases to better-quality emissions.

4. The differential

  A is located in the transmission.
  B is located in the clutch housing.
  C consists of three small bevel gears on the ends of the axle shafts.
  D consists of two small bevel gears on the ends of the axle shafts.

5. PCV is the abbreviation for

  A pollution control valve.
  B pollution valve control.
  C positive crankcase ventilation.
  D pollution control ventilator.

6. The formation of NO$_x$ in an engine is minimized by

A diluting the fuel/air mixture entering the combustion chamber.
B burning more fuel.
C using an alcohol-enriched fuel.
D not using a muffler.

7. With any two gears the gear with the greater number of teeth will

A turn slower than the smaller gear and produce less torque.
B always turn slower and produce greater torque.
C never produce much torque.
D always turn faster and products less torque.

8. The clutch is used to

A change compression ratios.
B stop the car.
C make it possible to change gears.
D drive the transmission.

9. First gear in a car is used

A at high speeds.
B in starting the car from a standstill.
C when the car is moving faster than 35 miles per hour.
D at speeds above 55 miles per hour.

10. The torque converter is found in

A the differential housing.
B the manual transmission housing.
C the engine compartment.
D in an automatic transmission.

11. Disc brakes are made with

A two pads and a rotating drum.
B two pads and a rotating disc.
C two brake shoes that slide along the inside drum mounted on the rear wheels.
D all-steel pads to stop the car quickly.

12. In a front-wheel-drive car the transmission

A is located in the rear of the car.
B is located in the engine compartment.
C has a long propeller shaft.
D has a short propeller shaft.

13. L$_0$ or L on the automatic transmission is the same as

A First gear in the manual transmission.
B Second gear in the manual transmission.
C Third gear in the manual transmission.
D Fourth gear in the manual transmission.

14. Park (P) position on an automatic transmission indicator means the transmission

A is in idle and can be towed.
B is in a locked position that prevents the car from moving.
C is in its highest speed position.
D is ready for pulling heavy loads.

15. The internal combustion engine can be best described as

A a high-torque engine even at low speeds.
B a low-torque engine even at low speeds.
C a low-speed engine.
D a high-speed engine.

MATHEMATICS KNOWLEDGE—SUBTEST 6

DIRECTIONS

This is a test of your ability to solve general mathematical problems. Each problem is followed by four answer choices. Select the correct response from the choices given. Then mark the space on your answer form that has the same number and letter as your choice. Use scratch paper to do any figuring that you wish.

Now look at this sample problem.

1. If $x + 8 = 9$, then x is equal to

   A 0.
   B 1.
   C -1.
   D 9/8.

The correct answer is 1, so B is the correct response.

Your score on this test will be based on the number of questions you answer correctly. You should try to answer every question. Do not spend too much time on any one question.

Start with question number 1 in Part 6. Mark your answer for this question next to number 1, Part 6, on your answer form.

THE ACTUAL TEST WILL SAY:

Do not turn this page until told to do so.

Mathematics Knowledge

Time: 24 minutes; 25 questions

1. Solve for x: $2x + 6 = 12 - x$.

   A 6
   B 9
   C 2
   D 3

2. From $8x^2 - 7x$ subtract $2x - 3x^2$.

   A $11x^2 - 9x$
   B $5x^2 - 5x$
   C $6x^2 - 4x$
   D $10x^2 - 10x$

3. What is the product of $2x^3y$ and $(3x^2y - 4)$?

   A $6x^5y^2 - 4$
   B $6x^5y^2 - 8x^3y$
   C $6x^6y^2 - 8x^3y$
   D $6x^6y - 8x^3y$

4. A worker can do 1/3 of a job by herself in one day, and her helper can do 1/5 of the job by himself in one day. What portion of the job can they do if they work together for one day?

   A 1/4
   B 8/15
   C 1/8
   D 2/15

5. A length of chain is 5 feet, 3 inches long. If a piece 3 feet, 9 inches in length is cut from the chain, what is the length of the remaining piece?

   A 2 feet, 6 inches
   B 1 foot, 1 inch
   C 1 foot, 4 inches
   D 1 foot, 6 inches

6. In a regular hexagon, all the angles are equal and one of them is 120 degrees. What is the sum of all the angles of the regular hexagon?

A 240 degrees
B 480 degrees
C 720 degrees
D 360 degrees

7. What is the product of $(3a - 2)$ and $(a + 3)$?

A $4a + 1$
B $3a^2 - 6$
C $3a^2 - 2a - 6$
D $3a^2 + 7a - 6$

8. If $x = 3$, what is the value of $|x - 7|$?

A 4
B -4
C 10
D -10

9. Solve the following system of equations for
$$x: 3x + y = 13$$
$$x - 2y = 2$$

A 18
B 4
C 3
D 6

10. How many feet are there in a length of y yards and i inches?

A $3y + i$
B $3y + 12i$
C $\dfrac{y + 12i}{3}$
D $\dfrac{36y + i}{12}$

11. Solve the following formula for F: $C = \dfrac{5}{9}(F - 32)$.

A $F = \dfrac{9}{5}C + 32$
B $F = \dfrac{5}{9}C + 32$
C $F = \dfrac{9C + 32}{5}$
D $F = \dfrac{9}{5}C + 288$

12. A woman travels 3 miles directly east and then travels 4 miles directly north. How many miles is she from her starting point?

A 7
B 5
C 25
D 3½

13. A line is drawn perpendicular to the base of an equilateral triangle at one of the vertices of a triangle. Find the number of degrees in the angle made by the perpendicular and the other side of the triangle that contains this vertex.

A 30 degrees
B 45 degrees
C 60 degrees
D 90 degrees

14. Solve the following inequality:
$$x - 6 \leq 5$$

A $x \leq 1$
B $x \leq 11$
C $x \geq 11$
D $x < 11$

15. A fence that had been installed around a rectangular field 40 feet long and 36 feet wide is torn down. The entire fence is then reused to completely enclose a square field. What is the length in feet of a side of the square field?

A 76
B 19
C 42
D 38

16. A cereal manufacturer packages breakfast cereal in individual-sized boxes measuring 2 inches by 3 inches by 4 inches. The same product is also packaged in large family-sized boxes measuring 3 inches by 8 inches by 12 inches. The contents of how many of the individual-sized boxes would be required to fill one family-sized box?

A 6
B 12
C 10
D 8

17. A wheel has a diameter of 14 inches. How many inches will the wheel roll along the ground during one rotation? (Use 22/7 as the value of π.)

A 44
B 22
C 14
D 28

18. In a right triangle whose hypotenuse has a length of 21 feet, the sine of one of the angles is 3/7. What is the length in feet of the side opposite this angle?

A 6
B 14
C 9
D 10

19. Find the value of $-x^4$ if $x = -0.1$.

A −0.1
B 0.0001
C −0.0001
D −0.4

20. Under the terms of a federal subsidy, a real estate developer is required to rent at least 30% of the apartments she builds to low-income families. If she plans on having 108 low-income apartments, what is the maximum number of apartments of all types that she can build?

A 360
B 252
C 324
D 396

21. A student has grades of 60% on each of two tests and a grade of 70% on a third test. What grade must he get on a fourth test to raise his average to 75%?

A 95%
B 85%
C 100%
D He cannot achieve a 75% average.

22. A motorist travels for 3 hours at 40 miles per hour and then travels for 2 more hours at 50 miles per hour. What is her average rate of speed in miles per hour for the entire trip?

A 45
B 44
C 43
D 90

23. A radar device is capable of detecting objects within the area around it up to a radius of 10 miles. If it is used to cover a 36 degree angular portion of this area, how many square miles of area will it cover? (Use 3.14 as the value of π.)

A 360
B 6.28
C 31.4
D 3.6

24. Solve for x: $x^2 + 2x = 15$.

    A $x = 3, x = 5$
    B $x = -3, x = 5$
    C $x = -5, x = 3$
    D $x = -15, x = 1$

25. 12 quarts of a radiator coolant contains 25% antifreeze and 75% water. How many quarts of water must be added to change the mixture to one containing 20% antifreeze?

    A 1
    B 2
    C 3
    D 4

MECHANICAL COMPREHENSION—SUBTEST 7

DIRECTIONS

This test has questions about general mechanical and physical principles. Pick the best answer to each question, then blacken the space on your separate answer form that has the same number and letter as your choice.

Here is a sample question.

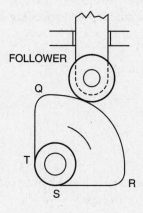

1. The follower is at its highest position between points

    A Q and R.
    B R and S.
    C S and T.
    D T and Q.

The correct answer is between Q and R, so you would blacken the space for A on your answer form.

Your score on this test will be based on the number of questions you answer correctly. You should try to answer every question. Do not spend too much time on any one question.

When you are told to begin, be sure to start with question number 1 in Part 7 of your test booklet and number 1 in Part 7 of your separate answer form.

THE ACTUAL TEST WILL SAY:

Do not turn this page until told to do so.

Mechanical Comprehension

Time: 19 minutes; 25 questions

1. Most of the lift on an aircraft's wings is because of

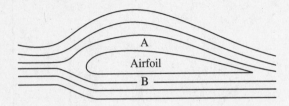

A. a decrease in pressure on the upper side, A.
B. a decrease in pressure on the bottom side, B.
C. a vacuum created under the wing at point A.
D. none of the above.

2. It is well known that oil rises in lamp wicks, melted wax rises in the wick of a candle, and water rises in a narrow tube. This phenomenon is called

A. wicking.
B. erosion.
C. capillarity.
D. osmosis.

3. Two strips of metal, one iron and one brass, are welded or riveted together to form a

A. heating element.
B. thermal bridge.
C. heat switch.
D. thermostat.

4. Which of the following metals expands the most when heated?

A. steel
B. aluminum
C. iron
D. tungsten

5. Clocks with pendulums tend to run faster when cold. This is caused by

A. the pendulum becoming longer when cold.
B. the pendulum becoming shorter when cold.
C. the air expanding and slowing the pendulum.
D. the air contracting and speeding up the pendulum.

6. Heat is a form of

A. energy.
B. motion.
C. thermal.
D. calories.

7. Which of the metals listed below is the best conductor of heat?

A. aluminum
B. copper
C. iron
D. silver

8. Heat is transferred from one place to another by conduction, convection, and

A. condensation.
B. evaporation.
C. radiation.
D. cooling.

9. When a salt is dissolved in water, it causes

A. an increase in the freezing point of the solution.
B. a decrease in the freezing point of the solution.
C. little or no difference in the freezing point.
D. the water to freeze and leave the salt.

10. When a liquid is changed to vapor, the process is called

A. evaporation.
B. dehydration.
C. pressurization.
D. condensation.

11. When water is heated and confined to a closed container so the steam cannot escape, the pressure inside increases and the temperature of the boiling water

A becomes lower.
B becomes higher.
C stays the same.
D does none of the above.

12. Crude petroleum is a mixture of many substances with different boiling points. The process of refining to obtain gasoline is called

A condensation.
B pressurization.
C dehydration.
D fractional distillation.

13. The speed of sound at 0 degrees has been found to be

A 1,492 meters per second.
B 3,500 meters per second.
C 1,086 feet per second.
D 186,000 miles per second.

14. The meter used to measure extremely high resistances is called a(n)

A ohmmeter.
B megger.
C resistance meter.
D ammeter.

15. In the figure below a hole is being drilled in 1. What is taking place in 2?

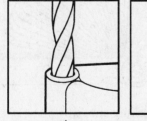 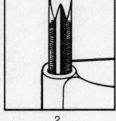

1　　　　2

A The hole is being reamed.
B The hole is being drilled.
C The hole is being tapped.
D The hole is being plugged.

16. The units shown are used on small gasoline engines as

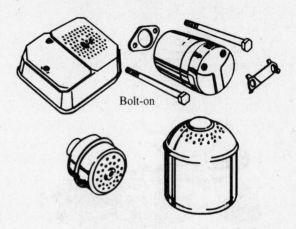

Bolt-on

A carburetors.
B filters.
C magnetos.
D mufflers.

17. The outboard engine shown is water-cooled and gets its cooling water from

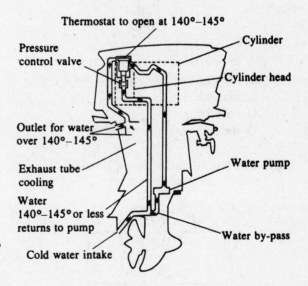

Thermostat to open at 140°–145°
Cylinder
Pressure control valve
Cylinder head
Outlet for water over 140°–145°
Exhaust tube cooling
Water pump
Water 140°–145° or less returns to pump
Water by-pass
Cold water intake

A its radiator.
B its oil cooler.
C the lake or river.
D its water holding tank.

18. In a small gasoline engine's fuel tank, the ball drops when suction stops. This prevents

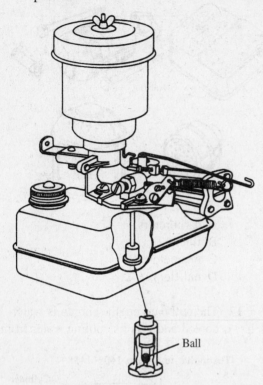

A the engine from running any more.
B the gasoline from running back into the tank.
C backfiring.
D the engine from exploding.

19. The type of cutter shown is called a

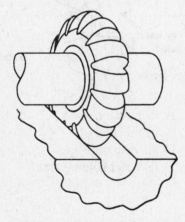

A convex cutter.
B single angle cutter.
C concave cutter.
D corner-rounding cutter.

20. In the figure shown the setup is being used to

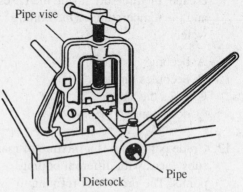

A ream a pipe.
B cut a pipe.
C thread a pipe.
D bore a pipe.

21. The tool shown is used in a

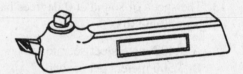

A lathe.
B grinder.
C shaper.
D drill press.

22. The thickness gage shown in the figure is used most often in

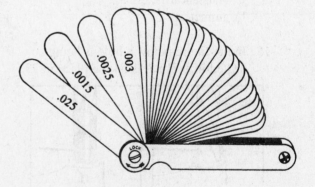

A woodworking shops.
B automotive work.
C plastics work.
D ceramics work.

23. The gage shown is used to measure the size of

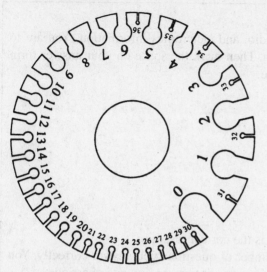

A wire.
B spark plug gaps.
C breaker point gaps.
D plastic rods.

24. A refrigerator's evaporator is located

A in the food compartment.
B under the refrigerator.
C outside the refrigerator.
D on top of the refrigerator.

25. Refrigerators and air conditioners made for homes use

A ammonia for a refrigerant.
B freon for a refrigerant.
C sulfur dioxide for a refrigerant.
D water as a refrigerant.

ELECTRONICS INFORMATION—SUBTEST 8

DIRECTIONS

This is a test of your knowledge of electrical, radio, and electronics information. You are to select the correct response from the choices given. Then mark the space on your answer form that has the same number and letter as your choice.

Now look at the sample question below.

1. What does the abbreviation AC stand for?

    A additional charge
    B alternating coil
    C alternating current
    D ampere current

The correct answer is alternating current, so C is the correct response.

Your score on this test will be based on the number of questions you answer correctly. You should try to answer every question. Do not spend too much time on any one question.

When you are told to begin, be sure to start with question number 1 in Part 8 of your test book and number 1 in Part 8 on your separate answer form.

THE ACTUAL TEST WILL SAY:

Do not turn this page until told to do so.

Electronics Information

Time: 9 minutes; 20 questions

1. Which of the following causes the inductance of a coil to decrease?

    A a copper core
    B an iron core
    C more turns of wire
    D shortening the length of the coil

2. Permeability is

    A a unit of measurement of magnetism.
    B a force field intensity measurement.
    C the ease with which magnetic lines of force distribute themselves throughout a material.
    D a property of a permanent magnet.

3. Which of the following is not a factor in determining capacitance of capacitor?

    A area of the plates
    B distance between the plates
    C material used as a dielectric
    D voltage applied to the plates

4. Capacitors placed in series produce

    A less capacitance.
    B a lower WVDC rating.
    C more capacitance.
    D higher reliability.

5. XC is equal to

    A $(1/2)\, \pi \times FC$
    B $(1/2)\, \pi \times FL$
    C $2\pi \times FL$
    D $2\pi \times FC$

6. Capacitors connected in parallel

A produce more capacitance.
B produce less capacitance.
C produce a higher WVDC rating.
D handle more voltage.

7. Impedance (Z) of a series *RL* circuit can be found by using

A $Z = \sqrt{R^2 + X_c^2}$
B $Z = \sqrt{R^2 + X_L^2}$
C $Z = \sqrt{R + X_L}$
D $Z = \sqrt{R + X_L^2}$

8. Parallel resonance occurs in a circuit when

A $Z = X_L$
B $Z = X_C$
C $X = 2\pi \times FC$
D $X_L = X_C$

9. A filter is used in a power supply to

A change AC to DC.
B change DC to AC.
C smooth out voltage variations.
D smooth out power surges.

10. Another name for a transistor is

A diode.
B semiconductor.
C crystal amplifier.
D integrated circuit.

11. Radio frequency amplifiers are used in

A audio amplifiers.
B differential amplifiers.
C operational amplifiers.
D receivers and transmitters.

12. A crystal microphone uses

A the piezoelectric effect.
B the pressure pack effect.
C magnetic waves to operate.
D a permanent magnet to operate.

13. The voice coil of a speaker has an impedance that is

A high.
B low.
C made of ceramic materials.
D made of ferrite materials.

14. A crossover network is used to

A direct the proper frequency range to the right speaker.
B eliminate noise.
C filter out high frequencies.
D filter out low frequencies.

15. The klystron is used in

A low-frequency transmitters.
B radar units.
C audio frequency amplifiers.
D frequency detectors.

16. There are two basic types of oscillators used for microwave generation. They are the magnetron and the

A klystron.
B op amp.
C Clapp oscillator.
D multivibrator.

17. There are two types of diodes used in electronics work. They are the semiconductor diode and the

A vacuum tube diode.
B full-wave diode.
C half-wave diode.
D zener diode.

18. Color television relies on three colors to produce the full color range needed for a good picture. These colors are red, blue, and

A gray.
B orange.
C yellow.
D green.

19. The folded dipole antenna has an impedance of

A 72 ohms.
B 300 ohms.
C 600 ohms.
D 75 ohms.

20. Television sets in the United States use a horizontal frequency of

A 525 hertz.
B 60 hertz.
C 15,750 hertz.
D 15,625 hertz.

SHOP INFORMATION—SUBTEST 9

DIRECTIONS

This test has questions about your knowledge of tools, as well as common shop terminology and practices. Pick the best answer for each question, then blacken the space on the answer form that has the same number and letter as your choice.

Here is a sample question.

1. A hammer is most commonly used for driving

  A nails.
  B Miss Daisy.
  C nine irons.
  D to Las Vegas.

A hammer is most commonly to drive nails, so A is the correct answer.

Your score on this test will be based on the number of questions you answer correctly. You should try to answer every question. Do not spend too much time on any one question.

When you are told to begin, be sure to start with question number 1 in Part 9 of your test booklet and number 1 in Part 9 on your separate answer form.

THE ACTUAL TEST WILL SAY:

Do not turn this page until told to do so.

Shop Information

Time: 8 minutes; 15 questions

1. Which of these tools breaks easily when twisted?

  A folding rule
  B ruler
  C yardstick
  D hand saw

2. Which type of saw is mounted in a mitre box?

  A rip saw
  B hack saw
  C cross-cut saw
  D back saw

3. In order to shape concrete it is placed in a

  A lake.
  B form.
  C hole.
  D large, round object.

4. In concrete work a "darby" is a

  A metal pole.
  B metal trowel.
  C type of wooden float.
  D stake to hold a form.

5. Nail sets are used for

  A driving tacks.
  B setting nails below the surface of the wood.
  C setting nails above the surface of the wood.
  D setting carpet tacks.

6. A tool used for marking wood is called a

  A saw.
  B plane.
  C screwdriver.
  D scratch awl.

7. In selecting the proper grinding wheel it is important to

   A choose the proper grain size for the job to be done.
   B choose the proper manufacturer.
   C choose the properly priced wheel.
   D choose the proper concrete binder.

8. Which of these metals can be made thinner than a coat of paint?

   A copper
   B aluminum
   C gold
   D silver

9. When making a hole in sheet metal, it is safer to

   A drill it.
   B punch it.
   C cut it.
   D burn it.

10. Rapid, uncontrolled drying of wood causes

   A checking and cracking.
   B warping.
   C no harmful effects.
   D discoloration only.

11. A bumping hammer is used to

   A perform final alignment on newly forged metal components.
   B indent or compress metal.
   C smooth out dents.
   D hammer out and form sheet metal elements.

12. Steel is an alloy of iron that

   A is made with carbon and magnesium.
   B does not rust.
   C has added strength.
   D all of the above.

13. Bolting and riveting provide

   A a permanent connection between two metals.
   B a temporary or semipermanent connection.
   C fused joins.
   D a soldered connection.

14. Gas welding uses

   A oxygen and acetylene to produce a flame.
   B oxygen and nitrogen to produce a flame.
   C chlorine and acetylene to produce a chemical reaction.
   D flux and acetylene to create an arc.

15. Plastics have

   A high corrosion resistance and excellent electrical insulating qualities.
   B high corrosion resistance and moderate electrical insulating qualities.
   C no corrosion resistance and excellent electrical insulating qualities.
   D high adhesive resistance and excellent corrosion insulating qualities.

ASSEMBLING OBJECTS—SUBTEST 10

DIRECTIONS

This test measures your ability to picture how an object will look when its parts are mentally put together. Each question shows you several separate shapes; you will then pick the choice that best represents how the pieces would look if they were all fitted together correctly. There is only one best answer for each shape. Pick the best answer for each question, then blacken the space on the answer form that has the same number and letter as your choice.

Here is a sample question.

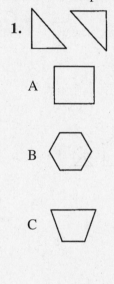

Choice A is the shape that will result when the two initial shapes are assembled correctly.

Your score on this test will be based on the number of questions you answer correctly. You should try to answer every question. Do not spend too much time on any one question.

When you are told to begin, be sure to start with question number 1 in Part 10 of your test booklet and number 1 in Part 10 on your separate answer form.

THE ACTUAL TEST WILL SAY:

Do not turn this page until told to do so.

Time: 20 minutes; 20 questions

1.

A

B

C

D

2.

A

B

C

D

3.

A

B

C

D

4.

A

B

C

D

5.

A

B

C

D

6.

A

B

C

D

7.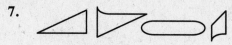

A

B

C

D

10.

A

B

C

D

8.

A

B

C

D

11.

A

B

C

D

9.

A

B

C

D

12.

A

B

C

D

13.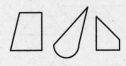

A

B

C

D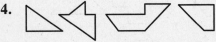

14.

A

B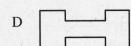

C

D

15.

A

B

C

D

16.

A

B

C

D

17.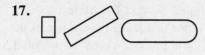

A

B

C

D

18.

A

B

C

D

19.

A

B

C

D

20.

A

B

C

D

ANSWERS AND ANSWERS EXPLAINED

GENERAL SCIENCE—SUBTEST 1
Answers

1. **D**	6. **C**	11. **A**	16. **C**	21. **C**
2. **C**	7. **B**	12. **C**	17. **B**	22. **D**
3. **D**	8. **B**	13. **B**	18. **D**	23. **B**
4. **C**	9. **D**	14. **B**	19. **B**	24. **C**
5. **B**	10. **C**	15. **C**	20. **C**	25. **D**

Answers Explained

1. **D** The sperm carries an X or Y chromosome, while all eggs normally have one X chromosome. An XX union results in a female, while the union of an X chromosome with a Y chromosome results in a male.

2. **C** Rocks do not conduct heat very quickly. If a rock becomes cold during the night but is rapidly heated during the day, the expansion and contraction may cause the outer layer to peel off. If water gets into a crack in the rock, freezing and thawing may cause the rock to split.

3. **D** Sand results from the weathering of igneous rock containing quartz crystals. Because of the relative hardness and insolubility of quartz, the crystals of quartz remain after other portions of the eroded rock have been dissolved or carried away.

4. **C** Vinegar contains acetic acid.

5. **B** All atoms of the same element have the same number of protons. In a neutral atom the number of electrons is the same as the number of protons. (Protons are inside the nucleus of an atom; electrons are outside it.) Atoms of the same element may differ in the number of neutrons.

6. **C** When heat is applied to a liquid at its boiling point, the added energy is used to separate the molecules from their neighbors, but no increase in the temperature of the liquid occurs. The molecules of vapor that leave the surface of the liquid possess increased potential energy because of the work done to overcome the forces acting on them.

7. **B** Nebulae are large clouds of gas and dust located between the stars. Our solar system is made up of the sun, the planets and their satellites, and asteroids.

8. **B** Space is a nearly perfect vacuum. The process by which solar energy (in the form of ultraviolet rays) is transmitted through space is called radiation.

9. **D** The gene for hemophilia lies on the X chromosome; this condition is therefore inherited as a sex-linked disorder.

10. **C** Only living things can duplicate themselves.

11. **A** The thermometer that indicates the freezing point of water at 0 degrees and the boiling point of water at 100 degrees is known as the centigrade, or Celsius, thermometer.

12. **C** A steep surface will increase runoff since the water will flow rapidly, giving it little time to be absorbed by the soil. Vegetation will make the surface more porous, decreasing the runoff and thereby decreasing erosion of the soil.

13. **B** The 25-pound force is the resultant of two forces acting at right angles to each other. The resultant can be represented as the hypotenuse of a right triangle, with one side representing the 15-pound force and the other side the unknown (x) force. Then, applying the Pythagorean Theorem,

$$\text{(hypotenuse)}^2 = \text{(side)}^2 + \text{(side)}^2$$
$$(25)^2 = (15)^2 + x^2$$
$$625 = 225 + x^2$$
$$400 = x^2$$
$$20 = x$$

14. **B** A hydrometer is used to test the specific gravity of the acid in a storage battery. The specific gravity is an index of the extent of charge of the battery.

15. **C** Fluorides are added to drinking water to reduce the incidence of dental caries (cavities).

16. **C** A reflex is a simple inborn response. An instinct involves a series of reflexes. A habit is an acquired trait. Phototropism is a response that occurs in plants.

17. **B** The Rh factor is an inherited characteristic of the blood.

18. **D** Iron is part of hemoglobin, the pigment of red blood cells.

19. **B** Land heats up rapidly in summer and cools off rapidly in winter. The result is the climate found in continental interiors where the winters are extremely cold and the summers extremely hot.

20. **C** All freely falling objects, regardless of their masses near the earth, fall toward the earth with equal acceleration. Any two objects at rest that begin to fall at the same instant will have equal velocities at the end of 3 seconds or any other time interval.

21. **C** Living things carry on respiration at all times. Respiration in plants goes on independently of photosynthesis, which occurs only in the presence of sunlight.

22. **D** Where a place is heated, the warm air rises on overflows, far above the earth, toward a colder region. Meanwhile other unheated air flows in to take its place. This causes a horizontal air current which, when close to the earth's surface, is called wind.

23. **B** Mammals appeared most recently on earth.

24. **C** White light is a mixture of all of the colors of the spectrum. With the aid of a prism it can be separated into the individual colors.

25. **D** A solution has a high ratio of solute to solvent if there is a large amount of solute dissolved in a small amount of solvent. Such a solution, by definition, is a concentrated solution.

ARITHMETIC REASONING—SUBTEST 2
Answers

1. **B**	7. **D**	13. **D**	19. **D**	25. **D**
2. **D**	8. **D**	14. **A**	20. **A**	26. **A**
3. **A**	9. **A**	15. **C**	21. **B**	27. **B**
4. **B**	10. **A**	16. **B**	22. **C**	28. **A**
5. **D**	11. **D**	17. **B**	23. **B**	29. **D**
6. **B**	12. **C**	18. **B**	24. **D**	30. **C**

Answers Explained

1. **B** This discount is 15% (or 0.15) of the marked price.
$$\$500 \times .15 = \$75$$
The cost is $500 - $75 = $425. Subtract the down payment to find the balance due.
$$\$425 - \$65 = \$360$$
Each installment is 1/2 of $360.
$$\frac{\$360}{12} = \$30$$

2. **D** 2 gallons will cover 1/4 acre. 4×2 gallons, or 8 gallons, will cover 1 acre. 10×8 gallons, or 80 gallons, will cover 10 acres. Since 2 gallons cover 1/4 acre, 2×2 gallons, or 4 gallons, cover 1/2 acre. 80 gallons + 4 gallons, or 84 gallons, will cover 10½ acres.

3. **A** The drawing and its enlargement will be similar. Therefore the lengths and widths will be in proportion.
$$\frac{\text{length of original}}{\text{length of enlargement}} = \frac{\text{width of original}}{\text{width of enlargement}}$$
$$\frac{18}{45} = \frac{12}{\text{width of enlargement } (x)}$$
Reduce 18/45 by dividing the numerator and denominator by 9.
$$\frac{2}{5} = \frac{12}{x}$$

To solve, cross-multiply the measurements.

$$2 \times x = 5 \times 12 = 60$$
$$x = \frac{60}{2}$$
$$x = 30$$

4. **B** Divide the number of acceptable products by the total number inspected. Then change your answer to a percentage.

$$\frac{266}{280} = \frac{133}{140} = \frac{19}{20}$$
$$\frac{19}{20} = \frac{95}{100} = 0.95 = 95\%$$

5. **D** If 3 pounds of candy cost $4.80, then 1 pound costs $4.80 ÷ 3, or $1.60.

There are 16 ounces in 1 pound.

1 ounce of the mix costs $\dfrac{\$1.60}{16} = \$0.10$

5 ounces cost

$$5 \times \$0.10 = \$0.50$$

6. **B** The perimeter of a square is the sum of the lengths of all four sides. But the four sides of a square are all equal in length.

The length of one side = 13 feet, 8 inches ÷ 4

Change 1 foot to 12 inches so that 13 feet, 8 inches becomes 12 feet, 20 inches.

12 feet, 20 inches ÷ 4 = 3 feet, 5 inches

7. **D** If 20% of the unit are officers, then the percent of enlisted men is
$$100\% - 20\% = 80\%$$
To find the number of enlisted men, multiply the total number by 80%.
$$360 \times 0.80 = 288.00$$
$$= 288 \text{ enlisted men}$$

8. **D** Her overtime is 10 hours – 8 hours regular work = 2 hours.

2 hours at "time and a half" is paid as 2 × 1½ hours, or 2 × 3/2 hours, or 6/2 hours, or 3 hours.

8 hours + 3 hours = 11 hours of pay. 11 × $8.50 = $93.50

9. **A** Find the relationship between each pair of numbers in the series. Thus,

$$(2\tfrac{1}{4};3\tfrac{3}{4})\ 2\tfrac{1}{4} + 1\tfrac{1}{2} = 3\tfrac{3}{4}$$
$$(3\tfrac{3}{4};3\tfrac{1}{4})\ 3\tfrac{3}{4} - 2\tfrac{1}{2} = 3\tfrac{1}{4}$$
$$(3\tfrac{1}{4};4\tfrac{3}{4})\ 3\tfrac{1}{4} + 1\tfrac{1}{2} = 4\tfrac{3}{4}$$

The pattern so far is

$$+ 1\tfrac{1}{2}, - 1\tfrac{1}{2}, + 1\tfrac{1}{2}$$

To continue the series, subtract 1/2 from the fourth member of the series.

$$4\tfrac{3}{4} - \tfrac{1}{2} = 4\tfrac{1}{4}$$

10. **A** Find the amount collected for adult tickets.

$$265 \times \$4 = \$1,060$$

Out of the $1,200 in receipts, the remainder came from the sale of children's tickets.

$$\$140 \div \$2 = 70 \text{ tickets}$$

11. **D** If she budgets 1/4 of her income for rent, she has 3/4 of her income left.

$$\frac{4}{4} - \frac{1}{4} = \frac{3}{4} \text{ (remainder)}$$

She then budgets 5 of this remainder for food.

$$\frac{2}{5} \times \frac{3}{4} = \frac{6}{20} = \frac{3}{10} \text{ (food)}$$

12. **C** The 3 who watched 2 hours each watched a total of 3 × 2 hours, or 6 hours. The 2 who watched 1 hour each watched a total of 2 × 1 hours, or 2 hours; 1 watched for 4 hours. Add the numbers of hours watched.

6 + 2 + 4 = 12 hours (total time spent).

Add the number of people.

3 + 2 + 1 = 6 persons were in the group.

Divide the total time spent by the number of persons in the group to find the average number of hours one person watches.

12 hours ÷ 6 persons = 2 hours per person average.

13. **D** Multiply the cost per yard by the length of the material in yards. 3 feet = 1 yard, so 2 feet = 2/3 yard.
3 yards, 2 feet = $3\frac{2}{3}$ yards.

$$\$9 \times 3\frac{2}{3} = \frac{9}{1} \times \frac{11}{3} = \$33$$

14. **A** Let x represent one of the 9 shares in which the profit must be divided. According to the ratio agreed on, the smaller partner's share is $4x$ and the larger partner's share is $5x$. Together the shares must add up to the \$63,000 profit. This can be written as an equation.
$$4x + 5x = 63,000$$
Solve by combining similar terms.
$$9x = 63,000$$
$$x = 7,000 \text{ (one share)}$$
Multiply the value of 1 share by the number of shares the smaller partner is to get
$$4x = 4 \times 7,000 = \$28,000$$

15. **C** The first courier will travel for 1 hour + 2 hours, or a total of 3 hours, before he is overtaken. Traveling 30 miles per hour for 3 hours will take the first courier 30×3 or 90 miles away.
The second courier must travel the 90 miles in 2 hours. Therefore, he must travel at a rate of $90 \div 2$ or 45 miles per hour.

16. **B** Find the discounted price paid by the merchant.
$$\$60 \times 25\% = \$60 \times 0.25$$
$$= \$15 \text{ (discount)}$$
$$\$60 - \$15 = \$45 \text{ (price paid by the merchant)}$$
Next find the merchant's selling price, based on an increase of 20% over the original wholesale price.
$$\$60 \times 20\% = \$60 \times 0.20 \text{ or}$$
$$\$60 \times 1/5 = \$12 \text{ (increase over wholesale price)}$$
$$\$60 + \$12 = \$72 \text{ (merchant's selling price)}$$
Finally, find the merchant's profit.
$$\$72 - \$45 = \$27$$

17. **B** To find the rate of speed when the distance and the time are known, divide the distance, x, by the time, y. x divided by y is expressed as $\frac{x}{y}$.

18. **B** Since the first 10 words cost \$1.50, the balance is left for the cost of the remaining words.
$$\$4.00 - \$1.50 = \$2.50$$
To find the number of words \$2.50 will pay for at \$0.05 per word, divide \$2.50 by \$0.05.
$$\$2.50 \div \$0.05 = 250 \div 5 \text{ (clearing decimals)}$$
$$250 \div 5 = 50 \text{ words}$$
50 words added to the first 10 words makes a total of 60 words.

19. **D** Since 1 inch represents 40 miles, divide 110 miles by 40 miles to find the number of inches required to represent it.
$$110 \div 40 = \frac{110}{40} = \frac{11}{4} = 2\frac{3}{4} \text{ inches}$$

20. **A** Multiply the purchase price of the home by the assessment rate to find the assessed value.
$$\$80,000 \times 75\% = \$80,000 \times \frac{3}{4} =$$
$$\frac{80,000}{1} \times \frac{3}{4} = \frac{20,000}{1} \times \frac{3}{1} =$$
$$\$60,000 \text{ (assessed value)}$$
Find the number of hundreds in the assessed value.
$$60,000 \div 100 = 600 \text{ (hundreds)}$$
Multiply the number of hundreds by the tax rate.
$$600 \times \$4.83 = \$2,898.00 \text{ (tax)}$$

21. **B** Set up a proportion.
$$\frac{\text{recipe sugar}}{\text{sugar actually used}} = \frac{\text{recipe flour}}{\text{flour actually used}}$$
$$\frac{\frac{3}{4}\text{cup}}{\frac{1}{4}\text{cup}} = \frac{4\frac{1}{2}\text{cups}}{x\text{ cups}} \text{ or } \frac{\frac{3}{4}}{\frac{1}{4}} = \frac{\frac{9}{2}}{x}$$

Simplify each side of the proportion.

$$\frac{3}{4} \div \frac{1}{4} = \frac{3}{4} \times \frac{4}{1} = \frac{3}{1}$$

$$\frac{9}{2} \div \frac{x}{1} = \frac{9}{2} \times \frac{1}{x} = \frac{9}{2x}$$

Solve the proportion by cross-multiplying.

$$6x = 9$$

Divide each side of the equation by 6 to find the value of x.

$$x = \frac{9}{6} = 1\frac{1}{2} \text{ cups of flour}$$

22. **C** Find the amount of the decline by subtracting.

$$1,200 - 1,044 = 156$$

To find the percent of decline, divide the amount of the decline by the original number of cars crossing the bridge.

$$156 \div 1,200 = \frac{156}{1,200} = \frac{13}{100} = 13\%$$

23. **B** First find the cost of 1 gallon. If 2 gallons cost $19.20, 1 gallon will cost $19.20 ÷ 2 or $9.60.
There are 4 quarts in 1 gallon. Divide the cost of 1 gallon by 4 to find the cost of 1 quart.

$$\$9.60 \div 4 = \$2.40$$

24. **D** Find the distance he drove on each leg of the trip by multiplying the rate in miles per hour by the time in hours.

$$50 \times 3 = 150 \text{ miles}$$
$$55 \times 2 = 110 \text{ miles}$$

Add the two distances to get the total distance he traveled.

$$150 + 110 \text{ miles} = 260 \text{ miles}$$

Divide the total distance traveled by the number of miles per gallon of gas to get the amount of gas used.

$$260 \div 20 = 13 \text{ gallons}$$

25. **D** First find the income from the $5,000 invested at 8%.

$$\$5,000 \times 0.08 = \$400.00$$

Next find the income desired from the total investment of $15,000.

$$\$15,000 \times 0.09 = \$1,350.00$$

Subtract the income from the first investment to find out how much income she must get from the second.

$$\$1,350 - \$400 = \$950$$

Divide the income, $950, by the investment, $10,000, to find the rate of interest.

$$\$950 \div \$10,000 = \frac{950}{10,000} = \frac{95}{1,000}$$
$$= 0.095 \text{ or } 9\frac{1}{2}\%$$

26. **A** Find the number of hours the generator operates.
From 9:15 A.M. to 3:15 P.M. is 6 hours.
From 3:15 P.M. to 3:55 P.M. is 40 minutes (or 2/3 of an hour).
6 hours + 40 minutes = 6⅔ hours.
Divide the total time run by the time provided by one fuel tank filling (1 hour, 20 minutes, or 1⅓ hours).

$$6\frac{2}{3} \div 1\frac{1}{3} = \frac{20}{3} \times \frac{3}{4} = 5 \text{ fillings}$$

27. **B** Find the total value of each kind of seed in the mixture.
10 pounds at $1.20 per pound is worth $10 \times \$1.20$, or $12.00.
8 pounds at $3.00 per pound is worth $8 \times \$3.00$, or $24.00.
Add the values of each kind to get the total value of the mixture.

$$\$12.00 + \$24.00 = \$36.00$$

Divide the total value of the mixture by the total number of pounds, 18, to get price per pound.

$$\$36.00 \div 18 = \$2.00 \text{ per pound}$$

28. **A** First multiply out the numerator.

$$\frac{0.02 \times 3}{0.001} = \frac{0.06}{0.001}$$

Clear the decimal in the divider by moving the decimal point in both numerator and denominator three places to the right.

$$\frac{0.06}{0.001} = \frac{60}{1} = 60$$

29. **D** Substitute the number values for the letters and then do the arithmetic operations.

$$1 + 5xy^2 - 3x^2y =$$
$$1 + (5 \times x \times y^2) - (3 \times x^2 \times y) =$$
$$1 + (5 \times 3 \times 2^2) - (3 \times 3^2 \times 2) =$$
$$1 + (5 \times 3 \times 3 \times 4) - (3 \times 9 \times 2) =$$
$$1 + 60 - 54 = 7$$

30. **C** Substitute the number values for P and R.

$$I = \sqrt{\frac{P}{R}}$$
$$I = \sqrt{\frac{48}{3}}$$
$$I = \sqrt{16}$$

The square root of 16 is the number that when multiplied by itself is 16; therefore $\sqrt{16} = 4$

$$I = 4$$

WORD KNOWLEDGE—SUBTEST 3
Answers

1. C	8. D	15. B	22. C	29. A
2. C	9. D	16. D	23. D	30. A
3. B	10. D	17. C	24. A	31. B
4. D	11. D	18. A	25. C	32. C
5. A	12. A	19. A	26. B	33. C
6. B	13. A	20. A	27. D	34. D
7. D	14. C	21. A	28. A	35. C

Answers Explained

1. **C** Tell, like **inform**, means to communicate knowledge or give information.
2. **C** **Crimson** is a vivid red or purplish red.
3. **B** **Caution** means forethought to avoid danger or harm; carefulness.
4. **D** **Intermittently** means starting and stopping, as in rain starting and stopping at irregular intervals.
5. **A** Event, like **occurrence**, means a happening or incident.
6. **B** Fraud, like **deception**, means the use of deceit.
7. **D** Stop, like **cease**, means to end.
8. **D** Applause, like **acclaim**, means enthusiastic approval.
9. **D** Construct, like **erect**, means to raise upright, as to erect or construct a building.
10. **D** Enjoy, like **relish**, means to take pleasure in.
11. **D** **Sufficient** means enough, adequate. Of the words given, sufficient most nearly means appropriate, as in a sufficient or appropriate amount.
12. **A** **Fortnight** means 2 weeks.
13. **A** A defect, like a **blemish**, is an imperfection or fault.
14. **C** To **impose** or require means to make compulsory.
15. **B** Scoff, like **jeer**, means to mock or poke fun at.
16. **D** An assumed name is an **alias**.
17. **C** Weaken, like **impair**, means to worsen or to damage.
18. **A** **Itinerant** means traveling, as in an itinerant salesperson.
19. **A** **Relinquish**, like abandon, means to give up possession.
20. **A** **Resolve** means to bring to a conclusion or end.
21. **A** Plentiful, like **ample**, means existing in great quantity.
22. **C** A **stench** is a foul odor, a stink.
23. **D** Angrily silent, like **sullen**, means resentful.
24. **A** **Rudiments** are fundamental skills or basic principles, like basic methods and procedures.
25. **C** To **conflict**, or clash, means to disagree or to be in opposition.
26. **B** **Camaraderie** means goodwill and rapport among friends.
27. **D** Cursory, like **superficial**, means hasty, not thorough.
28. **A** A **tapestry** is a fabric with multi-colored woven designs.
29. **A** **Terse**, or pointed, as in a terse or pointed comment, means brief but expressing a great deal.

30. **A** A combination of ingredients, as in cookery, is a **concoction**.
31. **B** Shortness, or **brevity**, means briefness of duration.
32. **C** Mercy, like **clemency**, means leniency, especially toward an offender or enemy.
33. **C** Disobedience, like **insubordination**, means failure to recognize authority or to accept the authority of a superior.
34. **D** **Preferential** means having or obtaining an advantage, as in receiving special or preferential treatment.
35. **C** Low spirits, like **doldrums**, are marked by listlessness, inactivity, or depression.

PARAGRAPH COMPREHENSION— SUBTEST 4
Answers

1. A   4. C   7. B   10. C   13. C
2. B   5. B   8. D   11. B   14. C
3. B   6. C   9. B   12. C   15. B

Answers Explained

1. **A** The main idea of this paragraph is given in the first sentence, which states that professional drivers have a low opinion of the average motorist.
2. **B** In this selection the word *shuddered* means shook.
3. **B** The paragraph clearly states that the Swedes and Finns (these two European peoples) were the first to use log cabins.
4. **C** The tone or mood of this passage is one of contentment. The man is described at rest with a smile on his face.
5. **B** This paragraph points out the favorable or good points about apprentice training. It does not discuss any negative or bad points, and it does not compare it to any other type of training.

6. **C** The paragraph states, "We never have enough closets no matter how many closets we have."
7. **B** A reactionary person looks to the past. The paragraph describes a liberal, using the key words *liberated* and *free*. The words *on the other hand* tell you that the description is about to shift from one way to another.
8. **D** You can infer from the passage that a conservation group wrote it. A lumber company or house-building company would more likely want to cut down the forest to use the lumber in its businesses. There is no reason to think that a religious group wrote the paragraph.
9. **B** The time for action suggests that the bridge should be built, but the paragraph makes it clear that official action—approval of bonds—must be taken first.
10. **C** The paragraph describes lightning as a "spark" and as a "release of energy."
11. **B** The paragraph clearly states that the morning rush hour starts 2 hours before 9 A.M.
12. **C** Acuity means sharpness. If you do not know the meaning of the word, you can figure it out from the context. You can immediately eliminate A; you can eliminate D because pressure is referred to in the phrase "eye pressure." You must then choose between strength and sharpness and in terms of the subject of this passage—vision—sharpness is more accurate.
13. **C** More than one seed of wheat has to be tested to form a conclusion.
14. **C** The last sentence states that bread and cereal provide 40% of the daily need for thiamine, one of the B vitamins.
15. **B** The second sentence states that most problems came from poor medical knowledge and lack of ways to fight disease.

AUTOMOTIVE INFORMATION— SUBTEST 5

Answers

1. **A**   6. **A**   11. **B**
2. **C**   7. **B**   12. **B**
3. **D**   8. **C**   13. **A**
4. **D**   9. **B**   14. **B**
5. **C**   10. **D**   15. **D**

Answers Explained

1. **A** The universal joint allows the drive shaft to move up and down as the road surface changes. At least one, and in most instances two, are needed for rear-wheel-drive cars and trucks.

2. **C** Much attention has been given to the pollutants emitted from today's cars. Nitrous oxides (NO_x) are of particular concern, and the air pump and the catalytic converter have been added to reduce these emissions. Hydrocarbons, carbon monoxide, and the oxides of nitrogen are of concern since they can contaminate the air and kill trees, plants, and small animals, as well as damage the lungs of humans.

3. **D** The catalytic converter eliminates some pollutants and reduces other pollutants. It reaches high temperatures and needs to be shielded from the body of the car by a heat deflector. An air pump is used on most late model cars to add to the combustion that takes place inside the converter and helps to reduce the amount of NO_x emitted from the exhaust pipe.

4. **D** The differential is located in the rear of the car when it is a rear-wheel-drive vehicle. It is located in front of the car on a front-wheel-drive vehicle. It consists of two small bevel gears on the ends of the axle shafts that are mounted in the differential frame. These bevel gears mesh with others to allow one wheel to turn faster than the other whenever the car makes a turn.

5. **C** The PCV valve is used to recirculate the fumes that would normally be exhausted to the atmosphere from the crankcase. By recirculating these fumes it is possible to cut down on the hydrocarbon contents of auto exhaust. This valve provides positive crankcase ventilation from the valve cover through the carburetor for recirculation.

6. **A** One of the ways to reduce the NO_x produced by the combustion of the internal combustion engine is to dilute the air/fuel mixture as it enters the combustion chamber.

7. **B** The number of teeth in a gear determines its speed when meshed with a second gear with similar teeth. The number of teeth in one gear is compared to the number of teeth in the one it meshes with. The number of teeth in the first gear as compared to the second is the gear ratio. If, for instance, one gear has 16 teeth and the one it meshes with has only 8, the gear ratio is 2:1 or 2 to 1. The gear with the greater number of teeth always turns slower and produces greater torque than the gear with the smaller number of teeth.

8. **C** The clutch is used to disconnect the engine from the wheels while the car is in neutral or when gears are being shifted.

9. **B** The first gear is used because of its ability to produce the starting torque needed to get the car moving from a standstill. The internal combustion engine is known as a fast engine. It must be revving up pretty fast to develop the torque needed to start the car rolling.

10. **D** The torque converter is located in the automatic transmission. It produces the torque needed to get the car started and to change speeds. Most torque converter transmissions also provide an intermediate and low gear range that can aid in braking the car when coming down steep hills and in hard pulling.

11. **B** Disc brakes use two pads to grasp the rotor that is attached to the wheel. The pads press against the rotor (disc) from both sides to make a faster and surer stop with little fading on hot days and with heavy braking.

12. **B** The transmission on front-wheel cars is located in the front engine compartment. It must be small enough to fit into the space allowed for the engine and the accessories. It took a few years to design a transmission to fit in front with the engine and leave space for the accessories needed to cause the engine to function properly.

13. **A** L_0 or L on older automatic transmissions were the same as first gear in manual transmissions. In most recent cars the L has been replaced by a 1 to indicate first gear and 2 to represent second gear instead of D1, S, or L2.

14. **B** Park (P) position on the automatic transmission gear selector indicator represents the position that locks up the transmission and prevents the wheels from rolling. The car is in neutral when placed in park and can be started only when in park or neutral.

15. **D** The internal combustion engine is best described as a high-speed engine. We cannot run an internal combustion engine at slow speed and get enough torque to get the vehicle moving. A higher speed engine is needed to produce the torque. That is where the transmission plays an important role in allowing the engine to speed up and still not have a very fast moving drive shaft connected to the wheels. The transmission's gear ratio plays a role in producing the torque needed to get the car moving from a resting position.

MATHEMATICS KNOWLEDGE— SUBTEST 6
Answers

1. **C**	6. **C**	11. **A**	16. **B**	21. **D**
2. **A**	7. **D**	12. **B**	17. **A**	22. **B**
3. **B**	8. **A**	13. **A**	18. **C**	23. **C**
4. **B**	9. **B**	14. **B**	19. **C**	24. **C**
5. **D**	10. **D**	15. **D**	20. **A**	25. **C**

Answers Explained

1. **C** First isolate all terms containing x on one side of the equation and all terms not containing x on the other side. To do this, add x to both sides of the equation and also subtract 6 from both sides of the equation. Remember to change the sign of any term when it is moved from one side of the equation to the other.

$$2x + x + 6 - 6 = 12 - 6 - x + x$$
$$3x = 6$$

Divide each side of the equation by 3 to undo the multiplication of 3 by x.

$$\frac{3x}{3} = \frac{6}{3}$$
$$x = 2$$

2. **A** Write the binomial to be subtracted underneath the binomial from which it is to be subtracted, placing similar terms in the same columns.

From $8x^2 - 7x$
Subtract $-3x^2 + 2x$

Change the signs of the terms in the bottom row (the subtrahend) and combine the similar terms in each column.

$$8x^2 - 7x$$
$$3x^2 - 2x$$
$$11x^2 - 9x$$

3. **B** Multiply $3x^2y$ by $2x^3y$ and also multiply -4 by $2x^3y$. To multiply $3x^2y$ by $2x^3y$, first multiply their numerical factors.

$$3 \times 2 = 6$$

To multiply powers of the same letter, add the exponents. Remember that y stands for y^1. Thus, $x^2 \times x^3 = x^5$ and $y \times y = y^2$.

$$2x^3y \times (3x^2y - 4) = 6x^5y^2 - 8x^3y$$

4. **B** Add the portions that each one does.

$$\frac{1}{3} + \frac{1}{5}$$

To add fractions, they must have a common denominator. The least common denominator for 3 and 5 is 15, the smallest number into which they both divide evenly. Change 1/3 and 1/5 to equivalent fractions having 15 as their denominator. Fractions with the same denominator may be added by adding their numerators.

$$\frac{5}{15} + \frac{3}{15} = \frac{8}{15}$$

5. **D** Subtract the length of the piece to be cut off.

5 feet, 3 inches
− 3 feet, 9 inches

Since we cannot subtract 9 inches from 3 inches, we borrow 1 foot from the 5 feet and convert it to 12 inches; thus 5 feet, 3 inches becomes 4 feet, 15 inches.

4 feet, 15 inches
− 3 feet, 9 inches
1 foot, 6 inches

6. **C** A hexagon is a polygon having 6 sides. If it has 6 sides, it must also have 6 angles. The sum of the 6 equal angles is 6 times the size of one of them.

$$6 \times 120° = 720°$$

7. **D** Set up the product like a multiplication example in arithmetic. Multiply each term of $(3a - 2)$ by a and write the results as the first line of partial products. Remember that the product of a positive number and a negative number is negative. Next multiply each term of $(3a - 2)$ by $+ 3$ and write the results as the second line of partial products. Add the partial products as you do in

arithmetic to get the final answer.

3a − 2
 a + 3
3a² − 2a
 + 9a − 6
3a² + 7a − 6

8. **A** Substitute 3 for x in the given expression.

$|x - 7|$ becomes $|3 - 7|$ or $|-4|$

$|-4|$ stands for the absolute value of -4. The absolute value of a number is its value without regard to sign. Thus, $|+4|$ equals 4, and $|-4|$ also equals 4.

9. **B** To solve these equations for x, we must eliminate y. First multiply both sides of the first equation by 2.

$$2 \times (3x + y) = 2 \times 13$$
$$6x + 2y = 26$$

Adding the original second equation to the new form of the first equation will eliminate y.

6x + 2y = 26
 x − 2y = 2
7x   = 28

Divide both sides of the equation by 7 to undo the multiplication of x by 7.

$$\frac{7x}{7} = \frac{28}{7}$$
$$x = 4$$

10. **D** Convert all units of measure to inches.

In 1 yard, there are 36 inches, so in y yards there are y times as many, or $36y$. The total length of y yards and i inches, expressed in inches, is $36y + i$ inches.

There are 12 inches in 1 foot. To find the number of feet in $36y + i$ inches, divide $36y + i$ by 12.

11. **A** The goal is to find an equation with

$$(36y + i) \div 12 = \frac{36y + i}{12}$$

F alone on one side and all other letters and numbers on the other side.

Begin by multiplying both sides of the formula by 9 to get rid of the fraction.

$$9 \times C = 9 \times \frac{5}{9}(F - 32)$$

$$9C = 5(F - 32)$$

Next remove the parentheses by multiplying each term inside them by 5.

$$9C = 5 \times F - 5 \times 32$$
$$9C = 5F - 160$$

To isolate the term containing F on one side of the equation, add 160 to both sides of the equation.

$$9C + 160 = 5F - 160 + 160$$
$$9C + 160 = 5F$$

To get an expression for F alone, divide both sides of the equation by 5.

$$\frac{9C + 160}{5} = \frac{5F}{5}$$

$$\frac{9}{5}C + 32 = F$$

The equation may be transposed to read

$$F = \frac{9}{5}C + 32.$$

12. **B** The path directly east forms a right angle with the path directly north. The distance from the starting point is measured on the third side (or hypotenuse) of the right triangle, which contains the paths to the east and to the north.

The Pythagorean Theorem states that in any right triangle, the square of the hypotenuse (c^2) equals the sum of the square of the other two sides, $a^2 + b^2$.

Thus, $c^2 = a^2 + b^2$
$$c^2 = 3^2 + 4^2$$

Perform the arithmetic operations.
$$c^2 = 9 + 16$$
$$c^2 = 25$$

To find c, take the square root of both sides of the equation. The square root of a number is another number which, when multiplied by itself, equals the original number.

Thus, the square root of 25 is 5, and the square root of c^2 is c.
$$c = 5$$

13. **A** The line perpendicular to the base of the triangle makes a right angle with the base; a right angle contains 90 degrees.

An equilateral triangle has 3 equal sides and 3 equal angles. Since the sum of all three angles of any triangle is 180 degrees, each angle of an equilateral triangle is 180°/3 or 60 degrees.

The 60-degree angle must be subtracted from the 90-degree angle to find the angle formed by the perpendicular and the other side of the triangle.

$$90° - 60° = 30°$$

14. **B** The inequality, $x - 5 \leq 5$, is a statement that x minus 6 is less than or equal to 5.

To solve this inequality, isolate x on one side of it by adding 6 to both sides.

$$x - 6 + 6 \leq 5 + 6$$
$$x \leq 11$$

The solution states that the inequality is true if x has any value less than or equal to 11. For example, suppose $x = 9$. Substitute 9 for x in the original inequality:

$$9 - 6 \leq 5 + 6$$
$$x \leq 11$$

The solution states that the inequality is true if x has any value less than or equal to 11. For example, suppose $x = 9$. Substitute 9 for x in the original inequality:

$$9 - 6 \leq 5$$

$3 \leq 5$, which is a true statement.

15. **D** If the same fence fits around the rectangle and the square field, then their perimeters are equal. The perimeter of a rectangle is the sum of the lengths of its four sides.

$$P = 40 + 36 + 40 + 36$$
$$= 152 \text{ feet}$$

The perimeter of a square is the sum of its four equal sides. Therefore, the length of one side is the perimeter divided by 4.

$$152 \div 4 = 38 \text{ feet}$$

16. **B** The volume of a rectangular box is equal to the length times the width times the height.

The volume of one individual-sized box = $3 \times 2 \times 4 = 24$ cubic inches.
The volume of one family-sized box = $8 \times 3 \times 12 = 8 \times 36 = 288$ cubic inches.
Divide the volume of the larger box by the volume of the smaller box.

$$288 \div 24 = 12$$

17. **A** Rotation of a wheel as it rolls on the ground has the effect of "laying out" its circumference along the ground. One rotation will move the wheel along by a distance equal to the circumference. The circumference, C, of a circle is given by the formula $C = 2 \times \pi \times R$, where R is the radius, or by the formula $C = \pi \times D$, where D is the diameter. If the first formula is used, R can be computed since the radius is one-half the diameter. However, it is easier in this case to use the second formula since we are given the diameter.

$$C = \frac{22}{7} \times 14 = \frac{22}{7} \times \frac{14}{1} = \frac{22}{1} \times \frac{2}{1} =$$

44 inches

18. **C** The sine of an angle in a right triangle is the ratio of the length of the side opposite the angle to the length of the hypotenuse. If the unknown length is x, the ratio of x to the length of the hypotenuse must be the same as the ratio 3/7.

$$\frac{x}{21} = \frac{3}{7}$$

To solve for x in this proportion, cross-multiply.

$$7 \times x = 3 \times 21$$
$$7x = 63$$

To undo the multiplication of 7 by x, divide both sides of the equation by 7.

$$\frac{7x}{7} = \frac{63}{7}$$

19. **C** $-x^4$ means $-(x)(x)(x)(x)$.
Substitute 0.1 for x.

$$-x^4 = -(0.1)(0.1)(0.1)(0.1)$$

To multiply $(0.1)(0.1)(0.1)(0.1)$, remember that the number of decimal places in the product is the total of the number of decimal places in the numbers being multiplied together.

$$-x^4 = -0.0001$$

20. **A** Change 30% to a decimal and let x represent the total number of apartments; 30% of x is 108.

$$0.30x = 108 \text{ or } 0.3x = 108$$

Clear the decimals by multiplying both sides of the equation by 10.

$$10 \times 0.3x = 10 \times 108$$
$$3x = 1,080$$

Undo the multiplication of 3 by x by dividing both sides of the equation by 3.

$$\frac{3x}{3} = \frac{1,080}{3}$$
$$x = 360$$

21. **D** Let x equal the mark on the fourth test. The average is obtained by dividing the sum of the four marks by 4.

$$\frac{60 + 60 + 70 + x}{4} = 75$$

To remove the fraction, multiply both sides of the equation by 4.

$$4 \times \frac{60 + 60 + 70 + x}{4} = 4 \times 75$$
$$60 + 60 + 70 + x = 300$$
$$190 + x = 300$$

To isolate x on one side, subtract 190 from both sides of the equation.

$$190 - 190 + x = 300 - 190$$
$$x = 110$$

He would need 110% on the fourth test, which is impossible.

22. **B** First find the distance traveled. Distance traveled is found by multiplying rate of speed by time.

3 hours × 40 miles per hour = 120 miles

2 hours × 50 miles per hour = 100 miles

The entire trip was 120 miles + 100 miles, or 220 miles.

The total time was 3 hours + 2 hours, or 5 hours.

The average rate of speed is obtained by dividing the total distance by the total time.

220 miles ÷ 5 hours = 44 miles per hour

23. **C** The radar is capable of covering a complete circle whose radius is 10 miles. First find the area of this circle, using the formula $A = \pi \times R^2$, where R is the radius.

$A = 3.14 \times 10^2 = 3.14 \times 100 = 314$ square miles

There are 360 degrees of rotation in the complete circle. If the radar is used to cover a portion of this, it covers 36/360 or 1/10 of the complete circle.

$$\frac{1}{10} \times 314 = 31.4 \text{ square miles}$$

24. **C** To solve a quadratic equation like $x^2 + 2x = 15$, first move all terms to the same side of the equation so that they equal 0 on the other side.

$$x^2 + 2x - 15 = 0$$

Find the two binomial factors that would multiply to produce the polynomial on the left side. The factors of the first term, x^2, are x and x. Use them as the first term in each of the binomial factors.

$$(x \quad)(x \quad) = 0$$

Now find the two numbers that would multiply together to give 15. They could be 15 and 1 or 5 and 3. Remember that when multiplying the two binomials together, $+2x$ must result for the middle term. This suggests that $+5x$ and $-3x$

were added to give $+2x$. Therefore, $+5$ and -3 are the factors to choose for -15.

$$(x + 5)(x - 3) = 0$$

The equation is now in a form in which the product of two factors equals 0. This is possible if either one or both of the factors equals 0.

$x + 5 = 0$	$x - 3 = 0$
$x = -5$	$x = 3$

These results may be checked by substituting them in the original equation.

$x^2 + 2x = 15$	$x2 + 2x = 15$
$(-5)^2 + 2(-5) = 15$	$(3)^2 + 2(3) = 15$
$25 - 10 = 15$	$9 + 6 = 15$
$15 = 15$	$15 = 15$

25. **C** First find the number of quarts of antifreeze in the original mixture.

0.25×12 or $\frac{1}{4} \times 12 = 3$ quarts of antifreeze

Let x equal the number of quarts of water to be added. The total mixture will now be $12 + x$ quarts; 20% of the new total mixture will be the 3 quarts of antifreeze still present in the mixture.

$0.20(12 + x) = 3$ or $0.2(12 + x) = 3$

Remove the parentheses by multiplying each term inside by .2.

$$2.4 + 0.2x = 3$$

Clear decimals by multiplying each term in the equation by 10.

$$10 \times 2.4 + 10 \times 0.2x = 10 \times 3$$
$$24 + 2x = 30$$

Isolate the term containing x by subtracting 24 from both sides of the equation.

$$24 - 24 + 2x = 30 - 24$$
$$2x = 6$$

Undo the multiplication of 2 by x by dividing both sides of the equation by 2.

$$\frac{2x}{2} = \frac{6}{2}$$
$$x = 3$$

MECHANICAL COMPREHENSION— SUBTEST 7

Answers

1. **A**   6. **A**   11. **B**   16. **D**   21. **A**
2. **C**   7. **D**   12. **D**   17. **C**   22. **B**
3. **D**   8. **C**   13. **C**   18. **B**   23. **A**
4. **B**   9. **B**   14. **B**   19. **A**   24. **A**
5. **B** 10. **A**   15. **C**   20. **C**   25. **B**

Answers Explained

1. **A** Air flowing over the top of the wing creates a vacuum, and the air underneath remains relatively the same. That means the upward push of the air under the wing into the vacuum above is rather easy. So, most of the lift on an aircraft's wing is because of a decrease in pressure on the upper side.

2. **C** *Capillary* action is responsible for the wax creeping up the wick and the water remaining on the sides of the small tube once the major portion of the water is back in a lower level. *Osmosis* is the gradual penetration of a shell or membrane. Erosion is the wearing away by wind or water or some gradual process.

3. **D** Two dissimilar metals put together expand at different rates, so they can be used to form a thermostat— to move a switch and turn a furnace or other object on or off as the temperature makes the metals expand or contract.

4. **B** Aluminum is the metal that expands the most of those listed. Tungsten expands very little even at high temperatures and is used for incandescent lamp filaments.

5. **B** As the cold causes the pendulum to contract, it is shortened. This shortened pendulum causes the clock to run faster since it moves back and forth more quickly.

6. **A** Heat is a form of energy. The calorie is one unit of measurement of heat. Thermals are usually upward movements of columns of air caused by heat rising.

7. **D** The best conductor of heat of the metals listed is silver. Aluminum expands rapidly, but it does not conduct heat as readily as does silver since it does not have its atoms as closely packed as silver.

8. **C** There are three ways of transferring heat from one place to another: conduction, convection, and radiation.

9. **B** Putting salt into water increases the specific gravity of the solution and lowers its freezing point.

10. **A** Changing a liquid to a gas or vapor is called *evaporation*. Boiling is one method of accomplishing the process.

11. **B** Adding heat to a container of boiling water that is totally enclosed increases the pressure of the steam inside the compartment or container and increases the temperature of the water. This can be very dangerous if the container is not capable of handling the pressure.

12. **D** Fractional distillation is the process used to produce gasoline, kerosene, tar, and heating oil, as well as other products from petroleum.

13. **C** Sound travels at 1,086 feet per second at 0°C. It travels at 1,492 meters per second in seawater and at 3,500 meters per second in copper. The speed of light is 186,000 miles per second.

14. **B** The meter used to measure extremely high resistances is called a *megger* since the units of measurement will be in the millions, or megs.

15. **C** The hole is being tapped with a tap. This tool is used to make threads in the drilled hole.

16. **D** The units shown are a few of the many types of devices used to muffle the noise made by small gasoline engines.

17. **C** Outboard engines use the lake, river, or water that they are placed in to obtain cooling water. The water pump pulls the water into the engine and circulates it to the areas that need cooling.

18. **B** The drop of the ball prevents all the gasoline from draining from the carburetor, so it can be easily started again if the need arises quickly after the loss of suction or a few days later.

19. **A** The shape of the cutter tells you its type. This type of cutter cuts a rounded groove. The groove cut is the opposite of the shape of the cutter itself. A concave-shaped cutter cuts a convex groove, and a convex cutter makes a concave-shaped groove.

20. **C** The die is mounted in the tool that fits over the end of the pipe. The die is then rotated to cut threads on the pipe.

21. **A** The tool holder shown here is made for use in a tool post on a lathe. The tool bit is shaped to do whatever job is desired.

22. **B** The thickness gage shown here is used most often in automotive work to set points, check clearances of valves, and check other tolerances.

23. **A** This is the American standard wire gage. It can also be used to check the gage of sheet metal and small diameter rods.

24. **A** The evaporator of the refrigerator is located inside the refrigerator in the food compartment or freezer, depending on the model. The evaporator allows the Freon to vaporize and take the heat inside the food compartment or freezer to the outside to be dissipated into the room.

25. **B** Freon is used as the refrigerant for all home equipment and air conditioners for cars. Sulfur dioxide is rarely used today. It was once used in ship cooling and freezing units. Water is used as a refrigerant in some large commercial and industrial processes. Ammonia is used in large freezer plants for making ice or freezing on a commercial scale.

ELECTRONICS INFORMATION— SUBTEST 8
Answers

1. **A** 5. **A**   9. **C** 13. **B** 17. **A**
2. **C** 6. **A** 10. **C** 14. **A** 18. **D**
3. **D** 7. **B** 11. **D** 15. **B** 19. **B**
4. **A** 8. **D** 12. **A** 16. **A** 20. **C**

Answers Explained

1. **A** When copper is inserted inside a coil, it makes the inductance decrease.

2. **C** Permeability is the ease with which magnetic lines of force distribute themselves throughout a material.

3. **D** The area of the plates, the distance between the plates, and the material of the dielectric all have a direct relationship on the capacitance of a capacitor. The voltage on the capacitor does not have an effect on its capacitance.

4. **A** When capacitors are placed in series, it is the same as placing the plates farther apart. This causes a decrease in the amount of capacitance for the series combination.

5. **A** Capacitive reactance is equal to the reciprocal of the product of $2\pi \times FC$.

6. **A** Capacitors connected in parallel effectively increase the plate area. That allows for more storage of electrons and more capacity or capacitance.

7. **B** The impedance of a series RL circuit can be found by taking the square root of the sum of the squares of the resistance and the inductance. The inductance is in henrys and the resistance is in ohms.

8. **D** Resonance occurs in any circuit when the inductive reactance and the capacitive reactance are equal.

9. **C** A filter is placed in the power supply to smooth out the voltage variations. In some cases a choke is used in the filter to smooth out the current variations.

10. **C** Another name for the transistor is the *crystal amplifier*. It has also been called the *transfer resistor*, from which it takes its name, *transistor*.

11. **D** Radio frequency amplifiers are used in receivers and transmitters to amplify frequencies above the human hearing range.

12. **A** A crystal microphone relies on the piezoelectric effect, where a pressure on a crystal produces an electric current.

13. **B** The voice coil of a speaker usually has a very low impedance. Some specially made speakers have higher impedances to match the system.

14. **A** A crossover network is designed to make sure that the right frequencies get to a speaker so it can reproduce them better.

15. **B** The klystron is used as a frequency source in microwave units—whether it be a microwave range for the kitchen or a radar unit for an aircraft.

16. **A** The two basic types of oscillators used in microwave installations are the klystron and the magnetron.

17. **A** The two general types of diodes are the semiconductor and the vacuum tube diode. Both types have particular applications and advantages.

18. **D** Color television uses red, blue, and green guns to direct electron streams toward the phosphors in the front of the picture tube. They produce the full-color spectrum when combined properly.

19. **B** The folded dipole antenna has an impedance of 300 ohms. It is the one most commonly used for home television reception. The dipole has an impedance of 72 ohms.

20. **C** Television sets in the United States use a horizontal frequency of 15,750 Hz, while those in Europe use 15,625 Hz. There are 525 lines that make up the television picture in the United States but 625 in Europe. The vertical oscillator frequency is 60 Hz in the United States but 50 in Europe.

SHOP INFORMATION—SUBTEST 9
Answers

1. **A**	6. **D**	11. **C**
2. **D**	7. **A**	12. **D**
3. **B**	8. **C**	13. **B**
4. **C**	9. **B**	14. **A**
5. **B**	10. **A**	15. **A**

Answers Explained

1. **A** The folding rule is well known for breaking easily when it is twisted even a little bit.

2. **D** The mitre box uses the back saw—the one with the metal band across the top of it—to cut angles as needed or provided by the type of mitre box being used.

3. **B** In order to shape concrete it is placed in a form.

4. **C** In concrete work the "darby" is made of wood and is used to float the concrete after it has set for the proper length of time.

5. **B** Nail sets are used to set nails just below the surface of the wood. Then a filler is added before painting or finishing so that there is a smooth surface.

6. **D** A scratch awl is used to do many things, one of which is to mark wood where you want to cut it. A saw is used to cut wood. A plane is used to smooth wood. A screwdriver is used to drive screws.

7. **A** In selecting the proper grinding wheel there are a number of things to be considered, one of the important being the proper grain size for the job to be done.

8. **C** Gold can be hammered into leaves so thin that it takes a fine camel hair brush to pick them up. This is usually the way gold is placed on the domes of state capitol buildings. Once placed on the surface, it is burnished or rubbed with a piece of smooth metal to make the extremely thin foil stick to the surface being coated.

9. **B** When making a hole in sheet metal, it is safer for the person performing the work to punch the hole rather than drill it. If the piece of sheet metal is not properly secured, the drill bit will catch and cause it to be whirled, possibly cutting the operator who may not be quick enough to get out of the way of the spinning object.

10. **A** Rapid, uncontrolled drying of wood causes checking and cracking, which is why new lumber is sometimes submerged in water until it is ready to be cut.

11. **C** A bumping hammer is used by auto body repair workers to smooth out dents. A peen or machinist's hammer is used for riveting or to indent or compress metal

12. **D** Steel is an alloy of iron made with carbon and magnesium that does not rust and that has added strength; therefore, the answer is "all of the above."

13. **B** Bolting and riveting provide a temporary or semipermanent connection. Welding produces a permanent connection between two metals.

14. **A** Gas welding uses an oxygen and acetylene mixture in a welding torch that produces a flame hot enough to melt and fuse metals.

15. **A** Plastics have a very high corrosion resistance and excellent electrical insulating qualities.

ASSEMBLING OBJECTS—SUBTEST 10
Answers

1. **B**	6. **C**	11. **A**	16. **C**
2. **A**	7. **D**	12. **B**	17. **B**
3. **D**	8. **A**	13. **D**	18. **B**
4. **B**	9. **C**	14. **D**	19. **A**
5. **A**	10. **B**	15. **D**	20. **D**

ANSWER SHEETS—Practice Examination Four

GENERAL SCIENCE—SUBTEST 1

1. Ⓐ Ⓑ Ⓒ Ⓓ	6. Ⓐ Ⓑ Ⓒ Ⓓ	11. Ⓐ Ⓑ Ⓒ Ⓓ	16. Ⓐ Ⓑ Ⓒ Ⓓ	21. Ⓐ Ⓑ Ⓒ Ⓓ
2. Ⓐ Ⓑ Ⓒ Ⓓ	7. Ⓐ Ⓑ Ⓒ Ⓓ	12. Ⓐ Ⓑ Ⓒ Ⓓ	17. Ⓐ Ⓑ Ⓒ Ⓓ	22. Ⓐ Ⓑ Ⓒ Ⓓ
3. Ⓐ Ⓑ Ⓒ Ⓓ	8. Ⓐ Ⓑ Ⓒ Ⓓ	13. Ⓐ Ⓑ Ⓒ Ⓓ	18. Ⓐ Ⓑ Ⓒ Ⓓ	23. Ⓐ Ⓑ Ⓒ Ⓓ
4. Ⓐ Ⓑ Ⓒ Ⓓ	9. Ⓐ Ⓑ Ⓒ Ⓓ	14. Ⓐ Ⓑ Ⓒ Ⓓ	19. Ⓐ Ⓑ Ⓒ Ⓓ	24. Ⓐ Ⓑ Ⓒ Ⓓ
5. Ⓐ Ⓑ Ⓒ Ⓓ	10. Ⓐ Ⓑ Ⓒ Ⓓ	15. Ⓐ Ⓑ Ⓒ Ⓓ	20. Ⓐ Ⓑ Ⓒ Ⓓ	25. Ⓐ Ⓑ Ⓒ Ⓓ

ARITHMETIC REASONING—SUBTEST 2

1. Ⓐ Ⓑ Ⓒ Ⓓ	7. Ⓐ Ⓑ Ⓒ Ⓓ	13. Ⓐ Ⓑ Ⓒ Ⓓ	19. Ⓐ Ⓑ Ⓒ Ⓓ	25. Ⓐ Ⓑ Ⓒ Ⓓ
2. Ⓐ Ⓑ Ⓒ Ⓓ	8. Ⓐ Ⓑ Ⓒ Ⓓ	14. Ⓐ Ⓑ Ⓒ Ⓓ	20. Ⓐ Ⓑ Ⓒ Ⓓ	26. Ⓐ Ⓑ Ⓒ Ⓓ
3. Ⓐ Ⓑ Ⓒ Ⓓ	9. Ⓐ Ⓑ Ⓒ Ⓓ	15. Ⓐ Ⓑ Ⓒ Ⓓ	21. Ⓐ Ⓑ Ⓒ Ⓓ	27. Ⓐ Ⓑ Ⓒ Ⓓ
4. Ⓐ Ⓑ Ⓒ Ⓓ	10. Ⓐ Ⓑ Ⓒ Ⓓ	16. Ⓐ Ⓑ Ⓒ Ⓓ	22. Ⓐ Ⓑ Ⓒ Ⓓ	28. Ⓐ Ⓑ Ⓒ Ⓓ
5. Ⓐ Ⓑ Ⓒ Ⓓ	11. Ⓐ Ⓑ Ⓒ Ⓓ	17. Ⓐ Ⓑ Ⓒ Ⓓ	23. Ⓐ Ⓑ Ⓒ Ⓓ	29. Ⓐ Ⓑ Ⓒ Ⓓ
6. Ⓐ Ⓑ Ⓒ Ⓓ	12. Ⓐ Ⓑ Ⓒ Ⓓ	18. Ⓐ Ⓑ Ⓒ Ⓓ	24. Ⓐ Ⓑ Ⓒ Ⓓ	30. Ⓐ Ⓑ Ⓒ Ⓓ

WORD KNOWLEDGE—SUBTEST 3

1. Ⓐ Ⓑ Ⓒ Ⓓ	8. Ⓐ Ⓑ Ⓒ Ⓓ	15. Ⓐ Ⓑ Ⓒ Ⓓ	22. Ⓐ Ⓑ Ⓒ Ⓓ	29. Ⓐ Ⓑ Ⓒ Ⓓ
2. Ⓐ Ⓑ Ⓒ Ⓓ	9. Ⓐ Ⓑ Ⓒ Ⓓ	16. Ⓐ Ⓑ Ⓒ Ⓓ	23. Ⓐ Ⓑ Ⓒ Ⓓ	30. Ⓐ Ⓑ Ⓒ Ⓓ
3. Ⓐ Ⓑ Ⓒ Ⓓ	10. Ⓐ Ⓑ Ⓒ Ⓓ	17. Ⓐ Ⓑ Ⓒ Ⓓ	24. Ⓐ Ⓑ Ⓒ Ⓓ	31. Ⓐ Ⓑ Ⓒ Ⓓ
4. Ⓐ Ⓑ Ⓒ Ⓓ	11. Ⓐ Ⓑ Ⓒ Ⓓ	18. Ⓐ Ⓑ Ⓒ Ⓓ	25. Ⓐ Ⓑ Ⓒ Ⓓ	32. Ⓐ Ⓑ Ⓒ Ⓓ
5. Ⓐ Ⓑ Ⓒ Ⓓ	12. Ⓐ Ⓑ Ⓒ Ⓓ	19. Ⓐ Ⓑ Ⓒ Ⓓ	26. Ⓐ Ⓑ Ⓒ Ⓓ	33. Ⓐ Ⓑ Ⓒ Ⓓ
6. Ⓐ Ⓑ Ⓒ Ⓓ	13. Ⓐ Ⓑ Ⓒ Ⓓ	20. Ⓐ Ⓑ Ⓒ Ⓓ	27. Ⓐ Ⓑ Ⓒ Ⓓ	34. Ⓐ Ⓑ Ⓒ Ⓓ
7. Ⓐ Ⓑ Ⓒ Ⓓ	14. Ⓐ Ⓑ Ⓒ Ⓓ	21. Ⓐ Ⓑ Ⓒ Ⓓ	28. Ⓐ Ⓑ Ⓒ Ⓓ	35. Ⓐ Ⓑ Ⓒ Ⓓ

PARAGRAPH COMPREHENSION—SUBTEST 4

1. Ⓐ Ⓑ Ⓒ Ⓓ	4. Ⓐ Ⓑ Ⓒ Ⓓ	7. Ⓐ Ⓑ Ⓒ Ⓓ	10. Ⓐ Ⓑ Ⓒ Ⓓ	13. Ⓐ Ⓑ Ⓒ Ⓓ
2. Ⓐ Ⓑ Ⓒ Ⓓ	5. Ⓐ Ⓑ Ⓒ Ⓓ	8. Ⓐ Ⓑ Ⓒ Ⓓ	11. Ⓐ Ⓑ Ⓒ Ⓓ	14. Ⓐ Ⓑ Ⓒ Ⓓ
3. Ⓐ Ⓑ Ⓒ Ⓓ	6. Ⓐ Ⓑ Ⓒ Ⓓ	9. Ⓐ Ⓑ Ⓒ Ⓓ	12. Ⓐ Ⓑ Ⓒ Ⓓ	15. Ⓐ Ⓑ Ⓒ Ⓓ

AUTOMOTIVE INFORMATION—SUBTEST 5

1. Ⓐ Ⓑ Ⓒ Ⓓ	4. Ⓐ Ⓑ Ⓒ Ⓓ	7. Ⓐ Ⓑ Ⓒ Ⓓ	10. Ⓐ Ⓑ Ⓒ Ⓓ	13. Ⓐ Ⓑ Ⓒ Ⓓ
2. Ⓐ Ⓑ Ⓒ Ⓓ	5. Ⓐ Ⓑ Ⓒ Ⓓ	8. Ⓐ Ⓑ Ⓒ Ⓓ	11. Ⓐ Ⓑ Ⓒ Ⓓ	14. Ⓐ Ⓑ Ⓒ Ⓓ
3. Ⓐ Ⓑ Ⓒ Ⓓ	6. Ⓐ Ⓑ Ⓒ Ⓓ	9. Ⓐ Ⓑ Ⓒ Ⓓ	12. Ⓐ Ⓑ Ⓒ Ⓓ	15. Ⓐ Ⓑ Ⓒ Ⓓ

MATHEMATICS KNOWLEDGE—SUBTEST 6

1. Ⓐ Ⓑ Ⓒ Ⓓ	6. Ⓐ Ⓑ Ⓒ Ⓓ	11. Ⓐ Ⓑ Ⓒ Ⓓ	16. Ⓐ Ⓑ Ⓒ Ⓓ	21. Ⓐ Ⓑ Ⓒ Ⓓ
2. Ⓐ Ⓑ Ⓒ Ⓓ	7. Ⓐ Ⓑ Ⓒ Ⓓ	12. Ⓐ Ⓑ Ⓒ Ⓓ	17. Ⓐ Ⓑ Ⓒ Ⓓ	22. Ⓐ Ⓑ Ⓒ Ⓓ
3. Ⓐ Ⓑ Ⓒ Ⓓ	8. Ⓐ Ⓑ Ⓒ Ⓓ	13. Ⓐ Ⓑ Ⓒ Ⓓ	18. Ⓐ Ⓑ Ⓒ Ⓓ	23. Ⓐ Ⓑ Ⓒ Ⓓ
4. Ⓐ Ⓑ Ⓒ Ⓓ	9. Ⓐ Ⓑ Ⓒ Ⓓ	14. Ⓐ Ⓑ Ⓒ Ⓓ	19. Ⓐ Ⓑ Ⓒ Ⓓ	24. Ⓐ Ⓑ Ⓒ Ⓓ
5. Ⓐ Ⓑ Ⓒ Ⓓ	10. Ⓐ Ⓑ Ⓒ Ⓓ	15. Ⓐ Ⓑ Ⓒ Ⓓ	20. Ⓐ Ⓑ Ⓒ Ⓓ	25. Ⓐ Ⓑ Ⓒ Ⓓ

MECHANICAL COMPREHENSION—SUBTEST 7

1. Ⓐ Ⓑ Ⓒ Ⓓ	6. Ⓐ Ⓑ Ⓒ Ⓓ	11. Ⓐ Ⓑ Ⓒ Ⓓ	16. Ⓐ Ⓑ Ⓒ Ⓓ	21. Ⓐ Ⓑ Ⓒ Ⓓ
2. Ⓐ Ⓑ Ⓒ Ⓓ	7. Ⓐ Ⓑ Ⓒ Ⓓ	12. Ⓐ Ⓑ Ⓒ Ⓓ	17. Ⓐ Ⓑ Ⓒ Ⓓ	22. Ⓐ Ⓑ Ⓒ Ⓓ
3. Ⓐ Ⓑ Ⓒ Ⓓ	8. Ⓐ Ⓑ Ⓒ Ⓓ	13. Ⓐ Ⓑ Ⓒ Ⓓ	18. Ⓐ Ⓑ Ⓒ Ⓓ	23. Ⓐ Ⓑ Ⓒ Ⓓ
4. Ⓐ Ⓑ Ⓒ Ⓓ	9. Ⓐ Ⓑ Ⓒ Ⓓ	14. Ⓐ Ⓑ Ⓒ Ⓓ	19. Ⓐ Ⓑ Ⓒ Ⓓ	24. Ⓐ Ⓑ Ⓒ Ⓓ
5. Ⓐ Ⓑ Ⓒ Ⓓ	10. Ⓐ Ⓑ Ⓒ Ⓓ	15. Ⓐ Ⓑ Ⓒ Ⓓ	20. Ⓐ Ⓑ Ⓒ Ⓓ	25. Ⓐ Ⓑ Ⓒ Ⓓ

ELECTRONICS INFORMATION—SUBTEST 8

1. Ⓐ Ⓑ Ⓒ Ⓓ	5. Ⓐ Ⓑ Ⓒ Ⓓ	9. Ⓐ Ⓑ Ⓒ Ⓓ	13. Ⓐ Ⓑ Ⓒ Ⓓ	17. Ⓐ Ⓑ Ⓒ Ⓓ
2. Ⓐ Ⓑ Ⓒ Ⓓ	6. Ⓐ Ⓑ Ⓒ Ⓓ	10. Ⓐ Ⓑ Ⓒ Ⓓ	14. Ⓐ Ⓑ Ⓒ Ⓓ	18. Ⓐ Ⓑ Ⓒ Ⓓ
3. Ⓐ Ⓑ Ⓒ Ⓓ	7. Ⓐ Ⓑ Ⓒ Ⓓ	11. Ⓐ Ⓑ Ⓒ Ⓓ	15. Ⓐ Ⓑ Ⓒ Ⓓ	19. Ⓐ Ⓑ Ⓒ Ⓓ
4. Ⓐ Ⓑ Ⓒ Ⓓ	8. Ⓐ Ⓑ Ⓒ Ⓓ	12. Ⓐ Ⓑ Ⓒ Ⓓ	16. Ⓐ Ⓑ Ⓒ Ⓓ	20. Ⓐ Ⓑ Ⓒ Ⓓ

SHOP INFORMATION—SUBTEST 9

1. Ⓐ Ⓑ Ⓒ Ⓓ	4. Ⓐ Ⓑ Ⓒ Ⓓ	7. Ⓐ Ⓑ Ⓒ Ⓓ	10. Ⓐ Ⓑ Ⓒ Ⓓ	13. Ⓐ Ⓑ Ⓒ Ⓓ
2. Ⓐ Ⓑ Ⓒ Ⓓ	5. Ⓐ Ⓑ Ⓒ Ⓓ	8. Ⓐ Ⓑ Ⓒ Ⓓ	11. Ⓐ Ⓑ Ⓒ Ⓓ	14. Ⓐ Ⓑ Ⓒ Ⓓ
3. Ⓐ Ⓑ Ⓒ Ⓓ	6. Ⓐ Ⓑ Ⓒ Ⓓ	9. Ⓐ Ⓑ Ⓒ Ⓓ	12. Ⓐ Ⓑ Ⓒ Ⓓ	15. Ⓐ Ⓑ Ⓒ Ⓓ

ASSEMBLING OBJECTS—SUBTEST 10

1. Ⓐ Ⓑ Ⓒ Ⓓ	5. Ⓐ Ⓑ Ⓒ Ⓓ	9. Ⓐ Ⓑ Ⓒ Ⓓ	13. Ⓐ Ⓑ Ⓒ Ⓓ	17. Ⓐ Ⓑ Ⓒ Ⓓ
2. Ⓐ Ⓑ Ⓒ Ⓓ	6. Ⓐ Ⓑ Ⓒ Ⓓ	10. Ⓐ Ⓑ Ⓒ Ⓓ	14. Ⓐ Ⓑ Ⓒ Ⓓ	18. Ⓐ Ⓑ Ⓒ Ⓓ
3. Ⓐ Ⓑ Ⓒ Ⓓ	7. Ⓐ Ⓑ Ⓒ Ⓓ	11. Ⓐ Ⓑ Ⓒ Ⓓ	15. Ⓐ Ⓑ Ⓒ Ⓓ	19. Ⓐ Ⓑ Ⓒ Ⓓ
4. Ⓐ Ⓑ Ⓒ Ⓓ	8. Ⓐ Ⓑ Ⓒ Ⓓ	12. Ⓐ Ⓑ Ⓒ Ⓓ	16. Ⓐ Ⓑ Ⓒ Ⓓ	20. Ⓐ Ⓑ Ⓒ Ⓓ

CHAPTER

14 Practice Examination Four

GENERAL SCIENCE—SUBTEST 1

DIRECTIONS

This test has questions about science. Pick the best answer for each question, then blacken the space on your separate answer form that has the same number and letter as your choice.

Here is a sample question.

1. The planet nearest to the sun is

   A Venus.
   B Mars.
   C Earth.
   D Mercury.

Mercury is the correct answer, so you would blacken the space for D on your answer form.

Your score on this test will be based on the number of questions you answer correctly. You should try to answer every question. Do not spend too much time on any one question.

When you begin, be sure to start with question number 1 in Part 1, and number 1 in Part 1 on your answer form.

THE ACTUAL TEST WILL SAY:

Do not turn this page until told to do so.

General Science

Time: 11 minutes; 25 questions

1. The function of an enzyme is to

   A provide energy for a chemical reaction.
   B speed up a chemical reaction.
   C become hydrolyzed during a chemical reaction.
   D serve as an inorganic catalyst.

2. The DNA of a cell is found mainly in its

   A membrane.
   B cytoplasm.
   C vacuoles.
   D chromosomes.

3. Most cells without a cell wall also lack

   A mitochondria.
   B chloroplasts.
   C cell membranes.
   D vacuoles.

4. The cells that can easily be scraped from the lining of the mouth make up

   A connective tissue.
   B epithelial tissue.
   C supporting tissue.
   D voluntary tissue.

5. The end product(s) of protein digestion consist(s) of

   A glucose.
   B fatty acids.
   C glycerol.
   D amino acids.

6. Blood circulation from the lungs goes directly to the

   A legs.
   B head.
   C heart.
   D digestive system.

7. The glucose content of the blood is regulated by

   A insulin and adrenaline.
   B nerve stimulation.
   C ACTH.
   D progesterone.

8. Erosion and depletion are problems associated with

   A blood circulation.
   B baldness.
   C soil conservation.
   D cardiovascular exercise.

9. The beneficial relationship between termites and the protozoa that inhabit their digestive systems is called

   A symbiosis.
   B parthenogenesis.
   C mitosis.
   D phagocytosis.

10. A viral infection in humans that has a very long time between the initial exposure and the exhibiting of symptoms is

    A AIDS.
    B measles.
    C pneumonia.
    D chicken pox.

11. Which substance can be used to treat drinking water of questionable purity?

    A ammonia
    B chlorine
    C hydrogen chloride
    D iodine

12. The number of atoms in a molecule of $CuSO_4 \cdot 5H_2O$ is

    A 15.
    B 18.
    C 21.
    D 29.

13. The reaction between sodium, metal, and water can be classified as

A decomposition.
B synthesis.
C single replacement.
D double replacement.

14. Nitrates are very useful as

A detergents.
B fertilizers.
C fuels.
D solvents.

15. A gaseous product of the fermentation of sugar is

A carbon monoxide.
B carbon dioxide.
C sulfur dioxide.
D oxygen.

16. The half-life of iodine-131 is 8 days. Approximately how long would it take for 1 milligram of I-131 to decay to 1/2 milligram of I-131?

A 4 days
B 8 days
C 2 weeks
D 1 month

17. A magnetic compass points in the direction of the

A true north.
B geographic North Pole.
C magnetic North Pole.
D local magnetic field.

18. The mass of 1 cubic meter of water is approximately

A 1 kilogram
B 10 kilograms
C 100 kilograms
D 1,000 kilograms

19. A 1-kilogram mass is dropped from a height of 1 meter. Its kinetic energy just before it hits the ground is

A 1 joule.
B 10 joules
C 100 joules
D 1,000 joules

20. A magnifying glass is what kind of lens used on objects how far away?

A convex lens used closer than one focal length
B concave lens used closer than one focal length
C convex lens used beyond one focal length
D concave lens used beyond one focal length

21. Frictional forces usually do NOT

A oppose motion.
B decrease kinetic energy.
C increase potential energy.
D produce wear.

22. A 120-volt electrical power supply produces 1/2 ampere to the load. The power delivered is

A 60 watts.
B 60 ohms.
C 240 watts.
D 240 ohms.

23. The category of weather system with the highest velocity winds is the

A thunderstorm.
B tornado.
C hurricane.
D sea breeze.

24. The member of the solar system with the shortest period of solar revolution is a

A planetary satellite.
B asteroid.
C planet.
D comet.

25. The ocean current that extends from Florida across the Atlantic Ocean to Europe is

A El Niño.
B the Japan Current.
C the Gulf Stream.
D the Southwest countercurrent.

ARITHMETIC REASONING—SUBTEST 2

DIRECTIONS

This test has questions about arithmetic. Each question is followed by four possible answers. Decide which answer is correct. Then, on your answer form, blacken the space that has the same number and letter as your choice. Use scratch paper for any figuring you wish to do.

Here is a sample question.

1. If 10 pounds of sugar cost $2.00, what is the cost of 1 pound?

A 90 cents
B 80 cents
C 50 cents
D 20 cents

The cost of 1 pound is 20 cents; therefore answer D is correct.

Your score on this test will be based on the number of questions you answer correctly. You should try to answer every question. Do not spend too much time on any one question.

Notice that Part 2 begins with question number 1. When you begin, be sure to mark your first answer next to number 1 in Part 2 on your answer form.

THE ACTUAL TEST WILL SAY:

Do not turn this page until told to do so.

Arithmetic Reasoning

Time: 36 minutes; 30 questions

1. A fire team is made up of four junior enlisted men and one noncommissioned officer as the team leader. A group of 64 privates fresh from basic training is to be divided into fire teams. How many team leaders will be needed?

A 8
B 10
C 12
D 16

2. A man working a part-time job earns $350.00 per week. His weekly check has $27.75 withheld for federal income taxes, $5.65 for FICA, and $12.87 for state income taxes. How much will his net pay for the week be?

A $314.73
B $304.73
C $303.73
D $313.73

3. Temperature readings on a certain day ranged from a low of –4°F to a high of 16°F. What was the average temperature for the day?

A 10°F
B 6°F
C 12°F
D 8°F

4. On a particular scale drawing, 1/4 inch represents 1 foot. How long would a line on the drawing have to be to represent a length of 3½ feet?

A 3/4 inch
B 7/8 inch
C 1⅞ inch
D 1¼ inch

5. An automobile manufacturer offers a 15% rebate on the list price of a new car. What would be the rebate on a car that lists for $13,620?

A $900.00
B $11,577.00
C $204.30
D $2,043.00

6. The price of gasoline rose from $1.90 to $2.08 per gallon. What was the percentage of increase?

A 4.2%
B 8.7%
C 10.5%
D 19.0%

7. A team won 70% of the 40 games it played. How many games did the team lose?

A 28
B 30
C 22
D 12

8. A flight is scheduled for departure at 3:50 P.M. If the flight takes 2 hours and 55 minutes, at what time is it scheduled to arrive at its destination?

A 5:05 P.M.
B 6:05 P.M.
C 6:15 P.M.
D 6:45 P.M.

9. How many 4-ounce candy bars are there in a 3-pound package of candy?

A 12
B 16
C 48
D 9

10. What if the fifth term of the series 2⅝, 3½, 4⅛, 4⅞, ...?

A 5⅛
B 5½
C 5⅝
D 6⅛

11. In a restaurant, a diner orders an entree with vegetables for $10.50, dessert for $1.50, and coffee for $0.50. If the tax on meals is 6%, what tax should be added to his check?

A $0.06
B $0.63
C $0.72
D $0.75

12. A 55-gallon drum of oil is going to be used to fill cans that hold 2 quarts each. How many cans can be filled from the drum?

A 55
B 27½
C 110
D 220

13. In a factory that makes wooden spindles, a lathe operator takes 45 minutes to do the finishing work on nine spindles. How many hours will it take him to finish 96 spindles at the same rate?

A 8
B 72
C 100
D 10

14. A triangle has two equal sides. The third side has a length of 13 feet, 2 inches. If the perimeter of the triangle is 40 feet, what is the length of one of the equal sides?

A 13 feet, 4 inches
B 26 feet, 10 inches
C 13 feet, 11 inches
D 13 feet, 5 inches

15. A lawn is 21 feet wide and 39 feet long. How much will it cost to weed and feed it if a gardening service charges $0.40 per square yard for this treatment?

A $109.20
B $36.40
C $327.60
D $24.00

16. A bonded courier drove for 7 hours on back roads at an average speed of 48 miles per hour. Her car gets 21 miles per gallon of gas. How many gallons of gas did she use?

A 24
B 14
C 18
D 16

17. Two partners operate a business that shows a yearly profit of $63,000. Their partnership agreement calls for them to share the profits in the ratio 5:4. How much of the profit should go to the partner who gets the larger share?

A $35,000
B $28,000
C $32,000
D $36,000

18. A purchaser paid $17.16 for an article that had recently been increased in price by 4%. What was the price of the article before the increase?

A $17.00
B $17.12
C $16.50
D $16.47

19. In a clothing factory, 5 workers finish production of 6 garments each per day, 3 others turn out 4 garments each per day, and 1 worker turns out 12 per day. What is the average number of garments produced per worker per day?

A 2⅗
B 6
C 4
D 7⅓

20. A man makes a 255-mile trip by car. He drives the first 2 hours at 45 miles per hour. At what speed must he then travel for the remainder of the trip in order to arrive at his destination 5 hours after he started?

A 31 miles per hour
B 50 miles per hour
C 51 miles per hour
D 55 miles per hour

21. A contractor bids $300,000 as her price for erecting a building. She estimates that 1/10 of this amount will be spent for masonry materials and labor, 1/3 for lumber and carpentry, 1/5 for plumbing and heating, and 1/6 for electrical and lighting work. The balance will be her profit. How much profit does she expect to make?

A $24,000
B $80,000
C $60,000
D $50,000

22. The list price of a TV set is $325, but the retailer offers successive discounts of 20% and 30%. What price does a customer actually pay?

    A $182.00
    B $270.00
    C $162.50
    D $176.67

23. A certain brand of motor oil is regularly sold at a price of two cans holding a quart each for $1.99. On a special sale, a carton containing six quart cans is sold for $5.43. What is the saving per quart if the oil is bought at the special sale price?

    A $0.27
    B $0.09
    C $0.54
    D $0.54¼

24. A worker earns $7.20 an hour. She is paid time and a half for overtime beyond a 40-hour week. How much will she earn in a week in which she works 43 hours?

    A $295.20
    B $320.40
    C $432.00
    D $464.40

25. A tree 36 feet high casts a shadow 8 feet long. At the same time, another tree casts a shadow 6 feet long. How tall is the second tree?

    A 30 feet
    B 27 feet
    C 24 feet
    D 32 feet

26. A company spends 3/5 of its advertising budget on newspaper ads and 1/3 on radio commercials. What portion of the advertising budget is left for TV commercials?

    A 1/2
    B 7/30
    C 1/15
    D 1/8

27. A VCR is programmed to record a TV show that lasts for a half hour. If the videotape can hold 180 minutes of recording, what percentage of the tape is used for this recording?

    A 16⅔%
    B 30%
    C 60%
    D 33⅓%

28. We bought 5 pounds of cashew nuts worth $1.80 per pound, mixed with 4 pounds of peanuts worth $1.62 per pound. What is the value per pound of the mixture?

    A $1.72
    B $1.71
    C $3.42
    D $1.82

29. A wall is 7 feet 8 inches in height; four vertical pieces of wallpaper are needed to cover the wall. Assuming there is no waste, what is the minimum length that a roll of wallpaper must be to cover the wall?

    A 29 feet, 2 inches
    B 31 feet, 2 inches
    C 31 feet
    D 30 feet, 8 inches

30. A night watchman is required to check in every 40 minutes while making his rounds. His tour of duty extends from 9:00 P.M. to 5:00 A.M. If he checks in at the start of his rounds and also when he finishes, how many times does he check in during the night?

A 12
B 13
C 8
D 20

WORD KNOWLEDGE—SUBTEST 3

DIRECTIONS

This test has questions about the meanings of words. Each question has an **underlined bold-face word**. You are to decide which one of the four words in the choices most nearly means the same as the underlined boldface word; then, mark the space on your answer form that has the same number and letter as your choice.

Now look at the sample question below.

1. It was a **small** table.

    A sturdy
    B round
    C cheap
    D little

The question asks which of the four words means the same as the boldface word, **small**. Little means the same as **small**. Answer D is the best one.

Your score on this test will be based on the number of questions you answer correctly. You should try to answer every question. Do not spend too much time on any one question.

When you begin, be sure to start with question number 1 in part 3 of your test booklet and number 1 in part 3 on your answer form.

THE ACTUAL TEST WILL SAY:

Do not turn this page until told to do so.

Word Knowledge

Time: 11 minutes; 35 questions

1. He reached the **pinnacle** of his career.

    A lowest point
    B final days
    C smallest salary
    D summit

2. **Brawl** most nearly means

    A trap.
    B fight.
    C speak.
    D provide.

3. She acted like a **pauper**.

    A poor person
    B slenderer
    C patriot
    D peculiar person

4. She has always been **punctual**.

    A a jokester
    B prompt
    C correct
    D prepared

5. **Segment** most nearly means

    A secret.
    B hermit.
    C part.
    D seep.

6. **Revere** most nearly means

    A esteem.
    B regulate.
    C reverse.
    D hold.

7. The speaker's audience appreciated **brevity**.

   A brilliance
   B illustrations
   C activity
   D conciseness

8. **Illogical** most nearly means

   A coherent.
   B illusive.
   C fallacious.
   D real.

9. **Excerpt** most nearly means

   A exam.
   B extract.
   C eventual.
   D superfluous.

10. The surface had a **sheen**.

    A color
    B luster
    C scratch
    D cover

11. **Divulge** most nearly means

    A divide.
    B fatten.
    C dissolve.
    D tell.

12. The attorney could **cite** examples.

    A cultivate
    B change
    C specify
    D grasp

13. I cannot **allay** your concerns.

    A ease
    B confirm
    C reverse
    D tempt

14. The animal had **vitality**.

    A liveliness.
    B viciousness.
    C cunning.
    D understanding.

15. **Defer** most nearly means

    A ascertain.
    B define.
    C abase.
    D delay.

16. I **deplore** your actions.

    A approve
    B applaud
    C regret
    D deprive

17. **Concur** most nearly means

    A defeat.
    B agree.
    C confine.
    D truth.

18. **Refute** most nearly means

    A refer.
    B disapprove.
    C disprove.
    D regard.

19. She served **copious** amounts of food.

    A unequal
    B small
    C uninviting
    D large

20. **Credulous** most nearly means

    A fantastic.
    B credit.
    C gullible.
    D awe-inspiring.

21. **Random** most nearly means

A haphazard.
B purpose.
C anger.
D ramble.

22. State the **salient** points.

A legal
B conspicuous
C less obvious
D missed

23. **Tangible** most nearly means

A illusory.
B tangent.
C concrete.
D tangle.

24. **Residue** most nearly means

A resident.
B part.
C rescue.
D remainder.

25. **Catastrophe** most nearly means

A violence.
B disorder.
C decision.
D disaster.

26. He promised us a **diagnosis**.

A analysis
B decision
C dialect
D diagram

27. Your reaction leaves me in a **quandary**.

A condition
B predicament
C certainty
D compunction

28. **Stilted** most nearly means

A bored.
B formal.
C stuffed.
D stifled.

29. The law says you must not **encroach**.

A enclose
B overreach
C trespass
D encounter

30. **Deter** most nearly means

A dissipate.
B detain.
C dispute.
D prevent.

31. **Falter** most nearly means

A die.
B fake.
C hesitate.
D fall.

32. Our meal was a **meager** one.

A sparse
B rich
C filling
D massive

33. **Stifle** most nearly means

A sign.
B suppress.
C shoot.
D stiff.

34. **Dearth** most nearly means

A lack.
B passing.
C ground.
D overabundance.

35. **Accord** most nearly means

A belief.
B accurate.
C settle.
D harmony.

PARAGRAPH COMPREHENSION—SUBTEST 4

DIRECTIONS

This is a test of your ability to understand what you read. In this section you will find one or more paragraphs of reading material followed by incomplete statements or questions. You are to read the paragraph and select one of four lettered choices that best completes the statement or answers the question. When you have selected your answer, blacken in the correct numbered letter on your answer sheet.

Now look at the sample question below.

In certain areas water is so scarce that every attempt is made to conserve it. For instance, for one oasis in the Sahara Desert the amount of water necessary for each date palm tree has been carefully determined.

1. How much water is each tree given?

    A no water at all
    B exactly the amount required
    C water only if it is healthy
    D water on alternate days

The amount of water each tree requires has been carefully determined, so answer B is correct.

Your score on this test will be based on the number of questions you answer correctly. You should try to answer every question. Do not spend too much time on any one question.

When you begin, be sure to start with question number 1 in Part 4 of your test booklet and number 1 in Part 4 on your answer form.

THE ACTUAL TEST WILL SAY:

Do not turn this page until told to do so.

Paragraph Comprehension

Time: 13 minutes; 15 questions

1. History tells us that Christopher Columbus once saved his own life because he knew from his almanac that there was going to be an eclipse of the moon. In 1504 Columbus was marooned in Jamaica with no food and unfriendly natives confronting him. The explorer threatened to turn off the light in the sky if the natives refused to give him food. Columbus kept his word; the natives gave him food.

The main idea of this paragraph is that

A natives rarely own almanacs or understand scientific facts.
B Christopher Columbus was in Jamaica in 1504 on his third voyage from Spain.
C on his arrival in Jamaica, Christopher Columbus had no food.
D Columbus saved his own life because he knew when there was going to be an eclipse of the moon.

2. One implied warranty required by state law is the "warranty of merchantability." This means that the seller promises that the product will do what it is supposed to do. For example,

A a car will never need repairs.
B a lawnmower will also cut bushes.
C a toaster will toast.
D your roof will last 75 to 100 years.

3. Railroads originating on both coasts of the United States were joined on May 10, 1869, when a golden spike was driven to join the last rail at Promontory Point, Utah. Great numbers of immigrants moved west to take up free homestead land or purchase tracts at low prices.

According to the passage, the settling of the American West

A made immigrants very wealthy from land ownership.
B followed the completion of the railroad.
C made it impossible for anyone to purchase land.
D was finished before the summer of 1869.

4. The most disadvantaged type in both countries was the single-parent, female-headed household, of which 38% in Canada and 61% in the United States were in need. Moreover, 44% of single females living alone in Canada and 51% in the United States were in housing need. By contrast, male single parents experienced about half the housing need of their female equivalents.

You can conclude from the paragraph that needy male single parents in housing need in the United States numbered approximately

A 61%.
B 30%.
C 44%.
D 22%.

5. In 1973, when the OPEC nations embargoed oil exports to the United States, their action signaled an unprecedented rise in oil prices. In fact, crude oil prices quadrupled, sending oil-dependent countries into a recession.

One of the results of the oil embargo was that

A the United States embargoed oil exports of OPEC nations.
B the price of crude oil declined.
C the price of crude oil doubled.
D oil-dependent countries experienced a recession.

6. Although they last no longer than a fraction of a second, voltage variations can cause problems with sensitive electronic equipment. Variation in voltage causes digital clocks to blink and timers to be thrown off schedule.

Computers are especially

A useful when you transfer data to memory.
B easy to protect from variations in voltage.
C useful in publishing.
D sensitive to voltage variations.

7. In 1948, the United Nations General Assembly adopted the resolution entitled the Universal Declaration of Human Rights. This resolution stresses personal, civil, political, social, cultural, and economic rights of people. In so doing, the article promotes

A financial well-being only.
B fundamental freedoms.
C social unrest.
D only one political party.

8. DNA, a nucleic acid contained in all living material, orders every cell to reproduce in a certain manner. In fact, DNA molecules determine both the form and function of all living cells.

DNA is

A found only in animals.
B one kind of cell.
C a nucleic acid.
D a nuclear device.

9. Garbage has become an alarming problem—and it won't go away. State landfills, as they are presently designed, are quickly filling up. Consequently, since 30% of trash being dumped can be recycled, it is time for communities to set up recycling programs.

Not all trash needs to be dumped. We know that

A a third of what we dump could be recycled.
B people could start their own landfills.
C recycling will never take place.
D 70% of trash can be recycled.

10. Sometimes a state legislature asks the voters to approve or reject a proposal called a referendum. The proposal may be a constitutional amendment, a plan for long-term borrowing, or a special law affecting a city. In effect, the question is "referred" to the voters. The Constitution of the United States was submitted to state conventions for approvals.

From the definition above, you can say that it was

A approved unanimously.
B approved by a form of referendum.
C rejected by a majority of the states.
D referred to the president of the United States.

11. Some pollutants that render air unsafe to breathe cannot be seen or smelled. Nitric oxide, carbon monoxide, and radon gas are examples. Other pollutants, such as formaldehyde, can be smelled at high levels only but are still unsafe to breathe even at lower levels.

You can conclude from the paragraph that formaldehyde

A is safer to breathe than nitric oxide.
B can never be seen or smelled.
C cannot be smelled at lower levels.
D is not one of the pollutants that renders air unsafe to breathe.

12. Pneumonia is caused by bacteria viruses, fungi, or mycoplasmas. Bacterial pneumonia is the main type of pneumonia that follows an attack of the flu and a major precipitator (beginning cause) of pneumonia deaths.

Which kind of pneumonia is the most deadly?

A bacterial
B viral
C fungi
D flu

13. Because the temperature of ocean water changes more slowly than the temperature of air, oceans affect the world's climate. As ocean water moves past land masses, it affects the climate by warming the air in winter and cooling it in summer.

The key idea in this paragraph is that

A ocean water moves past land masses.
B ocean water cools the air in winter.
C ocean water warms land masses in summer.
D the world's climate is affected by the temperature of the oceans.

14. Lasers and incandescent lights are different in an important way. Incandescent light from light bulbs emits light of different wavelengths and moves in many directions. On the other hand, laser beams are monochromatic, consisting of a single wavelength. They can travel great distances without spreading. Any comparison of laser and incandescent lights must include a discussion of

A small and large light bulbs.
B wavelengths.
C sound waves.
D echoes.

15. To get full value for your energy dollars, first arrange for an energy audit of your home. An audit will reveal such things as energy-sapping drafts, insufficient insulation, improper weatherstripping, and a need for storm windows and doors.

Installing storm windows may be energy-saving but should be preceded by

A an energy audit.
B storm doors.
C insulation.
D proper weatherstripping.

AUTOMOTIVE INFORMATION—SUBTEST 5

DIRECTIONS

This test has questions about automobiles. Pick the best answer for each question, then blacken the space on your separate answer form that has the same number and letter as your choice.

Here is a sample question.

1. The most commonly used fuel for running automobile engines is

    A kerosene.
    B benzene.
    C crude oil.
    D gasoline.

Gasoline is the most commonly used fuel, so D is the correct answer.

Your score on this test will be based on the number of questions you answer correctly. You should try to answer every question. Do not spend too much time on any one question.

When you are told to begin, be sure to start with question number 1 in Part 5 of your test booklet and number 1 in Part 5 on your separate answer form.

THE ACTUAL TEST WILL SAY:

Do not turn this page until told to do so.

Automotive Information

Time: 8 minutes; 15 questions

1. The piston of an internal combustion engine fits inside the

    A crankshaft.
    B cylinder.
    C radiator.
    D brake drum.

2. The flywheel is attached to the

    A crankshaft.
    B carburetor.
    C radiator.
    D differential.

3. There are three types of fuel injection used in cars today. They are multi-injector, mono-injector electronic, and

    A manual continuous electronic flow.
    B automatic continuous flow.
    C automatic convoluted flow.
    D manual continuous flow.

4. Most automobile engines are

    A two-stroke cycle engines.
    B three-stroke cycle engines.
    C four-stroke cycle engines.
    D six-stroke cycle engines.

5. When a spark plug fires, it is part of the

    A power stroke.
    B exhaust stroke.
    C intake stroke.
    D compression stroke.

6. If the universal joints are broken and the car is standing still, the car will

    A not move when the engine is revved up.
    B increase in speed.
    C work as usual.
    D become impossible to push.

7. When the clutch is engaged on a manual transmission, the clutch pedal will be

   A down.
   B up.
   C halfway down.
   D halfway up.

8. What gear is the transmission in when the engine is driving the car directly?

   A first gear
   B second gear
   C third gear
   D fourth gear

9. When the clutch is disengaged, the car will

   A be in reverse.
   B be in third gear.
   C be in neutral.
   D move quickly.

10. A four-wheel vehicle driving on all four wheels is known as a

    A 4×2.
    B 2×4.
    C 4×4.
    D 4×6.

11. If we increase the engine torque, we decrease the

    A RPMs.
    B weight.
    C power.
    D speed.

12. If the engine will not start, the problem could be

    A the clutch slipping.
    B a clogged oil filter.
    C too much carbon in the drain holes or slots.
    D a weak battery.

13. When the mixture of fuel and air burns in the cylinder, it creates a temperature of

    A 4000° to 4500°F.
    B 400° to 450°F.
    C 1000° to 2500°F.
    D 1250° to 1500°F.

14. The first emission control applied to automobile engines was called the

    A preventive combustion venturi system.
    B positive crankcase ventilation system.
    C pollution control ventilation system.
    D pollution combustion vertical system.

15. A tire that bears the code "P 185/70 R 14" is

    A a passenger-car tire that is 70 millimeters high.
    B a passenger-car tire that is 185 millimeters wide.
    C a radial tire that is 70 millimeters high.
    D a P-metric tire that is 70 millimeters wide.

MATHEMATICS KNOWLEDGE—SUBTEST 6

DIRECTIONS

This is a test of your ability to solve general mathematical problems. Each problem is followed by four answer choices. Select the correct response from the choices given. Then mark the space on your answer form that has the same number and letter as your choice. Use scratch paper to do any figuring that you wish.

Now look at this sample problem.

1. If $x + 8 = 9$, then x is equal to

   A 0.
   B 1.
   C –1.
   D 9/8.

The correct answer is 1, so B is the correct response.

Your score on this test will be based on the number of questions you answer correctly. You should try to answer every question. Do not spend too much time on any one question.

Start with question number 1 in Part 6. Mark your answer for this question next to number 1, Part 6, on your answer form.

THE ACTUAL TEST WILL SAY:

Do not turn this page until told to do so.

Mathematics Knowledge

Time: 24 minutes; 25 questions

1. What is 4% of 0.0375?

   A 0.0015
   B 0.9375
   C 0.0775
   D 0.15

2. What number multiplied by 2/3 will give a product of 1?

   A –2/3
   B –3/2
   C 3/2
   D 4/6

3. What is the value of the expression $x^2 - 5xy + 2y$ if $x = 3$ and $y = -2$?

   A –25
   B –27
   C 32
   D 35

4. Solve the following inequality: $x - 3 < 14$.

   A $x < 11$
   B $x < 17$
   C $x = 11$
   D $x > 17$

5. Multiply $7a^3b^2c$ by $3a^2b^4c^2$.

   A $10a^5b^6c^3$
   B $21a^5b^6c^2$
   C $21a^6b^8c^2$
   D $21a^5b^6c^3$

6. A floor is made up of hexagonal tiles, some of which are black and some of which are white. Every black tile is completely surrounded by white tiles. How many white tiles are there around each black tile?

   A four
   B five
   C six
   D eight

7. The value of 8^0 is

   A 8.
   B 0.
   C 1.
   D 1/8.

8. If $2x - 3 = 37$, what is the value of x?

   A 17
   B 38
   C 20
   D 80

9. An audience consists of M people, and 2/3 of the audience are adults. Of the adults, 1/2 are males. How many adult males are in the audience?

   A $\dfrac{1}{6}M$

   B $M - \dfrac{2}{3} - \dfrac{1}{2}$

   C $\dfrac{1}{3}M$

   D $M - \dfrac{1}{3}$

10. What is the value of $(0.2)^3$?

    A 0.008
    B 0.8
    C 0.006
    D 0.6

11. If $x^2 + x = 6$, what is the value of x?

    A 6 or –1
    B 1 or –6
    C 2 or –3
    D 3 or –2

12. What is the number of square inches in the area of a circle whose diameter is 28 inches? (Use 22/7 for the value of π.)

    A 616
    B 88
    C 44
    D 1,232

13. The expression $\dfrac{x^2 + 2x - 3}{x + 3}$ cannot be evaluated if x has a value of

    A 0.
    B –1.
    C 3.
    D –3.

14. If $\sqrt{x + 11} = 9$, what is the value of x?

    A –2
    B –8
    C 70
    D 7

15. The points $A(2,7)$ and $B(5,11)$ are plotted on coordinate graph paper. What is the distance from A to B?

    A 7
    B 5
    C 25
    D $\sqrt{14}$

16. Solve the following equation for y: $ay - bx = 2$.

    A $\dfrac{bx + 2}{a}$

    B $2 + bx - a$

    C $\dfrac{2}{a - bx}$

    D $\dfrac{2}{a} - bx$

17. For a special mission, one soldier is to be chosen at random from among three infantrymen, two artillerymen, and five tank crewmen. What is the probability that an infantryman will be chosen?

A 3/10
B 1/10
C 1/3
D 3/7

18. A cylindrical post has a cross section that is a circle with a radius of 3 inches. A piece of cord can be wound around it exactly seven times. How long is the piece of cord? (Use 22/7 as the value of π.)

A 66 inches
B 42 inches
C 198 inches
D 132 inches

19. A naval task force is to be made up of a destroyer, a supply ship, and a submarine. If four destroyers, two supply ships, and three submarines are available from which to choose, how many different combinations are possible for the task force?

A 9
B 24
C 8
D 12

20. The basis of a cylindrical can is a circle whose diameter is 2 inches. Its height is 7 inches. How many cubic inches are there in the volume of the can? (Use 22/7 for the value of π).

A 12⅔
B 22
C 44
D 88

21. A rectangular vegetable garden 16 yards long and 4 yards wide is completely enclosed by a fence. To reduce the amount of fencing used, the owner replaced the garden with a square one having the same area. How many yards of fencing did he save?

A 4
B 6
C 8
D 16

22. The value of $\sqrt{164}$ to the nearest integer is

A 18
B 108
C 42
D 13

23. What is the maximum number of boxes, each measuring 3 inches by 4 inches by 5 inches, that can be packed into a storage space measuring 1 foot by 2 feet by 2 feet, 1 inch?

A 120
B 60
C 15
D 48

24. A circle passes through the four vertices of a rectangle that is 8 feet long and 6 feet wide. How many feet are there in the radius of the circle?

A 14
B 2½
C 10
D 5

25. There are 12 liters of a mixture of acetone in alcohol that is 33⅓% acetone. How many liters of alcohol must be added to the mixture to reduce it to a mixture containing 25% acetone?

A 1
B 2
C 4
D 6

MECHANICAL COMPREHENSION—SUBTEST 7

DIRECTIONS

This test has questions about general mechanical and physical principles. Pick the best answer for each question, then blacken the space on your separate answer form that has the same number and letter as your choice.

Here is a sample question.

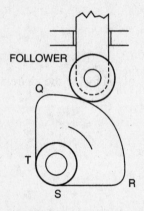

1. The follower is at its highest position between points

    A Q and R.
    B R and S.
    C S and T.
    D T and Q.

The correct answer is between Q and R, so you would blacken the space for A on your answer form.

Your score on this test will be based on the number of questions you answer correctly. You should try to answer every question. Do not spend too much time on any one question.

When you are told to begin, be sure to start with question number 1 in Part 7 of your test booklet and number 1 in Part 7 of your separate answer form.

THE ACTUAL TEST WILL SAY:

Do not turn this page until told to do so.

Mechanical Comprehension

Time: 19 minutes; 25 questions

1. Force is something that can change the velocity of an object by making it

   A start or stop.
   B speed up.
   C slow down.
   D all of the above.

2. The brakes on your car use the same force that stops your car if you just let it coast. This force is called

   A velocity.
   B gravity.
   C friction.
   D newton.

3. The SI (metric) term corresponding to pounds is

   A gram.
   B newton.
   C kilogram.
   D pascal.

4. If you drop something, it falls. The force acting on it is

   A gravity.
   B friction.
   C elastic recoil.
   D equilibrium.

5. When a rope is stretched, it is said to be in a state of

   A equilibrium.
   B tension.
   C buoyancy.
   D elastic recoil.

6. When a solid moves through a liquid, there is a frictionlike force retarding the motion of the solid. This is called

   A gravity.
   B friction.
   C elastic recoil.
   D viscous drag.

7. Weight is directly proportional to the acceleration due to

   A friction.
   B elastic recoil.
   C viscous drag.
   D gravity.

8. The force that acts in an upward direction on anything submerged in a liquid or a gas is called

   A friction.
   B viscous drag.
   C gravity.
   D buoyancy.

9. Forces exist only in pairs. These forces are sometimes called

   A action and interaction.
   B reaction and interaction.
   C action and reaction.
   D friction and gravity.

10. When forces act in pairs they are

    A equal in magnitude and opposite in direction.
    B equal in magnitude and in the same direction.
    C equal in magnitude.
    D unequal in magnitude.

11. If an object is in equilibrium, it is said to be

    A at rest.
    B moving.
    C at rest or moving at a constant speed and in a straight line.
    D moving upward only.

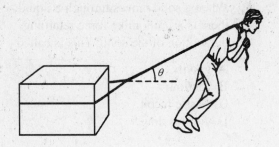

12. In the figure, the angle θ is important, since when it is

A 0 degrees the entire force is dragging the box.
B 90 degrees the entire force is lifting the box.
C both lifting and dragging between 10 degrees and 90 degrees.
D all of the above.

13. A good example of a simple machine is a

A manually operated pencil sharpener.
B doorknob.
C light switch.
D all of the above.

14. The effort times the effort distance is called

A the work input.
B the work output.
C the buoyancy.
D gravity.

15. The load times the load distance is called

A the work input.
B the work output.
C the buoyancy.
D gravity.

16. Work input is always more than work output because of

A gravity.
B buoyancy.
C friction.
D tension.

17. The ratio between work output and work input is called

A efficiency.
B work.
C leverage
D mass.

18. The amount of magnification that a machine produces is referred to as the

A effort arm.
B work.
C mechanical advantage.
D efficiency.

19. A ramp is a device commonly used to aid in

A lifting.
B lowering weights.
C high-efficiency situations.
D loading.

20. A screw consists of a single continuous spiral wrapped around a

A piston.
B cylinder.
C helix.
D square.

21. The distance between the ridges of screw threads is called the

A valley.
B peak.
C pitch.
D count.

22. A vise is a self-locking machine because its efficiency is considered to be

A near 100%.
B less than 50%.
C more than 50%.
D less than 25%.

23. The mechanical advantage of a winch is the ratio of the radius of the crank to the radius of the

A arm.
B lever.
C fulcrum.
D shaft.

24. The ideal mechanical advantage of a gear is the ratio of the number of teeth in the load gear to the number of teeth in the

A effort gear.
B loaded gear.
C lifting gear.
D spiral gear.

25. The rate at which work is done is called

A power.
B effort.
C watts.
D horsepower.

ELECTRONICS INFORMATION—SUBTEST 8

DIRECTIONS

This is a test of your knowledge of electrical, radio, and electronics information. You are to select the correct response from the choices given. Then mark the space on your answer form that has the same number and letter as your choice.

1. What does the abbreviation AC stand for?

    A additional charge
    B alternating coil
    C alternating current
    D ampere current

The correct answer is alternating current, so C is the correct response.

Your score on this test will be based on the number of questions you answer correctly. You should try to answer every question. Do not spend too much time on any one question.

When you are told to begin, be sure to start with question number 1 in Part 8 of your test booklet and number 1 in Part 8 on your separate answer form.

THE ACTUAL TEST WILL SAY:

Do not turn this page until told to do so.

Electronics Information

Time: 9 minutes, 20 questions

1. Electricity is defined as

    A flow of electrons along a conductor.
    B flow of ions along a conductor.
    C movement of charges.
    D static electricity.

2. A conductor is any material that

    A has no free electrons.
    B has many free electrons.
    C has free ions.
    D has free protons.

3. Convention current flow is from

    A + to +.
    B – to +.
    C + to –.
    D – to –.

4. Electron flow is from

    A + to +.
    B – to +.
    C + to –.
    D – to –.

5. An insulator is a material with

    A many free electrons.
    B few free electrons.
    C many free protons.
    D many free ions.

6. Opposition to current flow is measured in

    A ohms.
    B amps.
    C volts.
    D watts.

7. A watt is the power that gives rise to the production of energy at the rate of

    A 1 joule per minute.
    B 1 volt per second.
    C 1 amp per second.
    D 1 joule per second.

8. The Greek letter phi (φ) is used to

   A indicate ohms.
   B indicate angles or phases.
   C indicate volts.
   D indicate dielectric flux.

9. A parallel circuit with resistors of 10 ohms, 10 ohms, and 5 ohms has a total resistance of

   A 10 ohms.
   B 5 ohms.
   C 25 ohms.
   D 2.5 ohms.

10. Which of these is a symbol for a fuse?

   A ⎓⁓⁓⁓⎓
   B ⎓⁓⎓
   C ⎓⊣⊢
   D ⊛

11. The symbol for inductance is

   A X_L
   B I
   C L
   D X_C

12. Inductive reactance is found by using

   A $X_L = 2\pi\, FC$.
   B $X_L = 2\pi\, FL$.
   C $X_L = R$.
   D $X_L = Z$.

13. A capacitor of 100 microfarads has a capacity of

   A 100 picofarads.
   B 10 picofarads.
   C 100,000,000 picofarads.
   D 10,000 picofarads.

14. Impedance is represented by the symbol

   A X_L.
   B R.
   C X_C.
   D Z.

15. In electronics a CRT is a

   A constant radiation tube.
   B contrasting relief tube.
   C cathode ray tube.
   D conflicting relay tube.

16. A junction diode is used for

   A rectifying power-line frequencies and lower currents.
   B rectifying power-line frequencies and higher currents.
   C rectifying higher frequencies at lower currents.
   D rectifying higher frequencies at higher currents.

17. The SCR is a

   A specialized rectifier or diode.
   B special colored rectifier.
   C special controlled rectifier.
   D silicon-controlled relay.

18. In an FM receiver the AFC is

   A automatic frequency control for stabilizing the IF.
   B automatic frequency control for stabilizing the local oscillator.
   C automatic frequency control for tuning the incoming frequency.
   D automatic frequency control for the radio frequency amplifier.

19. Receivers with the ability to receive multiplexed signals are

   A FM.
   B FM-stereo.
   C AM.
   D AFC-FM.

20. The FM band covers

   A 550 to 1,600 kHz.
   B 88 to 108 MHz.
   C 100 to 200 MHz.
   D 550 to 1600 MHz.

SHOP INFORMATION—SUBTEST 9

DIRECTIONS

This test has questions about your knowledge of tools, as well as common shop terminology and practices. Pick the best answer for each question, then blacken the space on the answer form that has the same number and letter as your choice.

Here is a sample question.

1. A hammer is most commonly used for driving

    A nails.
    B Miss Daisy.
    C nine irons.
    D to Las Vegas.

A hammer is most commonly used to drive nails, so A is the correct answer.

Your score on this test will be based on the number of questions you answer correctly. You should try to answer every question. Do not spend too much time on any one question.

When you are told to begin, be sure to start with question number 1 in Part 9 of your test booklet and number 1 in Part 9 on your separate answer form.

THE ACTUAL TEST WILL SAY:

Do not turn this page until told to do so.

Shop Information

Time: 8 minutes; 15 questions

1. In concrete work, to butter a concrete block means to

    A put a finishing trowel to it.
    B put a hawk on it.
    C use a jointer on it.
    D put mortar on it.

2. Which of the following is a hard-wood?

    A oak
    B spruce
    C pine
    D fir

3. Which of the following is a softwood?

    A poplar
    B maple
    C pine
    D oak

4. To prevent rapid drying, freshly cut logs are often

    A submerged in oil.
    B placed in kilns.
    C submerged in water.
    D placed in sheds to dry slowly.

5. A bumping hammer is used to smooth out dents by a(n)

    A sheet metal duct worker.
    B autobody repairman.
    C bumper repairman.
    D none of the above.

6. A groover is used to

    A lock seams together.
    B make sheet metal seams.
    C open a seam.
    D fold a seam.

7. Sheet metal is formed into round cylinders by using a

   A squaring shear.
   B slip roll.
   C bar folder.
   D punch press.

8. The tip of a soldering iron is coated with solder before it is used. This process of coating the tip is called

   A welding.
   B brazing.
   C soldering.
   D tinning.

9. Punches are used in sheet metal work to

   A flatten the metal.
   B make holes in the metal.
   C groove the metal.
   D snip the metal.

10. A squaring shear is used to

   A cut metal off to a straight line.
   B square a piece of metal.
   C fold a piece of sheet metal.
   D punch a piece of sheet metal.

11. The term *penny* is used

   A to indicate the cost of a nail.
   B to indicate the size of a nail.
   C to designate a rosin-coated nail.
   D to indicate a galvanized nail.

12. Concrete reaches 98% of its strength in

   A 3 days.
   B 50 days.
   C 28 days.
   D 10 days.

13. A coping saw blade is placed in the saw

   A with the teeth pointing upward.
   B with the teeth pointing toward the handle.
   C so it cuts with the wood grain.
   D so it cuts across the wood grain.

14. Carpenters use

   A ball peen hammers.
   B chisel point hammers.
   C claw hammers.
   D planishing hammers.

15. A welding torch can also be used as

   A a light source.
   B an etching tool.
   C a cutting torch.
   D a pipe wrench.

ASSEMBLING OBJECTS—SUBTEST 10

DIRECTIONS

This test measures your ability to picture how an object will look when its parts are mentally put together. Each question will show you several separate shapes; you will then pick the choice that best represents how the pieces would look if they were all fitted together correctly. There is only one best answer for each shape. Pick the best answer for each question, then blacken the space on the answer form that has the same number and letter as your choice.

Here is a sample question.

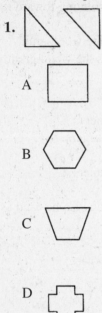

Choice A is the shape that will result when the two initial shapes are assembled correctly.

Your score on this test will be based on the number of questions you answer correctly. You should try to answer every question. Do not spend too much time on any one question.

When you are told to begin, be sure to start with question number 1 in Part 10 of your test booklet and number 1 in Part 10 on your separate answer form.

THE ACTUAL TEST WILL SAY:

Do not turn this page until told to do so.

Assembling Objects

Time: 20 minutes; 20 questions

1.

A

B

C

D

2.

A

B

C

D

3.

A

B

C

D

4.

A

B

C

D

5.

A

B

C

D

6.

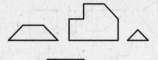

A

B

C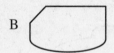

D

8.

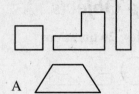

A

B

C

D

7.

A

B

C

D

9.

A

B

C

D

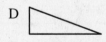

10.

A

B

C

D

11.

A

B

C

D

12.

A

B

C

D

13.

A

B

C

D

14.

A

B

C

D

15.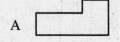

A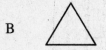

B

C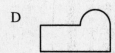

D

16.

A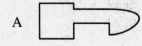

B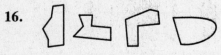

C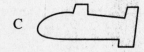

D

17.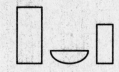

A

B

C

D

18.

A

B

C

D

19.

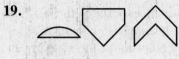

A

B

C

D

20.

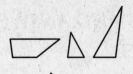

A

B

C

D

ANSWERS AND ANSWERS EXPLAINED

GENERAL SCIENCE—SUBTEST 1
Answers

1. B	6. C	11. D	16. D	21. C
2. D	7. A	12. C	17. D	22. A
3. B	8. C	13. C	18. D	23. B
4. B	9. A	14. B	19. B	24. C
5. D	10. A	15. B	20. A	25. C

Answers Explained

1. **B** Enzymes are organic (protein) catalysts that affect the speed of chemical reactions without being used up themselves.

2. **D** Chromosomes are composed of DNA and protein and are usually found in the nucleus.

3. **B** The cell wall, mainly composed of cellulose, is an important characteristic of plant cells. Chloroplasts contain energy-accumulating pigments and are found only in plant cells.

4. **B** Epithelial cells form the skin and inner lining for organs.

5. **D** Proteins are synthesized from a variety of amino acid "building blocks." Digestion breaks down the complex protein structures.

6. **C** The pulmonary circulation returns oxygenated blood from the lungs through the pulmonary veins to the left atrium of the heart.

7. **A** The relative concentration of glucose is maintained by the combined action of insulin from the pancreas and adrenaline from the adrenal medulla.

8. **C** Soil is eroded by the action of wind, water, and ice and/or is depleted by the removal of organic matter or minerals.

9. **A** Symbiosis is a nutritive relationship in which organisms of different species live together and benefit each other.

10. **A** A person exposed to the AIDS virus will take up to 6 months to show antibodies in the blood serum and 2 to 5 years to show externally observable symptoms.

11. **D** Iodine crystals in a small bottle of water make a saturated aqueous solution. A few milliliters of this solution added to a quart of water will destroy most organisms in an hour.

12. **C** The hydrate $CuSO_4 \cdot 5H_2O$ contains 6 atoms in the salt $CuSO_4$ (1Cu + 1S + 4O). The five loosely bonded water molecules contain 15 atoms (10H + 5O). The total number of atoms is 6 + 15 = 21.

13. **C** $2Na + 2HOH \rightarrow 2NaOH + H_2$ is a single replacement reaction where one sodium atom replaces just one of the hydrogen atoms in each water molecule.

14. **B** The nitrogen in the soil must be replaced by nitrogen-fixing bacteria in the roots of legumes or by artificial fertilizer containing nitrates.

15. **B** The fermentation of sugar by yeast produces ethyl alcohol and carbon dioxide.

16. **D** If the amount of I-131 is reduced by one-half every 8 days: 8 mg (8 days), 4 mg (8 days), 2 mg (8 days), 1/2 mg. It would take 32 days (approximately 1 month).

17. **D** A magnetic compass is influenced by all magnetic sources in its vicinity and aligns itself according to the net magnetic field at that location.

18. **D** One meter equals 100 centimeters. Therefore, 1 cubic meter equals 1,000,000 cubic centimeters. Since each cubic centimeter has a mass of 1 gram, the approximate total mass is 1,000 kilograms.

19. **B** Gravitational potential energy is converted to kinetic energy. The kinetic energy is equal to the mass of the object times the force of gravity times the height. Thus, mgh = 1 kilogram × 9.8 meters/second × 1 meter = (approximately) 10 joules.

20. **A** An object held closer than one focal length from a convex lens will produce a virtual magnified image.
21. **C** The friction force will tend to oppose motion, slow the object down, and produce wear between contacting surfaces.
22. **A** Power = voltage × current (in watts) = 120 volts × 1/2 ampe = 60 watts.
23. **B** Wind velocities of tornados have been measured in excess of 250 miles per hour.
24. **C** The planet Mercury orbits the sun in 88 days.
25. **C** No explanation required.

ARITHMETIC REASONING— SUBTEST 2
Answers

1. **D**	7. **D**	13. **A**	19. **B**	25. **B**
2. **C**	8. **D**	14. **D**	20. **D**	26. **C**
3. **B**	9. **A**	15. **B**	21. **C**	27. **A**
4. **B**	10. **B**	16. **D**	22. **A**	28. **A**
5. **D**	11. **D**	17. **A**	23. **B**	29. **D**
6. **C**	12. **C**	18. **C**	24. **B**	30. **B**

Answers Explained

1. **D** The number of privates in the group who have just graduated from basic training divided by the number in each fire team gives you the number of fire teams and therefore the number of team leaders needed.

$$64 \div 4 = 16$$

16 team leaders are needed, one for each position.

2. **C** Find the total of all the amounts withheld.
$27.75 + $5.65 + $12.87 = $46.27
Net pay is the salary for the week minus the total of all the withholdings.
Net pay = $350.00 – $46.27 = $303.73

3. **B** The average is the sum of the high and low temperatures divided by 2.

$$\text{Average} = \frac{-4° + 16°}{2} = \frac{12°}{2} = 6°$$

4. **B** If 1/4 inch represents 1 foot, then 3/4 inch will represent 3 feet. and 1/2 foot will be represented by one-half of 1/4 inch, or 1/8 inch. Thus, 3½ feet will be represented by 3/4 inch plus 1/8 inch.

$$\frac{3}{4} + \frac{1}{8} = \frac{6}{8} + \frac{1}{8} = \frac{7}{8}$$

5. **D** The rebate will be 15% (or 0.15) of the list price, $13,600.

$$\begin{array}{r} \$13,620 \\ \underline{0.15} \\ 681\ 00 \\ \underline{1\ 362\ 0} \\ \$2,043.00 = \text{rebate} \end{array}$$

6. **C** Find the rise in price by subtracting the original price from the new price per gallon.
Increase in price = $2.08 – $1.90 = $0.18
The percent of increase is the rise in price divided by the original price.

$$= \frac{0.18}{1.90} = \frac{18}{190} = \frac{2}{21} = 10.5\%$$

7. **D** The number of games won is 70% (or 0.70) of the number of games played, 40.
Number of games won = 0.70(40) = 28.00 = 28
The number of games lost is the total number played minus the number won.
Number of games lost = 40 – 28 = 12

8. **D** The time of arrival is 2 hours and 55 minutes after the departure time of 3:50 P.M. By 4:00 P.M., the flight has taken 10 minutes of the total flight time of 2 hours and 55 minutes. 2 hours and 45 minutes remain, and 2 hours and 45 minutes after 4:00 P.M. is 6:45 P.M.

9. **A** There are 16 ounces in 1 pound. Therefore, 4 of the 4-ounce candy bars will make 1 pound. A 3-pound package will hold 3 times 4 or 12 bars.

10. **B** Find the relationship between each pair of successive numbers in the series. It is helpful to change $3\frac{1}{2}$ to $3\frac{1}{6}$ in order to see the relationships.

For $\left(2\frac{5}{6}, 3\frac{1}{2}\right): 3\frac{1}{2} - 2\frac{5}{6}$

$= 3\frac{3}{6} - 2\frac{5}{6} = \frac{4}{6}$

For $\left(3\frac{1}{2}, 4\frac{1}{6}\right): 4\frac{1}{6} - 3\frac{1}{2}$

$= 4\frac{1}{6} - 3\frac{3}{6} = \frac{4}{6}$

For $\left(4\frac{1}{6}, 4\frac{5}{6}\right): 4\frac{5}{6} - 4\frac{1}{6}$

$= \frac{4}{6}$

Each term of the series is obtained by adding 4/6 to the preceding term. The fifth term is

$4\frac{5}{6} + \frac{4}{6} = 4\frac{9}{6}$

$= 4 + \frac{6}{6} + \frac{3}{6}$

$= 4 + 1 + \frac{1}{2}$

$= 5\frac{1}{2}$

11. **D** First add the prices of the three items ordered to get the cost of the meal before the tax.
$\$10.50 + \$1.50 + \$.50 = \$12.50$
The tax is 6% (or 0.06) of the cost of the meal.
$0.06 \times \$12.50 = \$.7500 = \$.75$

12. **C** There are 4 quarts in 1 gallon. A 55-gallon drum holds 4×55 quarts.
4×455 quarts = 220 quarts
If each can holds 2 quarts, the number of cans filled is 220 divided by 2.
$220 \div 2 = 110$ cans

13. **A** The number of minutes required to finish 1 spindle is the number of minutes, 45, taken for all 9 spindles, divided by their number, 9.
$45 \div 9 = 5$ minutes per spindle

The number of minutes to finish 96 spindles will be 96 times as much.
$5 \times 96 = 480$ minutes
There are 60 minutes in 1 hour. Divide the number of minutes by 60 to convert their number to hours.
$480 \div 60 = 8$ hours

14. **D** The perimeter, 40 feet, is the sum of the lengths of all three sides. The sum of the lengths of the two equal sides is the difference between the perimeter and the length of the third side.
Sum of lengths of 2 equal sides
= 40 feet − 13 feet, 2 inches
= 39 feet, 12 inches
− 13 feet, 2 inches
= 26 feet, 10 inches
The length of one side is obtained by dividing the sum by 2.
Length of one equal side

$= \dfrac{26 \text{ feet}, 10 \text{ inches}}{2}$

= 13 feet, 5 inches

15. **B** Since 3 feet = 1 yard, convert the length and width to yards by dividing their dimensions in feet by 3.

Width $= \dfrac{21}{3} = 7$ yards;

length $= \dfrac{39}{3} = 13$ yards

The area of a rectangle is the product of its length and width.
Area = $7 \times 13 = 91$ square yards
The cost for the entire lawn is obtained by multiplying the area in square yards by the cost per square yard.
$91 \times \$.40 = \$36.40$

16. **D** Find the number of miles traveled by multiplying the rate, 48 miles per hour, by the time, 7 hours.
$48 \times 7 = 336$ miles
The number of gallons of gas used is the number of miles driven divided by the number of miles per gallon.

$\dfrac{336}{21} = \dfrac{112}{7} = 16$ gallons

17. **A** If the profits are shared in the ratio 5:4, one partner gets 5/9 of the profits and the other gets 4/9. Note that 5/9 + 4/9 = 1, the whole profit. The larger share is 5/9 of the profit, $63,000.

$$\frac{5}{9} \times \frac{\$63,000}{1} = \frac{5}{1} \times \frac{\$7,000}{1}$$
$$= \$35,000$$

18. **C** Consider the original price as 100%. Then the price after an increase of 4% is 104%. To find the original price, divide the price after the increase, $17.16, by 104% (or 1.04).

$$\begin{array}{r} \$\ 16.50 = \text{original price} \\ 104\overline{)1716.00} \\ \underline{104} \\ 676 \\ \underline{624} \\ 520 \\ \underline{520} \end{array}$$

19. **B** 5 workers making 6 garments each
= 30 garments per day
3 workers making 4 garments each
= 12 garments per day
$\frac{1}{9}$ workers making 12 garments
$= \frac{12}{54}$ garments per day
Add the number of workers and the number of garments per day.
9 workers make 54 garments per day
To find the average number of garments per worker per day, divide the number of garments per day by the number of workers.
$\frac{54}{9} = 6$ garments per worker per day

20. **D** The distance traveled by driving at 45 mph for 2 hours is 2×45, or 90 miles.
The remainder of the 255 mile trip is 255 – 90, or 165 miles.
To finish the trip in 5 hours, the man has 5 – 2, or 3, hours still to drive. To find the rate of travel for a distance of 165 miles driven in 3 hours, divide the distance by the time.
$$\frac{165}{3} = 55 \text{ miles per hour}$$

21. **C**
$$= \frac{1}{10} \times \$300,000 \qquad = \$30,000$$
Cost of lumber and carpentry
$$= \frac{1}{3} \times \$300,000 \qquad = \$100,000$$
Cost of plumbing and heating
$$= \frac{1}{5} \times \$300,000 \qquad = \$60,000$$
Cost of electrical and lighting work
$$= \frac{1}{6} \times \$300,000 \qquad \underline{= \$50,000}$$
Total costs $\qquad \$240,000$
Profit $= \$300,000 - \$240,000$
$= \$60,000$

22. **A** The first discount of 20% means that a customer actually pays 80% (or 4/5) of the list price. The second successive discount of 30% means that a customer actually pays 70% (or 3/10) of the price determined after the first discount.
The price the customer actually pays is the list price multiplied by the portions determined from each discount.

$$\frac{\overset{13}{\cancel{\underset{65}{\$325}}}}{1} \times \frac{\overset{2}{\cancel{4}}}{\underset{1}{\cancel{5}}} \times \frac{7}{\underset{\underset{1}{5}}{\cancel{10}}} = \frac{26 \times 7}{1} = \$182$$

23. **B** At 2 quarts for $1.99, each quart costs
$$\frac{\$1.99}{2} = \$.99\frac{1}{2}$$
At 6 quarts for $5.43, each quart costs
$$\frac{\$5.43}{6} = \$.90\frac{1}{2}$$
The saving per quart is
$$\$.99\frac{1}{2} - \$.90\frac{1}{2} = \$.09$$

24. **B** For the regular 40 hours, the worker earns $7.20 × 40 = $288.00. If the regular wage is $7.20 per hour, then overtime paid at time and a half is $7.20 × 1½ or $7.20 × 3/2.

$$\frac{\overset{3.60}{\cancel{\$7.20}}}{1} \times \frac{3}{\underset{1}{\cancel{2}}}$$

$$= \frac{\$10.80}{1} = \$10.80 \text{ per hour}$$

If 43 hours are worked, 3 hours are overtime. Overtime pay = $10.80 × 3 = $32.40.

Add the regular pay for 40 hours to the overtime pay to find the total amount earned for the week. $288.00 + $32.40 = $320.40 = total pay

25. **B** The ratio of the heights of the two trees will be the same as the ratio of the lengths of their shadows. The ratio of the length of the shadow of the second tree to the length of the shadow of the first tree is 6/8 or 3/4.

Thus, the height of the second tree is 3/4 of the height of the 36 foot tree.

$$\frac{3}{\cancel{4}} \times \frac{\overset{9}{\cancel{36}}}{1} = \frac{27}{1} = 27 \text{ feet}$$

26. **C** Add the portion spent on newspaper ads and radio commercials.

$$\frac{3}{5} + \frac{1}{3} = \frac{9}{15} + \frac{5}{15} = \frac{14}{15}$$

The portion left for TV commercials is the entire budget, 1, minus the portion spent on newspaper and radio, $\frac{14}{15}$.

$$1 - \frac{14}{15} = \frac{15}{15} - \frac{14}{15} = \frac{1}{15}$$

27. **A** A half-hour is 30 minutes. The portion of 180 minutes represented by 30 minutes is 30/180 or 1/6. As a percentage, 1/6 is 16⅔%.

28. **A** 5 pounds of cashew nuts at $1.80 per pound is worth 5 × $1.80 = $9.00.

4 pounds of peanuts at $1.62 per pound is worth 4 × $1.62 = $6.48. The total value of the 9-pound mixture is $9.00 + $6.48 = $15.48. The value of the mixture per pound is found by dividing the total value by the number of pounds.

$$\frac{\$15.48}{9} = \$1.72$$

29. **D** If there are four pieces of wallpaper, each 7 feet, 8 inches long, the total length of the wallpaper is 4 × 7 feet, 8 inches, or 28 feet, 32 inches.

Since 12 inches = 1 foot, 32 inches = 2 feet, 8 inches. Thus, 28 feet, 32 inches = 30 feet, 8 inches.

30. **B** From 9:00 P.M. to 5:00 A.M. is a tour of duty of 8 hours. Since 60 minutes = 1 hour, when the watchman checks in every 40 minutes he checks in every 40/60, or every 2/3, of an hour.

$$\frac{8}{1} \div \frac{2}{3} = \frac{\overset{4}{\cancel{8}}}{1} \times \frac{3}{\underset{1}{\cancel{2}}} = \frac{12}{1} = 12$$

The watchman must check in once at the beginning of each of the twelve 40-minute periods, or 12 times. But he must also check in at the end of the last period. Thus, he checks in 12 + 1, or 13, times.

WORD KNOWLEDGE—SUBTEST 3
Answers

1. D	8. C	15. D	22. B	29. C
2. B	9. B	16. C	23. C	30. D
3. A	10. B	17. B	24. D	31. C
4. B	11. D	18. C	25. D	32. A
5. C	12. C	19. D	26. A	33. B
6. A	13. A	20. C	27. B	34. A
7. D	14. A	21. A	28. B	35. D

Answers Explained

1. **D** <u>**Pinnacle**</u>, like summit, means the highest point.

2. **B** **Brawl**, like fight, means a noisy quarrel.

3. **A** A **pauper** is an extremely poor person.

4. **B** **Punctual**, like prompt, means arriving or doing something exactly at the appointed time.

5. **C** **Segment**, like part, means a portion.

6. **A** **Revere**, like esteem, means to regard someone or something with great respect.

7. **D** **Brevity**, like conciseness, means of short duration.

8. **C** **Illogical**, like fallacious, means senseless.

9. **B** **Excerpt**, like extract, means something picked out from the total.

10. **B** **Sheen**, like luster, means shininess or brightness.

11. **D** **Divulge**, like tell, means to disclose or make known.

12. **C** **Cite**, like specify, means to bring information forward as proof.

13. **A** **Allay**, like ease, means to relieve.

14. **A** **Vitality**, like liveliness, means vigor or energy.

15. **D** **Defer**, like delay, means to postpone doing something.

16. **C** **Deplore**, like regret, means to feel or express disapproval.

17. **B** **Concur**, like agree, means to have the same opinion.

18. **C** **Refute**, like disprove, means to prove an argument or statement wrong.

19. **D** **Copious**, like large, means an ample or plentiful supply.

20. **C** **Credulous**, like gullible, means able to believe too readily.

21. **A** **Random**, like haphazard, means having no clear pattern.

22. **B** **Salient**, like conspicuous, means prominent or pronounced.

23. **C** **Tangible**, like concrete, means capable of being touched.

24. **D** **Residue**, like remainder, means what is left after the removal of something.

25. **D** **Catastrophe**, like disaster, means a great calamity or tragedy.

26. **A** **Diagnosis**, like analysis, means the opinion derived from examining the nature of something.

27. **B** **Quandary**, like predicament, means a dilemma or state of uncertainty.

28. **B** **Stilted**, like formal, means stiffly dignified.

29. **C** **Encroach**, like trespass, means to intrude.

30. **D** **Deter**, like prevent, means to restrain someone from doing something.

31. **C** **Falter**, like hesitate, means to waver.

32. **A** **Meager**, like sparse, means skimpy or scant.

33. **B** **Stifle**, like suppress, means to restrict.

34. **A** **Dearth**, like lack, means scarcity.

35. **D** **Accord**, like harmony, means agreement.

PARAGRAPH COMPREHENSION—SUBTEST 4
Answers

1. **D**	4. **B**	7. **B**	10. **B**	13. **D**
2. **C**	5. **D**	8. **C**	11. **C**	14. **B**
3. **B**	6. **D**	9. **A**	12. **A**	15. **A**

Answers Explained

1. **D** The main idea is stated in the first sentence of the paragraph. All of the other sentences contribute to the main idea by describing the circumstances under which Columbus was able to save his own life.

2. **C** When you apply the "warranty of merchantability," that is, that the product will do what it is supposed to do, you see that only one answer mentions a product (a toaster) and what it does (toasts).

3. **B** According to the passage, the settling of the American West took place after both coasts were joined by completion of the railroad.

4. **B** The paragraph states that 61% of single female parents were in hous-

ing need and that single male parents experienced half that housing need. Half of 61% is approximately 30%.

5. **D** The embargo caused the price of crude oil to quadruple. This increase, in turn, caused oil-dependent countries to experience a recession. Answers A, B, and C are all incorrect details.

6. **D** The paragraph talks about the effect of voltage variations on sensitive equipment. It is logical to conclude that computers, which are also sensitive equipment, would be affected by voltage variation.

7. **B** Answer B, fundamental freedoms, summarizes all the rights listed in the paragraph.

8. **C** The fact that DNA is a nucleic acid is stated in the first sentence. Answers A, B, and D are all incorrect details.

9. **A** The paragraph states that 30% of trash being dumped can be recycled. Another way of stating this detail is to say that a third of what we dump could be recycled.

10. **B** According to the paragraph's definition of a referendum, submitting the Constitution of the United States to the state conventions for approvals was a form of referendum.

11. **C** The paragraph states that unlike the other pollutants mentioned, formaldehyde can be smelled only at high levels. You can conclude that it cannot be smelled at lower levels.

12. **A** Sentence 2 states that bacterial pneumonia is a major precipitator (cause) of pneumonia deaths. Answers B, C, and D are all incorrect details.

13. **D** The key idea is found in the first sentence: The temperature of ocean water changes more slowly than that of the air; therefore, the oceans affect the world's climate.

14. **B** The purpose of the paragraph is to make a comparison between laser and incandescent light. The two are compared in one way, that is, in terms of their different wavelengths.

15. **A** The main idea of the paragraph is that an energy audit should be done as a first step toward saving energy dollars. The details that follow are some of the items an audit concentrates on. The question, however, asks you to identify what precedes, or comes before, the installation of an energy-saving device.

AUTOMOTIVE INFORMATION— SUBTEST 5
Answers

1. **B**	6. **A**	11. **D**
2. **A**	7. **B**	12. **D**
3. **D**	8. **C**	13. **A**
4. **C**	9. **C**	14. **B**
5. **A**	10. **C**	15. **B**

Answers Explained

1. **B** The piston is the object inside the engine that moves up and down inside the cylinder to produce the power needed.

2. **A** The flywheel is used to keep the engine running smoothly inasmuch as it has a tendency to smooth out the individual power surges generated by the various cylinders firing the fuel charge. The flywheel is attached to the crankshaft.

3. **D** The basic difference between a carburetor and fuel injection is an electrically operated fuel solenoid. It is electronically controlled and regulates the amount of fuel delivered to the engine. There are three types of fuel injection used in cars today: multi-injector, mono-injector electronic, and manual continuous flow.

4. **C** Lawn mowers and outboard engines are two-cycle. They are

used wherever horsepower is needed in a lightweight package. They
run very fast in order to produce
power. Four-cycle engines are used
in automobiles, where various conditions exist and load variations are
greater. One exception is the Mazda
auto. It uses a rotary engine for a
power plant.

5. **A** The spark plug fires, driving the
piston downward to produce power.
The intake stroke allows the fuel
and air mixture to enter the cylinder. The compression stroke com-
presses the air/fuel mixture. The
exhaust stroke allows the burnt
gases to be removed from the cylinder.

6. **A** Universal joints are needed to allow
the drive shaft to flex when the car
goes over a bump in the road. If the
universal joints are broken, the car
will be unable to move since the
drive shaft will not be connected to
the power source.

7. **B** The clutch pedal is pushed to the
floorboard in order to release the
engine from the drive train. Once
the pedal is released and spring
action returns it to the upward position, the clutch is engaged and the
engine is connected to the drive
train again.

8. **C** First gear is used to get the car
moving. Second gear is used to get
it moving a little faster. Then it is
placed in third gear when it has
reached a higher speed and needs
less power to make it move even
faster. When the third gear is
engaged, no gear reduction is taking place and the engine speed is
reflected in the speed at which the
wheels turn.

9. **C** Disengaging the clutch means placing the car in neutral since the
engine is disconnected from the
drive train.

10. **C** A four-wheel vehicle is called a 4 ×
4 if all wheels are driven. One with
six wheels with all six being driven
is called a 6 × 6, and one with six
wheels (like a truck) but only four
being driven is designated as a 4 ×
6.

11. **D** The engine furnishes power in the
form of a twisting force, and this
twist must be transmitted to a point
where it can turn the wheels. That
is the first requirement—to get
power from one place to another.
But this power must be changed
while it is being transmitted. We
increase the torque and decrease the
speed. We run the wheels at a slower speed than the engine, but with a
greater twisting force.

12. **D** A weak battery is the first thing to
check when the engine does not
start or turn over.

13. **A** When the mixture of fuel and air
burns in the cylinder, it creates a
temperature of 4,000° to 4,500°F.

14. **B** The first emission control device
for automobiles was the positive
crankcase ventilation (PCV) system.

15. **B** A tire that bears the code "P 185/70
R 14" is a passenger car tire that is
185 millimeters wide from sidewall
to sidewall.

MATHEMATICS KNOWLEDGE— SUBTEST 6
Answers

1. **A**	6. **C**	11. **C**	16. **A**	21. **C**
2. **C**	7. **C**	12. **A**	17. **A**	22. **D**
3. **D**	8. **C**	13. **D**	18. **D**	23. **A**
4. **B**	9. **C**	14. **C**	19. **B**	24. **D**
5. **D**	10. **A**	15. **B**	20. **B**	25. **C**

Answers Explained

1. **A** Multiply 0.0375 by 4% (or 0.04).
$0.0375 \times 0.04 = 0.001500 = 0.0015$
Note that the product has as many
decimal places as there are in
the multiplicand and multiplier
combined, but the two final zeros

may be dropped since they are to the right of the decimal point and at the end.

2. **C** If a number is multiplied by its reciprocal (also called its multiplicative inverse), the product is 1. The reciprocal of a fraction is found by inverting the fraction.

The reciprocal of 2/3 is 3/2, that is,

$$\frac{2}{3} \times \frac{3}{2} = 1.$$

3. **D** Substitute 3 for x and -2 for y in the expression $x^2 - 5xy + 2y$.

$$(3)^2 - 5(3)(-2) + 2(-2)$$
$$9 - 15(-2) - 4$$
$$9 + 30 - 4$$
$$35$$

4. **B** $x - 3 < 14$ is an inequality that states that x minus 3 is less than 14. To solve the inequality, add 3 to both sides of it.

$$x - 3 + 3 < 14 + 3$$
$$x < 17$$

The result says that the inequality is true for any value of x less than 17. Try it for some value of x less than 17, for example, $x = 10$.

$$10 - 3 < 14$$
$$7 < 14 \text{ is a true statement}$$

5. **D** To multiply $7a^3b^2c$ by $3a^2b^4c^2$, first multiply the numerical coefficients, 7 and 3.

$$7 \times 3 = 21$$

Powers of the same base, such as a^3 and a^2, are multiplied by adding their exponents; thus, $a^3 \times a^2 = a^5$.

$$(a^3b^2c) \times (a^2b^4c^2) = a^5b^6c^3$$

Note that c should be regarded as c^1 when adding exponents.

The combined result for $(7a^3b^2c) \times (3a^2b^4c^2) = 21a^5b^6c^3$

6. **C**

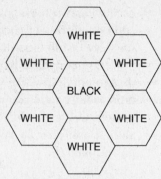

A hexagon has six sides. Each of the six sides of the black tile must touch a side of a white tile, so there are six white tiles surrounding each black tile.

7. **C** x^0 is defined as always equal to 1, provided that x does not equal 0. Therefore $8^0 = 1$.

8. **C** The equation $2x - 3 = 37$ means that "twice a number minus 3 is equal to 37." To arrive at a value for x, we first eliminate -3 on the left side. This can be done by adding 3 to both sides of the equation, thus undoing the subtraction.

$$2x - 3 + 3 = 37 + 3$$
$$2x = 40$$

To eliminate the 2 that multiplies x, we undo the multiplication by dividing both sides of the equation by 2.

$$\frac{2x}{2} = \frac{40}{2}$$
$$x = 20$$

9. **C** If 2/3 of M people are adults, then 2/3 M represents the number of adults. If 1/2 of (2/3)M are males, then $1/2 \times (2/3)M$ represents the number of adult males.

$$\frac{1}{\overset{2}{\underset{1}{\cancel{2}}}} \times \frac{\overset{1}{\cancel{2}}}{3} M = \frac{1}{3} M$$

10. **A** $(0.2)^3$ means $0.2 \times 0.2 \times 0.2$. Multiply the first two numbers:

$$0.2 \times 0.2 \times 0.2 = 0.04 \times 0.2$$

Now multiply the remaining two numbers: $0.04 \times 0.2 = 0.008$.

11. **C** Rewrite the equation as $x^3 + x - 6 = 0$. The left side of the equation can now be factored:

$$(x + 3)(x - 2) = 0$$

This result states that the product of two factors, $(x + 3)$ and $(x - 2)$, equals 0. But if the product of two factors equals 0, then either or both must equal 0:

$$x + 3 = 0 \quad \text{or} \quad x - 2 = 0$$

Subtract 3 from both sides of the left equation to isolate x on one side, and add 2 to both sides of the right equation to accomplish the same result:

$$x + 3 - 3 = 0 \qquad x - 2 + 2 = 0 + 2$$
$$x = -3 \qquad\qquad x = 2$$

12. **A** The area of a circle is πr^2, where $\pi = 22/7$ and r represents the length of the radius. A radius is one-half the length of a diameter. Therefore, if the diameter is 28 inches, the radius of the circle is 14 inches.

$$\text{Area of circle} = \frac{22}{7} \times \frac{14}{1} \times \frac{14}{1}$$

$$= \frac{22}{\underset{1}{\cancel{7}}} \times \frac{\overset{2}{\cancel{14}}}{1} \times \frac{14}{1}$$

$$= \frac{44}{1} \times \frac{14}{1}$$

$$= \frac{616}{1}$$

$$= 616 \text{ square inches}$$

13. **D** If $x = -3$, the denominator of

$$\frac{x^2 + 2x - 3}{x + 3}$$

will equal 0. Division of 0 is undefined, so x cannot equal –3.

14. **C** The given equation means that a number is added to 11, and then the square root of the result is taken and it equals 9. The square root sign (or radical sign) can be removed by squaring both sides of the equation.

$$\left(\sqrt{x + 11}\right)^2 = 9^2$$

$$x + 11 = 81$$

Isolate x on one side of the equation by subtracting 11 from both sides.

$$x + 11 - 11 = 81 - 11$$
$$x = 70$$

15. **B**

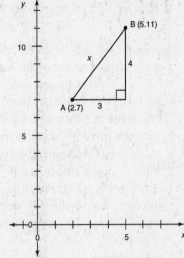

Plot the points. When a pair of numbers is given as the coordinates of a point, the first number is the x-value (or distance right or left from the origin). The second number is the y-value (or distance up or down). Form the right triangle shown in the diagram. The horizontal leg has a length of $5 - 2$, or 3; the vertical leg has a length of $11 - 7$, or 4. The distance A to B is the hypotenuse of the right triangle. Let $x = \overline{AB}$. By the Pythagorean Theorem, the square of the length of the hypotenuse equals the sum of the squares of the lengths of the legs.

$$x^2 = 3^2 + 4^2$$
$$x^2 = 9 + 16$$
$$x^2 = 25$$

The equation $x^2 = 25$ means that x times x equals 25. Therefore, $x = 5$.

16. **A** The given equation $ay - bx = 2$ is to be solved for y. Isolate the y-term on one side of the equation by adding bx to both sides.

$$ay - bx + bx = 2 + bx$$
$$ay = 2 + bx$$

y is multiplied by a. To obtain y

alone, undo the multiplication by dividing both sides of the equation by a.

$$\frac{ay}{a} = \frac{2+bx}{a}$$

$$y = \frac{2+bx}{a}$$

17. **A** The probability of an event occurring is the number of favorable outcomes divided by the total possible number of outcomes. Since there are three possible infantrymen to choose, there are three favorable outcomes for choosing an infantryman. Since a choice can be made from among 3 infantrymen, 2 artillerymen, and 5 tank crewmen, there are $3 + 2 + 5$, or 10, possible outcomes.

The probability of choosing an infantryman is 3/10.

18. **D** A length of cord that will wind around once is equal to the circumference of the circle whose radius is 3 inches. The circumference of a circle equals $2\pi r$ where $\pi = 22/7$ and r is the radius.

$$\text{Circumference} = \frac{2}{1} \times \frac{22}{7} \times \frac{3}{1}$$

$$= \frac{132}{7} \text{ inches}$$

If the cord can be wound around the post seven times, its length is seven times the length of one circumference.

$$\text{Length of cord} = \frac{132}{\overset{1}{\cancel{7}}} \times \frac{\overset{1}{\cancel{7}}}{1}$$

$$= 132 \text{ inches}$$

19. **B** There are four possible choices for the destroyer. Each of these choices may be coupled with any of the two choices for the supply ship. Each such destroyer-supply ship combination may in turn be coupled with any of the three possible choices for the submarine. Thus, there are $4 \times 2 \times 3$, or 24, different combinations possible.

20. **B** The volume of a cylinder is equal to the product of its height and the area of its base. The base is a circle. The area of a circle is πr^2, where $\pi = 22/7$ and r is the radius. Since the diameter is 2 inches, the radius (which is one-half the diameter) is 1 inch.

Area of circular base =

$$\frac{22}{7} \times \frac{1}{1} \times \frac{1}{1} = \frac{22}{7} \text{ square inches}$$

The height is 7 inches.

$$\text{Volume} = \frac{22}{7} \times \frac{7}{1} = 22 \text{ cubic inches}$$

21. **C**

The area of the rectangular garden is equal to the product of its length and width.

Area of rectangle = $16 \times 4 = 64$ square yards. In order for the square to have the same area, 64 square yards, its sides must each be 8 yards long, since $8 \times 8 = 64$ square yards.

The fence around the rectangular garden has a length of $16 + 4 + 16 + 4$, or 40, yards. The fence around the square garden has a length of 4×8, or 32, yards. The saving in fencing is $40 - 32$, or 8, yards.

22. **D** $\sqrt{164}$ stands for the square root of 164 or the number that when multiplied by itself equals 164. We know that $12 \times 12 = 144$ and that $13 \times 13 = 169$. Therefore, $\sqrt{164}$ lies between 12 and 13. It is nearer to 13 since 164 is nearer to 169 than it is to 144.

23. **A** The storage space measurements of 1 foot by 2 feet by 2 feet, 1 inch can be converted to inches as 12 inches by 24 inches by 25 inches. Boxes measuring 3 inches by 4 inches by 5 inches can be stacked so that four of the 3-inch sides make up the 12-inch storage dimension, six of the 4-inch sides fill the 24-inch storage dimension, and five of the 5-inch sides fill the 25-inch storage dimension.

There will be $4 \times 6 \times 5$, or 120, boxes packed into the storage space.

24. **D**

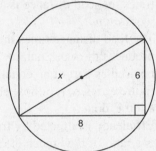

If the circle passes through all four vertices of the rectangle, its diameter will be a diagonal of the rectangle. Since a rectangle's angles are right angles, the diagonal forms a right triangle with two sides of the rectangle. Let x = the length of the diagonal. By the Pythagorean Theorem, in a right triangle the square of the length of the hypotenuse is equal to the sum of the squares of the legs.

$$x^2 = 8^2 + 6^2$$
$$x^2 = 64 + 36$$
$$x^2 = 100$$

$x^2 = 100$ means that x times $x =$ 100. Therefore $x = 10$ feet. But 10 is a diameter of the circle. A radius of a circle is one-half the diameter. Hence, the radius is 5 feet.

25. **C** If the original mixture is 33⅓% (or 1/3) acetone, then 1/3 of the mixture of 12 liters, or 4 liters, is acetone. The fraction 4/12 represents the ratio of acetone to total mixture. If the total mixture is increased by x liters, the ratio of acetone to total mixture becomes $4/(12 + x)$. This is to be equal to 25% (or 1/4).

$$\frac{4}{12 + x} = \frac{1}{4}$$

To undo the divisions on both sides of the equation, multiply both sides by 4 and also by $12 + x$.

$$\frac{4}{12 + x} \times \frac{4(12 + x)}{1} = \frac{1}{4} \times \frac{4(12 + x)}{1}$$

$$16 = 12 + x$$

To isolate x on one side of the equation, subtract 12 from both sides.

$$16 - 12 = 12 + x - 12$$
$$4 = x$$

MECHANICAL COMPREHENSION— SUBTEST 7
Answers

1. **D**	6. **D**	11. **C**	16. **C**	21. **C**
2. **C**	7. **D**	12. **D**	17. **A**	22. **B**
3. **B**	8. **D**	13. **D**	18. **C**	23. **D**
4. **A**	9. **C**	14. **A**	19. **A**	24. **A**
5. **B**	10. **A**	15. **B**	20. **B**	25. **A**

Answers Explained

1. **D** Force is something that can change the velocity of an object by making it start or stop, speed up, or slow down. This means that all the answers given are correct.

2. **C** Friction is used to stop a car. The brakes rub against the wheel drum or the disc to cause the car to stop. This rubbing is creating friction.

3. **B** Metric measurements are referred to as SI or international standards. The metric unit newton corresponds to our system unit of the pound.

4. **A** Gravity is the force that pulls things down whenever they are dropped. It is said that Isaac Newton discovered gravity while sitting under an apple tree and the obvious happened. Gravity is created by the mass of the

earth. The pull of gravity is much less on the moon than on earth.

5. **B** When a rope or string or anything is stretched, it is in a state of tension until the tension is released.

6. **D** Friction causes drag, or the holding back of an object being pulled along a surface or running through the air. When there is drag or a retarding motion on an object in a liquid, it is referred to as viscous drag.

7. **D** Weight is not a fixed property of an object; it varies with location. Your weight is slightly less at the North Pole than it is at the equator. Your weight is much less on the moon than on earth. Everything weighs less where the acceleration due to gravity is smaller. Weight is directly proportional to the acceleration due to gravity.

8. **D** Buoyancy is the force that makes ships float and helium-filled balloons rise. This means that the force that acts in an upward direction on anything submerged in a liquid or a gas is called buoyancy.

9. **C** It is impossible to exert a force unless there is something there to push back. Forces exist in pairs. For every action, then, there is a reaction.

10. **A** Inasmuch as it is impossible to have a force acting unless in pairs, it means that these forces must be equal in magnitude and opposite in direction.

11. **C** An object in equilibrium may or may not be at rest. If two or more forces act, their effects may eliminate each other. When this condition of equilibrium is reached, there is no net force and the velocity does not change. Equilibrium is reached when the object is at rest or moving at a constant speed and in a straight line.

12. **D** The angle of the rope determines if the box is being pulled along the floor or being lifted from the floor.

That means it can be both lifted and pulled along at any angle that is more than 0 degrees and less than 90 degrees.

13. **D** Simple machines are devices that make work easier. Some examples of simple machines are levers, hydraulic jacks, loading ramps, vises, and machines that spin — winches and gears. Door knobs, light switches, and manually operated pencil sharpeners are also simple machines.

14. **A** The effort times the effort distance is called the work *input*. The load times the load distance is called the work *output*.

15. **B** The load distance times the load produces the work output. This can be used as part of an equation to figure efficiency, or how efficiently a job is done.

16. **C** Efficiency is affected by friction. It is a ratio of how much effort went into a job compared to what was produced or outputted. Therefore, work input is more than the work output. Friction accounts for the loss in efficiency.

17. **A** In order to find out how well work was performed and how much effort was expended in getting the job done, the term *efficiency* is used to describe the ratio of work input to work output.

18. **C** By using a machine it is possible to multiply the amount of effort expended to get a job done. Mechanical advantage is the amount of magnification, or the ratio of load to effort.

19. **A** A ramp is a device commonly used to aid in lifting. The ramp is an inclined plane. The work output of an inclined plane is the work that would have to be done to lift the load directly. The work input is the actual force exerted in pushing the load up the ramp times the length of the ramp. An ideal mechanical

advantage of an inclined plane is equal to its length divided by its height.

20. **B** A screw is a simple device. It has been used for centuries as a means of lifting water out of wells and over the banks of irrigation canals. A screw consists of a single continuous spiral wrapped around a cylinder. The threads are cut into a rod in a spiral and make it possible to use the holding power of screw in fastening objects together.

21. **C** The distance between ridges on a screw is known as the pitch of its thread. Every time the screw makes one complete turn, the screw advances a distance equal to the pitch.

22. **B** The mechanical advantage of a screw (used in a vise) is equal to the length of the handle of the vise times 2π divided by the pitch of the thread. The vise is a high-friction device. It has to be, for it is the friction that keeps it from opening when you tighten it. A vise is a self-locking machine because its efficiency is considerably less than 50%.

23. **D** The principle of a winch is not much different from that of a lever. Since the crank and the shaft turn together, the torque exerted by the effort (the force on the handle) must be equal to the torque exerted by the load (the tension in the rope). The mechanical advantage then is the ratio of the radius of the crank to the radius of the shaft.

24. **A** In mechanical devices, gears are used to change torque. The ideal mechanical advantage of a gear is the ratio of the number of teeth in the load gear to the number of teeth in the effort gear.

25. **A** The English unit of power is foot-pound per second. It takes 550 foot-pounds to make 1 horsepower. The SI unit is the joule per second or watt. A horsepower is 746 watts. The rate at which work is done is called power. Power is work done per unit of time.

ELECTRONICS INFORMATION— SUBTEST 8
Answers

1. A	5. B	9. D	13. C	17. A
2. B	6. A	10. B	14. D	18. B
3. C	7. D	11. C	15. C	19. B
4. B	8. B	12. B	16. B	20. B

Answers Explained

1. **A** The definition of current electricity is the flow of electrons. Static electricity is conceived of as standing still or collecting on surfaces.

2. **B** Conductors have free electrons that are easily moved along with the right kind of push or force. There are a number of ways to cause these electrons to progress along a conductor. Heat, light, magnetism, chemicals, pressure, and friction can cause the generation of an EMF useful in causing electrons to move along a conductor.

3. **C** Conventional current flow is said to be from + to –. This idea was originally used by Ben Franklin to explain the conduct of lightning. This conventional flow is still used today by electrical engineers and people working in physics.

4. **B** Electron flow can be demonstrated to flow from – to +. The action that takes place in a vacuum tube indicates that the + attracts the – electron to cause it to move from – to +.

5. **B** An insulator is a material that has tightly held electrons and very few, if any, free electrons. This means that it can be used to protect the conductor since the insulator will not allow free electrons from the conductor to knock loose any tightly held electrons of the insulator material.

6. **A** The unit of measure for resistance or opposition to current flow is the ohm. It was agreed on many years ago and has aided in making the electrical field progress so rapidly.

7. **D** The watt is the unit of power in electrical work. It is defined as the production of energy at the rate of one joule per second (per second is the basis for all electrical work).

8. **B** The Greek alphabet is used almost in its entirety in the electrical field to represent various quantities and effects. The Greek letter phi(ϕ) is familiar if you have been looking at three-phase power. It is used to represent the phases of electrical power.

9. **D** Total resistance of a parallel circuit can be found two ways: by using the reciprocal formula or by using the product of two resistors divided by the sum of the two resistors divided by the sum of the two and then using it again to obtain the final answer in the case of three in parallel. In this case the two 10-ohm resistors will reduce to an equivalent of 5 ohms. This leaves, then, two 5-ohm resistors in parallel, which reduce to 2.5 or half of the value of one.

10. **B** The symbols shown are for the resistor, the fuse, and the capacitor, as well as for a lamp or light bulb. The one for the fuse is shown as in B.

11. **C** The symbol for inductance is L. The symbol for an inductor is a loop as in a coil of wire.

12. **B** The formula for finding inductive reactance has to utilize the L in inductance and the fixed constant 2π, as well as taking into consideration the frequency of the power applied to the circuit.

13. **C** A microfarad is 1 million pico-farads. Therefore, if you wish to convert microfarads to picofarads, you have to multiply by 1 million.

That means the answer is C because 100 times 1 million is 100 million.

14. **D** Impedance is the total opposition to current flow in a circuit. It has its own symbol, Z.

15. **C** A cathode ray tube (CRT) is familiar to anyone who watches television or a computer screen.

16. **B** A junction diode has a larger surface area than a point-contact diode, therefore it can be used to handle larger currents at power-line frequencies.

17. **A** The SCR is a special type of rectifier. It is used in control circuits. The name SCR was a descriptive one given it by General Electric Company engineers and it caught on in the literature. Its correct name is not silicon-controlled rectifier but thyrister.

18. **B** On an FM receiver the AFC is automatic frequency control. It keeps the receiver from drifting from the station it is tuned to. This is done by having part of the signal fed back to the local oscillator to keep it operating on the correct frequency and not drifting.

19. **B** A receiver made to receive multiplex signals is usually designated as a stereo receiver, which means it can receive the two signals needed to produce the stereo effect. These signals are multiplexed, or one signal is impressed on another to get it from the transmitter to the receiver.

20. **B** The FM band covers 88 to 108. The AM band covers 550 to 1600 kilohertz.

SHOP INFORMATION—SUBTEST 9
Answers

1. D	6. A	11. B
2. A	7. B	12. C
3. C	8. D	13. B
4. C	9. B	14. C
5. B	10. A	15. C

Answers Explained

1. **D** Buttering a concrete block means to put the mortar on it. This is usually done by taking the mortar from the hawk and applying it to the block's edges.

2. **A** Hardwood comes from deciduous trees such as the oak, maple, elm, and ash.

3. **C** Softwood comes from conifers, or trees with needles, usually called evergreens. Such trees are the pines, firs, and spruces.

4. **C** Sometimes logs are not cut into lumber immediately and must be kept from checking and splitting. This can be done by keeping them wet. At the sawmill the logs are kept floating in a pond until they are about ready to be used. This way they do not dry out too quickly and check or split.

5. **B** An auto repair collision worker uses a bumper hammer to take out some of the dents in a car's sheet metal. This hammer is ideally suited for the job.

6. **A** A groover is designed to cause the seams to become flattened and make a watertight seal.

7. **B** A squaring shear is used to cut sheet metal along a straight line. A bar folder is used to bend sheet metal, and a punch press makes holes in sheet metal. The slip roll is used to form the metal into round, cylindrical shapes.

8. **D** The tip of a soldering iron is tinned or coated with solder to make it more efficient in transferring the heat at the tip to the object being soldered. It also prevents copper oxide buildup on the tip.

9. **B** Punches are used in sheet metal for the same reason punches are used elsewhere—to punch holes.

10. **A** A squaring shear is used to cut sheet metal—usually keeping it square to one edge if properly aligned with the side of the unit. To shear means to cut.

11. **B** The term *penny* is an old English way to designate the size of a nail. It has no definite relation to today's measuring units. You can, however, keep in mind that the larger the number, the larger the nail.

12. **C** Concrete reaches 98% of its strength in 28 days.

13. **B** A coping saw blade is placed in the saw with the teeth of the blade facing the handle. That means you cut with a coping saw on the downward stroke. That also calls for a special type of vise to hold whatever it is you are cutting.

14. **C** Carpenters use claw hammers so they can remove nails if they don't go where they belong or are bent on the way into the wood. Machinists use ball peen hammers. Planishing hammers are used by people trying to flatten or shape sheet metal. There is no such thing as a chisel point hammer.

15. **C** A welding torch can be used as a cutting torch when the proper amount of oxygen is used.

ASSEMBLING OBJECTS—SUBTEST 10
Answers

1. B	6. C	11. C	16. C
2. A	7. B	12. D	17. A
3. D	8. D	13. B	18. A
4. B	9. C	14. A	19. C
5. A	10. A	15. C	20. D

PLANNING YOUR FUTURE

CHAPTER

15 Analyzing Your Test Scores and Job Opportunities

Chart Your Progress

After you take the first practice test, record your scores on the Progress Chart below. Find out the subjects in which you have the lowest scores and study those topics. Then take Practice Tests Two, Three, and Four and see your progress as your scores rise.

PROGRESS CHART
Your Number Correct

Subtest	Number of Questions	TEST ONE	TEST TWO	TEST THREE	TEST FOUR	Excellent	Good	Fair	Poor
1. General Science	25					25–23	22–21	20–19	18 or less
2. Arithmetic Reasoning	30					30–28	27–26	25–23	22 or less
3. Word Knowledge	35					35–32	31–29	28–26	25 or less
4. Paragraph Comprehension	15					15	14	13–12	11 or less
5. Automotive Information	15					15	14	13–12	11 or less
6. Mathematics Knowledge	25					25–23	22–21	20–19	18 or less
7. Mechanical Comprehension	25					25–23	22–21	20–19	18 or less
8. Electronics Information	20					20–19	18–17	16–15	14 or less
9. Shop Information	15					15	14	13–12	11 or less
10. Assembling Objects	20					20–19	18–17	16–15	14 or less

Study Guide

After you finish each test, determine your score, and record it on the Progress Chart. You should plan how and what to study to improve your scores.

➤ If you need improvement in Subtest 1, concentrate on Chapter 4—General Science Review.

➤ If you need improvement in Subtests 2 and/or 6, concentrate on Chapter 5—Mathematics Review.

➤ If you need improvement in Subtests 3 and 4, concentrate on Chapter 6—Paragraph Comprehension and Word Knowledge Review.

➤ If you need improvement in Subtest 5, concentrate on Chapter 10—Automotive Information Review.

➤ If you need improvement in Subtest 7, concentrate on Chapter 8—Basic Mechanics Review.

➤ If you need improvement in Subtest 8, concentrate on Chapter 7—Electronics Information Review.

➤ If you need improvement in Subtest 9, concentrate on Chapter 9—Shop Information Review.

➤ If you need improvement in Subtest 10, concentrate on Chapter 11—Assembling Objects.

Note: Consider yourself as needing improvement in a section if you receive other than an excellent rating in it.

Analyzing Your Job Opportunities

The ASVAB test, first administered in 1984, is designed to evaluate your potential for further formal education, as well as your aptitude for the different vocational-technical career fields. It does this by providing two types of composites: *academic* and *occupational*. Each type contributes to understanding your ASVAB results and their relation to career exploration and decision making.

The *academic composites* report your potential for further formal education and indicate performance in general areas requiring verbal and mathematical skills. The three *academic composites* are listed and defined below.

ACADEMIC COMPOSITES

Composite	Potential ✔	Subtest Composition	Purpose
VERBAL	—	(Word Knowledge + Paragraph Comprehension)* + General Science	Measures capacity for verbal activities
MATH	—	Mathematics Knowledge + Arithmetic Reasoning	Measures capacity for mathematical activities
ACADEMIC ABILITY	—	(Word Knowledge + Paragraph Comprehension)* + Arithmetic Reasoning	Measures potential for further formal education

*Subtests in parentheses are weighed as one unit.

The *occupational composites* report your aptitude in four career areas and can be used to make predictions about future occupational performance. The *occupational composites,* determined empirically as effective predictors of performance in military jobs, are listed below along with the subtests that make them up and examples of civilian counterparts of military jobs associated with each composite.

OCCUPATIONAL COMPOSITES

Composite	Potential ✔	Subtest Composition	Sample Occupational Groupings
MECHANICAL & CRAFTS	___	Arithmetic Reasoning +	Machinist Auto Mechanic
	___	Mechanical Comprehension +	Diesel Mechanic
	___	Automotive Information +	Sheet Metal Worker
	___	Shop Information +	Carpenter
	___	Electronics Information	
BUSINESS & CLERICAL	___	(Word Knowledge + Paragraph Comprehension)* +	Clerk-Typist Personnel Clerk Transport Agent Data Entry Operator
	___	Mathematics Knowledge	Paralegal Assistant

Composite	Potential ✔	Subtest Composition	Sample Occupational Groupings
ELECTRONICS & ELECTRICAL	___	Arithmetic Reasoning +	TV and Radio Repair
	___	Mathematics Knowledge +	Automatic Equipment Technician
	___	Electronics Information +	Line Installer- Repairer
	___	General Science	Electrician
HEALTH, SOCIAL, & TECHNOLOGY	___	(Word Knowledge + Paragraph Comprehension)* +	Medical Service Technician Computer Operator Police Officer
	___	Arithmetic Reasoning +	Dental Technician Firefighter
		Mechanical Comprehension	

*Subtests in parentheses are weighed as one unit.

You can determine your areas of greatest potential by analyzing your scores on the practice exams and then determining how these scores relate to the composites above. In order to do this, turn to the Progress Chart on page 471 and note the areas in which you did well on each test by putting a checkmark in the table below. (*Note:* Consider that you did well in a section only if you received an excellent rating in it. You will probably find that your scores have some consistency, and you will see checkmarks for the same subtests on each examination.)

FINDING YOUR BEST TEST AREAS

Subtests	Practice Exam One	Practice Exam Two	Practice Exam Three	Practice Exam Four
1. General Science				
2. Arithmetic Reasoning				
3. Word Knowledge				
4. Paragraph Comprehension				
5. Automotive Information				
6. Mathematics Knowledge				
7. Mechanical Comprehension				
8. Electronics Information				
9. Shop Information				
10. Assembling Objects				

Then, for all subtests for which you have placed a checkmark, place another checkmark in the tables labeled "Academic Composites" and "Occupational Composites." This will help you pinpoint your areas of greatest strength.

If you did better in the Academic Composites, seriously consider furthering your formal education. If you did better in the Occupational Composites, consider which occupation you might like. Regardless, remember that *a test **can't** tell everything about your abilities*. Don't think that a low score means a lack of aptitude. Many factors that have nothing to do with aptitude could have influenced your score, such as a lack of experience with the subject matter tested or the lack of school courses on the information tested. Nevertheless, the ASVAB can give you some ideas about careers and can show you a general pattern of occupational interest.

Military Occupations

The different branches of the U.S. military—Army, Navy, Air Force, Marines, and Coast Guard—use the ASVAB results (as well as your education level) in different ways to determine your aptitude or potential for a wide variety of military occupations. The overall ASVAB score is known as the AFQT score, or the Armed Forces Qualification Test score.

Your AFQT score is not derived from your score on the entire ASVAB. Instead, it is calculated based on only four areas of the ASVAB: Word Knowledge (WK), Paragraph Comprehension (PC), Arithmetic Reasoning (AR), and Mathematics Knowledge (MK). The score is computed as follows.

The first step is to determine your Verbal Expression (VE) score. This is done by adding the value of your ASVAB Word Knowledge (WK) score to your Paragraph Comprehension (PC) score. This result is then compared to a chart that gives you a scaled VE score.

The formula used to derive the AFQT raw score is 2VE + AR (Arithmetic Reasoning) + MK (Mathematics Knowledge).

Additionally, your AFQT score is not computed with the AR line score and the MK line score that you see on your ASVAB scores sheet. The AR and MK scores shown on the score sheet are based on the number of questions you answered correctly. However, the score used to compute your AFQT score is the weighted score, which takes into consideration the difficulty level of the question. This formula results in the AFQT raw score, which is then converted to a percentile score—that is, the percentage of the people whose score was not as high as yours who took the test at the same time you did. So, if you scored in the 51st percentile, that means that you scored higher than 50% of the people who took the test at the same time you did. If your percentile score was 99, then you are in the highest 1% bracket—99% of people who took the test when you did scored lower than you did.

For enlistment purposes, AFQT scores are divided into the following categories by percentile.

Category I: 93–100
Category II: 65–92
Category IIIA: 50–64
Category IIIB: 31–49
Category IVA: 21–30
Category IVB: 16–20
Category IVC: 10–15
Category V: 0–9

In the early 1990s, Congress passed a law stating that no Category V recruits could be accepted for enlistment in any of the military services and that no more than 20% of accessions could be in Category IV. Additionally, Congress required that any Category IV accessions had to be high school diploma graduates (no GEDs).

It's worthwhile here also to get a grasp of a little more military jargon. Each service has an official name for each specialty—such as infantryman, construction engineer, supply specialist, aviation mechanic, and so on—as well as names for their jobs in general. In the Army and Marines, this is known as your Military Occupational Specialty, or MOS; in the Air Force, it's known as your Air Force Specialty Code, or AFSC; and in the Navy and Coast Guard, it's referred to as your rating.

You read earlier that the ASVAB is used not only for identifying your aptitude and interest in different vocational fields but also for predicting your success in a particular military specialty. It's important to recognize that the military is somewhat different from a civilian employer. Even though a civilian company will advertise only for positions they have vacant and want filled—in that way the corporate world and the military are the same—you have the opportunity to pretty much come and go as you choose; if you want to quit, it's up to you (even though hopping from job to job will have negative consequences before long, it's your choice). In the military, you must sign a contract agreeing to serve for a specified time in a given specialty; even though there are sometimes opportunities to change specialties, you will be able to sign up only for a specialty and a location where there is a need, regardless of your qualifications. In other words, if you are qualified to serve as an electronics repairman in, for example, the Navy, but there are no vacancies for that rating at the time, you will not be offered that position. Instead, the recruiter will help you find another job that fits your interests *and* the Navy's needs; it also works the same way in the other services. The common phrase used to refer to this concept is "the needs of the service."

This concept holds true even in peacetime, but it is especially so in time of war—and although you may not realize it, the United States of America *is* at war. We are at war with a shifting group of terrorists who care nothing about human life—often not even their own—and who have no tolerance for other perspectives, religions, or cultures. They do not hesitate to kill noncombatants (civilians)—old people, babies, mothers with children, business people, teenagers—or even themselves if they think it will gain them some kind of advantage. In such a war, as in any war, the needs of the service change from the needs in peacetime, and they will evolve over time.

Also, we'll talk here about enlisted specialties only; officers have their own codes and terminology, which are mostly different.

AIR FORCE

ASVAB Score. Air Force recruits must score at least 40 points on the 99-point ASVAB scale. Exceptions are sometimes made, however, for a handful of high school graduates who can score as low as 21. But these Category IV (Cat IV) recruits (by regulation) cannot exceed more than 1% of all recruits per year.

In actuality, the number of Cat IV recruits the Air Force generally accepts each year is about 0.2% of the Air Force's annual accessions.

Education. Because the Air Force is perceived as more technically oriented, it can afford to be a little choosier in most cases, so non-high school graduates are probably out of luck. Even with a GED, their chances are not good. Only about 1/2 of 1% of all USAF enlistments each year are GED holders. To even be considered for one of these very few slots, a GED holder must score a minimum of 65 on the AFQT.

Composite Scores. The Air Force has four composite scores made up from the individual ASVAB subtests, known as MAGE. The four scores that make up MAGE are

- **Mechanical Aptitude Score**—Determined from General Science (GS), Mechanical Comprehension (MC), and Auto and Shop (AS).
- **Administrative Aptitude Score**—Determined directly from the VE score.
- **General Aptitude Score**—Determined from Arithmetic Reasoning (AR) and Verbal Expression (VE).
- **Electronics Aptitude Score**—Determined from General Science (GS), Arithmetic Reasoning (AR), Mathematics Knowledge (MK), and Electronics Information (EI).

The Air Force divides its AFSCs into the following overall categories: Operations, Maintenance and Logistics, Support, Medical and Dental, Legal and Chaplain, Finance and Contracting, and Special Investigations. Within these categories, AFSCs are further assigned to career fields. A career field may have one AFSC assigned to it, or it may have several. AFSCs with similar functions are grouped together in the same career field.

Specialty Codes

OPERATIONS
1A — Aircrew Operations
1C — Command and Control Systems Operations
1N — Intelligence
1T — Aircrew Protection
1S — Safety
1W — Weather

MAINTENANCE and LOGISTICS
2A — Manned Aerospace Maintenance
2E — Communications and Electronics
2F — Fuels
2G — Logistics Plans
2M — Missile and Space Systems Maintenance
2P — Precision Measurement Equipment Laboratory
2R — Maintenance Management Systems
2S — Supply
2T — Transportation and Vehicle Maintenance
2W — Munitions and Weapons

SUPPORT

3A — Information Management
3C — Communications and Computer Systems
3H — Historian
3M — Services
3N — Public Affairs
3P — Security Forces (Military Police)
3E — Civil Engineering
3S — Mission Support
3U — Manpower
3V — Visual Information

MEDICAL and DENTAL

4X — Medical
4Y — Dental

LEGAL and CHAPLAIN

5J — Paralegal
5R – Chaplain's Assistant

FINANCE and CONTRACTING

6C — Contracting
6F — Financial

SPECIAL INVESTIGATIONS

7S — Special Investigations (OSI)

ARMY

ASVAB Score. The Army requires a minimum AFQT score of 31 to qualify for enlistment. To qualify for enlistment incentives such as bonuses, an Army recruit must score a minimum of 50. The Army does allow a very few recruits (about 0.05%) to enlist each year with scores as low as 26, but these very few must have other exceptional qualifications.

Education. Those without a high school education need not apply. The Army allows no more than 10% per year of their enlistees to have a GED. To even be considered, a high school dropout (with a GED) must score at least a 50 on the AFQT.

Composite Scores. The Army determines job qualification from ten separate composite scores made up from various subtests of the ASVAB. The Army composite scores are

- **Clerical (CL)** —Determined from Verbal Expression (VE), Arithmetic Reasoning (AR), and Mathematics Knowledge (MK).
- **Combat (CO)** —Determined from Verbal Expression (VE), Auto and Shop (AS), and Mechanical Comprehension (MC).
- **Electronics (EL)** —Determined from General Science (GS), Arithmetic Reasoning (AR), Mathematics Knowledge (MK), and Electronics Information (EI).
- **Field Artillery (FA)** —Determined from Arithmetic Reasoning (AR), Mathematics Knowledge (MK), and Mechanical Comprehension (MC).
- **General Maintenance (GM)** —Determined from General Science (GS), Auto and Shop (AS), Mathematics Knowledge (MK) and Electronics Information (EI).
- **General Technical (GT)** —Determined from Verbal Expression (VE) and Arithmetic Reasoning (AR).
- **Mechanical Maintenance (MM)** —Determined from Auto and Shop (AS), Mechanical Comprehension (MC), and Electronics Information (EI).

- **Operators and Food (OF)**—Determined from Verbal Expression (VE), Auto and Shop (AS), and Mechanical Comprehension (MC).
- **Surveillance and Communications (SC)**—Determined from Verbal Expression (VE), Arithmetic Reasoning (AR), Auto and Shop (AS), and Mechanical Comprehension (MC).
- **Skilled Technical (ST)**—Determined from General Science (GS), Verbal Expression (VE), Mechanical Comprehension (MC), and Mathematics Knowledge (MK).

MARINE CORPS

ASVAB Score. Marine Corps recruits must have an AFQT score of at least 32. A small handful of exceptions are made (about 1%) for some recruits who are otherwise exceptionally qualified but have scores as low as 25.

Education. As with the Army and Air Force, those without a high school education are ineligible. The Marine Corps limits GED enlistments to no more than 5% per year. Those with a GED must score a minimum of 50 on the AFQT to even be considered.

Composite Scores

- **Clerical (CL)** —This composite score is no longer used. In 2002, all enlisted MOSs that had a requirement for a CL composite score were converted to GT scores.
- **Electronics Repair, Missile Repair, Electronics, and Communications (EL)** —Determined from General Science (GS), Arithmetic Reasoning (AR), Mathematics Knowledge (MK), and Electronic Information (EI).
- **General Maintenance, Construction, Utility, and Chemical Maintenance (MM)**— Determined from General Science (GS), Auto and Shop (AS), Mathematics Knowledge (MK), and Electronics Information (EI).
- **General Technical, Special, and Officer Programs (GT)** —Determined from Verbal Expression (VE) and Arithmetic Reasoning (AR).

NAVY

ASVAB Score. Navy recruits must score at least 35 on the AFQT. The Navy raised this requirement from 31 in 2003. Additionally, because of limited berths on ships, the Navy limits the number of women they can enlist each year. Quite often, when there are too many female applicants, the Navy requires a higher ASVAB score for females in order to decide which women get to enlist and which don't.

Education. Between 5% and 10% each year can be high school dropouts with a GED, but they must score a minimum of 50 on the AFQT. Additionally, high school dropouts must be at least 19 years of age and show a proven work history.

Job Qualification. The Navy uses direct ASVAB line scores for job qualification determination.

COAST GUARD

ASVAB Score. The Coast Guard requires a minimum score of 40 on the AFQT for those who took the ASVAB prior to July 1, 2004, and 36 for those who took the ASVAB after July 1, 2004. A waiver is possible if a recruit's ASVAB line scores qualify them for a specific job and the recruit is willing to enlist in that job.

Education. For a very few (about 5%) who will be allowed to enlist with a GED, the minimum AFQT score is 50.

Job Qualification. The Coast Guard uses direct ASVAB line scores for job qualification determination.

> Men think meanly of themselves for never having been a soldier.
> Samuel Johnson, 1709–1784

> People sleep peaceably in their beds at night only because
> rough men stand ready to do violence on their behalf.
> George Orwell, 1903–1950

Make no mistake, the military is an honorable calling—but you will have to prove your worth to be a member of this proud profession. Good luck.

INDEX

ANSWER SHEETS—Additional Practice

GENERAL SCIENCE—SUBTEST 1

1. Ⓐ Ⓑ Ⓒ Ⓓ	6. Ⓐ Ⓑ Ⓒ Ⓓ	11. Ⓐ Ⓑ Ⓒ Ⓓ	16. Ⓐ Ⓑ Ⓒ Ⓓ	21. Ⓐ Ⓑ Ⓒ Ⓓ
2. Ⓐ Ⓑ Ⓒ Ⓓ	7. Ⓐ Ⓑ Ⓒ Ⓓ	12. Ⓐ Ⓑ Ⓒ Ⓓ	17. Ⓐ Ⓑ Ⓒ Ⓓ	22. Ⓐ Ⓑ Ⓒ Ⓓ
3. Ⓐ Ⓑ Ⓒ Ⓓ	8. Ⓐ Ⓑ Ⓒ Ⓓ	13. Ⓐ Ⓑ Ⓒ Ⓓ	18. Ⓐ Ⓑ Ⓒ Ⓓ	23. Ⓐ Ⓑ Ⓒ Ⓓ
4. Ⓐ Ⓑ Ⓒ Ⓓ	9. Ⓐ Ⓑ Ⓒ Ⓓ	14. Ⓐ Ⓑ Ⓒ Ⓓ	19. Ⓐ Ⓑ Ⓒ Ⓓ	24. Ⓐ Ⓑ Ⓒ Ⓓ
5. Ⓐ Ⓑ Ⓒ Ⓓ	10. Ⓐ Ⓑ Ⓒ Ⓓ	15. Ⓐ Ⓑ Ⓒ Ⓓ	20. Ⓐ Ⓑ Ⓒ Ⓓ	25. Ⓐ Ⓑ Ⓒ Ⓓ

ARITHMETIC REASONING—SUBTEST 2

1. Ⓐ Ⓑ Ⓒ Ⓓ	7. Ⓐ Ⓑ Ⓒ Ⓓ	13. Ⓐ Ⓑ Ⓒ Ⓓ	19. Ⓐ Ⓑ Ⓒ Ⓓ	25. Ⓐ Ⓑ Ⓒ Ⓓ
2. Ⓐ Ⓑ Ⓒ Ⓓ	8. Ⓐ Ⓑ Ⓒ Ⓓ	14. Ⓐ Ⓑ Ⓒ Ⓓ	20. Ⓐ Ⓑ Ⓒ Ⓓ	26. Ⓐ Ⓑ Ⓒ Ⓓ
3. Ⓐ Ⓑ Ⓒ Ⓓ	9. Ⓐ Ⓑ Ⓒ Ⓓ	15. Ⓐ Ⓑ Ⓒ Ⓓ	21. Ⓐ Ⓑ Ⓒ Ⓓ	27. Ⓐ Ⓑ Ⓒ Ⓓ
4. Ⓐ Ⓑ Ⓒ Ⓓ	10. Ⓐ Ⓑ Ⓒ Ⓓ	16. Ⓐ Ⓑ Ⓒ Ⓓ	22. Ⓐ Ⓑ Ⓒ Ⓓ	28. Ⓐ Ⓑ Ⓒ Ⓓ
5. Ⓐ Ⓑ Ⓒ Ⓓ	11. Ⓐ Ⓑ Ⓒ Ⓓ	17. Ⓐ Ⓑ Ⓒ Ⓓ	23. Ⓐ Ⓑ Ⓒ Ⓓ	29. Ⓐ Ⓑ Ⓒ Ⓓ
6. Ⓐ Ⓑ Ⓒ Ⓓ	12. Ⓐ Ⓑ Ⓒ Ⓓ	18. Ⓐ Ⓑ Ⓒ Ⓓ	24. Ⓐ Ⓑ Ⓒ Ⓓ	30. Ⓐ Ⓑ Ⓒ Ⓓ

WORD KNOWLEDGE—SUBTEST 3

1. Ⓐ Ⓑ Ⓒ Ⓓ	8. Ⓐ Ⓑ Ⓒ Ⓓ	15. Ⓐ Ⓑ Ⓒ Ⓓ	22. Ⓐ Ⓑ Ⓒ Ⓓ	29. Ⓐ Ⓑ Ⓒ Ⓓ
2. Ⓐ Ⓑ Ⓒ Ⓓ	9. Ⓐ Ⓑ Ⓒ Ⓓ	16. Ⓐ Ⓑ Ⓒ Ⓓ	23. Ⓐ Ⓑ Ⓒ Ⓓ	30. Ⓐ Ⓑ Ⓒ Ⓓ
3. Ⓐ Ⓑ Ⓒ Ⓓ	10. Ⓐ Ⓑ Ⓒ Ⓓ	17. Ⓐ Ⓑ Ⓒ Ⓓ	24. Ⓐ Ⓑ Ⓒ Ⓓ	31. Ⓐ Ⓑ Ⓒ Ⓓ
4. Ⓐ Ⓑ Ⓒ Ⓓ	11. Ⓐ Ⓑ Ⓒ Ⓓ	18. Ⓐ Ⓑ Ⓒ Ⓓ	25. Ⓐ Ⓑ Ⓒ Ⓓ	32. Ⓐ Ⓑ Ⓒ Ⓓ
5. Ⓐ Ⓑ Ⓒ Ⓓ	12. Ⓐ Ⓑ Ⓒ Ⓓ	19. Ⓐ Ⓑ Ⓒ Ⓓ	26. Ⓐ Ⓑ Ⓒ Ⓓ	33. Ⓐ Ⓑ Ⓒ Ⓓ
6. Ⓐ Ⓑ Ⓒ Ⓓ	13. Ⓐ Ⓑ Ⓒ Ⓓ	20. Ⓐ Ⓑ Ⓒ Ⓓ	27. Ⓐ Ⓑ Ⓒ Ⓓ	34. Ⓐ Ⓑ Ⓒ Ⓓ
7. Ⓐ Ⓑ Ⓒ Ⓓ	14. Ⓐ Ⓑ Ⓒ Ⓓ	21. Ⓐ Ⓑ Ⓒ Ⓓ	28. Ⓐ Ⓑ Ⓒ Ⓓ	35. Ⓐ Ⓑ Ⓒ Ⓓ

PARAGRAPH COMPREHENSION—SUBTEST 4

1. Ⓐ Ⓑ Ⓒ Ⓓ	4. Ⓐ Ⓑ Ⓒ Ⓓ	7. Ⓐ Ⓑ Ⓒ Ⓓ	10. Ⓐ Ⓑ Ⓒ Ⓓ	13. Ⓐ Ⓑ Ⓒ Ⓓ
2. Ⓐ Ⓑ Ⓒ Ⓓ	5. Ⓐ Ⓑ Ⓒ Ⓓ	8. Ⓐ Ⓑ Ⓒ Ⓓ	11. Ⓐ Ⓑ Ⓒ Ⓓ	14. Ⓐ Ⓑ Ⓒ Ⓓ
3. Ⓐ Ⓑ Ⓒ Ⓓ	6. Ⓐ Ⓑ Ⓒ Ⓓ	9. Ⓐ Ⓑ Ⓒ Ⓓ	12. Ⓐ Ⓑ Ⓒ Ⓓ	15. Ⓐ Ⓑ Ⓒ Ⓓ

AUTOMOTIVE INFORMATION—SUBTEST 5

1. Ⓐ Ⓑ Ⓒ Ⓓ	4. Ⓐ Ⓑ Ⓒ Ⓓ	7. Ⓐ Ⓑ Ⓒ Ⓓ	10. Ⓐ Ⓑ Ⓒ Ⓓ	13. Ⓐ Ⓑ Ⓒ Ⓓ
2. Ⓐ Ⓑ Ⓒ Ⓓ	5. Ⓐ Ⓑ Ⓒ Ⓓ	8. Ⓐ Ⓑ Ⓒ Ⓓ	11. Ⓐ Ⓑ Ⓒ Ⓓ	14. Ⓐ Ⓑ Ⓒ Ⓓ
3. Ⓐ Ⓑ Ⓒ Ⓓ	6. Ⓐ Ⓑ Ⓒ Ⓓ	9. Ⓐ Ⓑ Ⓒ Ⓓ	12. Ⓐ Ⓑ Ⓒ Ⓓ	15. Ⓐ Ⓑ Ⓒ Ⓓ

MATHEMATICS KNOWLEDGE—SUBTEST 6

1. Ⓐ Ⓑ Ⓒ Ⓓ	6. Ⓐ Ⓑ Ⓒ Ⓓ	11. Ⓐ Ⓑ Ⓒ Ⓓ	16. Ⓐ Ⓑ Ⓒ Ⓓ	21. Ⓐ Ⓑ Ⓒ Ⓓ
2. Ⓐ Ⓑ Ⓒ Ⓓ	7. Ⓐ Ⓑ Ⓒ Ⓓ	12. Ⓐ Ⓑ Ⓒ Ⓓ	17. Ⓐ Ⓑ Ⓒ Ⓓ	22. Ⓐ Ⓑ Ⓒ Ⓓ
3. Ⓐ Ⓑ Ⓒ Ⓓ	8. Ⓐ Ⓑ Ⓒ Ⓓ	13. Ⓐ Ⓑ Ⓒ Ⓓ	18. Ⓐ Ⓑ Ⓒ Ⓓ	23. Ⓐ Ⓑ Ⓒ Ⓓ
4. Ⓐ Ⓑ Ⓒ Ⓓ	9. Ⓐ Ⓑ Ⓒ Ⓓ	14. Ⓐ Ⓑ Ⓒ Ⓓ	19. Ⓐ Ⓑ Ⓒ Ⓓ	24. Ⓐ Ⓑ Ⓒ Ⓓ
5. Ⓐ Ⓑ Ⓒ Ⓓ	10. Ⓐ Ⓑ Ⓒ Ⓓ	15. Ⓐ Ⓑ Ⓒ Ⓓ	20. Ⓐ Ⓑ Ⓒ Ⓓ	25. Ⓐ Ⓑ Ⓒ Ⓓ

MECHANICAL COMPREHENSION—SUBTEST 7

1. Ⓐ Ⓑ Ⓒ Ⓓ	6. Ⓐ Ⓑ Ⓒ Ⓓ	11. Ⓐ Ⓑ Ⓒ Ⓓ	16. Ⓐ Ⓑ Ⓒ Ⓓ	21. Ⓐ Ⓑ Ⓒ Ⓓ
2. Ⓐ Ⓑ Ⓒ Ⓓ	7. Ⓐ Ⓑ Ⓒ Ⓓ	12. Ⓐ Ⓑ Ⓒ Ⓓ	17. Ⓐ Ⓑ Ⓒ Ⓓ	22. Ⓐ Ⓑ Ⓒ Ⓓ
3. Ⓐ Ⓑ Ⓒ Ⓓ	8. Ⓐ Ⓑ Ⓒ Ⓓ	13. Ⓐ Ⓑ Ⓒ Ⓓ	18. Ⓐ Ⓑ Ⓒ Ⓓ	23. Ⓐ Ⓑ Ⓒ Ⓓ
4. Ⓐ Ⓑ Ⓒ Ⓓ	9. Ⓐ Ⓑ Ⓒ Ⓓ	14. Ⓐ Ⓑ Ⓒ Ⓓ	19. Ⓐ Ⓑ Ⓒ Ⓓ	24. Ⓐ Ⓑ Ⓒ Ⓓ
5. Ⓐ Ⓑ Ⓒ Ⓓ	10. Ⓐ Ⓑ Ⓒ Ⓓ	15. Ⓐ Ⓑ Ⓒ Ⓓ	20. Ⓐ Ⓑ Ⓒ Ⓓ	25. Ⓐ Ⓑ Ⓒ Ⓓ

ELECTRONICS INFORMATION—SUBTEST 8

1. Ⓐ Ⓑ Ⓒ Ⓓ	5. Ⓐ Ⓑ Ⓒ Ⓓ	9. Ⓐ Ⓑ Ⓒ Ⓓ	13. Ⓐ Ⓑ Ⓒ Ⓓ	17. Ⓐ Ⓑ Ⓒ Ⓓ
2. Ⓐ Ⓑ Ⓒ Ⓓ	6. Ⓐ Ⓑ Ⓒ Ⓓ	10. Ⓐ Ⓑ Ⓒ Ⓓ	14. Ⓐ Ⓑ Ⓒ Ⓓ	18. Ⓐ Ⓑ Ⓒ Ⓓ
3. Ⓐ Ⓑ Ⓒ Ⓓ	7. Ⓐ Ⓑ Ⓒ Ⓓ	11. Ⓐ Ⓑ Ⓒ Ⓓ	15. Ⓐ Ⓑ Ⓒ Ⓓ	19. Ⓐ Ⓑ Ⓒ Ⓓ
4. Ⓐ Ⓑ Ⓒ Ⓓ	8. Ⓐ Ⓑ Ⓒ Ⓓ	12. Ⓐ Ⓑ Ⓒ Ⓓ	16. Ⓐ Ⓑ Ⓒ Ⓓ	20. Ⓐ Ⓑ Ⓒ Ⓓ

SHOP INFORMATION—SUBTEST 9

1. Ⓐ Ⓑ Ⓒ Ⓓ	4. Ⓐ Ⓑ Ⓒ Ⓓ	7. Ⓐ Ⓑ Ⓒ Ⓓ	10. Ⓐ Ⓑ Ⓒ Ⓓ	13. Ⓐ Ⓑ Ⓒ Ⓓ
2. Ⓐ Ⓑ Ⓒ Ⓓ	5. Ⓐ Ⓑ Ⓒ Ⓓ	8. Ⓐ Ⓑ Ⓒ Ⓓ	11. Ⓐ Ⓑ Ⓒ Ⓓ	14. Ⓐ Ⓑ Ⓒ Ⓓ
3. Ⓐ Ⓑ Ⓒ Ⓓ	6. Ⓐ Ⓑ Ⓒ Ⓓ	9. Ⓐ Ⓑ Ⓒ Ⓓ	12. Ⓐ Ⓑ Ⓒ Ⓓ	15. Ⓐ Ⓑ Ⓒ Ⓓ

ASSEMBLING OBJECTS—SUBTEST 10

1. Ⓐ Ⓑ Ⓒ Ⓓ	5. Ⓐ Ⓑ Ⓒ Ⓓ	9. Ⓐ Ⓑ Ⓒ Ⓓ	13. Ⓐ Ⓑ Ⓒ Ⓓ	17. Ⓐ Ⓑ Ⓒ Ⓓ
2. Ⓐ Ⓑ Ⓒ Ⓓ	6. Ⓐ Ⓑ Ⓒ Ⓓ	10. Ⓐ Ⓑ Ⓒ Ⓓ	14. Ⓐ Ⓑ Ⓒ Ⓓ	18. Ⓐ Ⓑ Ⓒ Ⓓ
3. Ⓐ Ⓑ Ⓒ Ⓓ	7. Ⓐ Ⓑ Ⓒ Ⓓ	11. Ⓐ Ⓑ Ⓒ Ⓓ	15. Ⓐ Ⓑ Ⓒ Ⓓ	19. Ⓐ Ⓑ Ⓒ Ⓓ
4. Ⓐ Ⓑ Ⓒ Ⓓ	8. Ⓐ Ⓑ Ⓒ Ⓓ	12. Ⓐ Ⓑ Ⓒ Ⓓ	16. Ⓐ Ⓑ Ⓒ Ⓓ	20. Ⓐ Ⓑ Ⓒ Ⓓ

ANSWER SHEETS—Additional Practice

GENERAL SCIENCE—SUBTEST 1

1. Ⓐ Ⓑ Ⓒ Ⓓ	6. Ⓐ Ⓑ Ⓒ Ⓓ	11. Ⓐ Ⓑ Ⓒ Ⓓ	16. Ⓐ Ⓑ Ⓒ Ⓓ	21. Ⓐ Ⓑ Ⓒ Ⓓ
2. Ⓐ Ⓑ Ⓒ Ⓓ	7. Ⓐ Ⓑ Ⓒ Ⓓ	12. Ⓐ Ⓑ Ⓒ Ⓓ	17. Ⓐ Ⓑ Ⓒ Ⓓ	22. Ⓐ Ⓑ Ⓒ Ⓓ
3. Ⓐ Ⓑ Ⓒ Ⓓ	8. Ⓐ Ⓑ Ⓒ Ⓓ	13. Ⓐ Ⓑ Ⓒ Ⓓ	18. Ⓐ Ⓑ Ⓒ Ⓓ	23. Ⓐ Ⓑ Ⓒ Ⓓ
4. Ⓐ Ⓑ Ⓒ Ⓓ	9. Ⓐ Ⓑ Ⓒ Ⓓ	14. Ⓐ Ⓑ Ⓒ Ⓓ	19. Ⓐ Ⓑ Ⓒ Ⓓ	24. Ⓐ Ⓑ Ⓒ Ⓓ
5. Ⓐ Ⓑ Ⓒ Ⓓ	10. Ⓐ Ⓑ Ⓒ Ⓓ	15. Ⓐ Ⓑ Ⓒ Ⓓ	20. Ⓐ Ⓑ Ⓒ Ⓓ	25. Ⓐ Ⓑ Ⓒ Ⓓ

ARITHMETIC REASONING—SUBTEST 2

1. Ⓐ Ⓑ Ⓒ Ⓓ	7. Ⓐ Ⓑ Ⓒ Ⓓ	13. Ⓐ Ⓑ Ⓒ Ⓓ	19. Ⓐ Ⓑ Ⓒ Ⓓ	25. Ⓐ Ⓑ Ⓒ Ⓓ
2. Ⓐ Ⓑ Ⓒ Ⓓ	8. Ⓐ Ⓑ Ⓒ Ⓓ	14. Ⓐ Ⓑ Ⓒ Ⓓ	20. Ⓐ Ⓑ Ⓒ Ⓓ	26. Ⓐ Ⓑ Ⓒ Ⓓ
3. Ⓐ Ⓑ Ⓒ Ⓓ	9. Ⓐ Ⓑ Ⓒ Ⓓ	15. Ⓐ Ⓑ Ⓒ Ⓓ	21. Ⓐ Ⓑ Ⓒ Ⓓ	27. Ⓐ Ⓑ Ⓒ Ⓓ
4. Ⓐ Ⓑ Ⓒ Ⓓ	10. Ⓐ Ⓑ Ⓒ Ⓓ	16. Ⓐ Ⓑ Ⓒ Ⓓ	22. Ⓐ Ⓑ Ⓒ Ⓓ	28. Ⓐ Ⓑ Ⓒ Ⓓ
5. Ⓐ Ⓑ Ⓒ Ⓓ	11. Ⓐ Ⓑ Ⓒ Ⓓ	17. Ⓐ Ⓑ Ⓒ Ⓓ	23. Ⓐ Ⓑ Ⓒ Ⓓ	29. Ⓐ Ⓑ Ⓒ Ⓓ
6. Ⓐ Ⓑ Ⓒ Ⓓ	12. Ⓐ Ⓑ Ⓒ Ⓓ	18. Ⓐ Ⓑ Ⓒ Ⓓ	24. Ⓐ Ⓑ Ⓒ Ⓓ	30. Ⓐ Ⓑ Ⓒ Ⓓ

WORD KNOWLEDGE—SUBTEST 3

1. Ⓐ Ⓑ Ⓒ Ⓓ	8. Ⓐ Ⓑ Ⓒ Ⓓ	15. Ⓐ Ⓑ Ⓒ Ⓓ	22. Ⓐ Ⓑ Ⓒ Ⓓ	29. Ⓐ Ⓑ Ⓒ Ⓓ
2. Ⓐ Ⓑ Ⓒ Ⓓ	9. Ⓐ Ⓑ Ⓒ Ⓓ	16. Ⓐ Ⓑ Ⓒ Ⓓ	23. Ⓐ Ⓑ Ⓒ Ⓓ	30. Ⓐ Ⓑ Ⓒ Ⓓ
3. Ⓐ Ⓑ Ⓒ Ⓓ	10. Ⓐ Ⓑ Ⓒ Ⓓ	17. Ⓐ Ⓑ Ⓒ Ⓓ	24. Ⓐ Ⓑ Ⓒ Ⓓ	31. Ⓐ Ⓑ Ⓒ Ⓓ
4. Ⓐ Ⓑ Ⓒ Ⓓ	11. Ⓐ Ⓑ Ⓒ Ⓓ	18. Ⓐ Ⓑ Ⓒ Ⓓ	25. Ⓐ Ⓑ Ⓒ Ⓓ	32. Ⓐ Ⓑ Ⓒ Ⓓ
5. Ⓐ Ⓑ Ⓒ Ⓓ	12. Ⓐ Ⓑ Ⓒ Ⓓ	19. Ⓐ Ⓑ Ⓒ Ⓓ	26. Ⓐ Ⓑ Ⓒ Ⓓ	33. Ⓐ Ⓑ Ⓒ Ⓓ
6. Ⓐ Ⓑ Ⓒ Ⓓ	13. Ⓐ Ⓑ Ⓒ Ⓓ	20. Ⓐ Ⓑ Ⓒ Ⓓ	27. Ⓐ Ⓑ Ⓒ Ⓓ	34. Ⓐ Ⓑ Ⓒ Ⓓ
7. Ⓐ Ⓑ Ⓒ Ⓓ	14. Ⓐ Ⓑ Ⓒ Ⓓ	21. Ⓐ Ⓑ Ⓒ Ⓓ	28. Ⓐ Ⓑ Ⓒ Ⓓ	35. Ⓐ Ⓑ Ⓒ Ⓓ

PARAGRAPH COMPREHENSION—SUBTEST 4

1. Ⓐ Ⓑ Ⓒ Ⓓ	4. Ⓐ Ⓑ Ⓒ Ⓓ	7. Ⓐ Ⓑ Ⓒ Ⓓ	10. Ⓐ Ⓑ Ⓒ Ⓓ	13. Ⓐ Ⓑ Ⓒ Ⓓ
2. Ⓐ Ⓑ Ⓒ Ⓓ	5. Ⓐ Ⓑ Ⓒ Ⓓ	8. Ⓐ Ⓑ Ⓒ Ⓓ	11. Ⓐ Ⓑ Ⓒ Ⓓ	14. Ⓐ Ⓑ Ⓒ Ⓓ
3. Ⓐ Ⓑ Ⓒ Ⓓ	6. Ⓐ Ⓑ Ⓒ Ⓓ	9. Ⓐ Ⓑ Ⓒ Ⓓ	12. Ⓐ Ⓑ Ⓒ Ⓓ	15. Ⓐ Ⓑ Ⓒ Ⓓ

AUTOMOTIVE INFORMATION—SUBTEST 5

1. Ⓐ Ⓑ Ⓒ Ⓓ	4. Ⓐ Ⓑ Ⓒ Ⓓ	7. Ⓐ Ⓑ Ⓒ Ⓓ	10. Ⓐ Ⓑ Ⓒ Ⓓ	13. Ⓐ Ⓑ Ⓒ Ⓓ
2. Ⓐ Ⓑ Ⓒ Ⓓ	5. Ⓐ Ⓑ Ⓒ Ⓓ	8. Ⓐ Ⓑ Ⓒ Ⓓ	11. Ⓐ Ⓑ Ⓒ Ⓓ	14. Ⓐ Ⓑ Ⓒ Ⓓ
3. Ⓐ Ⓑ Ⓒ Ⓓ	6. Ⓐ Ⓑ Ⓒ Ⓓ	9. Ⓐ Ⓑ Ⓒ Ⓓ	12. Ⓐ Ⓑ Ⓒ Ⓓ	15. Ⓐ Ⓑ Ⓒ Ⓓ

MATHEMATICS KNOWLEDGE—SUBTEST 6

1. Ⓐ Ⓑ Ⓒ Ⓓ	6. Ⓐ Ⓑ Ⓒ Ⓓ	11. Ⓐ Ⓑ Ⓒ Ⓓ	16. Ⓐ Ⓑ Ⓒ Ⓓ	21. Ⓐ Ⓑ Ⓒ Ⓓ
2. Ⓐ Ⓑ Ⓒ Ⓓ	7. Ⓐ Ⓑ Ⓒ Ⓓ	12. Ⓐ Ⓑ Ⓒ Ⓓ	17. Ⓐ Ⓑ Ⓒ Ⓓ	22. Ⓐ Ⓑ Ⓒ Ⓓ
3. Ⓐ Ⓑ Ⓒ Ⓓ	8. Ⓐ Ⓑ Ⓒ Ⓓ	13. Ⓐ Ⓑ Ⓒ Ⓓ	18. Ⓐ Ⓑ Ⓒ Ⓓ	23. Ⓐ Ⓑ Ⓒ Ⓓ
4. Ⓐ Ⓑ Ⓒ Ⓓ	9. Ⓐ Ⓑ Ⓒ Ⓓ	14. Ⓐ Ⓑ Ⓒ Ⓓ	19. Ⓐ Ⓑ Ⓒ Ⓓ	24. Ⓐ Ⓑ Ⓒ Ⓓ
5. Ⓐ Ⓑ Ⓒ Ⓓ	10. Ⓐ Ⓑ Ⓒ Ⓓ	15. Ⓐ Ⓑ Ⓒ Ⓓ	20. Ⓐ Ⓑ Ⓒ Ⓓ	25. Ⓐ Ⓑ Ⓒ Ⓓ

MECHANICAL COMPREHENSION—SUBTEST 7

1. Ⓐ Ⓑ Ⓒ Ⓓ	6. Ⓐ Ⓑ Ⓒ Ⓓ	11. Ⓐ Ⓑ Ⓒ Ⓓ	16. Ⓐ Ⓑ Ⓒ Ⓓ	21. Ⓐ Ⓑ Ⓒ Ⓓ
2. Ⓐ Ⓑ Ⓒ Ⓓ	7. Ⓐ Ⓑ Ⓒ Ⓓ	12. Ⓐ Ⓑ Ⓒ Ⓓ	17. Ⓐ Ⓑ Ⓒ Ⓓ	22. Ⓐ Ⓑ Ⓒ Ⓓ
3. Ⓐ Ⓑ Ⓒ Ⓓ	8. Ⓐ Ⓑ Ⓒ Ⓓ	13. Ⓐ Ⓑ Ⓒ Ⓓ	18. Ⓐ Ⓑ Ⓒ Ⓓ	23. Ⓐ Ⓑ Ⓒ Ⓓ
4. Ⓐ Ⓑ Ⓒ Ⓓ	9. Ⓐ Ⓑ Ⓒ Ⓓ	14. Ⓐ Ⓑ Ⓒ Ⓓ	19. Ⓐ Ⓑ Ⓒ Ⓓ	24. Ⓐ Ⓑ Ⓒ Ⓓ
5. Ⓐ Ⓑ Ⓒ Ⓓ	10. Ⓐ Ⓑ Ⓒ Ⓓ	15. Ⓐ Ⓑ Ⓒ Ⓓ	20. Ⓐ Ⓑ Ⓒ Ⓓ	25. Ⓐ Ⓑ Ⓒ Ⓓ

ELECTRONICS INFORMATION—SUBTEST 8

1. Ⓐ Ⓑ Ⓒ Ⓓ	5. Ⓐ Ⓑ Ⓒ Ⓓ	9. Ⓐ Ⓑ Ⓒ Ⓓ	13. Ⓐ Ⓑ Ⓒ Ⓓ	17. Ⓐ Ⓑ Ⓒ Ⓓ
2. Ⓐ Ⓑ Ⓒ Ⓓ	6. Ⓐ Ⓑ Ⓒ Ⓓ	10. Ⓐ Ⓑ Ⓒ Ⓓ	14. Ⓐ Ⓑ Ⓒ Ⓓ	18. Ⓐ Ⓑ Ⓒ Ⓓ
3. Ⓐ Ⓑ Ⓒ Ⓓ	7. Ⓐ Ⓑ Ⓒ Ⓓ	11. Ⓐ Ⓑ Ⓒ Ⓓ	15. Ⓐ Ⓑ Ⓒ Ⓓ	19. Ⓐ Ⓑ Ⓒ Ⓓ
4. Ⓐ Ⓑ Ⓒ Ⓓ	8. Ⓐ Ⓑ Ⓒ Ⓓ	12. Ⓐ Ⓑ Ⓒ Ⓓ	16. Ⓐ Ⓑ Ⓒ Ⓓ	20. Ⓐ Ⓑ Ⓒ Ⓓ

SHOP INFORMATION—SUBTEST 9

1. Ⓐ Ⓑ Ⓒ Ⓓ	4. Ⓐ Ⓑ Ⓒ Ⓓ	7. Ⓐ Ⓑ Ⓒ Ⓓ	10. Ⓐ Ⓑ Ⓒ Ⓓ	13. Ⓐ Ⓑ Ⓒ Ⓓ
2. Ⓐ Ⓑ Ⓒ Ⓓ	5. Ⓐ Ⓑ Ⓒ Ⓓ	8. Ⓐ Ⓑ Ⓒ Ⓓ	11. Ⓐ Ⓑ Ⓒ Ⓓ	14. Ⓐ Ⓑ Ⓒ Ⓓ
3. Ⓐ Ⓑ Ⓒ Ⓓ	6. Ⓐ Ⓑ Ⓒ Ⓓ	9. Ⓐ Ⓑ Ⓒ Ⓓ	12. Ⓐ Ⓑ Ⓒ Ⓓ	15. Ⓐ Ⓑ Ⓒ Ⓓ

ASSEMBLING OBJECTS—SUBTEST 10

1. Ⓐ Ⓑ Ⓒ Ⓓ	5. Ⓐ Ⓑ Ⓒ Ⓓ	9. Ⓐ Ⓑ Ⓒ Ⓓ	13. Ⓐ Ⓑ Ⓒ Ⓓ	17. Ⓐ Ⓑ Ⓒ Ⓓ
2. Ⓐ Ⓑ Ⓒ Ⓓ	6. Ⓐ Ⓑ Ⓒ Ⓓ	10. Ⓐ Ⓑ Ⓒ Ⓓ	14. Ⓐ Ⓑ Ⓒ Ⓓ	18. Ⓐ Ⓑ Ⓒ Ⓓ
3. Ⓐ Ⓑ Ⓒ Ⓓ	7. Ⓐ Ⓑ Ⓒ Ⓓ	11. Ⓐ Ⓑ Ⓒ Ⓓ	15. Ⓐ Ⓑ Ⓒ Ⓓ	19. Ⓐ Ⓑ Ⓒ Ⓓ
4. Ⓐ Ⓑ Ⓒ Ⓓ	8. Ⓐ Ⓑ Ⓒ Ⓓ	12. Ⓐ Ⓑ Ⓒ Ⓓ	16. Ⓐ Ⓑ Ⓒ Ⓓ	20. Ⓐ Ⓑ Ⓒ Ⓓ

ANSWER SHEETS—Additional Practice

GENERAL SCIENCE—SUBTEST 1

1. Ⓐ Ⓑ Ⓒ Ⓓ	6. Ⓐ Ⓑ Ⓒ Ⓓ	11. Ⓐ Ⓑ Ⓒ Ⓓ	16. Ⓐ Ⓑ Ⓒ Ⓓ	21. Ⓐ Ⓑ Ⓒ Ⓓ
2. Ⓐ Ⓑ Ⓒ Ⓓ	7. Ⓐ Ⓑ Ⓒ Ⓓ	12. Ⓐ Ⓑ Ⓒ Ⓓ	17. Ⓐ Ⓑ Ⓒ Ⓓ	22. Ⓐ Ⓑ Ⓒ Ⓓ
3. Ⓐ Ⓑ Ⓒ Ⓓ	8. Ⓐ Ⓑ Ⓒ Ⓓ	13. Ⓐ Ⓑ Ⓒ Ⓓ	18. Ⓐ Ⓑ Ⓒ Ⓓ	23. Ⓐ Ⓑ Ⓒ Ⓓ
4. Ⓐ Ⓑ Ⓒ Ⓓ	9. Ⓐ Ⓑ Ⓒ Ⓓ	14. Ⓐ Ⓑ Ⓒ Ⓓ	19. Ⓐ Ⓑ Ⓒ Ⓓ	24. Ⓐ Ⓑ Ⓒ Ⓓ
5. Ⓐ Ⓑ Ⓒ Ⓓ	10. Ⓐ Ⓑ Ⓒ Ⓓ	15. Ⓐ Ⓑ Ⓒ Ⓓ	20. Ⓐ Ⓑ Ⓒ Ⓓ	25. Ⓐ Ⓑ Ⓒ Ⓓ

ARITHMETIC REASONING—SUBTEST 2

1. Ⓐ Ⓑ Ⓒ Ⓓ	7. Ⓐ Ⓑ Ⓒ Ⓓ	13. Ⓐ Ⓑ Ⓒ Ⓓ	19. Ⓐ Ⓑ Ⓒ Ⓓ	25. Ⓐ Ⓑ Ⓒ Ⓓ
2. Ⓐ Ⓑ Ⓒ Ⓓ	8. Ⓐ Ⓑ Ⓒ Ⓓ	14. Ⓐ Ⓑ Ⓒ Ⓓ	20. Ⓐ Ⓑ Ⓒ Ⓓ	26. Ⓐ Ⓑ Ⓒ Ⓓ
3. Ⓐ Ⓑ Ⓒ Ⓓ	9. Ⓐ Ⓑ Ⓒ Ⓓ	15. Ⓐ Ⓑ Ⓒ Ⓓ	21. Ⓐ Ⓑ Ⓒ Ⓓ	27. Ⓐ Ⓑ Ⓒ Ⓓ
4. Ⓐ Ⓑ Ⓒ Ⓓ	10. Ⓐ Ⓑ Ⓒ Ⓓ	16. Ⓐ Ⓑ Ⓒ Ⓓ	22. Ⓐ Ⓑ Ⓒ Ⓓ	28. Ⓐ Ⓑ Ⓒ Ⓓ
5. Ⓐ Ⓑ Ⓒ Ⓓ	11. Ⓐ Ⓑ Ⓒ Ⓓ	17. Ⓐ Ⓑ Ⓒ Ⓓ	23. Ⓐ Ⓑ Ⓒ Ⓓ	29. Ⓐ Ⓑ Ⓒ Ⓓ
6. Ⓐ Ⓑ Ⓒ Ⓓ	12. Ⓐ Ⓑ Ⓒ Ⓓ	18. Ⓐ Ⓑ Ⓒ Ⓓ	24. Ⓐ Ⓑ Ⓒ Ⓓ	30. Ⓐ Ⓑ Ⓒ Ⓓ

WORD KNOWLEDGE—SUBTEST 3

1. Ⓐ Ⓑ Ⓒ Ⓓ	8. Ⓐ Ⓑ Ⓒ Ⓓ	15. Ⓐ Ⓑ Ⓒ Ⓓ	22. Ⓐ Ⓑ Ⓒ Ⓓ	29. Ⓐ Ⓑ Ⓒ Ⓓ
2. Ⓐ Ⓑ Ⓒ Ⓓ	9. Ⓐ Ⓑ Ⓒ Ⓓ	16. Ⓐ Ⓑ Ⓒ Ⓓ	23. Ⓐ Ⓑ Ⓒ Ⓓ	30. Ⓐ Ⓑ Ⓒ Ⓓ
3. Ⓐ Ⓑ Ⓒ Ⓓ	10. Ⓐ Ⓑ Ⓒ Ⓓ	17. Ⓐ Ⓑ Ⓒ Ⓓ	24. Ⓐ Ⓑ Ⓒ Ⓓ	31. Ⓐ Ⓑ Ⓒ Ⓓ
4. Ⓐ Ⓑ Ⓒ Ⓓ	11. Ⓐ Ⓑ Ⓒ Ⓓ	18. Ⓐ Ⓑ Ⓒ Ⓓ	25. Ⓐ Ⓑ Ⓒ Ⓓ	32. Ⓐ Ⓑ Ⓒ Ⓓ
5. Ⓐ Ⓑ Ⓒ Ⓓ	12. Ⓐ Ⓑ Ⓒ Ⓓ	19. Ⓐ Ⓑ Ⓒ Ⓓ	26. Ⓐ Ⓑ Ⓒ Ⓓ	33. Ⓐ Ⓑ Ⓒ Ⓓ
6. Ⓐ Ⓑ Ⓒ Ⓓ	13. Ⓐ Ⓑ Ⓒ Ⓓ	20. Ⓐ Ⓑ Ⓒ Ⓓ	27. Ⓐ Ⓑ Ⓒ Ⓓ	34. Ⓐ Ⓑ Ⓒ Ⓓ
7. Ⓐ Ⓑ Ⓒ Ⓓ	14. Ⓐ Ⓑ Ⓒ Ⓓ	21. Ⓐ Ⓑ Ⓒ Ⓓ	28. Ⓐ Ⓑ Ⓒ Ⓓ	35. Ⓐ Ⓑ Ⓒ Ⓓ

PARAGRAPH COMPREHENSION—SUBTEST 4

1. Ⓐ Ⓑ Ⓒ Ⓓ	4. Ⓐ Ⓑ Ⓒ Ⓓ	7. Ⓐ Ⓑ Ⓒ Ⓓ	10. Ⓐ Ⓑ Ⓒ Ⓓ	13. Ⓐ Ⓑ Ⓒ Ⓓ
2. Ⓐ Ⓑ Ⓒ Ⓓ	5. Ⓐ Ⓑ Ⓒ Ⓓ	8. Ⓐ Ⓑ Ⓒ Ⓓ	11. Ⓐ Ⓑ Ⓒ Ⓓ	14. Ⓐ Ⓑ Ⓒ Ⓓ
3. Ⓐ Ⓑ Ⓒ Ⓓ	6. Ⓐ Ⓑ Ⓒ Ⓓ	9. Ⓐ Ⓑ Ⓒ Ⓓ	12. Ⓐ Ⓑ Ⓒ Ⓓ	15. Ⓐ Ⓑ Ⓒ Ⓓ

AUTOMOTIVE INFORMATION—SUBTEST 5

1. Ⓐ Ⓑ Ⓒ Ⓓ	4. Ⓐ Ⓑ Ⓒ Ⓓ	7. Ⓐ Ⓑ Ⓒ Ⓓ	10. Ⓐ Ⓑ Ⓒ Ⓓ	13. Ⓐ Ⓑ Ⓒ Ⓓ
2. Ⓐ Ⓑ Ⓒ Ⓓ	5. Ⓐ Ⓑ Ⓒ Ⓓ	8. Ⓐ Ⓑ Ⓒ Ⓓ	11. Ⓐ Ⓑ Ⓒ Ⓓ	14. Ⓐ Ⓑ Ⓒ Ⓓ
3. Ⓐ Ⓑ Ⓒ Ⓓ	6. Ⓐ Ⓑ Ⓒ Ⓓ	9. Ⓐ Ⓑ Ⓒ Ⓓ	12. Ⓐ Ⓑ Ⓒ Ⓓ	15. Ⓐ Ⓑ Ⓒ Ⓓ

MATHEMATICS KNOWLEDGE—SUBTEST 6

1. Ⓐ Ⓑ Ⓒ Ⓓ	6. Ⓐ Ⓑ Ⓒ Ⓓ	11. Ⓐ Ⓑ Ⓒ Ⓓ	16. Ⓐ Ⓑ Ⓒ Ⓓ	21. Ⓐ Ⓑ Ⓒ Ⓓ
2. Ⓐ Ⓑ Ⓒ Ⓓ	7. Ⓐ Ⓑ Ⓒ Ⓓ	12. Ⓐ Ⓑ Ⓒ Ⓓ	17. Ⓐ Ⓑ Ⓒ Ⓓ	22. Ⓐ Ⓑ Ⓒ Ⓓ
3. Ⓐ Ⓑ Ⓒ Ⓓ	8. Ⓐ Ⓑ Ⓒ Ⓓ	13. Ⓐ Ⓑ Ⓒ Ⓓ	18. Ⓐ Ⓑ Ⓒ Ⓓ	23. Ⓐ Ⓑ Ⓒ Ⓓ
4. Ⓐ Ⓑ Ⓒ Ⓓ	9. Ⓐ Ⓑ Ⓒ Ⓓ	14. Ⓐ Ⓑ Ⓒ Ⓓ	19. Ⓐ Ⓑ Ⓒ Ⓓ	24. Ⓐ Ⓑ Ⓒ Ⓓ
5. Ⓐ Ⓑ Ⓒ Ⓓ	10. Ⓐ Ⓑ Ⓒ Ⓓ	15. Ⓐ Ⓑ Ⓒ Ⓓ	20. Ⓐ Ⓑ Ⓒ Ⓓ	25. Ⓐ Ⓑ Ⓒ Ⓓ

MECHANICAL COMPREHENSION—SUBTEST 7

1. Ⓐ Ⓑ Ⓒ Ⓓ	6. Ⓐ Ⓑ Ⓒ Ⓓ	11. Ⓐ Ⓑ Ⓒ Ⓓ	16. Ⓐ Ⓑ Ⓒ Ⓓ	21. Ⓐ Ⓑ Ⓒ Ⓓ
2. Ⓐ Ⓑ Ⓒ Ⓓ	7. Ⓐ Ⓑ Ⓒ Ⓓ	12. Ⓐ Ⓑ Ⓒ Ⓓ	17. Ⓐ Ⓑ Ⓒ Ⓓ	22. Ⓐ Ⓑ Ⓒ Ⓓ
3. Ⓐ Ⓑ Ⓒ Ⓓ	8. Ⓐ Ⓑ Ⓒ Ⓓ	13. Ⓐ Ⓑ Ⓒ Ⓓ	18. Ⓐ Ⓑ Ⓒ Ⓓ	23. Ⓐ Ⓑ Ⓒ Ⓓ
4. Ⓐ Ⓑ Ⓒ Ⓓ	9. Ⓐ Ⓑ Ⓒ Ⓓ	14. Ⓐ Ⓑ Ⓒ Ⓓ	19. Ⓐ Ⓑ Ⓒ Ⓓ	24. Ⓐ Ⓑ Ⓒ Ⓓ
5. Ⓐ Ⓑ Ⓒ Ⓓ	10. Ⓐ Ⓑ Ⓒ Ⓓ	15. Ⓐ Ⓑ Ⓒ Ⓓ	20. Ⓐ Ⓑ Ⓒ Ⓓ	25. Ⓐ Ⓑ Ⓒ Ⓓ

ELECTRONICS INFORMATION—SUBTEST 8

1. Ⓐ Ⓑ Ⓒ Ⓓ	5. Ⓐ Ⓑ Ⓒ Ⓓ	9. Ⓐ Ⓑ Ⓒ Ⓓ	13. Ⓐ Ⓑ Ⓒ Ⓓ	17. Ⓐ Ⓑ Ⓒ Ⓓ
2. Ⓐ Ⓑ Ⓒ Ⓓ	6. Ⓐ Ⓑ Ⓒ Ⓓ	10. Ⓐ Ⓑ Ⓒ Ⓓ	14. Ⓐ Ⓑ Ⓒ Ⓓ	18. Ⓐ Ⓑ Ⓒ Ⓓ
3. Ⓐ Ⓑ Ⓒ Ⓓ	7. Ⓐ Ⓑ Ⓒ Ⓓ	11. Ⓐ Ⓑ Ⓒ Ⓓ	15. Ⓐ Ⓑ Ⓒ Ⓓ	19. Ⓐ Ⓑ Ⓒ Ⓓ
4. Ⓐ Ⓑ Ⓒ Ⓓ	8. Ⓐ Ⓑ Ⓒ Ⓓ	12. Ⓐ Ⓑ Ⓒ Ⓓ	16. Ⓐ Ⓑ Ⓒ Ⓓ	20. Ⓐ Ⓑ Ⓒ Ⓓ

SHOP INFORMATION—SUBTEST 9

1. Ⓐ Ⓑ Ⓒ Ⓓ	4. Ⓐ Ⓑ Ⓒ Ⓓ	7. Ⓐ Ⓑ Ⓒ Ⓓ	10. Ⓐ Ⓑ Ⓒ Ⓓ	13. Ⓐ Ⓑ Ⓒ Ⓓ
2. Ⓐ Ⓑ Ⓒ Ⓓ	5. Ⓐ Ⓑ Ⓒ Ⓓ	8. Ⓐ Ⓑ Ⓒ Ⓓ	11. Ⓐ Ⓑ Ⓒ Ⓓ	14. Ⓐ Ⓑ Ⓒ Ⓓ
3. Ⓐ Ⓑ Ⓒ Ⓓ	6. Ⓐ Ⓑ Ⓒ Ⓓ	9. Ⓐ Ⓑ Ⓒ Ⓓ	12. Ⓐ Ⓑ Ⓒ Ⓓ	15. Ⓐ Ⓑ Ⓒ Ⓓ

ASSEMBLING OBJECTS—SUBTEST 10

1. Ⓐ Ⓑ Ⓒ Ⓓ	5. Ⓐ Ⓑ Ⓒ Ⓓ	9. Ⓐ Ⓑ Ⓒ Ⓓ	13. Ⓐ Ⓑ Ⓒ Ⓓ	17. Ⓐ Ⓑ Ⓒ Ⓓ
2. Ⓐ Ⓑ Ⓒ Ⓓ	6. Ⓐ Ⓑ Ⓒ Ⓓ	10. Ⓐ Ⓑ Ⓒ Ⓓ	14. Ⓐ Ⓑ Ⓒ Ⓓ	18. Ⓐ Ⓑ Ⓒ Ⓓ
3. Ⓐ Ⓑ Ⓒ Ⓓ	7. Ⓐ Ⓑ Ⓒ Ⓓ	11. Ⓐ Ⓑ Ⓒ Ⓓ	15. Ⓐ Ⓑ Ⓒ Ⓓ	19. Ⓐ Ⓑ Ⓒ Ⓓ
4. Ⓐ Ⓑ Ⓒ Ⓓ	8. Ⓐ Ⓑ Ⓒ Ⓓ	12. Ⓐ Ⓑ Ⓒ Ⓓ	16. Ⓐ Ⓑ Ⓒ Ⓓ	20. Ⓐ Ⓑ Ⓒ Ⓓ